MULTICULTURALISM, CRIME, AND CRIMINAL JUSTICE

MULTICULTURALISM, CRIME, AND CRIMINAL JUSTICE

SECOND EDITION

Robert McNamara

Ronald Burns

NEW YORK   OXFORD
OXFORD UNIVERSITY PRESS

Oxford University Press is a department of the University of Oxford.
It furthers the University's objective of excellence in research, scholarship,
and education by publishing worldwide. Oxford is a registered trade mark of
Oxford University Press in the UK and certain other countries.

Published in the United States of America by Oxford University Press
198 Madison Avenue, New York, NY 10016, United States of America.

Library of Congress Cataloging-in-Publication Data

Names: McNamara, Robert Hartmann, author. | Burns, Ronald G., 1968- author.

Title: Multiculturalism, crime, and criminal justice / Robert McNamara,
    Ronald Burns.
Description: Second edition. | New York : Oxford University Press, [2021] |
    Includes bibliographical references and index. | Summary:
    "Multiculturalism, Crime, and Criminal Justice provides a clear overview
    of the most controversial issues facing African Americans, Hispanics,
    women, and the LGBTQ community among others as offenders, victims, and
    practitioners within the context of the criminal justice system"—
    Provided by publisher.
Identifiers: LCCN 2020004526 (print) | LCCN 2020004527 (ebook) | ISBN
    9780190078652 (paperback) | ISBN 9780190078669 (epub) | ISBN
    9780190078720 (ebook)
Subjects: LCSH: Discrimination in criminal justice administration—United
    States. | Criminal justice, Administration of—United States. |
    Multiculturalism—United States.
Classification: LCC HV9950 .M427 2021 (print) | LCC HV9950 (ebook) | DDC
    364.30973—dc23
LC record available at https://lccn.loc.gov/2020004526
LC ebook record available at https://lccn.loc.gov/2020004527

9 8 7 6 5 4 3 2

Printed by Sheridan Books, Inc., United States of America

DEDICATION

To Carey, who sees no color; and to Connor, who I hope
follows in his mother's footsteps.

To Lisa, Ryan, Lily, and all others who make the world a better place.

BRIEF CONTENTS

CONTENTS

CHAPTER **13**   **Corrections and Multiculturalism**   *363*

PREFACE

The creation of this work stemmed from the absence of a thorough work on diversity, multiculturalism, crime, and justice. There are many insightful existing works that address crime, multiculturalism, or criminal justice, but relatively few that combine all three important issues. We sought to address that void with the goal of drawing attention to the interconnectedness of these topics.

Many developments and incidents in relation to the topics prompted us to develop a book that comprehensively addresses the issues in a reader-friendly manner. Consider, for instance, the incidents and developments in the last several years, and how justice-based practices have impacted police-community relations and perceptions of justice. The name "Ferguson" no longer simply refers to a city in Missouri. Instead, it conjures images of questionable justice–based actions that exist throughout our country and elsewhere. Some of these events are startling reminders of the fragility of human life and the delicate nature of the relationships we form with others. In thinking about these issues, which are discussed in each chapter, we note that there is increasingly more evidence and research being done on disproportionality within the justice process and why it occurs. Unfortunately, much of the evidence is mixed or inconclusive and the answers to why discrimination occurs, and how it impacts our society, continue to elude researchers, policy makers, and practitioners. Questions still remain about whether the system is biased against minorities, whether offenders tend to come primarily from minority groups, or whether they are so heavily represented in crime statistics due to greater attention given to certain neighborhoods by the police, a situation which leads to more arrests, convictions, and punishment.

We hope that this second edition contributes to the multiculturalism narrative, particularly as it relates to crime and justice. The significance of this book is evidenced by events such as the recent episodes of White officers shooting Black men, and the subsequent backlashes, including the killing of police officers—some of whom, ironically, were protecting protestors at a demonstration against the excessive use of force by police officers. Other events, such as the debate about whether transgender people should be allowed to use the bathroom of their choice, have also had an impact on public policy and the public's perception of race, gender, discrimination, and other issues. Race, ethnicity, crime, and discrimination continue to be central topics of discussion in political campaigns, policy formation, social interactions, and many other areas. All of these events shape and define this country's understanding of diversity and multiculturalism and their economic, social, and political impacts on its occupants.

This book focuses on marginalized groups and expands understanding of multiculturalism to the entire criminal justice field. Particularly, the work addresses the ways in which different groups are impacted by law enforcement, the courts, and correctional agencies, including discussion of the unique problems and issues each group faces. Most significant for this book is coverage of how multiculturalism affects officials within the criminal justice system. Thus, the chapters include coverage of the unique problems members of minority groups face as individuals who work within the system.

The book provides a comprehensive view of multiculturalism as well as the problems stemming from it in relation to all dimensions of the system. The updates and additions, including "checkpoints" provided throughout the chapters to ensure that readers grasp the key points, make the book an even more valuable tool for professors teaching a wide array of courses. The book is focused on multiculturalism, crime, and criminal justice, but even those who strictly use it for courses on diversity and multiculturalism will find it a compelling and comprehensive resource for their students. Perhaps equally important, the book, while empirically accurate and balanced in its presentation of various issues, is written in a style that is easy for students to understand, and instructors will find it helpful for generating classroom discussion.

Within the discussion of the experiences of the various groups, some of the most controversial and celebrated topics within criminal justice are explored. Examples include the impact of police shootings upon minority communities, disparities in sentencing for African Americans, drug trafficking and Hispanics, hate crimes against gays and lesbians, the increased involvement of females and the elderly in crime, and gang problems and human trafficking among Asian Americans. In addition, attention is given to the cultural and social biases found in the processing of offenders, as well as the host of internal problems faced by different employees within the criminal justice system.

The book is divided into three logically organized parts that would likely be the outline for a course on this topic. Part I deals with developing an understanding of the difficulty in defining multiculturalism, race, and ethnicity. These topics are critical to laying the foundation of the problems various groups face in American society. There is also discussion of the structure and process of group dynamics, the various ways people communicate and develop ideas, and the ways in which this leads to a perception of different groups and cultures. We also address how these tendencies translate into problems for disenfranchised groups.

Part II of the book addresses cultural specifics in the criminal justice system. It consists of several chapters that include descriptions of cultural groups that are most likely to experience problems within the criminal justice system. These include African Americans, Hispanic/Latinos, Asian American, Native Americans, women, the LGBT community, the elderly, and juveniles. The problems each group experiences are discussed in each of these chapters, for instance as they relate to profiling, sentencing disparities, jurisdictional issues, child trafficking, misuse of powers, hate crimes, health concerns (e.g., for elderly inmates), sexual harassment, and immigration issues.

Part III of the book addresses the means by which multiculturalism affects criminal justice personnel in particular and the system as a whole, preparing for and addressing multiculturalism through policies and training, and the future of multiculturalism in the criminal justice system. With chapters on police, courts, and corrections, the book addresses key components of problems internal to the criminal justice system. This is true not only of the particular problems certain groups might face but also of how and in what ways criminal justice personnel interact with other cultural groups. In Part III we also address responses to diversity and multiculturalism with particular concern for training and policies. The final chapter offers a look to the future of multiculturalism, crime, and criminal justice, which provides a suitable concluding chapter of the book.

Throughout the book, a comprehensive assessment of the issues and problems for each group or topic are presented, with an eye toward a balanced description of the material. Updated and recent research findings provide empirical support for the content. This approach is useful for instructors who wish to explore individual topics in more depth and generate lively discussion. Thus, rather than simply being a historical account of each group or simply a collection of characteristics of them, the problems and issues come alive in the context of a discussion, which allows students to grasp the underlying factors that contribute to the problems.

This book has many strengths not found in similar works focused on multiculturalism, diversity, and criminal justice. To begin with, it offers a thorough grounding in the foundational chapters about the nature of social interaction, group dynamics, and communication. This foundation provides context for the remaining chapters, which focus on a variety of different groups and their involvement in crime and the criminal justice system. Second, carefully constructed boxed inserts conveying important issues and incidents alert students to how these themes recur. These boxed inserts provide short examples of the issues in the chapter, and are accompanied by critical thinking questions. The aforementioned "checkpoints" provide guidance for readers.

Further, boxed inserts titled "You Make the Call" provide examples of dilemmas as they relate to multiculturalism. These scenarios challenge students to appreciate the complexity and difficulty of decisions that are made regarding multiculturalism in the criminal justice system. The organization of the book also sets it apart from many other books, as it is divided into three logically organized sections. In Part 2, in particular, our work differs from others in the sense that we devote entire chapters to particular groups with regard to crime and criminal justice. Particularly, we focus closely on African Americans, Hispanic Americans, Asian Americans, Native Americans, women, the LGBT community, the elderly, and juveniles. Other books comment on these groups, however our directed focus on each sets this work apart.

Both authors have published scholarly works addressing issues pertaining to multiculturalism and crime/justice, and are familiar with the historical and recent research literature in the area. As such, recent, relevant research is shared throughout the text to help ensure that the content is "bias free." The focus in writing the first edition of this work and updating it for a second edition was to let sound, recent research be the basis of the work.

Each chapter has learning objectives, a list of key terms, key terms in bold type, discussion questions, and suggestions for further reading. There is also a complete list of references; a companion website that acts as a student study guide with chapter outlines, study questions, and update features; and an instructor's guide and test bank to assist professors in the design and implementation of the course. Also, PowerPoint slides and transparencies exist for each chapter.

One merely needs to consider recent events around the country to recognize the significance of multiculturalism and diversity as they relate to crime and the criminal justice system. This book addresses these and many other issues, while enlightening readers regarding three very important areas: crime, multiculturalism, and criminal justice. Alone, these areas have historically challenged our country. Combined, they have generated additional areas of necessary attention.

Many social issues currently challenge our society; however, some pose more obstacles than others. This book covers key aspects of important contributors to many of society's concerns, and does so in a manner that brings the issues to life. We hope you enjoy reading it, and that it encourages you to give due consideration to how injustices occur, what can be done to prevent them, and how each one of us can continue to make the world a better place.

ACKNOWLEDGMENTS

A project of this magnitude cannot be accomplished without a substantial amount of assistance. While authors often get all the credit, success usually comes from those behind the scenes making things happen for them. This is true in our cases, where we had many people picking up the slack while we were distracted and encouraging us to work harder. From a professional standpoint, we cannot express enough gratitude to Steve Helba and Kora Fillet from Oxford University Press for their support, encouragement, and belief in both the project and us. We also owe our families a debt of gratitude for their patience and understanding while completing this project. Families of academics often bear a considerable cost that is often overlooked and it is something we wish to acknowledge, and we would like to express our thanks for the gift of being able to pursue our passions. We would also like to thank our colleagues and those who used the first edition of the work. Your support is greatly appreciated, and all feedback designed to make the next edition even better is appreciated. Finally, we wish to thank the following reviewers for their input: Hasmik Arakelyan, California State University Los Angeles; Dianna Carmenaty, University of the Southwest; Nicole Doctor, Ivy Tech Community College; Emily Horowitz, St. Francis College; Rebecca Katz, Morehead State University; Emil J. Kolick, Rosemont College; Ray Nickson, Fresno Pacific University; James Pitts, California State University, Fresno; and, Michele Stacey, East Carolina University.

ABOUT THE AUTHORS

Robert Hartmann McNamara is currently a professor of criminal justice at the Citadel. He is the former associate provost and dean of the graduate college at the Citadel, the former founding associate dean of evening undergraduate studies at the Citadel, and founding director of the 2 + 2 program in criminal justice. He is the author of twenty-five books, including: *Juvenile Delinquency: Bridging Theory to Practice*; *Problem Children: Special Populations in Delinquency*; *Multiculturalism in the Criminal Justice System*; *Homelessness in America*, 3 vols.; *The Lost Population: Status Offenders in America*; *In My Father's Hands*; *Boundary Dwellers: The Lives of Homeless Women in Transitional Housing*; *A New Look at American Society*; *Perspectives on Social Problems*; *Understanding Contemporary Social Problems*; *Crossing the Line: Interracial Couples in the South*; *Crime Displacement: The Other Side of Prevention*; *The Times Square Hustler: Male Prostitution in New York City*; *Sex, Scams, and Street Life: The Sociology of New York City's Times Square*; *Beating the Odds: Crime, Poverty, and Life in the Inner City*; *Police and Policing*; *The Urban Landscape: Selected Readings*; and *Social Gerontology*. Dr. McNamara has also served as a senior research fellow for the National Strategy Information Center, the Policy Lab, the Police Executive Research Forum in Washington, DC, and the Pacific Institute for Research and Evaluation in Baltimore, Maryland.

Dr. McNamara has also published numerous articles on a variety of topics and has been a consultant for state, federal, and private agencies on topics such as AIDS, drug abuse, urban redevelopment, homelessness, policing, gangs, and healthcare. He worked with the Regional Community Policing Institute at Eastern Kentucky University to study school safety in eight high schools across the state. He also worked with the Mexican government and the National Strategy Information Center to develop an anti-corruption curriculum in their public schools. In 2015, Dr. McNamara was a fellow at the American Council on Education as part of the Emerging Leaders program, and was a fellow at the Executive Leadership Academy at the American Leadership Institute in Washington, DC. He has extensive leadership training and has worked with a number of institutions in higher education on a variety of issues. Dr. McNamara holds a PhD in sociology from Yale University.

Ronald Burns is the department chair and a professor of criminal justice at Texas Christian University (TCU). He has published over seventy-five articles in areas such as multiculturalism in the criminal justice system, the criminal justice system, policing, and white-collar crime. He is the author, coauthor, or editor of eight books, including *Multiculturalism in the Criminal Justice System; Environmental Law, Crime, and Justice* (2nd edition); *Federal Law Enforcement; Policing: A Modular Approach; Critical Issues in Criminal Justice; The Criminal Justice System; Environmental Crime: A Sourcebook*, and *Policing and Violence*. Dr. Burns graduated from Florida State University in 1997 and has been at TCU ever since.

PART

I

AN INTRODUCTION TO MULTICULTURALISM

CHAPTER 1

INTRODUCTION

CHAPTER OBJECTIVES

After reading this chapter, you should be able to:

- Define the issues surrounding race and ethnicity in the United States
- Define concepts such as race, ethnicity, minority groups, multiculturalism, prejudice, and discrimination as they are used in the social science literature
- Contrast the debate of whether or not multiculturalism is a valuable idea in American society
- Understand how race and ethnicity play a role in the criminal justice system

  - According to a report by the Anti-Defamation League, White supremacist propaganda nearly tripled in 2018. This propaganda ranged from veiled White supremacist language to explicit racist, anti-Semitic, and Islamophobic fliers, stickers, banners, and posters.[1]
  - In Charlottesville, Virginia, what began as a protest by White nationalists of the removal of a Confederate statue resulted in riots and the death of a young woman. Two days after the incident, Trump stated:
    "I think there is blame on both sides....You had some very bad people in that group. But you also had people that were very fine people, on both sides." A year later, Trump attempted to walk back his controversial comments by tweeting: "The riots in Charlottesville a year ago resulted in senseless death and division. We must come together as a nation. I condemn all types of racism and acts of violence. Peace to ALL Americans!"[2]
  - In Texas in 2018, a man was charged with kidnapping and conspiracy for his involvement in attempts to lure gay men around the Dallas area for the purpose of carjacking, robbery, and hate crimes.[3]
  - In January 2019, three men were convicted of conspiracy to blow up an apartment complex in an attempt to kill Somali Muslim immigrants who lived there.[4]

Incidents such as these suggest that the United States has a long history of tension between different groups, particularly as they relate to race, ethnicity, sexual orientation, and religion. While many refer to America as a **melting pot**, or a society that blends together a variety of backgrounds and cultures into a cohesive whole, this is actually a misnomer. While there is a great deal of diversity in the United States, there is also considerable intergroup conflict. According to the U.S. Census Bureau, there are approximately 322 million people living in America, many of whom come from a host of different backgrounds.[5] This diversity is one of the defining features of American culture, and, at the same time, presents one of its more difficult and enduring problems.

On one hand, living in a society where everyone is the same has advantages. For instance, in small, **homogeneous societies**, people tend to know each other more intimately; they tend to see the world the same way, making disagreements less common; and the sense of conformity and treatment of others is more equitable. People in societies such as this tend to be figuratively "on the same page" with regard to social life. People also feel more connected to the larger society.

The downside to living in such a place, however, is that change happens slowly, if at all.

Additionally, people can be too intimately involved in each other's day-to-day lives, making privacy difficult. Ask anyone who lives in a small town: one of the things they like the most, and, at the same time, the least, about living there is that they are known by most people. In general, social control is easier to achieve in small towns because there is general agreement about what is right or wrong, good or bad, legal or illegal. It is what sociologist Émile Durkheim called the **collective conscience**.[6] In other words, the morality of a society is stronger because there is greater consensus on the meaning and importance of social life.

In contrast, in **heterogeneous societies**, people come from a wide range of backgrounds and experiences. They may come from other countries and participate in cultures with different attitudes, values, norms, and belief systems, and there tends to be a lower degree of consensus on how people should meet their social responsibilities. In other words, the

Life in small towns can be characterized as having a strong sense of social cohesion and collective conscience.

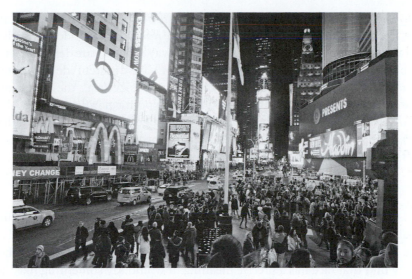

As life becomes more diverse, such as in major cities, there are different ideas about what is appropriate and acceptable. This can sometimes lead to disagreements about elements of social life.

people living in diverse societies tend to have different ideas about how the world works as well as their place in it. In Durkheim's terms, the collective conscience tends to be weaker since there is a lack of consensus as well as a generally lower degree of connectedness to the larger group.[7]

This also means that people tend to think of social relationships in a different way. Instead of building trust and intimacy, people tend to interact based on what the people around them can offer in meeting their individual needs. It is this distinction that surrounds much of the efforts relating to community policing. How does the government or the police department generate a sense of community in places where little collective conscience exists? How can police officers bring people together in a neighborhood to solve problems in the spirit of cooperation?

Living in a diverse society also means that some groups are going to acquire more economic, social, and political power than others. In fact, that is often how groups distinguish themselves: by their ownership or control of scarce resources. How does living in a diverse society create problems for groups that do not have much power? How are they treated? What are the consequences for being placed in a less powerful status? Much of these discussions relate to criminal justice in that differences in crime statistics, sentencing practices, the use of police discretion, and the overall treatment of minority group members are all symptoms of larger issues. While this book does not attempt to solve the problems of the unequal treatment of some groups, it does explore how some groups are treated when they come to the attention of the criminal justice system. This book also examines what it is like to be a member of a minority group and work within the system itself.

Prior to any discussion of how some groups are treated with regard to crime and criminal justice, a number of terms must be defined. In research methodology, this is called **operationalization**. In simple terms, it refers to the way concepts are defined. For example, when people talk about minority groups, they might have different ideas about what that really means. Some might think in terms of numerical size (e.g., the fewest number of redheads in a group of people), or they might focus on political influence (e.g., they do not have a lot of political power so they are not able to change policy or laws regulating certain behaviors). In the next few sections, we will spend some time defining our terms to ensure that readers understand what we mean by them.

RACE

Race has a variety of meanings, which can make its discussion confusing and difficult. In fact, probably the only thing about race that is clear is that people are confused about the proper use of the term. If one looked at the definition of race in a biology textbook, they would likely find that race has a precise meaning. It would say something like, "a biological race is a genetically isolated group characterized by a high degree of inbreeding that leads to distinctive gene frequencies. This distinctiveness is made most apparent by the presence of inherited physical characteristics that differentiate members of a group from others."[8] What does that mean? It means that, essentially, you can see the differences between people from different races.

However, it is very difficult to consider race in a strictly biological sense. Given that people have migrated over a wide range of geographic areas for hundreds of years, pure genetic types have not existed for some time, if ever. Think about it for a minute. Are there mutually exclusive races? Can you really tell where one race begins and another race ends? If so, on what basis is that difference identified? It is not as though a person can take a blood test to determine their race; such measures do not work with any real accuracy. Given interbreeding of races over the sweep of history, where, for example, many African Americans are light-skinned and a large number of Whites have African American ancestry, is it even possible to tell where to draw the line between races?

As an illustration, several years ago, Reverend Al Sharpton, a Black community activist who has spent his career exposing racism and the mistreatment of African Americans, was discovered to be related to former U.S. senator Strom Thurmond, a conservative Republican from South Carolina who spent a good part of his career maintaining the White-dominated status quo in the South.[9] This ironic familial tie serves as an example of the difficulty in separating races.

Though race is not a useful biological category, it is clear there are certain groups with similar traits. What is important is that race becomes significant, not because it matters in a biological sense, but because society has constructed it in such a way to symbolize certain attitudes, values, and beliefs about members who possess those physical traits. Race matters, in other words, because society has made it matter. This is sometimes referred to as the **social construction of race**. Every culture must determine which physical features are used to define membership in certain races (Americans typically use skin color) and also determine which attitudes and values are associated with a particular race. Simply put, people attach significance to the concept of race and consider it a real and important way to categorize people. As long as people believe that differences in certain physical traits are meaningful, they will act on those beliefs, which influence how they see and interact with others. Unfortunately, in doing so, people often rely on stereotypes to determine the behavior patterns of certain groups.

Another problem with using the term "race" is that it often suggests a type of homogeneity among the different races. When Americans talk about "Blacks" in the United States, they typically think of African Americans, or those whose ancestry dates back to American slavery. However, there are a host of differences between Jamaicans, Haitians, and even immigrants from various parts of Africa, which have little in common with African Americans. Similarly, another example might be to use the term "Whites" as if all are part of the same cultural group. There are significant differences between Polish Americans and Jewish Americans as well as Irish Americans and Italian Americans, yet we often do not see those differences when using those labels.[10]

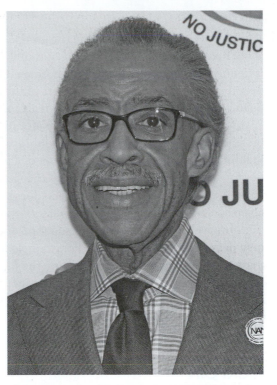

Al Sharpton, one of the more controversial figures in American society, actually has a historical linkage to a prominent and ultra-conservative Southern White family.

ETHNICITY

In its most simplistic form, an ethnic group is a collection of individuals and organizations identified by national origin, cultural distinctiveness, racial characteristics, or religious affiliation. This gets a bit tricky since most textbooks define ethnicity as being a distinction based on cultural heritage and racial groups based on physical features. However, because of the problems and disagreement on its scientific validity, many social scientists have avoided using the term "race" and instead use "ethnic group" to describe those groups commonly defined as racial. In the United States, African Americans, Chinese Americans, and Native Americans all have the elements of ethnic groups: a unique culture and in some cases even physical territory. But at the same time, most members of these groups are physically differently from Americans of European origin. Calling these groups "ethnic" seems reasonable because there are always consistent and significant cultural traits that set them apart from other groups.[11]

MINORITY GROUPS

This seems simple enough, right? The group with the fewest members. But minority status is not necessarily the result of being outnumbered. In the social sciences, a minority group is defined as a subordinate group whose members have significantly less control or power over their own lives than the members of the dominant group. While numerical size may be important and related, the issue is really one of power.[12]

In one sense, the idea of minority groups seems fair to people. After all, this is a democracy and the majority rules. The subordination of a minority, however, is more than its inability to rule over society. A member of a minority group experiences fewer opportunities for education, wealth, and success that go beyond any personal shortcoming they may have. In other words, a minority group does not share in proportion to its numbers what a given society defines as valuable.[13]

Moreover, being numerically superior does not guarantee power, control over one's own destiny, or majority status. For example, think of the Republic of South Africa during the apartheid regime. During that era, the majority of people in South Africa were Black, but under the apartheid system of government, Blacks did not have any significant control over their lives. In terms of making sense of minority groups, the following are important characteristics to consider.

CHECKPOINT

- It is very difficult to consider race in a strictly biological sense. Given that people have migrated over a wide range of geographic areas for hundreds of years, pure genetic types have not existed for some time, if ever. In its most simplistic form, an ethnic group is a collection of individuals and organizations identified by national origin, cultural distinctiveness, racial characteristics, or religious affiliation. In the social sciences, a minority group is defined as a subordinate group whose members have significantly less control or power over their own lives than the members of the dominant group. While numerical size may be important and related, the issue is really one of power.

DISTINGUISHING PHYSICAL OR CULTURAL TRAITS

Each society has its own arbitrary standard for determining which characteristics are most important in determining if a person belongs to a minority group. Examples might include skin color (as in the case of African Americans in the United States) or fluency in a certain language (as in the case of Hispanics/Latinos).

UNEQUAL TREATMENT BY THOSE IN POWER

As mentioned, minorities experience unequal treatment and have less power over their lives than members of a dominant group. Social inequality may be created or maintained in a variety of ways including prejudice, discrimination, and/or segregation. In extreme cases, the dominant group attempts to eliminate minorities completely; this is sometimes referred to as **extermination**.

During apartheid, Blacks in South Africa, who constituted a majority of the population, had little control over their own lives.

INVOLUNTARY MEMBERSHIP

Membership into a minority group is not voluntary. Often this involuntary membership is not changeable either. This is particularly true in American society, where skin color and other physical features often identify a minority.

SOLIDARITY OF MEMBERS

Perhaps due to the mistreatment or denial of equality, minority members are very conscious of their status. They also tend to be more sympathetic to other, similarly stigmatized groups. This can explain some of the relationships minority groups form with each other (e.g., women as a discriminated group and the LGBT community). At the same time, minority groups can also be hostile toward each other. An example might be some of the tension between African Americans and Hispanics, who, because of their unequal treatment, feel a sense of competition for power, however little it might be. Thus, there is a sense of exclusivity to most groups, but particularly those that have been mistreated or denied equal status in society. Because of their position in society, there is a need for affiliation.

In prisons, for example, inmates often segregate themselves by ethnicity. Let's say that a White male inmate is new to the prison but does not wish to join the Aryan Brotherhood gang (the noted White supremacist prison gang), preferring to remain on his own. The norm of gang solidarity is so strong that members from every gang in the prison will attempt to victimize that inmate until he makes the decision to join a particular gang. If the inmate does join the Aryan Brotherhood, his contact with African American or Hispanic gangs will be limited because they are perceived as a threat to him. However, all gang members in the prison, regardless of race, generally oppose the correctional staff and the administration. In this example, being a member of a group not only increases the cohesion between members and demonstrates the tension between the groups, it also identifies the commonality of the groups as they come together against a common adversary.

IN-GROUP MARRIAGE

As a general rule, most people marry people a lot like themselves in terms of religious background, educational levels, occupational levels, and ethnicity. A member of a dominant group is often unwilling to join a supposedly inferior minority group by marrying one of its members. Moreover, the group's sense of solidarity encourages marriages within the group and discourages out-group marriages.[14] This is why for so many years interracial marriage, particularly when Blacks married Whites, was considered unacceptable to many Americans.[15] This has since changed and interracial marriage is far more common today than in the past, but at one time there were laws that prohibited Blacks from marrying Whites.[16]

TYPES OF MINORITY GROUPS

In making the distinction between different types of minority groups, there is an immediate problem: what are the boundaries between the criteria? While race as a concept is defined by the physical distinctions between one group of people and another, there are instances where physical features are insufficient. For example, Hispanics/Latinos have some clearly defined physical features, but they are generally considered an ethnic group rather than a racial one. Similarly, Jews would normally be categorized as a religious group, but because their culture is such an essential component to their identity, experts tend to classify them as an ethnic group. This is why, as mentioned earlier, using the term "ethnicity" seems more reasonable. However, the thing to remember is that this distinction is used as a general way of categorizing minorities and should not be taken as definitive or complete.

RACIAL GROUPS

This term is reserved for those minorities who are classified according to obvious physical differences. The crucial words are "obvious" and "physical." What is obvious? Hair color? Earlobe shape? As mentioned, each society defines that which is considered obvious. In the United States, skin color is perhaps the main characteristic in determining the difference between one race and another. In the United States, minority races include Blacks, Native Americans, and Asian Americans.

ETHNIC GROUPS

Minority groups who are designated by their ethnicity are distinguished from the dominant group on the basis of cultural differences such as language, attitudes toward marriage, food habits, and so on. Ethnic groups are set apart from others because of their national origin or distinctive cultural patterns. Ethnic groups in the United States include a grouping that we refer to collectively as *Hispanics* or *Latinos*. While there are distinguishing physical features that might cause someone to consider this group a racial category, because language and heritage is such a fundamental part of the Hispanic and Latino experience, they are classified as an ethnic group instead. This includes Puerto Ricans, Cubans, Mexicans, and other Latin Americans in the United States. European ethnic groups include: Irish, German, Polish, Norwegian, and Italian, among others.

RELIGIOUS GROUPS

The third basis for minority status is association with a religion other than the dominant faith. As mentioned, Jews are excluded from this category and placed among ethnic groups because in their case, culture is a more important defining trait than religious ideology. Jews share a cultural tradition that goes beyond theology. In this sense, it is appropriate to view them as an ethnic group rather than as members of a religious faith.

GENDER GROUPS

The final attribute that divides dominant and subordinate groups is gender: males are the social majority and females, although more numerous, are relegated to the position of social minority. Women are a minority even though they do not exhibit all the characteristics outlined earlier. For instance, women encounter prejudice and discrimination and are physically visible. Group membership is involuntary and women who are members of racial and ethnic minorities face special challenges to achieving equality. They suffer from a form of double jeopardy because they belong to two separate minority groups: a racial or ethnic group plus a subordinate gender group.[17]

CHECKPOINT

- Minority groups who are designated by their ethnicity are distinguished from the dominant group on the basis of cultural differences such as language, attitudes toward marriage, food habits, and so on. Ethnic groups are set apart from others because of their national origin or distinctive cultural patterns. A racial group consists of those minorities who are classified according to obvious physical differences. The third basis for minority status is association with a religion other than the dominant faith. The final attribute that divides dominant and subordinate groups is gender: males are the social majority and females, although more numerous, are relegated to the position of social minority.

CREATING SUBORDINATE GROUPS

You might be wondering how this all happens. How did society get to a point where there are all these groups and some of them are mistreated? You may be also wondering why such groups might stay in this country, given the way they have been treated. These are good questions and some of the answers are found in how some minority groups came to this country in the first place. There are really three situations that are likely to lead to the construction of a minority group: migration, annexation, and colonialism.

MIGRATION

"Migration" is the general term to describe any transfer of population. There are really two types of migration, where people come into a country. **Voluntary migration** consists of those people who immigrate to a new country willingly, looking for a better life. Upon arrival however, they often find themselves in the position of social minority. The immigrant is often set apart from the dominant group by cultural or physical traits and/or religious affiliation.

Although many may come to the new country voluntarily, the choice to leave the home country is often due to a lack of options. Wars, political unrest, or economic disasters in native countries (such as the potato crop failure in Ireland and Germany in the 1840s,) are often the catalysts behind migration. In contrast, **involuntary migration** occurs, for instance, when individuals have been brought into a new land as slaves.

ANNEXATION

There are times when countries will attach land as part of a war victory or conquest. An example would be the treaty that ended the Mexican-American war in 1848, which gave the United States California, Utah, Nevada, most of New Mexico, and parts of Arizona, Wyoming, and Colorado. When annexation occurs, the dominant group usually makes a considerable effort to force a change in the attitudes, values, and beliefs of the minority groups.

COLONIALISM

This is the most frequent way for one group of people to dominate another. Colonialism is the cultural, political, economic, and social domination of a people by a foreign power for an extended period of time. Unlike annexation, it does not involve physical incorporation into the dominant people's nation. Relations between the colonial nation and the colonized people are similar to those between a dominant group and exploited subordinate groups. The colonial subjects are generally limited to menial jobs, and the profits from their labor and from natural resources benefit members of the ruling class. Interestingly, while most of the countries that were colonies prior to World War I have achieved political independence, many of them could not develop their own industries and technology. As a result, they remained dependent on their dominators long after they separated from them politically. This dependence and domination is known as **neocolonialism**.[18]

CHECKPOINT

- How did society get to a point where there are all these groups and some of them are mistreated? You may be also wondering why such groups might stay in this country, given the way they have been treated. Three main reasons are: migration, which is the general term to describe any transfer of population; annexation, such as in those instances when countries will attach land as part of a war or conquest; and colonialism, which is the cultural, political, economic, and social domination of a people by a foreign power for an extended period of time.

THE CONSEQUENCES OF SUBORDINATE GROUP STATUS

What consequences do members feel as being a part of a minority group? Essentially, there are six outcomes for minority groups: extermination, expulsion, secession, segregation, fusion, and assimilation.

Extermination is the most extreme way of dealing with a subordinate group. Today the term **genocide** is used to describe the deliberate, systematic killing of an entire people group or nation. While it has been associated with Nazi Germany, other forms of ethnic cleansing have occurred in other parts of the world. **Expulsion** is another extreme consequence of being a minority group. As will be discussed in the chapter on Native Americans, essentially, the U.S. government in the nineteenth century drove many tribes out of their tribal land and forced them to live in uninhabitable locations. This created problems with the physical health of many Native Americans that actually resulted in the death of many members of this group, which might be considered a form of extermination.[19]

Secession is another strategy, whereby minority groups sometimes want to depart from their country or at least have an opportunity to create their own society. For example, Pakistan was created in 1947 when India was partitioned. The predominantly Muslim areas in the north became Pakistan, making India predominantly Hindu.

Segregation of minority groups usually occurs when the other strategies are not possible or effective. This happens when the dominant group is forced to coexist with the minority group. However, the way the problem is addressed is to simply limit contact between the dominant group and minority members. In the United States the extent of racial isolation at one time was significant, especially between Whites and African Americans. An analysis of the 2010 census showed that neighborhood segregation is still problematic despite increases in diversity in the United States. This is especially true in the largest U.S. cities over the past twenty years. African Americans remain concentrated in segregated neighborhoods and immigrants still settle into particular neighborhoods where others like them are located.[20] This pattern is not limited to impoverished inner cities: they include all-Black middle-class or affluent suburban neighborhoods as well. Moreover, residential segregation exists for other minorities, such as Hispanics and Asian Americans, but the trend is usually less profound than that for African Americans.[21]

Cultural fusion is the goal of multiculturalism, where minority and majority groups come together to form an entirely new group. An example of cultural fusion occurred

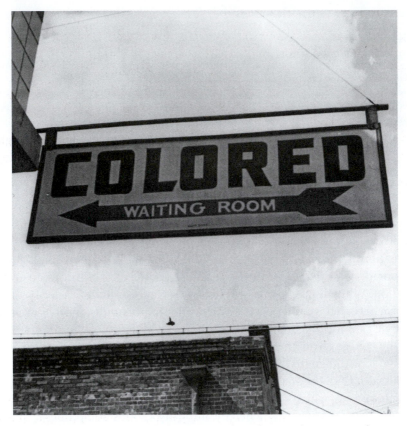

Even when minority groups attempt to assimilate, there can be an unequal access to opportunities for success.

during the first part of the twentieth century, where the public believed that the United States was a cultural melting pot. The public became convinced that America should meld all of its unique cultures into one unifying ideology. This, people said, would eliminate racism, bigotry, discrimination, and inter-group conflict. However, as mentioned, despite the use of the term in popular culture, it is a mistake to think of the United States as an ethnic mixing bowl. While there are superficial signs of fusion, more significant trends indicate that Americans may think little of the contribution of subordinate groups.[22]

Finally, **assimilation** is the process by which the subordinate group takes on the characteristics of the dominant group and is eventually accepted as part of that group. In the United States assimilation is difficult because the group must give up their cultural traditions to become a part of a different and often condescending culture. Members of minority groups often discover that even when these changes are made, the dominant culture still casts them in a secondary position. The result leaves the minority member in a position of marginality: they do not belong to the dominant culture, nor are they accepted completely by their native one.[23]

PREJUDICE AND DISCRIMINATION

Prejudice and discrimination are closely intertwined, so much so that people are likely to view them as the same thing. In reality they are quite distinct. **Prejudice** is a negative attitude toward certain people based solely on their membership in a particular group. Individuals are "prejudged" on the basis of whatever undesirable characteristic the whole group is assumed to have. **Discrimination** refers to behavior, particularly the unequal treatment of people, based on their membership in a particular group.[24]

The relationship between prejudice and discrimination is complex. Although they are likely to go together, as Robert K. Merton demonstrated in the following typology, sometimes they do not. In fact, there are four different ways or permutations, that people may combine prejudice and discrimination. The **unprejudiced non-discriminator** is the most desirable from the point of view of American political and social values. This individual accepts other racial or ethnic groups both in belief and in practice. They embrace the idea of difference, of cultural diversity as a healthy concept, and do not try to impose their own cultural and social ideas on to others. The **prejudiced discriminator** has negative feelings toward a particular group or groups and translates these sentiments into unequal and negative treatment of people in that group. Examples might include members of the Neo-Nazi Party or members of the Ku Klux Klan. White supremacists in general typically have strong attitudes against Blacks and other minority groups, and they advocate segregated schools and neighborhoods.

These two types are relatively easy to understand. One is a person who accepts all people as they are, without any judgment, while the other is a person who discriminates against others. Hate groups are smaller in size but intense in their feelings toward anyone other than people like themselves. More subtle forms of discrimination and prejudice emerge with the latter two linkages. For instance, the **prejudiced non-discriminator** is the type of person who might be called a "closet bigot"—someone who is prejudiced against members of some groups but does not translate these attitudes into discriminatory practices. A landlord, for example, may be prejudiced against Asian Americans yet still rent apartments to them because of laws forbidding housing discrimination.

Perhaps the most difficult to grasp is the **unprejudiced discriminator**. A person in this category treats members of some groups unequally not because they have any personal animosity toward them but simply because it is advantageous to do so.[25] In the 1970s, for example, it was common for real estate agents to engage in "steering" of minority clients. Steering involves efforts to convince minorities to buy homes in predominantly minority neighborhoods as homeowners in all-White communities feared a decline in property values if African Americans moved in. Since real estate agents wanted return business from affluent Whites who would likely buy more property in the future, agents tried to avoid showing homes in some neighborhoods or highlighting the advantages to a minority couple of living in a more mixed community.[26]

While Merton's typology helps to gain a better sense of the relationship between prejudice and discrimination, what it does not account for is what is referred to as **institutional discrimination**, which is the type of discrimination built into the structure of society. This is dangerous because it is the type of mistreatment of certain groups whereby the people engaging in the behavior do not realize they are doing it. In fact, people who engage in institutional discrimination might even think that they are treating everyone fairly.

For example, at one time in the United States many police departments and fire departments had height and weight requirements for their candidates. Because they treated all potential candidates similarly, civil service commissions felt that they did not discriminate against any particular group. However, what we now know is that the criteria were biased. Obviously, women, Hispanics, Asians, and others were being systematically excluded from those jobs even though there was no legitimate reason for doing so. Institutional discrimination is dangerous because it can be deceptive and give the appearance that everyone is treated fairly. As a result of lawsuits, many police and fire departments were required to remove any criteria that were not clearly related to the performance of duty.[27]

RACISM

What about racism? This is perhaps one of the most commonly used terms in the discussion of minority groups and is the basis for a great deal of social policy in this country with regard to their treatment. **Racism** is the belief that people are divided into distinct hereditary groups that are innately different from each other in their behavior and abilities.[28] Such a definition also means that groups can be ranked as superior or inferior on the basis of those abilities and behavior. The presumed superiority of some groups is used

---

ENVIRONMENTAL RACISM

A chemical manufacturing company wishes to relocate its new factory in your small town. You initially think of the social and economic benefits that will accompany the relocation, including better schools and more jobs. However, the chemical waste produced by the company may have detrimental impacts on your community, including harmful impacts on the river in which you and your children swim and the water you drink. You begin to realize that you cannot enjoy the social and economic benefits without your health. Your initial optimism wanes, and you and your neighbors protest against the relocation of the company. The company offers financial incentives for all residents if permission to relocate is granted. Most of your neighbors have little money, and eventually they cease protesting and support the relocation.

Historically, the United States and most other countries have shown considerable neglect of environmental protection. Recent societal concerns regarding global warming have drawn attention to protecting the environment. Part of the neglect of the environment involved the under-regulation of environmental waste sites. Perhaps the most famous incident of environmental neglect is Love Canal, in Niagara Falls, New York, where extensive dumping of hazardous waste led to numerous health problems among residents in the area.

The location of hazardous waste sites has been controversial. Unfortunately for many minorities and lower-class citizens, hazardous waste sites have historically been placed in their neighborhoods. With limited financial and political power to fight against this practice, poor minorities have disproportionately been the target of what is called **environmental racism**. This involves the under-regulation of environmental laws, and the disproportionate placement of hazardous materials in minority neighborhoods. Similarly, **environmental justice** refers to attempts to treat all groups, regardless of race, ethnicity, or income, equally with regard to environmental protection and laws. Efforts toward environmental justice also include meaningful involvement on behalf of individuals who are potentially or currently affected by environmental harms.

The environmental justice movement began in the 1960s during the civil rights movement; however, it wasn't until the 1990s that the federal government took substantial action to correct injustices. The Office of Environmental Equity within the U.S. Environmental Protection Agency (EPA) was created in 1992. In 1994 the name was changed to the Office of Environmental Justice. The federal government, specifically the EPA, has made notable progress in correcting environmental injustices; however, there is still concern among researchers that the least powerful groups in society continue to be the target of harmful environmental under-regulation.

to legitimate the unequal distribution of resources as well as the mistreatment of groups thought to be inferior to others. Because these traits are innate, a misguided conclusion that is drawn by some people is that since the traits are unchangeable, those at the top are given their position by some sort of natural selection process. In other words, those that have power "deserve" it while those who are not successful are used as examples of the group's inferiority.

While inherently **ethnocentric**—that is, having the tendency to judge other cultures by the standards of one's own, thinking the latter is superior[29]—racist thought is not confined only to those groups where the physical and social abilities are distinct, as is the case with the differences between Whites and Blacks in the United States. Rather, racist beliefs are those that describe any behavior that justifies superiority or attributes hatefulness or exploitation to hereditary traits. In this way, racism is not confined only to racial groups but is applicable to any ethnic group. Racism can pertain to Italian Americans, French Canadians, Jewish Americans, or Polish Americans just as easily as it can apply to African Americans or Asian Americans. In light of this, some experts have called for omitting the term "racism" for the same reasons that the term "race" is too vague. Rather, these experts contend that the use of the term **ethnicism** is more appropriate, because racism applies to all types of ethnic groups.[30]

CHECKPOINT

- Prejudice is a negative attitude toward certain people based solely on their membership in a particular group. Individuals are "prejudged" on the basis of whatever undesirable characteristic the whole group is assumed to have. Discrimination refers to behavior, particularly the unequal treatment of people, because they are members of a particular group. Racism is the belief that people are divided into distinct hereditary groups that are innately different in their behavior and abilities

WHERE DOES MULTICULTURALISM FIT INTO THE DISCUSSION?

At this point you may be confused about all the terms that define certain groups and you may be wondering how it all relates to the differences in arrests, sentences, and other aspects of the criminal justice process. You may even be wondering why we cannot all just get along. You might even wonder why we should be thinking about multiculturalism and why people in America have trouble living here. After all, people from different cultures should be able to simply adapt to our standards and culture, right? Is multiculturalism bad since it means there is no one standard to follow, or is it a good thing to hear and be exposed to different perspectives on the same issues? After all, the world is a pretty boring place if everyone thinks, believes, and acts the same way. These are great questions and we will try to present this debate, although it is part of a much larger discussion. The remainder of this book highlights the issues stemming from the differential treatment of certain groups and how it impacts not only crime and criminal justice, but the time, energy, and resources dedicated to dealing with them. Thus, it is in everyone's interest to at least know what the problems are, how extensively they affect people, and the predictions for the future. We hope that by the end of this text, you will have a greater understanding of the issues.

IS MULTICULTURALISM IN AMERICA A GOOD THING?

While some experts argue that cultural diversity enhances the social harmony that exists in society, other experts contend that the diversity serves not as a uniting point for Americans, but as a source of racial tension and conflict. One of the challenges Americans face is the tendency to engage in ethnocentrism—Americans tend to believe that their culture is far superior to all others in the world. Americans also tend to be ethnocentric within their own borders as well in comparing one group to another.

On one hand, ethnocentrism can be a unifying mechanism, as was the case in the September 11, 2001, terrorist attacks against the United States. As a result of the attack, most Americans united against the terrorists, and a strong sense of compassion and cohesion was created in the United States. However, at the same time, the September 11 attacks also created problems when many Americans began to believe that anyone who was from the Middle East (or even looked like they were from there) suddenly became suspected of being a terrorist. It is interesting to note that prior to 9/11, racial profiling of African Americans by police officers was one of the most controversial topics in criminal justice. However, after the attacks, the profiling of people of Middle Eastern descent appeared to be acceptable to many Americans.

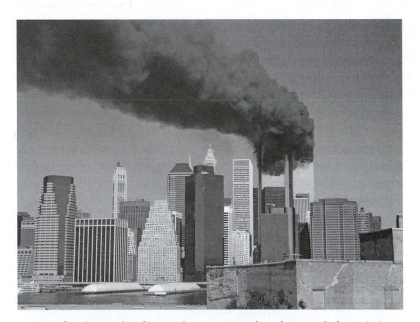

As seen after the attacks of September 11, 2001, when threatened, the majority group often targets all members of a minority group, not just the individuals responsible.

Thus, the discussion of the value of **multiculturalism**, which can be defined in many ways, but includes the embracing of cultural diversity, a willingness to coexist with people from different backgrounds and cultures, and the celebration of difference, centers on whether it divides a society or unifies it.

Multiculturalism Divides People

In many countries, such as the United States, there exists a strong national identity or national character. This means that as Americans, people can identify with being part of the larger collectivity. While there are people from many different backgrounds and preferences, there remains a unifying theme that unites them. It is similar to baseball fans: people may support different teams and/or players, but they are all united by the love of the game. However, some people feel that as a society grows more diverse, that national character or identity loses its influence over people. This is especially true for people who are already afraid that the country's character is being diluted for the sake of diversity and individualism.

Critics of multiculturalism argue that when a society becomes more heterogeneous, cultural standards—the very essence that gives a country its character and identity—begin to fall. They argue that in the interest of protecting the different backgrounds and abilities of its members, educational standards are reduced, resulting in a decline in talent and innovative thinking. Opponents to multiculturalism also argue that this threatens the economic and political viability of the United States, as mediocrity becomes the norm rather than demanding excellence from everyone. In this view, it is only when minority groups are taught to accept and validate the majority culture that any type of success can be achieved. This is particularly important as the discussion turns to language, one of the most important components to a country's culture.[31] In sum, opponents of multiculturalism argue that the celebration of cultural differences does little to foster a sense of cultural identity; leads to the reduction of important educational, economic, and political standards of accountability; and weakens the overall collective conscience or morality of a society.

Multiculturalism Fosters Discrimination

A second and related area that critics of multiculturalism point to is that discrimination between groups is more likely. As multiculturalism celebrates differences in backgrounds and experiences, it also segregates people into categories or groups. While the intended goal, of course, is to strengthen and validate minority groups and their values, attitudes, and belief systems, the result is that making distinctions between groups may hasten hatred rather than promoting appreciation of the differences between groups. At the very least, it creates a climate where inequality and discrimination based on membership in those groups are more likely. Opponents to multiculturalism argue that if society desires to reduce discrimination, prejudice, and inequality, it comes not by celebrating the differences but by galvanizing around the similarities.

Related to this is the problem of **reverse discrimination**. As societies attempt to remedy past mistakes in the treatment of minority groups, one solution is to have current members provide some sort of restitution or compensation for deeds of the past. This form of payback can easily create a climate of tension rather than of restoration. An example of such practices includes programs like **affirmative action**, which were designed to remedy the historical mistreatment of some groups by providing various types of preferential treatment. While the current practice of affirmative action is not what was originally intended, the result has led some people to feel they are being punished for something over which they had no control. In effect, they are being asked to remedy the behaviors of their ancestors, and this breeds hostility rather than harmony and equality toward minority members.

Related to this is the fact that multiculturalism also creates a climate in which minority groups can adopt a victim mentality. This means that as society calls for more equity and the fair distribution of economic, social, and political power, some minority group members may use that as a justification for failing to meet their responsibilities. An example might be that an individual or group might contend that the reason they have not found adequate employment is due to the legacy of slavery when, in fact, it is a result of their unwillingness to look for jobs. Such an attitude can cause even the most ardent defender of past injustices to feel they are now being exploited.

Multiculturalism Prevents Equality

A third argument against multiculturalism is that it places too heavy an emphasis on the differences between groups rather than their similarities. This discourages assimilation by minority groups and encourages them to remain isolated from the larger society. This isolation can result in people being less willing or less able to get along with people from other ethnic, racial, or religious backgrounds. As this isolationism increases, it leads certain groups to feel as though they need less from the larger society in terms of skills, talents, education, and opportunities. As a result, members do not pursue these opportunities and remain locked into certain professions or jobs and do not become upwardly mobile. This not only creates an ethnic distinction between minority groups and others, it also promotes class distinctions. This is significant because there are many experts who argue that social class, not race or ethnicity, is the key to achieving social, economic, and political equality.[32]

The Value of Multiculturalism

The preceding discussion can easily be taken out of context to mean that everyone should think, look, and act like everyone else, lest society go into a cultural tailspin. Of course, there are challenges to living in a culturally diverse society, but this is a far cry from saying that unless we limit differences, we are doomed to a culture without an identity.

The other side of the debate about multiculturalism is that it creates a climate in which difference is not something to fear or reject—it actually promotes innovative thinking. America has been and continues to be a culturally diverse society. This leaves us with only a few options: to remove everyone who does not think, look, and act like the majority, which is unrealistic and socially dangerous (e.g., who gets to decide?), or we can find a way to use people's different backgrounds and talents toward something positive and useful. While it can be tempting to sit around and complain about what is bad about diversity, it serves little constructive purpose. Rather, the more productive way appears to be to accept that it exists and find ways to use it to society's advantage.

In reality, there are many experts who believe that America's national identity is the composition of a collection of regional and local cultures. What makes America unique, they say, is that while there may be something of a national identity, it is made up of so many different backgrounds and cultural preferences that to section out certain parts would be virtually impossible. Perhaps more importantly, cultural diversity is central to the tenets of living in a democratic society. How can people claim to be free if they are constrained in terms of what they think and believe simply because it is different from the majority? Further, there is a historic precedent in this country for tolerating ethnic diversity. While we also have a history of the mistreatment of certain groups, we have, at least in theory, always accepted people from different cultures.

In its purest form, the arguments in favor of multiculturalism center on integration and social cohesion. While it is true that many Americans, especially those living in large American cities, can feel isolated and lacking in a sense of community, who do not know their neighbors and feel disconnected in general, one of the things that binds people together is their commonality. One of those strands might be religion while another could be ethnicity. Ethnic ancestry is said by some experts to give minorities a feeling of community—making ethnic identities a method by which a national identity can occur. Thus, not only does ethnic group membership help the individual to psychologically feel more connected to his or her larger community, it can bind them into a larger sense of what some call "peoplehood." For example, a person with an Italian background might feel better connected to their neighbors if they lived near a neighborhood comprised mostly of Italian Americans, such as the Little Italy enclave in New York City. By being better integrated at a local level, the person might also begin to affiliate with other groups, such as the local Catholic Church, which further expands their circle and sense of identity. The person then begins to consider their place in the larger society as a New Yorker or more generally as an American, which further stimulates their integration to the larger society. The process begins, however, at the micro level, where the person uses their cultural heritage as a starting point to affiliate with others and to begin to feel as though their place in the world matters.[33]

In the end, the process of multiculturalism has a host of implications for society. While at extremes it can become problematic, in this age of globalization, where every country is connected politically, socially, and economically to every other one, society in general will continue to diversify. This can be healthy growth, where Americans learn to celebrate differences and to evaluate others not on their differences but on their commonality, or we can fear change and difference and compartmentalize their lives because they feel threatened by some groups. The misuse of power or the tendency to exploit or take advantage of others begins with an initial perception of other groups. Many times impressions of people are based on small bits of information or on stereotypes of what is known about some members of particular groups.

In the next chapter we will discuss group dynamics and how we interpret people's behavior, which influences our interactions with them. As we will see, and as the subsequent chapters on the treatment of other minority groups in the criminal justice system show, often our initial perceptions lead us to believe certain groups have attitudes, values, and beliefs regardless of whether any evidence exists to verify that perception. Unfortunately, when such perceptions translate into social policy, judicial and police practices, or in how juries decide the facts of a case, the consequences are significant and can even be life-threatening for minorities.

For those students interested in criminology or the study of the causes of crime, many of the theories can be used not only to explain why a particular person engages in unlawful acts, but also to understand the way minority groups are treated. That is, some theories argue that because they are exploited or denied opportunities to achieve success, some minority groups engage in criminal acts either to achieve some level of success (e.g., strain or disorganization theories) or out of frustration for the way they have been identified by others (e.g., labeling theory).

Other theories offer insight into the way people's perceptions of minority groups influence their lack of understanding of cultural differences (e.g., cultural conflict theory) or suggest that the person engaging in an unlawful act has rejected mainstream society and made a poor choice when they decided to commit a crime (e.g., Hirschi and Gottfredson's general theory of crime). Still other explanations for the involvement of minorities in the criminal justice system may be due to the perceptions of minorities by participants in the system, such as the police, judges, or even the public when they serve as jurors. Thus, our goal in this text is not to contend that criminals are not responsible because they were oppressed or mistreated over the sweep of history, or to say that the criminal justice system is hopelessly racist. Rather, we believe that there are a host of factors that explain the trends in crime data, including racism and social history, that get us closer to understanding the interplay between crime, minorities, and criminal justice.

Do minorities get arrested because they commit more crimes? Maybe, but it could also be due to the fact that the police spend more time looking for criminals, and minorities fit the profile officers have been trained to identify. Do African Americans get different sentences for similar crimes as Whites? In some cases, but the reasons for that may not simply be that judges are racist and intentionally hand out tougher sentences because they do not like African Americans. Human behavior is very complex and the reasons why people act as they do is difficult to determine. Unlike other scientific disciplines, where the laws regulating the universe have been discovered, social behavior remains a mystery in many ways. What is known is that a variety of factors play into a person's decision to engage in certain acts and some of these factors have historical, economic, political, and social influences. As the next chapter describes, one of the most important factors in understanding social behavior is found in the way people communicate with each other. As you will see, interaction often consists of symbolic cues that must be interpreted correctly in order for communication to be effective. However, a crucial component of that process is an understanding of the meaning of those cues and gestures. Misunderstandings, miscommunications, and preconceived ideas about what a person means are not only the basis of poor relationships, they are at the heart of problems such as discrimination, racism, and the mistreatment of certain groups.

One final important point is needed. Americans live in an information-saturated age. Scholars, reporters, practitioners, and the general public are much more educated about issues and problems now than at any other time in our history. As a result, they increasingly demand "proof" or "data" to support claims of a practice, a trend, or the effectiveness of a particular strategy, or to justify a change in resource allocation. Consequently, researchers have spent a great deal of time studying the criminal justice system and the problems contained within it.

However, as you will see in some of the chapters, although we use the most current data available to describe trends and patterns, in some cases the research is limited or dated. It may come as some surprise to students to learn that there are times when the information on a particular topic is sparse or has not been updated in recent years. This is particularly true with some government publications. However, know that we have reviewed the literature and what we offer is based on what is currently known.

SUMMARY

The issue of race and ethnicity in the United States remains an important factor in understanding social interaction, relationships, and the fabric of American culture. While many people like to think that issues such as racism, discrimination, and prejudice are a thing of the past, there is ample evidence to suggest that these problems remain a critical component of social life. It is also the case that many people misunderstand or misuse certain terms when discussing race-related issues. This chapter outlined the way social scientists operationalize terms such as "prejudice," "discrimination," "minority groups," "racism," "race," and "ethnicity." It also attempted to explain how minority groups are created, how and why they are mistreated, and the debate about the value of multiculturalism in American society. On one hand, some experts believe that too diverse a society dilutes its national identity and the social cohesion that comes from people seeing the world similarly. On the other hand, multiculturalism celebrates people from different backgrounds and offers insight into human nature as well as how groups can coexist peacefully and equitably. For students of criminal justice, the treatment of minority groups is central to understanding criminal behavior and how the administration of justice affects people without power. Many of the theories to explain crime can be used in part to describe the motivation of some offenders, but they also are framed in light of criminals' minority status. Thus, any discussion of crime in American society must contain some attention to the way certain groups are treated by the dominant culture.

YOU MAKE THE CALL

Imagine you are on vacation for the first time in a foreign country. You are sitting in a restaurant with your partner trying to figure out the menu when another customer comes in to the dining area, loudly complaining about why the menu is not in English and why so many things are different from American culture. The restaurant server looks at you and asks if you know this person...probably because they are American as well. How do you respond to the server, knowing that your answer might impact the quality of the service and the food you receive?

Do you: Offer insight into the nature of ethnocentrism, prejudice, and discrimination? Or do you plead ignorance and say you don't know the person at all? Or do you confront the other patron and remind them that their behavior impacts you as well? What are the possible consequences of each possibility?

KEY TERMS

affirmative action

assimilation

collective conscience

cultural fusion

discrimination

environmental justice

environmental racism

ethnicism

ethnocentric

expulsion

extermination

genocide

heterogeneous society

homogeneous society

institutional discrimination

involuntary migration

melting pot

multiculturalism

neocolonialism

operationalization

prejudice

prejudiced discriminator

prejudiced non-discriminator

racism

reverse discrimination

secession

segregation

social construction of race

unprejudiced discriminator

unprejudiced non-discriminator

voluntary migration

DISCUSSION QUESTIONS

1. What role does diversity play in the strength of the collective conscience or morality of a society?
2. Why is it so difficult to identify examples of institutional discrimination? If rules apply to everyone, shouldn't that be enough to prevent unfair treatment? Can you give examples of institutional discrimination?
3. Are Americans inherently ethnocentric? Do Americans always believe their culture is better than everyone else's? Why or why not?
4. Is multiculturalism really a bad thing, as some experts have suggested? Does it really dilute the "American identity"? Why or why not?

FOR FURTHER READING

Duneier, M. *Ghetto: The Invention of a Place, the History of an Idea.* New York: Farrar, Straus, and Giroux, 2016.

Durkheim, E. *The Division of Labor in Society.* New York: The Free Press, 1893.

West, C. *Race Matters.* Boston, MA: Harvard University Press, 2000.

Wilson, W. J. *When Work Disappears.* Chicago, IL: University of Chicago Press, 1997.

NOTES

1. Claire Hanson, "White Supremacist Propaganda Efforts Skyrocketed in 2018," *U.S. News and World Report*, March 5, 2019. Available at: https://www.usnews.com/news/national-news/articles/2019-03-05/white-supremacist-propaganda-efforts-skyrocketed-in-2018
2. Rick Klein, "Trump Said 'Blame on Both Sides' in Charlottesville, Now the Anniversary Puts Him on the Spot," *ABC News*, August, 12, 2018. Available at: https://abcnews.go.com/Politics/trump-blame-sides-charlottesville-now-anniversary-puts-spot/story?id=57141612
3. U.S. Department of Justice, Federal Bureau of Investigation, *Hate Crime Examples*, March 28, 2019. Available at: https://www.justice.gov/hatecrimes/hate-crimes-case-examples

4. Ibid.

5. Robert Schlesinger, "The Size of the U.S. and the World in 2016," *US News & World Report*, January 5, 2016. Available at: http://www.usnews.com/opinion/blogs/robert-schlesinger/articles/2016-01-05/us-population-in-2016-according-to-census-estimates-322-762-018

6. D. Jary and J. Jary, *Collins Dictionary of Sociology* (New York: Harper Collins, 1991), 93.

7. Ibid.

8. J. Scott and G. Marshall, *A Dictionary of Sociology*, 3rd ed. (New York: Oxford University Press, 2005). Available at: http://www.oxfordreference.com/view/10.1093/acref/9780199533008.001.0001/acref-9780199533008-e-1859?rskey=BVTpmt&result=1859

9. R. Shulman, "Sharpton's Ancestor Was Owned by Thurmond's," *Washington Post*, February 26, 2007, A01.

10. Scott and Marshall, *Dictionary of Sociology*.

11. Ibid.

12. Ibid.

13. Ibid.

14. Ibid.

15. See, e.g., R. McNamara, M. Tempenis, and B. Walton, *Crossing the Line: Interracial Couples in the South* (Westport, CT: Praeger, 1999).

16. Ibid.

17. Ibid.

18. Scott and Marshall, *Dictionary of Sociology*.

19. Ibid.

20. Jeff Nesbit, "Study of Census Data Finds a Segregated America, Especially for Blacks," *US News & World Report*, July 24, 2012. Available at http://www.usnews.com/news/blogs/at-the-edge/2012/07/24/study-of-census-data-finds-a-segregated-america-especially-for-blacks

21. Scott and Marshall, *A Dictionary of Sociology*.

22. Ibid.

23. Ibid.

24. Ibid.

25. R. K. Merton, "Discrimination and the American Creed," in Robert MacIver (ed.), *Discrimination and National Welfare* (New York: Harper and Row, 1949), 99–126.

26. CivilRights.Org staff, *Report: Racial Steering into Segregated Neighborhoods Most Prevalent Form of Housing Discrimination* (April 7, 2006). Accessed July 25, 2007, at http://www.civilrights.org/fairhousing/laws/report-racial-steering-into-segregated-neighborhoods-most-prevalent-form-of-housing- discrimination-1.html

27. See, e.g., Smith v. City of East Cleveland, 363 F. Supp. 1131 (N.D. Ohio 1973).

28. Scott and Marshall, *Dictionary of Sociology*.

29. Ibid.

30. Ibid.

31. Ibid.

32. W. J. Wilson, *When Work Disappears* (Chicago: University of Chicago Press, 1997). See also W. J. Wilson, *The Declining Significance of Race* (Chicago: University of Chicago Press, 2012).

33. Tepperman and Blain, *Think Twice*.

CHAPTER 2

GROUP DYNAMICS, COMMUNICATION, AND SOCIAL INTERACTION

CHAPTER OBJECTIVES

After reading this chapter, you should be able to:

- Recognize Erving Goffman's contribution to our understanding of social interaction
- Understand what constitutes a group
- Understand the basics of communication and the communication process
- Discuss the significance of verbal and nonverbal communication in the criminal justice system
- Identify the importance of status and roles in justice-based practices

Part of the problem with discrimination, prejudice, racism, and other forms of mistreatment of people is a result of a poor or limited understanding of the values, attitudes, and beliefs of the members of different groups. Limited or no contact with various groups can lead to stereotypical ideas about the motives, beliefs, and behaviors of these groups. Conversely, if the interaction that takes place between different groups tends to be negative, this can lead to problems in understanding behavior. Recall that in the first chapter we mentioned that a great deal of social interaction is ambiguous: we do not always know what people are thinking or intending; all we see is their behavior. This means that the lens through which we filter those actions becomes critical to how we understand and respond to their behavior.

An important thing to remember is how people present themselves when they act. Most of the time we are trying to convey a symbolic message with our words, facial expressions, and body language. However, there are a host of instances when what we want to convey and how that is interpreted are incongruent or misunderstood. While we can easily understand the problems that occur when groups from different cultures interact, we should note that all of us have trouble at times interacting with each other, even those we know. Many conflicts originate from the failure to effectively communicate, or misinterpretation of communication. For instance, consider a time when you texted or emailed someone who misinterpreted the meaning of your message. You may have meant one thing, but the receiver interpreted your message in another way. Certainly, many misinterpreted messages do not end in conflict, but there are times when they do. We begin this chapter with recognition of the work of Erving Goffman, who undoubtedly changed the way we recognize and understand human interaction. His work helps us to understand the interactions between the criminal justice system and those who enter the system.

ERVING GOFFMAN AND THE NATURE OF SOCIAL INTERACTION

In trying to explain the nature of social interaction, Erving Goffman, in his classic book *The Presentation of Self in Everyday Life*, tried to shed light on the nature of social interaction, particularly in a group setting. In order to maintain a stable self-image, people perform for their social audiences. As a result of this interest in performance, Goffman focused on **dramaturgy**, or a view of social life as a series of dramatic performances like those performed on stage.[1]

Goffman assumed that when individuals interact, they want to present a certain sense of self that will be accepted by others. However, even as they present that self, actors are aware that members of the audience can disturb their performance. For that reason, actors need to control the audience, especially those elements that might be disruptive. They hope that the sense of self they present will cause the audience to voluntarily act as the actors intend for them to. Goffman characterizes this central interest as *impression management*, which involves techniques that actors use to maintain certain impressions in the face of problems they are likely to encounter and methods they use to cope with the problems.

Following this analogy, Goffman spoke of a "front stage," as compared to a "backstage." The front stage is that part of the performance that generally functions in rather fixed and general ways to define the situation for those who observe the performance. Several key components of the front stage include the **setting**, which refers to the physical scene that ordinarily must exist if the actors are to perform. Without a setting the actors usually cannot perform. For instance, a correctional officer requires a prison, just like an ice skater needs ice. **Personal fronts** consist of those items of equipment that the audience identifies with the performers and expects them to carry into the setting. For instance, a police officer is expected to wear a uniform and carry weapons, much as a surgeon is expected to dress in a medical gown and have certain instruments. Pertinent to one's personal front are appearance and manner. **Appearance** includes those items that tell us the performer's social status (e.g., the police officer's uniform). **Manner** tells the audience what sort of role the performer expects to play in the situation (e.g., physical mannerisms, demeanor). A brusque manner and a meek manner may indicate quite different kinds of performances. In general, we expect appearances and manner to be consistent.

Goffman's most interesting insights lie in the domain of the interaction. He argued that because people generally try to present an idealized picture of themselves in their front stage performances, they inevitably feel that they must hide things in their performance. Accordingly, Goffman also discussed a "backstage," which is usually adjacent to the front stage but it is also cut off from it. Performers expect that no members of their front audience will appear in the back. For instance, roll call in a police department is often conducted behind the scenes, away from the public. The information shared during roll call is typically reserved for police officers and consists of brief training periods and briefings on issues such as crime problems and community concerns. Officers tend to view roll call as "their time" away from the public, where they can speak freely with each other and not have to be concerned about members of the general public being privy to the discussion. The backstage involves several processes, including:

1. **Concealing secret pleasures**, which includes activities engaged in prior to the performance or in past lives that are incompatible with their performance. For instance, a judge may wish to prevent others from knowing that he uses recreational drugs.
2. **Concealing errors** that have been made in the preparation of the performance as well as steps that have been taken to correct these errors. For example, a police officer may seek to hide the fact that he or she wrongfully stopped someone.
3. **Showing only the end product** and concealing the process of producing it. An officer may wrongfully stop someone but then justify the stop upon finding illegal drugs.[2]

Goffman also argued that the audiences themselves may try to cope with the falsity so as not to shatter their idealized image of the actor. This reveals the interactional character of all performances. A successful performance depends on the involvement of all parties. Actors also try to make sure that all parts of any performance blend together. In some cases, a single flaw can disrupt a performance. However, performances vary in the amount of consistency required. For instance, a slip by a priest on a sacred occasion would be very disruptive, but a taxi driver making a wrong turn would not damage his or her overall performance.

Goffman's discussion of how individuals present themselves is related to recent discussions of explicit and implicit biases in the criminal justice system. **Explicit bias** refers to the beliefs or attitudes an individual maintains at a conscious level. The actions associated with this type of bias are apparent to the individuals and the audience, for instance when a correctional officer uses a racially derogatory term toward an African American inmate. **Implicit bias** involves less overt cognitive processes that shape attitudes and stereotypes while operating at a below-conscious level. The individual is not consciously aware of their biased behavior, but it exists, for instance, when police assume that some individuals, based primarily on their race or ethnicity, are more likely to commit crime.

IMPRESSION MANAGEMENT

Goffman closed *Presentation of Self in Everyday Life* with some additional insights on the art of impression management (IM). In general, IM is oriented to guarding against a series of unexpected actions, such as unintended gestures, inopportune intrusions, as well as intended actions such as making a scene. Goffman was interested in the various methods of dealing with such problems. Two important components of IM are dramaturgical discipline and dramaturgical circumspection. **Dramaturgical discipline** is defined as concise execution of the performance. This includes such things as having the presence of mind to avoid slips, maintaining self-control, and managing facial expressions and the tone of voice of one's performance. Related to this is **dramaturgical circumspection**, which involves the logistical planning involved in carrying out the performance. Examples include planning for emergencies, making only brief appearances (which limits the potential for mistakes and errors), and preventing audiences access to private information (which might be used to discredit the performance in some way).[3]

One of Goffman's most interesting books is *Stigma: Notes on the Management of Spoiled Identity*. He was interested in the gap between what a person ought to be, or what he calls their "virtual social identity," and what a person actually is: their "actual social identity." Anyone who has a gap between these two identities is stigmatized. The book focuses on the dramaturgical interaction between stigmatized people and "normals."[4] The nature of that interaction depends on which of the two types of stigma an individual possesses. In the case of **discredited stigma**, the actor assumes that the differences are known by the audience members or are evident to them. An example would be a paraplegic or someone who has lost a limb. Here the dramaturgical problem is how to hide the fact of the obvious stigma and demonstrate that the person is just like everyone else. The IM techniques here are called "covering." This is often accomplished by "proving" that the person can do everything a person without the disability can do. In the case of someone confined to a wheelchair, the person may go to great lengths to demonstrate their independence.

A discreditable stigma is one in which the differences are neither known by audience members nor perceivable by them. An example might be a gay man trying to hide his lifestyle in a heterosexual environment. This is often referred to as "passing," as in passing oneself off as something one is not. For someone with a discredited stigma, the basic dramaturgical problem is managing tension produced by the fact that people know of the problem. A problem for someone with a discreditable stigma is managing information so that the problem remains unknown to the audience. For instance, historically it was difficult for gay police officers to reveal their lifestyle preference to other officers. It was, and in some cases remains, feared that other officers wouldn't be accepting. In recent years, however, officers have increasingly shared their preferences with other officers, and the stigma his dissipated.

Goffman devotes much of *Stigma* to people with obvious, often grotesque stigmas. However, as the book unfolds, one begins to realize that Goffman is really saying that we are all stigmatized at one time or another or in one setting or another. His examples include Jews "passing" in a predominantly Christian community, the obese person in a group of people of normal weight, and the individual who has lied about his past and must be constantly sure that the audience does not learn of his history.

The significance of Goffman's work is found in the nature of social interaction. We spend a great deal of time trying to present ourselves in a favorable light, and we tend to evaluate people on the basis of how *they* present themselves. It should be obvious, then, that many of our interactions are not smooth or successful because we are using very little information with which to determine who someone really is. It is also the case that we make mistakes that can have serious consequences for some individuals.[5]

CHECKPOINT

- Erving Goffman explained social interaction as a series of events in which people engage in performances in efforts to present certain images.
- Impression management, according to Goffman, focuses on social interactions in which individuals guard against unanticipated actions. Dramaturgical discipline and dramaturgical circumspection are key components of impression management.

SOCIAL INTERACTION AND THE CRIMINAL JUSTICE SYSTEM

In light of Goffman's account of social interaction, consider the following scenario as it relates to the criminal justice system:

> A young African American man is escorted into a courtroom for his initial appearance, dressed in state-issued attire (i.e., prison garb). Handcuffed and shackled, the young man appears before a judge who informs him of his rights and the charges against him. The young man discouragingly listens with his head down, staring at the ground as the judge reads the charges. The judge begins to get frustrated by the suspect's seeming disinterest in the proceedings and suggests that the individual "look the court in the eye." The young man grudgingly lifts his head and looks at the agitated judge. "Your disinterest in this case reflects your apparent disinterest in the law," says the judge. He adds: "I've read you your rights and informed you of the charges against you. I suggest you take things seriously or you'll find yourself spending a good portion of your life in state prison."

This account of one man's experience in a courtroom exemplifies the power of verbal and nonverbal communication in today's criminal justice system. Let's deconstruct this situation to identify the presumptions made by the two participants. Let's begin with the presence of a young African-American male in the courtroom. Author Jeffrey Reiman discusses how, despite the more severe harms resultant from white-collar offenders, society recognizes young, urban, poor, African American males as the "typical criminal." Reiman notes that the image of the typical criminal, who instills fear in most law-abiding Americans, is created and perpetuated by government practices (e.g., focusing on street crime) and media and government reports suggesting that this group commits an unreasonable amount of crime.[6] The individual entering the court in our scenario undoubtedly fits the mold of the "typical criminal."

The individual in our scenario enters the court handcuffed and shackled in state-issued attire. This look, fitting for a dangerous individual who could violently react without warning, is ascribed to an individual who is legally "innocent until proven guilty." Remove yourself from this situation and consider walking around the general public, for instance in a mall, dressed as the young man in our example. What impressions would the public have of you? Would they recognize you as "innocent"? On the other hand, do we want allegedly violent individuals to remain unconstrained in a stressful environment such as the courtroom? Needless to say, the appearance of many who enter our courts suggests they are indeed guilty as opposed to "innocent until proven guilty."

We could also question the accuracy of the judge's belief that the suspect was disinterested in the case, and ultimately the law, simply because he was not making eye contact with the judge. The significance of multicultural studies is evident in this particular exchange, as it is possible that the suspect was showing the judge respect by not looking him in the eye. It is considered rude in some cultures (e.g., in many Asian cultures) to look someone in the eyes, whereas some other cultures consider it respectful to maintain limited eye contact. Americans, however, view eye contact as a sign of respect. For instance, Americans maintain almost three times as much eye contact as Japanese persons.[7] The judge was clearly speculating and engaging in an ethnocentric manner when commenting on the motives behind the suspect's behavior.

Ethnocentrism involves believing that one's culture or group is superior to others.[8] The judge seemingly interpreted the suspect's behavior according to personal cultural beliefs, which is not uncommon. Sociologist Robert Young suggests, "Precisely because everyday patterns of behavior are culture specific, culture serves the function of binding us to those who share our culture and alienating us from those who do not." He adds, "Those who are part of the same culture will tend to behave in similar ways and have tastes and preferences similar to each other and at the same time different from those of different cultural backgrounds."[9]

The situation in our scenario could be interpreted differently from the perspective of the judge. For instance, the judge is likely familiar with nonverbal communication given the amount of time judges spend interacting with various individuals in a courtroom. It is possible that judges can, with accuracy, recognize the differences between cultural practices and disinterest. It is also possible for judges to misinterpret actions. Further, should we expect the judge to understand all cultures and respond to each, or should the judge expect all who enter the courtroom to conform to the culture the judge finds most appealing? To do so requires the judge (and all criminal justice practitioners) to familiarize themselves with, and accept, the many cultural backgrounds entering our criminal justice system. While we hope that we can reach complete understanding and acceptance of cultural differences, the limitations of human behavior regularly enter into criminal justice practices and lead to differential treatment of various group members. Recognizing and responding to the expectation of one cultural community often leads us to violate the expectations of another.[10] Finding common ground can be difficult.

The same challenges and opportunities for misinterpretation, or miscommunication, discussed in our scenario could easily be applied to all facets of criminal justice. We could easily replace the courtroom scenario with a police officer reacting notably punitively upon encountering a group of young adults who don't speak English, or a prison officer who fails to respect the rights of prisoners by disrupting the privacy of those who wish to pray several times a day. To understand our criminal justice system we must recognize that the system is composed of individuals who act within specific guidelines established by individuals.

As the United States has become increasingly diverse, criminal justice agencies have made many efforts to help employees understand and properly respond to cultural differences. For instance, recruits in the New York City police academy are provided a manual

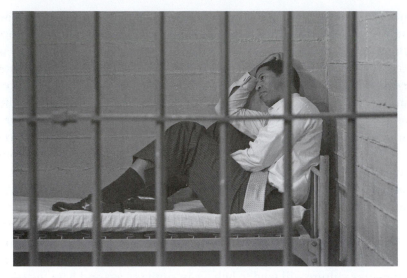

The American public's perception of the criminal population is biased toward African Americans.

titled "Policing a Multicultural Society," which provides tips for recruits who will graduate and work in New York, a very diverse city. The manual provides various communication tips that assist officers dealing with diverse groups. For instance, it notes that police officers should not assume that Arab immigrants speaking loudly are arguing, given that Arabs generally do speak loudly, or that failing to make eye contact with an officer is a sign of disrespect, since, for instance, immigrants from rural Mexico generally avoid making eye contact with authority figures. Further, the manual instructs officers who are interacting with Latin American and Asian immigrant groups to direct their questions to the head of the household if possible, and it teaches that Arab Americans are offering a gesture of courtesy when they immediately get out of their car upon being pulled over.[11]

CHECKPOINT

- Various factors influence social interactions in the criminal justice system. Some of these interactions are impacted by ethnocentrism, a lack of understanding of other groups, and shortcuts sometimes taken by those who work in—and are caught up in—the system.

THE CRIMINAL JUSTICE "SYSTEM"?

The compilation of practices that involve identifying and responding to crime and delinquency is often termed a "system." Some argue that our criminal justice system is indeed a true system in its current form, although it may not be a fine-tuned one. In other words, our system does something . . . maybe not the most effective thing, but something. Others would suggest it is a finely tuned system. Some suggest it is not a system at all. In light of accepted definitions of the term "system," which include mention of terms such as "correlation," "coordination," and "orderly," our system of justice looks nothing like a system. Our decentralized practices of dispensing criminal justice often result in uncorrelated, uncoordinated practices at local, county, state, and federal levels. While there is greater cooperation and correlation among the levels of criminal justice practices today than there has ever been, much work remains before we could safely call ours a true system.

On paper, our system of justice seems well-designed and well-planned (Figure 2.1 depicts the steps of the criminal justice system). One merely needs to examine the recorded steps of the criminal justice system to see that protocol is in place for those accused and convicted of breaking the law. Simply using the term "system" conjures images of a smoothly working entity that encounters problematic situations on rare occasions and maintains proper corrective actions for mishaps. One typically thinks of material objects as systems (e.g., an automobile or an air conditioning unit), which typically function in a more mechanical, predictable manner than does an abstract system composed of individuals. The fact that our system of criminal justice is decentralized and composed of human interactions provides several challenges for those who believe it is truly a system.

The effectiveness of the system, despite how fluid it looks on paper, is influenced by human practices. Humans participate on both sides of the law in the criminal justice system. Accordingly, the system is vulnerable to limitations and/or problems associated with human behavior. To clarify, it is often asked whether or not the criminal justice system is racist or biased. The clear and simple answer is "no." The system, *as diagrammed*, does not have arrows pointing one way for minorities and another way for nonminorities. The system does not formally treat groups differently. However, humans create laws that are then enforced by police officers and interpreted by courtroom personnel and enforced again by corrections personnel. Individuals influence how justice is determined throughout these and related processes. The system is not biased. But some individuals impacting the system are biased. Fortunately, their impact is not as strong as it once was because one could make a strong argument that today's criminal justice system is more culturally sensitive than at any time in history.

Biases in criminal justice hamper the effectiveness of the system and can result in injustices. Injustices have been abundant in the criminal justice system, as evidenced in the U.S. Supreme Court's landmark decision in the 1972 case *Furman v. Georgia*.[12] In *Furman*, the Court ruled that the death penalty, as it was being administered, constituted cruel and unusual punishment and was in violation of the Eighth and Fourteenth Amendments. The majority of justices ruled that the procedures used at that time in applying the death penalty were arbitrary and unfair. The Court did not rule that death as punishment in and of itself was unfair; instead, the Court found problems with the manners in which the penalty was being applied. Thirty-eight states introduced new capital punishment statutes following *Furman*. As evidenced, the criminal justice system often takes steps to correct injustices. Other examples of corrective actions include the introduction of truth-in-sentencing laws, mandatory-minimum sentencing practices, and the use of sentencing guidelines. Nevertheless, the introduction of these actions demonstrates that the system occasionally needs corrective action given its differential treatment of groups, although some have questioned the fairness involved in each of these "corrective" approaches and

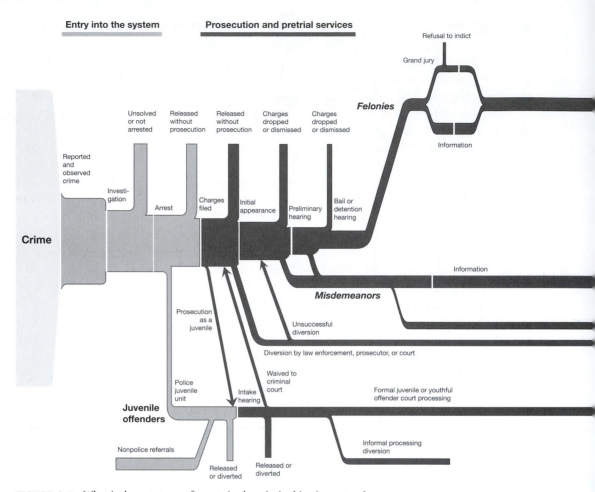

FIGURE 2.1   What is the sequence of events in the criminal justice system?

Note: This chart gives a simplified view of caseflow through the criminal justice system. Procedures vary among jurisdictions. The weights of the lines are not intended to show actual sizes of caseloads.

sentencing practices in general.[13] Criminal justice policies have both direct and indirect impacts on the daily lives of ethnic and racial groups.[14]

Just how do humans *prevent* the criminal justice system from truly operating as a system? One primary obstacle in producing a bias-free criminal justice system involves understanding the varied cultural backgrounds of those entering and working in the system. How does the multicultural society in which we live impact simple, everyday exchanges between individuals, specifically within the criminal justice system? This remainder of this chapter addresses these questions by specifically focusing on three critical topics: groups, communication, and social interaction. Comprehension of this material helps set the stage for the discussions in the chapters that follow. These issues clearly relate to one another and help to explain how the criminal justice system is not necessarily a smooth-functioning

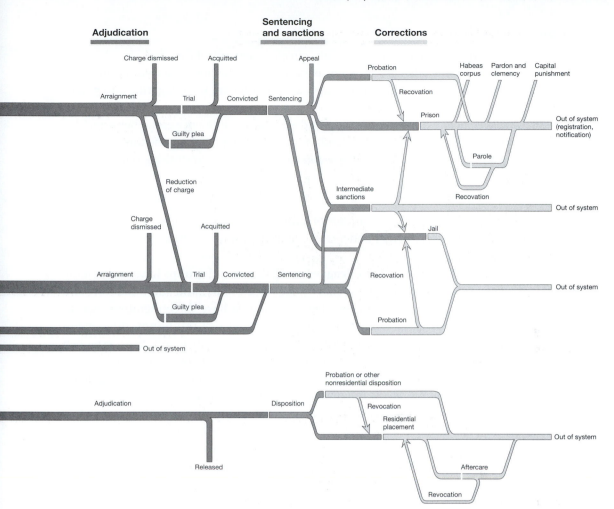

system, per se, as much as it is a behemoth entity filled with justice-seeking personnel, the accused, and the convicted. This chapter helps readers understand how and why multiculturalism is one of the most controversial issues within criminal justice.

CHECKPOINT

- There are various opinions regarding whether or not we truly have a criminal justice "system," and how effectively our justice systems truly work. As designed, our system appears straightforward; however, in practice there are obstacles that impede its effectiveness.

GROUPS

We all belong to groups. Whether it's our family, our close network of friends, a church group, an athletic group, or some other group, we all associate with other individuals in varying contexts. Participants in the criminal justice system are no different. We categorize into groups those who engage in criminal justice: police officers, prosecutors, prison wardens, and the like. Yet, what specifically constitutes a group, and what factors influence group behavior? Are the students who sit in the back of the classroom considered a group? Are the three individuals communicating with each other as they walk out of a department store a group?

WHAT CONSTITUTES A GROUP?

Prominent among the varied definitions of groups include references to group size, whether or not there exists interdependence of members, group identity, group goals, and group structure.[15]

Sociologists William Hickey and colleagues noted that **social groups** have two or more people who interact in patterned ways, "have a feeling of unity, and share interests and expectations."[16] Other researchers suggest that groups must have three members. For instance, Professor Joann Keyton notes that a group must have, at minimum, three members, for these primary reasons: (1) providing the opportunity for members to establish coalitions in which two members side against the third, (2) enabling the opportunity for hidden communication to take place, and (3) determining how roles are assigned.[17] Regardless of the minimum size, the maximum size of a group is dependent on the context of the group. For instance, athletic teams are limited to a set number of participants, while some groups (e.g., pro-environmental groups) seek all the support they can muster. The appropriate size of a group is largely determined by the group's ability to achieve its goals.[18]

Cross-cultural relations have improved as the United States has become more diverse.

Interdependence of members is also vital to establishing a group. Members of a group must rely on group or individual actions for the group to accomplish its task(s). Individuals join groups primarily to enjoy the company of others and accomplish tasks they could not do alone. Group members rely on one another for direction, support, and interaction. Groups must also include an identity through which members identify themselves. Group members who identify with one another and the group's goals accept the values and norms of the group, which subsequently increases the motivations and abilities of group members to interact and proceed effectively.

The final characteristics central to the definition of groups are group goals and group structure. As the name suggests, **group goals** are agreed-upon tasks or activities that the group seeks to complete or accomplish. Goals are varied in nature (e.g., short-term vs. long-term; financial vs. nonfinancial), and not all members of the group have to appreciate the goal. However, there must be a shared understanding of the goal and group members must perceive it as being worthwhile.[19] Groups must also involve structure, which can be informal (e.g., classmates) or formal (e.g., a police department). **Group structure**, which is largely determined by group roles, typically evolves in accordance with, or from, group norms and rules.[20] The structure is vulnerable to change as norms, goals, and other factors impacting the group change. Table 2.1 summarizes the characteristics of a group.

As noted, groups come in all sizes and shapes and there is some subjectivity in determining a group. Often, we hear of group member counts, which are sometimes used to gauge support for a particular group and its goal(s). However, simple counts do not suggest that all who are counted are active members of the group. Subjectivity enters when one makes determinations of group membership, for instance, through members paying dues, active participation, or being listed on a current roster.

Subgroups often emerge as groups become larger and group goals become distorted. Subgroups, or factions of group members that exist within the larger group, sometimes emerge and maintain the possibility of breaking off from the larger group to form an independent group. The existence of subgroups can both help and hinder the larger group as goals are sometimes more easily achieved when individuals work together with limited input and interference. Subgroups, however, may ultimately detach from the larger group, for instance, if they believe their identity or goals differ significantly from the larger group, or problems may occur if the subgroup is not receptive to direction from the larger group.

TABLE 2.1 CHARACTERISTICS OF GROUPS

Group Size – Should have at least three members

Interdependence of Members – Members of a group must rely on group or individual actions for the group to accomplish its task(s)

Group Identity – Group members who identify with one another and the group's goals accept the values and norms of the group

Group Goal – Agreed-upon tasks or activities that the group seeks to complete or accomplish

Group Structure – It is largely determined by group roles, and typically evolves in accordance with, or from, group norms and rules

GROUPS IN THE CRIMINAL JUSTICE SYSTEM

Given the elements necessary for the existence of a group, what groups exist within the criminal justice system? To be sure, there are many groups existing at various levels working toward different goals. For starters, we could loosely identify the nearly 2.5 million individuals working in our nation's justice system as a group that has the ultimate goal of ensuring justice.[21] We could also recognize each component of the criminal justice system as a group (i.e., police, courts, and corrections), and further identify groups as we observe different levels of justice (e.g., local, state, and federal). We could take it further to group individuals working particular beats, in particular courtrooms, or in specific cell blocks.

An example of a group within the criminal justice system is the **courtroom workgroup**, which is recognized as a group of individuals who work on a regular basis in a courtroom setting. The familiarity of courtroom personnel contributes to the local legal culture in the sense that there's a shared understanding of norms, practices, and expectations among courtroom practitioners. The courtroom workgroup emerges as individuals (including judges, prosecutors, and defense attorneys), working within a jurisdiction, come to understand and anticipate particular behaviors from other members of the workgroup. For instance, those regularly acting within a courtroom typically have a clear understanding of the **"going rate,"** or the penalties one can expect to be associated with particular offenses. A defense attorney can share with his or her client information culled from previous interactions with other members of the workgroup. In turn, suspects have an understanding of what to expect upon entering the courtroom. Among other things, the familiarity among members of the courtroom workgroup helps plea bargain negotiations, which is typical of proceedings in the courtroom, for instance, as the large majority of criminal court cases (roughly 85 percent to 95 percent), are resolved via plea bargaining, as opposed to criminal trials.

Recognition of suspects as members of particular groups undoubtedly affects criminal justice practices, as identified in the criminal justice research literature and throughout this book. While suspects in general do not meet the criteria of the definition of a group, primarily due to the lack of cohesiveness or organization of suspects, they undoubtedly belong to some group (e.g., based on affiliation with a gang membership or a culture-based group) and are typically pre-judged and treated in various manners.

CHECKPOINT

- Groups exist in various shapes and sizes, and for various reasons. There are many different groups found within our justice systems.
- Groups must have at least three members for the purposes of providing the opportunity for members to establish coalitions in which two members side against the third, enabling the opportunity for hidden communication to take place, and determining how roles are assigned.
- The various groups within our justice systems impact the extent to which justice is served. Among the largest groups are those who work in law enforcement, the courts, and corrections.

COMMUNICATION

Communication is at the core of human interaction. It guides, conveys, directs, suggests, and so on. Effective communication is vital to the effective functioning of any group, and has saved more than one police and correctional officer's life. Communication is perhaps the most important, yet often overlooked, aspect of the criminal justice system. Take, for instance, a police officer who bases their decision to draw and shoot their firearm on interpersonal communication. Consider the prison officer who interprets an inmate's behavior as unruly and proceeds to forcefully remove the inmate from his cell. With regard to parole, author/editor Marsha Bailey suggests, "In dealing with Hispanic offenders, parole officers should be direct and to the point when instructing, and should expect to see more reaction from parolees" as "Hispanics generally are more immediate and vocal in communication; sometimes the dialogue sounds more intimidating than it really is."[22] Miscommunication is the basis for some interpersonal conflict and the cause for some criminal injustice, which explains, for instance, why 91 percent of state and local law enforcement training academies include communications among their major subject areas of instruction. The median number of hours of training at the academies is about 15.[23]

Communication comes in two forms: verbal and nonverbal. Verbal communication consists of the words we speak. Nonverbal communication entails all non-vocal acts that convey a message. The judge that was mentioned at the beginning of this chapter based his assumptions of the suspect upon nonverbal cues, and offered his input via verbal communication. The visible power differential in the courtroom, for example, with the judge dressed in a robe and sitting above the courtroom actors, is also a form of nonverbal communication (e.g., the judge expects respect).

THE COMMUNICATION PROCESS

To understand the impact of communication in the criminal justice system one could deconstruct the communication process. Deconstructing verbal communication provides a starting point for understanding nonverbal communication. Understanding verbal communication begins with the thought process of the individual sending the verbal message (the sender). At the most basic level, the sender interprets or analyzes a situation and generates thoughts. Part of the interpretation and analysis involves determining what message the sender wishes to transmit and how he or she wishes to send it. There is a filter involved, as we all sometimes think about saying things yet refrain from doing so. Some of us have a more restrictive or porous filter than others, which explains why some folks are quiet, others speak their mind, and why some are constantly putting their foot in their mouth.

Once the message is created in the sender's mind, the individual targets others (receivers) whom he or she wishes to hear the message. It sometimes occurs that we wish to convey a message to some individuals present, yet exclude others from the message, which is why we sometimes whisper or speak coyly. Upon locating proper targets, the sender conveys the message via some channel, typically either verbally or in writing. Failing to properly organize thoughts has prompted many misunderstandings and controversies. Aside from the spoken words, the pitch and tone of one's verbal message certainly influences verbal communication.

Receivers encode the message through receiving, interpreting, and analyzing the message. Proper listening is key to verbal communication. Although the act of hearing is physical in nature, listening is a mental exercise. Effective listeners often maintain the ability to lead the conversation. Many people, however, are not effective listeners, and the proliferation of distractions, for instance in the form of electronic devices (e.g., cell phones), has hampered communication.[24]

Upon hearing and listening to the message, receivers generate a response regarding how they received, interpreted, and understood the message. For instance, the message could generate a series of verbal and nonverbal reactions, including a return message, smile, frown, punch, and/or gunshot. The communication process continues until one or all participants find a suitable point for conclusion. Of particular importance in this exchange are one's ability to generate thoughts into words or actions (including the filtering process) and the ability of others to receive, interpret, and adequately respond to the message. Former president Ronald Reagan was deemed the "Great Communicator" for his ability to inspire many with his words and actions. Figure 2.2 depicts the communication process.

Of particular concern with regard to any form of communication is the message being sent. Mostly, the communication process succeeds and receivers understand the sender's message. The message, however, may generate a reaction, or series of reactions. For instance, **hate speech** includes communication that attacks individuals or groups on the basis of specific attributes, such as race, ethnicity, gender, sexual orientation, religion, or disability. Such communication can be in the form of speech, conduct, writing, gestures, or displays directed against specific groups. Some cities and colleges in the United States have adopted policies that ban hate speech; however, such acts have generated claims that the bans violate First Amendment protections with regard to the freedom of speech.

NONVERBAL COMMUNICATION

Nonverbal communication also involves reception, interpretation, and reaction. One merely needs to view commercial advertising to understand the power of nonverbal communication and symbolic cues. Advertisements including vehicles driving in idealistic

FIGURE 2.2 The communication process

Effective communication requires messages to be sent clearly, and listeners to be receptive of the message.

environments or individuals drinking beer on an exotic island suggest to consumers that purchase of a particular products will enable them to live such lifestyles. Much research and consideration goes into commercial advertising, so at some point during the advertising development phase a marketing group determined that nonverbal cues such as a hammock and a beach would entice consumers to drink their beer.

Nonverbal cues such as clothing, body posture, eye contact, and physical aggression are significant forms of communication that generate and dictate much action within the criminal justice system. Nonverbal communication begins with the nonverbal message transmitted by a sender, which can be in the form of body movements, facial expressions, and gestures. The message is then received and interpreted by the receiver, who evaluates the message and the sender and then reacts. Similar to verbal communication, the message being sent isn't always the message received.

Interpretation and analyses of nonverbal communication pose particular obstacles due to the greater amount of subjectivity involved, especially since a message isn't being directly conveyed like a verbal exchange would be. This obstacle is evident in the earlier passage when the judge interprets the suspect's behavior of failing to make eye contact as a sign of disrespect. The significance of nonverbal cues is also recognized in police departments that use a force continuum to guide officer decision-making when encountering potentially violent situations. The **continuum of force** is a concept that guides officer behavior with respect to use of force. Officers are expected to consider the continuum of force in their attempts to adequately interpret and respond to suspect behavior. For instance, officers are legally permitted to use deadly force only when they perceive suspects as posing deadly threats to the officer and/or others. The perception aspect of the laws surrounding deadly force involves officers interpreting nonverbal (and sometimes verbal) cues. Failure to react accordingly could result in death(s), civil and criminal litigation, and the officer's dismissal from the force.

Of particular importance in any discussion of communication are kinesics, vocalics, and proxemics.[25] **Kinesics** refers to body language, including gestures, facial expressions, eye behavior, and body movements. **Vocalics**, or paralanguage, refers to vocal characteristics such as inflection, tone, accent, rate, pitch, volume, and vocal interrupters. **Proxemics** refers to the space between the communicator and his or her audience. The actions within the criminal justice system take place at all levels of space. For instance, police officers are sometimes required to physically detain suspects through invasion of the individual's intimate space, while communications between prison officers and prisoners may occur within personal space. Judges sitting in a courtroom typically conduct business from a public distance. The varying levels of acceptable or expected interaction among cultures sometimes leads to misunderstandings and perhaps violence.

THE CONFEDERATE FLAG AND ITS MEANING

In June 2015, a White gunman killed nine people in a Black church in Charleston, South Carolina. The gunman, Dylann Roof, was captured and faced thirty-three federal hate crime charges and, among other charges, nine counts of murder by the State of South Carolina. He received the death penalty for his actions, and became the first federal hate crime defendant to receive capital punishment. The mass murder reignited arguments that South Carolina should no longer fly the Confederate flag over its State Capitol building. Following his arrest, photos of Roof appeared depicting him wrapped in a Confederate flag accompanied by a hate-filled account with his racist comments. He appeared in other photos displaying the flag.

The debate over displaying the Confederate flag has continued for decades. Some feel it is a symbol of free speech, provides recognition of the soldiers who fought for the Confederacy, and it is a proud sign of Southern heritage. They argue that displaying the flag is their right under the First Amendment. Others feel it is a symbol of White supremacy, hate, racial intolerance, and slavery. The flag means different things to different people, and has generated controversy throughout the United States for some time. In July 2015, the Confederate flag was removed from the South Carolina State Capitol. Politicians felt pressure from many groups, and decided that the removal of the flag would help with recovery efforts from the tragedy in Charleston.

The debate over displaying the flag continues, however, as South Carolina was certainly not the only state having to address the issue, and flying the flag over the State Capitol was not the only case. For example, on the same day as the Charleston shooting, the U.S. Supreme Court ruled that Texas did not violate the First Amendment by refusing to create specialty license plates displaying the flag.[26] At the time, the flag appeared on license plates in several southern states; however, the Court's ruling allows the states to ban the plates. Further, some states (e.g., Alabama, Georgia, Arkansas, Florida) have images or symbols on their flags that reflect the Confederacy. Mississippi's state flag actually features the Confederate emblem, although in 2019 the state offered an alternative flag that does not include the emblem. Debates over the meaning of the Confederate flag and the Constitutionality of portraying it will continue, as the flag means different things to different people and highlights the importance of symbolism in everyday life.

OBSTACLES AFFECTING COMMUNICATION

Many obstacles or hurdles exist in the communication process, as effective communication involves an expectation that all parties clearly understand each other. One must bear in mind that we often use words, which are human creations, to convey a message and rely on the perception of others to correctly interpret the message. The meanings of words exist in people, not in the actual spoken words.[27]

Perception refers to the act of becoming aware or apprehending something via the senses. As such, word selection is vital to effective communication, as there is an assumption that all receivers have the same interpretation of the word. For instance, individuals, specifically suspects, are sometimes deemed "dangerous" or "threatening" to others. Such a classification generally prompts a rapid, punitive response; yet, we must ask several questions before we act too rashly. For instance, we must ask, "How are they dangerous?" and "To whom are they dangerous or threatening?" For example, there was a great sense of insecurity in the United States following the terrorist attacks of September 11, 2001. In response, the criteria for perceptions of "dangerous" and "threatening" differed following the attacks, and it is argued that a substantial number of individuals were inaccurately deemed "dangerous." Ethnic profiling has become increasingly recognized in the United States since the attacks.[28]

Prominent among the hurdles involved in communication is the fact that the human body is limited in its intake capacity, and interference can certainly play a role in miscommunication. The limited capacity of the human brain prevents us from fully ingesting and interpreting all societal cues.[29] Physical challenges such as color-blindness, deafness, blindness, and speaking with a thick accent also restrict successful communication.

Of particular significance to criminal justice is the expectation that conveyed messages will be received and interpreted in the proper context. The multicultural society in which we live poses significant challenges given the numerous languages spoken and the varied values, beliefs, and expectations associated with the grouping and interactions of individuals from various cultures. The ability to speak a second (or third) language is becoming increasingly important for criminal justice professionals, particularly since language is a primary identifying feature of a culture.[30] Table 2.2 depicts results from the U.S. Census Bureau's survey of the languages spoken in U.S. households. Related, Table 2.3. depicts the top-ten most spoken languages in the world.

The popularity of social media has changed communication practices in both positive and negative ways. The benefits of social media in relation to communication include the ability to connect and instantly interact with people from all over the world. We can receive real-time news and other information in a fast and convenient manner. Ultimately, it enables us to connect and learn much more effectively.

TABLE 2.2 LANGUAGES SPOKEN AT HOME IN THE UNITED STATES, 2010–2014

Subject	Total
Population age 5 years and older	294,133,373
Speak only English	79.1%
Speak a language other than English	20.9%
Spanish	13.0%
Other Indo-European languages	3.7%
Asian and Pacific Island languages	3.3%
Other languages	.9%

Source: U.S. Census Bureau, 2010–2014 American Community Survey 5-Year Estimates.

TABLE 2.3　TOP TEN MOST SPOKEN LANGUAGES IN THE WORLD

Language	Total speakers
Chinese	1,311 million
English	850 million
Spanish	500 million
Arabic	490 million
Hindi	380 million
Bengali	271 million
Russian	260 million
Portuguese	250 million
French	220 million
Malay	220 million

Source: Statista.com, "The Most Spoken and Most Popular Languages Worldwide." Accessed online at: https://www.statista.com/statistics/266808/the-most-spoken-languages-worldwide/

Despite these and other benefits, the use of social media has negatively impacted communication. Too often we communicate via technology instead of personal interaction, and messages sometimes get distorted or misinterpreted. Interacting online eliminates the nonverbal messages that are notably important when communicating. The use of emojis (e.g., a smiley face) helps contextualize information, but it is less impactful than the nonverbal cues present in offline interaction. Further, the physical distance between online communicators may encourage individuals to state harmful things that they otherwise would have avoided. This, in turn, can lead to conflict.

The limitations inherent in communication are sometimes addressed through restating, or re-emphasizing the message, as we often hear senders state, "Let me clarify . . . ," or "Put simply . . . ," or "For example. . . ." Understanding how individuals react to miscommunication and how to resolve miscommunication should be of utmost importance to criminal justice practitioners and scholars. Understanding our reactions to miscommunication is perhaps as important as recognizing the reasons why we miscommunicate.

DIFFERENTIAL TREATMENT AND SYMBOLISM

The criminal justice literature is filled with studies examining differential treatment of groups based on symbolic cues. **Symbols**, or items used to represent something else, are evident throughout the criminal justice system. For instance, the police officer's badge, the judge's gown, and the scales of justice are but a few of the many symbols used by criminal justice personnel to represent something else. The use of symbols, of course, requires that all who encounter the symbol understand what it is being symbolized.

Criminal justice personnel not only display symbols, they interpret them as well. Two well-documented examples of symbolism influencing police discretion include the concept of "symbolic assailants" and, more recently, racial profiling. Years ago scholar Jerome Skolnick used the term **symbolic assailant** to refer to particular individuals, as perceived

Tattoos, clothing, and a host of related symbols influence our perceptions. Which of these two individuals threatens you more? What is it about his appearance that leads you to believe that one is more threatening than the other? Which of these two men would likely be treated more leniently by criminal justice officials?

by police officers, who appear as potential sources of violence or as enemies to be reckoned with. Skolnick described symbolic assailants as "persons who use gesture, language, and attire that the policeman has come to recognize as a prelude to violence."[31]

Scholars recently identified two groups that could be deemed symbolic assailants. Particularly, it was argued that the high-profile deaths of several African American men (e.g., Tamir Rice and Philando Castile) at the hands of the police exemplify the historical view of Black men as symbolic assailants.[32] Further, researchers noted that there is little evidence demonstrating a relationship between immigration and crime, even though immigrants have been portrayed as symbolic assailants who pose threats to national security and must be strictly controlled via our justice systems.[33]

Racial profiling, which involves recognizing individuals as suspects based merely upon race, has existed in society since groups of different backgrounds interacted. It is among the hot topics in policing and society in general. The relatively short history of the United States is rife with accounts of racial profiling, not the least of which involves the Anglo settlers confronting Native Americans prior to and following the Revolutionary War. It has only recently been the topic of much discussion from a research and policy standpoint, particularly in light of accounts of African American motorists being targeted by law enforcement and the differential treatment of those of Middle-Eastern descent following the terrorist attacks of September 11, 2001.[34] Racial profiling exemplifies how images and stereotypes of various racial, cultural, and ethnic groups influence formal social control efforts.[35]

Racial profiling is often thought to primarily involve police officers targeting motorists based on their race. However, profiling based upon one's race extends far beyond roadways; the terms "Flying while Black" and "Shopping while Black" are used to describe how African Americans have drawn the attention of authorities largely based on race. For instance, interviews with African American shoppers found that the majority felt they had been unfairly targeted as a shoplifter or thief (59 percent) or had received poor or no service (52 percent) based upon their race.[36]

Further, racial profiling is not always targeted toward minority groups and is not always based on race. Police officers often note that crime detection is sometimes an advanced version of the children's game "One of These Things Is Not Like the Others." Specifically, officers identify individuals or objects that don't "fit" within the context of the situation. Examples include expensive automobiles in low-income areas, a minority person loitering in a predominantly nonminority neighborhood, or a nonminority person loitering in a predominantly minority neighborhood. In other words, officers use symbolic cues to base their actions. Proponents of racial profiling argue that categorizing individuals based on appearance is necessary for solid police work, while opponents argue that appearance alone should not dictate perceptions of one's behavior.

Researchers used booking photos, criminal histories, and sentencing information to assess the relationships between physical appearance, threat perceptions, and criminal punishment. Among other findings, they noted that Blacks or offenders with visible

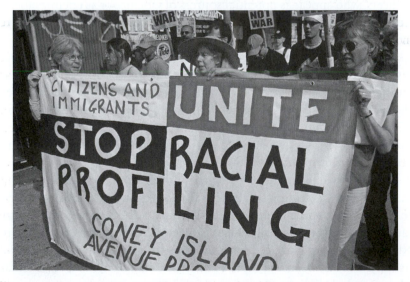

Racial profiling occurs in many contexts and has drawn much public attention in recent years. Some view it as an effective yet illegal tool for law enforcement, while others cite the discrimination inherent in its use.

tattoos or scars were more likely than their counterparts to be perceived as more threatening in appearance. Asian Americans and offenders who were baby-faced or more attractive were perceived to be less threatening in appearance.[37] These findings have implications regarding how different groups are treated throughout our justice systems.

This base-level account of verbal and nonverbal communication is elaborated upon in the communications studies literature. We've only scratched the surface of the intricate nature of interpersonal communication in an understanding of how individuals communicate, how communications can become distorted, and the significance of miscommunication.

CHECKPOINT

- Communication is inherent within social interaction. It is particularly important in the criminal justice system, in which miscommunication can result in serious repercussions, including the loss of life. Communication can be both verbal and nonverbal.
- The communication process can be broken down, on a basic level, as the sender transmitting a message to the receiver, who must effectively interpret the message through various forms of interference.

- Nonverbal communication is an often overlooked, yet very important aspect of the communication process.
- Various obstacles impede our efforts to communicate. Words are human constructs and are subject to various interpretations.
- Symbolic cues used to make judgements have historically impacted justice-based practices. Symbols, racial profiling, and reactions to the symbolic assailant are examples.

SOCIAL INTERACTION AND MULTICULTURALISM

Social interaction is the process through which individuals act and react in relation to other individuals. Volumes have been written on the complex nature of social interaction, and we can be sure that many more works are forthcoming. Our discussion of social interaction is restricted to the dynamics and complexities involving human interaction in a multicultural society, with particular emphasis on the criminal justice system.

A primary challenge of a multicultural society involves group members' ability to effectively coexist. To understand social interaction in a multicultural society requires recognition of what constitutes culture. Historically, a White, male, European worldview has defined and controlled the majority culture in the United States.[38] However, the world is becoming increasingly diverse as society grows and national borders continuously open. Sociologist John Macionis stated that "Multiculturalism represents a sharp change from the past, when our society downplayed cultural diversity and defined itself primarily in terms of well-off European and especially English immigrants."[39]

Social interaction is regulated by norms that are primarily determined by our culture. However, people act out norms in various means. Cultural norms provide guidance for our behavior. **Culture** refers to the learned beliefs, values, norms, behaviors, and material goods that collectively constitute a people's manner of life. Culture shapes what we do and shapes our personalities.[40] It is often categorized into two categories: material and nonmaterial. **Material culture** consists of objects that are real to the senses (e.g., a baton, handcuffs, a judge's gavel). **Nonmaterial culture** is largely composed of our shared beliefs and values, and the social expectations individuals have for one another. Because nonmaterial culture is not able to be seen, it is particularly problematic when cultures interact.[41]

Despite the conflicts that develop, people in the United States take great pride in its status as a "melting pot," in which individuals from all cultures are welcome and expected to contribute to the greater good. In turn, the United States is a notably diverse and heterogeneous society consisting of individuals from many different backgrounds and cultures. The extensive diversity in the United States continues to increase. Annually, roughly 1 million people from other countries come to the United States. In contrast, historic isolation has made Japan the most monocultural of all high-income nations. Intense immigration has contributed to the United States becoming the most multicultural of all high-income countries. A century ago most immigrants to the United States hailed from Europe, but today most immigrants arrive from Asia and Latin America.

STATUS AND ROLES

Understanding social interaction requires recognition of both status and role. **Status** involves the social position maintained by an individual. **Role** refers to the behavior that is expected of an individual who maintains a particular status. Status is part of our everyday behavior and helps dictate our relationship with those with whom we interact. We each hold a status set which entails the different statuses we maintain at a given time. Statuses are subject to change over time. For instance, one could be a student, a correctional officer, and a father. The multiple statuses that we maintain at a given time dictate the roles we play in everyday life. We could play the role of judge, jury member, probation officer, or therapist. Roles refer to the actions or activities that constitute one's status.

We sometimes encounter role conflict. For instance, consider the dilemma of the police officer who is hanging out at a bar with a group of friends. The officer notices that one guy in the group may be unfit (i.e., too drunk) to drive home, even though he says he's "fine" and the others in the group see no problem letting him drive. The officer is faced with role conflict in that he took an oath to serve and protect, yet he wants to remain "one of the guys," not the "police officer friend" in the group. How should the officer handle this situation?

Statuses and roles are noticeably evident in the criminal justice system. For example, prison officers expect, based on their status, to be treated with respect by inmates. Inmates often expect the same treatment; however, their status as "offenders" leaves them in a position to receive limited respect. There are clear hierarchies in many criminal justice agencies that specifically designate one's status in the system.

SOCIALLY CONSTRUCTING REALITY

Some researchers argue that individuals don't understand society in a truly objective manner. Instead, it is argued that people mentally construct ideas about phenomena and thus create a reality, in what is recognized as the **social construction of reality**.[42] Through interacting with one another we creatively mold a reality that could vary according to the interpretations of participants. Social interaction involves complex negotiations of reality. Most of us can agree about what occurs in everyday life; however, we may all have different perceptions of what happens. Such differences, particularly as they exist in the criminal justice system and with regard to various cultures, could lead to significant miscommunication and uncomfortable interactions.

It is often argued that issues are socially constructed with particular ideologies in mind. For instance, the war on drugs has disproportionately impacted young, minority males, leading some researchers to question the identified intentions of the war. More generally, one could argue that society's preoccupation with street crime, as opposed to white-collar crime, stems from the status and power differentials of the groups primarily involved in each type of crime. Street crime arrests typically involve lower-class minority males, while white-collar crimes are recognized as predominantly involving wealthy non-minorities. Some argue that the constructed images of the "typical criminal" and the "war on (street) crime" enable the more powerful in society to maintain status quo with regard to the discrepancy in power.

Sports-talk radio provides an example of competing constructions of the world. Consider, for example, discussions of college football rankings. Put simply, college football rankings are highly subjective. The manner by which teams are evaluated and ranked is highly suspect, at times political, and sometimes responsible for schools earning or losing millions of dollars. To say that one team should be ranked higher than another ("higher" meaning "better"), when in fact the teams have not played each other or a common opponent, leads to much discussion and argument. Sports-radio hosts and their guests debate how the teams should be ranked, all the while sharing their constructed reality that often differs from the reality created by others.

Subjectivity is inherent in communication, and in a multicultural society subjectivity becomes critical in human interaction. Consciously or subconsciously, we all incorporate subjectivity during social interaction. Sometimes, unfortunately, the subjectivity involves characteristics that hamper the coexistence of various groups and acceptance of others. Social interaction is grounded in the belief that messages conveyed will be interpreted in the manner intended. We know, however, that social interaction is often clouded by mis-hearings, mis-speaks, misinterpretations, and various other misunderstandings.[43]

CHECKPOINT

- Social interaction in diverse societies is challenged by cultural differences, including material culture and nonmaterial culture.
- Statuses and roles are key aspects of social interactions. Status pertains to the social position of an individual, while roles involve the behavior of an individual who maintains a particular status.
- It is suggested that we each construct our own version of reality, which contributes to differences among groups and individuals.

SUMMARY

The significance of cultural diversity in the criminal justice system is evidenced in a Bureau of Justice Statistics report, which noted that 95 percent of state and local law enforcement training academies offered training in cultural diversity and human relations, while 78 percent trained cadets with regard to hate/bias crimes.[44] The median number of hours for cultural diversity training was 12, while the median number of hours devoted to hate/bias crimes was 3. The need for more effective interaction with the various cultural groups entering the criminal justice system is well documented. Many solutions have been offered in response, including promotion of multiculturalism in criminal justice education.

Researcher William Calathes argues that "criminal justice education has missed much by promulgating a 'melting pot' philosophy. Our students think in terms of White monoculturalism, the assumption that we all belong to one system, which is that of White Anglo-Europeans."[45] The changing nature of society encourages greater recognition of multiculturalism in criminal justice curriculums, as today's criminal justice students are tomorrow's justice professionals.

At any stage during the suspect-turned-offender's journey through the criminal justice system, he or she could very easily encounter someone who doesn't view society in the same manner as he or she does. For instance, cultural differences may result in a jury rendering an unfavorable verdict based on preferences or prejudices. The opportunity for miscommunication increases as the number of contacts throughout case processing increases. In turn, there's a greater chance of misunderstanding and misguided behaviors because the suspect/offender encountered a greater number of individuals. An overriding goal of the criminal justice system, then, should be to eliminate, or at least reduce, the likelihood of injustices occurring from improper personal interactions.

Addressing cultural differences as they exist throughout the system is a vital first step toward addressing the issue, as evidenced, for example, in the training provided correctional officers at the New Mexico Corrections Training Academy. The Academy requires cadets to recognize and practice facial expressions, posture, positioning, and distance. Such training, which is not restricted to the New Mexico Corrections Training Academy, helps cadets understand various aspects of nonverbal communication.[46]

The criminal justice system is, by nature, supported by human interaction. Consider the various contexts of human interaction found at all steps involved in criminal case processing. To begin, a crime is committed and someone contacts the authorities. The police investigate primarily through interviewing witnesses and suspects. An arrest may ultimately be made, and the suspect is turned over to the courts where he or she will interact with judges, prosecutors, defense attorneys, and possibly jurors. If convicted, the offender is turned over to the supervision of some correctional group and will encounter many different situations involving individuals from various backgrounds.

The manner in which social interaction takes place in the criminal justice system is influenced by the technological revolution society is currently experiencing. For instance, computers eliminate much of the busywork previously associated with running background checks on individuals and vehicles. The need to communicate with a dispatcher is reduced as mobile computer units are found in many police cars. In corrections, global positional satellite monitoring (GPS) is used to track some offenders serving their penalties in the community. For instance, South Carolina governor Mark Sanford earlier signed a bill that mandates GPS monitoring for sex offenders convicted of certain offenses. This form of electronic monitoring will likely increase in the criminal justice system, as the number of face-to-face contacts required as part of probation and parole plans are likely reduced. Email and texting have significantly changed the manner in which many of us interact, as it is easier for many of us to send an email or text than to make a phone call or personally visit our target recipient. In the end, understanding and comprehending technology-based communications is becoming increasingly important.

YOU MAKE THE CALL
SYMBOLISM AND POLICING

Consider the following scenario. Debate the pros and cons of all options and decide what you would do.

You're a rookie police officer teamed with an experienced officer on patrol. You're both White males on patrol in a predominantly Asian neighborhood. Racial tensions between the police and the residents were enhanced last week when a White officer was accused of using excessive force on a young Asian suspect. As you patrol, you and your partner notice a young Asian male wearing a shirt that states "I hate pigs" and has a picture of a gun pointing at a police officer. You let it roll off your back, as you've been trained to do. Your partner, however, tells you to pull over. He suggests the "punk needs to show a little respect." Your partner approaches the Asian youth and tells him to get into the car. The youth complies and your partner tells you to drive off. While driving around, your partner threatens to violently beat the youth and make sure that nobody knows about it. You're taken aback by what's going on, as you expected more from your colleague. The youth is crying, fearful for his life. He says his older brother made him wear the shirt. After a while, your partner tells you to pull over and lets the youth out. He's about two miles from where you picked him up, and is left to find a ride home. While pulling away, the officer tells the boy that if anything is said of this encounter, the officer will follow through on his threats.

Questions

1. Should our laws regarding freedom of expression permit individuals to wear hate-based, threatening clothing?
2. What type of social interaction and nonverbal communication instigated this incident?
3. Should you and your fellow officer have responded at all to the symbolism found on the youth's shirt?
4. What steps should you have taken to address this troubling situation? How would your actions have impacted your role and status as a police officer?

KEY TERMS

appearance	going rate
concealing errors	group goals
concealing secret pleasures	group structure
continuum of force	hate speech
courtroom workgroup	implicit bias
culture	kinesics
discredited stigma	manner
dramaturgical circumspection	material culture
dramaturgical discipline	nonmaterial culture
dramaturgy	perception
ethnocentrism	personal front
explicit bias	proxemics

racial profiling   social interaction
role   status
setting   symbolic assailant
showing only the end product   symbol
social construction of reality   vocalics
social group

DISCUSSION QUESTIONS

1. Discuss how those who enter the courtroom as "innocent until proven guilty" may not be recognized as such.
2. Identify and discuss the five characteristics of a group. Would you consider the members of a
   football team a group? Why or why not?
3. What do you believe are the most significant impediments to communication? Do you feel
   some groups are better communicators and listeners than others?
4. Describe the verbal communication process and note how miscommunication occurs.
5. Describe the similarities between the "typical criminal" and the "symbolic assailant." Do you
   believe it is effective police practice for officers to identify individuals as threats based on demographic profiles? Do you believe it is fair for officers to do so?

FOR FURTHER READING

Beauchamp, S. R., and S. J. Baran. *Introduction to Human Communication: Perception, Meaning, and
   Identity*. New York: Oxford University Press, 2015.
Berger, Peter L., and Thomas Luckmann. *The Social Construction of Reality: A Treatise in the Sociology of
   Knowledge*. New York: Penguin Books, 1991.
Goffman, E. *The Presentation of Self in Everyday Life*. New York: Doubleday, 1959.
Reiman, J., and P. Leighton. *The Rich Get Richer and the Poor Get Prison: Ideology, Class, and Criminal
   Justice*. 11th ed. New York: Routledge, 2017.
Rothwell, J. D. *In the Company of Others*. 5th ed. New York: Oxford University Press, 2016.

NOTES

1. E. Goffman, *The Presentation of Self in Everyday Life* (New York: Doubleday, 1959).
2. Ibid.
3. Ibid.
4. E. Goffman, *Stigma: Notes on the Management of Spoiled Identity* (Englewood Cliffs, NJ: Prentice-
   Hall, 1963).
5. Ibid.
6. J. Reiman and P. Leighton, *The Rich Get Richer and the Poor Get Prison: Ideology, Class, and Criminal
   Justice*, 10th ed. (Boston, MA: Allyn and Bacon, 2013).
7. John L. Graham and Yoshihiro Sano, *Smart Bargaining: Doing Business with the Japanese*
   (Cambridge, MA: Ballinger, 1984).
8. Robert L. Young, *Understanding Misunderstandings: A Practical Guide to More Successful Human
   Interaction* (Austin, TX: University of Texas Press, 1999), 122.
9. Ibid., 102.

10. Ibid., 103.

11. J. Goldstein, "Little-Known Guide Helps Police Navigate a Diverse City," *New York Times*, June 10, 2013. Available at: http://www.nytimes.com/2013/06/11/nyregion/a-not-for-tourists-guide-to-navigating-a-multicultural-city.html?_r=0

12. Furman v. Georgia, 408 U.S. 238 (1972).

13. See, e.g., Charles Crawford, Ted Chiricos, and Gary Kleck, "Race, Racial Threat, and Sentencing of Habitual Offenders," *Criminology* 36, no. 3 (1998): 481–511.

14. Nancy Rodriquez, "The Nexus Between Race and Ethnicity and Criminal Justice Policy," in *Images of Color, Images of Crime: Readings*, 3rd ed. (Los Angeles, CA: Roxbury, 2006), 249.

15. Joann Keyton, *Communicating in Groups: Building Relationships for Group Effectiveness*, 3rd ed. (New York: Oxford University Press, 2006), 4, 5.

16. W. E. Thompson, J. V. Hickey, and M. L. Thompson, *Society in Focus: An Introduction to Sociology*, 8th ed. (Lanham, MD: Rowman & Littlefield, 2016), 143.

17. Keyton, *Communicating in Groups*, 5.

18. Ibid., 7.

19. Ibid., 10.

20. Ibid., 10, 11, 13.

21. D. W. Neubauer and H. F. Fradella, *America's Courts and the Criminal Justice System*, 12th ed. (Boston, MA: Cengage, 2017), 7.

22. Marsha Bailey, "Georgia Parole Officers Confront Language and Cultural Barriers," *Corrections Today* (December 1991): 118, 121.

23. B. A. Reaves, *State and Local Law Enforcement Training Academies, 2013*. U.S. Department of Justice, Bureau of Justice Statistics, 2016, NCJ 249784, 5.

24. B. Sullivan and H. Thompson, *The Plateau Effect: Getting from Stuck to Success* (New York: Dutton, 2013).

25. Keyton, *Communicating in Groups*.

26. Walker v. Texas Division, Sons of Confederate Veterans, 576 U.S. (2015).

27. Ronald D. Hunter, Thomas Barker, and Pamela D. Mayhall, *Police-Community Relations and the Administration of Justice*, 7th ed. (Upper Saddle River, NJ: Prentice Hall, 2008).

28. D. Johnson, D. Brazier, K. Forrest, C. Ketelhut, D. Mason, and M. Mitchell, "Attitudes Toward the Use of Racial/Ethnic Profiling to Prevent Crime and Terrorism," *Criminal Justice Policy Review* 22, no. 4 (2011): 422–27.

29. C. Ray Jeffery, *Criminology: An Interdisciplinary Approach* (Englewood Cliffs, NJ: Prentice Hall, 1990).

30. Gary Cesarz and Joyce Madrid-Bustos, "Taking a Multicultural World View in Today's Corrections Facilities," *Corrections Today* 53, no. 7 (December 1991): 68–71.

31. Jerome H. Skolnick, *Justice Without Trial: Law Enforcement in a Democratic Society*, 4th ed. (New Orleans, LA: Quid Pro, 2011).

32. Jeannine Bell, "Dead Canaries in the Coal Mines: The Symbolic Assailant Revisited," *Georgia State University Law Review* 34 (2018): 513–79.

33. Jize Jiang and Edna Erez, "Immigrants as Symbolic Assailants: Crimmigration and Its Discontents," *International Criminal Justice Review* 28, no.1 (2017): 5–24.

34. See, e.g., Richard Lundman and Robert L. Kaufman, "Driving While Black: Effects of Race, Ethnicity, and Gender on Citizen Self-Reports on Traffic Stops and Police Actions," *Criminology* 41, no. 1 (2003): 195–220.

35. Rodriguez, "The Nexus Between Race and Ethnicity."

36. Cassi Pittman, "'Shopping While Black': Black Consumers' Management of Racial Stigma and Racial Profiling in Retail Settings," *Journal of Consumer Culture* (2017): 1–20.

37. Brian D. Johnson and Ryan D. King, "Facial Profiling: Race, Physical Appearance, and Punishment," *Criminology* 55, no. 3 (2017): 520–47.

38. Linda S. Miller and Karen M. Hess, *The Police in the Community: Strategies for the 21st Century*, 3rd ed. (Belmont, CA: Wadsworth, 2002).

39. J. J. Macionis, *Sociology*, 15th ed. (Upper Saddle River, NJ: Pearson, 2014), 48.

40. Thompson et al., *Society in Focus*.

41. Young, *Understanding Misunderstandings*, 101.

42. Peter L. Berger and Thomas Luckmann, *The Social Construction of Reality: A Treatise in the Sociology of Knowledge* (New York: Anchor, 1966).

43. Young, *Understanding Misunderstandings*.

44. Reaves, *State and Local Law Enforcement Training Academies*.

45. William Calathes, "The Case for a Multicultural Approach to Teaching Criminal Justice," *Journal of Criminal Justice Education* 5, no. 1 (1994): 1.

46. Cesarz and Madrid-Bustos, "Taking a Multicultural World View."

CULTURAL SPECIFICS IN THE CRIMINAL JUSTICE SYSTEM

CHAPTER 3

AFRICAN AMERICANS AND THE CRIMINAL JUSTICE SYSTEM

CHAPTER OBJECTIVES

After reading this chapter, you should be able to:

- Identify the role slavery and Reconstruction played in the history of the African American experience in this country
- Understand the current state of African Americans, particularly the rise of the Black middle class
- Describe the ways in which African Americans perceive the police
- Understand the overrepresentation of African Americans in the criminal justice system, including arrests, use of force, deadly force, sentencing, and the death penalty

The African American experience in the United States is perhaps best understood by examining their present position in American culture as well as the historical context in which this diverse group of people came to this country. While many experts recognize the varying degrees of difference among Hispanic or Latino Americans, the diversity of African Americans is often overlooked. This is particularly true as many African Americans have transcended social class, educational, and political boundaries. This chapter explores the presence of African Americans in the social, political, and economic development of the United States and offers insight into how and in what ways they become involved in the criminal justice system.

HISTORICAL BACKGROUND

There is little disagreement among historians, sociologists, and anthropologists about the fact that African Americans played a significant role in the development of the United States. Black people accompanied the first explorers to this country in the early 1600s, and a Black man was among the first to die in the American Revolution.[1] In fact, over five thousand Blacks fought in the American Revolution and over two hundred thousand fought during the Civil War.[2] In the 1960s, the mistreatment of African Americans resulted in numerous riots and other violent episodes in many cities across America.[3] However, the most significant event in American history as it relates to the African American experience was slavery.

SLAVERY

The significance of slavery in the United States is argued by many experts to be the basis for most of the racism, discrimination, and prejudice experienced by African Americans today. Thus, slavery was not simply a single tragic event in the development of a country; rather, slavery has been an essential part of this country's social, political, and economic fabric for nearly four hundred years. In fact, for nearly half of America's history, slavery was not only tolerated, it was legally protected by the Constitution and the United States Supreme Court.[4] As slavery developed in colonial America, **slave codes**, or laws regulating slave behavior, were created to clarify the position of slaves. Because they were legal and binding, and carried the support of the law, slave codes controlled and determined all aspects of the lives of enslaved Africans, including how slaves were to think, act, and believe.[5]

In an effort to quell potential uprisings by slaves, owners often used religion as a tool to foster compliance. While African religions were forbidden, slave owners introduced slaves to a distorted version of Christianity that taught that complete obedience to one's master—and to Whites in general—led to salvation and eternal happiness. According to this version, to do otherwise (such as questioning slavery) would be to question God's will, resulting in everlasting damnation.[6] While clearly designed by slave owners to gain compliance and to reduce conflict, religion served another valuable purpose. Nightly prayer meetings and singing gave slaves a sense of unity and made their lives more bearable.[7]

THE POST-SLAVERY ERA

For a generation after the American Revolution, restrictions on slaves increased as Southerners accepted slavery as a permanent feature of the economic and social landscape. In order to appease the South, writers of the Constitution legitimized slavery's existence by allowing a slave to be counted as three-fifths of a person in determining representation in the House of Representatives.[8] **Abolitionists** contended that slavery was morally objectionable, and slaves made the problem worse by not participating in protests. Many Southern states responded to this passive acceptance of slavery by enacting the **Fugitive Slave Act**, which required that slaves who had escaped, even to a free state, must be returned to their owners.[9]

In 1863, the **Emancipation Proclamation** was signed; however, the proclamation freed slaves only in the Confederacy. Two years later abolition became a reality when the Thirteenth Amendment abolished slavery nationwide.[10] From 1867 to 1877, a period known as **Reconstruction**, a new social, political, and economic portrait of the South was created. Because the federal government recognized that Southern states would not likely comply with the parameters of Reconstruction, The **Reconstruction Act of 1867** was passed to require compliance. According to the act, each Southern state was controlled by

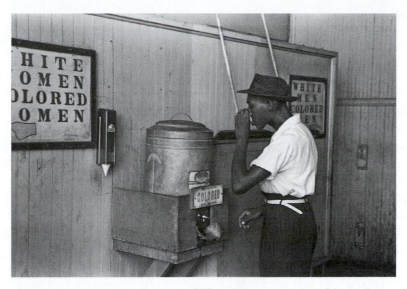

Blacks were segregated in all aspects of life, and this was the law of the land as late as 1896 and beyond.

a military governor until a new state constitution could be written.[11] This meant that until each state created a constitution that recognized Blacks as equal, the federal government would retain control over that state. Added to the problems of Reconstruction was the resistance Blacks felt from Whites after Reconstruction ended. Evidence of this resistance was found in the **Jim Crow** era. Jim Crow was a slave who entertained people through song and dance. White performers imitated him in singing and dancing style, and some used makeup to look like Jim Crow. The term "Jim Crow" eventually became a label for the social, political, and legal separation of Whites and Blacks in all aspects of society.[12]

By the end of the nineteenth century, with the legalization of segregation, discrimination against Blacks became more evident. In 1896, the U.S. Supreme Court ruled in *Plessy v. Ferguson* that state laws requiring separate but equal accommodations, such as drinking fountains or restrooms, for Blacks were a reasonable use of state government power.[13] In 1898, the Supreme Court ruled in *Williams v. Mississippi* that the use of poll taxes, literacy tests, and residential requirements were constitutional. Clearly these measures were used to discourage Blacks from voting, but even these measures did not prevent voting completely.[14] The South created a one-party system, which excluded Blacks from voting. This was considered constitutional because the party was defined as a private organization free to define its own membership.[15]

In response to the way they were treated in the South, many Blacks—nearly one million between 1914 and 1920—moved to the North in the hope of a better life.[16] However, those who thought life would be better in the North were met with a similar form of discrimination and prejudice by Whites, which led to the **civil rights movement**, which began in the 1960s.

THE CIVIL RIGHTS MOVEMENT

Perhaps in hopes of achieving equality or at least some level of respect from Whites, over one million Blacks served in the military during World War II.[17] However, Blacks soon found that discrimination also existed in the military. Training for Blacks was minimal, troops were separated by color, and most of the tasks given to Blacks were menial.[18] After the war ended, there were many opportunities for jobs due to the growth of a number of industries. As a result, many people moved to the cities for work, causing schools to become overcrowded and housing to become limited. As problems stemming from congestion escalated, the courts decided cases related to segregation issues, arguably the most important of which focused on the education of Black children.

The civil rights movement was essentially the culmination of many attempts by African Americans to secure equality following World War II. Several U.S. Supreme Court decisions during this period suggested a shift in thinking away from tolerating racial inequalities. The White primary and one-party system in the South was finally challenged and declared unconstitutional in the 1944 case of *Smith v. Allwright*. However, many states simply passed laws that used other measures to frustrate African American voters.[19] One such measure was **restrictive covenants**, a private contract between neighborhood property owners, which stipulated that property could not be sold or rented to certain minority groups, thus ensuring that minorities could not live in the area. In 1948, in *Shelly v. Kraemer*, the Supreme Court ruled that such covenants were unconstitutional.

While there were demonstrations and lawsuits since 1942, perhaps the most noted event for the start of the civil rights movement was the 1954 U.S. Supreme Court's decision in *Brown v. Board of Education*. However, the *Brown v. Board of Education* case was not the only attack on White supremacy. There are many examples of rebellion by African

The civil rights movement was one of the most significant events in the history of this country and was an attempt to secure equal protections under the law for African Americans.

Americans as early as 1942, but by 1954, unequal treatment for African Americans was a common feature of the social landscape.[20]

For the majority of Black children, public education meant attending segregated schools. Some school districts assigned children to school by race rather than by neighborhood, which is the practice that was challenged in the *Brown* case. Seven-year-old Linda Brown was not permitted to enroll in the grade school four blocks from her home in Topeka, Kansas. The policy of the local school board dictated that she attend the Black school almost two miles from her home. The NAACP Legal Defense Fund filed a lawsuit on behalf of Linda and twelve other Black children.

The NAACP argued that the Fourteenth Amendment should rule out segregation in public schools. Thurgood Marshall argued the case for the NAACP, and he went on to become a member of the United States Supreme Court.[21] The issue for the NAACP was simply that Blacks should be allowed to go to school with Whites. Given their conditions, funding, and size, all-Black schools could never be equal to all-White schools. The result was that Black children were denied the protections of the due process clause of the Fourteenth Amendment.[22]

The reaction to the *Brown* decision to desegregate public schools "with all deliberate speed," was angry and swift. Some state legislators in the South called for the impeachment of all the Supreme Court justices, others petitioned Congress to declare the Fourteenth Amendment unconstitutional, and some cities even closed schools rather than comply with the ruling. In Little Rock, Arkansas, the governor enlisted the National Guard to prevent Black students from entering previously all-White high schools.[23]

The most enduring resistance to *Brown* was found in the formation of White Citizens' Councils. Founded in Mississippi, these councils spread throughout the South and claimed as many as a half-million members. The groups began opening private all-White **Freedom Schools** that enrolled an estimated 300,000 White children by 1970. All of this effort was done with the sole intent of evading the *Brown* decision.[24]

In 1962, school desegregation took another fascinating turn when Mississippi National Guardsmen and federal authorities clashed over the admission of James Meredith, who was the first African American admitted to the University of Mississippi. A year later, Governor George Wallace "stood in the schoolhouse door" to block two Blacks from enrolling in the University of Alabama. In response to such outlandish opposition to federal law, President Kennedy federalized the Alabama National Guard in order to guarantee that the students would be admitted to campus.[25]

CIVIL DISOBEDIENCE

On December 1, 1955, Martin Luther King Jr. began his campaign of civil disobedience after the famous Rosa Parks episode. In 1955, in Montgomery, Alabama, Parks refused to comply with a bus driver's demand to give up her seat in the "colored" section of a public bus because the "White" section was already full of passengers. This led to Parks's arrest.[26] In response, King and his followers boycotted the bus system in Montgomery, Alabama. The bus boycott was the first of many instances in which nonviolent direct action was employed as a means of obtaining rights for Blacks. While the *Brown* decision may have awakened America to the level and scope of racial injustice experienced by African Americans, the Montgomery boycott marked a significant shift away from the historic reliance on the NAACP court battles and focused on concrete action to effect social change.[27] Under King's leadership, civil disobedience gained a measure of acceptability among some prominent Whites. King hoped that by emphasizing nonviolence, southern Blacks would express their hostility to racism and undercut any violent reactions by Whites.

MARTIN LUTHER KING JR. AND THE RIOTS

In 1963, President Kennedy submitted legislation to Congress to secure voting rights and broaden government protection of African Americans' civil rights. In August 1964, more than two hundred thousand people participated in the March on Washington for Jobs and Freedom, which is considered the high point of the civil rights movement. It was at this march that King delivered his famous "I Have a Dream" speech.[28]

In January 1964, the Twenty-Fourth Amendment to the U.S. Constitution was ratified, outlawing the poll tax that had prevented Blacks from voting. The enactment of the Civil Rights Act, which provided equal rights to African Americans, was hailed as a major victory and provided the illusion of equality.[29] The **Voting Rights Act** was also passed, which encouraged Blacks about their role in the political process. However, the significance of this event was overshadowed by violence in the Watts section of Los Angeles.[30] In the worst riot since 1943, the Watts riot in L.A. in 1965 was shocking in its intensity and left thirty-four people dead. Many Americans believed that racial harmony had been addressed through the passing of federal legislation; however, the events in Watts were a marker of the tension felt all over the country.[31]

In fact, many scholars point to the series of riots that devastated certain cities across America as the end of the civil rights movement. Between 1965 and 1967, major riots were witnessed in Cleveland, Ohio; Newark, New Jersey; and Detroit, Michigan. A presidential commission on the causes of violence estimated that, for 1967 alone, there were 257 civil disorders in 173 cities, killing 87 and injuring 2,500, leading to 19,000 arrests. In April 1968, after the assassination of Martin Luther King Jr., more cities witnessed violence.[32]

THE RISE OF BLACK POWER

In 1966, following the passage of the Voting Rights Act, James Meredith marched from Memphis, Tennessee, to Jackson, Mississippi, in an effort to encourage fellow Blacks to vote.[33] During the march, Stokely Carmichael, an activist, proclaimed to a cheering Black crowd, "What we need is Black power!" By advocating **Black Power**, Carmichael encouraged Blacks to create new institutions and emulate the political path followed by many European immigrant groups such as the Italians and the Irish, in previous generations. Prominent Black leaders opposed the concept because they feared that Whites would retaliate even more violently than before. While the civil rights movement tried to end segregation, it was fairly evident that White society was not interested in equality in any meaningful sense. In contrast, Black Power contended that the only way for African Americans to ever gain a political, economic, or social influence was to be more assertive.[34]

THE NATION OF ISLAM AND BLACK IDENTITY

Few recent social movements have gained as much attention and reaction as **Black nationalism**, the philosophy that encourages Blacks to see themselves as Blacks first rather than as Americans. An important part of this movement for the individual is a transformation that leads Blacks to control their own destiny and to resist any attempts to continue their own subordination.

As mentioned, Southern slave owners encouraged and often required their slaves to attend church and to embrace a distorted version of Christianity. Black nationalism, as a general rule, rejects this ideology. An example of Black nationalism is found in the **Nation of Islam**, which became known as the Black Muslims, and has attracted a large number of followers. The Muslim religion was first introduced to Black America in 1930 by W. Fard Muhammad in Detroit, Michigan.[35]

Under the leadership of Elijah Muhammad, W. Fard Muhammad's successor, the Black Muslims became a well-known and controversial organization. Malcolm X became the most powerful voice of this group in the 1960s.[36] In 1977, a Muslim sect led by Louis Farrakhan broke with the current leadership of the Nation of Islam and created his own group, adopting the more orthodox ideals of Elijah Muhammad, such as Black moral superiority.[37]

CHECKPOINT

- The following take-home messages are important in understanding this section: slavery is perhaps one of the most traumatic and enduring challenges for African Americans. This is true even after slavery was abolished. Jim Crow laws and other forms of discrimination, some of which were declared legal and constitutional, led to the civil rights movement. Along with significant political activism, including the work of Dr. Martin Luther King Jr. and the development of the Black Power movement and the Nation of Islam as a militant group, the efforts to obtain equal rights has been a long-standing challenge in American society.

AFRICAN AMERICANS TODAY: THE RISE OF THE BLACK MIDDLE CLASS

Some critics of African American history have attacked the generalizations of African American families, arguing that historians overemphasize the poorest segment of the Black community. Instead, many scholars focus on the growth of the **Black middle class** as a testimony to the success many African Americans have achieved in overcoming a legacy of racism. However, this description of African Americans today would be equally inaccurate. Rather, a true understanding of the African American experience must include a balanced view of both the success and failure of this group to achieve some semblance of the American Dream.[38]

A clearly defined Black middle class has emerged. According to the most recent census, nearly one-third of African Americans earned more than the median income for Whites. Yet many African Americans are more likely than Whites to be first-generation middle-class, who depend on two or more sources of income and live precariously close to the lower class.[39]

In 2005, in testimony before the U.S. Commission on Civil Rights, David Besharov, a research fellow at the Enterprise Institute, a think tank in Washington, DC, argued that since 1980, while the absolute numbers had increased, the Black middle class had hardly grown as a percentage of African Americans. As evidence, Besharov pointed to data on median family income for Whites and Blacks. He found that between 1980 and 2003, the percentage of Black households with incomes greater than the 1980 median income of all American households increased by one-third, from about 29 percent to about 40 percent. However, at the same time, White incomes had increased, leaving the gap about the same. Thus, while there are an increasing number of African Americans who might fit into the middle-class category, the number of Whites who are in that category has also increased. The reason for this continued stagnation has a great deal to do with the lack of educational progress for many African Americans.[40]

As some scholars have pointed out, the migration of the middle-class Blacks out of the ghetto in the 1970s and 1980s left a vacuum. Middle-class Blacks may still care about the problems of the poor, but they are no longer present as role models. As social class becomes more salient in the lives of African American families, particularly those that have gained some measure of economic and even political success, the relationship of social class, race, and poverty becomes important.[41]

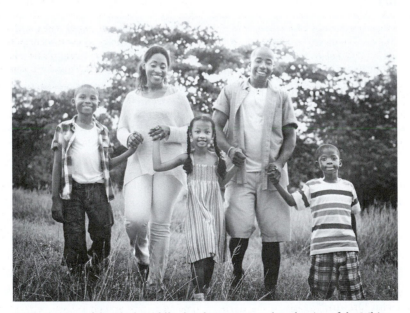

While the size of the Black middle class has grown, so has the size of the White middle class. Despite the fact that some Blacks have done well by any societal standard, there still remains a large number who feel the effects of discrimination despite their success.

Social scientists have long recognized the importance of class. It is a difficult concept to define, as many disagree on the boundaries of where one class category begins and another ends, not to mention the problems of determining a sufficient number of class categories. However, few experts argue that social class is not an important variable in the discussion of issues such as poverty, employment, healthcare, housing, and criminal justice.[42]

The complexity of relative influence of race and class was apparent in the controversy surrounding William Julius Wilson's (1978) *The Declining Significance of Race*. Pointing to the increasing influence of African Americans, Wilson concludes that class has become more important than race in determining life chances or opportunities for Blacks' success in the modern world. His conclusions suggest that programs must be developed to confront class issues rather than ethnic and racial discrimination. Wilson argues that the legacy of discrimination is still alive, as reflected in the disproportionate number of Blacks who are poor, less educated, and who live in inadequate housing. However, he contends that the evidence shows that many segments of the African American population are able to effectively compete with segments of the White population.[43]

THE BLACK LIVES MATTER MOVEMENT

The relationship between race and crime, particularly for African Americans, is often seen in comments made by policy makers and political figures. Recently, the group Black Lives Matter has been at the center of a great deal of controversy surrounding the shooting of police officers. They focus their attention on the disenfranchisement of all Blacks—including those with an LGBT focus and the elderly—and the structures of society that attempt to continue to oppress Blacks. The website offers further commentary:

It goes beyond the narrow nationalism that can be prevalent within Black communities, which merely call on Black people to love Black, live Black and buy Black, keeping straight Black men in the front of the movement while our sisters, queer and trans, and disabled folk take up roles in the background or not at all.

Black Lives Matter affirms the lives of Black queer and trans folks, disabled folks, Black undocumented folks, folks with records, women and all Black lives along the gender spectrum. It centers those that have been marginalized within Black liberation movements. It is a tactic to (re)build the Black liberation movement.

What Does #BlackLivesMatter Mean?

When we say Black Lives Matter, we are broadening the conversation around state violence to include all of the ways in which Black people are intentionally left powerless at the hands of the state. We are talking about the ways in which Black lives are deprived of our basic human rights and dignity.[44]

Interestingly, unlike the Civil Rights Movement of the 1960s, the Black Lives Matter movement does not have a single leader and has instead opted to have many organizers and activists shape its direction and cause. The rationale is that, should a leader leave, as in the case of the assassination of Martin Luther King Jr., which left the Civil Rights Movement without a direction or long-term commitment, the same fate could befall the Black Lives Matter movement as well. As Fredrick Harris of *Dissent Magazine* points out:

They are rejecting the charismatic leadership model that has dominated Black politics . . . and for good reason. . . . This older model is associated with Martin Luther King. . . . Black Lives Matter activists today recognize that granting decision-making power to an individual . . . poses a risk to the durability of a movement—charismatic leaders can therefore weaken them, even lead to their collapse.[45]

Another distinction between the Black Lives Matter movement and the civil rights movement of the 1960s involves the use of social media. In a previous era, the ability to message a broad audience was limited, given the technology of the time. Today, with the advent of Facebook, Twitter, Snapchat, and Instagram, the Black Lives Matter advocates can instantaneously broadcast their message worldwide, thereby engaging a much wider audience of potential supporters.

Critics of the movement argue that this is an inflammatory group that gives attention only to certain types of lives. Others claim that they promote violence against society and the police, as evidenced by the assassination of police officers in Dallas, Texas. In response to the creation of Black Lives Matter, other

(*continued*)

(continued)

groups have been created, such as the "All Lives Matter" effort or the "Blue Lives Matter" in response to the murder of police officers, often by African Americans, some of whom claim affiliation and association with the Black Lives Matter group.

It is also important to note that not all African Americans embrace the Black Lives Matter movement. According to a 2016 poll from the Pew Research Center, about 12 percent of African Americans oppose the movement (with about 5 percent strongly in opposition to it) and about 20 percent of African American adults think it will be effective. Young White adults are more enthusiastic about the movement than older Whites, suggesting that perhaps a Millennial interest is involved in the effort. While there may continue to be debate about what the goals of the organization might be, there can be little doubt that the Black Lives Matter group will remain a part of the multicultural narrative, particularly as it relates to the involvement of African Americans in the criminal justice system.

CHECKPOINT

- The emergence of a sizeable Black middle class may indicate to some people that the history of discriminatory treatment and prejudice has passed. As we have seen, however, the rise of the black middle class is not a simple concept, and the injustices against African Americans continues. This is what led to the emergence of the Black Lives Matter movement, which attempts to call attention to the unequal treatment of Blacks by the police and the criminal justice system.

THE HISTORICAL TREATMENT OF AFRICAN AMERICANS IN THE CRIMINAL JUSTICE SYSTEM

Any discussion of the African American experience in this country is incomplete without including what some experts have referred to as a byproduct of the legacy of slavery. That so many African Americans are under the supervision of the criminal justice system, with many others touched by its extensively long hand, illustrates the social position of African Americans in the United States.

In his book, *No Equal Justice: Race and Class in the American Criminal Justice System*, David Cole (1999) argues that historically, African Americans were mistreated by the criminal justice process. This exploitation begins with the ratification of the U.S. Constitution in 1788, where, prior to the ratification of the Constitution, women could not vote and enslaved Africans counted as three-fifths of a person and had no fundamental rights of citizenship. Prior to the ratification of the U.S. Constitution, slavery had a two-hundred-year history in the colonies. The institution of slavery simultaneously was built on the tenet that Africans brought to America "had no rights which the White man was bound to respect," as articulated by the U.S. Supreme Court in the landmark case of *Dred Scott v. Sandford* in 1857 (60 U.S. 393; 1857).

The ratification of the Thirteenth, Fourteenth, and Fifteenth Amendments and Reconstruction, which was purported to offer a glimmer of hope for equality and citizenship, led many African Americans to believe that equality was within their grasp. However, violence by groups such as the Ku Klux Klan kept most African Americans away from the polls.[46] Cole makes an interesting argument concerning the way the Thirteenth

Amendment was written to increase the likelihood that African Americans would continue to be legally exploited despite the abolition of slavery. He states that as a legal loophole, the Thirteenth Amendment provided for the continued enslavement of individuals based on their status as a *criminal offender.*[47]

Cole also points out that during the Jim Crow era of the late nineteenth century, African Americans were convicted of crimes at a much higher rate than Whites. As evidence of this, Cole points to statistics from Georgia, where, in 1908, Black prisoners outnumbered White prisoners 10 to 1, and the majority of the Black prisoners were convicted of nonviolent property crimes.[48]

Other scholars raise similar concerns about decisions by the U.S. Supreme Court.[49] Two of the most well-known Supreme Court decisions on criminal justice do not in practice protect African Americans. In 1963 in the case of *Gideon v. Wainwright* (372 U.S. 335; 1963), the Court held that states must provide a lawyer at state expense to all defendants charged with a serious crime who cannot afford to hire one. Three years later, in *Miranda v. Arizona* (384 U.S. 436; 1966), the Court required the police to provide poor suspects with an attorney at state expense and to inform all suspects of their rights before questioning them in custody.

Some experts argue that in these landmark decisions, the Court sought to ameliorate societal inequalities that undermined the criminal justice system's promise of equality. As the Court stated in *Miranda*, "[w]hile authorities are not required to relieve the accused of his poverty, they have the obligation not to take advantage of indigence in the administration of justice."[50] These decisions were decided by the Supreme Court under Chief Justice Earl Warren, at a time when the Court was solidly liberal and strongly committed to racial and economic equality. It is also argued that at virtually every juncture since *Gideon* and *Miranda*, the Supreme Court has undercut the principle of equality reflected in those decisions.[51]

These same scholars contend that *Gideon* is a symbol of equality unrealized in practice; poor defendants are entitled to the assistance of counsel at trial, but the Supreme Court has failed to demand that the assistance be meaningful. Cole says, "Lawyers who have slept through testimony or appeared in court drunk have nonetheless been deemed to have provided their indigent clients 'effective assistance of counsel.'"[52] These experts argue that today's Court has so diluted *Miranda* that the decision has had little effect on actual police interrogation practices.[53]

More generally, the problems of exploitation and inequality in the criminal justice system are driven by the need to balance two fundamental and competing interests: the protection of Constitutional rights and the protection of law-abiding citizens from crime. For example, without a Constitutional requirement that police have probable cause and a warrant before they conduct searches, police officers would be far more effective in rooting out and stopping crime. Without jury trials, criminal justice administration would be much more efficient. But without these safeguards, we would live in a police state, with no meaningful privacy protection. Absent jury trials, the community would have little check on overzealous prosecutors.[54]

Much of the public and academic debate about criminal justice focuses on where we should draw the line between law enforcement interests and Constitutional protections. Liberals and conservatives agree, at least in principle, that the line should be drawn in the same place for everyone. However, some experts suggest that there appears to be an inconsistency when and where that line is drawn, which results in an unfair burden placed on African Americans.[55]

AFRICAN AMERICANS AND THE CRIMINAL JUSTICE SYSTEM TODAY

THE POLICE

Perhaps the most controversial interaction that African Americans have with the criminal justice system relates to the police. Much has been said and written about police-minority relations, the use of force by police officers against African Americans, and **racial profiling**. As described below, there are a number of sensational cases in which the police have mistreated members of minority groups. There also appears to be a long record of such activity involving African Americans. The following accounts are illustrative:

FERGUSON, MISSOURI. On August 9, 2014, a police officer was on patrol and encountered eighteen-year-old Michael Brown and a friend walking down a street. An altercation ensued between Officer Wilson and Brown, who at the time was standing at the window of the vehicle. Officer Wilson fired two shots from inside the vehicle, one likely grazing Brown's thumb, and the other missing him. Brown then ran away and Officer Wilson pursued him on foot. Brown stopped and turned toward Officer Wilson, who also stopped. Brown then moved toward Officer Wilson, who fired several shots, fatally wounding Brown. According to the county prosecutor, Brown suffered at least seven gunshot wounds. His body lay in the street for four hours before it was removed. Wilson fired a total of twelve times, though investigators were unclear exactly how many struck Brown. Riots lasted for days in the city of Ferguson after Brown's death, as members of the African American community felt the actions of Officer Wilson were unjustified.

In November, a St. Louis County grand jury and the U.S. Justice Department failed to find enough evidence to bring charges against Officer Wilson. The panel of jurors was composed of twelve citizens: six White men, three White women, one African American man, and two African American women. Much of the evidence from witnesses was contradictory. Some of it had supported Officer Wilson's version of events. Other witness statements had appeared to support the account of Dorian Johnson, Brown's friend who was with him when he died. St. Louis County prosecutor Robert McCulloch did not recommend any charges against Officer Wilson to the jury. This caused anger in Ferguson and around the U.S. as critics said it showed an unwillingness to prosecute.[56]

BALTIMORE, MARYLAND. On April 12, 2015, Freddie Gray, a twenty-five-year-old male, was arrested by the Baltimore Police Department for allegedly possessing what was said to be an illegal switchblade. Gray was put into a police van; while in transit to the police station, he became unresponsive and fell into a coma. Gray was taken to a trauma center where he died four days later. In the video shot by a bystander, Gray shouts in pain as he is dragged into a police van. While being handled by police, the video shows that Gray's leg appears injured. From the scene where he was arrested to the police station, Gray suffered a neck and spinal injury. When taken to the trauma center, Gray was treated for three fractured vertebrae and a crushed larynx (voice box). The doctors at the trauma center said that Gray's injuries were consistent with those that might be sustained by someone who was in a car accident. Just like in Ferguson, riots ensued and lasted for days. Gray's death was ruled a homicide and six officers had legal charges brought against them for second-degree murder (Caesar Goodson, Garrett Miller, Edward Nero, William Porter, Brian Rice, and Alicia White). The officers were ultimately acquitted of all charges.[57]

CHICAGO, ILLINOIS. On October 20, 2014, Laquan McDonald, a seventeen-year-old male, was shot sixteen times by Chicago police officer Jason Van Dyke. McDonald was being pursued by the Chicago Police after calls and complaints reported him to be carrying a knife and breaking into cars parked in a trucking yard. When confronted by police, McDonald took out his knife and slashed the tires of a police patrol car and damaged the windshield. He was told by the police to drop the knife but he continued to walk away. A police cruiser's dash-cam captured the last few minutes of McDonald's life. He is seen walking away and avoiding all officers on the scene when he is shot by Van Dyke, who fired all sixteen rounds in the magazine of his weapon. The video shows that McDonald's limp body was shot while he was lying on the ground. According to the toxicology report, McDonald had PCP in his system, which contributed to his erratic behavior. Officer Van Dyke was charged with first-degree murder a few hours after the video was released, and he turned himself in to authorities. He was indicted for six counts of first-degree murder and one count of official misconduct.[58] In 2019, Van Dyke was convicted of second-degree murder and sixteen counts of aggravated battery. He was sentenced to more than six years in prison.[59]

STATEN ISLAND, NEW YORK. On July 17, 2014, Eric Garner, a forty-three-year-old Black male, was being questioned and pursued by police for selling untaxed cigarettes, something for which he had been reprimanded numerous times in the past. After confronting a verbally combative Garner, several police officers went to arrest him. When White Officer Daniel Pantaleo took Garner's wrist behind his back, Garner resisted. Pantaleo then put his arm around Garner's neck and pulled him backward and down onto the ground. After Pantaleo removed his arm from Garner's neck, he then pushed Garner's face into the ground while four officers moved to restrain Garner. Throughout the video, which was recorded by a bystander, who was also a friend of Garner, Garner is heard repeating, "I can't breathe," during the altercation and while lying face down on the sidewalk. After he lost consciousness, officers turned Garner onto his side to help ease his breathing. Garner remained lying on the sidewalk for seven minutes while the officers waited for an ambulance to arrive. Neither police officers nor the EMTs performed CPR because they believed him to still be breathing.

According to the medical examiner, Garner was killed by the compression to his neck, but there was no damage to his windpipe or his spine. While Officer Pantaleo would not be indicted, a separate investigation of the entire department in regards to police brutality resulted in the Garner family settling their lawsuit with the city for $5.9 million. This ruling ignited protests that led to the shooting of two Brooklyn police officers.[60]

CHARLESTON, SOUTH CAROLINA. On April 4, 2015, Walter Scott, a fifty-year-old Black male, was fatally shot by a White North Charleston police officer, Michael Slager. Scott was stopped by Slager for a minor traffic violation. After Slager approached the car and was heading back to his patrol car, Scott exited his car and fled from the scene. Slager pursued Scott on foot. After hitting Scott with his Taser, Slager then pulled out his handgun and fired eight rounds at Scott, hitting him five times. Controversy arose after the video was released showing Slager planting his Taser on Scott. Slager's reasoning for shooting Scott was that Scott had taken his Taser and Slager feared for his safety.

After reviewing the video, Officer Slager was arrested and charged with murder. He was later indicted for the charge. In January 2016, Slager was released on a $500,000 bond and was under house arrest until his trial in October 2016.[61] In December 2016, a mistrial was declared in the case after jurors could not unanimously agree on a verdict. The jurors deliberated for four days and had three options: murder, voluntary manslaughter, or acquittal. One juror declared that he refused to convict Slager of anything and several other jurors were conflicted about a decision during deliberations as well.[62] Slager was ultimately convicted on federal charges and sentenced to twenty years in prison.[63]

BATON ROUGE, LOUISIANA. In July 2016, two White officers were arresting Alton B. Sterling, a Black man, after responding to a call about an armed man. The caller allegedly told police that a Black man in a red shirt selling music CDs outside a convenience store had threatened him with a gun. Mr. Sterling had a long criminal record, including convictions for battery and illegal possession of a gun, but it is not clear whether the officers knew any of that when they tried to arrest him. As the officers wrestled with Mr. Sterling and brought him to the ground, someone in the video can be heard saying "He's got a gun! Gun!" and one officer can be seen pulling his weapon. While there is more than one video, and the facts of the case have not been conclusively determined, the officers shot Sterling, killing him. The incident prompted protests and demonstrations in cities across the country. A federal investigation has also been launched.[64] Several days later, in response to the shooting, three police officers were killed and three others were wounded by a former U.S. Marine. The suspect, who was Black (the officers killed were White), was killed by police.[65]

DALLAS, TEXAS. In July 2016, in response to deadly shooting incidents in Baton Rouge, Louisiana, and suburban St. Paul, Minnesota, police officers were ambushed by a sniper with a rifle in Dallas, Texas. Five police officers were killed and seven officers and two civilians were wounded. These officers were killed while providing protection to demonstrators who were protesting police violence against Black people. The suspect, Micah X. Johnson, a former soldier and an alleged supporter of the Black Lives Matter movement, died after a standoff with police. The suspect said he was upset about the recent police shootings of African Americans in Baton Rouge, Louisiana, and in Minnesota.[66] While the details of each episode are still under investigation, the situations raise questions about the appropriateness of police actions as well as perceptions of African Americans by police officers.[67]

ST. PAUL, MINNESOTA. On July 6, 2016, in a suburb of St. Paul, Minnesota, Jeronimo Yanez, a Hispanic police officer, pulled over Philando Castile, a Black male. Castile fit the description of an armed robbery suspect that the police were searching for. Castile told

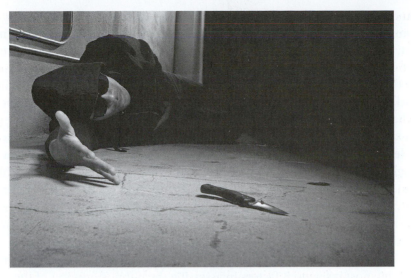

Tensions between the police and the Black community stem from the perception of excessive violence by officers against African American males.

officer Yanez that he had a gun permit and was armed. As he was allegedly reaching for his ID, officer Yanez shot Castile. Castile's girlfriend videotaped the incident and streamed it on Facebook. In response, protestors marched, causing traffic jams on Interstate 35 in Minneapolis and Interstate 94 in St. Paul, causing an estimated $1.5 million in damages. In all, more than 150 arrests were made as a result of the demonstrations.[68]

On almost any given day, we hear of instances like the ones just described. These dramatic episodes raise questions about the role of the police in our society, particularly in their interactions with minority groups. These individuals argue that situations like the ones described above are indicators that the police target minorities and treat them differently. Is there any truth to these assertions? Are the police racist? Do they treat minorities differently? How does the public perceive the police?

Public Opinion and the Police

According to a 2013 Justice Department report, an estimated sixty-three million people in the United States—about 26 percent of the population—have some form of contact with the police every year. This contact is about equally likely to be initiated by residents as by the police. The latter include traffic stops or stopping persons in public places. The majority of persons in contact with the police thought the police behaved properly during the contact. Approximately 93 percent of those who requested police assistance, 88 percent of drivers pulled over in traffic stops, and 71 percent of persons involved in street stops felt the actions of officers were appropriate.

As it related to traffic stops, Black drivers (13 percent) were more likely than White and Hispanic (10 percent each) to be pulled over by police in a traffic stop; however Blacks,

Whites, and Hispanics were equally likely to be stopped in a street stop. This is quite different from data in the early 1990s that reflected a tendency to "stop and frisk" minorities more often than Whites. Further, about 80 percent of drivers in traffic stops and 60 percent of those involved in street stops believed they were stopped for a legitimate reason.[69]

While this latest study from the Department of Justice shows some promising trends, it is important to note that these findings have been consistent since 2005.[70] These figures indicate that, in general, a significant proportion of the population thinks the police are doing a good job; however, minorities generally feel less confident in the police and are generally less satisfied with police services. Another important factor is the characteristic of the neighborhood. One study found that people living in high-crime neighborhoods and low-income communities tend to have more contact with the police and report less overall satisfaction. Furthermore, because minorities tend to live in these types of neighborhoods, it is not surprising that the confidence in the police is lower for them than it is among Whites.[71]

A 2003 study found that neighborhood characteristics and interactions with police officers were the most influential factors in assessing the public's opinion of the police. The study, conducted in four diverse neighborhoods in Los Angeles, found that residents from neighborhoods perceived to be crime-ridden, dangerous, and disorderly were less likely to approve of the police. In contrast, residents who had informal personal contact with police were more likely to express approval.

While race and ethnicity had been cited as influential factors in other studies, neither was as important as the level of social and physical disorder in the community in determining the public's satisfaction with police. Where race and ethnicity did matter was in the perception of how the police treated minorities. For example, African Americans were more likely to say that officers had acted unprofessionally toward them than were Whites. This study also found that the media had little influence on public opinion of the police. While limited in its ability to make an overall assessment of the public's opinion of the police, this study nevertheless raised a number of questions about how to change the public's perception of police officers.[72]

Why do police officers have more contact with low-income and minority neighborhoods? Part of the answer is that this group makes greater use of police services than other groups. Police departments assign more patrol officers to these neighborhoods because of greater calls for service and because minority groups in these areas have higher crime rates. Another reason is that minorities and low-income people are more likely to call the police to solve a variety of non-criminal matters. Compared to middle-class Americans, for instance, people in the low-income category are more likely to call the police for assistance with medical emergencies and family problems. This means that the police are more actively and intrusively involved in the daily lives of people from these areas. Greater contact also means that the decisions made by officers may not be what the members of these neighborhoods prefer, resulting in lower levels of satisfaction. In sum, evidence suggests differential treatment of minorities by police on a variety of indicators, including violent crime, deadly force, arrests, and other minor forms of abuse.[73]

Violent Crime

Perhaps due to the distortion of crime and criminals in the media, as well as their own experiences with crime, many people, including the police, believe that African Americans and other minorities are more involved in violent crime than Whites. Moreover, this perception affects how officers respond to violent crimes. For instance, using data from the *National Crime Victimization Survey*, one study examined the relationship between the victim and the offender's race on three measures of police responses to robbery and aggravated assault. The variables considered were the response time to the scene, the amount of effort made by officers to investigate these crimes at the scene, and the likelihood of arrest.[74]

Officers were quicker to respond and invested more effort in the investigation (e.g., searches) when the incident consisted of African American offenders and White victims. This relationship held even when variables such as poverty, the victim's gender, and whether or not the victim was injured were taken into account. With regard to aggravated assault, particularly those involving strangers, officers were more likely to be more thorough at the scene if it involved a White victim and an African American offender. Officers were also more likely, all other things being equal, to respond more quickly and to put forth a more determined effort if there was an injury to the White victim, particularly by an African American offender. None of these findings applied when the victim was an African American and the offender was White. Thus, evidence suggests that the race of the victim and the offender plays a role in how the police respond to violent crime. If the crime involves a White victim and an African American offender, officers seem to respond more quickly to the scene of the crime and investigate it more thoroughly, and arrests are more likely to occur.[75]

Arrests

Is race a factor in the arrest of a suspect? The answer appears clear as minorities are arrested out of proportion to their representation in the population. According to the Uniform Crime Reports, in 2017, African Americans represented about 14 percent of the population but approximately 27 percent of all arrests and 38 percent of arrests for violent crime (see Table 3.1). Also in 2017, approximately 69 percent of all individuals arrested were White, about 27 percent were Black, with the remaining 4 percent from other races. White individuals were arrested more often for violent crimes than individuals of any other race and accounted for approximately 59 percent of those arrests. Of adults arrested for murder, about 53 percent were Black and 44 percent were White, with other races making up the remaining percentage (see Table 3.2). As it relates to juveniles, Blacks comprised nearly 51 percent of all juveniles arrested for violent crime while White juveniles accounted for nearly 57 percent of all juveniles arrested for property crimes.[76]

However, there is a great deal of controversy surrounding this issue. What are the reasons for this apparent differential treatment? Do police officers arrest African Americans more frequently due to racial bias or because Blacks commit more crimes? What variables are considered in the decision to arrest?

In his famous article "The Social Organization of Arrest," Donald Black (1971) found that, in general, the decision to arrest was predicated on a number of factors, including the strength of the evidence, the seriousness of the crime, whether or not the complainant or

TABLE 3.1   ARRESTS BY RACE 2017

Race	Arrests
White	5,626,140
Black or African American	2,221,697
American Indian or Alaska Native	196,908
Asian	97,049
Hawaiian or Pacific Islander	21,055
Total Arrests:	8,162,849

Source: U.S. Department of Justice, Federal Bureau of Investigation (2018). *Crime in the United States 2017*, Table 43. Available at: https://ucr.fbi.gov/crime-in-the-u.s/2017/crime-in-the-u.s.-2017/tables/table-43

TABLE 3.2   ARRESTS BY RACE AND TYPE OF CRIME

Crime	Whites	Black or African American
Murder	4,188 (44.2%)	5,025 (53.1%)
Rape	12,187 (67.5%)	5,182 (28.7%)
Robbery	32,128 (43.6%)	40,024 (54.3%)
Aggr. Assault	188,087 (62.1%)	101,513 (33.5%)
Burglary	104,671 (67.5%)	46,227 (29.8%)
Larceny	501,231 (67.7%)	215,650 (29.1%)
MV Theft	46,621 (66%)	21,415 (30.3%)
Arson	5,051 (71.3%)	1,788 (25.2%)
Violent Crime	236,590 (58.5%)	151,744 (37.5%)
Property Crime	657,574 (67.6%)	285,080 (29.3%)

Source: U.S. Department of Justice, Federal Bureau of Investigation (2018). *Crime in the United States 2017*, Table 43. Available at: https://ucr.fbi.gov/crime-in-the-u.s/2017/crime-in-the-u.s.-2017/tables/table-43

victim wanted the suspect arrested, and whether the suspect was disrespectful toward the officer. The decision to arrest was also based on the relationship between the victim and the offender. If the suspect was a stranger to the victim, the officers were more likely to arrest him or her.[77]

Interestingly, Black found that race was not a factor in the decision to arrest. He did find that African Americans were arrested more often than Whites, but this was mainly due to the fact that Whites were more likely to show deference to the officer. As he describes, this creates a vicious cycle, where the African American men who are arrested more often have negative feelings toward the police. When these feelings are demonstrated, they are more likely to be arrested, which increases the hostility felt by African Americans.[78]

Much research following Black's earlier work found that race does matter. In the 1980s, for instance, race was considered in terms of the decision to arrest. One study found that in those instances where the suspect was African American and the victim was White, officers were more likely to make an arrest.[79] Similar to Black's findings, in these situations, officers were also more likely to arrest the suspect upon the victim's request to do so.[80]

Another study found that African Americans and Hispanics were more likely to be arrested on less evidence than Whites. The study also found that Blacks and Hispanics were more likely to be released without the case going to the prosecutor. While at first glance this may appear to be advantageous, arrest still represents a form of punishment even though formal charges may not be filed.[81]

Another study examined 718 police officers in Ohio and examined the extent to which a suspect's race influenced an officer's behavior. The results of the study showed that officers did not feel race was a significant factor in determining the officer's behavior. What was significant was the suspect's demeanor—how they acted toward the officer. However, care should be taken in interpreting this finding since it may be related to race in that African Americans may be more likely to have a negative attitude toward the police, which can lead to a similar outcome. The evidence seems to suggest, then, that the race of the victim and of the offender play an important role in the decision to arrest.[82]

Use of Force

The Rodney King example is perhaps the most visible and memorable reminder of excessive use of force by police officers. King, who was driving while intoxicated, led the police on a high-speed car chase in 1991. After he eventually stopped, four officers were videotaped beating King, while several other officers observed the beating. The video, one of the first of its kind, was sent to the media and resulted in the arrest of four officers, who were charged with assault with a deadly weapon and excessive use of force. Three officers were eventually acquitted of all charges and the fourth officer was acquitted of the assault charge, but the jury deadlocked 8–4 in favor of acquittal on the excessive use of force. These decisions were said to be the reason for the subsequent riots that occurred in Los Angeles that led to millions of dollars in property damage and other crimes. After the state trial, federal charges were brought against the officers for violating King's civil rights. The result was that two of the officers were acquitted again and two officers were found guilty.[83]

However, prior to 1991, there was considerable academic interest in the use-of-force topic prior to the King incident.[84] In his classic study of the police, Albert J. Reiss (1971) found that race, per se, was not a determining factor in the use of excessive force. Instead, "class rather than race determines police misconduct."[85] The typical victim of excessive force is a lower-class male, regardless of race. Others, however, disagree and see excessive use of force as particularly prevalent against African American men. According to a 1999 Bureau of Justice Statistics report on police-citizen contacts, there were substantial racial and ethnic disparities in police use of force. African Americans were three times as likely to experience force or threatened force than Whites. Hispanics were more likely than Whites but less likely than African Americans to experience police use of force.[86]

The implications of this trend are particularly significant for African Americans. Even if the overall rate of the use of force comprises 1 percent of all police-citizen encounters, if those incidents are concentrated in low-income neighborhoods and consist of lower-class men, who are likely to be African American, the effects of these incidents accumulate over time to create a perception that the police routinely harass African Americans.[87] The symbolic significance of the excessive use of force should not be overlooked. As representatives of the larger system, police officers who engage in excessive use of force serve as a reminder of the larger problems of discrimination and exploitation felt by African Americans.[88] More recently, according to a U.S. Department of Justice report, large state and local law enforcement agencies received approximately 26,000 complaints from citizens about the excessive use of force by officers. This number translates into a rate of about 6.6 complaints per 100 full-time sworn officers. About 8 percent of these complaints were officially sustained, meaning there was sufficient evidence to justify disciplinary action against the officer or officers; about 34 percent were not sustained; 25 percent were declared unfounded or the complaint was not supported by the facts (or the incident did not occur); and 23 percent ended in exonerations because the officers acted properly.[89]

Deadly Force

Despite the notoriety when such events occur, there has been a general decline in the incidence of deadly force by the police.[90] However, a great deal of attention has been given to the frequency with which police officers use deadly force against minorities.[91] When compared with their numbers in the population, African Americans are disproportionately killed by the police. However, these findings also suggest that when compared with rates of police-citizen contacts, arrest rates, and resistance to or attacks upon the police, there is no apparent racial disparity in the use of deadly force by the police.[92]

By the mid-1980s, when many departments adopted a defense-of-life rule, which allows officers to use deadly force only when attempting to protect themselves or the lives of others, the number of persons shot and killed by the police decreased significantly. Part of the reason for the general decline in the use of deadly force has come from more restrictive policies at the departmental level as well as from the Supreme Court decision in *Tennessee v. Garner*.[93] One study found that from 1970 to 1984, the police use of deadly force declined substantially, particularly against African Americans.[94] More recently, the data indicate that the racial disparity in the number of people shot and killed by the police has decreased from about seven African Americans for every White to about three to one.[95]

Another situation in which deadly force is justified occurs when the officer prevents the escape of a person who is extremely dangerous.[96] In *Tennessee v. Garner* (471 U.S. 1 (1985)), two officers used deadly force against an African American juvenile who was fleeing the scene of a burglary. At that time, the officers were justified in using deadly physical force against a fleeing felon. However, the Court ruled that this was no longer acceptable. As a result, many departments were required to modify their policies concerning use of force against fleeing felons. Thus, while there was a time when officers were given wide latitude in using deadly force, since 1980 departments all over the country have changed their policies regarding the use of force and the number of incidents has declined considerably.

In 2011, the U.S. Department of Justice released a report on arrest-related deaths, which noted that between 2003 and 2009, 4,813 persons died during or shortly after law enforcement personnel attempted to arrest or restrain them. About 60 percent were classified as homicides by law enforcement personnel and 40 percent to other manners of death, such as suicide, death by intoxication, accidental injury, or natural causes.

Of those person who died during the process of arrest, 95 percent were male, about 42 percent were White, 32 percent were Black, and 20 percent were Hispanic or Latino. More than 55 percent were between the ages of twenty-five and forty-four. And among male arrest-related deaths 62 percent were attributed to homicide. Of those who committed suicide during the process of arrest, 60 percent were White, 15 percent were Black and 20 percent were Hispanic or Latino. Among those deaths by intoxication, 41 percent were Black while 34 percent were White, with Hispanics comprising 21 percent.[97]

Profiling and Other Forms of Abuse

The issue surrounding discriminatory treatment of African Americans extends beyond serious offenses. In fact, one might argue that it is the minor forms of abuse that create a climate of fear and hostility between the police and minorities. These indignities, or what sociologist Elliot Liebow has referred to as the "little murders of everyday life,"[98] characterize the attitudes the police have toward minorities in some circumstances. The difference between this type of abuse and the others discussed, however, is that there is no tangible reminder that the incident occurred.

Minor forms of abuse such as profiling usually end with the interaction between the officer and the suspect. These forms of abuse usually occur on the street and typically involve no witnesses. This makes sustaining allegations very difficult and results in continued tension between the police and minorities.[99]

In the mid-1990s, the New Jersey State Police were investigated for allegedly ordering officers to concentrate on stopping Black drivers. Three state troopers stated they were instructed by their superiors to single out African American drivers for traffic stops. Additionally, a 1992 study of traffic stops in Florida found that while 5 percent of the drivers on the road were African American or Hispanic, nearly 70 percent of those stopped and 80 percent of those searched were African American or Hispanic. Further, nationally, from January 1993 to August 1995, almost 90 percent of the individuals subjected to search-and-seizure operations on buses and trains were people of color. Another study of all reported federal decisions from 1993 to 1995 involving bus and train sweeps found that nearly 90 percent of those targeted were minorities.[100]

About ten years later, another controversy was created when, in April 2005, a report on racial profiling was scheduled to be released by the Department of Justice's Bureau of Justice Statistics. Based on interviews with 80,000 people in 2002, the study found that White, Black, and Hispanic drivers nationwide were stopped by the police that year at about the same rate, roughly 9 percent. But, the Justice Department report also found that once they were stopped, Hispanic drivers were searched or had their vehicles searched by the police 11.4 percent of the time and Blacks 10.2 percent of the time, compared to only 3.5 percent for White drivers. The study found that officers were more likely to threaten or use force against Blacks and Hispanics than Whites, and the police were much more likely to issue tickets to Hispanics rather than simply giving them a warning.

The authors of the study said they were not able to draw any conclusions about the reason for the differing rates, but they said the gaps were notable. The research "uncovered evidence of Black drivers having worse experiences—more likely to be arrested, more likely to be searched, more likely to have force used against them—during traffic stops than White drivers." The inflammatory nature of these findings allegedly led the Justice Department to try to suppress some of the information or to change the findings. While strenuously arguing that the results should not be altered for political purposes, the director of the Bureau of Justice Statistics was demoted.[101] What should also be considered in reviewing the trends cited in the earlier studies is the more recent data highlighted at the beginning of this chapter. While it may be reasonable to assume that some form of profiling may exist at an individual officer level, the fact that the trends are far different from what was discovered during the 1990s indicates that the changes were made in police practices as it relates to police-citizen interactions.

Another study explored the extent to which there are racial differences in getting hassled as well as what the researchers identify as **vicarious hassling**—knowing someone who has experienced this type of treatment by the police. The main finding of the study was that African Americans are more likely to perceive they are being hassled by the police individually and vicariously. Nearly one-half of African Americans in the study had experienced a negative police interaction, and two-thirds knew someone who'd had a similar experience, compared to the 10 percent of Whites who experienced this type of treatment in the same way. While such a discrepancy could be a result of different patrol practices, which focus on minority neighborhoods, it could also be that some of these perceptions are a result of frequent police contact. A third explanation may be that there exists a perception by officers that African Americans and other minorities are more likely to commit crimes and thus are potential offenders that warrant police attention.[102]

Finally, there is verbal abuse. Many complaints are filed each year against officers who verbally abuse citizens. The **Christopher Commission**, created to investigate allegations of abuse in Los Angeles following the beating of Rodney King by White officers, found that officers frequently used abusive language. This may have occurred during the interaction with citizens or it may have happened between officers. For example, the Commission's investigation discovered computer messages sent between officers that contained racially offensive comments.

Research on police behavior suggests that derogatory comments and the stigmatizing labeling of people is a way for officers to control suspects. Profanity serves several functions: to gain the individual's attention when interacting with officers, to keep them at a social distance while the interaction occurs, and to psychologically dominate the individual.[103]

What does all this tell us? It should remind us that the relationship between the police and African Americans is complex. As some conservative researchers, such as Heather MacDonald, have pointed out, African Americans may be arrested disproportionately, in part, because of their more pronounced involvement in criminal activities;[104] it may also have to do with the way African Americans respond to police contact. Structural issues such as poverty and overcrowding in urban areas may contribute to greater police contact, in that the problems experienced in those areas require a more frequent police presence. Minority involvement with the police may also have something to do with the attitudes of police officers—some officers believe minorities are more likely to become involved in criminal activities, so they merit greater police attention. Finally, African American overrepresentation in the criminal justice system may also have something to do with the perceptions of the police, which tend to inflame the nature of the interaction between the two groups.

In response to problems stemming from police interactions in low-income African American communities, and after being accused of racially motivated excessive use of force, some officers in several cities around the country have employed **de-policing** as a strategy. De-policing is a tactic employed by some officers who answer only 911 calls instead of engaging in routine patrol. This is done to avoid contact with minorities and to prevent routine situations from escalating into charges of racial profiling or discriminatory treatment of minorities. By only answering emergency calls, such contact is limited, but crime rates also increase dramatically.[105]

Some experts have noted that some officers are responding to anti-police riots and media coverage in a similar fashion, which is showing up in crime data. Other anecdotal evidence reflects the concerns about the potential backlash. In August 2015, a Birmingham, Alabama, detective pulled over a car because of erratic behavior by the driver. The officer told the driver to stay in the car while he called for backup. Instead, the driver got out and confronted the officer, repeatedly asking him why he had been stopped. The driver, a convicted felon, then allegedly grabbed the detective's gun and pistol-whipped him, knocking him unconscious. The driver, who fled the scene but was later arrested, has a long record of felony convictions including robbery, assault, and attempted murder. The officer later stated that he hesitated in how he handled the situation because he was concerned about how the police are being portrayed in the media and did not want to be responsible for additional negative publicity. He added, "A lot of officers are being too cautious because of what's going on in the media. I hesitated because I didn't want to be in the media like I am right now."[106]

As mentioned, the concern by law enforcement about its relationship with community residents is seen in crime data. In Baltimore, for example, according to some observers, following the riots and the indictment of six officers for the death of drug dealer Freddie Gray, arrests saw a 60 percent decrease compared with arrests the previous year. In New York City, criminal summonses, which are an important tool for the police to maintain order, decreased by 24 percent through July 2015, compared with the same period the previous year; and the total number of arrests decreased by 16.5 percent.[107]

These problems are particularly troubling given that the media does not appear to cover attacks on the police with the same enthusiasm or dedication as they do when an officer is perceived to have attacked a citizen. There have been several incidents where officers have been attacked and killed by citizens, such as the assassination of two NYPD officers in New York City, Wenjian Liu and Rafael Ramos, who were shot and killed while sitting in their patrol car in Brooklyn. This extraordinary event occurred as a result of retaliation for the deaths of Michael Brown in Ferguson, Missouri, and Eric Garner in Staten Island, New York. The suspect, Ismaaiyl Abdullah Brinsley, had written that he would be "putting wings on pigs today" to avenge Brown and Garner's death. "They take one of ours . . . let's take two of theirs." Curiously, the media coverage was not nearly as extensive as it would have been if the officers had shot Brinsley, but the impact this could have on police-community relations is significant. A similar sentiment was felt after police officers were ambushed in Dallas and other officers were killed in Baton Rouge, Louisiana, in apparent retaliation for incidents involving the deaths of African Americans.[108]

What seems to be missing from the discussion of the perception that White officers are racist and are on a mission to kill Blacks, a sentiment that created the Black Lives Matter movement, is the data about the extent of this trend. As one article points out, in New York City, which has had a Civilian Review Board, created in the 1990s to address police abuse of authority and excessive force, the data for 2014 indicate that the number of complaints filed against the police had decreased 10 percent and the number of excessive force claims had decreased by 11 percent. Additionally, profanity accusations dropped by 20 percent. Further, according to the NYPD's 2013 Annual Firearms Discharge Report, NYPD officers killed eight people in 2013, and five of those cases involved a suspect with a handgun, one of whom fired six times at two officers on a subway, one with a knife. In comparison, in New York City in 2013, 335 citizens were murdered, and in 63 percent of those cases the suspect was Black. According to the Uniform Crime Reports for 2013, 90 percent of Black murder victims nationally are killed by Black assailants.[109]

So while questions about police misconduct are worthy of an in-depth discussion and require specific action by departments and other agencies, it is not completely clear to what extent the police are responsible for the number of Blacks killed each year. Some data show, for instances, that while Blacks were more than six times likelier than Whites to have been murder victims, Blacks were also almost eight times likelier than Whites to have committed murder.[110] Thus, care must be taken to ensure that all of the data has been presented and interpreted in a fair and unbiased way. To do otherwise is to create a climate of mistrust, fear, and an unwillingness to work collaboratively to solve the larger problems in the Black community.

CHECKPOINT

- The relationship between the police and the Black community is a thorny one that calls attention to many forms of unequal treatment. From racial profiling to increased likelihood of arrest, use of force, as well as the likelihood of Blacks being more likely to be stopped, frisked, and searched by officers, several unfortunate incidents between police officers and Black suspects has created a great deal of mistrust and suspicion.

THE COURTS AND AFRICAN AMERICANS: SENTENCING ISSUES

Not only is there some evidence to suggest that Blacks are more likely than Whites to be stopped, searched, arrested, and killed by police officers, they are also likely to receive harsher treatment once they arrive in court. In fact, there are many who contend that the War on Drugs is really a war on African Americans.[111] For instance, there is evidence to suggest that African Americans are likely to receive harsher penalties and sentencing than Whites for similar crimes. This is most apparent in the different penalties for selling crack cocaine compared to powder cocaine, designer drugs, or even steroids. The federal sentencing guidelines are substantially harsher than the penalties provided by many state statutes, suggesting that state prosecutors are more likely to refer crack cases involving racial minorities to the federal system for prosecution.[112]

In fact, an analysis of sentences by the U.S. Sentencing Commission found that prison sentences of Black men were almost 20 percent longer than those of White men for similar crimes.[113] The Sentencing Commission report recommended that federal judges give the guidelines more significance. This analysis has come under some scrutiny, where one law professor claims racial disparity has not increased since 2005, when the U.S. Supreme Court struck down the 1984 federal law that required judges to use the federal sentencing guidelines. In the case of *U.S. v. Booker*, the Court ruled that the law, while originally designed to address disparity in sentencing, limited judges in rendering decisions that were based on laws that were inherently biased in the first place. The most common example used involved federal law that created longer sentences for crack cocaine offenses compared to sentences for powder cocaine offenses, which were more frequently committed by Whites.

While Congress reduced the disparity in 2010, in 2007 sentences of Blacks were about 15 percent longer than those of similarly convicted Whites. The latest study by the U.S. Sentencing Commission, in 2018, found that the majority of those convicted in federal court were Hispanics (54.3 percent), while Whites and Blacks made up 21 percent each. As it relates to Hispanic offenders, about 85 percent of the sentences were either for immigration violations (74 percent) or drug trafficking (15.6 percent). The report also showed that the majority of federal offenders were U.S. citizens (57 percent) who received a prison sentence about 83 percent of the time. In contrast, while non-citizens represented less than half of the offenders, in 96 percent of the cases they received a prison sentence.[114]

A previous Commission report found that Black males were serving about 20 percent longer sentences than Whites for similar crimes and that Black males were 25 percent less likely than Whites to receive a sentence below the guidelines' range. While this study does not, by itself, prove that judicial discretion caused greater Black-White federal sentencing disparity, it nevertheless is an improvement in the understanding of what happens to similar types of offenders in terms of the outcome of their cases.[115]

Part of the explanation for the dramatically different punishment for cocaine and crack is likely a result of the fear of drugs and those who sell drugs rather than pure discrimination and prejudice. Because of the perception by members of mainstream culture that crack cocaine represents a more serious and immediate threat to way of life, particularly when crack cocaine left the inner-city and appeared in the suburbs, more punitive measures were easily justified. Given that African Americans were already perceived to be responsible for the "drug problem" nationwide, the perceptions that the problem was being brought into middle-class suburbia resulted in panic and more punitive actions.[116] The 2018 report by the Commission shows that the average sentence for offenders who are caught with crack cocaine is comparable to the sentence for those caught with its powder form (73 months vs. 78 months on average). In comparison, the average length of sentence for a conviction for methamphetamine was 95 months, while heroin convictions resulted in an average sentence of 69 months. [117]

A related conclusion appears in murder cases. Researchers found that when the level of seriousness is controlled for, such as the degree of severity and the number of persons killed, prosecutors and juries are more likely to demand the death penalty if the victim is White and the offender is Black than in any of the other possible racial combinations (e.g., White offender/Black victim; Black offender/Black victim; White offender/White victim).[118]

Further, a number of studies indicate that Whites receive a higher proportion of plea-bargain deals than Blacks. One study found that Whites were more successful in getting charges reduced or dropped, diversion, probation, or fines instead of incarceration.[119] However, other studies indicate inconsistent results with regard to the effects of race on plea bargaining and prosecution strategies.[120]

A number of studies demonstrate racial bias in sentencing. A study in thirty-nine states found that Blacks typically serve longer sentences than Whites for robbery, rape, and murder.[121] A growing body of research indicates that in many cases the key factor is the race of the victim. Preliminary evidence suggests that when the victim of rape or robbery is White, the sentence is likely to be more severe.[122] More recently, a meta-analysis of 85 research studies revealed that, after taking into account the defendant's criminal history and the seriousness of the offense, Blacks and Latinos were generally sentenced more harshly than Whites. However, the research available on sentencing patterns of Whites compared to those of Asians or Native Americans does not reveal significant differences between these groups. In general, there appears to be some evidence to suggest that disparities in sentencing still occur, even involving sentencing guidelines.[123]

In 1991, the seventeen-member New York State Judicial Commission on Minorities, composed of judges, lawyers, law professors, and an official from the New York State Department of Education, concluded that the state court system showed signs of racism. The commission found that minority group members were less likely than Whites to receive favorable actions from the courts; that judges and prosecuting attorneys, more than other court employees, were more hostile and racially biased toward minorities; and that minority lawyers were often subjected to opposing attorney's racial stereotyping and racist jokes.[124]

Further, a recent report from the Sentencing Project, a nonprofit organization that conducts research on criminal justice issues, noted that part of the challenge of understanding the sentencing disparity issue relates to how people in general perceive Blacks and their involvement in crime. For instance, one of the findings form the report indicates that, based on their 2010 survey, Whites overestimate the proportion of crimes committed by people of color and associate people of color with criminality.

In fact, the survey showed that this overestimation ranges between 20 percent and 30 percent for burglaries, drug sales, and juvenile crime. Similarly, the report showed that Whites, who associate crime with Blacks and Latinos, are also more likely to support punitive policies, including capital punishment and mandatory minimum sentencing. The report also showed disparities in police stops, prosecutorial decision-making, and issues relating to bail and sentencing, which suggests an implicit racial bias within the criminal justice system.[125]

The conclusions from such findings, naturally, explain varying racial perceptions of crime and criminals, and foster the basis of understanding why Blacks and Latinos, while accounting for 30 percent of the general population, account for nearly 60 percent of the prison population. These perceptions also drive the belief by some groups that the criminal justice system is biased against Blacks. Such a belief is underscored by the results of the survey, which showed that over two-thirds of African Americans saw the system as biased, compared to only 25 percent of Whites.[126]

THE DEATH PENALTY AND AFRICAN AMERICANS

African Americans' overrepresentation in sentencing and incarceration is also found among those sentenced to death. According to the Bureau of Justice Statistics, in 2013 about 42 percent of inmates on death row were Black. This percentage has been consistent since 1968, and 53 percent of all people executed since 1930 have been African American.[127]

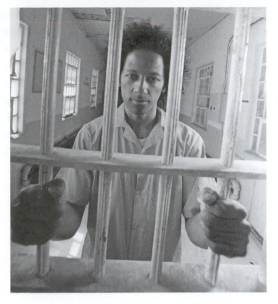

A large proportion of Black men are under the supervision of the criminal justice system.

Perhaps the most graphic illustration of the relationship between race and criminal justice involves the use of capital punishment. When the *Furman v. Georgia* (408 U.S. 238; 1972) decision was first handed down by the Supreme Court, many scholars interpreted the finding as the abolition of capital punishment in the United States. However, in 1976 the Court heard three cases, the most important of which is *Gregg v. Georgia* (428 U.S. 153; 1976). In this case, the state of Georgia provided the Court with a set of procedural safeguards designed to guide the discretion of the judge or jury when faced with a capital case. For instance, the Georgia statute provided an automatic appeal of all death penalty cases. It was argued that separate trials, one trial to determine guilt and another for punishment, guarded against irrelevant evidence that might influence sentencing decisions. The Georgia statute made it mandatory that the death penalty could not be imposed unless a jury unanimously (and beyond a reasonable doubt) found that the offender used excessive force or engaged in behavior that escalated the severity of the crime. The Court argued in *Gregg* that capital punishment does not necessarily amount to cruel and unusual punishment as long as certain procedural safeguards are carried out that are designed to curb arbitrary and capricious application of the death. In short, where discretion is reasonable and controlled, capital punishment is constitutionally permissible for the crime of murder.

Studies have revealed that, despite the significance of this case, the guidelines established in *Gregg* have not eliminated racial disparities in capital cases. One study examined patterns of death sentencing in Florida, Texas, Ohio, and Georgia. In each of these states, killers of Whites were sentenced to death more consistently than killers of Blacks. Also, Black defendants with White victims were more likely to receive the death penalty than

White defendants with Black victims. The implication, of course, is that the decision to execute in these states reflects the same arbitrariness that has characterized the imposition of the death penalty in the past.[128] Federal statistics show that 84 percent of White victims and 93 percent of Black victims between 1980 and 2008 were murdered by someone of the same race. However, although roughly half of all U.S. homicide victims are Black, more than three-quarters of victims of death-row defendants executed since 1976 were White.[129]

Another study found a clear pattern of racial disparity in South Carolina death penalty cases when the race of the offender and the race of the victim were considered together. This study found that Blacks who killed Whites had over 4.5 times greater risk of having the death penalty sought than did Black killers of Blacks. Whites who killed Blacks were 1.1 times more likely to have the death penalty sought by the prosecutor than Whites who killed other Whites. This study concluded that the race of the victim may be a more important consideration of public prosecutors than the race of the offender.[130]

In *McCleskey v. Kemp* (481 U.S. 279; 1981), Warren McClesky, a Black man, was convicted in Fulton County, Georgia, of murdering a White police officer during the armed robbery of a furniture store. The conviction was consistent with the Georgia statute concerning aggravating circumstances. At trial, McClesky failed to present any mitigating evidence to the jury and was subsequently sentenced to death.

On appeal to the U.S. Supreme Court, McCleskey claimed that the Georgia capital sentencing process is administered in a racially discriminatory manner which violated the protections provided by the Eighth Amendment to the U.S. Constitution. He also argued that the discriminatory system violated the Fourteenth Amendment's equal protection clause. To support his claim, McCleskey offered the results of an empirical study documenting evidence of a racial bias against African Americans. The study showed that from 1973 to 1979 there were 2,484 murder and non-negligent manslaughter cases in Georgia. Defendants who killed Whites were sentenced to death in 11 percent of the cases, while defendants who killed Blacks were sentenced to death in only about 1 percent of the cases.[131]

This study also discovered that the death penalty was imposed in 22 percent of the cases where an African American defendant was convicted of murdering a White victim; 8 percent of the cases with a White defendant and a White victim; 3 percent of the cases with a White defendant and a Black victim, and only 1 percent of the cases involving a Black defendant and a Black victim. In this detailed analysis, the researchers controlled for some 230 nonracial variables and found that none could account for the racial disparities in capital sentences among the different racial combinations of defendant and victim. People who killed Whites were 4.3 times more likely to be sentenced to death than those who killed Blacks.[132]

McCleskey claimed that race had infected the administration of capital punishment in Georgia in two ways. First, offenders who murder Whites were more likely to be sentenced to death than offenders who murder Blacks. Secondly, Black murderers were more likely to be sentenced to death than White murderers.

In 1987 the Supreme Court handed down its 5–4 decision. The essential question before the Court was whether a complex statistical study that indicates a risk that racial consideration enters into capital sentencing determinations is unconstitutional under the Eighth and Fourteenth Amendments. The Court held that the study does not prove that the administration of the Georgia system violates these amendments.

The essence of the Court's ruling is that there are acceptable standards of risk of racial discrimination in imposing the death penalty. The Court held that the study simply shows that discrepancies appear to correlate with race in imposing death sentences, but that, according to the Court, the statistics did not prove that race is a factor in any capital sentencing decisions, nor that race was a factor in this particular one.[133] The Court was also concerned that a finding for the defendant would open other claims that "could be extended to other types of penalties and to claims based on unexplained discrepancies correlating to membership in other minority groups and even to gender." The dissenters in the ruling argued that whether McCleskey could prove racial discrimination in his particular case is totally irrelevant in evaluating his claim of a constitutional violation because the Court has long recognized that a pattern of substantial risk of arbitrary and capricious capital sentencing suffices for a claim of unconstitutionality.

CHECKPOINT

- This section shows that minorities, particularly African Americans and more recently Hispanics, are disproportionately convicted of crimes and are more likely to serve time in prison compared to other types of offenders. There is also an unequal distribution of sentences in capital punishment cases, where, compared to offenders with similar offenses, a disparity exists for African Americans and Hispanics.

CORRECTIONS AND AFRICAN AMERICANS

There is a long history of disproportionality in the criminal justice system with regard to race, and this is clearly reflected in statistics regarding incarceration. In 2014, according to the U.S. Department of Justice, there were an estimated 1,561,500 prisoners in state and federal correctional facilities, a decrease of 1 percent from 2013. At the end of 2017, there were 1,489,363, a decrease of about 2 percent from the previous year.

Further, the imprisonment rate for sentenced offenders under state or federal jurisdiction decreased about 2 percent from 2016, from 450 to 440 sentenced prisoners per 100,000 U.S. residents. This rate represents the lowest figure since 1997. It seems evident, by any measure, that African Americans are disproportionately incarcerated. While they represented approximately 14 percent of the overall population in this country in 2018, African Americans represented 36 percent of those incarcerated in state and federal prisons. Whites represented about 75 percent of the total population, yet they only constituted 34 percent of the inmate population. Hispanics represented about 17 percent of the U.S. population, but about 22 percent of those incarcerated in 2014.[134]

According to the Bureau of Justice Statistics, in 2017, while the imprisonment rate for sentenced Black adults decreased by 4 percent from 2016 and by nearly a third since 2007, compared to other prisoners of other races, the imprisonment rate for Black males was 2,336 per 100,000 U.S. residents, which is nearly six times higher than for White males (397 per 100,000 U.S. residents). Among female prisoners, the imprisonment rate for Black females in 2017 (92 per 100,000 U.S. residents) was twice that of White females (49 per 100,000 U.S. residents), and a third higher than that of Hispanic females (66 per 100,000 U.S. residents).[135]

Types of offenses also varied by race and ethnicity, although compared to violent and property offenders in state prisons, those serving time for drug offenses had very little racial disparity. Overall, about 48 percent of White male prisoners, 57 percent of Black, and 59 percent of Hispanic male inmates were convicted of violent offenses. However, White offenders were more likely serving time for a property offense (25 percent) compared to Blacks (16 percent) and Hispanics (14 percent). As was mentioned, drug offenders were about evenly distributed, with Blacks representing the largest percentage of offenders (16 percent) followed by Whites and Hispanics equally (14.5 percent each).

THE MASS INCARCERATION OF AMERICA

It might be tempting to conclude that current immigration policy efforts, including the widespread use of detention, are part of a larger strategy designed to rid the country of illegal immigrants. While there may be some truth to such a position, the United States has been embarking upon the use of incarceration as a mainstay strategy in criminal justice for decades. The term "mass incarceration," like the phrase "sanctuary city," has no precise meaning and the criteria used to make assertions about what it is, or how much it needs to be reduced, are relatively arbitrary. As Pfaff (2017) points out, the general use of the term suggests that mass incarceration implies that we have been using jails in prisons for all manner of problems and the rates of incarceration needs to be reduced.[136]

As a starting point of this discussion, it is important to note that mass incarceration is inextricably linked to a larger discussion about race in the United States. That is, the disproportionality of African Americans, and of Hispanics and Latinos, is found at every stage of the criminal justice system. Blacks, who represent about 14 percent of the population, are more likely to be stopped, frisked, arrested, formally charged, sentenced to longer periods of incarceration, denied parole, and executed than whites, even when charged with similar crimes.[137]

While this trend can be part of a larger discussion of the role of race in crime in general, in this section we will focus more on the role of race in incarceration trends. Parenthetically, it is worth noting that any discussion of race in criminal justice can be a source of considerable debate. Normally debates about social problems like crime inevitably include criticism of the data, the methodology of a given study, or its findings. However, in the case of the disproportionality of African Americans and Hispanics/Latinos in the criminal justice system, there are few if any disputes about whether the trends actually exist. Instead, it is in the explanations of why the disproportionality exists that the disagreements become heated.

As it relates to race and incarceration rates, there are essentially three schools of thought. First, there is what Pfaff (2017) calls the "Standard Story," which argues that the mass incarceration of minorities is the result of attention paid to policy decisions and practices that resulted in the incarceration of many low-level drug dealers as part of the War on Drugs. Such policies, it is argued, paid special attention to African Americans since the use, sale, and distribution of drugs typically occurred in inner-city neighborhoods where many African Americans live. Moreover, this position argues that drug transactions typically occur in public spaces, which made them more susceptible to police surveillance.

In contrast, whites, who have similar drug use patterns and sell and distribute drugs at similar rates as African Americans, have the resources to avoid such open-air transactions and lived in neighborhoods that did not attract the attention of the police. Thus, while whites were as actively involved in drug use and dealing as African Americans, they escaped the attention of the police. Additionally, polices and laws created during the 1980s in response to the War on Drugs resulted in longer prison sentences, with mandatory minimums, which resulted in a dramatic increase in the prison population.

This school of thought argues that the focus on the systematic discrimination of African Americans in the justice process ensures that this group remains marginalized and prohibited from achieving any level of upward social mobility. With arrest records and felony convictions, African Americans, primarily males, are permanently unable to achieve some level of societal success and are also more likely to remain under the control of the system. This is the position most often associated with Michelle Alexander (2012), in her book *The New Jim Crow: Mass Incarceration in the Age of Colorblindness*.[138]

Alexander argues that the criminal justice system imposed racially motivated social controls on African Americans through convictions for nonviolent crimes, mainly drug crimes. She also argues that the reasons for these efforts was to circumvent the rights afforded to African Americans as part of the civil rights movement of the 1960s. In what is sometimes referred to as the "racial hierarchy argument," the objective was to create a caste system whereby African Americans would be segregated from society via the criminal justice system. While not overtly racist or discriminatory, such policies and laws created under the rubric of accountability, law and order, and maintaining the safety and security of communities became the vehicle by which more subtle and nuanced forms of discrimination and racism could occur.[139]

Thus, the racism that existed during the Jim Crow era, when prejudice and discrimination were more overt, made the mistreatment of Blacks appear justified given their status in society. Today, however, Alexander argues, a more subtle form of racism has emerged. By using a law-and-order campaign, one that appeals to people's sense of reasonableness (after all, it is understandable that people want to feel safe and to hold accountable those who do not abide by the rules), Blacks can still be discriminated against and relegated to a marginalized status. This is accomplished through the use of incarceration and social labeling that prohibits them from obtaining jobs, housing, the ability to vote in the democratic process, and other opportunities.

This marginalization is further accomplished by recasting minor drug offenses into major crime categories, such as President Clinton's "three strikes and you're out" laws, along with elevating possession-of-drug charges to distribution and trafficking offenses. It is also seen at the federal level with longer prison sentences for crack cocaine convictions compared to those for the possession of powder cocaine. Capitalizing on the public's fear, along with a rise in crime rates, these changes were seen as a reasonable response to a growing epidemic of crime and drug use.[140] Alexander's point, in agreement with other scholars, is that in the short term, the fundamental problem of the mass incarceration of Blacks is one of selective enforcement by concentrating on where they live and what they do. If Whites and Blacks use and sell drugs at similar rates, but the police focus on those places where Blacks are more likely to live and engage in these activities, then this group is far more likely to end up in prison than whites who do not live there.

In the long term, the problems of mass incarceration become more enduring. If it becomes part of conventional wisdom that Blacks are more likely to be involved in criminal activity, it is reasonable to think that the people working within the system, along with the general public, will normalize the criminalization of Blacks so that they are typically seen and labeled as criminals. Once the formal label is applied and the person has a record of imprisonment, the chances that they will be able to participate in society as an equal is virtually eliminated. This consequence of the social labeling results in a return to crime since they cannot obtain good jobs, live in good neighborhoods, and associate with good people who can offer them the opportunities to succeed.[141]

Interestingly, these changes related to incarceration occurred at a time when experts and policymakers were reconsidering the purpose and value of prison as a form of punishment. Until the 1980s, most experts questioned the value of incarceration as a crime control effort, believing that prison should be a last resort for offenders since the deleterious effects of incarceration often resulted in criminals becoming worse upon their release. This is based on the notion that inmates could not be imprisoned forever, and if the offender is more of a risk to the community upon their release than prior to their sentence, what value does prison actually have?[142]

Additionally, the 1970s witnessed the closing of several federal prisons and the elimination of mandatory minimum sentences for low-level drug offenses because the prevailing view was that drug addiction should be seen as a public health problem rather than a criminal justice one. However, the 1980s brought with it a change in perception about crime, criminals, and the value of incarceration.[143]

Instead, the philosophy of punishment shifted from one involving the notion of rehabilitation as the goal, to one involving just desserts. This was politically popular since it gave politicians an opportunity to demonstrate that they were being hard on criminals and holding them accountable for their actions. This was important because at the time the country was coming off a period where rehabilitation was seen as ineffective, and it was thought that the nation coddled criminals and gave them too many incentives to continue to commit crime.[144]

Policymakers and politicians created a climate of fear and then capitalized on it by passing laws and policies that ramped up the punishment of criminals. Such strategies also resulted in the massive construction of prisons, which was seen as a means to reduce unemployment and put people back to work. This "get tough on crime" approach resulted in changing laws that made offenders eligible for longer prison sentences; mandatory minimum sentences, particularly for drug offenses; and redefining certain offenses as eligible for incarceration. As a result of these and other changes, incarceration rates dramatically increased, leading to the need for the construction of additional prisons and jails.[145]

In sum, the racial hierarchy argument points out that the decline in economic opportunities for Blacks, in part due to deindustrialization and the elimination of many semi-skilled jobs, particularly in inner cities around the country, led to increases in unemployment, poverty, and other challenges. In an effort to contain and control displaced workers, who were largely African American, some of whom became involved in crime, the get-tough approach to crime was seen as a reasonable reaction.[146]

However, not everyone agrees with this position, best characterized in Alexander's book. For instance, Barry Latzler, whose book *The Rise and Fall of Violent Crime in America*, takes issue with much of what Alexander offers as an explanation of why African Americans were the subject of so much discussion of the mass incarceration in America.[147] Latzler argues that the main thrust of Alexander's argument, that mass incarceration is a result of political factors rather than actual crime increases, is incongruent with other research that shows support for tougher sanctions against African Americans by Black leaders.[148]

Latzler points to James Forman's book, *Locking Up Our Own*, which describes how fear in the Black community led many to support the punitive approach that resulted in the increases in incarceration rates among African Americans.[149] Latzler argues that the increase in incarceration rates were not simply Whites attempting to control Blacks. Rather, it was residents and communities responding to increases in violent crimes; those people living in poor and minority neighborhoods, along with Black leaders, were concerned about the increase in crime as it related to all neighborhoods—that Blacks were killing other Blacks with alarming frequency—so much so that they needed to support a more strict law-and-order campaign.[150]

Latzler (2016) also points out, as do Forman (2017) and Pfaff (2017), that while drugs were a part of that discussion, unlike Alexander's, the data suggest that drug offenses made up only a small part of the increases in incarceration. Instead, violent crime was increasing and the longer sentences and incarceration of Blacks was a reflection of and a response to the data that suggested that people were—and had reason to be—afraid. Perhaps more importantly, Latzler points out that homicide-victimization rates *doubled* between 1960 and 1980 and did not begin a consistent decline until the mid-1990s. Additionally, though Blacks represented approximately 12 percent of the U.S. population during this period, they were nearly *half* of the homicide victims and 60 percent of the suspected perpetrators.[151]

Additionally, Latzler questions Alexander's claim about the majority of sentences being related to drug offenses. He argues that among state offenders, drug crimes were about 20 percent of all sentences, whereas sentences for violent crimes were anywhere from 46 percent to 59 percent of all sentences. Among federal offenders, drug sentences amounted to more than half of all sentences, but federal offenders made up only about 7 percent of the total prison population. More importantly, federal offenders tended to be higher level drug dealers, not the street-level offenders, who tended to be African Americans. Finally, Latzler questions Alexander's claims that the massive increase in incarceration was an abysmal failure. Latzler points out that while the increase in incarceration was not the only reason for reductions in crime, it had some role to play in the decrease in crime rates.[152]

There is little question about the increase in incarceration rates. According to a Prison Policy Initiative report in 2019, the American criminal justice system holds almost 2.3 million people in 1,719 state prisons, 109 federal prisons, 1,772 juvenile correctional facilities, 3,163 local jails, and 80 Indian Country jails as well as in military prisons, immigration detention facilities, civil commitment centers, state psychiatric hospitals, and prisons in the U.S. territories (See Figure 3.1).[153]

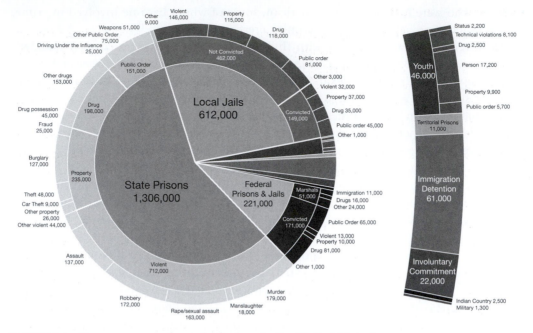

FIGURE 3.1   How many people are locked up in the United States?
The United States locks up more people per capita than any other nation, at the staggering rate of 698 per 100,000 residents. But to end mass incarceration, we must first consider *where* and *why* 2.3 million people are confined nationwide. *Source:* https://www.prisonpolicy.org/reports/pie2019.html

The number of inmates in state-run facilities is large; despite the fact that it has seen decreases in recent years, it remains at 1.3 million people, a significantly large number by any account.

Interestingly, the Prison Policy Initiative report identifies local jails as playing a significant role in the mass-incarceration phenomenon. What is important to note about local jails is that those incarcerated there often have not been convicted of a crime—some may have just been arrested and cannot afford bail, so they remain incarcerated until their trial. According to the report, every year, over 600,000 people enter *prison* gates, but people go to *jail* 10.6 million times each year. Only a small number (less than 150,000 on any given day) have been convicted, and are generally serving misdemeanor sentences under a year.[154]

CHECKPOINT

- There is considerable debate about the mass incarceration of Blacks and Hispanics in the United States, but the data also demonstrate a consistent pattern where these two groups are much more likely than White offenders to experience incarceration as a result of a conviction.

RACE, FEAR, AND CRIME

Given evidence that clearly suggests that African Americans are stopped, frisked, arrested, prosecuted, convicted, sentenced to longer prison terms, and more likely to be given the death penalty, how can such a distinctive set of trends be explained?

One theory is that African Americans are more likely to engage in criminal activity, more likely to get caught, and, given their repeated patterns of behavior, likely to receive harsher treatment at every level of the criminal justice system. This is perhaps the most popular theory since it focuses the blame squarely on the people who are adversely affected. Arguably, African Americans are punished more because they commit more acts against society and this is reflected in the arrest, conviction, and incarceration statistics.

Another theory places the blame for the misrepresentation of African Americans in the criminal justice system on the structure of society and on the system itself. Arguments on this side contend that the system is racist, and African Americans are treated unfairly largely because of public fears. As a result, a self-fulfilling prophecy develops. Motivated by the perception that African Americans represent a greater threat than White offenders, police, judges, and other court officials treat African Americans more harshly. Blacks, in turn, perceive this treatment as biased and are likely to become a more substantial threat than they would have been without exposure to racism in the criminal justice system. This reinforces the public's fears that African Americans pose a greater threat to safety than White people.

IS THE CRIMINAL JUSTICE SYSTEM RACIST?

In contrast to the prevailing view about the system being biased against African Americans in particular, and minorities in general, William Wilbanks, in his book *The Myth of a Racist Criminal Justice System* (1987), presents a somewhat different argument about the relationship of race to the criminal justice system. He contends that the explanation is not found in a racist system that systematically singles out Blacks for special treatment. Rather, there are other factors at play that contribute to the involvement of Blacks in the justice system—namely, poverty, negligence, and previous involvement in crime. It seems fairly clear that Whites and Blacks differ sharply over whether the criminal justice system is racist. The vast majority of Blacks appear to believe that the police and the courts unfairly discriminate against Blacks, whereas a majority of Whites reject this charge. This disparity also appears to exist among those who work in the system.

Some Blacks have suggested that the criminal justice system is so characterized by racism that Blacks are outside the protection of the law. A sizable minority of Whites, in contrast, think that the system actually discriminates *for* Blacks out of fear of being charged with racism from the Black community. White police officers have reported often ignoring criminal activity by Blacks out of a fear of criticism from the department, the Black community, and/or the media.[155]

Wilbanks contends that these contrasting perceptions regarding the fairness of the system have at least four important consequences. First, research shows that Blacks may turn to criminality or engage in more crime because of a perception that the criminal law and its enforcement is unfair and even racist. Thus, in a way, Blacks believe they are justified in breaking the law. The second consequence relates to civil disturbances. Many riots occur because of a perception that the system is unfair and unjust. The Kerner Commission, which investigated the civil disturbances in American cities in the 1960s, found a widespread belief among Blacks that the criminal justice system was racist and concluded that negative perceptions of Blacks by the agents of the criminal justice system, particularly the police, were a major cause of the violence.

A third consequence of these opposing perceptions is a heightened sense of hostility toward the police. As mentioned, many Blacks view the criminal justice system as racist and the police as prejudiced. The greater intrusiveness by police officers into the lives of people in low-income areas often leads to heightened tensions and resentment of the police. It also creates an impression that the police are intentionally harassing people in these neighborhoods, looking for a reason to arrest them.[156]

The fourth consequence is that the White backlash to civil rights programs such as affirmative action and racial quotas may be due in part to a White perception that Blacks complain about racism, when, in fact, Whites provide excessive preferential treatment to African Americans. Wilbanks takes the position that the perception of the criminal justice system as racist is a myth. He argues that the question of whether the criminal justice system is racist must not be confused with Blacks committing crimes at a higher rate than Whites because of discrimination in employment, housing, education, and so forth. It may be that racial discrimination produces a gap in offending between Blacks and Whites, but this gap is not increased as Black and White offenders move through the system. If the gap does not increase after the point at which offenses occur, the system cannot be held responsible for the gap that results at the end of the system (e.g., prison).

Wilbanks says that Blacks believe the system is racist for several reasons, the most important of which he calls **negative attribution**. This suggests that, in response to the history of how Blacks have been treated, African Americans have developed a negative view of Whites that attributes evil motives and traits to them. They see Whites as an "out group" intent on denying Blacks equal rights and opportunities. This attribution leads to the tendency to look for "facts" to confirm this view of Whites.

Second, Wilbanks explains that the suspicions of African Americans of the entire criminal justice system are not an abstract or intellectual argument. The mistrust of the system in general, and of the police in particular, come from their direct personal experiences with police officers. Such personal experiences tend to confirm what people commonly hear in the Black community; thus, Blacks often express the view that they do not need statistical proof of racial discrimination since they have experienced it.

In short, Wilbanks offers the idea that the disparity in the legal system has more to do with poverty levels than race. The argument suggests that crimes like assault, drugs, burglary, and robbery are a function of the adversity families and individuals are facing as a result of being poor. Empirical support for this position was offered in the 1990s when researchers noted that a decrease in poverty levels was related to reductions in crime rates, particularly in the early part of the twentieth century. To be fair, some studies suggested a link between poverty and crime, but other evidence began to emerge that suggested race was playing a role in the justice process. Thus, while Wilbanks's approach garnered some credibility for a time, and perhaps today with conservative thinkers, the weight of the evidence suggests that something is amiss with regard to the relationship between race and the justice process.

A third position is offered by Walker, Spohn, and DeLone (1996). After an extensive review of the literature, they suggested a more moderate theory that contends that the system is neither completely free of racial bias nor does it contain the type of systematic bias that other experts assert. Walker and his colleagues agree that racial and ethnic groups are, in fact, treated more harshly at some (or many) stages of the system, but at other points they are not singled out compared to Whites who are going through the justice process.[157]

SUMMARY

This chapter explored the historical experience of African Americans in the United States and how this group has found itself in a disadvantaged position for some time. From the early days of slavery to discrimination as they fought in world conflict to the civil rights movement, the African American has played an important role in the history of the United States. Reconstruction also played a role in the current position of African Americans, as many formal and informal norms and laws were created to distance African Americans from Whites even when they were forced to live in close proximity to one another. The legacy of slavery, Jim Crow, segregation, and the denial of equal protection under the law, as found in U.S. Supreme Court cases, has fundamentally shaped the position of African Americans in the United States. A byproduct of this treatment and legacy of slavery is seen in the disproportionate representation of African Americans in the criminal justice system.

While the topic remains controversial, there can be little doubt that African Americans are overrepresented in crime statistics. This is true despite the fact that there is a growing Black middle class of educated, professional, and politically savvy African Americans. Whether it involves arrest, use of force, searches, convictions, sentences, or executions, Blacks are disproportionately represented in the criminal justice system. Not only do Blacks have different experiences with the criminal justice system than Whites, there is a general sense of mistrust of the system in general and of the police in particular.

In many low-income neighborhoods there is a significant amount of tension between African Americans and the police. Part of the reason for this mutual mistrust is due to the fact that police officers intervene into the lives of many African Americans perhaps more often than Whites living in suburban neighborhoods. As a result, not only do African Americans perceive the police as intrusive, but this frequent contact can also make it more likely that they become involved in the criminal justice system.

The reasons for the overrepresentation of African Americans in the criminal justice system range from individualistic theories, which contend that African Americans commit more crimes, get caught, and are punished, to structural explanations, which suggest there are factors outside the control of the individual which result in their involvement in the system. Finally, as Wilbanks points out, there also exists a debate concerning the racism embedded in the criminal justice system itself.

YOU MAKE THE CALL

Consider the following scenario. Debate the pros and cons of all options and decide what you would do.

You are a White, middle class, male police officer with less than one year's experience in law enforcement. You have been assigned to a high-crime, low-income neighborhood. There are many calls for service and a significant amount of violent crime in this area. In fact, several times this year the SWAT team has been called to rescue officers who have been attacked by armed residents. Your partner is an eight-year veteran officer who has been involved in many disturbances in this neighborhood and dislikes many of the citizens who live in this neighborhood. In fact, during the course of several conversations, your partner uses racial epithets against African Americans and talks about "nuking the entire area" and starting all over with a group of "civilized" people. In the eleven months since you've been a police officer, you have heard rumors that this officer has engaged in acts of excessive violence toward citizens and has even planted evidence on suspects in order to arrest them.

While working late one night, the two of you answer a call from a resident that a domestic disturbance is taking place. Your partner says, "I know these people, we get called here all the time. I'll handle this." You enter the home of an African American family and your partner rushes into another room. Three shots are fired and when you come into the room, you find a Black man lying on the floor with gunshot wounds to his chest. Your partner is standing over him with his weapon drawn, smoke coming from the barrel of his pistol. He tells you that the dead man reached for a gun, but none is found. The man's family begins to scream that your partner shot an unarmed man.

Later, when detectives take your statement, they ask if your partner used excessive force against the victim. The investigators also tell you that the deceased family members claim they did not own a gun and one was not found at the scene. Does your partner's attitudes toward African Americans factor into his behavior? Do you think your partner might be prejudiced against minorities in general? What about in this particular case? How do you know? What do you say to the detectives?

KEY TERMS

abolitionist

Black middle class

Black nationalism

Black Power

Christopher Commission

Civil Rights Act of 1964

Civil rights movement

de-policing

Emancipation Proclamation

Freedom Schools

Fugitive Slave Act

Jim Crow

Nation of Islam

negative attribution

racial profiling

Reconstruction

Reconstruction Act of 1867

restrictive covenants

slave codes

vicarious hassling

Voting Rights Act

DISCUSSION QUESTIONS

1. Why do you think African Americans are overrepresented in the crime statistics? Is it because they commit more crimes, or is it due to greater police presence in their communities?

2. What role, if any, does the legacy of slavery play in the involvement of African Americans in crime?

3. Do you think the criminal justice system is racist toward African Americans, or does it show that individual people within the system discriminate against African Americans?

4. What role do the media play in assessing the importance of race and the criminal justice system?

5. What role do you think the Black middle class should play in resolving some of the problems in low-income neighborhoods?
6. Assume you are a U.S. Supreme Court Justice and are hearing a case on the death penalty. Do you think studies examining the race factor in executions should be used to determine if discrimination exists? Why or why not?

FOR FURTHER READING

Hay, J., ed. *The Montgomery Bus Boycott*. New York: Greenhaven Press, 2011.
Alexander, M. *The New Jim Crow: Mass Incarceration in the Age of Color Blindness*. New York: The New Press, 2012.
Isenberg, N. *White Trash: The 400-Year Untold History of Class in America*. New York: Viking, 2016.
Stuart, F. *Down, Out, and Under Arrest: Policing and Everyday Life in Skid Row*. Chicago, IL: University of Chicago Press, 2016.

NOTES

1. J. Scott and G. Marshall, *A Dictionary of Sociology*, 3rd ed. (New York: Oxford University Press, 2005), 183. Available at: http://www.oxfordreference.com/view/10.1093/acref/9780199553008.001.0001/acref-9780199553008-e-1859?rskey=BVTpmt&result=1859
2. M. Tarver, S. Walker, and H. Wallace, *Multicultural Issues in the Criminal Justice System* (Boston, MA: Allyn and Bacon, 2002), 33–40.
3. J. H. Franklin and A. A. Moss, *From Slavery to Freedom: A History of African Americans*, 8th ed. (New York: McGraw-Hill, 2000), 220–43.
4. W. E. B. Dubois, *The Negro American Family* (Cambridge, MA: MIT Press, 1970), 18.
5. Ibid.
6. F. Frazier, *The Negro Church in America* (New York: Schocken, 1974), 20–29; K. Stampp, *The Peculiar Institution: Slavery in the Ante-Bellum South* (New York: Vintage, 1956/1989), 322.
7. G. P. Rawick, *From Sundown to Sunup: The Making of the Black Community* (Westport, CT: Greenwood Press, 1972), 123.
8. Franklin and Moss, *From Slavery to Freedom*.
9. J. Oakes, "Slavery," in M. K. Clayton, E. J. Gorn, and P. W. Williams (eds.), *Encyclopedia of American Social History* (New York: Scribners, 1993), 1407–19.
10. L. M. Killian, *The Impossible Revolution? Phase 2: Black Power and the American Dream* (New York: Random House, 1975), 57.
11. Ibid.
12. R. D. Abrahams, *Singing the Master: The Emergence of African American Culture in the Plantation South* (New York: Pantheon, 1992), 22; M. D. Free, *African Americans and the Criminal Justice System* (New York: Garland, 1996), 88.
13. L. Bennett, "The White Problem in America," *Ebony* (August, 1965): 29–45.
14. D. Lacy, *The White Use of Blacks in America* (New York: McGraw-Hill, 1972), 83–98.
15. P. Lewinson, *Race, Class, and Party: A History of Negro Suffrage and White Politics in the South* (New York: Universal Library, 1965), 94, 157; Lacy, *The White Use of Blacks in America*.
16. Free, *African Americans and the Criminal Justice System*.
17. Tarver et al., *Multicultural Issues in the Criminal Justice System*.
18. Scott and Marshall, *Dictionary of Sociology*.

19. A. Oberschall, "The Los Angeles Riot of August 1965," *Social Problems* 15 (1968): 322–41. doi:10.2307/799788

20. Ibid.

21. R. Kluger, *Simple Justice* (New York: Random House, 1998).

22. Oberschall, "The Los Angeles Riot."

23. Killian, *The Impossible Revolution*.

24. Oberschall, "The Los Angeles Riot."

25. J. S. Butler, "The Return of Open Debate," *Society* 33 (March/April 1996): 11–18.

26. "What If I Don't Move to the Back of the Bus?" Available at: https://www.thehenryford.org/explore/stories-of-innovation/what-if/rosa-parks/

27. Franklin and Moss, *From Slavery to Freedom*.

28. Ibid.

29. Scott and Marshall, *A Dictionary of Sociology*.

30. Oberschall, "The Los Angeles Riot."

31. Ibid.

32. Ibid.

33. Scott and Marshall, *Dictionary of Sociology*.

34. K. Cleaver, "How TV Wrecked the Black Panthers," *Channels of Communication* (November–December 1982): 98–99.

35. T. Watnabe, "Righting Islam's Image in America," *Los Angeles Times*, May 18, 1999, B2.

36. Ibid.

37. Ibid.; E. Allen, "Religious Heterodoxy and Nationalist Tradition: The Continuing Evolution of the Nation of Islam," *Black Scholar* 26, no. 3/4 (1996): 2–34.

38. J. P. Crank, *Understanding Police Culture* (Cincinnati, OH: Anderson, 1998).

39. Scott and Marshall, *Dictionary of Sociology*.

40. D. J. Besharov, "The Economic Stagnation of the Black Middle Class," Testimony before the U.S. Commission on Civil Rights, July 2005.

41. W. J. Wilson, *The Truly Disadvantaged* (Chicago: University of Chicago Press, 1987); E. Anderson, *Streetwise* (Chicago: University of Chicago Press, 1990).

42. J. P. Crank, "Understanding Police Culture," *American Journal of Criminal Justice* 24, no. 1 (September 1999): 151–54.

43. W. J. Wilson, *The Declining Significance of Race* (Chicago: University of Chicago Press, 1978).

44. See the Black Lives Matter website at: http://blacklivesmatter.com/about/

45. F. C. Harris, "The Next Civil Rights Movement?" *Dissent Magazine*, Summer 2015. Accessed from https://www.dissentmagazine.org/article/black-lives-matter-new-civil-rights-movement-fredrick-harris

46. D. Cole, *No Equal Justice: Race and Class in the American Criminal Justice System* (New York: The Free Press, 1999), 88–109.

47. Ibid.

48. Ibid.

49. Ibid.

50. J. Harris, "Fathers Behind Bars and on the Street," Prison Fellowship. Available at: https://www.prisonfellowship.org/2014/10/fathers-behind-bars-the-problem-solution-for-americas-children/

51. Ibid.

52. Ibid.

53. Ibid.

54. Ibid.

55. Cole, *No Equal Justice*; Harris, "Fathers Behind Bars."

56. Emily Brown, "Timeline: Michael Brown Shooting in Ferguson, Mo.," *USA Today*, August 14, 2014. Available at: http://www.usatoday.com/story/news/nation/2014/08/14/michael-brown-ferguson-missouri-timeline/14051827/

57. L. Bui, "Baltimore Officer Acquitted of Murder, Other Charges in Freddy Gray Case," *The Washington Post*, June 23, 2016. Available at: https://www.washingtonpost.com/local/public-safety/judge-to-deliver-verdict-for-police-officer-charged-with-murder-in-freddie-gray-case/2016/06/22/7a0e015b-3b12-4294-8b72-84a36e1715cd_story.html?utm_term=.64a0a51371f5; P. Hermann and J. W. Cox, "A Freddie Gray Primer: Who Was He, How Did He Die, Why Is There So Much Anger?" *Washington Post*, April 28, 2015. Available at: https://www.washingtonpost.com/news/local/wp/2015/04/28/a-freddie-gray-primer-who-was-he-how-did-he-why-is-there-so-much-anger/; Kevin Rector, "The 45-Minute Mystery of Freddie Gray's Death," *Baltimore Sun*, April 25, 2015. Available at: http://www.baltimoresun.com/news/maryland/freddie-gray/bs-md-gray-ticker-20150425-story.html

58. Annie Sweeney and Jason Meisner, "A Moment-by-Moment Account of What the Laquan McDonald Video Shows," *Chicago Tribune*, November 25, 2015. Available at: http://www.chicagotribune.com/news/ct-chicago-cop-shooting-video-release-laquan-mcdonald-20151124-story.html; Anne Swaney, "Chicago Police Officer Jason VanDyke Charged with 1st-Degree Murder in Laquan McDonald Shooting," *ABC7 Eyewitness News*, November 24, 2015. Available at: http://abc7chicago.com/news/cop-charged-with-1st-degree-murder-in-laquan-mcdonald-shooting/1097312/

59. Madhani, Aamer, "Chicago Cop Jason Van Dyke Sentenced to more than 6 years for Murder of Laquan McDonald," USA Today, January 18, 2019. Available at: https://www.usatoday.com/story/news/2019/01/18/laquan-mcdonald-jason-van-dyke-sentencing/2602213002/

60. "Medical Examiner Rules Eric Garner's Death a Homicide, Says He Was Killed by Chokehold," *NBC4 New York*, August 21, 2014. Available at: http://www.nbcnewyork.com/news/local/Eric-Garner-Chokehold-Police-Custody-Cause-of-Death-Staten-Island-Medical-Examiner-269396151.html; Al Baker, J. David Goodman, and Benjamin Mueller, "Beyond the Chokehold: The Path to Eric Garner's Death," *New York Times*, June 13, 2015. Available at: http://www.nytimes.com/2015/06/14/nyregion/eric-garner-police-chokehold-staten-island.html

61. Catherine Shoichet, "Walter Scott Shooting Case: Court Documents Reveal New Details," *CNN*, September 10, 2015. Available at: http://www.cnn.com/2015/09/08/us/south-carolina-walter-scott-shooting michael-slager/; Alex Johnson, "Michael Slager, S.C. Cop Who Killed Unarmed Motorist Walter Scott, Released on $500,000 Bond," *NBC News*, January 4, 2016. Available at: http://www.nbcnews.com/storyline/walter-scott-shooting/michael-slager-s-c-cop-who-killed-unarmed-motorist-walter-n490066; Andrew Knapp, "Feds Seek to Charge North Charleston Police Officer in Walter Scott Shooting," *Post and Courier*, December 3, 2015. Available at: http://www.postandcourier.com/article/20151204/PC16/151209762

62. A. Knapp, "Federal Civil Rights Trial for Michael Slager Anticipated This Spring," *Post and Courier*, December 14, 2016. Available at http://www.postandcourier.com/news/federal-civil-rights-trial-for-michael-slager-anticipated-this-spring/article_c7f64bd2-c183-11e6-b628-373f 8053c64c.html

63. Matthew Vann and Erik Ortiz, "Walter Scott Shooting: Michael Slager, Ex-officer, Sentenced to 20 years in Prison," *NBC News*, December 7, 2017. Available at: https://www.nbcnews.com/storyline/walter-scott-shooting/walter-scott-shooting-michael-slager-ex-officer-sentenced-20-years-n825006

64. R. Fausset, R. Perez-Pena, and C. Robertson, "Alton Sterling Shooting in Baton Rouge Prompts Justice Department Investigation," *New York Times*, July 6, 2016. Available at: http://movile.nytimes.com/2016/07/06/alton-sterling-baton-rouge-shooting.html?

65. B. Jansen, "Three Police Officers Fatally Shot in Baton Rouge; Dead Suspect Identified," *USA Today*, July 7, 2016. Available at: http://www.usatoday.com/story/news/2016/07/17/reports-baton-rouge-police-officers-shot/87218884/

66. G. Lopez, J. Williams, and L. Nelson, "Dallas Shooting Kills Multiple Police Officers: What We Know," *Vox*, July 9, 2016. Available at: http://www.vox.com/2016/7/7/12125740/dallas-shooting-police-protests.html

67. See Lopez et al., "Dallas Shooting"; Jansen, "Three Police Officers Fatally Shot"; Fausset et al., "Alton Sterling Shooting."

68. K. Potter and A. Forliti, "AP News Guide: More Unrest as Police Shooting Probe Goes On," *Los Angeles Times*, July 28, 2016. Available at: http://www.latimes.com/nation/sns-bc-us-police-shooting-minnesota-news-guide-20160727-story,amp.html

69. L. Langton and M. Durose, *Police Behavior During Traffic and Street Stops* (Washington, DC: Bureau of Justice Statistics, 2013). Available at http://www.bjs.gov/content/pub/pdf/pbtss11.pdf

70. M. R. Durose, E. L. Smith, and P. A. Langan, *Contacts Between the Police and the Public 2005*, April 2007. Available at: https://www.bjs.gov/content/pub/pdf/cpp05.pdf

71. D. A. Smith and C. Visher, "Street-Level Justice: Situational Determinants of Police Arrest Decisions," *Social Problems* 29, no. 2 (1981): 167–77.

72. C. Maxon, K. Hennigan, and D. Sloane, *Factors That Influence Public Opinion of the Police* (Washington, DC: National Institute of Justice, 2003). Available at: https://www.ncjrs.gov/pdf-files1/nij/197925.pdf

73. S. Walker, C. Spohn, and M. Delone, *The Color of Justice: Race, Ethnicity and Crime in America* (Belmont, CA: Wadsworth, 2004), 108–32.

74. R. Bachman, "Victims' Perceptions of Initial Police Responses to Robbery and Aggravated Assault: Does Race Matter?" *Journal of Quantitative Criminology* 12, no. 4 (1996): 363–90.

75. Ibid.

76. Federal Bureau of Investigation, *Crime in the United States 2017*, Table 43, U.S. Department of Justice, 2018. Available at: https://ucr.fbi.gov/crime-in-the-u.s/2017/crime-in-the-u.s.-2017/tables/table-43

77. D. Black, "The Social Organization of Arrest," *Stanford Law Review* 23 (1971): 1087–11.

78. Ibid.

79. Smith and Visher, "Street-Level Justice."

80. Ibid.

81. J. Petersilia, *Racial Disparities in the Criminal Justice System* (Santa Monica, CA: RAND, 1983). Available at: http://www.rand.org/pubs/reports/R2947.html

82. I. S. Son, M. Davis, and D. M. Rome, "Race and Its Effect on Police Officers' Perceptions of Misconduct," *Journal of Criminal Justice* 26, no. 1 (1998): 21–28.

83. Public Broadcasting System. "The Legacy of Rodney King," *Frontline*, May 2001. Available at: http://pbs.org/wgbh/pages/frontline/shows/lapd/race/king.html

84. R. J. Friedrich, "Police Use of Force: Individuals, Situations, and Organizations," *Annals of the American Academy of Political and Social Science* 452 (1980): 82–97; K. Adams, "Measuring the Prevalence of Police Abuse of Force," in William Geller and Hans Toch (eds.), *And Justice for All* (Washington, DC: The Police Executive Research Forum, 1995); H. Cohen and L. Sherman, "Exploiting Police Authority," *Criminal Justice Ethics* (Summer/Fall 1986): 23–31.

85. A. Reiss, *The Police and the Public* (New Haven, CT: Yale University Press, 1971),122.

86. Adams, "Measuring the Prevalence."

87. Walker et al., *The Color of Justice*.

88. Ibid.

89. M. Hickman, *Citizen Complaints About Police Use of Force*, U.S. Department of Justice, Bureau of Justice Statistics, June 2006. Available at: https://www.bjs.gov/content/pub/pdf/ccpuf.pdf

90. Ibid.

91. J. G. Shoop, "National Survey Suggests Racial Disparity in Police Use of Force," *Trial* 34, no. 1 (1998): 97; J. J. Fyfe, "Police Use of Deadly Force: Research and Reform," *Justice Quarterly* 5, no. 2 (1988): 165–205; R. Dunham and G. Alpert, *Critical Issues in Policing: Contemporary Readings* (Cincinnati, OH: Waveland, 1992); W. Westley, *Violence and the Police: A Sociological Study of Law, Custom, and Morality* (Cambridge, MA: MIT Press, 1970).

92. Fyfe, "Police Use of Deadly Force"; W. A. Geller and M. S. Scott, "Deadly Force: What We Know," in C. B. Klockars and S. D. Mastrofski (eds.), *Thinking About Police* (New York: McGraw-Hill, 1993), 446–76.

93. Walker et al., *The Color of Justice*.

94. Cohen and Sherman, "Exploiting Police Authority."

95. Walker et al., *The Color of Justice*.

96. R. R. Roberg and J. Kuykendall, *Police and Society* (Belmont, CA: Wadsworth, 1993).

97. A. Burch, *Arrest-Related Deaths 2003–2009*. U.S. Department of Justice, Bureau of Justice Statistics, November 2011. Available at: https://www.bjs.gov/content/pub/pdf/ard0309st.pdf

98. E. Liebow, *Tell Them Who I Am* (Chicago, IL: University of Chicago Press, 1999).

99. Walker et al., *The Color of Justice*.

100. Cole, *No Equal Justice*.

101. E. Lichtblau, "Profiling Report Leads to Demotion," *New York Times*, August 24, 2005, B1.

102. S. L. Browning, F. T. Cullen, L. Cao, R. Kopache, and T. J. Stevenson, "Race and Getting Hassled by the Police: A Research Note," *Police Studies* 17, no. 1 (1994): 1–11.

103. M. F. White, T. C. Cox, and J. Basehart, "Theoretical Considerations of Officer Profanity and Obscenity in Formal Contacts with Citizens," in T. Barker and D. L. Carter (eds.), *Police Deviance*, 2nd ed. (Cincinnati, OH: Anderson, 1991), 275–97.

104. H. MacDonald, *The War on Cops* (New York: Encounter Books, 2015). See also T. Lynch: "The 'War on Cops': Flawed Logic and Fantasy," *Newsweek*, July 31, 2016. Available at: http://www.newsweek.com/war-cops-flawed-logic-fantasy-485546

105. R. Sutton, "The Dangers of Depolicing: Will Cops Just Stand Down?" *New York Post*, May 5, 2015. Available at: http://nypost.com/2015/05/05/the-dangers-of-de-policing-will-cops-just-stand-down/

106. H. McDonald, "Officer Beaten by a Convicted Felon Hesitated for Fear of Being Called Racist: Welcome to Post-Ferguson Policing," *The National Review*, August 16, 2015. Available at: http://www.nationalreview.com/article/422605/Birmingham-cop-beaten-unconscious-feared-racism-charge

107. Ibid.

108. See Lopez et al., "Dallas Shooting"; Jansen, "Three Police Officers Fatally Shot"; Fausset et al., "Alton Sterling Shooting."

109. D. Murdock, "An Assassination of Truth," *National Review*, January 8, 2015. Available at: http://www.nationalreview.com/article/395919/assassination-truth-deroy-murdock.html

110. Ibid.

111. Tarver et al., *Multicultural Issues in the Criminal Justice System*.

112. Walker et al., *The Color of Justice*.

113. J. Palazzolo, "Racial Gap in Men's Sentencing," *Wall Street Journal*, February 14, 2013. Available at: http://www.wsj.com/articles/SB10001424127887324432004578304463789858002

114. U.S. Sentencing Commission, *FY 2018 Overview of Federal Crime Cases*, 2019. Available at: https://www.ussc.gov/sites/default/files/pdf/research-and-publications/research-publications/2019/FY18_overview_federal_criminal_cases.pdf

115. Ibid.
116. C. Crawford, T. Chiricos, and G. Kleck, "Race, Racial Threat and Sentencing of Habitual Offenders," *Criminology* 36, no. 3 (1998): 481–511.
117. U.S. Sentencing Commission, *FY 2018 Overview of Federal Crime Cases*.
118. S. Ekland-Olson, "Structured Discretion, Racial Bias, and the Death Penalty: The First Debate after Furman in Texas," *Social Science Quarterly* 69 (December 1988): 853–73.
119. R. Weitzer and S. A. Tuch, "Race, Class and Perceptions of Discrimination by the Police," *Crime and Delinquency* 45, no. 4 (1999): 494–507.
120. Tarver et al., *Multicultural Issues in the Criminal Justice System*.
121. A. Hacker, "Affirmative Action: The New Look," *New York Review of Book*s 36 (October 12, 1989): 63–68.
122. G. LaFree, "The Effect of Sexual Stratification by Race on Official Reactions to Rape," *American Sociological Review* 45 (October 1980): 842–54.
123. O. Mitchell and D. L. MacKenzie, *The Relationship Between Race, Ethnicity, and Sentencing Outcomes: A Meta-Analysis of Sentencing Research* (Washington, DC: National Institute of Justice, 2014). Available at: https://www.ncjrs.gov/pdffiles1/nij/grants/208129.pdf
124. J. Gray, "Panel Says Courts Are Infested with Racism," *New York Times*, June 5, 1991, B1.
125. N. Ghandnoosh, *Race and Punishment: Racial Perceptions of Crime and Support for Punitive Policies* (The Sentencing Project, 2014). Available at: http://sentencingproject.org/doc/publications/rd_Race_and_Punishment.pdf
126. Ibid.
127. Walker et al., *The Color of Justice*.
128. W. J. Bowers and G. Pierce, "Deterrence or Brutalization: What Is the Effect of Executions?" *Crime and Delinquency* 26 (1980): 453–84.
129. M. Ford, "Racism and the Execution Chamber," *Atlantic*, June 23, 2014. Available at: http://www.theatlantic.com/politics/archive/2014/06/race-and-the-death-penalty/373081/
130. R. Paternoster, "Prosecutorial Discretion in Requesting the Death Penalty: A Case of Victim-Based Racial Discrimination," *Law and Society Review* 18 (1984): 437–78.
131. D. Baldus, G. Woodworth, and C. A. Pulaski, *Equal Justice and the Death Penalty: A Legal and Empirical Analysis* (Boston: Northeastern University Press, 1990).
132. Ibid.
133. *McCleskey v. Kemp*, 481 U.S. 279 (1981).
134. Jennifer Bronson and E. Carson, "Prisoners in 2017," U.S. Department of Justice, Bureau of Justice Statistics, April 2019. Available at: http://www.bjs.gov/content/pub/pdf/p14.pdf
135. Ibid.
136. John F. Pfaff *Locked In: The True Causes of Mass Incarceration and How to Achieve Real Reform* (New York: Basic Books, 2017).
137. See Robert McNamara and Ronald Burns, *Multiculturalism, Crime, and Criminal Justice*. New York: Oxford University Press, 2017.
138. Michelle Alexander, *The New Jim Crow: Mass Incarceration in the Age of Colorblindness* (New York: The New Press, 2012).
139. Ibid.
140. Ibid.
141. Ibid.

142. Barry Latzler, "Why Michelle Alexander Is Wrong About Mass Incarceration," *National Review*, April 22, 2019. Available at: https://www.nationalreview.com/magazine/2019/04/22/michelle-alexander-is-wrong-about-mass-incarceration/

143. Ibid.

144. Pfaff, *Locked In*.

145. Ibid.

146. Ibid.

147. Barry Latzler, *The Rise and Fall of Violent Crime in America* (New York: Encounter Books, 2016).

148. Ibid.

149. Barry Forman, *Locking Up Our Own: Crime and Punishment in Black America* (New York: Farrar, Straus, and Giroux, 2017).

150. Latzler, "Why Michelle Alexander Is Wrong."

151. Ibid.

152. Ibid.

153. Wendy Sawyer and Peter Wagner, "Mass Incarceration: The Whole Pie 2019," *Prison Policy Initiative*, March 29, 2019. Available at: https://www.prisonpolicy.org/reports/pie2019.html

154. Ibid.

155. See, e.g., MacDonald, *War on Cops*, 105.

156. Walker et al., *The Color of Justice*.

157. Ibid.

CHAPTER 4

HISPANIC AMERICANS AND THE CRIMINAL JUSTICE SYSTEM

CHAPTER OBJECTIVES

After reading this chapter, you should be able to:

- Understand the significance of the Hispanic/Latino influence in America
- Understand the historical importance of immigration for Chicanos, Cubans, Puerto Ricans, and those from Central and South America
- Describe the current position in American society for Chicanos, Cubans, and Puerto Ricans
- Describe the overrepresentation of Hispanic Americans in the criminal justice system, including arrests and sentencing

The group label "Hispanic Americans" includes a population of people who share a common language heritage but have many significant differences. More than one in eight people in the U.S. population are of Spanish or Latin American origin.[1] Collectively this group is called "Hispanics" or "Latinos," terms we will use interchangeably in this chapter. The U.S. Census Bureau estimates that by 2060, Hispanics will constitute 119 million people, about 29 percent of the U.S. population. According to the Census Bureau, in 2017 there were 58.9 million people of Hispanic origin in the United States, making it one of the nation's largest ethnic or racial minorities. Hispanics constituted 18.1 percent of the nation's population. About 64 percent of those identifying with Hispanic heritage were Mexican, followed by about 10 percent who were of Puerto Rican background, about 4 percent who were Cuban, and about 10 percent who were from other Central American countries.[2]

Financially, the median household income for Hispanics in the United States in 2017 was $47,675 with a poverty rate of about 20 percent. Nearly 29 percent of Hispanics age twenty-five and older had at least a high school education. Mexicans had one of the lowest graduation rates, at 28 percent, followed by Puerto Ricans at 29 percent, and Cubans, who had the highest graduation rates at 30 percent. Others from Central America had the lowest rates of education, at 27 percent. About 32 percent had a bachelor's degree or higher. About 63 percent of Hispanics or Latinos sixteen years and older were in the labor force in 2017 and 38 percent worked in management, business, science, or artistic occupations.[3]

The problems of identity are evident from the outset of the discussion. How does one define this group of diverse people—are they Hispanic, Latino, or something else? People of Spanish or Latin origin share the group labels "Hispanic" or "Latino" and a common ancestral home, Central and South America. The Hispanic label combines the offspring of colonized natives, the *Hispanos*, with the descendants of foreigners, and with political and economic refugees.[4] The term "Hispanic" is not universally used, and some people, particularly from Latin America, prefer the term "**Latino**." Also, even among the cultures of Latin America, significant differences exist.[5]

In addition to the countries of origin, some sense of the Hispanic population can be made by examining where different groups tend to live. Chicanos, those who are Americans of Mexican origin, for example, are found primarily in the Southwest, whereas Puerto Ricans tend to live in the New England area, and Cubans tend to congregate in Florida. Given their diversity both in background and regionalism, groups in the West tend to use the term "Latino" whereas the term "Hispanic" is more often used in the East.[6]

There is even diversity found in the one area thought to be common for all Hispanics: language. Because of different dialects and nuances in pronunciation, while "Spanish-speaking" might be a way to generally identify the group, perhaps it is more accurate to say that Hispanics or Latinos are a "non–English speaking" group.

CHICANOS AND MEXICANS

Chicanos, who are Americans of Mexican origin, are the largest ethnic group in the United States, numbering more than 39 million, with more than 55 percent living in California, Florida, and Texas in 2014. About 15 million live in California. Chicanos have a long history in the United States, dating back to the early days of European exploration. The Chicano people trace their ancestry to the merging of Spanish settlers with Native Americans of Central America. In fact, evidence of Chicano history can be traced to the Mayan and Aztec civilizations.[7] Thus, the Spaniards conquered the land and merged with Native Americans over several centuries to form the Mexican people.

In 1821 Mexico obtained its independence, but domination from the north began less than a generation later. After the conclusion of the Mexican-American War, treaties were signed which gave the United States Texas, California, and most of Arizona and New Mexico for $15 million. In exchange, the United States granted citizenship to about 75,000 Mexicans.[8]

The beginning of the Chicano experience was varied, but the one thing they had in common was that they were regarded as a vanquished people. Although maltreatment and discrimination existed, more serious issues arose when Whites began to encroach on Chicano land. Prior to 1869, Chicanos in California owned all parcels of land valued at more than $10,000. By the 1870s they owned only 25 percent of the land. A widely accepted, and ironic, explanation for this trend was that many Whites felt justified in taking Chicano land because of the land grabbing that some Mexican governors perpetrated against American Indians. That Whites perpetuated this same type of behavior against American Indians somehow is lost in the justification of the treatment of Chicanos.[9]

IMMIGRATION

Immigration from Mexico is unique in several respects. From about 1901 to 1913, large numbers of Mexicans came into the country to work in the growing agricultural industry. The Mexican population grew significantly after the Mexican Revolution of 1909–1922, which brought even more refugees into the United States. When World War I began, fewer people from Europe came to this country, which opened the proverbial door in the labor market for Mexican workers. More Mexicans emigrated to the United States after the Mexican Revolution, due to the political conflicts in their native country.[10]

The influx of Mexicans into the United States slowed after 1929 as the Great Depression was felt all over the country. Consequently, Mexicans were not needed for labor and the ones already in the United States were considered competition for existing jobs. In an attempt to reduce the labor force, the government embarked upon a deportation program, referred to as **Repatriation**, to effectively send Chicanos back to Mexico.[11]

The legal justification for Repatriation was that deportation only applied to illegal immigrants. However, one of the problems this program created stemmed from the poorly kept records concerning immigrants prior to 1930. Because the United States at that time had little interest in whether Mexicans entered with the proper credentials, preferring their labor to their papers, many Mexicans who could be classified as illegal aliens had resided in the United States for decades. And, because many Mexicans had children who were citizens at birth, technically, they could not be legally deported. Regardless, many Chicanos were deported because they could not produce sufficient documentation that they were U.S. citizens.[12]

As a result, about a half-million people were deported to Mexico. The Chicanos and Mexicans who were allowed to remain could not find work, and many lost the property they owned because they were unable to pay taxes. As a result, a large number of Chicanos flocked to growing concentrations of segregated areas, called **barrios**, of the Southwest.[13]

When the Depression ended, Mexican laborers again became attractive to industry. In 1942 the United States and Mexico agreed to a program allowing migration across the border by contracted workers called **Los Braceros**. Minimum standards were maintained for the transportation, housing, wages, and healthcare of the Braceros. Ironically, these safeguards placed the Braceros in a better economic situation than Chicanos, who often worked alongside the protected Mexican nationals.[14]

CHICANOS TODAY

Perhaps the two most significant areas that demonstrate the current status of Mexican Americans in this country relate to education and healthcare. Both Mexican Americans and Puerto Ricans have seen some progress in terms of educational achievement; however, both groups lag behind Whites.

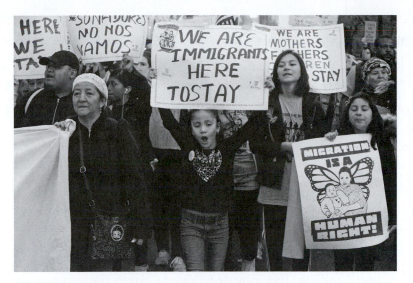

Many of the problems experienced by African Americans are also felt by the Hispanic/Latino community.

Particularly in the 1960s and 1970s, strong campaigns were launched to ensure that Whites and Blacks were provided equal educational opportunities. The momentum for equality had lessened at a time when more Hispanics were entering congested, minority-dominated schools.[15]

Not surprisingly, Mexican Americans and Puerto Ricans are underrepresented in higher education. As an illustration, according to the U.S. Census, in 2017, 63.8 percent of Mexican Americans and 79.8 percent of Puerto Ricans age twenty-five and over had completed high school or higher. Cubans had the highest percentages of those who graduated high school or higher at 81.2 percent. Those from Central American countries had the lowest rate of high school graduation, with 58.5 percent. This compares with 89 percent of non-Hispanic Whites.[16]

Hispanics are also adversely affected by issues surrounding healthcare. According to the U.S. Census Bureau, despite the efforts to improve the number of Americans who have health insurance, and despite the fact that Hispanics and Latinos have seen an increase in the number of people who have obtained it, there still exists a sizeable portion of the population that remain uninsured. According to a 2018 report, *Health Insurance Coverage in the United States*, in 2017, Hispanics had the highest uninsured rate in 2017, at 16.2 percent.[17] Not only is the quality of healthcare limited for many Hispanics, particularly those who are poor, there is no continuity of care since they must often rely on clinics for their medical needs. It also means preventive healthcare is limited. An added problem is the language barrier. Even with translators, communication with Hispanic patients is difficult for English speakers, since many medical terms are not easily translatable, particularly for interpreters who are not familiar with medical terminology.[18]

CHECKPOINT

- There is a long history of involvement of the Chicano population in the United States, and this trend continues today. However, while some progress has been made to improve the educational, healthcare, and employment statuses of many Mexicans, they still lag far behind Whites in many categories.

CUBANS

Third in population only to Chicanos and Puerto Ricans, Cuban Americans represent a significant ethnic minority in the United States. The Cuban influence in this country was seen as early as 1831, with small, close-knit communities organized around a single enterprise such as a cigar manufacturing factory.[19]

Until recently, however, the number of Cuban Americans was relatively small. In 1960 79,000 people who were born in Cuba lived in the United States. By 1990, this number had grown to over 1 million. This increase followed Castro's rise to power after the 1959 Cuban Revolution. Since then, immigration to the United States has come in four distinct waves. First, there was an initial exodus of approximately 200,000 following Castro's claim to power. The first wave lasted for a period of about three years and ended as a result of the Cuban missile crisis in 1962.[20]

The second stage of immigration was informal, but important. Between 1962 and 1965, there was no direct sanctioned transportation, but nearly 30,000 Cubans came via private planes, boats, and other forms of transportation. The third stage occurred between 1965 and 1973, when the Cuban government permitted approximately 300,000 of its citizens to emigrate to the United States.[21]

The fourth wave has been the most controversial. In 1980, more than 124,000 refugees fled Cuba to Key West, Florida, seeking asylum in the United States. President Carter, reflecting the nation's hostility toward Cuba's communist government, welcomed the refugees "with open arms and an open heart." Castro saw President Carter's claim as an opportunity to deport a host of inmates, criminals, and drug addicts. However, while refugees from this last wave of immigration have been somewhat historically stigmatized, it should be noted that the majority of refugees were not social deviants.[22]

Unfortunately, this group of refugees was given the name **Marielitos**. The word, meant to suggest that they were undesirable, refers to Mariel, the fishing port west of Havana where Cuban authorities herded people onto boats. The negative reception by the Cubans who were already here, coupled with the group's lack of formal education, resulted in a great deal of difficulty for many Marielitos in adjusting to life in America.[23]

CUBANS TODAY

Compared to other recent immigrant groups, and to Hispanics as a whole, Cuban Americans have made a successful transition to American culture. Unemployment rates are low for Cuban American women, who are less likely than other groups to seek employment.

The close-knit structure of Cuban American families encourages women to follow traditional roles of homemaker and mother.

Probably no ethnic group has had more influence on the fortunes of a city in a short period of time than the Cubans have had on Miami. It is the only city in the country where more than 57 percent of the inhabitants, an estimated two million Cuban Americans, are foreign-born. This is an increase from the 1.2 million in 2000.[24] The early immigrants were generally well educated, and many had professional or managerial backgrounds. Consequently, many Cubans used their talents and skills in the United States to achieve economic success.

However, the recent wave of immigration from Cuba, more than 500,000 since 1990, according to the U.S. Department of Homeland Security, has changed the fabric of the Cuban experience and Cuban American views of Cuba. While Cuban immigrants who came to the United States before 1990 generally think there is little in common between Cuban Americans and people living in Cuba, in 2013 almost half of current immigrants think that Cuban Americans and people living in Cuba have a lot in common.[25]

According to a 2018 study by the Cuban Research Institute at Florida International University, almost 80 percent of Cubans living in Miami-Dade County do not believe the economic embargo has worked. In fact, only a slight majority of Cubans oppose continuing the embargo, and a large majority favor diplomatic relations with Cuba, with nearly 70 percent of respondents in favor of lifting the travel restrictions from the United States to Cuba. Additionally, nearly 90 percent of the respondents support the Cuban Adjustment Act. This law, which began in 1966, states that Cuban citizens and their spouses and children may get a green card and become residents of the United States one year after

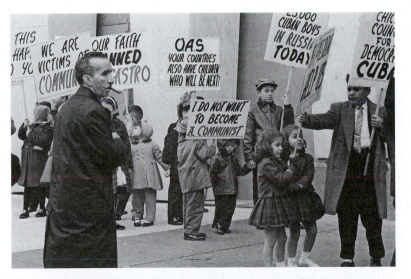

While relations have improved between the United States and Cuba, many Cuban Americans are still concerned about human rights violations in their home country.

arriving in the country. This automatic application is unusual for other immigrant groups. Additionally, a large majority of respondents (48 percent) favor the "wet foot/dry foot" immigration policy—that is, Cubans who leave by raft or boat are sent back to Cuba if they are caught before they reach U.S. soil.[26]

These demographic shifts are seen in political views. About 57 percent of recent Cuban immigrants say they identify with or "lean toward" the Democratic Party, while 19 percent feel that same way about the Republican party. In contrast, about half of older immigrants—those who arrived before 1990—say they are Republican, while 35 percent identify with Democrats.[27] This is a significant shift since, among Latinos, those of Cuban origin have some of the highest voter turnout rates. In 2012, more than two-thirds of Cuban Americans voted nationally. This is far lower than the 48 percent of Latinos overall.[28]

According to data by the Cuban Research Institute, in 2018 only 54 percent of registered Cuban voters say they identify with the Republican Party, down from 64 percent in 2003. While only about 22 percent identified themselves as Democrats in 2003, in 2018 that number was 19 percent, with about 26 percent stating they are Independent. In 2004, for example, George W. Bush won 78 percent of the Cuban vote in Florida, but in 2012 the Cuban vote was split, with 49 percent supporting Barack Obama and 47 percent supporting Republican Mitt Romney.[29] In 2016, about 41 percent of Cubans voted for President Trump.

As was mentioned, this political shift is related to shifts in immigration patterns. While the wave of Cubans who arrived in the 1960s benefited from the changes taking place in Miami and the state as a whole, the slowly recovering economy in South Florida, coupled with an influx of uneducated and less fluent Cubans, has led to greater poverty among the current wave of Cuban immigrants. A 2014 poll conducted by the Robert Wood Johnson Foundation, the Harvard School of Public Health, and NPR, showed that 45 percent of Cuban Americans say their finances are not so good or poor. Cuban Americans now see themselves as financially troubled at higher rates than other Latinos, and nearly two-thirds were worried about possible unemployment. Of those who find work, it is often in the lowest-paying sectors of the labor market.[30]

In 2015, President Obama announced that he planned to visit Cuba, and he did so in 2016. This was the first time in ninety years that a sitting U.S. president visited the island. This came on the heels of breaking the diplomatic freeze between the two countries. In addition, both the United States and Cuba reopened embassies in both Washington, DC, and Havana, and the Obama administration developed a series of rule changes to allow U.S. businesses to export products to Cuba. Additionally, a deal was also reached regarding the reestablishment of commercial airline flights and cellular service by U.S. companies.[31]

According to a report by the Migration Policy Institute, the decision by U.S. President Barack Obama and Cuban President Raúl Castro to normalize relations opened a new era for Cuban migration. Anticipating an end to their special immigration treatment, Cuban arrivals more than doubled from about 24,000 in fiscal year 2014 to 56,400 in 2016. Additionally, during the final days of his presidency in January 2017, President Obama ended the "dry-foot" aspect of the policy, which had resulted in thousands of Cubans making their way through Central America and Mexico to reach the U.S. border.[32]

However, not everyone embraced the Obama plan. Opponents of this change in relations between the two countries cite the continued human rights violations and political persecutions that remain a feature of life in Cuba. According to the Cuban Commission of Human Rights and National Reconciliation, there were 8,616 arrests of Cuban citizens who were deemed political prisoners in 2015, slightly less than the 8,899 arrests in 2014.[33]

According to research by the Cuban Research Institute, since 2016 the Trump administration has not made many policy changes toward Cuba since the Obama administration, but the relationship between the two countries has changed. As it seems to be with all Latino nations, the national narrative toward Cuba is one of hostility rather than engagement; confrontation rather than negotiation. According to the Trump administration, in response to a "sonic attack" on U.S. Embassy personnel in Havana, the administration placed a travel restriction on Cuba and limited personnel at the U.S. Embassy in 2019. Under the current immigration policy, Cubans requesting visas to visit relatives in the United States must travel to U.S. embassies in a third country to make an appointment for visa applications. Still, over 63 percent of respondents in the latest poll by the Cuban Research Institute favor supporting diplomatic relations with Cuba, and 57 percent favor unrestricted travel by all to and from Cuba.[34]

CHECKPOINT

- While the Cuban experience in the United States has been a product of several waves of immigration, the most noted group is the Marielitos during the 1980s, who were considered criminals and deviants by the Castro administration. Cubans today have a wide range of experiences, with some coming to the United States and achieving some success, but others continue to struggle. While historically considered politically conservative, the latest polls indicate that many Cuban Americans now lean more toward liberal policies.

PUERTO RICANS

Puerto Rico represents an interesting case because they are a group left in limbo with regard to their status in the United States. The island was taken by the United States during the Spanish-American War in 1898. During the time Spain controlled the island, which lasted for about four centuries, slavery was prominent as many Puerto Ricans were enslaved by the Spanish and there was an influx of Africans to the island. This legacy of slavery and intermarriage can be seen in the skin tone of many Puerto Ricans, who appear darker than other Hispanic or Latino groups.

The subsequent economic, social, and political colonization, which was enhanced in 1948 when Puerto Rico became a commonwealth, left the people in a state of ambiguity in terms of status. While they are United States citizens and elect their own governor, Puerto Ricans cannot vote in presidential elections and have no representation in Congress. However, they are subject to military service and all federal laws.[35]

Historically, many Puerto Ricans came to the mainland during World War II to work on railroads and in manufacturing. New York City represented a haven for many Puerto Ricans since there was a large group who had already settled there. More recently, while many Puerto Ricans remain in New York City, others have migrated to New Jersey, Florida, Connecticut, and Pennsylvania. This latter group of Puerto Ricans is much more familiar and comfortable with American culture, making the migration easier. Perhaps most significant has been the loss of manufacturing jobs in many cities, necessitating a move to other areas of the country.[36] Puerto Ricans who return to the island after spending time away, typically in New York, have come to be called **Neoricans**. This group represents a better-educated, more affluent segment of the population who returned to Puerto Rico.[37]

However, recent changes have impacted all of Puerto Rico. A slow economic recovery has led many Puerto Ricans to leave the island for the United States in the largest numbers since World War II. The Census Bureau calls attention to the impact this massive migration has had on the island, showing its first sustained population decline since the island became a U.S. territory. While the number of Puerto Ricans living on the mainland reached a record 4.9 million in 2012, since 2006 it has exceeded the number of those living on the island (3.5 million in 2012). In fact, the overall population in Puerto Rico was 3.6 million in 2013—a significant decline from the 4.5 million in 2000.[38]

Puerto Ricans who arrived from the island since 2000 are less likely than earlier migrants to settle in the Northeast and more likely to live in the South, particularly Florida. This new wave of immigrants differs from its counterpart of the past, according to a recent study by the Pew Research Center. These individuals are more likely to live in poverty than earlier groups and are more likely to have been born on the island.[39]

The challenges facing the island, both in terms of negative migration and economic challenges, stems from a nearly decade-old recession, during which the public debt reached over $72 billion and unemployment reached 14 percent, higher than any U.S. state. In January 2016, Puerto Rico defaulted on its $37 million payment due on bonds issued by two government agencies. Still, the Commonwealth was able to pay off the $328 million in general obligation debt, but it had to use more than $100 million in reserve funds to make the payments.[40]

Unlike a state in a severe economic decline, however, Puerto Rico cannot declare bankruptcy. This mountain of debt impacts its ability to jumpstart the economy and put people back to work. Tax laws were once generous to U.S. companies seeking to do business in Puerto Rico, which generated the growth of factories and jobs on the island, particularly in textiles and pharmaceuticals. But after a phase-out of these incentives, coupled with the worldwide recession, the number of jobs dwindled. In response to these challenges, little was done to ensure Puerto Rico's future. Deficits increased and pensions absorbed much of the government's revenue. In 2006, the government ordered a two-week shut down because it could not meet its financial obligations. The governor reduced taxes and instituted massive layoffs, and the government began to borrow in order to pay its expenses.[41]

The impact of these decisions was seen in the employment and poverty rates of Puerto Rican citizens. According to one estimate in 2015, the per capita income was $15,200, half

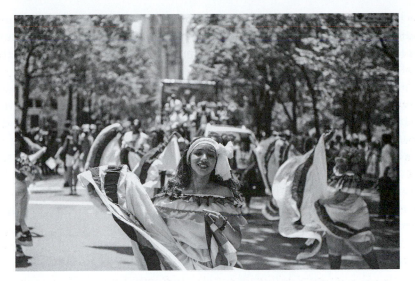

Historically and currently, many Puerto Ricans came to New York in search of jobs and a better life, but they have maintained their Puerto Rican heritage.

that of Mississippi, the poorest state in the United States. Moreover, 37 percent of all households in Puerto Rico received food stamps. This is in contrast to Mississippi, where that figure was 22 percent. And while jobs were scarce, pension benefits continued to shrink, all leading to a sense of malaise about the future of the island. This is what triggered the massive migration to the mainland.[42] In short, in virtually all social areas, such as housing, healthcare, and education, Puerto Rico falls far short of acceptable minimal standards.[43]

The problems that existed in Puerto Rico were exacerbated in 2017 when Hurricane Maria hit the island on September 20. The devastation was considerable, with over $100 million in damages to the island, which was without power for over a year—in August 2018, the government-owned power company announced that it had officially restored electricity to the island.

The U.S. Government Accountability Office said 54 percent of federal emergency personnel were not qualified to do the rescue work in October 2017. The report also states there were logistical challenges due to the location of Puerto Rico and that the Federal Emergency Management Agency (FEMA) had to assume many of the local government's responsibilities given the loss of power and communications. However, this study was not the only one published in the wake of Hurricane Maria that touched upon the storm's level of devastation.

Another study by George Washington University determined 2,975 people died on the island following the storm—far more than the official death toll of 64 given by the island's government. However, on September 13, 2018, President Donald Trump posted a controversial tweet in which he denied that an estimated 3,000 people had died on the island in the aftermath of the hurricane. In his tweet, Trump rejected the death toll presented by the George Washington University study and also claimed that Democrats intentionally inflated the death toll to make him "look as bad as possible."[44]

The lack of support by the federal government, which was slow to respond, resulted in the migration of many Puerto Ricans to the mainland. In fact, in 2018, Census Bureau data show that the island lost nearly 4 percent of its population after the hurricane, the largest decrease of people in its history.

The data show that 129,848 people left the island between July 2017 and July 2018. While disputes occur about the actual number of deaths as a result of the hurricane, the Census Bureau points to deaths and emigration to account for the population decreases. The Census data show that there were 6,440 more deaths than births during 2017 and 2018, which is considered a normal figure, even though there were several thousand more deaths than normal following the hurricane. While many of the deaths from the hurricane were likely of the sick and elderly, largely because of the lack of electricity and access to medical care and fresh water, there is no discounting the long-term effects of the population decreases, particularly in major metropolitan areas like San Juan.[45]

CHECKPOINT

- The history of Puerto Rico has been a complicated one; Puerto Rico is not a state and therefore is not given the same rights and authority as a state. A history of mismanagement has led to persistent economic challenges on the island and a steady exodus of people to the mainland. The recent effects of Hurricane Maria, along with the lack of effective responses by the federal government to help the island recover, have only further exacerbated the problems there.

THE INFLUENCE OF CENTRAL AND SOUTH AMERICA

When most people think of Hispanics and Latinos, they usually think only of the groups mentioned thus far in this chapter. However, an essential part of the Hispanic and Latino presence in this country is is made up of immigrants and citizens with a background from Central and South America. In fact, as was mentioned, the influence of this group on the culture of Little Havana in Miami, or even the changing face of New York City, is considerable.

For instance, people from Chile and Costa Rica have very little in common with other Hispanic and Latino groups other than the Spanish language and geographic location. In the case of Brazil, natives do not speak Spanish; their official language is Portuguese. For some reason, Americans tend to lump groups from Central and South America into a single category despite a wide range of cultural differences. In addition, instead of making distinctions between group membership based on light or dark skin tones, as is done in this country, Latin Americans make distinctions in terms of group membership based on a light-to-dark skin continuum sometimes called a **color gradient**. These differences are significant in terms of identifying social class and religious differences between South American and Central American groups. Thus, not only do people from these regions of the world not fit into a simple category of "Hispanic" or "Latino" but there are enough differences to render any type of generalization difficult.[46]

HISPANICS, ILLEGAL IMMIGRATION, AND THE CRIMINAL JUSTICE SYSTEM

Given the attention it has received on almost a daily basis, it is difficult to read the newspaper or scan the internet and not see a story or development about immigration. As with all social problems, it is important to separate fact from fiction, and the debate swirling about immigration is no exception. What we offer in this section is an assessment of how the current immigration policies, which heavily focus on enforcement and the deportation of immigrants, fall heavily on those who are Latino and Hispanic. Another common theme is that the federal government has taken liberties with justifications and rationalizations to engage in what we are calling the criminalization of immigration. Much of these "alternative facts" that are offered by immigration officials about the criminal acts of immigrants is incongruent with the actual research, making the enforcement efforts questionable at many levels.

In April 2019, the director of the Department of Homeland Security, Kirstjen Nielsen, abruptly resigned after President Trump demanded more from the agency in terms of its ability to address the influx of immigrants to the United States. Included in those discussions was the reviving of the decision to separate children from families of detained immigrants, as well as extending how long children could be detained. It also included denying applications for asylum and forcing people who were seeking asylum to wait in Mexico while their cases are being reviewed, which is a violation of federal law.[47]

Within hours of Neilson's resignation, the director of the U.S. Secret Service was informed that he would be relieved of his duties (the Secret Service director reports directly to the Department of Homeland Security, or DHS). Additionally, the Acting Deputy Director of the DHS, Claire Grady, also resigned. Such a dramatic shakeup, along with resignations across the Trump administration, raised questions about what exactly was being asked of employees and their respective agencies. Critics pointed out that many of Trump's demands and policies were, in fact, illegal, leading those directors to refuse to carry out those orders, attempt to convince the president to modify his stance on particular issues, or resign. This was especially true of Trump's decision to revise the family separation policy that drew such heavy criticism from members of Congress and the general public.[48]

These policy changes, including the harsh treatment of immigrants, have escalated, including the heavy reliance on deportation and detention, and reflect a negative perception of immigrants by the Trump administration. This is what we are referring to as "the criminalization of immigration," where the status of being an immigrant makes one vulnerable to a wide range of sanctions, and the recalibration and defining of certain acts increases criminal prosecution. However, this process, while purportedly applied to all immigrants who attempt to enter this country illegally, as well as those who are already here, appears to result in a greater proportion of attention given to immigrants of color.

IMMIGRANTS AND THE CRIMINAL JUSTICE SYSTEM

Given the recent stepped-up enforcement of immigration policies by the Trump administration, there has been an increase in the number of immigrant apprehensions, deportations, and prosecutions of illegal immigrants who have committed crimes. In fact, there are more apprehensions of non-Mexicans than Mexicans at the border. In 2017, apprehensions of Central Americans at the border exceeded those of Mexicans for the third time since 2014.[49]

In 2018, according to the Migration Policy Institute, the Border Patrol reported 404,142 apprehensions at both southern and northern borders in 2018, a significant increase from 310,531 in 2017, and closer to the 415,816 apprehensions in 2016. The vast majority of apprehensions, 98 percent, occurred along the southwest border. While apprehensions were up in 2018, they remained a small share of the 1.6 million that occurred during the peak year of 2000.[50]

Within the United States, where ICE is responsible for the internal enforcement of immigration policy, ICE made 158,581 administrative arrests in 2018, up 11 percent from a year earlier. It should be noted that an administrative arrest is the arrest of an individual for a civil violation of U.S. immigration law, which is subsequently adjudicated by an immigration judge or through other administrative processes.[51]

The Deportation of Immigrants

When discussing the topic of deportation, the terms often associated with that practice include what are known as "removals" and "returns," which are the movement of immigrants who are deemed to be deportable or inadmissible to the United States for one reason or another. Both the Border Patrol and ICE conduct removals and returns, and in 2018 there were 256,085 removals and returns carried out by ICE, an increase of 13 percent from 2017 (data on the number of removals or returns by the Border Patrol were not available for 2017 or 2018 at the time of this writing).[52]

In 2016, according to the Pew Research Center, around 340,000 immigrants were deported from the U.S. in 2016, slightly increased from 2015. Overall, the Obama administration deported about three million immigrants between 2009 and 2016, a significantly higher number than the two million immigrants deported by the Bush administration between 2001 and 2008.

The Detention of Immigrants

Detaining non-citizens is not a new strategy in the United States. At the turn of the century, about 20 percent of immigrants who were examined at Ellis Island were detained due to health concerns or because of legal questions about their status.[53] By the early 1950s, detaining migrants no longer seemed necessary. European and Asian migration had fallen drastically as a result of the Immigration Act of 1924 and the Great Depression. In 1954, government officials felt that a majority of migrants could be released while their cases were being reviewed. Detention was reserved for migrants who were deemed likely to flee or who posed some sort of threat to the country. This position changed in the 1980s with the migration of Cubans and Haitians into the United States.[54]

During the 1980s, Americans came to see Cuban exiles as a dangerous threat, and this led to the use of detention as a primary strategy to deal with immigration. As part of the Mariel Boatlift, approximately 125,000 Cubans fled for the United States, many of whom were not criminals but were labeled "antisocial" by Cuban officials. Thousands of immigrants were placed in military bases while they waited to be sponsored by someone who agreed to take care of them until they could become self-sufficient.[55]

As the months went by, most exiles left the military bases, but those who had no family members or acquaintances in the United States often had difficulty finding sponsors. Without sponsorship, the only way they could leave the camps was by leaving the United States. But government officials could not deport them because the Castro government refused to take them back.[56]

By 1982, about four hundred Mariel Cubans who still had not been sponsored were sent to prison, primarily to a maximum-security penitentiary in Atlanta. This trend, coupled with a fear of another large migrant group coming into the United States, led to the development of a policy that focused more on detention as a default strategy than the policy of allowing immigrants to remain free while their cases were being handled. Added to this was the fact that it was an era of "getting tough" on criminals in general, where there was an unprecedented level of incarceration of all types of offenders in the United States.

During the first term of the Obama administration, an average of more than thirty thousand immigrants were held in detention per day. This was the result of a "detention bed quota" imposed by Congress, and enhanced efforts to target immigrants with criminal convictions, many of whom were subject to mandatory detention. During the Trump administration, the use of detention has grown considerably as a result of interior immigration enforcement as well as stepped-up efforts at the Mexican border. This trend continues, and U.S. policy reflects the growth of detention as a strategy and the development of privately run prisons.[57] In 2018, ICE reported that the average daily number of the detained immigrant population was 38,106 per day; this had increased to 49,447 by March 2019.[58]

In 2019, President Trump took another dramatic step in the immigration conflict by asserting that he was seriously considering releasing detained immigrants into sanctuary cities. Such a decision was considered by many experts to be a political ploy designed to punish Democrats for their failure to support Trump's efforts to build a border wall. Others who were not in favor of such a shift in policy pointed to the logistics involved, along with the potential liability issues such a decision would create. More importantly, those who were not supportive of this latest idea argued that such a strategy would do little to stem the flow of undocumented people into the United States. By offering them sanctuary in cities where they would want to go in the first place, President Trump's plan could exacerbate the problem rather than curtail it.

In fact, according to some experts, most large sanctuary cities would not be adversely impacted by a massive influx of detained immigrants. By one estimate, even a million additional immigrants would not significantly impact the infrastructure of social services that would be needed to accommodate those individuals. Where it might be more problematic, however, is in smaller cities and towns, where a large and dramatic increase in immigrants could overtax the ability of that city's or town's infrastructure.

In general, most immigrants would likely prefer to be placed in a larger urban area, simply because the job opportunities there would be much more plentiful, along with a greater presence of people with similar cultural backgrounds to theirs. Thus, if anything, a decision by Trump to place immigrants in sanctuary cities would likely do little to reduce the number of illegal immigrants in the United States; in fact, it might have exactly the opposite effect.[59]

CHECKPOINT

While there has always been a flow of immigrants from Mexico into the United States, and while undocumented immigration has been a persistent problem in the United States, particularly since comprehensive immigration reform has not occurred, the recent enforcement efforts by the Trump administration have created the criminalization of immigrants and a sense of tension and hostility toward Hispanics/Latinos.

TRUMP, IMMIGRATION, AND NATIONAL EMERGENCIES

It is important to note that while the Trump immigration policies are perhaps intensive, intrusive, and insensitive, his efforts are similar to what other presidents have done with regard to immigration in this country. This is not a defense of those efforts or of the language used to describe and promote them, but it would be unfair to criticize only President Trump for the failure to pass a comprehensive immigration policy that reflects a reasonable and responsible effort to address the problem.

Trump's position on nationalism has been a consistent one. In a speech before the United Nations in 2018, President Trump actually doubled down on his claim that he is against globalization and committed to a pattern of isolationism as part of his domestic and international policies.[60] As evidence of his commitment to such a position, President Trump promised to build a border wall along the Mexican border that would stem the flow of illegal immigration. Trump also promised that the Mexican government would pay to build the wall, something that the country has consistently refused to do. In 2018, Trump made claims that the construction of the wall had begun, but funds approved by Congress were to replace sections of the existing border fence that needed repair, not the construction of a new, state-of-the-art wall, with an estimated cost of $25 billion. [61]

In fact, the federal government experienced the longest shutdown in its history as a result of a standoff between the president and Congress over the funding. In early 2019, Trump attempted to circumvent Congress by declaring a national emergency at the border, which would allow him to use funds not approved by Congress to build the wall. This was a widely controversial move, one that even caused some Republicans and Trump supporters to disagree with such a measure. Lawsuits were filed, and legal challenges will likely delay the construction of the wall until after 2020.

However, in May 2019, a federal judge rejected a lawsuit filed by Congress that attempted to block Trump's plan to divert funds for the wall. The judge ruled that the House of Representatives did not have legal standing to sue President Trump for using funds approved by Congress for a different purpose. House Democrats, who brought the lawsuit, argued that diverting the funds violated the separation-of-powers doctrine of the U.S. Constitution.[62]

The decision to declare a national emergency comes on the heels of a two-month-long effort, where Trump attempted to convince Congress of the need to build a wall along the Mexican border. As part of the funding package approved by Congress, the legislative branch, which constitutionally determines funding for government projects, granted $1.375 billion for about fifty-five miles of fencing. Mr. Trump signed the package into law to avoid a second government shutdown after a thirty-five-day shutdown of many federal agencies that left eight hundred thousand workers without pay.[63]

In response, Trump threatened to declare a national emergency and use his executive powers as president to divert funds from other military projects and use them to build the wall. The emergency declaration, according to White House officials, enables the president to divert $3.6 billion from military construction projects to the wall. Mr. Trump will also use presidential discretion to tap $2.5 billion from counter-narcotics programs and $600 million from a Treasury Department asset forfeiture fund. Combined with $1.375 billion authorized for fencing in the spending package, Mr. Trump would have about $8 billion in all for barriers, significantly more than the $5.7 billion he unsuccessfully demanded from Congress.[64]

Despite the concerns expressed by members of his own party, Trump did just that in early 2019. Trump stated: "We're going to confront the national security crisis on our southern border, and we're going to do it one way or the other," he said. "It's an invasion," he added. "We have an invasion of drugs and criminals coming into our country."[65]

Critics question the need for a wall, often referring to it as a vanity project by the president to fulfill a campaign promise. Others claim the crisis is a manufactured effort to gain public approval and to set up Trump's bid for reelection. As evidence, in 2018 critics pointed out that illegal border crossings had dramatically decreased in recent years, to 400,000 in 2018 from a peak of 1.6 million in 2000.[66] However, in 2019, there was a significant increase in attempts to cross the border, where in the first few months of the 2019 fiscal year, which began in October 2018, the Border Patrol detained 136,150 families traveling with children. This was a significant increase from the previous year, where there were 107,212 families detained.[67]

Others point out that Trump himself recognized the absence of any real emergency when he stated: "I didn't need to do this, but I'd rather do it much faster," he said. "I just want to get it done faster, that's all."[68] Critics also point out that the general public generally disagrees with such an approach. Most Americans oppose Mr. Trump's emergency declaration, according to polls. A *Fox News* poll in 2019 found 56 percent against it, including 20 percent of Republicans.[69]

Supporters of Trump's decision pointed out that the declaration of national emergencies has been used by presidents in the past. Presidents have declared national emergencies nearly sixty times in the past, but most of them dealt with foreign crises and involved freezing property, blocking trade or exports, or taking other actions against national adversaries. In fact, in only two other instances have presidents acted without legislative approval.[70]

George Bush did so in 1990 in anticipation of the war in the Persian Gulf, and in 2001, George W. Bush spent funds just after the 9/11 terrorist attacks. In those instances, however, the president appropriated military funds for military action against an identified enemy and those actions had not occurred after Congress had rejected the president's course of action.[71]

Finally, Trump was a vocal critic of President Obama's use of executive authority during his administration. When President Obama failed to gain consensus on an immigration policy, he essentially prevented millions of illegal immigrants from being deported. In 2014, Trump tweeted "Repubs must not allow Pres Obama to subvert the Constitution of the US for his own benefit & because he is unable to negotiate w/ Congress."[72]

Closing the Border and a National Emergency

In March 2019, President Trump made another dramatic announcement: that unless Mexico did something to address the growing immigration crisis, he would consider closing the border completely. While Trump had made similar claims in the past, the latest threat of closing the Mexican border completely was an extraordinary step in a long line of immigration-related decisions. While most experts pointed out that closing the border could have a significant impact on both countries' economies, where an estimated $1.7 billion in goods and services flow back and forth across the border between the two countries daily,[73] Trump remained committed to the idea.

In April 2019, President Trump reconsidered his plan, stating it was due to the fact that the Mexican government had taken some steps to secure its own border. However, his admonition to the Mexican government was to do more to arrest migrants and address drug trafficking. If Mexico failed to demonstrate significant improvement in these areas, Trump threatened to impose tariffs on automobiles produced in Mexico.[74] About a month later, in May 2019, President Trump followed up on his threat and imposed a 5 percent tariff on Mexican goods, with the promise to increase the tariff to 25 percent until the immigration crisis was resolved.

In response, Mexican President Lopez Obrador stated that he was committed to finding an acceptable solution to the problem and sent envoys to Washington to reach an agreement that would avoid tariffs. He also reiterated that Mexico had stepped up its immigration enforcement policies. According to some reports, Mexico is now detaining double the number of migrants per day than a year ago, when the Mexican government opted to give visas to Central Americans, hoping they would stay in Mexico.[75]

Similarly, Trump threatened to cut aid, an estimated $500 million, to several Central American countries that were said to be the source of the rise in illegal immigrants into the United States. While most experts note that a viable solution to the problem is to address the political and economic crises in those countries that propel people toward the United States in the first place, Trump argued that these countries, primarily Honduras, Guatemala, and El Salvador, had not done enough to warrant continued support. He stated, "We're not paying them anymore because they haven't done anything for us."[76]

At the present time, the decision is still pending, and although Trump cannot eliminate all the aid to those countries because the funds have been appropriated by Congress, he does have the authority to limit it to some degree. Most experts note that reducing the funding would not stem the flow of immigrants to the United States; rather, it would increase it since the problems people are experiencing in those countries would increase in the absence of U.S. aid. [77]

CHECKPOINT

- It is fairly evident that since his election, President Trump has made immigration a foundational issue for his presidency. The stepped-up enforcement efforts, with an emphasis on detaining and deporting undocumented immigrants, along with his controversy with Congress over the funding of the border wall, remain important issues in the discussion of Hispanic involvement in the Criminal Justice System.

The DREAM Act and DACA

During his administration, President Obama attempted to provide temporary legal relief to many undocumented immigrants. In 2012, a program known as *Deferred Action for Childhood Arrivals (DACA)* offered renewable, two-year deportation deferrals and work permits to undocumented immigrants who had arrived in the United States as children and had no criminal records.

Obama argued that DACA was an intervening solution but attempted to influence Congress to pass the Dream Act, which first began in 2001, that would have benefited many of the same people. The first version of the *Development, Relief, and Education for Alien Minors (DREAM)* Act was introduced in 2001. As a result, young undocumented immigrants have since been called *Dreamers*. Since its creation, there have been multiple versions of the legislation, each of which outlines a pathway for undocumented immigrants who came into the United States as minors. Despite support in Congress from various Senators and Congressmen, none of the versions of the legislation has become law.[78]

In 2012, DACA was created by then–Secretary of Homeland Security Janet Napolitano. DACA provides temporary relief from deportation (deferred action) to certain young undocumented immigrants brought to the United States as children. DACA has enabled almost eight hundred thousand eligible young adults to work lawfully, attend school, and plan their lives without the constant threat of deportation. However, unlike federal legislation, DACA does not provide a permanent legal status to individuals and must be renewed every two years. In 2017, Acting Secretary of Homeland Security Elaine Duke ended the 2012 DACA program. Since then, no new applications for DACA have been accepted but current DACA beneficiaries whose status was set to expire before March 5, 2018, were permitted to renew their status for an additional two years. Any person for whom DACA expired on March 6, 2018, or later will no longer have deferred action or employment authorization.[79]

As it relates to DACA beneficiaries and undocumented youth attempting to obtain a college degree to enhance their job opportunities, there remain significant barriers to completing a degree. Colleges and universities each have their own policies about admitting undocumented students; some deny them admission while others allow them to attend. However, even when undocumented students are allowed to attend college, the tuition is often too expensive for them to remain on campus. Given that undocumented students do not qualify for financial aid, it is unlikely students can afford to attend even a public university. To address part of the challenges for undocumented students, some states have created the opportunity for them to receive in-state tuition. However, while this mitigates one dimension of the problem, the absence of financial aid makes this challenging as well.

In 2014, Obama attempted to extend DACA benefits to undocumented parents of U.S. citizens and permanent residents. However, nearly half of U.S. states sued his administration, alleging that the program, known as *Deferred Action for Parents of Americans (DAPA)*, violated federal immigration law and the U.S. Constitution. The U.S. Supreme Court ruled in 2016 that the program was unconstitutional.

Despite these efforts, the Obama administration removed more than three million people during his tenure, higher than what President George W. Bush and Bill Clinton achieved. In fact, according to one researcher, Obama has been referred to as the "deporter in chief," a disparaging term of word play on the president's role as commander in chief.[80] However, Obama's advocates have pointed out that his efforts focused on illegal immigrants who had committed serious crimes.[81]

In addition, the Trump administration attempted to limit the flow of legal immigrants into the United States by reducing the number of refugees admitted and making it more difficult for people to obtain political asylum. In early 2018, the Trump administration implemented a zero-tolerance policy, where all illegal immigrants would be arrested and criminally prosecuted. As a result, thousands of children were detained, separately from their parents or guardians. In response to widespread protests and criticisms, Trump ended the family separation policy.[82]

Sanctuary Cities and Immigration

The federal government is generally responsible for enforcing immigration laws, but it may delegate some immigration-control duties to state and local law enforcement. However, the degree to which local officials are obliged to cooperate with federal authorities is a subject of intense debate. Proponents of tougher immigration enforcement have labeled state and local jurisdictions that limit their cooperation with federal authorities as "sanctuary cities." There is no official definition or count of sanctuary cities, but the Immigrant Legal Resource Center identifies more than six hundred counties with such policies.[83]

President Trump issued an executive order to block federal funding to sanctuary cities and attempted to reinstate the Secure Communities program, in which state and local police provide fingerprints of suspects to federal immigration authorities and transfer individuals to federal authorities who were assumed to be illegal immigrants. He also ordered the expansion of enforcement partnerships among federal, state, and local agencies. Several cities are challenging Trump's order in court. In March 2018, the Justice Department filed a lawsuit against California, alleging that several of the state's laws obstruct federal immigration enforcement. The main issue is whether state and municipal agencies can be controlled by the federal government.[84]

CHECKPOINT

- A critical part of the discussion of President Trump's efforts to control the flow of immigrants into the United States from Mexico and Central America center on how children who were brought to the United States illegally are handled. DACA and Dreamers, as they are called, had no control over the decision of their parents to cross the border, yet their status in the United States remains controversial. Similarly, those cities that have resisted the federal government's efforts to collaborate in the escalated enforcement of immigration laws, known as sanctuary cities, remain a highly controversial topic.

SEPARATING FACT FROM FICTION IN IMMIGRATION

Another interesting pattern regarding illegal immigration is that once people cross the border into the United States, they tend to find jobs and build lives for themselves. According to research by the Pew Research Center, more than half of the undocumented have lived in the country for more than a decade, and nearly one-third are the parents of U.S.-born children.[85]

What is also noteworthy is that while the controversy surrounding border security continues, with President Trump shutting down the federal government because he did not receive funding for his proposed border wall, most of the undocumented population in this country are what are known as **overstayers**, or people who obtained visas legally and simply remained in the United States once it expired.[86]

President Trump has also consistently claimed that illegal or undocumented immigrants are responsible for drug trafficking. In fact, the research on this subject consistently shows that the vast majority of illegal drugs that come into this country occur at legal border checkpoints. Thus, the image of illegal immigrants serving as couriers of the drug cartels, who bring drugs into this country when they cross the border, represents very little of the actual problem relating to drug trafficking. The United States might be better suited to address the challenges at legal border checkpoints than to consider that stemming the flow of illegal immigrants will resolve the drug problem in this country.[87]

Similarly, the claim made by President Trump and his supporters about the criminal activity of illegal immigrants is questionable. This is not to say that a proportion of illegal immigrants do not commit crimes once they arrive in the United States, but one can compare the rate of criminal activity committed by undocumented immigrants to those of U.S.-born residents, along with comparisons to all immigrants who reside in the United States, to see that the portrayal of immigrants as criminals is an exaggeration.

While the rhetoric and narrative offered by President Trump and other politicians and policymakers attempt to sway public opinion about stemming the "invasion" of immigration into this country, where they are characterized as rapists, murderers, and animals,[88] contribute to drug trafficking,[89] or are linked to terrorists,[90] in the vast majority of cases what has occurred is that certain minor offenses have been elevated in seriousness, such as traffic offenses or what had previously been administrative offenses.

By elevating minor offenses to crimes, and by making the offenses retroactive, more immigrants are eligible to be detained, deported, and labeled as criminals. Repeat offenses, known as "aggravated felonies," escalates the stigma and justifies longer and more severe punishment. However, as the data show, immigrants—even those who are undocumented or who crossed the border illegally—constitute a small percentage of all criminals and far less than U.S.-born offenders.[91] Why? Because immigrants do not come to the United States to commit crimes; rather, they come to this country in search of a better life—and most of them find it. This is underscored by the length of time most immigrants stay in the United States and by the fact that they buy homes, pay taxes, and build lives for themselves reflective of the American dream.

CHECKPOINT

- As part of an overall zero-tolerance policy toward immigrants, the federal government has changed its policies in an effort to target what they consider to be violent and dangerous criminals who entered the United States illegally. In the process, however, the government has amended its policies on determining how an immigrant is defined as a felon or criminal, thereby making more of them eligible for deportation.

OTHER HISPANIC INVOLVEMENT IN THE CRIMINAL JUSTICE SYSTEM

The impact of the criminal justice system on the Hispanic population has been studied since the 1970s. Several significant studies have been conducted including the following: a report by the U.S. Commission on Civil Rights entitled *Mexican Americans and the Administration of Justice in the Southwest* (1970); a report from the National Minority Advisory Council on Criminal Justice entitled *The Inequality of Justice: A Report on Crime and the Administration of Justice in the Minority Community* (1982); and a report by the Population Research Institute at Penn State University entitled *Hispanics Penalized More by Criminal Justice System Than Whites and Blacks* (2001). In these reports, the involvement and treatment of Hispanics in the criminal justice process has been highlighted and has shown a consistent trend of discrimination.

In 2002, Charles Kamasaki, Senior Vice President of the National Council of La Raza, testified before the U.S. Sentencing Commission on the impact of drug sentencing and the Latino community. He argued that there was increasing evidence that Hispanics were being held to a standard of accountability far exceeding any other segment of the population in the criminal justice system. For instance, the 2010 census showed that Latinos represented 17 percent of the U.S. population, but according to the U.S. Sentencing Commission, they constituted 52 percent of the total number of offenders in 2014.[92]

Additionally, Kamasaki argued that Hispanics were discriminated against at every stage of the criminal justice process. For example, Hispanic and Black federal defendants were more likely than White defendants to be charged with drug offenses. Compared to 29 percent of Whites charged with drug offenses in U.S. District Courts, 46 percent of Hispanic offenders and 48 percent of Black offenders were charged with drug offenses. Perhaps most important, three times as many Hispanic men ages 25 to 29 were sentenced to prison than Whites. Additionally, Hispanic men were a third less likely to be released before trial than Whites—approximately 23 percent of Hispanics were released before trial compared to 63 percent for non-Hispanic defendants. As further evidence of this disparity, half of Hispanic federal prison inmates had no previous criminal history, compared to 29 percent of Blacks and 38 percent for Whites. Finally, of all federal inmates to receive some type of substance abuse treatment, Hispanics were least likely to receive treatment. Compared to 54 percent of Whites and 48 percent of African Americans, only 36 percent of Hispanics received any type of substance abuse treatment.[93]

In sum, Kamasaki argued that despite the fact that Latinos were no more likely than other groups to use illegal drugs, they were more likely to be arrested and charged with drug offenses and less likely to be given pre-trial release. Once convicted, Latinos received harsher sentences even though the majority of offenders had no criminal history.[94]

In October 2004, a report issued by the **National Council of La Raza**, the nation's largest Hispanic civil rights organization, also found more systematic discrimination against Hispanics in the criminal justice system. The report, entitled *Lost Opportunities: The Reality of Latinos in the U.S. Criminal Justice System*, was heralded as the first comprehensive examination of Hispanics in every facet of the criminal justice system. The study was based on data from government sources, including the Bureau of Justice Statistics and the U.S. Census Bureau, and was coauthored by the Center for Youth Policy Research and Michigan State University's Office of University Outreach and Engagement.[95]

Among the many key findings from the report was that Hispanics experienced discrimination during arrest, prosecution, and sentencing and were more likely to be incarcerated than Whites when charged with the same offense. Some of the findings related to the circumstances surrounding police contact with Hispanics, which can often lead to arrest, but Hispanics were also disproportionately represented by public defenders, who are often overwhelmed with cases. Compared to defendants with private attorneys, 71 percent who were represented by public counsel, compared to 54 percent with private attorneys, were sentenced to incarceration. The report also highlighted problems stemming from harsh mandatory minimum sentences, which give prosecutors the upper hand in plea negotiations and are inconsistent with the severity of the offense. The report was also critical of courts that do not provide documents written in Spanish or who fail to provide translators to defendants.[96]

Another important finding of this study was that Hispanics were disproportionately charged with nonviolent, low-level drug offenses. Similar to a report in 2002, where health statistics showed similar rates of drug use, Hispanics were three times more likely to be arrested for drug offenses than Whites and accounted for nearly half of all offenders convicted of drug offenses in 2000.[97]

Since the publication of the La Raza study in 2004, these trends have continued to reveal a pattern of a problem. According to a 2014 report by the Tomas Rivera Policy Institute at the University of Southern California, research showed that Latinos receive harsher treatment in arrests, pretrial proceedings, and sentencing than Whites, even when they were charged with the same offense.[98] Other key findings include that Latinos were murdered in California at twice the rate of Whites (5.1 per 100,000, compared to 2.4). In California, Latinos of any age were more likely than Whites to have been killed by strangers (40.5 percent vs. 26.1 percent of homicide victims). Latinos were also more likely to experience multiple crimes—a 2013 survey found that 43 percent of Latinos had experienced three or more crimes within the past five years, compared to 36 percent of crime victims overall.[99]

A report from the Bureau of Justice Statistics shows that from 1994 to 2011, Latinos were more likely to be shot than Whites[100] and had generally higher burglary rates than Whites.[101] Being victimized is exacerbated by a fear of reporting the crime. However, some data indicate that Latinos are reluctant to report a crime even when they have experienced one. In a 2012 survey, 44 percent of Latinos said they would be hesitant to report being victimized for fear that the police would ask them or others about their immigration status.[102]

As offenders, there appears to be some evidence to suggest unequal treatment of Latinos/Hispanics in the criminal justice system. For instance, a 2011 meta-analysis of forty different reports found that suspects of color were more likely to be arrested than White suspects.[103] Another study found that police officers search Latino/Hispanic drivers more often than White male drivers and White officers conducted more searches than African American and Latino police officers.[104] A 2014 study found that 80 percent of Latinos in California felt that racial disparities in drug enforcement were a serious problem.[105]

As it relates to Latino/Hispanic experiences with the courts, one study of felony defendants found that Latinos/Hispanics were less likely to be released on their own recognizance and when they were offered bail, it was approximately $25,000 higher than that for African Americans or Whites in similar cases.[106] At the sentencing stage, a 2011 study by the U.S. Sentencing Commission found that Hispanics and Latinos were more likely than any other group to be convicted of a crime with a mandatory sentence.[107]

According to the Bureau of Justice Statistics, in 2013 there were 1,158 Latino men in prison for every 100,000 in the United States, 2.5 times the rate for White men. This does not include those who are in county jails or cannot make bail. In California, nearly 70 percent of prison inmates were Latino or Black, with the former comprising 41 percent of those in prison. Whites made up 23 percent, according to the California Department of Corrections and Rehabilitation.[108] Additionally, California Latinos pointed to the amount of money spent on prisons and the use of incarceration for minor crimes as their main concern with the criminal justice system.[109]

According to the Uniform Crime Reports in 2017, the latest data available, in comparing Hispanic arrests to Non-Hispanics, overall Hispanics were arrested for approximately 18 percent of all arrests. Of the total 6,584,533 arrests based on ethnicity, Hispanics/Latinos made up 1,190,671 of arrests. About 82 percent, or 5,393,862 arrests, involved non-Hispanic offenders, which includes whites, blacks, and others. A review of the overall violent crime rates indicate that Hispanics/Latinos accounted for about 24 percent of violent crime and about 16 percent of property crime arrests. The highest percentage of arrests by Hispanics/Latinos in 2017 was rape at 27 percent (see Table 4.1).

In recent years there has been a general decline in prison populations overall, however, according to research from the Pew Research Center, the disproportionality of African Americans and Hispanics has remained (see Figure 4.1).[110]

TABLE 4.1 PERCENTAGE OF HISPANIC/LATINO ARRESTS 2017

Total Arrests		Ethnicity	
		Hispanic/Latino	Non-Hispanic
6,584,533		1,190,671 (18.1%)	5,393,862
Crime	**Arrests**		
Murder	7,031	1,462 (20.8%)	5,569
Rape	14,025	3,787 (27%)	10,238
Robbery	59,680	12,722 (21.3%)	46,958
Aggr. Assault	255,056	61,107 (24%)	193,949
Burglary	123,671	24,873 (20.1%)	98,798
Larceny	563,359	78,921 (14%)	484,438
MV Theft	55,723	14,525 (26.1%)	41,198
Arson	5,594	1,073 (19.2%)	4,521
Violent Crime	335,792	79,078 (23.5%)	256,714
Property Crime	748,347	119,392 (16%)	628,955

Source: U.S. Department of Justice, Federal Bureau of Investigation. (2018). *Crime in the United States 2017,* Table 43. Available at: https://ucr.fbi.gov/crime-in-the-u.s/2017/crime-in-the-u.s.-2017/topic-pages/tables/table-43

FIGURE 4.1 **Blacks, Hispanics make up larger shares of prisoners than of U.S. population. U.S. adult population and U.S. prison population by race and Hispanic origin, 2017.**

Note: Whites and Blacks include those who report being only one race and are non-Hispanic. Hispanics are of any race. Prison population is defined as inmates sentenced to more than a year in federal or state prison.

Source: U.S. Census Bureau, Bureau of Justice Statistics.

Like their African American counterparts, Hispanics are significantly overrepresented in many of the crime statistics in this country. The same arguments that are used to explain why African Americans are overrepresented in the crime figures can be applied to Hispanics/Latinos. That is, on one hand, the treatment of Hispanics and Latinos demonstrates the fact that the system discriminates against minority groups. A counterargument is that Hispanics and Latinos have fewer opportunities to obtain well-paying jobs, have poorer educational experiences, and have fewer overall chances to succeed than Whites. All of these factors, in turn, result in some segments of the population turning to crime.

SUMMARY

This chapter explored the changing face of American society as an increasing number of Hispanics, both legal and illegal, become a fixture of the social landscape. Estimates by the Census Bureau suggest that Hispanics will constitute the largest minority group by 2050. The Latin and Hispanic influence on American culture can be seen in a host of ways. Perhaps the best example exists in Miami, which has been transformed by the influx of Cuban immigrants over the years. Moreover, the way that Hispanics and Latinos have been historically treated in this country has resulted in many subgroups remaining mired in a life of poverty and crime. As we have seen, part of the problem for Chicanos stems from the isolation they experience with regard to education as well as the limited access to quality healthcare in this country. For Puerto Ricans, the main issue is also related to economics and the poor economy on the island. These challenges, along with a lack of optimism for the future, have led many foreign-born residents to flee the island for the mainland.

As it relates to criminal justice, Hispanics, as a general category, are overrepresented in virtually every area of criminal justice. Whether it is treatment by the police, sentences relating to drugs, or the increase in the number of Hispanic inmates in prison, clearly the trend with this group's experience in the criminal justice system looks remarkably like that of their African American counterparts. Recent changes to immigration policy has impacted Hispanics/Latinos in a particular way, especially the elevation of certain offenses to constitute aggravated felonies. These changes, along with an aggressive enforcement policy, has increased the number of Hispanics/Latinos who are in detention.

YOU MAKE THE CALL
PRESIDENT TRUMP'S IMMIGRATION POLICY

Imagine that you are a police chief in a city that contains a large number of Hispanics and Latinos. Under President Trump's new immigration policy, there is no sanctuary for illegal immigrants, even for children born in the United States to undocumented immigrants. President Trump has threatened to withhold federal funding to any state or municipality that does not support his position and he demands that your department collaborate with federal ICE agents to "round up" undocumented and other immigrants. The mayor is a member of Trump's party and has pledged his support for the effort, but you feel that this is not only an unreasonable use of your officers (since the department is responsible for dealing with crime in your city, not addressing the immigration problem), and you feel that the policy violates the constitutional protections of citizens born in this country even though their parents might have entered illegally. However, you work at the pleasure of the mayor, who orders you to comply. What do you do?

Questions

1. Can you refuse a direct order from a superior? Will it lead you to be terminated from your position?
2. What happens if you comply with the order but it negatively impacts morale within the department?
3. If you decide to cooperate, what steps could you consider that would fulfill your responsibilities but would not embrace the policy? In other words, can you put forth a half-hearted effort to demonstrate cooperation but not yield much success? Is such a tactic ethical?
4. What role do you think the media could play in this situation that might assist you in leveraging your opposition to the policy?

KEY TERMS

barrios

Chicano

color gradient

Latino

Los Braceros

Marielitos

National Council of La Raza

Neorican

overstayers

Repatriation

sanctuary cities

DISCUSSION QUESTIONS

1. Why have Cubans been so successful in assimilating into American society yet retaining elements of their native culture?
2. How can the high rates of illegal immigration be curtailed? Is simply granting citizenship to those who have entered illegally the solution? Why or why not?
3. Why is drug use so high among Hispanic adolescents?
4. Why do you think some Hispanic groups continue to struggle economically, politically, and socially in the United States? Is it the language barrier or some other set of factors?
5. What do you think is needed for Hispanic/Latino groups to assimilate and be accepted by mainstream society? Why does it appear that Americans are reluctant to treat them fairly?
6. Are the experiences of African Americans similar to or different from that of Hispanics in this country? Give several examples from your point of view.

FOR FURTHER READING

Song-Ha Lee, S. *Building a Latino Civil Rights Movement: Puerto Ricans, African Americans, and the Pursuit of Racial Justice in New York City*. Chapel Hill, NC: University of North Carolina Press, 2014.

Foley, N. *Mexicans in the Making of America*. Cambridge, MA: Belknap Press, 2014.

Logan, J. *The New Latinos: Who They Are, Where They Are*. Albany, NY: Lewis Mumford Center for Comparative Urban and Regional Research, 2001.

Rodriquez, C. E. *Puerto Ricans: Born in the USA*. Boston, MA: Unwin Hyman, 1989.

Abrahamson, M. *Urban Enclaves: Identity and Place in America*. New York: St. Martin's Press, 1996.

NOTES

1. J. Logan, *The New Latinos: Who They Are, Where They Are* (Albany, NY: Lewis Mumford Center for Comparative Urban and Regional Research, 2001), 1. Available at http://mumford.albany.edu/census/HispanicPop/HspReport/MumfordReport.pdf
2. United States Census Bureau, *American Fact Finder*, ACS Demographic and Housing Estimates, 2010–2014 American Community Survey 5-Year Estimates, U.S. Department of Commerce, 2018. Available at: https://factfinder.census.gov/faces/tableservices/jsf/pages/productview.xhtml?src=bkmk
3. Ibid.
4. J. Scott and G. Marshall, *A Dictionary of Sociology*, 3rd ed. (New York: Oxford University Press, 2005). Available at http://www.oxfordreference.com/search?btog=chap&pageSize=10&q0=hispanic&sort=relevance&source=%2F10.1093%2Facref%2F9780199553008.001.0001%2Facref-9780199553008

5. D. Gonzalez, "What's the Problem with 'Hispanic'? Just Ask a 'Latino.'" *New York Times*, November 15, 1992, E6.

6. Scott and Marshall, *Dictionary of Sociology*.

7. Logan, *The New Latinos*.

8. Z. Vargas, *Crucible of Struggle: A History of Mexican Americans* (New York: Oxford University Press, 2011), 152.

9. Ibid., 102.

10. Ibid., 144–65.

11. Ibid., 213–36.

12. Ibid.

13. Ibid.

14. Scott and Marshall, *Dictionary of Sociology*.

15. H. A. Moore and P. Iadicola, "Resegregation Processes in Desegregated Schools and Status Relationships for Hispanic Students," *Aztlan* 12 (September 1981): 39–58.

16. Scott and Marshall, *Dictionary of Sociology*.

17. Jessica C. Barnett and Marina S. Vornovitsky, U.S. Census Bureau, *Health Insurance Coverage in the United States: 2015*, Open-file report 2016, U.S. Department of Commerce, 2016. Available at: https://www.census.gov/content/dam/Census/library/publications/2016/demo/p60-257.pdf

18. R. P. McNamara and K. M. McNamara, *Hispanic Healthcare Needs in Greenville, South Carolina* (Center for Social Research, Furman University, 2001), Executive Summary.

19. R. J. Chaskin, "Urban Enclaves: Identity and Place in America," *Social Science Review*, 70, no. 4 (December 1996): 662–64.

20. L. Perez, "Growing Up in Cuban Miami: Immigrants, the Enclave, and New Generations," in R. G. Rumbaut and A. Portes (eds.), *Ethnicities* (Berkeley, CA: University of California Press, 2001), 91–125.

21. Ibid.

22. Ibid.

23. M. Clary, "Black, Cuban Racial Chasm Splits Miami," *Los Angeles Times*, March 23, 1997, A1, A20.

24. M. H. Lopez, "As Cuban American Demographics Change, So Do Views of Cuba," Pew Research Center, December 23, 2014. Available at http://www.pewresearch.org/fact-tank/2014/12/23/as-cuban-American-demographics-change-so-do-views-of-cuba/; see also G. Allen, "Poll Findings: On Cuban Americans and the Elusive 'American Dream,'" *Morning Edition*, National Public Radio, January 22, 2014.

25. Ibid.

26. G. J. Grenier and H. Gladwin, *Cuba Poll: How Cuban Americans in Miami View U.S. Policies Toward Cuba* (Miami: Florida International University, Cuban Research Institute, 2014). Available at: https://cri.fiu.edu/research/cuba-poll/2014-fiu-cuba-poll.pdf

27. M. H. Lopez, "As Cuban American Demographics Change, So Do Views of Cuba," Pew Research Center, December 23, 2014. Available at: http://www.pewresearch.org/fact-tank/2014/12/23/as-cuban-American-demographics-change-so-do-views-of-cuba; see also G. Allen, "Poll Findings: On Cuban Americans and the Elusive 'American Dream,'" *Morning Edition*—National Public Radio, January 22, 2014.

28. Ibid.

29. Ibid.

30. Allen, "Poll Findings."

31. Alan Gomez and G. Korte, "Obama Reportedly Plans to Visit Cuba Soon," *USA Today*, February 18, 2016, 2.

32. Jeanne Batalova and Jie Zong, "Cuban Immigrants in the United States," Migration Policy Institute, November 9, 2017. Available at: https://www.migrationpolicy.org/article/cuban-immigrants-united-states

33. Ibid.

34. Florida International University, "How Cuban Americans in Miami View U.S. Policies Toward Cuba," *FIU Cuba Poll 2018*, Cuban Research Institute, 2019. Available at: https://cri.fiu.edu/research/cuba-poll/2018-fiu-cuba-poll.pdf

35. D. Christopulos, "Puerto Rico in the Twentieth Century: A Historical Survey," in A. Lopez and J. Petras (eds.), *Puerto Rico and Puerto Ricans: Studies in History and Society* (New York: Wiley, 1974), 123–66.

36. M. Navarro, "Puerto Rican Presence Wanes in New York," *New York Times*, February 28, 2000, A1, A20.

37. C. G. Muschkin, "Consequences of Return Migrant Status for Employment in Puerto Rico," *International Migration Review* 27, no. 4 (1993): 13; C. G. Muschkin, "With a Vote for 'None of the Above' Puerto Ricans Endorse Island's Status Quo," *New York Times*, December 14, 1998, A12.

38. D. Cohn, E. Patten, and M. H. Lopez, "Puerto Rican Population Declines on Island, Grows on U.S. Mainland," Pew Research Center, August 6, 2014. Available at: http://www. pewhispanic.org/2014/08/11/puerto-rican-population-declines-on-island-grows-on-u-s-mainland/ph-2014-08-11-puerto-rico-0-01/

39. Ibid.

40. J. Zarroli, "Puerto Rico Says It Will Miss $37 Million in Bond Payments this Week," *The Two-Way*—National Public Radio, December 30, 2015.

41. L. Alvarez, "Economy and Crime Spur New Puerto Rican Exodus," *New York Times*, February 8, 2014. Available at: http://nyti.ms/1aHmGNS

42. Ibid.

43. D. A. Hemlock, "Puerto Rico Loses Its Edge," *New York Times*, September 21, 1996, 17, 30.

44. "A Year Later: A Look at Hurricane Maria and Its Aftermath. *NBC News.* September 20, 2018. Available at: https://www.nbcwashington.com/news/national-international/Hurricane-Maria-Storm-Year-Later-Anniversary-Puerto-Rico-Island-US-Trump-Aftermath-493725371.html?amp=y&_osource=AMP

45. "New Data Shows 4% Drop in Population Since Maria." (2019). *Associated Press*, April 19, 2019. Available at: https://www.apnews.com/df63a2f9186a4eaaaa531d69d59adf4e

46. A. Orlov and R. Ueda, "Central and South Americans," in S. Thernstrom (ed.), *Encyclopedia of American Ethnic Groups* (Cambridge, MA: Belknap Press, 1980), 210–17.

47. Colleen Long and Jill Colvin, "Trump: Not Looking to Reinstate Family Separation Policy," *Associated Press*, April 10, 2019. Available at: https://news.yahoo.com/trump-says-not-looking-reinstate-family-separation-policy-164139863--politics.html

48. Zamira Rahim, "Trump Told Border Agents to Break the Law but Bosses Told Them to Ignore Him, Report Claims," *The Independent*, April 9, 2019. Available at: https://www.yahoo.com/news/trump-told-border-agents-break-084555838.html

49. G. Lopez, K. Bialik, and J. Radford, "Key Findings about U.S. Immigrants," Pew Research Center, 2018.

50. Jie Zong, Jeanne Batalova, and Micayla Burrows, "Frequently Requested Statistics on Immigrants and Immigration in the United States," Migration Policy Institute, March 14, 2019. Available at: https://www.migrationpolicy.org/article/frequently-requested-statistics-immigrants-and-immigration-united-states#Enforcement

51. Ibid.

52. Ibid.

53. Katie Sullivan and Jeff Mason, "Immigration Detention in the United States—A Primer," *Bipartisan Policy Center*, April 24, 2019. Available at: https://bipartisanpolicy.org/blog/immigration-detention-in-the-united-states-a-primer/

54. Michael Clemens, "What the Mariel Boatlift of Cuban Refugees Can Teach Us about the Economics of Immigration: An Explainer and a Revelation," *Center for Global Development*, May 22, 2017. Available at: https://www.cgdev.org/blog/what-mariel-boatlift-cuban-refugees-can-teach-us-about-economics-immigration

55. Ibid.

56. Ibid.

57. Ibid.

58. Sullivan and Mason, "Immigration Detention in the United States."

59. Susan Crabtree, "Trump's Sanctuary Threat Could Answer Immigrants' Prayers," *Real Clear Politics*, April 17, 2019. Available at: https://www.realclearpolitics.com/articles/2019/04/17/trumps_sanctuary_threat_could_answer_immigrants_prayers_140073.html

60. See, e.g., Julian Borger, "Trump Urges World to Reject Globalism in U.N. Speech That Draws Mocking Laughter," *The Guardian*, September 26, 2018. Available at: https://www.theguardian.com/us-news/2018/sep/25/trump-united-nations-general-assembly-speech-globalism-america

61. Jane Timm, "Fact Check: Trump Says His Wall Is Under Construction. It Is Not," *NBC News*, July 3, 2018. Available at: https://www.nbcnews.com/politics/donald-trump/fact-check-trump-say-his-border-wall-under-construction-it-n888371

62. Eric Beech, "U.S. Judge Denies Democrats' Lawsuit to Stop Border Wall Funds," Reuters, June 4, 2019. Available at: https://news.yahoo.com/u-judge-denies-democrats-suit-012109670.html?soc_src=newsroom&soc_trk=com.apple.UIKit.activity.Mail&.tsrc=newsroom

63. Peter Baker, "Trump Declares a National Emergency and Creates a Constitutional Clash." *New York Times*, February 15, 2019. Available at https://www.nytimes.com/2019/02/15/us/politics/national-emergency-trump.html

64. Ibid.

65. Ibid.

66. Ibid.

67. Miriam Jordan, "More Migrants Are Crossing the Border This Year. What's Changed?" *New York Times*, March 5, 2019. Available at: https://www.nytimes.com/2019/03/05/us/crossing-the-border-statistics.html

68. Ibid.

69. Ibid.

70. Ibid.

71. Ibid.

72. Ibid.

73. Meredith McGraw and Jordyn Phelps, "Trump Backs Off Threat to Close Border, Gives Mexico One Year Warning," *ABC News*, April 4, 2019. Available at: https://abcnews.go.com/Politics/trump-backs-off-threat-close-border-mexico-year/story?id=62170562

74. Ibid.

75. Steve Holland and Dave Graham, "Trump Says U.S. Likely to Go Ahead with Tariffs on Mexico over Immigration," *Reuters*, June 4, 2019. Available at: https://www.yahoo.com/finance/news/mexicos-ebrard-eyes-common-ground-124018622.html

76. Conor Finnegan, "Trump Cuts All Direct Assistance to Northern Triangle Countries: Honduras, El Salvador, Guatemala, *Good Morning America*, March 30, 2019. Available at: https://www.yahoo.com/gma/trump-cuts-direct-assistance-northern-triangle-countries-honduras-043000627--abc-news-topstories.html?soc_src=newsroom&soc_trk=com.apple.UIKit.activity.Mail&.tsrc=newsroom

77. Ibid.

78. American Immigration Council, "The Dream Act, DACA, and Other Policies Designed to Protect Dreamers. Fact Sheet," September 6, 2017. Available at: https://americanimmigrationcouncil.org/research/dream-act-daca-and-other-policies-designed-protect-dreamers

79. Ibid.

80. Tanya Golash-Boza, *Deported: Immigrant Policing, Disposable Labor, and Global Capitalism* (New York: New York University Press, 2015.)

81. Ibid.

82. Ibid.

83. Ibid.

84. Ibid.

85. G. Lopez, K. Bialik, and J. Radford, "Key Findings about U.S. Immigrants," Pew Research Center, 2018.

86. Ibid.

87. Jana Winter, "Trump Says Border Wall Will Stop Drugs. Here's What a DEA Intel Report Says," *Foreign Policy*, August 29, 2017. Available at: https://foreignpolicy.com/2017/08/29/trump-says-border-wall-will-stop-drugs-heres-what-a-dea-intel-report-says/; see also David Bier, "New CATO Report: A Border Wall Won't Stop Drug Smuggling: Marijuana Legalization Has," *CATO Institute*, December 19, 2018. Available at: https://www.cato.org/blog/new-cato-report-border-wall-wont-stop-drug-smuggling-marijuana-legalization-has

88. Gregory Korte and Alan Gomez, "Trump Ramps Up Rhetoric on Undocumented Immigrants 'These Aren't People, These are Animals,'" *USA Today*, May 16, 2018. Available at: https://www.usatoday.com/story/news/politics/2018/05/16/trump-immigrants-animals-mexico-democrats-sanctuary-cities/617252002/

89. Michelle Ye Hee Lee, "Donald Trump's False Comments Connecting Mexican Immigration and Crime," *Washington Post*, July 8, 2019. Available at: https://www.washingtonpost.com/news/fact-checker/wp/2015/07/08/donald-trumps-false-comments-connecting-mexican-immigrants-and-crime/?utm_term=.73b65664434d

90. Jennifer Epstein and Justin Sink "Trump Admits He Has No Proof Terrorists Are in the Migrant Caravan," *Time*, October 23, 2018. Available at: http://time.com/5432702/trump-no-proof-terrorists-migrant-caravan/

91. See B. Gonzalez O'Brien, L. Collingwood, and S. El-Khatib, S., "The Politics of Refuge: Sanctuary Cities, Crime, and Undocumented Immigration." *Urban Affairs Review*, May 17, 2017. Available at: http://journals.sagepub.com/doi/abs/10.1177/1078087417704974?journalcode=uarb; Golash-Boza, *Deported*; David C. Brotherton and Phillip Kretsedemas (eds.), *Immigration Policy in the Age of Punishment* (New York: Columbia University Press, 2017), 1–34.

92. U.S. Department of Justice, U.S. Sentencing Commission, Annual Report, 2014. Available at: http://www.ussc.gov/sites/default/files/pdf/research-and-publications/annual-reports-and-sourcebooks/2014/2014-Annual-Report.pdf

93. C. Kamasaki, *Testimony on Drug Sentencing and Its Effects on the Latino Community. U.S. Sentencing Commission*, February 25, 2002. Available at: http://www.ussc.gov/sites/default/files/pdf/amendment-process/public-hearings-and-meetings/20020225–26/kamasaki.pdf

94. Ibid.

95. National Council of La Raza, *Lost Opportunities: The Reality of Latinos in the Criminal Justice System*, Executive Summary, 2004, ix.

96. Ibid.

97. Ibid.

98. Californians for Safety and Justice, *Latino Voices: The Impacts of Crime and Criminal Justice Policies on Latinos* (California: Tomas Rivera Policy Institute, University of Southern California, 2014), Executive Summary, ix.

99. David Binder Research, *California Crime Victims' Voices: Findings from the First-Ever Survey of California Crime Victims and Survivors*, Quantitative Research Summary, 2013. Available at: http://www.njjn.org/uploads/digital-library/CA_CSJ_CA-Crime-victims-voices_March-2014.pdf

100. *Firearm Violence, 1993–2011*, U.S. Department of Justice, Bureau of Justice Statistics, 2013.

101. *Household Burglary, 1994–2011*, U.S. Department of Justice, Bureau of Justice Statistics 2013.

102. N. Theodore, *Insecure Communities: Latino Perception of Police Involvement in Immigration Enforcement* (Chicago: University of Illinois at Chicago, 2013), Executive Summary, i. Available at: http://www.policylink.org/sites/default/files/INSECURE_COMMUNITIES_REPORT_FINAL.PDF

103. T. R. Kochel, D. B. Wilson, and S. D. Mastrofski, "Effect of Suspect Race on Officers' Arrest Decisions," *Criminology* 49, no. 2 (2011): 473–512.

104. B. L. Withrow, "Race-Based Policing. A Descriptive Analysis of the Wichita Stop Study," *Police Practice and Research* 5, no. 3 (2004): 223–40.

105. Adrian D. Pantoja, "Poll Shows Major Support Among Latinos for Sentencing Reform," *Latino Decisions* (blog), May 1, 2014.

106. T. Schlesinger, "Racial and Ethnic Disparity in Pretrial Criminal Processing," *Justice Quarterly* 22, no. 2 (2005): 170–92.

107. U.S. Sentencing Commission, *Report to the Congress: Mandatory Minimum Penalties in the Federal Criminal Justice System*, 2011, Executive Summary, i–ix.

108. E. Ann Carson, "Prisoners in 2013." U.S. Department of Justice, Bureau of Justice Statistics, September 30, 2014. Available at: https://www.bjs.gov/content/pub/pdf/p13.pdf; State of California, Legislative Analyst's Office, "California's Criminal Justice System: A Primer," January 17, 2013. Available at: https://lao.ca.gov/reports/2013/crim/criminal-justice-primer/criminal-justice-primer-011713.aspx

109. David Binder Research, *California Latino Voters and Criminal Justice Reforms* (research brief), 2014. Available at: http://safeandjust.uscmediacurator.com/key-finding-1-california-realignment/

110. See Pew Research Center,. "Shrinking Gap Between Number of Blacks and Whites in Prison," April 30, 2019. Available at: https://www.pewresearch.org/fact-tank/2019/04/30/shrinking-gap-between-number-of-blacks-and-whites-in-prison/ft_19-04-29_prisonracegapsupdate_2_updated/

CHAPTER 5

ASIAN AMERICANS AND THE CRIMINAL JUSTICE SYSTEM

CHAPTER OBJECTIVES

After reading this chapter, you should be able to:

- Understand the differences between Far East Asians, Southeast Asians, and Pacific Islanders, and why this distinction is important
- Understand the historical importance of immigration for Chinese, Japanese, Korean, Filipino, and other Asian groups
- Understand the current position in American society for Japanese, Chinese, Korean, Southeast Asians, and Pacific Islanders
- Understand the representation of Asian Americans in the criminal justice system, including involvement in different forms of criminal activity such as drugs, gangs, human smuggling, and transnational crime

The U.S. Census uses the label "Asian American" to refer to people from the Far East (including China, Japan, and Korea), Southeast Asia (including Thailand, Cambodia, Vietnam, Laos, Malaysia, and Indonesia), and the Indian subcontinent (including India, Pakistan, Burma, Sri Lanka, Bangladesh, and Nepal). The term "Pacific Islander" refers to people who have origins in Hawaii, Guam, Samoa, or other Pacific Islander groups.[1]

Asian Americans, like Hispanics/Latinos and Native Americans, represent a vast array of people who are quite diverse in their customs, languages, and cultures. However, as with most minority groups in this country, those differences tend to be simplified, and groups are often put into a generic and overly broad category.

In fact, the term "Asian American" covers a wide breadth of people, who, in some cases, are nothing like each other. This collection of individuals from different backgrounds is one of the fastest growing segments of the U.S. population. One of the topics this chapter will explore is the differences between these groups and their impact on American culture. Like other groups, Asian Americans have made a concerted and successful effort at assimilating into mainstream America. Unfortunately, there are many

Americans who have stereotypical perceptions of Asian Americans and this has overshadowed the hard work, determination, and sacrifice many members of these populations have contributed.

In some ways, then, Asian Americans are different from other minority groups in the sense that they have made the transition and retained much of their native culture, and while some are involved in criminal activity, Asian Americans are one of the minorities that is generally underrepresented in crime statistics. This underrepresentation not only means they do not appear to represent a large portion of the data collected on crime, it also means that Asian Americans have not been studied in as much depth as other minority groups in terms of their involvement in crime. In terms of their participation in the criminal justice system, there is less of a presence than, say, African Americans, Whites, or Hispanics. Specifically, this chapter will discuss Chinese Americans, Japanese Americans, Southeast Asians—specifically Vietnamese Americans—and Asian Indians. Because they represent the largest group of Pacific Islanders in this country, Hawaiians and Filipinos will also be discussed.

In a recent report by the Pew Research Center, Asian Americans surpassed Hispanics/Latinos as the fastest growing immigrant group in the United States. In fact, the Asian American population in the United States grew by 72 percent between 2000 and 2015, the largest of any major racial or ethnic category. In comparison, the Hispanic population grew by 60 percent during the same time period. In 2017, there were an estimated 20 million people listed under the category of Asian/Pacific Islander, which constitutes about 5.8 percent of the U.S. population.[2]

Of this group, there were about 5 million Chinese Americans; 4 million Filipinos; 4 million from India; 1.9 million Vietnamese; 1.8 Korean; and 1.4 million Japanese Americans (see Table 5.1). This represents the five largest groups under this classification. The Census Bureau expects that the Asian American population in the United States will be about 38 million people by 2050, which will constitute about 9 percent of the total U.S. population.[3] Some of this growth will be attributed to immigration by certain groups, while another source of this increase will be due to higher birth rates.

TABLE 5.1   ASIAN AMERICAN POPULATION IN THE UNITED STATES, 2015

Group	Population
Chinese	4.9 million
Filipino	3.9 million
Indian	4.0 million
Vietnamese	1.9 million
Korean	1.8 million
Japanese	1.4 million
Other	2.5 million
Total	20.4 million

Source: U.S. Census Bureau, "Selected Population Profile in United States," American Community Survey, 2016. Available at: https://factfinder.census.gov/faces/tableservices/jsf/pages/productview.xhtml?src=bkmk

The influx of Asians in the United States can be divided into two distinct periods. The first occurred roughly from the middle of the 1800s to the early years of the twentieth century. The Chinese were the first Asian group to arrive, followed by the Japanese, with Koreans and Filipinos arriving in much smaller numbers afterward. The first wave of immigrants was mostly recruited for construction and work in the agricultural industry.

The second wave of immigration was different from the first in that most of the new immigrants came from a higher socioeconomic status. Changes in immigration laws prevented many Asians from entering into this country until after 1965.[4] This latter group of immigrants has also been more diverse in national origin, coming from all areas of Asian society.[5]

A BRIEF PROFILE OF ASIAN AMERICANS

Generally speaking, according to a 2019 survey by the Pew Research Center, people who identify as Asian Americans value hard work, are highly educated, have higher median incomes than the general population, and believe their outlook for the future is bright. They generally believe in the value of hard work as a pathway to success, and while some have experienced discrimination, the group has a tendency not to see these experiences as inhibiting their drive toward success.[6]

Asian Americans collectively also have median family incomes higher than the general population: $73,060 compared to $53,600 for the rest of the United States. Moreover, Asian Americans are more likely than the rest of the general population to hold a bachelor's degree or higher (50 percent vs. 28 percent). Asian Americans have a poverty rate as a group that is slightly lower than the national average (12.1 percent vs. 15.1 percent).[7] About 30 percent of Asian Americans have married a non-Asian, and about half of all Asian Americans say they are comfortable with the idea of a family member marrying a non-Asian.[8]

There is also a strong emphasis on family relations, and Asian children are more likely than any other group to live in a household with two married parents. Asian Americans place a higher priority on having a successful marriage than the general population. Asian Americans are also more likely to vote Democrat than Republican (50 percent vs. 28 percent).[9]

While there are a number of promising trends for some Asian Americans, for others the transition to the United States has resulted in more difficult circumstances. A number of issues have arisen for all Asian Americans, particularly those who have achieved some level of societal success. These issues include the model minority myth, the glass ceiling in the labor market, hate crimes, and racial profiling.

MODEL MINORITY MYTH

The **model minority myth** states that Asian Americans constitute an ideal minority because they have endured political, economic, and social obstacles. Some experts even argue that Asian Americans are no longer considered a marginal minority.[10] However, to effectively determine whether the apparent success can be extended across all Asian American groups, we must examine the data.

Although the term "model minority" might seem to be complimentary, at one time many Asian Americans saw it as a condescending and damaging stereotype. Some Asian Americans have pointed out that this positive image tends to minimize or ignore some of the social and economic problems that continue to prevent many Asian Americans from succeeding. This is particularly true of Southeast Asian refugees, who remain poor, uneducated, and relatively unsuccessful.[11] Additionally, approximately 12 percent of Asian American families live below the poverty line, compared to 15 percent of White families. Thus, in many ways, when President Ronald Reagan called Asian Americans the model minority, he set in motion a series of expectations that ignored the wide diversity of educational talent among this segment of the population.

However, given the recent data from the Pew Research Center, where most Asian Americans self-identify as their respective group, rather than as Asian Americans, and given recent opinion data that suggest that their belief in the value of hard work is a key component to success, many Asian Americans do not appear to embrace this categorization.

INCOME DATA

Another sign of the apparent success of Asian Americans is the information concerning median family incomes. While the median family income of Asian Americans might seem significant to many outsiders, the total number of family members working should also be factored into the analysis. The reason for this is that the median family income figure

The model minority myth suggested that many Asian Americans had adequately assimilated into American society.

DOES EDUCATION PAY OFF FOR ALL ASIAN AMERICANS?

While most Americans agree that education is the path out of poverty and is the best way for minorities to achieve success, some evidence exists that problems occur even when minority groups embrace education. Asian Americans have been identified as an ethnic minority group that has successfully overcome racism and achieved the American dream, primarily through education. It is true that more than half of all Asian American adults have at least a college degree, the highest of all the major racial and ethnic groups. It's also common for Asian American students to have the highest test scores and/or GPAs within any given high school or college cohort.[12] However, Southeast Asians are still struggling to adapt to their lives in the United States. For example, Vietnamese Americans have a college-degree attainment rate of 29 percent, only about a third the rate for other Asian American ethnic groups and about on par with Whites. Further, Laotians, Cambodians, and Khmer only have rates around 13 percent. Those Asian Americans who are struggling tend to be immigrants who have limited English proficiency. Most are relatively fluent in English but a large portion are not.[13] Therefore, similar to other immigrant minority groups, Asian Americans still have a need for bilingual education that is also culturally sensitive to their immigration experiences and family situations.

Even for those who make it to college, challenges have been presented. Beginning in the 1980s, many more Asian Americans were applying to college than before. Soon, it became common for 10 percent, 15 percent, or more of a given university's student population to be of Asian ancestry at a time when Asians were only about 3 percent of the general population. Many universities responded by rejecting Asian students once their Asian student population reached 10 percent to 15 percent of the student body. Soon, Asian Americans were accusing universities such as U.C.–Berkeley, UCLA, Stanford, Harvard, Princeton, and Brown of imposing a quota or upper limit on their admission numbers. After several protests and investigations, these universities admitted that there were problems with these admission procedures but never admitted any deliberate wrongdoing.[14] Thus, Asian Americans may appear to be succeeding in assimilating into American society, but the reality is that many still face a host of problems.

only counts total family income, not the number of people working within that family. It is one thing if a family consists of a single parent earning most of the money, such as a corporate executive, which should suggest a certain socioeconomic position for that family. However, in many Asian American families, the total family income requires several people, all working full-time, to earn that same amount. This suggests a different economic picture for that family.

There is also the issue of the **glass ceiling** in business. While it appears promising that Asian Americans work in the same professions as Whites, Asian immigrants are found disproportionately in the lower paying service occupations. Even in managerial positions, few Asian Americans ever reach the very top of the corporate ladder.[15]

In an effort to explain this unusual trend, Jane Hyun, whose book *Breaking the Bamboo Ceiling: Career Strategies for Asians*, offers her insight into why so few Asian Americans obtain top management positions. She says that part of the reason is cultural. Many Asian American employees are taught to respect authority. Consequently, they remain quiet in meetings, and this is interpreted by their White colleagues as aloofness, arrogance, or inattention, when it is simply a general Asian habit of respecting authority.[16]

Thus, while Asian Americans have done well in small businesses, because of the long hours, the income from these businesses may be below prevailing wages. Examples include Chinese restaurants, Korean American convenience stores, and Asian Indian–owned motels and gasoline stations.[17] In sum, while it might appear that Asian Americans are doing well, this is an oversimplification of the diversity of the group and its experiences. Further, this simplification also changes the public's perceptions of the need to help many

Many Asian American executives experience a glass ceiling, or limited opportunities.

Asian Americans in terms of social programs.[18] A recent study of the United States Equal Employment Opportunity Commission examining 2013 employment data from Google, Yahoo, and Facebook revealed more evidence of a glass ceiling for executive positions in those companies. In this study, while Asian Americans made up one-third of the workforce of these three companies, far surpassing the representation of African Americans or Hispanic/Latinos, Asian Americans were significantly underrepresented in leadership roles. The analysis of the data shows that there were both race and gender implications regarding Asian Americans. Overall, White males had a 42 percent advantage over White women when it came to being promoted to the executive level, and a 260 percent advantage over Asian women. Whites generally had a 150 percent advantage over Asians regardless of gender, suggesting the presence of a glass ceiling at the higher levels of business.[19]

HATE CRIMES AND RACIAL PROFILING

The perception that Asian Americans are accepted in the United States is not completely congruent with their experiences in America. For instance, reports by the National Asian Pacific American Legal Consortium demonstrate an anti-Asian sentiment in this country. Moreover, the hostility against Asian Americans is not limited to violent episodes or individual hate crimes. Part of the problem stems from the apparent success of many Asian Americans in education, business and professions, which creates a backlash of resentment from Whites.

Another reason for the resentment of Asians by Whites was due to the economic growth of some Asian countries, such as Japan, in the early 1990s. So strong was the resentment that ad campaigns were launched that encouraged people to buy "American," meaning American-made products, in order to save American jobs.

The trend of hate crimes against Asian Americans can be seen in official statistics. According to the Uniform Crime Reports in 2017, approximately 47 percent of the hate crimes in this country are motivated by racial bias. In 2017, law enforcement agencies reported 8,437 hate crime offenses. Of these offenses, about 2 percent were due to an anti-Asian/Pacific Islander bias. In terms of offenders, of the total hate crime offenses committed in 2017, 44 percent of the offenders were White, while 14.3 percent were African American. Hispanics comprised three percent of offenders, and Asian offenders constituted only 22 offenses, or less than one half of one percent of hate crime offenders, the lowest of any group.[20]

Many Asian Americans also report evidence of a new form of **racial profiling**. A 2014 poll by the *Los Angeles Times* indicated that many Asian Americans support the position of Blacks and Hispanic/Latinos on perceptions of police effectiveness and racial profiling. While 18 percent of Whites felt that the police were ineffective, 47 percent of Blacks, 40 percent of Latinos, and 24 percent of Asians felt that way about the police. The findings of this study are similar to results about the attitudes toward the policy by Asian Americans nearly thirty years ago. However, these perceptions are not necessarily based on negative interactions between Asian Americans and the police.

While 28 percent of African Americans and 20 percent of Latinos said they had been treated unfairly by the police, only about 11 percent of Asians had had similar experiences. Approximately12 percent of Whites had had experiences or interactions with the police where they felt they had been treated unfairly.[21]

Thus, while it may appear that Asian Americans have succeeded in their attempts to assimilate into mainstream American society, there are noticeable differences between the groups as well as a tendency to overgeneralize the level of success they have achieved. Perhaps the way to begin is to examine a selection of these groups that make up Asian Americans and explore their history as well as their current situations.

CHECKPOINT

- It is important to remember that "Asian American" as a category covers a wide range of groups, with varying degrees of education, income, and overall success. There is also an enduring belief in the model minority myth, where people assume that all Asian Americans are successful. In reality, this is true for some groups, but others struggle with poverty, lower educational achievement, and a glass ceiling even when they are successful in the business world. There is also evidence of racial profiling among Asian Americans as well as hate crime data to indicate that there remains a certain amount of animosity toward Asian Americans.

FAR EAST ASIAN AMERICANS

CHINESE AMERICANS

Early immigration from China into the United States was initiated largely because of economic and political unrest in China coupled with discovery of gold in California in the 1840s. Added to this was the construction of the transcontinental railroads, which drew many Chinese immigrants to the United States.[22] At the time, Chinese immigrants were welcomed because they provided a sizeable group of hard-working employees. In a very short time, however, the influx of Chinese workers created a backlash of anti-Chinese sentiment. Based partly on a perceived threat felt by White workers, the hostility toward Chinese immigrants led to the passage of the **Chinese Exclusion Act**, which lasted in various forms for more than sixty years. Enacted by Congress in 1882, the Chinese Exclusion Act outlawed Chinese immigration for ten years. The act also denied naturalization rights to immigrants already in the United States. There was little debate over it in Congress, in part because of the general belief in the threat the Chinese posed to American workers.[23]

In 1892, Congress extended the Exclusion Act for another ten years and added that Chinese laborers had to obtain certificates of residence within a year or face deportation. The ban against the Chinese was made permanent in 1907, and marked a significant moment in United States history when for the first time a specific group was formally prohibited from entering the country.[24]

When the act was initially passed in 1882, there were approximately 125,000 Chinese immigrants in the United States. By 1910 the number of immigrants had dropped to about 70,000, and did not really change until after 1965. Part of the reason for this had to do with the fact that most of the people coming into this country at that time were males. By one estimate, before 1882, more than 100,000 men but fewer than 9,000 women had emigrated to the United States from China.[25] Because of this imbalance between the sexes, it was quite difficult for Chinese immigrants to create ethnic communities. As a result of this sense of isolation, both from the discrimination felt by larger society as well as feeling disconnected ethnically, many were forced to live in urban ghettos or Chinatowns. In fact, many immigrants did not leave Chinatowns in great numbers until after the end of World War II.[26]

After the Exclusion Act was repealed in 1943, Chinese nationals were gradually permitted to enter the United States, first as spouses of servicemen and later as college students who were allowed to complete their education. Immigration continued slowly until the 1965 Immigration Act was passed, allowing more Chinese citizens to immigrate into the United States. The influx has recently become fairly robust, with numbers approaching 100,000 annually. In fact, in the 1990s the number of Chinese immigrants entering the United States actually exceeded the total number of those already within United States that were present in 1980.[27] Today, as was mentioned, Chinese Americans represent the largest subgroup of Asian Americans, totaling nearly four million immigrants.

At least on the surface, Chinese Americans appear to have lower unemployment rates and are represented in many professional occupations. However, most of the jobs are found in Chinatowns around the country. The reason for this had to do with the fact that Chinese

Chinatowns have played an important part in the assimilation of many Asian immigrants since they have provided places where many Asians already lived and worked.

Americans were prohibited for generations from working anywhere else. While Whites did not object to Chinese immigrants in domestic occupations, largely because White men were unwilling to participate in such menial jobs, for the most part, Chinese Americans had few opportunities to work outside of the Chinatowns in most large urban areas.

CHECKPOINT

- Despite efforts to assimilate according to the cultural and legal standards established by the federal government, many Chinese Americans still struggle to gain social, economic, and political acceptance. Evidence of an anti-Chinese sentiment is found in the Chinese Exclusion Act, which limited the number of Chinese immigrants who could migrate into the United States. The reason for this is that many citizens felt that Chinese immigrants, who would work harder and for less pay, presented a threat for American jobs.

JAPANESE AMERICANS

The Japanese American experience in the United States is a fascinating case of how minority groups appear to be a threat to the mainstream way of life even when they have made efforts to assimilate and belong. While it appears that fears about the "threat" of minority groups often drives our decisions about whether or not to allow certain immigrant groups into this country, what is more fascinating is the source of those fears and how they dictate our perception of certain groups. As we will see, the **yellow peril** was largely based on fear of Asians. This "threat" actually resulted in strict immigration laws and the imprisonment of American citizens.

The First Wave of Anti-Japanese Resentment

The Japanese who immigrated to the United States in the 1890s took jobs as laborers at low wages with poor working conditions. Their industriousness in these situations made them popular with employers but unpopular with unions and other employees. The Japanese had the misfortune of arriving just as bigotry toward the Chinese had been formalized in the Chinese Exclusion Act of 1882. While this legislation limited opportunities for Chinese workers, Japanese workers, at least initially, replaced the dwindling number of Chinese laborers in some industries, especially agriculture. Over time, however, once the threat and presence of Chinese workers disappeared, it was replaced with an anti-Japanese sentiment.

In 1913 California enacted the **Alien Land Act**. The act prohibited anyone who was ineligible for citizenship to own land, and it limited leases to three years. The land laws drove many first-generation Japanese into cities. However, government and union restrictions prevented Asian immigrants from taking jobs. As a result, many Japanese immigrants embarked upon self-employment to earn a living. More than any other group, Japanese immigrants opened grocery stores and other types of small businesses. The Japanese differed in many respects from the Chinese in terms of how they were treated. For instance, Japanese Americans had the benefit of witnessing what had happened to the Chinese and were able to understand what changes had to occur for their treatment to be different from the experiences of the Chinese.

Second, Japanese Americans were much more vocal about the unfair treatment they received. First- and second-generation Japanese Americans often organized demonstrations, held boycotts, and enlisted the support of sympathetic Whites. Finally, in their native land, Japan took a more active interest in what was happening to its citizens in the United States than did China. The knowledge of how Japan felt about the treatment of their immigrants in this country, coupled with a fear of retaliation for the way Japanese Americans had been treated, led many Americans to be concerned about Japanese Americans' loyalty once Japan attacked Pearl Harbor on December 7, 1941.

The Second Wave: Internment

Almost immediately after the attack on Pearl Harbor, fear and concern about the war led people to feel threatened by Japanese Americans living on the West Coast. Many feared that Japanese Americans would fight on behalf of Japan, resulting in a successful invasion of the United States. Rumors mixed with racist bigotry, rather than facts, explain the events that followed. Japanese Americans in Hawaii were alleged to have cooperated in the attack by using signaling devices to assist pilots in locating their targets. Newspapers covered in detail FBI arrests of Japanese Americans allegedly assisting the attackers. They were accused of poisoning drinking water, cutting sugar cane fields to form arrows directing enemy pilots to targets, and blocking traffic along highways to the harbor. None of these charges was substantiated despite thorough investigations.[28]

The executive order signed by President Franklin D. Roosevelt authorized the removal of anyone considered a threat to national security in defined strategic military areas. All people on the West Coast of at least one-eighth Japanese ancestry were taken to assembly centers for transfer to concentration camps. This order covered 90 percent of the 126,000 Japanese Americans on the mainland. Of those evacuated, two-thirds were American citizens and three-fourths were under the age of twenty-five. Ultimately 120,000 people were interned in the camps: 113,000 from the mainland, 1,100 evacuated from Hawaii, about 200 voluntary residents (Caucasian spouses), and 5,900 who were born in the camps.[29]

What is interesting is that the evacuation order did not arise from any court action. No trials took place, no indictments were issued. Merely having a Japanese great-grandparent was enough to mark an individual for involuntary confinement. Perhaps even more fascinating is the fact that many Japanese Americans did not fight the order. The governing body for Japanese Americans and immigrant groups, the Japanese American Citizens League, believed that, given the emotional climate surrounding the attack as well as the suspicions of Japanese Americans, if any of those interned tried to flee or defied the order, it would likely confirm that Japanese people could not be trusted.

Those that were to be interned were instructed to carry only personal items. No provision was made for shipping their household goods. The federal government took a few steps to safeguard the belongings internees left behind, but the evacuees assumed all risks and agreed to turn over their property to the government for an indeterminate length of time. Internment caused merchants, farmers, and business owners to sell their property at any price they could get. Precise figures of the loss in dollars are difficult to obtain, but the Federal Reserve Bank estimated it to be approximately $400 million by 1941 standards. Today that amount would easily be in the billions of dollars.[30]

A few Japanese Americans resisted the evacuation and took legal action. Several cases arising out of the evacuation and detention reached the United States Supreme Court during the war. The Court upheld lower court decisions on Japanese Americans without

As a result of fears that Japanese Americans would side with Japan during World War II, the government required that many Japanese Americans live in internment camps for the duration of the war.

even raising the issue of the constitutionality of the internment. Finally, in *Mitsuye Endo v. the United States*, the Supreme Court ruled that the defendant, and, presumably all evacuees, must be granted their freedom. Two weeks later, Japanese Americans were allowed to return to their homes for the first time in three years.[31]

As the *Endo* case demonstrates, our attitudes about the appropriateness of internment remained steadfastly strong. No legal action granting compensation to the evacuees for property lost was taken until 1948, with the Japanese Americans Evacuation Claims Act. Even when Americans recognized the injustice, little was done to remedy the problem. Two years after the Evacuation Claims Act's passage, only seventy-three people had received any money. Eventually there were approximately 23,000 claims and the government paid $38 million, less than 10 percent of the Federal Reserve Bank's estimate of the cost to Japanese Americans. All claims were settled with no interest or consideration of the increase in land values. Moreover, the settlements were delayed so that by 1967, when the final payments were made, many of the claimants had died.[32]

In the late 1970s, President Carter created the Commission on Wartime Relocation and Internment of Civilians. The final Commission recommendation in 1983 was for a formal apology from the government and a tax-free payment of $20,000 to each of the approximately 66,000 surviving internees. Congress began hearings in 1986 on the bill and President Reagan signed the Civil Liberties Act in 1988, which authorized the payments.[33] Still, the payments were slow in coming, and the internees were dying at a rate of two hundred per month. In 1990, the first checks were finally issued, accompanied by President George Bush's letter of apology.[34]

Today, only about a third of Japanese Americans are foreign-born, and they have a median family income of $65,000 per year. This group is highly educated, with 16 percent having earned advanced degrees and 31 percent having earned a bachelor's degree. More than half, or 55 percent intermarry, often to non-Asians.[35]

CHECKPOINT

- Like their Chinese American counterparts, Japanese Americans were feared by many U.S. citizens, particularly during World War II, when there were concerns about a Japanese attack. This led to the internment of hundreds of thousands of Japanese Americans, many of whom were U.S. citizens, as well as the forfeiture of their land, assets, and businesses.

KOREAN AMERICANS

In the early part of the twentieth century, a few thousand Koreans were recruited to work the sugar plantations in Hawaii. They were needed, in fact, to replace the Chinese workers who had been prohibited from remaining in the United States by the 1882 Chinese Exclusion Act. Still, the number of Korean immigrants remained small until after the Korean War in the 1950s, when many came either as refugees or as spouses of American servicemen returning home. However, the growth of the population exploded in the

1970s. Between 1970 and 1980, the Korean American population increased fivefold, from 70,000 to 355,000. According to the 2010 Census, Korean Americans numbered over 1.7 million.[36] However, in the late 1990s many Korean Americans chose to return to Korea. Part of the reason had to do with the political and economic growth in Korea, while for others who'd had difficulty adapting to American culture, the chance to feel "at home" was very appealing. For still others, operating a small business was considered too risky as tensions between Koreans and African Americans rose during the Los Angeles riots in 1992.[37]

In L.A.'s poor areas, the only shops in which to buy groceries or liquor or gasoline were owned by Korean immigrants. They had largely replaced the White-owned businesses. Scores of White business owners had left the ghetto area after the 1965 Watts riots. African Americans were well aware of the dominant role Korean Americans played in their local retail market. Many African Americans expressed resentment that had been previously fueled by the 1991 shooting of a fifteen-year-old Black girl by a Korean grocer. The resentment grew when the grocer, convicted of manslaughter, had her prison sentence waived by a judge in favor of five years of probation.[38]

During the riots, one thousand Korean businesses valued at $300 million were destroyed. In a post-riot survey of African Americans who were arrested, 80 percent said that they felt that Korean Americans were disrespectful, compared to 56 percent who felt similarly about Whites. Korean Americans' desire to succeed led them to the inner-city, where they did not face competition from Whites, but it also meant that they had to deal on a daily basis with the frustration of African Americans.[39]

Recent Census data indicate that nearly 80 percent of Korean Americans in the United States are foreign-born, with about 40 percent who speak English well. Korean Americans are also more likely to marry other Koreans (61 percent) than other Asian American groups. Korean Americans have a median family income of approximately $50,000 per year.[40]

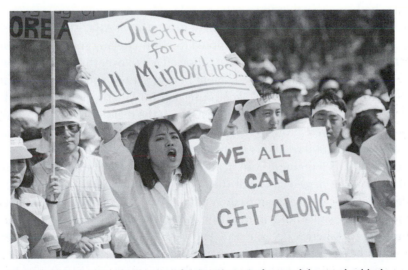

During the L.A. riots, many Korean businesses were damaged due to a backlash against Korean Americans by African American residents.

CHECKPOINT

- By many accounts, the efforts put forth by Korean Americans have resulted in moderate levels of success, in terms of economic, educational, and social acceptability. However, anti-Korean sentiments were particularly evident during the famous L.A. riots, especially among low-income Blacks who felt that they were competing with Korean Americans for jobs.

SOUTHEAST ASIAN AMERICANS

The people of Southeast Asia—the Vietnamese, Cambodians, and Laotians—were once part of the former French Indochinese Union. "Southeast Asian" is only a term of convenience, especially since the people of these areas are ethnically and linguistically different from each other. Numbering more than 2.8 million in 2010, Vietnamese Americans are the largest group with 1.9 million, which is approximately 9 percent of the total Asian American population.[41]

The catalyst to understanding this group of people for many Americans has been the Vietnam War. Historically, Southeast Asia consisted of many different tribes and countries such as Vietnamese, **Hmong tribes**, Cambodians, and ethnic Khmer. These and many other tribal groups came together in the early 1860s under the label "Indochina" as the French colonized the region. Because of dissatisfaction with the political, cultural, economic, and social dominance by the French, civil wars broke out and communist influence began to take hold in the mid-1950s. In 1954, the United States sent 16,000 military advisors and support personnel in an effort to prevent communism from taking over South Vietnam. By 1962, military involvement had escalated in the forms of air strikes and the use of Special Forces units to infiltrate the area. By 1964, most Americans believed that the United States had an obligation to free the people of Vietnam.[42]

By 1965 over 550,000 troops had been sent to Southeast Asia. At about the same time, the communist government in Laos attempted to eliminate any support for United States efforts in that country. The civil unrest that followed led to over three million Cambodians being killed by the Khmer Rouge government between 1975 and 1979. The United States withdrew from Southeast Asia in 1975, counting 58,000 American soldiers dead and thousands more wounded. While the U.S. withdrawal left the region under communist control, thousands of refugees were brought into this country.[43] In 2015, Hmong and Cambodians represented about 600,000 residents in the United States.[44]

The problems for Vietnamese Americans, like that of all immigrant groups, were essentially based on the perceived threat they posed to Americans. This was the case even though the initial U.S. involvement in the Vietnam War was intended to protect the South Vietnamese from the spread of communism. When the war ended and the idea of many refugees coming to America became a reality, public opinion about the presence of the Vietnamese was negative and hostile.

Some people thought that allowing more immigrants from different cultures would cause the United States to lose its identity as a country. This same attitude was found in the mid-1970s with regard to Southeast Asians. Some experts believed that the news media created an unflattering image of the South Vietnamese, which led Americans to believe the Vietnamese were not worth saving.[45]

Approximately one million refugees fled Vietnam after the war in an attempt to escape religious persecution. In a scene similar to what was experienced in the 1980s and 1990s in Cuba, many of the people attempting to leave their native country took to the ocean in overcrowded vessels, hoping that some ship would pick them up and offer sanctuary. Hundreds of thousands were placed in other nations or remained in overcrowded refugee camps administered by the United Nations.[46] In fact, like Cuban immigrants, there were four distinct waves of immigration to the United States from Vietnam.

The first wave, which occurred between 1975 and 1977, resulted in over 130,000 refugees, the vast majority of which were Vietnamese. For the most part, these were people from upper and middle-class backgrounds. Educated and professional, this group had perhaps the easiest time making the adjustment to life in a new country.

The second wave occurred between 1978 and 1979, bringing nearly 60,000 Vietnamese, Chinese from Vietnam, Cambodians, and Hmong to the United States. Because this group of immigrants was more diversified in terms of their social class and educational backgrounds, the difficulty in transitioning to America was considerable. The third wave, which occurred between 1980 and 1981, had perhaps the greatest impact on American society. This group of immigrants consisted of peasants, farmers, and others who had no formal education or experience with Western culture.[47] Included in this wave of immigrants were nearly 200,000 Hmong tribal members. This is a group that lived in the highlands of Laos, Vietnam, and Cambodia and was intimately involved in the U.S. efforts in Laos. In fact, some estimates indicate that the Hmong experienced nearly a 50 percent casualty rate during the war. Because the Hmong tend to migrate and had no written language until the 1950s, this group experienced significant problems in adjusting to American culture.[48]

The fourth wave of immigration is associated with people who lived in refugee camps in Thailand and other relocation centers. Between 1987 and 1993, the number of refugees admitted from Vietnam was 173,116, from Laos (including the Hmong) 75,554, and from Cambodia approximately 9,000.[49] Fortunately, Hmong children in these camps were exposed to English and American culture at an early age, which made their transition to America easier.

Despite the fact that it has been over thirty years since the end of the Vietnam War, Americans still seem to have mixed feelings about Southeast Asians. Surveys in the late 1980s and early 1990s show that although few Americans regarded this group as undesirable, about 50 percent still worried that they would be an economic drain. Even though most Southeast Asian children spoke no English upon arrival here, they have done extremely well in school. Many families place a heavy emphasis on education for their children.[50] However, many adult immigrants have experienced what is called **downward social mobility**. This means that the jobs Southeast Asian immigrants take are often occupationally below what they were doing in their native country.

However, Census Bureau data suggest that refugees from Vietnam have increased their family incomes when compared to what they made back home. Part of the reason for this, however, may be due to working longer hours or having more members of the family working full-time.[51] According to recent Census data, this group has one of the highest percentages of foreign-born residents, at approximately 84 percent, and one of the lowest percentages of members who feel they speak English well, at 29 percent. Further, the median family income is one of the lowest of all Asian American groups ($60,000 compared to $73,060 for all Asian Americans).[52]

CHECKPOINT

- Southeast Asian Americans have a long history in the United States, particularly the Hmong tribes, which fought alongside American soldiers during the Vietnam War. While achieving lower levels of education and financial success, this group continues to work toward becoming a more mainstream group and assimilating into American culture.

PACIFIC ISLANDER AMERICANS

HAWAIIANS

Historically, Hawaiians have been very tolerant of missionaries and plantation operators. Hawaiians were united under a monarchy, were respected by European immigrants, and enjoyed a spirit of goodwill with their European and American residents. In the late 1800s, however, a revolution occurred and the Hawaiian monarchy was overthrown. The United States got involved and five years later, Hawaii was annexed as a territory to the United States. During that time, citizenship had a mixed impact. Laws were passed that granted civil rights to all those born on the islands, but the anti-Asian laws still applied, which excluded the Chinese and Japanese from voting or running for office.

Hawaii has since become a strategic military outpost, and while most demographers contend that people marry others with similar backgrounds, sometimes known as **endogamy**, a high incidence of marrying outside one's group, called **exogamy**, can be taken as an indicator of acceptance of other groups. In Hawaii, there is a general acceptance of intermarriage or exogamy. The rate of intermarriage varies by group but consists of about 45 percent of all marriages in Hawaii, 62 percent of which include at least one Chinese American spouse.[53]

But Hawaii has its share of social problems. The pineapple and sugar cane plantation legacy persists, and native Hawaiians tend to struggle financially, often working land they do not own. The economy is dominated by Japanese Americans. Chinese Americans have had some success in business in Hawaii, but the top positions are almost all filled by Whites. The conclusion from these trends suggests that, in an absolute sense, Hawaii is not a racial paradise. The future of race relations in Hawaii is uncertain, but relative to the mainland and much of the world, its race relations more closely resemble harmony than bigotry.[54]

CHECKPOINT

- Despite a long-standing commitment to diversity and multiculturalism, as evidenced by the tendency toward endogamy with other groups, Hawaiians have achieved some level of success, particularly since they are identified as a state within the United States.

FILIPINOS

Few people think of Filipinos when they consider Asian Americans, yet this group is the second-largest of the Asian American population. During the past thirty years, only Mexicans have outnumbered Filipinos as immigrants to the United States.[55] After the Spanish-American War the United States took possession of the Philippines. Following the country's independence in 1946, political ties with the United States remained close. As evidence, English is one of the country's major languages and is spoken by most educated people. Moreover, like the early Koreans, Filipinos were brought to Hawaii as agricultural workers to replace the excluded Chinese, and many immigrated to the mainland in the 1920s.

Interestingly, because the Philippines was a U.S. territory at the time, immigrants were considered American nationals and as such, they were not subjected to the same kind of restrictions and resentment as were other Asian groups.[56] Added to the gentler attitude toward Filipinos was the fact that the Philippines became an important ally in the Pacific war against Japan. Consequently, Americans were much more tolerant of immigrants from this country than perhaps any other.

The long history and cultural compatibility, not to mention the U.S. military presence in the Philippines over the last forty years, resulted in a great deal of overlap between the two cultures.[57] This is reflected in the percentage of Filipinos who feel they speak English well—at 82 percent, it is significantly higher than most other Asian groups and higher than the overall Asian American average of 53 percent. This group has one of the highest median family incomes, approximately $80,000 per year, and is generally open to inter-marriage, particularly with non-Asians.[58]

CHECKPOINT

- Perhaps the most successful of all Asian American groups, Filipinos have higher levels of education and median family income than other groups. This group is also one that embraces diversity and inter-marriage.

INDIAN SUBCONTINENT

ASIAN INDIANS

Like the Asian American category as a whole, it is important to understand that people classified as **Asian Indian** represent a wide range of populations. India itself is a diverse nation with dozens of languages and ethnic enclaves. While most observers of India might note the religious divisions of Hindus, Muslims, and Sikhs, there are many other distinctions as well. The majority of Asian Indian immigrants have come from India, but sizable numbers come from Pakistan, Bangladesh, and Sri Lanka as well as other countries, such as Trinidad and Tobago and Guyana.[59]

As with other Asian groups, changes in immigration policies in the 1960s allowed many Asian Indians to enter the United States legally. Those who have come in recent times have been highly educated and from professional classes in their native countries. In fact, many Asian Indian immigrants have been students at American universities who find employment in the United States after graduation. This is particularly true in the computer industry.[60]

Like some other immigrant groups, Asian Indians have witnessed two types of experiences once arriving in the United States. On one hand, Asian Indians have played a significant role as entrepreneurs in the small business sector. For instance, by one estimate, more than half of all motels in the United States are owned by Asian Indians.[61] This group has the highest median family income of all Asian Americans—$100,000 per year—and is the best educated: 38 percent have advanced degrees, compared to 20 percent for all Asian Americans and 10 percent for Americans in general. Additionally, 32 percent of Asian Indians have bachelor's degrees. This compares to 29 percent for all Asian Americans and 18 percent of Americans in general.[62] On the other hand, there is a segment of this population that has not fared as well, being relegated to the lower paying industries such as restaurant workers, taxi drivers, and truck drivers. As one study concluded, Asian Indians are as likely to be cab drivers or managers of convenience stores as they are to be physicians or college professors. Many of the jobs in the service sector place them at higher risk for victimization by crime.[63]

CHECKPOINT

- This section offers an account of the experiences of several Asian American groups and their experiences with U.S. culture. As we have seen, whether it is the Chinese Exclusion Act, the internment of Japanese Americans during World War II, or the mistreatment of Koreans during the L.A. riots, there is a pattern of discriminatory and unequal treatment of this group.

ASIAN AMERICANS AND THE CRIMINAL JUSTICE SYSTEM

CRIME STATISTICS

According to the Uniform Crime Reports for 2017, Asian Americans represented 97,049 of the 8,162,849 arrests made by the police. This represents 1.2 percent of all arrests, even less than Native Americans, who represent 2.4 percent of all arrests for that year (see Table 5.2). This low representation in crime statistics has been a consistent trend for many years. Essentially, Asian Americans are a small proportion of those arrested by the police. Further, the percentage of arrests committed by Asian American or Pacific Islander juveniles was similar to that for all offenses, approximately 1.1 percent of all arrests for those eighteen years old and younger. Further, while Asian Americans represent about 4 percent of the total population in this country, they represent only about 1 percent of those arrested.[64] Unlike African Americans, Hispanics/Latinos, or even Native Americans, Asian Americans are underrepresented in the crime statistics.

Since 1990 the literature on crime and offenders has changed its focus from the larger minority groups, such as African Americans and Hispanics, to smaller groups of minorities, such as Native Americans and Asian Americans. While there is still a great deal less information, scholars and experts have begun to examine the criminal behavior patterns among Asian Americans,[65] and some of the evidence from these studies shows that certain Asian groups are more likely to be involved in criminal activity than others.

One study examined the odds of arrest for various offenses of seven different Asian groups. The findings revealed that Southeast Asian immigrants were more likely to be arrested for criminal activity than Whites. Vietnamese immigrants were overrepresented in every arrest category, while Cambodians, Laotians, and Vietnamese were more likely to be arrested for property crimes such as larceny and auto theft.[66]

A few trends also appear when examining the data on Asian Americans as victims of crime. However, one of the problems in assessing the victimization rates among Asian Americans is that the indicator used, primarily the National Crime Victimization Survey (NCVS), collapses all the categories of Asian Americans into one group. As we have seen, there is a great deal of difference in the types of groups under this heading, and aggregating the cases obscures their differences and minimizes the overall impact of any single group. In fact, the NCVS collapses all racial groups into three categories: White, Black, and Other. It also includes a separate category comparing Hispanics to non-Hispanics. Because of the aggregation of the data, any real analysis of Asians is virtually impossible, but the information does suggest that Asians are not victimized to the same extent as other groups.

As was mentioned, data from the Uniform Crime Reports in 2017 show a low level of involvement in reported crime. Only about 100,000 arrests of Asian offenders occurred, representing less than 1 percent of all arrests. What is important to note is that a comparison with Uniform Crime Report data since 2013 shows that this trend has been consistent for more than five years.[67]

Thus, while Asian Americans as a group are underrepresented in crime statistics, both as offenders and as victims, some attention has been given to the types and extent of criminal activity perpetrated by some Asian American groups.

TABLE 5.2   FIVE-YEAR ARREST TREND FOR ASIAN AMERICANS

Year	Total Arrests	Asian American Arrests	Percentage
2017	8,162,849	97,049	1.2%
2016	8,421,481	103,244	1.2%
2015	8,248,709	101,064	1.2%
2014	8,730,665	100,067	1.1%
2013	9,014,635	105,109	1.2%

Source: Federal Bureau of Investigation, *Crime in the United States*, U.S. Department of Justice, 2014, 2015, 2016, 2017, Table 43.

ASIAN GANGS

Growing concern about Asian crime stems from several factors, including the legal and illegal immigration of Asians into the United States over the past twenty years. This has provided new opportunities for immigrants to engage in criminal activities such as youth gangs.[68] Some research suggests that younger Chinese Americans, unlike their elders, are not content to be grateful for what they have been given in exchange for their labor but expect the full rights and privileges of citizenship. More than their parents, they refuse to tolerate continued discrimination and unemployment.[69] Upward mobility is not in the future for many of these alienated and angry youth who, with the prospect of low-wage work in restaurants and laundries, turn to gangs to achieve some level of success.

Chinese Gangs

In perhaps one of the most thorough examinations on the subject, Ko-Lin Chin, a professor at Rutgers University in New Jersey and an expert on Chinese culture, describes what is known about Chinese gangs. While there is some research to contradict Chin's findings, Chin argues that Chinese gangs are closely associated with, and are controlled by, powerful community organizations. In other words, they are an integral part of community life. These gangs are also influenced, to a great extent, by Chinese secret societies and the norms and values of the **triad subculture**.[70]

The primary activity of Chinese gangs is making money. Members invest a considerable amount of money in legitimate businesses and spend a lot of time negotiating business deals. Chinese gangs develop in communities in which adult criminals serve as role models and mentors for gang members. In keeping with their entrepreneurial efforts, drug use among Chinese gang members is rare. Although involved in drug trafficking, gang members rarely use drugs. In fact, if a member begins using drugs, he is expelled from the

Asian gangs are closely connected to the triad subculture.

gang. Thus, unlike Black and Hispanic gangs, the establishment of Chinese gangs is not based on illicit drug use or fads.

Additionally, Chin found that Chinese gangs do not experience the deterioration and poverty that is prevalent with other types of gangs. Rather, Chinese gangs grow and become economically prosperous by maintaining ties with the economic and political structures of their communities. In other words, there is a cultural component to the success of Chinese gangs: they have a certain legitimacy within the community based on the historical experience of the **triad societies**.[71]

More recently, a study in New York City found that, like Chin's findings, Chinese gangs are characterized by a highly structured and disciplined manner. However, unlike the conclusions drawn by Chin, while Chinese gangs maintain close ties to adult organizations they are not controlled by them. Adult criminals also provide opportunities for gang members to advance within the larger criminal organization and to become apprentices of crime.[72]

Chinese gangs also typically engage in nonviolent forms of extortion of merchants in the area. The pervasiveness of extortion comes from a cultural understanding that extortion is a part of regular business activity. When gang violence is evident, it usually involves intergang rivalries. Popular wisdom about gang wars stemming from drug trafficking or gangs being used to leverage political control is not supported by empirical research. Also popular but unsupported by the research is the organized nature of human trafficking. While the activity is fairly common, it is not controlled by gangs. Rather, human smuggling is often a loosely organized, entrepreneurial activity.[73]

Vietnamese Gangs

While still part of an overall "Asian" category, Vietnamese youth gangs, especially in Southern California, are quite different in their characteristics from Chinese gangs. This group of immigrants, having experienced racism and discrimination both in the job market as well as in the classroom, has had a number of significant problems assimilating into mainstream American culture. Essentially, the following three themes best characterize Vietnamese gangs: mistrust, hiding, and self-control.

A pervasive cultural theme of mistrust runs through Vietnamese communities, one that gang members exploit. For example, many members of the Vietnamese community distrust American banks and, as a result, keep their valuables and money at home. This creates a host of opportunities for gangs to rob Vietnamese citizens. As a result, robbery is a primary activity for gangs. Drug dealing in Vietnamese gangs is perceived as too risky and is avoided; thus, very few Vietnamese gang members are involved in drug dealing. Drug use, however, is heavy. The drug of choice is cocaine, while heroin is avoided since it is perceived to make one unreliable and crazy.

Vietnamese gang members continue their low-profile approach to social life by avoiding conspicuous gang tattoos or hand signs. Those that are used as indicators of gang affiliation (such as tattoos) are designed so that they can be easily concealed. Moreover, in regard to dress, Vietnamese gangs tend to opt for clothing similar to other youth in Southern California. In this way, they are able to blend in to the social landscape and more easily avoid the attention of the police. Finally, the structure of Vietnamese gangs tends to be unorganized and fluid. Membership changes constantly, and the rituals and practices of traditional gangs are noticeably absent.[74]

A recent study of Laotian/Hmong gangs in California reveals that these groups have become one of the latest threats to social life in Southern California. Laotian and Hmong gangs are an understudied area in the gang literature, yet they appear to have a greater willingness to engage in violence. Members of these gangs have been involved in homicide, armed robbery, and aggravated assaults, making them a cause for considerable concern.[75]

In sum, Vietnamese gangs are loosely defined in terms of an organizational structure, disdain drug trafficking, and an attempt to conceal their gang affiliation to others. Vietnamese gangs do not claim turf, do not adopt similar modes of dress, and in some cases, avoid the use of gang names and "signs."[76]

HUMAN SMUGGLING

As was mentioned, one of the main areas of criminal activity for Asian Americans involves illegal immigration. For Chinese immigrants in particular, the problems are similar to illegal entry into the United States by Mexicans. Given the distance that must be traveled, however, as well as the unique nature of the activity, some attempts have been made to learn more about human smuggling organizations, particularly in China.[77] While human smuggling into the United States has been going on for more than twenty years, its prevalence is based on the overwhelming numbers of Chinese nationals who wish to enter this country. As a result, when legitimate avenues were blocked, illegitimate opportunities were created.

People who leave China illegally are often called "**human snakes**." Chinese human smugglers who lead illegal immigrants across the borders are called **snakeheads**. This has actually become an industry term to describe human smugglers either in China or overseas. As was mentioned, few have studied this subject empirically, largely because of the difficulties of finding and interviewing research subjects.

There are three main smuggling methods with estimated costs ranging from $35,000 to $65,000 to transport each illegal immigrant. Often, these methods are used in combination to transport Chinese nationals into the United States. One method is to travel to Mexico or Canada and then illegally cross the border into the United States. This method would be similar in many respects to what illegal immigrants in Mexico do to enter the country. There, the term "coyote" is used to describe the guides or facilitators who bring Mexican immigrants into the country. A second method is to have immigrants obtain false documents certifying that they are citizens of another country, and then fly into the United States through transit points outside China. A third method, the one best popularized in the media and Hollywood movies, is to use fishing trawlers or freighters to smuggle immigrants into the United States.[78]

While conventional wisdom suggests that this type of activity would be sponsored and carried out by organized crime syndicates, largely because of the logistical details involved, the research seems to suggest that human smuggling is run by individual entrepreneurs, most of whom operate independently. That is, snakeheads come from a host of different backgrounds and occupations, do not affiliate with any particular organized crime group, and individual teams of smugglers may work together, usually in groups no larger than five, largely based on their particular skill or networks at different points in the smuggling process.[79] In addition to the loose affiliation many snakeheads have in terms of cooperation, they also generally do not remain involved in smuggling for longer than six years, making discovery, study, or even prosecution of snakeheads exceptionally difficult.[80] Finally, the absence of a figurehead or leader of this activity, what some researchers have called a "godfather," prohibits the police from any meaningful intervention to minimize this type of criminal activity.

TRANSNATIONAL ORGANIZED CRIME

In 2012, in an attempt to assess the impact of Asian transnational organized crime in the United States, as well as to lay the foundation for a research agenda that would help the United States better understand the potential threats of international crime, two researchers, Ko-Lin Chin and James Finckenauer, conducted a study to explore the extent of Asian transnational organized crime.[81] While agreement on the particular problems as well as an assessment of the scope of activities relating to organized crime is difficult to achieve, leading experts on organized crime in eight Asian countries (Cambodia, China, Hong Kong, Japan, Macau, the Philippines, Taiwan, and Thailand) have agreed that there are a few common issues.

In China, for example, law enforcement officials and other authorities consider drug distribution to be the most serious problem in that country. The increase in the number of heroin addicts in China has led officials to believe that local drug syndicates are importing heroin from the Golden Triangle area (Burma, Thailand, and Cambodia) and distributing it locally. Gambling is also considered a serious problem in China. According to officials, even though the problems of gambling and prostitution were thought to be eradicated when China began a communist reign in 1949, today these two industries appear to be thriving. Finally, Chinese authorities are concerned about the escalating levels of violence in their country. Perhaps more importantly, the violence extends beyond criminal gangs or organized crime syndicates and is affecting ordinary citizens and business owners.[82] Chinese officials are also concerned about the problems stemming from the human smuggling industry.[83]

In Japan, the most serious organized crime problem relates to that country's version of organized crime, the **yakuza**. Their involvement in gambling, prostitution, drug trafficking—particularly in amphetamines—and extortion are cause for considerable concern by authorities. Additionally, because of its large number of wealthy businessmen, Japan has become a major destination for women in the sex industry.[84]

In the Philippines, the main concerns relate to human trafficking and kidnapping for ransom, the drug trade, and illegal gambling and firearms smuggling. While the country recently passed an anti-trafficking law, little priority is given to enforcing such laws despite the sexual exploitation that occurs there. Thus, while the official position is that something needs to be done about these crimes, the reality is that little emphasis is being given to solving the problem.

With regard to the drug trade, in response to improved law enforcement interdiction efforts to control the influx of amphetamines from China, Filipino authorities have discovered local laboratories that have been established to manufacture the drugs. Thus, the problems in the Philippines relating to drugs have shifted from an international focus to a local concern. Authorities contend that much of this trade, like a great deal of criminal activity in general, is controlled by organized crime syndicates who are protected by local politicians.[85]

In 2018, the United Nations Office on Drugs and Crime (UNODC) issued a report on human trafficking. Similar to the trends discovered ten years earlier, the challenges involved in identifying and prosecuting traffickers remains at the present time, along with a wide variety of organizations and structures. One of the more recent trends has been the involvement of women as offenders as well as their traditional role as victims of human trafficking. The UNODC reports that about a third of all offenders are now women.[86]

Additionally, about 50 percent of victims are adult women, although this number may be skewed since girls are not counted in the tabulation. According to the UNODC, in 2018, children represented about one-third of all trafficking victims, two-thirds of whom are girls. Further, while sex remains one of the primary activities of human trafficking victims, forced labor is also a common feature, as is the recruitment of children as forced combatants by countries wracked by civil unrest. While women are typically victimized for sexual purposes, with male victims usually involved in forced labor, in China many women are used for the purposes of forced labor as well.[87]

The UNODC also found that only four in ten countries have reported ten or more convictions for human trafficking, with about 15 percent of countries reporting no convictions at all. Part of the challenge relates to the discovery and prosecution of human trafficking crimes, but given the enormous profits generated from this industry, one could also assume that some countries have ignored human trafficking for economic reasons.[88]

ARE WE OVERLOOKING ASIAN INVOLVEMENT IN THE CRIMINAL JUSTICE SYSTEM?

While it seems that Asian Americans are less represented in crime statistics, which suggests that they are not extensively involved in criminal activity, a recent report by the Urban Institute raises interesting questions about whether this is in fact the case. As reported by that agency, one of the problems seen in the data is that many organizations fail to include "Asian" as a category for reporting purposes. This can lead to artificial decreases in crime figures. For example, the report offers the observation that Asian Americans and Pacific Islanders (AAPI) as a group represents about five percent of the total population but only about 1 percent of the federal prison population. A Prison Policy Institute study found that incarceration rates of Native Hawaiian/Pacific Islanders in Hawaii was four times higher than that of non-Hispanic whites. The reason for this underreporting is that correctional facilities often use flawed methods of recording data.

Another example is found in the Urban Institute report, which uses data from state and federal agencies to point out that while AAPIs represent more than 35 percent of the overall population, the data suggest that Asian involvement in the juvenile justice system is minimal—representing a bit more than 10 percent of all the youths age 10 to 17 who were arrested and booked by San Francisco police (see Figure 5.1).

However, when the data involving Asians is examined more carefully, it shows that Samoan youth represent less than 1 percent of the age group but about 5 percent of those who were arrested and booked in 2010 (see Figure 5.2). The significance of these findings points to an often overlooked assumption about Asian Americans as a generalized category, and these data can identify a variety of policy issues when examining the involvement of AAPI in the criminal and/or juvenile justice system.[89]

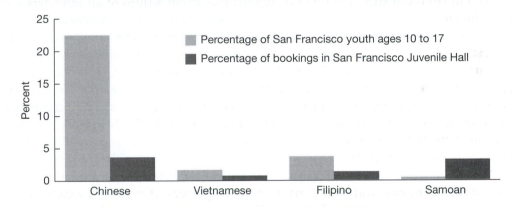

FIGURE 5.1 Juvenile justice system involvement of AAPIs in San Francisco.
Source: San Francisco Juvenile Probation Department and 2010 American Community Survey.

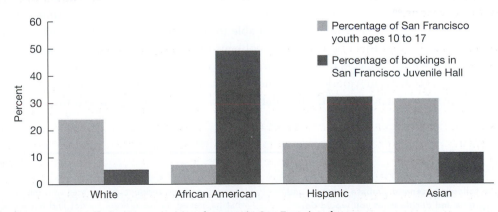

FIGURE 5.2 Juvenile justice system involvement in San Francisco by race.
Source: San Francisco Juvenile Probation Department and 2010 American Community Survey.

CHECKPOINT

- As we have seen in this section, there is ample evidence that Asian Americans are underrepresented in crime data—where there is a consistent pattern of the lack of involvement in the criminal justice system, either as offenders or as victims. That said, it does not mean that certain Asian groups are not involved in crime. Evidence of Asian gangs, whether as part of the Chinese triads, Japanese yakuza, or Vietnamese gangs, is seen in the literature. However, even in these instances, criminal offenders are sometimes able to avoid involvement in the criminal justice system by concealing much of their activity. From a data perspective, we also need to be mindful of the way we collect crime information about Asian Americans. The tendency to lump all Asian Americans into a single category or to omit the identification of this group at all, can have a significant impact on our understanding of the trends identified in the literature.

SUMMARY

This chapter explored several of the most common Asian American groups in the United States. Many of these groups listed under the general heading of "Asian American" cover a broad spectrum of groups, with different attitudes, values, beliefs, and languages, making the category more of convenience than actual understanding. Additionally, diversity is evident in the experiences of Asian Americans and success in assimilating into mainstream American culture. Historically, most of these groups, particularly the Chinese and Japanese, were initially perceived as beneficial since they provided cheap labor in expanding industries. However, as immigrants demonstrated their willingness to work hard and work for very little money, the group became perceived as threatening to American workers. As a result, legislation was passed to limit their immigration into the United States.

The willingness to work hard, sacrifice, and persevere has resulted in some success for groups of Asian Americans, particularly in the area of education. In fact, in more recent times, Asian Americans were given the label "model minority" to describe how well they assimilated into American culture. This label is a myth, largely because it does not address the wide range of experiences for Asian Americans. While some have achieved a level of societal success, there are other groups who remain mired in poverty and discrimination. Some groups of Asian Americans have been able to successfully integrate themselves into American society; for others however, the problems of poverty and crime are readily self-evident. Thus, while it appears from an examination of the crime statistics as well as victimization surveys that Asian Americans are underrepresented in terms of their involvement in crime, there remains a portion of the population that is actively involved in criminal activity.

YOU MAKE THE CALL

Consider the following scenario. Debate the pros and cons of all options and decide what you would do.

You are a young prosecutor with only two years of experience trying criminal cases. A gang fight erupts in an Asian neighborhood which results in the deaths of two rival gang members. Upon interviewing residents of the area who might have seen what happened, police officers cannot find anyone willing to make a statement. They, do, however, recover substantial physical evidence that links two particular suspects to the crime. While you are trying to decide what to do, local Asian Americans protest the treatment citizens receive from police officers, causing a major uproar at City Hall. As a result, your supervisor tells you to drop the case since it will likely result in a political disaster. Given that the gang problem has become a topic of interest for the police and is of some concern to the courts as well, what do you do? Assume also that you have what you think to be enough evidence to obtain a warrant for the arrest of the suspects.

Questions

1. What do you do? Do you proceed despite your supervisor's orders? What is the dilemma for you?

2. What kind of repercussions might you experience if you decide to continue with the case? What would they be if you decided to drop it?

3. Why would the police chief, the district attorney, and the mayor want you to drop the case?

4. Can a group such as Asian Americans, which typically represent a small percentage of the crime statistics and are usually less vocal than other minority groups, really have an impact on local politics? How?

KEY TERMS

Alien Land Act
Asian Indian
Chinese Exclusion Act
downward social mobility
endogamy
exogamy
glass ceiling
Hmong tribes

human snakes
model minority myth
racial profiling
snakeheads
triad society
triad subculture
yakuza
yellow peril

DISCUSSION QUESTIONS

1. What do Chinese, Japanese, and Koreans all have in common in terms of their immigration into the United States?
2. How do the media contribute to the model minority myth for many Asian American groups?
3. Why do you think Asian Americans are underrepresented in the crime statistics? Is it that they commit fewer crimes, are simply better at avoiding the police, or other factors?
4. Do you think that hate crimes against Asian Americans are common? Why is it that when people think of hate crimes, they usually think of African Americans?

FOR FURTHER READING

Hyun, J. *Breaking the Bamboo Ceiling: Career Strategies for Asians*. New York: HarperCollins, 2005.
Long, P. D., and L. Ricard. *The Dream Shattered: Vietnamese Gangs in America*. Boston, MA: Northeastern University Press, 1996.
Takaki, R. *A Different Mirror: A History of Multicultural America*. New York: Back Bay Books, 2008.
Weglyn, M. *Years of Infamy: The Untold Story of America's Concentration Camps*. New York: Quill, 1976.

NOTES

1. K. Humes, and J. McKinnon, *The Asian and Pacific Islander Population in the United States: Population Characteristics*, U.S. Census Bureau, Current Population Reports, 2000.
2. Abby Budiman, Anthony Cilluffo, and Neil G. Ruiz, "Key Facts About Asian Origin Groups in the United States," Pew Research Center, May 22, 2019. Available at: https://www.pewresearch .org/fact-tank/2019/05/22/key-facts-about-asian-origin-groups-in-the-u-s/

3. Budiman, Cilluffo, and Ruiz, "Key Facts About Asian Origin Groups"; See also *From the Mideast to the Pacific: A Profile of the Nation's Asian Foreign-Born Population*, United States Census Brief 100–4, 2000.

4. American Immigration Center, *Asian American History Timeline*. Available at: https://www. us-immigration.com/asian-american-history-timeline/

5. Ibid.

6. Budiman, Cilluffo, and Ruiz, "Key Facts About Asian Origin Groups."

7. Gustavo Lopez, Neal G. Ruiz, and Eileen Patten, "Key Facts About Asian Americans: A Diverse and Growing Population," Pew Research Center, September 8, 2017. Available at: https://www .pewresearch.org/fact-tank/2017/09/08/key-facts-about-asian-americans/

8. Ibid.

9. Ibid.

10. J. Guo, "The Real Reasons the U.S. Became Less Racist Toward Asian Americans," *Washington Post*, November 29, 2016. Available at https://www.washingtonpost.com/news/wonk/wp/2016/11/29/ the-real-reason-americans-stopped-spitting-on-asian-americans-and-started-praising-them/?utm_term=.30b90a7a5d7e.

11. J. Calma, "Forty Years After Resettlement, Thousands of Southeast Asian Refugees Face Deportation," *NBC News*, November 23, 2015. Available at: http://www.nbcnews.com/news/asian-america/ forty-years-after-resettlement-thousands-southeast-asian-refugees-face-deportation-n466376

12. Lopez, Ruiz and Patten, 2017.

13. Ibid.

14. Ibid.

15. T. Lien, "Asian Americans Face Glass Ceiling at Tech Firms, Report Shows," *Los Angeles Times*, May 6, 2015. Available at: http://www.latimes.com/business/la-fi-tech-diversity-asians-20150507-story.html

16. J. Hyun, *Breaking the Bamboo Ceiling: Career Strategies for Asians* (New York: HarperCollins, 2005), 73–92.

17. T. Varadarajan, "A Patel Motel Cartel?" *New York Times Magazine*, July 4, 1999. Available at: http://www.nytimes.com/1999/07/04/magazine/a-patel-motel-cartel.html

18. Ibid.

19. See, e.g., T. Lien, "Asian Americans Face Glass Ceiling."

20. Federal Bureau of Investigation, *Crime in the United States, Incidents and Offenses Hate Crime Statistics 2017*, U.S. Department of Justice, 2017. Available at: https://ucr.fbi.gov/hate-crime/2017/ topic-pages/tables/table-5.xls

21. "Asian Americans Side with Blacks and Latinos in Opinions About Police Effectiveness and Racial Profiling," Reappropriate.co, September 14, 2014. Available at: http://reappropriate.co/2014/09/ asian-americans-side-with-blacks-latinos-not-whites-in-opinions-on-police-effectiveness-racial-profiling/

22. *Chinese Exclusion Act*, National Archives, 2017. Available at: https://www.archives.gov/research/ chinese-americans

23. Ibid.

24. Ibid.

25. I. Light, "Chinese Americans," *American Journal of Sociology* 81, no. 2 (September, 1975): 432–35.

26. Chinese Historical Society of South Carolina, "Chinatowns in the United States of America." Available at: http://www.chssc.org/History/ChinatownsInAmerica.aspx

27. J. Batalova and A. Terrareas, "Frequently Requested Statistics on Immigrants and Immigration in the U.S.," *Migration Policy Institute*, December 9, 2010. Available at: http://www.migrationpolicy.org/article/frequently-requested-statistics-immigrants-and-immigration-united-states-1

28. Ibid.

29. M. Weglyn, *Years of Infamy: The Untold Story of America's Concentration Camps* (New York: Quill, 1976), 316.

30. S. Caudill and F. Mixon, "Human Capital Investment and Internment of Japanese Americans During WWII: A Public Choice Approach," *International Journal of Applied Economics* 9, no. 1 (2012): 1–14.

31. Ibid.

32. Ibid.

33. "Redress to WWII Internees Complete," *Chicago Tribune*, September 11, 1998. Available at: http://articles.chicagotribune.com/1998-09-11/news/9809110328_1_civil-liberties-act-internees-japanese-americans

34. Commission on Wartime Relocation and Internment of Civilians, *Recommendations*, June 1983. Available at: https://archive.org/details/Personal-Justice-Denied

35. Lopez, Ruiz and Patten, 2017.

36. Ibid.

37. Ibid.

38. S. Mydans, "Shooting Puts Focus on Korean-Black Frictions in Los Angeles," *New York Times*, October 6, 1991, available at http://www.nytimes.com/1991/10/06/us/shooting-puts-focus-on-korean-black-frictions-in-los-angeles.html

39. Lopez, Ruiz and Patten, 2017.

40. Ibid.

41. Ibid.

42. Ibid.

43. J. Zong and J. Batalova, "Vietnamese Immigration in the U.S.," *Migration Policy Institute*, June 8, 2016. Available online at http://www.migrationpolicy.org/article/vietnamese-immigrants-united-states

44. Lopez, Ruiz and Patten, 2017.

45. C. B. Luce, "Refugees and Guilt," *New York Times*, May 11, 1975, E19.

46. Zong and Batalova, "Vietnamese Immigration in the U.S."

47. Ibid.

48. F. Ng, "Towards a Second Generation Hmong History," in *Adaptation, Acculturation, and Transnational Ties Among Asian Americans* (New York: Garland, 1998), 99–117.

49. A. Portes and R. G. Rumbaut, *Immigrant America: A Portrait*, 2nd ed. (Berkeley: University of California Press, 1996).

50. F. Ng, "Towards a Second Generation Hmong History."

51. J. Zong and J. Batalova, "Vietnamese Immigration in the U.S."

52. Lopez, Ruiz and Patten, 2017.

53. Ibid.

54. Zong and Batalova, "Vietnamese Immigration in the U.S."

55. Ibid.

56. Ibid.

57. Ibid.

58. Lopez, Ruiz and Patten, 2017.

59. Zong and Batalova, "Vietnamese Immigration in the U.S."

60. B. Boxall, "Asian Indians Remake Silicon Valley," *Los Angeles Times*, July 6, 2001.

61. Varadarajan, "A Patel Motel Cartel?," 36–39.

62. Lopez, Ruiz and Patten, 2017.

63. Varadarajan, "A Patel Motel Cartel?"

64. Federal Bureau of Investigation, *Crime in the United States 2017*, Uniform Crime Reports, U.S. Department of Justice, 2019. Available at https://ucr.fbi.gov/crime-in-the-u.s/2017/crime-in-the-u.s.-2017/tables/table-43

65. E. B. Penn and S. L. Gabbidon, "Race and Justice," *Criminal Justice Studies* 18, no. 1 (2005): 1–121.

66. A. J. Kposowa and G. T. Tsunokai, "Offending Patterns Among Southeast Asians in the State of California," *Journal of Ethnicity in Criminal Justice* 1, no. 1 (2003): 93–113.

67. Federal Bureau of Investigation, *Crime in the United States*, 2014, 2015, 2016, 2017. Table 43. U.S. Department of Justice.

68. J. Z. Wang, "Asian Gangs: New Challenges in the 21st Century," *Journal of Gang Research* 8, no. 1 (2000): 51–62.

69. Ibid.; see also K. Chin, "Chinese Gangs and Extortion," in C. Ron Huff (ed.), *Gangs in America* (Newbury Park, CA: Sage, 1990), 129–45.

70. D. Joe and N. Robinson, "Chinatown's Immigrant Gangs," *Criminology* 18 (1980): 337–45; K. Joe, "Myths and Realities of Asian Gangs on the West Coast," *Humanity and Society* 18, no. 2 (1994): 3–18; P. Takagi and T. Platt, "Behind the Gilded Ghetto," *Crime and Social Justice* 9, no. 2 (1978): 2–25. See also Chin, "Chinese Gangs and Extortion."

71. Chin, "Chinese Gangs and Extortion"; see also V. Webb, L. Ren, and J. Z. Zhao, "A Comparative Study of Youth Gangs in China and the United States," *International Criminal Justice Review* 21, no. 3 (2011): 225–52.

72. See Federal Bureau of Investigation, *2011 National Gang Threat Assessment*, U.S. Department of Justice, 2012. Available at: https://www.fbi.gov/stats-services/publications/2011-national-gang-threat-assessment/2011-national-gang-threat-assessment; Wang, "Asian Gangs."

73. Federal Bureau of Investigation, *2011 National Gang Assessment*.

74. P. Wyrick, *Vietnamese Youth Gang Involvement* (Washington, DC: Office of Juvenile Justice Delinquency Prevention, 2000). Available at: https://www.ncjrs.gov/pdffiles1/ojjdp/fs200001.pdf; J. D. Vigil, "Cholos and Gangs: Culture Change and Street Youth in Los Angeles," in Huff, *Gangs in America*, 106–28; J. D. Vigil and Steve Chong Yun, "Vietnamese Youth Gangs in Southern California," in Huff, *Gangs in America*, 146–62.

75. J. Z. Wang, "A Preliminary Profile of Laotian/Hmong Gangs: A California Perspective." *Journal of Gang Research* 9, no. 4 (2002): 1–4.

76. P. D. Long and L. Ricard, *The Dream Shattered: Vietnamese Gangs in America* (Boston, MA: Northeastern University Press, 1996).

77. See U.S. Department of State, *Trafficking in Persons Report*, June 2014. Available at: https://www.state.gov/j/tip/rls/tiprpt/2014/index.htm.

78. Ibid.

79. Ibid.

80. Ibid.

81. K.-L. Chin and J. O. Finckenauer, *Selling Sex Overseas: Chinese Women and the Realities of Prostitution and Global Sex Trafficking* (New York: NYU Press, 2012).

82. Ibid.

83. Sheldon Zhang and Ko-Lin Chin, *Characteristics of Human Smugglers* (Washington, DC: National Institute of Justice, Research in Brief, 2002). Available at: https://www.ncjrs.gov/pdffiles1/nij/204989.pdf.

84. Chin and Finckenauer, *Selling Sex Overseas*.

85. Ibid.

86. United Nations Office on Drugs and Crime, *Trafficking in Persons*, United Nations, 2018. Available at: https://www.unodc.org/documents/data-and-analysis/glotip/2018/GLOTiP_2018_BOOK_web_small.pdf

87. Ibid.

88. Ibid.

89. Cathy Hu and Sino Esthappen, "Asian American and Pacific Islanders, a Missing Minority in Criminal Justice Data," *The Urban Institute*, May 23, 2017. Available at: https://www.urban.org/urban-wire/asian-americans-and-pacific-islanders-missing-minority-criminal-justice-data

CHAPTER 6

NATIVE AMERICANS AND THE CRIMINAL JUSTICE SYSTEM

CHAPTER OBJECTIVES

After reading this chapter, you should be able to:

- Identify the significance of the historical treatment of American Indians in this country
- Understand the importance of federal intervention in the form of laws and agencies in regulating life both on and off the reservation
- Describe the current condition of many Native Americans in this country
- Understand the involvement of Native Americans in the criminal justice system, particularly in light of the tension between self-governance of tribes and the influence of federal laws

As with the other groups discussed thus far, it is impossible to describe the many American-Indian cultures of North America, let alone those in Central and South America and the islands of the Caribbean. The term "Indian culture" is a generic term that includes a vast array of cultures and ways of life of the group we call "American Indians." For simplicity's sake, the terms "Native American" and "American Indian" will be used interchangeably, but, as we saw with the discussion of Hispanics and Latinos, know that there are a host of differences that make any sweeping generalizations impractical.

HISTORICAL PRESENCE OF NATIVE AMERICANS

The United States has had a stormy history with Native Americans. In 1500, the number of American Indians north of the Rio Grande was estimated at about 7 million. This number gradually decreased as food sources disappeared or they died due to diseases such as measles and small pox. Between 1800 and 1900, the Native American population was reduced from about 600,000 to approximately 250,000.[1]

The government's policy toward Native Americans has historically been one of expediency. If the needs of the tribes interfered with Whites' needs or desires, the sentiment was that Native Americans should capitulate to Whites. The tribes were viewed as separate nations to be dealt with by government treaties. While one may think this is a civilized approach, history clearly shows that American Indians were either exploited by cooperating with the federal government or eliminated if they refused to give up their land.[2]

For instance, as settlers moved west, the need for land increased. The government believed that Indians had no right to interfere with societal progress. To that end, the **Indian Removal Act of 1830** called for the relocation of all Eastern tribes to west of the Mississippi River. The act not only disrupted Native American culture, but it did not move the tribes far enough to stay ahead of the growing population of settlers. In an effort to elicit cooperation, peace commissioners were sent out in 1867 in an attempt to create reservations for Native American tribes.[3]

The nineteenth century proved to be a difficult time for Native Americans as the U.S. government continued to claim land that belonged to tribes. The treatment of the Sioux Nation serves as an example of this insensitivity. In 1868, the U.S. government signed the **Fort Laramie Treaty** with the Sioux. The government agreed to keep Whites from hunting or settling on the newly established Great Sioux Reservation, which included all of the land that is now South Dakota. In exchange, the Sioux relinquished most of the remaining land they occupied at that time.[4]

Urged on, perhaps, by George Custer's claims of gold in the Black Hills, a flood of White people eventually infiltrated the Sioux reservation. As one might expect, conflict between the Sioux and Whites occurred. In response, the U.S. violated the parameters of the Fort Laramie Treaty and demanded that the Sioux move out of the Black Hills. When the Sioux failed to move, General George Custer was sent into the area to remove them physically. Custer underestimated the strength of the Sioux warriors, which led to the now famous **Battle at Little Big Horn** in 1876, where Custer and his men were defeated.

The Battle of Little Big Horn was a historic moment in the history of the treatment of Native Americans.

Afterward, the army redoubled its efforts to eliminate the Sioux. The tribe eventually sold the Black Hills to the federal government and agreed to the reduction of the Great Sioux Reservation to five smaller reservations.[5] The Sioux had a difficult time adjusting to life on the reservation. They sought escape through the **Ghost Dance religion**, a religion that included dances and songs proclaiming the return of the buffalo and the resurrection of dead ancestors in a land free of the White people. Although the Ghost Dance was essentially harmless, Whites feared that the social solidarity encouraged by the movement would lead to renewed warfare. As a result, more troops were summoned to areas where the Ghost Dance had become popular.[6]

In late December 1890, anticipating that a massive Ghost Dance would occur, a cavalry division arrived at a reservation of Sioux at Wounded Knee Creek on the Pine Ridge in South Dakota. While an exact account of what happened is not known, a battle ensued that left about 300 Sioux and 25 U.S. soldiers dead. This conflict is known as the **Battle of Wounded Knee**. The event was not the deadliest for Native Americans, but the battle is heralded by historians as significant because it extinguished the hope of the Sioux Nation of ever returning to a life of freedom.[7]

LEGISLATING FOR THE PEOPLE

As the death toll mounted and the conflict between Native Americans and White settlers continued, the federal government attempted a different strategy: assimilation. The idea was that if cultural differences were the source of the problem, meaning that the attitudes, values and beliefs of the tribes were in conflict with the progressive ideas of the government and settlers, then the solution was to weaken the influence of tribal culture. If tribal institutions were weakened, then Native Americans would be more likely to assimilate and subscribe to the ideas the federal government proposed. Evidence of assimilation strategy was seen in the General Allotment Act of 1887, also known as the **Dawes Act**.[8]

The General Allotment Act proposed to make landowners of individual tribe members without consulting tribal leaders. Advocated largely by community activists who sought to empower tribal members by helping them to become more like Whites, each family was given 160 acres of land. However, like programs for the poor that attempt to empower families as homeowners but do not properly equip them with the skills necessary to maintain a home, no effort was made to acquaint Native Americans with the skills necessary to make the land productive. As a result, eventually much of the land initially deeded under the act came into the possession of Whites when Native Americans became victims of fraudulent land transfers. By 1934 Native Americans had lost approximately 90 million of the 138 million acres in their possession prior to the General Allotment Act.[9]

John Collier was appointed head of the Bureau of Indian Affairs during President Franklin D. Roosevelt's first term. Collier proposed major changes in Indian policy that included the preservation of Native American culture. Perhaps most significant was his proposal to end the allotment system. In 1934 Congress passed the Indian

Reorganization Act, which, among other things, prohibited further allotments of tribal lands and encouraged Native Americans to create self-governing systems within their tribes.[10]

TERMINATION

In the mid-1940s, Whites realized the significance of mistreating Native Americans, especially those who lived on reservations. However, instead of improving the quality of life on reservation land, many Americans mistakenly thought that part of the solution was to force Native Americans to assimilate into mainstream society.[11] This was accomplished by simply eliminating official recognition of tribes. The **Termination Act** was passed by Congress in 1953 which led to the termination of thirteen tribes between 1945 and 1962. The Termination Act also meant that certain tribes would lose tax-exempt status for their lands. Consequently, many tribal members who lost their status had to sell their land to pay the taxes on it and to pay for health and educational services for their communities.[12] Consequently, termination laws forced nearly 35,000 displaced former land owners into urban areas. The Bureau of Indian Affairs Employment Assistance Program offered reimbursement for transportation, low-cost housing, and incidental expenses to Native Americans who agreed to resettle in cities. Soon, Indian populations in cities exceeded those of some reservations. According to the Census Bureau, in the 1960s more than half of all Native Americans lived in cities. Most Native Americans strongly resisted the Termination Act, realizing that tribes would lose their lands as well as their native culture.

During the 1970s the **Red Power movement**, which was similar to the Black Power movement for African Americans in that they tried to gain economic, social, and political equality for Native Americans, pressured the federal government to address Native Americans' concerns and to reaffirm tribal rights as set out in the Indian Reorganization Act. The effect was a renewed effort by the U.S. government to give more control back to the tribes.

The more radical American Indian Movement (AIM), which became the most visible reminder of the Red Power movement, was originally to monitor the police and to document evidence of police brutality. Eventually, AIM turned their attention to solving problems within the Native American community like programs that focused on reducing the high incidence of alcoholism among Native Americans as well as educational programs for Native American children to improve academic performance.

The 1970s, a time of great protest in the United States, was also a time when Native Americans made dramatic efforts to have their rights preserved. Perhaps the most dramatic confrontation between Native Americans and the federal government occurred in 1973. Known as the Battle of Wounded Knee II, the leader of AIM and nearly three hundred supporters began a seventy-day standoff with authorities in Wounded Knee, South Dakota, the site of the first famous battle with General Custer in 1890. While the event drew a great deal of media attention, it had little effect on the federal government's policy on Native Americans.[13]

GOVERNMENT INVOLVEMENT IN INDIAN AFFAIRS

In recent years, many of the policies instituted by the Bureau of Indian Affairs, the primary regulatory arm of the federal government as it relates to Native Americans, have been designed with the idea that the government should be less involved in Indian life. In an attempt to relinquish control over Indian affairs the federal government formed the Indian Claims Commission (ICC) to handle disputes. Until 1946, Native Americans could not bring any land claim against the federal government without a special act of Congress. Although not an official U.S. court, the ICC operates somewhat like one in that lawyers present evidence for both sides in a disagreement. If the commission agrees with the tribe, it then determines the value of the land at the time it was illegally seized. This is of critical importance since the value of the land at the time of loss could be pennies an acre. Payments are then decreased by what are called setoffs. These are deductions from the money due equal to the cost of federal services provided to the tribe. It is not unusual to have a case decided in favor of the tribe only to have its settlements exceeded by the setoffs.[14] In other words, while the tribe may have won the moral and legal victory by having the case decided in their favor and being entitled to compensation, the costs of using government services often left tribes in a deficit because the value of the land was not calculated at current market value.

More recently, but particularly in the 1980s, which is recognized as a decade of progress in Indian Law, Native Americans have increasingly succeeded in winning their lawsuits. The U.S. Supreme Court ruled on nearly eighty cases between the 1960s and 1980s, most of which were decided in favor of the tribes and reasserted such basic principles as tribes as separate governments. The 1990s were heralded as a time of new tribal sophistication,

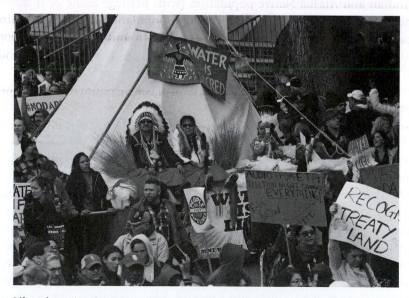

Like other minority groups, many Native Americans have protested the government's discrimination against them.

where **Tribal Courts** were increasing in quantity and in political standing, spawned perhaps by the economic wealth of some tribes due to casino gambling.[15] Tribal courts are courts of jurisdiction designed to allow the tribes the authority to hear and decide cases relating to life on the reservation without interference of traditional U.S. Courts.

CHECKPOINT

- Historically, the treatment of Native Americans by the federal government has consisted of a series of events where land was taken from them and treaties that had been signed were invalidated and ignored. The level of exploitation includes the elimination of tribes.

NATIVE AMERICANS TODAY

We must again emphasize the diversity of Native Americans. Besides the variety of tribal heritages, it is important to recognize that there is a distinction between Native Americans that live on and off reservations, as well as tribal members who live in small towns and in central cities, and those living on one coast or the other. Native American life has generally shifted from several hundred reservations to small towns and big cities. Life in these places is quite different, but there are enough similarities to draw a few broad conclusions about the status of Native Americans in the United States today. Let's look at a couple of dimensions.

EMPLOYMENT AND INCOME

According to the 2017 American Community Survey conducted by the U.S. Census, the American Indian and Alaska Native population (with heritage alone or in combination with another race) hit just over 2 percent. The total population in 2017, according to the Census report estimate, is 325,719,178. American Indian and Alaska Native population numbers (alone or in combination) are 6,795,785 or 2.1 percent, and American Indian and Alaska Native population (alone) is 4,104,295 or 1.3 percent of the population. According to 2010 Census numbers, American Indian and Alaska Native populations were just below 2 percent of the total population.[16]

According to Census officials, the number of people who self-identify in this category is growing. There were 170,110 people who identified as Sioux in the 2010 census. The largest group, Cherokee, consisted of 819,105 people. Of those who identified as Native American or Alaska Native as their only race, about one-third live on reservations or tribal lands. Among all American Indians and Alaska Natives, about 22 percent live on reservations or tribal lands.[17]

In terms of identifying with a particular tribe, with 43 percent living on reservations, the Cherokee, followed by the Navajo and Sioux, are the largest tribes today. The increase in population size over the past twenty years is primarily due to a greater willingness for Native Americans to claim their heritage, either by moving back to reservations or by simply claiming their heritage within an official survey. Some experts contend that the increases are due to the growth of the casino gambling industry.[18]

By the U.S. standard of living, Native Americans are quite poor. In an absolute sense of dollars earned or quality of housing, Native Americans are no worse off now than in the past. However, when making comparisons between minority groups and the larger society, most experts always use a relative standard, not an absolute one. In other words, poverty is not defined by the percentage of people who have no food, clothing, or housing. Poverty is determined by a standard that is relative to some larger group. In a relative sense, Native Americans are far behind on all standards of income and occupational status when compared to Whites. In the 1980s, for example, according to the U.S. Census, Native American families were three times more likely to live below the poverty level and much less likely to have anyone in that family working full-time. When Congress passed the Personal Responsibility Work Reconciliation Act in 1997, more commonly known as welfare reform, a major part of the act focused on chronic poverty, which many Native Americans experience. Today, the problems seem to be getting worse for Native Americans, who generally have higher poverty and unemployment rates than the national average. According to the U.S. Census Bureau, the median income of the American Indian and Alaska Native group in 2017 was $41,882—in contrast, the median income for the entire population was $60,336.[19]

About 25 percent of American Indians and Alaska Natives were living in poverty in the United States in 2017. This compares to about 15 percent of the population as a whole.[20]

Another marker of economic success is home ownership. According to the U.S. Census, only 54 percent of American Indian and Alaska Native householders owned their own home in 2017—compared to 64 percent of the overall population. Additionally, the value of that home is lower than the national average. In 2017 the median home value for Native Americans was $135,200 compared to $217,600 for the rest of the population. Also, while about 9 percent of the country lacked health insurance in 2017, the percentage of American

Poverty rates on Native American reservations are alarmingly high, largely due to the lack of employment opportunities.

Indians and Alaska Natives who lacked health insurance was nearly 20 percent. Even considering Native Americans who acquired private health insurance, the proportion was lower than the rest of the population. In 2017 43 percent of Native Americans had private health insurance, compared to 67.6 percent of the rest of the population.[21]

People living on reservations also have the highest rates of unemployment in the United States. Some of the most commonly cited reasons for high unemployment among Native Americans are lack of education, discrimination, and the scarcity of jobs and industry on and near reservations. In fact, many American Indians move to cities in search of better schooling, improved housing, and higher-paying jobs. Despite the fact that many American Indians want to obtain an education, few are prepared to do so.

High school graduation rates continue to improve. According to the National Center for Educational Statistics, in 2017 the national average graduation rate for White students was 88.6 percent, for Asian students it was 91.2 percent; for Hispanics it was about 80 percent, and for African American students it was 77.8 percent. However, American Indian and Alaska Native students had the second-lowest high school graduation rate of any racial or ethnic group; at 72.4 percent.[22] For Native American students, there are particular factors at play. According to Theresa Pouley, the chief judge of the Tulalip Tribal Court in Washington: "Their substance abuse rates are higher. They're twice as likely as any other race to die before the age of 24. They have two times the rate of abuse and neglect."[23]

Some of the challenge of enhancing educational achievement relates to access to the internet. According to a recent report by the U.S. Census Bureau, only about 53 percent of Native Americans living on reservations or other tribal lands with a computer have access to the internet. In contrast, subscription rates in general hovered above 67 percent for people who do not identify as American Indian or Alaska Natives. Part of the reason for this is infrastructure; the terrain on reservations makes constructing cell towers expensive and difficult. In addition, the lack of federal funding from the Federal Communications Commission (FCC) has hampered tribes' ability to acquire internet services. According to one report, less than 1 percent of federal funding from the FCC and the Department of Agriculture's Rural Utilities Services has been awarded directly to tribes or service providers owned by tribes. As a result, many companies do not want to invest in the endeavor since it would affect profits. In response to these challenges, school-age children attempt to use internet service at local libraries, tribal offices, or at school.[24]

CHECKPOINT

- By most measures, Native Americans are more likely to live in poverty and to not graduate high school. These factors also result in the lack of adequate employment as well as suffering from an assortment of health-related problems. Native Americans are also less likely to own their own home, compared to Whites. Even when they are homeowners, the value of Native American homes is far lower than the median value of homes for Whites.

INSULTS, MASCOTS, AND NATIVE AMERICANS IN SPORTS

There is little question that racism affects all aspects of American society. On one hand, Americans seem willing to avoid the use of derogatory terms because they evoke such a strong and offensive reaction on the part of the targeted group. Americans have also become more sensitive to racial slights in sports and advertising, where depictions of African Americans and Hispanics that, in the past, would seem funny or entertaining, are now no longer considered so. However, the same sensitivity seems to be lacking with regard to Native Americans.

For example, would anyone ever consider naming a sports team the Frito Banditos or the Little Black Sambos? Would any team consider using those characters as mascots? It does not seem likely. Yet colleges and universities as well as professional sports teams frequently use Native American terms to do just that. This is particularly true in professional baseball and football. Examples include the Cleveland Indians and the Atlanta Braves, who are famous for their tomahawk chop to rally the team. Professional football uses Native American logos for the Kansas City Chiefs and the Washington Redskins.

It would be unconceivable to purposely insult the racial and religious values of African Americans, Hispanics, or even women. However, according to the National Coalition on Racism in Sports and Media, very little progress has been made to educate teams, fans, coaches, and the general public about the offensive nature Native American logos and mascots present. The public has historically been conditioned by the sports industry, educational institutions, and the media to trivialize indigenous culture as common and harmless entertainment. These groups somehow fail to recognize that using Native American names and depictions to identify teams, particularly caricatures, shows a lack of respect for the history of Native Americans and diminishes the importance of certain social positions, such as the tribal leader or "chief."

Apparently this inconsistency is being noticed, and at least six universities have changed their logos and/or mascots of the university athletic program, including the University of Illinois. Perhaps Americans are realizing that the historical insensitivity toward Native Americans has to stop and that they should be treated like other minority groups in this country.

While urban areas provide better opportunities for some, as evidenced by the lower unemployment rates for Native Americans who live in cities compared to those on the reservation, moving to these locations often entails other costs. Native Americans in cities do not always improve their standard of living because housing, food, clothing, and healthcare are more expensive in urban areas.[25]

CASINO GAMBLING

One area that has served as a respite for some tribal members has been the increase of gambling casinos on reservations. For many tribes, commercial gambling is the only viable source of employment and revenue. Under the 1988 Gaming Regulatory Act, states must negotiate gambling agreements with reservations and cannot prohibit any gambling already allowed under state law. In 2000, 201 tribes in over twenty-one states were operating a variety of gambling operations, such as blackjack, roulette tables, sports betting, slot machines, and high stakes bingo. In 2013, according to the National Indian Gaming Commission, about 250 tribes and villages operated casinos. The booming gambling industry netted almost $11 billion in 2000, $22 billion in 2006, $28 billion in 2013,[26] and nearly $31 billion in 2018.[27]

While some tribes have done well, some recent research has found that casino revenue can actually increase the poverty of some tribal members. Many of the factors discussed earlier play a role in steady employment, such as poor health—Native Americans have the highest rates of obesity and diabetes of any group, and more than 14 percent of Native Americans are in poor health, according to the Department of Health and Human Services, compared with 10 percent of the general population. Added to this problem is the lack of access to adequate medical care—27 percent of Native Americans under the age of 65 lack health insurance, compared to 17 percent for non-Native Americans, and the realities of steady employment become apparent. However, even those tribes that have been successful with casino gambling may be inadvertently contributing to the problem. As the casinos have become more successful, whereby tribal members receive their share of the profits, the incentive to find steady employment decreases. This problem becomes readily apparent if the profits received are not sufficient to live on.

A few successful casinos have had staggering success, like the 493 members of the Connecticut Mashantucket Pequot Indians, whose Foxwoods Resort Casino provides generous benefits to anyone who can establish that he or she is at least one-sixteenth Pequot. In fact, the impact of the Pequot casino extends far beyond individual tribal members. The casino is now one of the largest taxpayers in the state and also one of its largest employers.[28] The tribe has also donated money to a variety of charities and paid for many improvements in the state's infrastructure, such as roads leading to the casino and being indirectly responsible for a host of ancillary industries surrounding the area.

In other states, Native American casinos have contributed money to create childcare programs, housing, roads, scholarships, health clinics, and water systems for their people. Revenues also fund tribal law enforcement, firefighting, and other services.

While the success of casinos owned by Native Americans seems readily apparent, the National Indian Gaming Association states that the tribes that make substantial profits from gambling amounts to less than 1 percent of total Native Americans. The more typical picture is of moderately successful gambling operations associated with tribes whose social and economic needs are overwhelming.[29]

The main criticism against Indian casinos is the concern that organized crime will infiltrate the industry, and that casinos will become a magnet for other criminal activities. While only limited research exists on a direct relationship between Indian gaming and criminal justice on reservations, limited evidence does exist that shows the relationship between Indian gaming and organized crime.[30]

Allegations of corruption, money laundering, and loan sharking have been made against various tribes. For example, Asian-based organized crime has been linked to loan sharking and other forms of exploitation of Asian customers at the Mohegan Sun and Foxwoods Casinos in Connecticut.[31] An added problem, critics point out, is that Indian casinos are self-regulated, and the supervision offered by the National Indian Gaming Commission, the Internal Revenue Service, and other regulatory agencies is limited due to funding and jurisdictional issues.[32] Despite these claims, no definitive evidence exists of a connection between Indian gaming and organized crime.[33]

What is significant about the research linking Native American gaming and crime on reservations relates to the delay between the startup of a tribally owned casino and a large increase in crime and gambling in counties near an Indian casino.[34]

Despite the public's perception that Native American casinos earn huge profits, only a few tribes see substantial rewards for their efforts.

Indian-Controlled Casinos and Sports Betting

A recent issue related to casino gambling involves the legality of sports betting. For nearly thirty years, federal law allowed the tribes to operate casinos dominated by slot machines and blackjack tables. A 2017 Supreme Court decision made it possible for states to allow legal gambling on sports. However, such a decision could impact those states that already have agreements in place with Native American tribes that give them exclusive control over gambling. This is particularly true in places like Connecticut, where the Mashantucket Pequot and Mohegan Tribes, who operate large casinos, argue that they have the exclusive right to offer sports betting. Should the state decide to offer this option to other businesses, it would violate the compact agreement between the tribes and the government. Given that the tribes paid the state nearly $275 million in 2017 and represents one of the largest employers in the state, the implications are significant. Under the agreement, as long as the state does not allow any other slot machines or commercial casinos, the tribes are obligated to share 25 percent of their slot machine revenue with the state.[35]

CHECKPOINT

- One of the more promising pathways for success of Native Americans relates to casino gambling. The data indicate that while some tribes are enormously successful, often becoming the largest employer in some states, recent legislative efforts to legalize sports betting represents a challenge to the monopoly that many tribes have had with states regarding this practice.

EDUCATIONAL ACHIEVEMENT

As it has been with the rest of their lives, education for Native Americans has been in the control of the federal and state governments. Unfortunately, the lack of understanding of the social, cultural, political, and economic differences between Native Americans and other groups has resulted in poor management of Native American children's educational experiences. Part of the problem has been funding; Indian education programs are typically ignored or underfunded. Additionally, there are few Native American teachers, and curriculum decisions do not take into account the unique position of Native American students. As with the way Whites have always treated this group, U.S. educational policies appear to reflect the insistence that Native Americans should assimilate and ignore the celebration of their heritage. It is not surprising that Native American students have the highest dropout rate of any racial or ethnic group. According to the Postsecondary National Policy Institute, in 2018: only 10 percent of Native Americans attain bachelor's degrees and only 17 percent attain associate's degrees. According to the available data, enrollment numbers and participation rates for Native Americans—already lower than any other measured group—continue to decline. For instance, the higher education participation rate of Native American students went from 23 percent in 2015–2016 to just 19 percent in 2016–2017. Additionally, in 2000, about 30 percent of Native Americans age 25 to 29 had attained at least an associate's or bachelor's degree. In 2017, that number fell to 27 percent. Moreover, the percentage of Native Americans who had attained an associate's degree or higher in 2017 was 27 percent, compared to 54 percent for White students. Compared to White students, about 42 percent of whom attained at least a bachelor's degree in 2017, only about 16 percent of Native American students achieved that level of success.

Additionally, completion rates for Native American students fall below those of their White counterparts. For instance, about 23 percent of first-time, full-time Native American students attending four-year institutions beginning in 2008 graduated within four years, compared to nearly 44 percent for White students. Approximately 41 percent of Native American students graduated within six years, compared to nearly 63 percent of White students. Native American students are less likely to be prepared for college as they are more likely to attend high schools that offer little to no access to Advanced Placement or college prep courses. They are also more likely to need financial aid than white students and are most likely to be the first person in their family to attend college.[36]

This comes at a time when the national graduation rate for public schools is at an all-time high of 74.7 percent. A 2013 report titled *Second Chances: Turning Dropouts into Graduates* shows that there has been considerable success in addressing dropout rates since 2000. In fact, from 2000 to 2010, the graduation rates for African Americans increased more than 16 percent, while for Hispanic/Latino students, it increased 13 percent. The only group that did not narrow the gap with White students was Native Americans. Even today, Native Americans have the lowest high school graduation rates of any group, at 46 percent. The next lowest group is that of Hispanics/Latinos at 63 percent.[37]

In response to this problem, federal legislation was enacted to create institutions that recognize the importance of Native American culture. In 1968 the Navajo Nation created the first tribally controlled college, now called Diné College. Other tribal colleges quickly developed.

Most of these tribal colleges began as two-year institutions and have open admissions policies. However, the data indicate that even with the benefits of attending a Tribal College, completion rates still lag behind those of White students.

HEALTHCARE

From the beginning of their interactions with Whites, Native Americans have been susceptible to disease and illness. In the early part of the twentieth century, there were a number of epidemics, particularly tuberculosis, that killed thousands of American Indians. By the end of the twentieth century, the health of Native Americans improved due to increased standards of living and an increase in immunizations. While physical diseases such as measles and diphtheria were brought under control, social problems have gripped this population. Alcoholism, domestic violence, and mental disorders have plagued Native Americans, particularly in the 1980s and 1990s.[38]

For instance, in the late 1980s, the Indian Health Service, a division of the U.S. Public Health Service, reported that the number of deaths of Native Americans due to alcoholism was four times greater than what was reported for the general population. Additionally, suicide rates among Native Americans were 77 percent higher than the national average. More recently, diabetes and HIV have become prominent issues for Native Americans.

In the mid-1990s, the Indian Health Service reported that Native Americans were about three times more likely to be diagnosed with diabetes than Whites. Healthcare is provided by the Indian Health Service, which itself is a division of the Department of Health and Human Services.

Today, according to the Indian Health Service, the American Indian and Alaska Native people have long experienced lower health status when compared with other Americans. Lower life expectancy and the disproportionate disease—for example, heart disease, unintentional injuries, and diabetes—are leading causes of American Indian and Alaska Native deaths. American Indians and Alaska Natives born today have a life expectancy that is 5.5 years less than the U.S. all-races population (73.0 years to 78.5 years, respectively). American Indians and Alaska Natives continue to die at higher rates than other Americans in many categories, including chronic liver disease and cirrhosis, diabetes mellitus, unintentional injuries, assault/homicide, intentional self-harm/suicide, and chronic lower respiratory diseases.[39]

In addition, about 20 percent of American Indians and Alaska Natives have two or more chronic health problems, including obesity, diabetes, smoking, and alcoholism. American Indians and Alaska Natives have an infant death rate that is 60 percent higher than the rate for Whites and in 2017, the tuberculosis rate for American Indians was more than six times the rate for Whites.[40] While these health problems are primarily related to lifestyle, meaning they can be effectively remedied, the challenge is that most American Indians and Alaska Natives have limited or no access to health care. According to the Indian Health Service, more than 40 percent of American Indians have no access to medical care.[41]

It is important to note that not all Indian Health Service facilities meet the healthcare needs of Native Americans. Moreover, not all reservations or communities have medical clinics or hospitals, and the ones that exist are often small with outdated equipment.[42] Part of the problem stems from a lack of funding. Because of the poor salaries and inadequate equipment, there is a shortage of doctors, nurses, and pharmacists in clinic reservations which affects the quality and continuity of healthcare for Native Americans. For example, according to a report by the United States Commission on Civil Rights, the mental health challenges facing Native Americans, including suicide, depression, and other needs, are considerable. This calls for mental health professionals to treat such conditions. However, Native Americans have approximately 101 mental health professionals per 100,000 people, compared to 173 per 100,000 people for Whites.[43]

As it relates to healthcare, substantial increases are proposed to address the lack of adequate facilities and equipment, along with improved sanitation facilities to address chronic health problems in communities without adequate sanitation, along with the augmentation of the Purchase/Referred Care program, which is designed to provide essential healthcare services to tribal members. In all, this ambitious effort attempts to address many of the challenges Native Americans currently face.[44]

CHECKPOINT

- By virtually any measure, Native Americans continue to lag behind all other categories, including other minorities. Native Americans are more likely to be poor, unemployed, and have a variety of health-related problems; they are least likely to have health insurance, and are less likely to graduate high school or college than Whites, Blacks, Hispanics, or Asians. Moreover, while some tribes have benefited from the development of casino gambling, a recent ruling by the Supreme Court opens the door for states to legalize sports betting beyond the confines of the tribes that own casinos.

NATIVE AMERICANS AND THE CRIMINAL JUSTICE SYSTEM

One of the more intriguing aspects about Native Americans relates to the study of crime. While there is data collected on victims, arrests, crimes known to the police, and information on inmates, one must remember that these individuals are typically not those who live on reservations. Rather, they are Native Americans and Alaska Natives who live off the reservation. This may seem like a subtle difference, but crime reporting and the administration of justice on tribal lands is a different proposition than what occurs in U.S. cities and towns. While data is collected on crime that occurs on tribal land, and while the FBI does get involved in criminal cases on reservations, historically, accurate data has been difficult to come by.

Fortunately, in 2010, the Tribal Law and Order Act was signed into law, which requires the Bureau of Justice Statistics to create a tribal data collection system and to support tribal participation in national records-keeping. The law requires the director to consult with Indian tribes to determine the best ways of collecting the data, who then must report to Congress about what is known about tribal crime. In one of the first technical reports, published in July 2015, the Bureau of Justice Statistics found that at midyear 2014, a total of

566 tribes in the 48 contiguous states and in Alaska participated in the project. The tribes, in turn, were eligible for funding and services from the Bureau of Indian Affairs.

The tribal justice system in Indian country varies across tribal nations and regions. The authority to prosecute, to make arrests, and other jurisdictional matters, along with whether or not the reservation is a federally recognized one, if there exist tribal communities and identified trust lands, all contribute to how a crime is investigated and prosecuted. What also matters is the type of crime committed, whether the offender or the victim(s) is a tribal member, and the state in which the offense occurred. Because federally recognized tribes are sovereign, crimes committed in Indian country are often subject to concurrent jurisdictions among multiple agencies.[45]

In 2017 the Office of Inspector General issued a report about the Department of Justice's efforts with regard to the Tribal Law and Order Act. It found that there continues to be a lack of coordination between federal authorities and tribes in accordance with the act. The report also found that federal agents assigned to reservations were not adequately trained in either the Act or the jurisdictional issues created by it. The report also found that many of the problems that existed with regard to the lack of prosecution of violent crimes, along with standardized data collection procedures, continued to be problematic despite the Act and the government's promises of collaboration.

Perhaps most importantly, a 2018 report indicated that U.S. Attorneys declined to prosecute about half of all cases on reservations prior to the Tribal Law and Order Act. In 2016, the latest figures available, the data show that about 46 percent of cases were declined by U.S. Attorneys. While this is an improvement by four percent, it is only a marginal one. These cases included more than 550 for assault (which includes domestic violence) and sexual assault cases, more than any other type of crime. Prosecutors explained that the decision not to prosecute these cases was the result of a lack of evidence.[46]

The Bureau of Justice Statistics also produced a report in 2014 using some of the data collected in an effort to examine crimes in the federal system. This report showed that the FBI investigated about half of the 6,137 Indian-country suspects on various incidents referred to the U.S. Attorney's office from 2009 to 2011. The number of suspects in such cases increased from 1,940 to 2,220 between 2009 and 2011. Additionally, the number of defendants in forty-eight federal district courts increased from 1,235 in 2009 to 1,395 in 2011. These figures suggest that the cooperation between tribes and the federal authorities has improved since the tribes were willing to have an increased number of cases resolved in federal court rather than in tribal ones. However, the report in 2017 raises questions about the actual level of improvement that has taken place.[47]

An important element of tribal self-government is jurisdiction over incidents that take place on reservations. For instance, there are currently separate laws governing the prosecution of Native American and non-Native American offenders for crimes that take place on reservations. Another area of concern involves the lack of attention paid to the victimization of Native Americans. As the data show, the rate of violent crime against Native Americans is substantially higher than for other minority groups. A third area of concern relates to the type and frequency of crimes committed by Native Americans. Clearly, crime appears to have become a consistent feature of social life for Native Americans.

CRIME RATES

There is substantially less information regarding Native Americans and crime compared to African Americans and Hispanics. In a report issued by the U.S. Department of Justice in 1997, the homicide rate for Native American males was almost three times higher than that for White males. Between 1992 and 1996, while the rest of the country was experiencing a decline in violent crime, the Native American population witnessed a dramatic increase in violent crime. According to the Bureau of Justice Statistics, the annual average violent crime rate among Native Americans was twice as high as that of Blacks (50 per 1,000 persons), 2.5 times higher than that for Whites (41 per 1,000 persons), and 4.5 times than that for Asians (22 per 1,000 persons).[48]

In 2017, according to the Uniform Crime Reports, American Indians and Alaskan natives committed crimes that resulted in 171,185 of the estimated 8,421,481 arrests, about 2 percent of the total non-reservation arrests. This population was responsible for about 1.8 percent of arrests for violent crime and 1.7 percent of arrests for property crimes. The most common types of arrests included those for drunkenness (30,632), assault (17,062), DUI (15,950), drug abuse (15,038), liquor law violations (9,705), and larcenies (13,242).[49] These crimes relate to alcohol, which will be discussed in a section later in the chapter.

VICTIMIZATION

According to information collected by the Bureau of Justice Statistics (BJS), during the 1990s, American Indians were likely to experience violent crimes at more than twice the rate of all other U.S. residents. The BJS reported that between 1992 and 1996 the average annual rate of violent victimizations among Indians (including Alaska Natives and Aleuts) was 124 per 1,000 residents age twelve years old and older, compared to 61 violent victimizations per 1,000 Blacks, 49 per 1,000 Whites, and 29 per 1,000 Asians.[50]

More recently, a BJS report on Native American crime between 1992 and 2002 found that the violent crime rate in every age group below thirty-five was significantly higher for Native Americans than for all persons. The report also found that among Native Americans age twenty-five to thirty-four, the rate of violent crime victimization was more than 2.5 times the rate for all persons the same age. Rates of violent victimization for both males and females were higher for Native Americans than for all races. Further, the rate of violent victimization among Native American women was more than double that among all women.[51] According to a study by the Bureau of Justice Statistics, the most recent data available on victimization rates for Native Americans, with regard to age, in all age groups Native Americans had higher rates of violent crime victimization than other groups. The rate was highest at 155 per 1,000 people for Native Americans ages eighteen to twenty-four, compared to the highest rate in the twelve-to-seventeen age group for all races (94 per 1,000). Among the elderly, Native Americans age fifty-five or older had a violent crime rate that was three times that for all races (22 per 1,000 compared to 8 per 1,000).[52]

As previously mentioned, in terms of the race of the offender and the relationship with the victim, Native Americans who were victims of violent crime were more likely to be victimized by a stranger than an intimate partner. Strangers committed 42 percent of the violent crimes against Native Americans from 1992 to 2001, while an acquaintance committed about one-third of all violence against Native Americans. Only about 20 percent of the victimizations of Native Americans came as a result of a relationship between the victim and the offender.[53]

With regard to race, crime against Native Americans also tends to be interracial, whereas other forms of victimization with other races tends to be intraracial. Nearly 88 percent of the victimizations against Native Americans were committed by White or African American offenders. Victims stated that Asians and other Native Americans were responsible for only13 percent of violent acts.

The problems relating to criminal behavior by Native Americans is not episodic; rather, it reflects the chronic condition many members of this population experience. For example, the recidivism rate of Native Americans was similar to those for all offenders, whether for a new arrest, conviction, or sentence to prison. An estimated 60 percent of Native Americans are arrested for a new crime—a felony or a serious misdemeanor—within three years of their release from state prison. Related to this is the fact that over one-third of Native Americans released from prison were returned to prison due to a parole or probation violation.[54]

THE ROLE OF ALCOHOL AND NATIVE AMERICAN CRIME

Alcohol use among Native Americans is not a recent development. Historically its use was limited to ceremonies and religious rituals.[55] Some tribes, for example, believed that drunkenness brought a purification of one's mind and heart which would also produce rain for crops.[56] However, the impact of alcohol abuse among Native Americans can be seen in physical diseases. One study found that alcoholism kills Native Americans at a rate five times higher than other Americans. It also kills people between the ages of twenty-five and thirty-five at ten times the rate of other young adults.[57] The relationship between alcohol consumption and violence is particularly noteworthy among Native Americans. Crimes such as rape, homicide, and suicide occur with a much higher frequency among this segment of the population than other segments. Alcohol is also involved in 75 percent of all fatal accidents, a number three times higher than that for non-Native Americans.[58]

Unfortunately, there is no single explanation for alcohol abuse among Native Americans. One of the most prevalent theories is that it is due to the loss of their culture. That is, in an attempt to deal with the psychological problems relating to being isolated by society and unable to achieve their goals, many Native Americans use alcohol to relieve feelings of anxiety and depression. The living conditions for many Native Americans also contribute to the need for self-medication through alcohol.

On the other hand, there are experts who contend that Native Americans do not live in a cultural vacuum. That is, every culture undergoes changes and even though Native Americans might have lost their culture over generations of time, it could also be the case that as they assimilate and move to cities, their identification with American culture can ease the stress they are experiencing because they have some type of cultural mooring.[59] This school of thought argues that alcohol abuse is more of a function of poor choices than a coping mechanism for dealing with the loss of one's culture.

According to some researchers, the government's response to alcohol abuse among Native Americans has been minimal despite the physical and social risks related to it. The government often criminalizes the byproduct behavior that comes as a result of alcohol abuse, such as homelessness, public intoxication, and liquor law violations.[60] Unfortunately, the solution then becomes arresting and incarcerating people for these symptomatic behaviors instead of addressing the larger issue of alcoholism and its causes.

QUESTIONING THE RELATIONSHIP BETWEEN NATIVE AMERICANS AND CRIME STATISTICS

A number of researchers question the official statistics regarding Native American crime. In fact, some go so far as to question whether Native Americans are actually overrepresented in the crime data. One group of scholars is critical of a widely cited report published by the Bureau of Justice Statistics (BJS) entitled *American Indians and Crime.* This report contends that American Indians over the age of twelve are twice as likely to be victims of violent crime than are members of all other racial and ethnic categories combined. Critics of this report contend that the actual rates of arrests for violence among American Indian youth are the same as those for White youth, and the murder rates of Indian people has remained constant for the last twenty years. Further, one must consider that American Indian victims of violent crime are most likely attacked by non-Indian offenders—which makes the prosecution of crimes against American Indians difficult, especially if it occurs on Indian land. Finally, critics of the BJS report argue that the highest rates of violence occur in urban settings, not on reservations. Nevertheless, the perception that Native Americans perpetuate a higher proportion of crime is a common assertion in the media.[61]

Some experts even believe that federal surveys may not be the most effective tool to measure crime among Native Americans on reservations due to a host of logistical and methodological problems. For instance, the number of crimes known among Native Americans and the size of the population on the reservation used to calculate arrest rates can produce exaggerated crime estimates.[62] This can easily create the impression that crime is more common, and a more serious problem, on reservations than in other places.

In an attempt to remedy the methodological problems stemming from using aggregated data, particularly with small populations, an in-depth analysis of a decade of arrest data for one tribe on one reservation was conducted by a team of researchers. The findings showed that violent and non-violent juvenile crime was far below the estimates in the BJS report. They also showed that juvenile crime in this community, like many communities across the country, was the result of a small group of repeat offenders.[63]

NATIVE AMERICANS AND THE POLICE

Perhaps the most fascinating—and complicated—issue surrounding Native Americans relates to the jurisdiction and composition of tribal courts. When Congress passed Public Law 280 (PL 280) in 1953, criminal and civil jurisdiction over tribal lands was transferred to local governments. This gave local law enforcement the authority over Indian communities. In places where PL 280 did not apply, either the Bureau of Indian Affairs or the tribal councils were to provide law enforcement officers.[64]

As was mentioned, these varying jurisdictional boundaries present problems related to the prosecution of offenders depending on whether the person is a Native American, whether the crime took place on Indian land, and whether local law enforcement, tribal councils, or the Bureau of Indian Affairs has authority over that particular area. Problems emerge, for example, when a non–Native American commits a crime on Indian land. In those situations, a criminal act normally prosecuted by state and local governments is considered an Indian issue, rendering no criminal charges against the offender. When a Native American commits a crime on Indian land and is convicted by tribal courts, the Indian Civil Rights Act of 1968 usually applies, which means tribal criminal sentences can last no more than one year in custody and a $5,000 fine, regardless of the crime.[65] Clearly both sets of circumstances are not in the interest of justice, nor do they send the appropriate message about accountability of offenders' behavior.

According to the National Congress of American Indians, law enforcement on tribal lands is difficult to say the least. Police in Indian country not only have jurisdictional challenges, meaning they must answer to multiple authorities, but they patrol some of the most desolate parts of the country, often without resources or backup. For instance, there are only 2,380 Bureau of Indian Affairs and tribal uniformed officers available to serve millions of Native Americans covering over 56 million square miles. It is estimated that in order to provide a minimum of coverage to this area, at least 4,290 officers are needed. Compared to officers in non-Indian communities, tribal lands have half the number of officers per 1,000 residents.

Law enforcement authority varies by the location of where the crime was committed, whether or not the victim and/or the offender is a tribal member, and the nature of the crime (whether a felony or a misdemeanor was committed). Officers who have jurisdiction on reservations include the following:

> *Tribal Security Officers.* These are employed by the tribe and have security-related duties. At times they are given the ability to enforce tribal law and order codes by the tribal government, but they do not have arrest powers.
>
> *Tribal Police Officers* are also employed by tribal governments, but these officers have arrest powers over tribal members committing violations of tribal law and other codes committed on reservations. Such officers are trained at a formal police academy.
>
> *Federally Deputized Police Officers.* These officers present a type of hybrid police presence in that they are hired by the tribal governments but are also deputized by and work for federal agencies, such as the Bureau of Indian Affairs and Special Law Enforcement Commissions. They are able to enforce federal laws both on and off the reservation and can arrest non-Indians and Indians for violation of federal laws.[66]

THE ADMINISTRATION OF JUSTICE: TRIBAL COURTS

There are also differences in philosophy between tribal courts and American criminal courts. Over the past two hundred years, the federal government has established a pattern of taking over the jurisdiction of an increasing number of crimes, removing them from tribal authority, and giving itself the power to punish offenders. This contradicts the parameters of treaties signed by the federal government giving Native tribes the right to have their own separate system of justice.[67] In 1953, Congress passed Public Law 280, without tribal consent, which offered states the opportunity to assume jurisdiction over reservations within their borders. This law stipulates that law enforcement for Native reservations is typically handled by state police and county or state courts rather than through the tribe. This law has created concern that courts are treating Native people and Whites unequally.[68]

As sovereign entities, Native tribes have the right to organize and maintain their own laws and law enforcement agencies; however, not every tribe in the United States has the funding for their own tribal court or police system. Essentially, a Tribal Court is established for American Indian and Alaska Native tribes for resolving civil, criminal, and other legal matters. There is significant variation in the types of tribal courts and how they apply tribal laws. Some are like non-Indian courts, where court procedures are used, while others use traditional Native means of solving disputes.

Finally, there are also a number of Courts of Indian Offenses. These are established by the Bureau of Indian Affairs for those tribes who do not have their own tribal courts. In 2012, 39 of the 109 federally recognized tribes in California either had a tribal court or had access to one through a tribal coalition. The number of tribal courts in California has more than doubled since 2002, from nine to twenty-two.[69]

NATIVE AMERICANS AND THE CORRECTIONAL SYSTEM

According to the Bureau of Justice Statistics, in 2016 there were an estimated 2,540 inmates were held in eighty Indian country jails, up 1.2 percent from the 2,510 inmates at midyear 2015 in seventy-six facilities. During June 2016, the number of inmates admitted into Indian country jails (9,640) was nearly four times the average daily population (ADP) at 2,480. Most persons held in Indian country jails were convicted inmates, and fewer than half were awaiting court action on a current charge.

Since 2010, about a third of Indian country jail inmates have been held for a violent offense, a decline from 40 percent in 2007. At midyear 2016, domestic violence (14 percent) and aggravated or simple assault (10 percent) accounted for nearly one-fourth of all inmates. Inmates held for rape or sexual assault (1 percent) and other violent offenses (5 percent) accounted for an additional 6 percent of the jail population. Inmates held for DWI/DUI declined from 16 percent of the total inmate population in 2000 to 7 percent at midyear 2016. From 2010 to 2015, approximately 5 percent of inmates were held for a drug law violation. By midyear 2016, the percentage of inmates held for a drug violation had increased to 8 percent. At midyear 2016, 23 percent of inmates were held for public intoxication. Although males accounted for the largest proportion of the inmate population in Indian country jails, the percentage of female jail inmates increased from 20 percent of all inmates in 2000 to 27 percent in 2016.[70]

SUMMARY

This chapter examined the history of Native Americans in this country as well as the ways in which they become involved in the criminal justice system. The position of Native Americans is rather unique in that while they are supposed to have a separate system of justice to address problems relating to crime, increasingly, the federal government is encroaching upon tribal authority to handle a variety of tasks. We have also seen that in many ways Native Americans are a forgotten people. Historically, the United States seems to have had a sense of entitlement when it came to taking land that belonged to Native Americans. Social progress was seen as more important than preserving the heritage and authority of Native Americans. Even when treaties were signed that stipulated the rights and privileges of Native Americans, Whites historically ignored the agreements and used force when Native Americans refused to capitulate.

Control over Native Americans has historically fallen to the federal government, which has created the Bureau of Indian Affairs to regulate most of the aspects of life on and off the reservation. Other agencies, such as the Department of Health and Human Services, the Public Health Service, and the Indian Health Service, all attempt to address the many issues surrounding Native Americans.

While Native Americans have made an effort to assimilate, their experiences have resulted in a number of social problems. Many Native Americans still lag behind Whites economically and educationally. There are higher dropout rates for Native Americans than other minority groups, fewer who graduate from college, and even fewer in professional careers. Moreover, a large percentage of Native Americans live at or below the poverty level. Native Americans also suffer from a variety of health problems, including tuberculosis, alcoholism, mental illness, and other disorders.

Many of these limitation and problems result in a significant involvement with the criminal justice system, either as victims or as offenders. As was mentioned, jurisdictional problems confuse the issues of justice. Thus, while not a large segment of the population in terms of victimization or as offenders, like their African American and Hispanic counterparts, this group is overrepresented in the crime statistics.

YOU MAKE THE CALL

NATIVE AMERICAN INMATES AND THEIR RELIGIOUS RITUALS

Consider the following scenario. Debate the pros and cons of all options and decide what you would do.

Imagine you are the Cultural Diversity Officer with the Federal Bureau of Prisons. Part of your job centers around ensuring that correctional institutions remain sensitive to the cultural and religious needs of inmates. You receive a complaint from a Native American inmate in a federal correctional institution who states that his religious beliefs are being denied. This particular inmate, along with several other Native Americans in the institution, practice what is known as the Pipe Religion. Pipe Religion revolves around the use of the Sacred Pipe in seven specific rituals, in particular the sweat lodge ceremony, which is the traditional way of cleansing the body, mind, and spirit. By sweat and prayer, Native Americans cleanse their bodies of toxins and their minds of negativities, heighten their spirits, and come into a balanced relationship with themselves, the earth, and everything that surrounds them.

Although other correctional facilities provide a sweat lodge for Indian inmates, the prisoners are restricted as to when and how long the sweat lodges can be used. As a result, Sacred Pipe ceremonies—that normally span several days—cannot be performed.

Many correctional officials and other experts hold the position that freedom of religion is inferior to the state's interest in maintaining security and order within the prison.

Questions

1. How do you respond to the inmate's complaint? Do you allow the religious practice, or do you argue that inmates lose some of their constitutional protections once they are convicted?
2. What liability does the institution bear if someone becomes ill or injured during the course of one of these rituals?
3. Should taxpayer money be used to allow inmates to practice their religion?
4. Are correctional officials as well as the public at greater physical risk by denying inmates the opportunity to practice their religion?

KEY TERMS

Battle at Little Big Horn
Battle at Wounded Knee
Bureau of Indian Affairs
Dawes Act
Fort Laramie Treaty
Ghost Dance religion
Indian Claims Commission

Indian Health Service
Indian Removal Act 1830
Red Power movement
setoffs
Termination Act
tribal court

DISCUSSION QUESTIONS

1. What role, if any, does casino gambling have on improving the lives of Native Americans? Is it really a solution to the problems relating to poverty and unemployment that is characteristic of Native Americans?
2. In the recent era of celebrating individual differences and cultures, why do you think the federal government has forced Native Americans to assimilate into mainstream American culture? What impact do you think this has on the preservation of Native American culture?
3. Should there be a separate system of justice for Native American tribes, or should the federal government retain authority to hear all cases? Should there be a distinction between crimes committed on reservations and those outside them?
4. Do you think Native Americans should have their own educational system, such as tribal colleges? Why or why not?
5. Should Native Americans who commit crimes on reservations be judged differently from those off the reservation? Why or why not?
6. What obligation, if any, should the federal government have to improve the lives of Native Americans on reservations? Defend your position one way or the other.

FOR FURTHER READING

Brown, D. *Bury My Heart at Wounded Knee*. New York: Holt, Rinehart and Winston, 1971.

Nagel, J. *American Indian Ethnic Renewal: Red Power and the Resurgence of Identity and Culture*. New York: Oxford University Press, 1996.

Nielsen, M. O., and R. A. Silverman, eds. *Native Americans, Crime and Justice*. Boulder, CO: Westview Press, 1996, 58–74.

Ross, Luana. *Inventing the Savage: The Social Construction of Native American Criminality*. Austin: University of Texas Press, 1998.

NOTES

1. R. Strickland, "The Eagle's Empire: Sovereignty, Survival, and Self-Governance in Native American Law and Constitutionality," in R. Thornton (ed.), *Studying Native America: Problems and Prospects* (Madison, WI: University of Wisconsin Press, 1998), 247–70.
2. Ibid.
3. Ibid.
4. R. Thornton, "Demographic Antecedents of the 1890 Ghost Dance," *American Sociological Review* 46 (February 1981): 88–96.

5. B. Duran, E. Duran, and M. Yellow Horse Braveheart, "Native Americans and the Trauma of History," in Thornton, *Studying Native America*, 60–78.

6. Ibid.

7. Ibid.

8. Henry C. Dennis, *The American Indian 1492–1970: A Chronology and Fact Book* (Dobbs Ferry, NY: Oceana, 1971).

9. Indian Land Tenure Foundation, *General Allotment Act*. Available at: https://www.iltf.org/resources/land-tenure-history/allotment

10. Native Voices, "President Roosevelt Signs the Indian Reorganization Act," Available at: https://www.nlm.nih.gov/nativevoices/timeline/452.html

11. Ibid.

12. Judith Nies, *Native American History: A Chronology of the Vast Achievements of a Culture and Their Links to World Events* (New York: Ballantine Books, 1996), 357.

13. W. Washburn, "A Fifty-Year Perspective on the Indian Reorganization Act," *American Anthropologist* 86 (1984): 279–89.

14. J. Nagel, *American Indian Ethnic Renewal: Red Power and the Resurgence of Identity and Culture* (New York: Oxford University Press, 1996); D. Drabelle, "The Trade of the Tribes," *Washington Post National Weekly Edition* 24 (September 8, 1997): 34.

15. S. W. Perry, *Tribal Crime Data Collection Activities*, U.S. Department of Justice, Office of Justice Programs (Washington, DC: Bureau of Justice Statistics, 2015). Available at: https://www.bjs.gov/index.cfm?ty=pbdetail&iid=5323

16. Schilling, Vincent, "Census Releases Latest Population Numbers: Native Americans are at 2.09%, " Indian Country Today. Available at: https://newsmaven.io/indiancountrytoday/news/census-releases-latest-population-numbers-native-americans-are-at-2-09-uf7gL2XbP0SRzFmI-7jXUXQ/

17. Jens Manuel Krogstad, "One in Four Native Americans and Alaska Natives Are Living in Poverty," Pew Research Center, June 13, 2014. Available at: http://www.pewresearch.org/fact-tank/2014/06/13/1-in-4-native-Americans-and-alaska-natives-are-living-in-poverty/

18. Luana Ross, *Inventing the Savage: The Social Construction of Native American Criminality* (Austin: University of Texas Press, 1998), 16–19.

19. U.S. Department of Commerce, "American Community Survey 2017," American Fact Finder, U.S. Census Bureau, 2019. Available at: https://factfinder.census.gov/faces/tableservices/jsf/pages/productview.xhtml?src=bkmk

20. Ibid.

21. Ibid.

22. National Center for Education Statistics, "Fast Facts," 2018. Available at: https://nces.ed.gov/fastfacts/display.asp?id=805

23. Ibid.

24. Hansi Lo Wang, "Native Americans on Tribal Lands Are 'The Least Connected' to High Speed Internet," National Public Radio, December 6, 2018. Available at: https://www.npr.org/2018/12/06/673364305/native-americans-on-tribal-land-are-the-least-connected-to-high-speed-internet

25. Ibid.

26. "Of Slots and Sloth: How Cash Casinos Make Native Americans Poorer," *The Economist*, January 17, 2015. Available at: http://www.economist.com/news/united-states/21639547-how-cash-casinos-makes-native-Americans-poorer-slots-and-sloth

27. Kevin Draper, Tina Arango, and Alan Blinder, "Indian Tribes Dig In to Gain Their Share of Sports Betting," *New York Times*, May 21, 2018. Available at: https://www.nytimes.com/2018/05/21/sports/sports-betting-indian-casinos.html

28. F. Carstensen, *Economic Impact of the Mashantucket Pequot Tribal Nation Operations in Connecticut* (Storrs: Connecticut Center for Economic Analysis, 2000).

29. Ibid.

30. M. Rezendes, "Gambling and Crime," *CitizenLink*, December 27, 2000. Available at: http://www.family.org; J. Unseem, "The Big Gamble: Have American Indians Found Their New Buffalo?" *Fortune*, October 2, 2000.

31. M. Burgard and R. Green, "More Arrests in Loan Scheme: Casino Patrons Are Victimized," *Hartford Courant*, March 13, 2002.

32. Rezendes, "Gambling and Crime."

33. H. M. Buffalo, "Indian Gaming Success in the North," in *Oklahoma Supreme Court Sovereignty Symposium 2002: Language and the Law* (Oklahoma City: Supreme Court of Oklahoma, 2002), III 22-III, 40; G. A. Fine, *Review of Indian Gaming Crimes*, Office of Inspector General, Report Number 1-2-1-06, July 3, 2001.

34. W. N. Evans and J. H. Topeleski, "The Social and Economic Impact of Native American Casinos," National Bureau of Economic Research Working Paper 9198, 2002. Available at: http://wnetc.mcc.ac.uk/WoPEc/data/Papers/nbrnberwo9198.html

35. Draper, Arango, and Blinder, "Indian Tribes Dig In."

36. Postsecondary National Policy Institute. *Factsheets: Native American Students*, 2019. Available at: https://pnpi.org/native-american-students/#

37. Diplomas Count, *Second Chances: Turning Dropouts into Graduates*, 2013. Available at http://www.edweek.org/media/diplomascount2013_release.pdf

38. L. Gould, "Alcoholism, Colonialism, and Crime," in *Native Americans and the Criminal Justice System*, ed. J. I. Ross and L. Gould (Boulder, CO: Paradigm Publishing, 2006), 87–102.

39. Bureau of Indian Affairs, Indian Health Services. *Fact Sheets: Disparities in Health*. Available at: https://www.ihs.gov/newsroom/factsheets/disparities/

40. Bureau of Indian Affairs, Indian Health Services. *Minority Health*. Available at http://minorityhealth.hhs.gov/omh/browse.aspx?lvl=3&lvlid=62

41. U.S. Department of Health and Human Services, Office on Women's Health. *American Indians/Alaska Natives*, July 16, 2012. Available at: http://www.womenshealth.gov/minority-health/American-indians/

42. R. Garcia Cano, "Watchdog: Staff Issues Affect Care at Reservation Hospitals," Associate Press, October 7, 2016. Available at https://apnews.com/68b5a09034c24c9a8a29fc4c46773889/watchdog-staff-issues-affect-care-reservation-hospitals

43. United States Commission on Civil Rights, *Broken Promises: Evaluating the Native American Healthcare System*, 2012. Available at: https://www.law.umaryland.edu/marshall/usccr/documents/cr122004024431draft.pdf

44. Ibid.

45. Ibid.

46. Associated Press, "Native American Women Still Facing Higher Rates of Crime," September 5, 2018. Available at: https://nypost.com/2018/09/05/native-american-women-still-facing-high-rates-of-crime/

47. Ibid.

48. L. Greenfield and S. K. Smith, *American Indians and Crime*, U.S. Department of Justice, Office of Justice Programs, Bureau of Justice Statistics, February 1999, NCJ 173386. Available at: https://www.bjs.gov/content/pub/pdf/aic.pdf

49. Federal Bureau of Investigation, *Crime in the United States 2017*, Table 43. U.S. Department of Justice, 2019. Available at: https://ucr.fbi.gov/crime-in-the-u.s/2017/crime-in-the-u.s.-2017/topic-pages/tables/table-43

50. Greenfield and Smith, *American Indians and Crime.*

51. Steven W. Perry, *A BJS Statistical Profile 1992–2002: American Indians and Crime* (Washington, DC: U. S. Bureau of Justice Statistics, 2004). Available at: https://www.bjs.gov/content/pub/pdf/aic02.pdf

52. Ibid.

53. Ibid.

54. Ann L. Pastore and Kathleen Maguire, *Sourcebook of Criminal Justice Statistics* (Washington, DC: U.S. Bureau of Justice Statistics, 2004). Available at: https://www.ncjrs.gov/pdffiles1/Digitization/208756NCJRS.pdf.

55. R. Snake, G. Hawkins, and S. LaBoueff, *Report on Alcohol and Drug Abuse: Final Report to the American Indian Policy Review Commission* (Washington, DC: U.S. Government Printing Office, 1976).

56. J. H. Parry, "Spanish Indian Policy in Colonial America: The Ordering of Society," in J. J. TePaske (ed.), *Three American Empires* (Durham, NC: Duke University Press, 1967), 109–26.

57. C. Grim, *Responding Through Collaborations*, a report delivered at the Tribal Leader Summit on Alcohol and Substance Abuse, Albuquerque, New Mexico, 2002.

58. Gould, "Alcoholism, Colonialism, and Crime."

59. S. Saggers and D. Gray, *Dealing with Alcohol: Indigenous Usage in Australia, New Zealand and Canada* (Cambridge, UK: Cambridge University Press, 1998).

60. Gould, "Alcoholism, Colonialism, and Crime."

61. Eileen Luna-Firebaugh, *Tribal Policing: Asserting Sovereignty, Seeking Justice* (Phoenix: University of Arizona Press, 2007).

62. R. A. Silverman, "Patterns of Native American Crime," in M. O. Nielsen and R. A. Silverman, (eds.), *Native Americans, Crime and Justice* (Boulder, CO: Westview Press, 1996), 58–74.

63. Luna-Firebaugh, *Tribal Policing.*

64. Ibid.

65. Ibid.

66. Hon. Marcy L. Khan, *New York Federal-State-Tribal Courts and Indian Nations Justice Forum*, 2014–2015. Available at: http://www.courts.ca.gov/documents/forum-20140821-materials.pdf

67. Ross, *Inventing the Savage.*

68. Ibid.

69. Khan, *New York Federal-State-Tribal Courts.*

70. Bureau of Justice Statistics, *Tribal Crime Data Collection Activities 2016–2018*, U.S. Department of Justice, 2018. Available at: https://www.bjs.gov/content/pub/pdf/tcdca1618.pdf

CHAPTER 7

WOMEN AND THE CRIMINAL JUSTICE SYSTEM

CHAPTER OBJECTIVES

After reading this chapter, you should be able to:

- Understand how women are a distinct culture
- Recognize the differences between male and female criminality and victimization
- Understand how females have overcome—and also continue to face—barriers with regard to being accepted as law enforcement officers
- Contrast the roles of males and females with regard to courtroom practices
- Understand the particular challenges facing women under correctional supervision

Women have faced much adversity in their fight for equal rights. Toward this end, much progress has been made, yet much work remains. Regarding criminal justice, females have historically been treated as an afterthought, with a few "evil women" entering the system. The situation is much different today. An increasing number of females are entering the criminal justice system, in turn providing distinct challenges for the system and multiple hurdles for female offenders.

THE FIGHT FOR RIGHTS

Females were largely taken for granted in the early part of U.S. history. The limited consideration of females is evidenced in the prohibition of women from voting, serving on juries, holding property, or making legal contracts. Further, the 1776 Declaration of Independence noted that all *men* are created equal, and the only reference to sexual category in the Constitution is in the **Nineteenth Amendment**, signed in 1920, which gave women the right to vote. Women were not considered persons protected by the Fourteenth Amendment to the Constitution, which provides equal protection of the law.[1]

The advancement of females in relation to these and related restrictions is largely attributable to **feminist movements**, which generally promote the idea that males and females should be politically, socially, and economically equal. The beginning of the first feminist movement of the nineteenth century is traced to a convention in Seneca Falls, New York, attended by roughly three hundred women intent on achieving equal rights for women. The group's focus was on property and suffrage. Attendees adopted a women-specific Declaration of Independence highlighting women's concerns. In the end, their efforts went formally unrecognized[2]; however, their voices were heard, in turn opening the doors for additional women's rights movements and the ultimate advancement of female interests.

Other forms of activism in support of woman's rights emerged following the gathering in Seneca Falls. For instance, in 1916, a group of feminists, then known as suffragists, organized into the National Women's Party and picketed the White House. This group of feminists consisted of two factions with differing goals. One faction sought reform of all institutions of society, while the other faction focused on winning the right to vote for females. The latter faction dominated the movement, and with passage of the 1920 amendment that gave women the right to vote, the group disintegrated. The United States lagged behind many other countries in granting women the right to vote, including New Zealand (women were first permitted to vote in 1893), Norway (1913), Canada (1917), Germany (1918), the United Kingdom (1918), and Sweden (1919).

Support for women's rights re-emerged in the 1960s and continues today. This wave has broad goals ranging from increasing employment opportunities for females to reducing the amount of violence against women. This movement is focused on meeting the needs of today's women and continues to shape public policy as it relates to gender equality. These movements have paid off in terms of the advancement of females. Table 7.1 highlights the accomplishments of several females who significantly impacted the criminal justice system.

To be sure, many other females have impacted the development of the criminal justice system. The individuals featured in the table are among those who have made the most significant contributions.

TABLE 7.1   INFLUENTIAL FEMALES IN THE HISTORY OF U.S. CRIMINAL JUSTICE

Mary Weed – The first woman administrator in U.S. corrections, Weed was the principal keeper of the Walnut Street Jail in 1793.

Charlotte E. Ray – In 1872 Ray became the first African-American woman admitted to the bar in the United States.

Lola G. Baldwin – In 1908 Baldwin became one of the United States' first female policewomen.

Alice Stubbins Wells – In 1910 Wells became one of the United States' first female policewomen.

Jane Addams – Addams's work improving social and living conditions for the poor was among the contributions that earned her a Nobel Peace Prize in 1931.

Dorothea Dix – During the nineteenth century Dix was extremely influential in advocating humanitarian reform in American mental institutions.

Sandra Day O'Connor – In 1981 O'Connor began serving as the first female Associate Justice of the Supreme Court of the United States.

Penny Harrington – In 1985 Harrington became the first woman in the United States to become chief of police in a large city when she was appointed to head the Portland (Oregon) Police Bureau.

Despite all this progress, females continue to face discrimination and challenges involving the criminal justice system. Among the problems currently faced by females are increased levels of drug addiction, poverty, racism, and incarceration. These troubles are pronounced with regard to the marginalized females in society.[3]

CHECKPOINT

- Females have had to overcome many barriers to obtain rights and to become more generally ingrained in society, particularly within the criminal justice system.

Many influential females have helped pave a path for future generations of women.

WOMEN AS A DISTINCT CULTURE

Family therapist and author John Gray published the best-selling book *Men Are From Mars, Women Are From Venus*. In the book, Gray discusses the differences between males and females, suggesting that men and women are as distant as planets of the solar system, and offers advice on how the differences between males and females can be overcome. Whether one agrees with Gray's assertions that there are substantial differences between men and women is their own prerogative. However, it cannot be denied that men and women are different in several forms and fashions.

There is some debate regarding whether or not women's culture is distinct from men's culture. At the most basic level, **culture** involves the sharing of norms, language, beliefs, values, behaviors, and material objects. Thus, the question is asked, do females differ from males with regard to culture? Researchers have identified differences between males and females with regard to each of these criteria, yet are the differences significant enough to warrant a women's culture distinct from men's culture? We believe there indeed exists a distinct women's culture, thus a chapter on females is included in this book. Nevertheless, we recognize the great number of similarities between males and females and appreciate the arguments of those who suggest that females are not culturally distinct from males. The deciding factor in our decision to include a chapter on females in this work was the distinct nature, treatment, and plight of females entering the criminal justice system. In many ways, the females who enter the justice system are different from the males who do so. Accordingly, females are worthy of directed scholarly attention.

Gender is a master status, as it cuts across all walks of life. It is a social characteristic that varies from one group to another and refers to femininity or masculinity. We are all labeled either "male" or "female," and with that label comes expectations of our behavior and images of what we are like. The labels often guide our behavior. Related to gender is **sex**, which relates to the biological characteristics that distinguish between males and females. You inherit your sex; you are socialized into your gender by the expectations and standards of the culture in which you live.

Females are considered a minority group in the United States despite there being more females than males in the population. How can this be? As mentioned earlier in this book, a minority group consists of a group of individuals who face discrimination based on members' cultural or physical characteristics. While progress has been made with regard to societal acceptance of women as equal to men, there remains a great deal of discrimination against females solely on the basis of gender.

The distinction between sex and gender generates debate regarding whether human behavior is mostly a product of biological influences or sociological ones. For instance, are females distinct from males in many ways due to biological factors, or are the differences attributable to the manner in which society treats both males and females? This issue of nature versus nurture is alive and well.

Aside from the obvious biological differences, females differ from males in a variety of ways. The psychological, biological, and sociological research literatures are filled with studies highlighting differences between males and females. Differences between males and females with regard to social factors are evident and relevant to the study of crime and justice. For instance, along with education levels, a major predictor of poverty is the sex of the individual who heads the family. Females, compared to males, are more likely to be poor, and poverty rates are highest for families headed by single women. Figure 7.1 depicts the income disparities for males and females. Divorce, births to single women, and the lower wages paid to females largely contribute to the increased level of poverty among females. These factors ultimately contribute to increased incarceration rates.

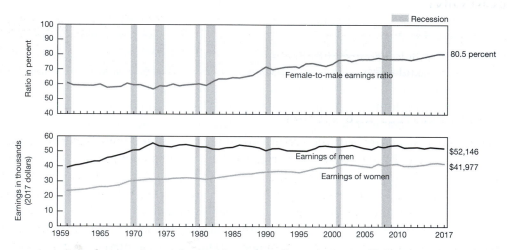

FIGURE 7.1 **Female-to-male earnings ratio and median earnings of full-time, year-round workers fifteen years and older by sex: 1960 to 2017**

Note: The data points are placed at the midpoints of the respective years. Data on earning on full-time, year-round workers are not readily available before 1960.

Source: U.S. Census Bureau, Current Population Survey, 1961 to 2018 Annual Social and Economic Supplements.

The criminal justice system has been mixed in its approach to recognizing distinctions between male and female criminals and crime. For example, there exists a wealth of research suggesting that females, to a greater extent than males, are given preferential treatment by police, prosecutors, and judges. On the other hand, the lack of consideration of female needs in prison and the belief that what explains male crime also explains female crime suggest that criminal justice professionals and criminologists believe females are no different from males.

The continuously emerging field of feminist criminology has aptly changed society's interpretation of differences between males and females regarding criminality. Too often, females are considered as only a control variable in criminological research.[4] While the consideration of male/female differences is appropriate, merely including females as a control variable says little about the distinct nature of female involvement in crime and criminal justice practices. The fields of criminology and criminal justice lag behind many other disciplines with regard to the acceptance of female scholarship as vital to the field of study. While feminist scholarship has grown in the past three decades, much of the work has been marginalized and relegated to specialty journals.[5] Females have been underrepresented in sociological and criminological journals dating back to 1895, with both male and female researchers more likely to focus on males than on females.[6]

CHECKPOINT

- There is debate regarding whether or not there is a distinct women's culture that differs from men's culture. Regardless, there are many differences between males and females, including females being considered a minority group.

FEMALE ARRESTEES AND VICTIMS

Females have historically been underrepresented in criminal behavior. Recent evidence suggests increased female involvement in crime; however, males continue to be responsible for the bulk of criminal behavior. Data from the 2017 Uniform Crime Report (UCR) suggest that females constituted 27 percent of all arrests. There was a notable difference in arrest patterns with regard to violent and property crimes. Specifically, females constituted roughly 36 percent of arrests for property crimes, yet only 20.5 percent of arrests for violent crimes. Females accounted for 24.3 percent of arrests for drug abuse violations.[7]

Arrest trend data highlight the increased level of female involvement in crime and the criminal justice system. Nationwide, there was a substantial decrease in the number of people arrested between 2008 and 2017. There were, however, substantial differences between males and females. The number of males arrested decreased 25.1 percent

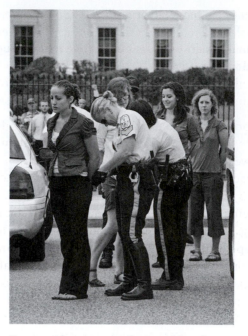

Recent evidence suggests increased female
involvement in crime compared to males.

between 2008 and 2017, compared to a decrease of only 14.2 percent in the number of
females arrested. During the same time frame, the number of males arrested for violent
crime fell 14 percent, yet the number of females arrested for violent crime decreased by
only 1.7 percent.[8] Again, despite these changes, it remains the case that men constitute
the bulk of offenders and arrestees. Nevertheless, these findings must be considered in
light of the fact that arrests do not necessarily explain criminal behavior. For instance,
it is believed by some researchers that despite increased arrests for females committing violent crimes, the typical female offender has not become increasingly violent
in recent history.[9] Arrests are largely influenced by police officer discretion, which certainly influences arrest statistics.

Increased female involvement in the criminal justice system has not happened by
chance. To be sure, there are several explanations for the fact that females are increasingly
represented in arrest statistics. Prominent among the explanations for recent trends in
female arrests are the following:

- Less-biased responses by criminal justice practitioners to criminal behavior
- Changes in law enforcement practices targeting less serious offenses
- Gender equality and more desire and opportunity to commit crime
- Increased economic marginalization of women
- Increased inner-city community disorganization

- Expanded opportunities for female-type crimes, for instance as they relate to increased consumerism
- Changes in the criminal underworld, for instance the reduced supply of male crime partners due to increased incarceration
- Trends in drug dependency, with drug addiction encouraging income-generating crime[10]

Each of these items helps explain the rise in female involvement in the criminal justice system, and each is worthy of greater empirical evaluation to determine the extent to which they have impacted females and the criminal justice system.

The distinction between males and females in the criminal justice system is obvious with regard to victimization rates, for instance, as females are notably more likely than males to be victimized by someone known to them rather than a stranger. The increased likelihood of women being violently victimized during domestic abuse cases largely contributes to these findings. Females are also far more susceptible to sex offenses than are males. **Acquaintance rape**, which involves an individual raping an acquaintance; **marital rape**, in which a man or woman rapes their spouse; and sexual abuse (including that against children) are of particular concern to females, who are also particularly vulnerable to specific types of violent crime, such as domestic violence and stalking. Females in some countries are not protected from domestic violence to the extent they are in the United States; for example, some Latin American countries excuse a man who murders his wife if she is caught engaging in adultery, and many countries around the globe offer limited protection for females in domestic violence cases. Such cases are often viewed and treated as private family matters.[11]

Females are more likely to be victimized by someone they know than by a stranger.

CHECKPOINT

- Males are arrested far more often than females; however, female involvement in the criminal justice system (including arrests) is increasing. Victimization rates also differ to some extent, particularly with regard to crime type.

WOMEN AND POLICING

There is debate regarding who deserves the title of the first female police officer. Alice Stebbens Wells arguably became the world's first policewoman when she began her career with the Los Angeles Police Department in 1910. Others claim that Portland's Lola Baldwin became the nation's first policewoman following her 1908 appointment as an officer in Portland, Oregon, and more recently it was suggested Marie Owens was the first policewoman in the United States when she was employed as a police officer in Chicago in the 1890s.[12] Regardless of who deserves the distinction, female involvement in policing prior to the time of Wells was restricted to roles as jailers and police matrons. By 1915 female police officers worked in twenty-five different U.S. cities, and in 1918 Ellen O'Grady became Police Commissioner of New York City.[13] The pioneering work of these and other female officers has paved the way for enhanced female involvement in policing, yet for several reasons, females remain very underrepresented in policing. A primary reason for the underrepresentation of females in policing is the nature of police work. It is likely that many females may not wish to work in policing. Females and minorities have historically been underrepresented on police forces, although proactive efforts by police departments have sought to increase the representation of both groups.

Females have made great progress in policing since the **Civil Rights Act of 1964**, which prohibited discrimination in hiring on the basis of color, race, sex, religion, or national origin, and the **Equal Employment Opportunity Act of 1972**, when protections of women and minorities were extended to local governments. Women have moved beyond primarily assuming the administrative assignments and matron-like duties to increasingly engaging in traditional police officer practices. Nevertheless, much work remains.

Females remain underrepresented in all ranks of policing, constituting only about 12 percent of local law enforcement officers as of 2016. This percentage has remained about the same in recent years, although it is much higher than it was decades ago (it was 8 percent in 1987). Figure 7.2 notes female representation among full-time sworn personnel from 1997 to 2016.[14]

Higher percentages of female officers are generally found in larger departments rather than small, rural departments. Research in the area notes that females have higher levels of representation in departments that emphasize community policing, have higher

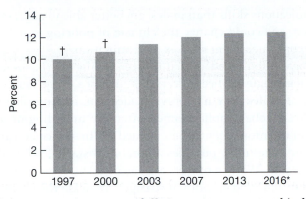

FIGURE 7.2   Female representation among full-time sworn personnel in local police departments, 1997–2016

*Comparison group.
†Significant difference from comparison group at the 95% confidence level.
Source: Bureau of Justice Statistics, Law Enforcement Management and Administrative Statistics survey, 1997–2016.

education requirements, have more incentives and benefits, do not have physical fitness screening criteria, and have no collective bargaining rights. They are also more likely to be employed by departments that serve larger and more racially and ethnically diverse communities.[15] Females are more represented in non-sworn law enforcement positions (e.g., as dispatchers).[16] Unfortunately, some male officers and members of the general public maintain the misperception that females are unsuited for the difficulties associated with police work.

Females are underrepresented in federal law enforcement, constituting roughly 14 percent of all federal law enforcement officers in 2016, a decrease from 15.5 percent in 2008.[17] They did not enter federal law enforcement until 1971[18], although it was not until 2002 that a woman headed a federal law enforcement agency, when Teresa Chambers became the chief of the U.S. Park Police.[19] In a study of female federal law enforcement officers, it was noted that all respondents (*N* = 168) reported at least one occupational barrier in the workplace, with 24.1 percent of respondents citing negative attitudes from male colleagues, and over half (59.1 percent) noting the lack of female role models. Other concerns included the perceived glass ceiling to promotions (19.4 percent), sexual discrimination (21.3 percent), and non-family-friendly care policies (34 percent).[20]

POLICEWOMEN

Despite the perception of some individuals in society and some male police officers, females have much to offer police work. For instance, the research literature in policing suggests that females tend to use less force, and thus face fewer excessive-force complaints, have better communications skills than males, are better able to address situations of violence against women, and could change the climate of policing to reduce the number of claims regarding sexual harassment and sex discrimination.[21]

Policewomen have often faced difficulty overcoming the barriers associated with being accepted as "legitimate" police officers. For instance, some male officers (and their wives) perceive that females may not provide adequate backup during dangerous encounters. Some officers believe policewomen often are unwilling or unable to provide the appropriate level of enforcement when needed.[22] The police culture, which emphasizes masculinity and toughness, provides a notable obstacle for females wishing to be accepted among the ranks. Women officers are perceived by some in policing and general society to lack the physical and emotional strength to tackle the rigors of police work.[23] Females are sometimes required to "prove" themselves and mitigate traditional stereotypes early in their careers by using force in the presence of male officers.[24] Research examining officer use of force in St. Petersburg, Florida, and Indianapolis, Indiana, suggests that compared to male officers, female officers were not reluctant to use physical force, and few differences were found with regard to the extent to which officers used verbal and physical violence and the reasons for doing so.[25] Another study examining female officer use of force found no statistically significant differences between male and female officers with regard to the overall rate of force or the rate of unarmed physical force.[26] Table 7.2 highlights several barriers females have had to overcome in being accepted as a police officer.

Female officers from other minority groups sometimes face a sense of **double marginality** when their race and gender pose particular challenges not faced by many other officers.[27] Hostility, separation, intimidation, and implicit and explicit discriminatory behaviors of

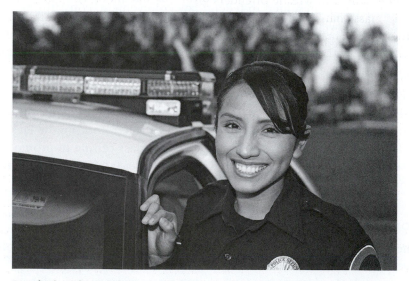

Females have become increasingly involved in policing, although they remain largely underrepresented compared to males.

TABLE 7.2   BARRIERS TO FEMALES IN POLICING

- Stereotypes—for instance, that females are not strong enough for police work
- Discrimination in the hiring process
- Sexual harassment
- Social isolation
- A double-standard in performance evaluations, as females feel they must outperform their male counterparts
- Receiving less desirable assignments
- Limited opportunities for promotion
- Lack of family-friendly policies such as those pertaining to child care.

Source: P. S. Harringtonand K. A. Lonsway, "Current Barriers and Future Prospects for Women in Policing," in B. R. Price and Natalie J. Sokoloff (eds.), *The Criminal Justice System and Women: Offenders, Prisoners, Victims, & Workers,* 3rd ed. (New York: McGraw-Hill, 2004).

fellow male officers contribute to the underrepresentation of African American female officers on many forces.[28] Double marginality is not restricted to African American females in policing, as female officers from other minority groups face similar challenges. For instance, researchers found that lesbian police officers in a large municipal police department faced a notable sense of social exclusion and overt sexist and anti-gay behavior from co-workers. Lesbian officers in a small department, however, sensed that their greatest barriers were attributable to their gender rather than their sexual orientation.[29]

The misperception that females are less effective police officers than males hampers efforts of females to become more ingrained in policing. Very few individuals in society would seek to work in an area where one's colleagues and "customers" are skeptical of one's abilities to perform the job. The term "misperception" is used as it is well documented that females perform as well as, or better than, males in particular aspects of policing. To be sure, there are aspects of policing that are better suited to males. For instance, males are generally better suited to wrestle offenders given the likelihood of male officers having more muscle mass than females. Yet, wrestling offenders is a small, albeit important, aspect of the job. The inability of females to physically interact with offenders on par with males is tempered by the fact that some male offenders won't engage in physical contact with females, and female officers are better able than male officers to verbally, as opposed to physically, quell a confrontational situation.

THE INTERNATIONAL ASSOCIATION OF WOMEN POLICE

In 1915 the International Policewomen's Association was established to support the advancement of females in policing. The group would later reorganize and change its name to the International Association of Women Police (IAWP). Among other contributions to supporting women's involvement in policing, the IAWP annually hosts a five-day forum for researchers and practitioners from around the world to share their views and disseminate information on females in policing. Currently, the IAWP has members from more than sixty different countries.

The IAWP, like other professional associations that promote the advancement of females in policing, offers its members educational, networking, and mentoring opportunities. Further, the IAWP seeks to enhance the prestige and professionalism of policewomen, encourage officers to learn new things about themselves and their career, and provide a sense of belonging for the officers. Primary among the goals of the IAWP are to promote fairness and equity in workplaces and to encourage a work environment that is free of harassment and discrimination.[30]

(continued)

(continued)

The adoption of an international component of a professional policewomen's association demonstrates the awareness of the need to promote cross-national interaction in policing, particularly with regard to females. Understanding the challenges faced by female officers in other countries, and the responses to those challenges, provides numerous benefits to policing in general. Along these lines, the existence of the IAWP and other professional associations designated for policewomen (such as the National Association of Women Law Enforcement Executives, the National Center for Women and Policing, and various state- and regional-level groups) provides valuable support for female officers and demonstrates the significant advancement of females in policing.

INTERACTION WITH THE POLICE

It is well established in the criminology literature that males commit the bulk of crime in society. Accordingly, it is expected that males would more often be in contact with the police. In 2015, over 53.3 million U.S. residents (or 21 percent) over the age of fifteen had one or more contacts with the police. Females were far less likely than males to be the targets of both street and traffic stops.[31]

Most police-citizen encounters occur while officers are on patrol. Patrol is considered the backbone of policing. Among other functions, patrol enables officers to quickly respond to calls, promotes positive police-community relations, deters would-be offenders, and helps control crime through traffic stops. The U.S. Bureau of Justice Statistics noted that male drivers were more likely than females to experience a vehicle or personal search or to be arrested during a traffic stop.[32] During all types of contacts (including street and traffic stops), males were far more likely than females to have force used against them.[33] These numbers do not prove differential treatment of males and females, as one must consider the actions and behaviors of the motorists stopped by, and individuals in contact with, the police. Nevertheless, the numbers do suggest that interactions between police and motorists differ based on gender.

CHECKPOINT

- Females have historically been underrepresented in policing. The percentage of females in policing steadily increased since the 1960s until recently, when the figure generally stabilized at about 12 percent.

- Female police officers face certain obstacles not encountered by their male counterparts. Females have proven themselves very capable of being police officers.
- Females are less likely than males to have contact with the police.

FEMALES AND THE COURTS

Discretion is inherent in the criminal justice system, and is perhaps most obvious in the legal arena where critical decisions are often made. The decision to file charges, grant pretrial release (including the nature of the release), engage in plea bargaining, convict or acquit, and impose a punitive or soft sentence are among the most critical decisions made by courtroom personnel. To be sure, consideration of cultural factors influences some decisions. For instance, the double marginality faced by minority females in the criminal justice system, based on their status as both female and minority, dictates that courts ought to make concerted efforts to release female minority defendants on their own recognizance since they are often low-income and unable to post bail.[34] If bail is required, it should be reasonable given that many minority females who enter the criminal justice system are single parents and detention would have secondary effects on the defendants' children.[35] Similarly, poor minorities entering our courts also face challenges, as a lack of resources increases the difficulties associated with, among other things, obtaining competent representation and/or securing release from detention.

Gender-based decisions are notably obvious in the legal arena, as evidenced in the criminal justice research literature and our discussion of females and the courts. We focus on several critical areas of gender differences as they exist in the courts. Specifically, we examine decision-making and gender as it relates to sentencing and the imposition of capital punishment. The section concludes with a look at the nature and challenges of females working in the courtroom.

SENTENCING

Historically, female offenders generally received more lenient sentences than their male counterparts. The difference was more pronounced with regard to less serious crimes, as more serious, violent crimes decreased the likelihood of differential treatment. Some research suggests there is no gender neutrality in the sentencing process, as females face much lower odds than males of being incarcerated. Female offenders are sometimes viewed as less culpable, less likely to re-offend, and more amenable to rehabilitation than male offenders, and are sentenced accordingly.[36] There is debate, however, regarding whether or not females continue to receive preferential treatment in the courts, and whether or not paternalism or chivalry on behalf of criminal justice officials persists. In light of the increasing number of females entering the criminal justice system, some researchers suggest that females are no longer treated differently from males.

It appears that with regard to judicial decision-making and sentencing decisions, judges consider both legally relevant and irrelevant factors when sentencing females, yet only legally relevant factors when sentencing males.[37] Judges typically consider dangerousness, blameworthiness, and social costs in their sentencing decisions, with the latter consideration most often benefiting female defendants. Judges are more likely to take child care into consideration in processing females convicted of less serious crimes.[38] **Sentencing guidelines**, designed to provide consistency and parity in sentencing decisions, are sometimes undermined by judges who deviate from the sentencing schedule while treating females more leniently than males.[39] Nevertheless, sentencing guidelines have largely contributed to the increased rate of female incarceration in the states that use them.

CAPITAL PUNISHMENT AND FEMALES

In 1998 Karla Faye Tucker generated worldwide attention. Tucker, a born-again Christian, was scheduled for execution in Texas. Prior to the execution, Waly Bacre Ndiaye (of the United Nations Commission on Summary and Arbitrary Executions), Pope John Paul II, Italian Prime Minister Romano Prodi, and others offered support for Tucker, who was convicted of committing murder with a pickaxe. Why the controversy, given that Texas executes many offenders? For starters, Tucker was to be the first female executed in Texas since the Civil War. To be sure, other females in Texas had committed offenses worthy of capital punishment between the Civil War and 1998. So why hadn't they faced execution? Karla Faye Tucker was executed on February 3, 1998.

It is suggested that receiving the death penalty (i.e., capital punishment) is akin to a crapshoot which is dependent upon a variety of variables. Judicial discretion, jury makeup, and the state in which the capital offense was committed largely contribute to one's likelihood of being executed. Needless to say, capital punishment remains one of the more controversial issues in society. The small number of females executed or facing execution in relation to the number of males adds to the controversy; however, males undoubtedly commit more violent crime and more capital offenses than females. Thus, it is not surprising that only 1.8 percent of the roughly 2,800 inmates sentenced to death in 2016 were female.[40]

FEMALE COURTROOM PERSONNEL

Courtroom personnel have traditionally consisted of White males, although recent trends suggest an increase in the numbers of women assuming law-related careers as public defenders, prosecutors, and judges.[41] For instance, the percentage of female lawyers increased from 23 percent in 1994 to 35 percent in 2017, and female attorney salaries as a percentage of their male counterparts' have increased.[42] Further, the enrollment of females in law school has increased and females constituted over half (52.3 percent) of all law school enrollments in 2018.[43] Until the 1950s and 1960s, women had been denied entry to some law schools, which contributed to them constituting less than 5 percent of the legal profession as late as 1970.[44]

Females have increasingly become represented as judges, as they comprise over one-third (35 percent) of the U.S. Supreme Court Justices, federal Circuit Courts of Appeals judges, and federal District Court judges.[45] They comprise roughly 33 percent of all state court judges in the United States.[46] An increasing number of females have assumed positions as federal judges beginning with Jimmy Carter's presidency, with females constituting 18 percent of former president Bill Clinton's nominations to the federal judiciary.[47] President Barack Obama nominated two females to the U.S. Supreme Court: Justice Sonia Sotomayor and Justice Elena Kagan. Over one-fourth (28 percent) of the judges President Trump appointed to the federal courts were female, which is well below the 42 percent appointed by President Obama, yet still higher than many former presidents.[48] Ultimately, females remain underrepresented as practitioners in the legal system.

The lack of representation in the legal arena is pronounced for minority females, who face the double marginality of being female and a minority group member. For instance, as of 2014, only 7.4 percent of attorneys were women of color.[49] Research on this population noted that compared to White men, women attorneys of color felt excluded from informal and formal networking opportunities, were more likely to believe they met with clients only when their gender or race would be advantageous to the firm, and more often felt that their accomplishments didn't receive due consideration.[50]

Unfortunately, women of all races who have "broken the barrier" and entered the inside world of working within the courts continue to face particular challenges such as limited advancement opportunities due to stereotyping females and lack of access to the male socialization process.[51] Gender bias is primary among the concerns addressed by the women's rights movement, and certainly is evident in our courts as the U.S. legal system is by no means exempt from such claims. Task forces were created in thirty-six states to investigate gender bias in the legal system. Such bias can come in the form of decision-making based on stereotypes regarding gender, such as, for instance, believing that domestic violence is a private matter that should be addressed at home. Gender bias also comes in the form of comments and actions toward individuals based on gender. Referring to female attorneys by their first names or making sexist remarks or jokes fall in this category and were common among the claims addressed by the task forces. Bias based on gender is also evident in claims that females face more difficulty than males in being hired and promoted, and that they are paid less than their male counterparts.[52]

The increased number of females working in the legal arena may or may not lead to changes in our courtrooms. The possibility and/or extent of these changes is open to debate. Particularly, some feel that gender differences will result in differential treatment of those entering our courts. There is also the possibility that any possible differences due to gender would be tempered by the background of the females entering the courts and the socialization process found in our courts. Put simply, there is uncertainty regarding if and how biological (i.e., differences due to gender) or sociological factors (e.g., the influences of law school and working directly within the court system) will influence future courtroom practices in light of the increasing number of females working in our courts.

Of particular interest with regard to the increased number of females working within our courts is the changing practices associated with judicial discretion. Speculation and assumptions regarding the behaviors of female judges tend to suggest that female judges are less punitive than male judges, although more likely than male judges to act harshly toward sex offenses. There is also the belief that male judges are more paternalistic than female judges toward female defendants. However, limited empirical research has examined the on-the-job differences between male and female judges. To address the lack of research in the area, professors Darrell Steffensmeier and Chris Hebert examined the sentencing practices of male and female judges and found both similarities and differences in the sentencing practices of males and females on the bench. Particularly, they found that female judges were somewhat more punitive and more considerate of defendant characteristics (specifically, race, sex, and age) and prior record than male judges. They also found that female judges were more punitive than male judges when sentencing repeat Black offenders.[53]

CHECKPOINT

- Females have become increasingly ingrained in courtrooms, both as defendants and employees.
- It is believed the females historically received less severe punishments compared to males. There is debate as to whether or not that is still the case.

- Females are notably underrepresented on death row, simply because males commit the large majority of capital offenses.
- Females, compared to males, have historically been underrepresented as judges and attorneys. They have increasingly assumed these and other courtroom positions.

FEMALES AND CORRECTIONS

As more females are arrested and convicted, it follows that a greater percentage of women will be under correctional supervision. The increased presence of females in correctional facilities and under correctional supervision provides particular challenges to correctional staff and administration. Females under correctional supervision have needs that are distinct from those of male offenders. Female prison and jail administrators must continue to consider the particular needs of female inmates and ensure that the goals of the correctional agency or institution are met. Too often in corrections, it is believed that simply applying male-based correctional practices to females will suffice. This approach is limited at best.

The increased number of incarcerated females has encouraged corrections officials to adjust to a series of issues and concerns as they relate to females. For instance, many female inmates have children they must care for while incarcerated. Traditional correctional practices and procedures are not well suited to address the different needs of females. Addressing, at least in part, the challenges posed by an increasingly female correctional population has changed the face of corrections and has helped address what has been termed **collateral damage**, or the harms suffered by children of incarcerated parents.[54] At the very least it has forced correctional agencies to consider ways to best adapt to the changing demographics of their population.

FEMALE INCARCERATION

The United States has experienced a dramatic increase in its incarceration rate, beginning in the early 1980s. Increased incarceration of both males and females has impacted females in several ways. For example, the high cost of building prisons takes resources away from the social services from which females often benefit. Further, enhanced focus on incarceration takes resources from social services which are typically offered by female professionals. In turn, there are fewer professional employment opportunities for women.[55]

One of the more notable developments in society pertains to the increased number of females incarcerated in U.S. prisons and jails. Although the number of males incarcerated far outnumbers the number of females, the percentage of incarcerated females is increasing at a higher rate than males. Three competing hypotheses are offered to explain the increased rate of female incarceration: the demise of chivalry or the paternalistic treatment of women; women becoming increasingly involved in crime; and the equal treatment of females and males.[56]

Primary among the reasons for the increased presence of females in the criminal justice system are the substantial impact the war on drugs has had on females, and the merging of society's move to become tough on crime with a backlash against women's equality.[57] Other factors influencing the increased number of females being incarcerated include:

- Increased poverty of women
- Income inequality
- Selective enforcement of drug crimes disproportionately targeting minority and the poor

- An overall more punitive societal and criminal justice system approach to crime
- Increased use of sentencing guidelines and less use of judicial discretion
- Increased drug use and addiction among women
- A political switch to the right in which criminal behavior is believed to be caused by evil self-will
- Racism, sexism, homophobia, and class bias[58]

With regard to prison statistics, men, at year-end 2017, were roughly twelve times more likely than females to be incarcerated. However, the male prison population decreased at a higher rate (7.1 percent) than that of females (2.6 percent) between 2007 and 2017. Females comprised approximately 7 percent of the prison population in 2017, compared to 6.1 percent at year-end 2000.[59]

The increased presence of females noted in the prison population is also found with regard to jails. One doesn't get to prison without having first passed through jail. Accordingly, the female jail population has also recently increased. Although there are nearly 6 males for every female in prison, the rate of male inmates dropped from 448 to 394 per 100,000 male residents between 2005 and 2017, while the rate of females increased from 63 to 69.[60]

With regard to race and gender, minority females are more likely than White females to be incarcerated. There were more White women than Black or Hispanic women in state and federal prisons at year-end 2017; however, the rate of incarceration for Hispanic women (66 per 100,000) and Black women (92 per 100,000) was higher than it was for White women (49 per 100,000).[61] This discrepancy is largely attributable to the war on drugs, which has been very influential on women's involvement in the criminal justice system. The war has had a particular influence on Black and Latina women. Along these lines, women of color are more often the mothers of dependent children, and economically marginalized and disadvantaged. The increased level of female incarceration has heavily impacted Black and Latina women.[62]

WOMEN IN JAIL

With a relatively transient population, jails offer more limited treatment opportunities and services than prisons. This problem has been compounded by the increasing number of females incarcerated. Jails have been forced to adapt to a changing inmate population. While several areas of policy and procedure in jails remain constant regardless of inmate gender (e.g., searches, housing, and transportation), special accommodations are needed for females. Inmate mental and physical well-being is of concern, as is the need to consider that many female inmates are single parents who must consider the well-being of their children. These considerations are by no means restricted to jails, as female prison inmates face these and other struggles.

Jails need to consider several issues as related to the increasing involvement of females in the criminal justice system. Particularly, females generally have a more difficult time than males raising money for pretrial release, and female inmates may not receive proper medical and mental health attention, as jails have traditionally been structured toward serving male inmates. Visiting hours with their children is also of concern, as are appropriate jail-issued clothing, hygiene supplies, recreational activities, work training programs, and inmate worker positions.[63]

These concerns have not always been addressed. For example, in 1999 the U.S. General Accounting Office published a report, *Women in Prison: Issues and Challenges Confronting U.S. Correctional Systems*, which highlighted the failure of the state to meet the special needs of women and provide adequate medical care.[64] Again, many of these issues also apply to females in prison, but these concerns are more likely to be addressed in prison than in jails given that those in prison stay for longer periods of time and the problems may be more noticeable and more likely to be addressed in prison. Unfortunately, females in jail have been referred to as an "afterthought" that pose burdens on the staff.[65] Experienced jail staff who convey to new recruits the stereotype that women in jail are difficult perpetuate a culture of bias.[66]

FEMALES IN PRISON

Female prisoners were housed in institutions designed for males until the early nineteenth century. In some institutions females were housed in separated sections. The initial step toward creating prisons specially designed for women didn't occur until 1835, when a prison for females was attached to Sing Sing, a male prison in Mount Pleasant, New York. The twentieth century brought about females being incarcerated exclusively in female prisons, which were less threatening and smaller than male prisons. The relatively small number of female prisoners compared to males resulted in a limited number of female prisons.[67]

Prisons contain inmates facing long-term stays (one year or more). Accordingly, the opportunity for inmates to receive specialized treatment and recognition of cultural differences is generally of greater consideration in prison than in jails. However, the burden is on prison officials to provide the specialized treatment and recognize and respond to the various cultural differences.

One of the more notable differences between male and female prisons concerns the social world of prison life. The social structure of male prisons is largely built around the ideas of masculinity, manhood, and homophobia, while female prisons are more structured around kinship, open expression of affection, and family-type structures.[68] **Prison play-families**, in which inmates assume the roles of different family members, are more often found in female prisons than in male institutions, where such structural arrangements are frowned upon. Latina prisoners are particularly active in play-families given their likelihood of being from families with strong kinship ties outside of prison.[69]

Concern for familial ties extends beyond the prison walls. Of particular concern regarding female prison inmates is care for their children. Roughly two-thirds of the women in prison in the United States have a child under age eighteen.[70] While female jail inmates must also contend with caring for their children while incarcerated, prison stays are longer than the time spent in jail and, accordingly, family concerns are amplified

The female inmate population has increased in recent history. Female prisons differ to some extent from male prisons, for instance in terms of the social atmosphere, health needs, and programming.

among female prisoners. The social, psychological, and economic effects of an increasing number of children with incarcerated parents will have significant societal impacts for years and generations to come.[71] More children are likely to encounter the incarceration of a father rather than a mother, however, children of female inmates are more likely than their counterparts to suffer from problems associated with being separated from their parent as well as more trauma, as the mother is often the primary caregiver.[72] Pertinent among the factors influencing the ability of a child with an incarcerated mother to avoid involvement with the criminal justice system include the age of the child at the time of the mother's incarceration, the child's relationship with their custodian, the strength of the mother-child bond, the type of crime committed by the mother, and the length of the mother's sentence.[73]

The increasing number of parents, particularly mothers, incarcerated leads to two concerns: What becomes of the children upon incarceration of their parent(s), and how can prisons facilitate continued parental contact with their children? The children of inmates most often live with the child's other parent. However, there is a notable difference between male and female inmates with regard to who assumes custody of their children while the parent is incarcerated. Particularly, the children of male inmates are most often cared for by the child's mother, whereas females most often leave their children in the care of the child's grandparent.[74] The large number of males being incarcerated leaves behind a greater percentage of troubled children living in single-parent families with marginal economic resources.

Female inmates are more often in contact with their children than are males. The bond between mothers and their children is particularly important for newborns, yet it is often difficult for women who give birth while incarcerated to establish and maintain that bond.

Some prisons take efforts to address this concern; ten states permit mothers with infant children to care for them in prison nurseries.[75] Criminal justice officials concerned with promoting close contact between incarcerated parents and their children need to consider placement issues, with the goal of keeping parents as close as possible to their children while maintaining the goals of incarceration. Close family ties during incarceration are related to lower recidivism, improved mental health of inmates, more enhanced unification of the family following release, and enhanced success on parole.[76]

Avenues to address the negative impacts upon children of incarcerated parents include:

- Crisis nurseries to address acute trauma such as a parent's incarceration
- Crisis intervention counseling following the arrest of a parent
- Therapeutic interventions to help children address the effects of disturbing situations and promote coping skills
- Therapeutic visitation to reduce the likelihood of domestic violence upon reentry
- Community-based mother-infant correctional programs to foster maternal bonding
- Parent-child visitation programs to encourage positive interactions between child and incarcerated parent
- Children's support groups, which help children confront the concerns they may face while having an incarcerated parent[77]

The varied cultural backgrounds of incarcerated females generate several issues of concern. Consideration of cultural concerns regarding Latina, African American, and Asian American female inmates is documented in the criminology and criminal justice literature. For instance, Native American females were identified as having several unmet needs while in prison, despite the fact that females and Native Americans are among the groups with the fastest growing incarceration rate. Unfortunately, little is known about Native American female inmates. In response, Native American scholar Luana Ross studied the troubles faced by Native American women in a Montana prison and noted how these inmates resist prison due to the institutional lack of recognition or honoring of Native American culture. Ross found that Native American female inmates lacked access to native spiritual leaders and culturally relevant betterment programs in prison. The desistance of these women led to them receiving more punitive treatment in the facility.[78] To be sure, these and related cultural challenges exist not only within the institution Ross studied but in many other correctional institutions as well. Further, cultural concerns are not restricted to Native American females, as other groups also face a variety of challenges.

Treatment, counseling, and other therapeutic approaches in correctional facilities have historically been designed and targeted toward male offenders. Further, prison staff should be well-versed in multicultural counseling awareness, training, and sensitivity as they pertain to females. Failure to recognize and address the specific needs of females, in conjunction with a lack of concern for aftercare, contributes to the re-incarceration of female (and other) offenders.[79] Females entering the criminal justice system are more likely than other women to have substance abuse problems, yet correctional institutions often lack adequate substance abuse treatment. In some cases, substance abuse counseling is offered absent additional treatment approaches such as group therapy, family counseling, reunification programs, and mental health assistance.[80] Greater focus on issues such as violence against females, childhood sexual abuse, and caring for children while incarcerated is needed in today's prisons.

Our discussion of females under correctional supervision has centered primarily on institutional corrections. However, we should not neglect the substantial and increasing number of females under correctional supervision in the community. As expected in light of the increasing number of females being arrested and convicted, women are increasingly being supervised in the community. The increased presence of females in the criminal justice system is evident in the percentage of females on probation and parole. For instance, at year-end 2016, females constituted 25 percent of all probationers, which was an increase from 22 percent in 2000.[81] The percentage of females on probation increased from 21 percent in 1995 to 23 percent in 2005.[82] Further, the percentage of females on parole increased from 10 percent to 12 percent of all parolees between 1995 and 2005, and was at 13 percent in 2016.[83]

To be sure, females face particular challenges and issues both as offenders under community corrections and as professionals supervising offenders in the community. Consider the particular challenges faced in supervising Hispanic males in the community. The emphasis on machismo in the Hispanic community may pose particular challenges for female probation officers. For example, it is suggested that female probation officers initially establish their official role due to Hispanic males often basing their relationship with women according to roles.[84] Further, understanding cultural differences with regard to language can facilitate interactions with clients. Hispanics are typically more immediate in their vocal communications, which may, inaccurately, sound intimidating to some. Interactions are enhanced if parole officers are concise and to the point when communicating with Hispanic clients.[85] Women face particular issues when working in all areas of corrections, particularly prisons.

FEMALES WORKING IN CORRECTIONS

While not completely absent from correctional facilities, females working in prisons were historically restricted to clerical duties. Things changed with Title VII of the Civil Rights Act of 1964, which prohibited sex discrimination by governments in hiring and promotion practices. Among many other accomplishments, this act enabled females to increasingly assume positions in correctional facilities. By 1998, females constituted over 20 percent of the correctional officers in U.S. prisons.[86] By 2005, the percentage of females working in federal and state correctional institutions increased to 33 percent.[87] More recently, there were more female than male probation officers or correctional treatment specialists (52.9 percent compared to 47.1 percent), females comprised about 27 percent of the staff in the Federal Bureau of Prisons in 2019 (a percentage that has consistently increased), and just under one-fourth (24.1 percent) of jailers were female in 2016.[88]

Females have had to overcome a series of obstacles to gain acceptance as correctional officials. They were notably under-represented in the ranks of jail employees until the 1980s and 1990s.[89] Despite the increase in numbers, females have not been particularly well received as employees working in jails. Discrimination, harassment, and the belief that females are unable to fulfill the need for authoritativeness and occasional aggressiveness are but a few of the factors working against females employed in jails.

The introduction of female staff members into male prisons initially generated controversy among inmates and (male) prison staff. Much of the controversy stemmed from the belief that female prison officers were not strong enough to guard male inmates, and that they were more sympathetic to inmate causes.[90] Further, some male officers believe the long shifts and the need to put in overtime as a correctional officer render females unsuitable for the job, primarily because women are viewed as having to be accountable to family needs.[91] Among other effects, the resentment faced by early female corrections officers limited their opportunities to learn from the social networks established by experienced male officers.[92] These and related concerns subsided over time, yet some believe corrections remains the most male-dominated, sex-segregated component of the criminal justice system.[93]

Inmates had their own set of concerns with regard to the presence of females on the prison staff. Some male prisoners were sensitive to having to use toilets and showers in plain view of female correctional officers. Sexual harassment of female officers also generated concern, as inmates (and male correctional officers) would have to learn, and abide by, the rules surrounding sexual harassment.[94] Today, female and male prison officers are viewed by prisoners as similar with regard to arbitrariness, fairness, and empathy.[95]

Consider the struggles of a female warden at a male prison. Females have historically been absent from the top level of administration in prisons, although more females today are assuming positions as wardens of men's (and women's) prisons.[96] Tekla Miller, who was appointed warden of the maximum-security Huron Valley Men's Facility in Michigan, documented the challenges she faced upon assuming the role.[97] Male prison staff, some of whom were opposed to female employees in a male prison, viewed the appointment of Miller as warden with disdain. Miller was able to successfully overcome the opposition of the officers by remaining diplomatic and encouraging a team-oriented approach from her subordinates. In general, females have had success as wardens of male (and female) prisons.[98] However, the number of female wardens will remain low until females are more openly accepted among the ranks of correctional officers, an important stepping stone for one who wishes to become a warden. Females have had a much easier time being accepted among the ranks of probation and parole officers.

Probation emerged from the treatment model of corrections in the early part of the twentieth century, and was led by White female probation officers who had backgrounds in social services. Probation took a slight turn in focus during the late 1960s and early 1970s when the emphasis on rehabilitative services turned toward **reintegration**, or helping offenders adjust as they re-entered society. In the 1980s and 1990s the focus of probation would change again, this time adopting an emphasis on risk assessment and increased surveillance. The latter change has negatively impacted probation officer morale and involvement.[99]

Through all of these changes, female probation officers have remained active in probation services. For several reasons, female probation officers have not faced the same level of rejection and harassment they face in law enforcement and, to a lesser degree, the legal arena. First, male probation and parole officers have not established a culture that excludes females.

Second, the need for treatment and professionally trained social workers in probation and parole bodes well for the acceptance of females. Third, probation has never truly been recognized as a male-dominated profession; therefore, male officers often have little concern when working with female colleagues.[100]

Increased diversification in correctional staff provides greater encouragement for multicultural training. For instance, correctional agencies were forced to offer specialized training for prison officers upon the increased presence of females in male prisons. Issues such as sexual harassment, supervising men in prison, and management strategies increasingly became part of correctional officer and administrator training programs.[101] Similar training concerns appeared as more racial and ethnic minorities joined prison staffs. There has been a notable increase in the overall number of African American females working in criminal justice, particularly in corrections. Among the reasons for this increase are civil rights legislation, welfare reform, national and local changes in public assistance programs, and national movements promoting awareness and support for diversity and inclusion.[102]

CHECKPOINT

- Females have become more ingrained in all aspects of corrections as both offenders and employees.
- Various factors have influenced the increased presence of females under correctional supervision. The war on drugs has had a notable influence on the involvement of women of color in the criminal justice system.
- The increased percentage of females in jails has highlighted the need for jails to be more accommodating to female inmate needs.

- The increased presence of females in prisons has highlighted the different needs of female inmates in relation to males. Childcare and healthcare are among the issues that differ between male and female prisons.
- Females have historically been underrepresented among those who work in corrections. They have increasingly assumed positions within the field, but remain particularly underrepresented with regard to supervisory positions.

SUMMARY

Women may or may not be culturally distinct from males. Regardless of one's view on this, females are distinct from males when it comes to crime and justice. As both practitioners and "participants" in the system, females face specific hurdles not faced by their male counterparts.

Criminal justice in the United States is undergoing significant changes that will impact generations to come. Prominent among the changes is the increased involvement of women in all aspects of our justice systems. Females are increasingly assuming roles as police officers, police chiefs, attorneys, judges, probation officers, parole officers, correctional officers, wardens, defendants, inmates, and clients. Responding to these changes has been and continues to be a work in progress that we hope will result in fruitful benefits for all. As practitioners, females have much to offer the criminal justice system. The goal is to recognize and utilize the many benefits females have to offer. Equally important is the need to recognize and respond to the fact that male and female offenders differ and accommodations for these differences should not be ignored.

YOU MAKE THE CALL
FEMALE CORRECTIONAL OFFICER

Consider the following scenario. Debate the pros and cons of all options and decide what you would do.

As a female, you are a bit apprehensive about becoming a prison officer. Particularly, you wonder how the inmates will treat you. You know that tension exists between prison officers and prisoners, but you don't expect tension from your colleagues. As you begin your career in corrections, several male officers make off-the-cuff comments about you being a female prison officer. One officer asks you why you want to do a "man's job." Not one to put up with such shortsightedness, you report their behavior to your supervisor. The supervisor notes that the officers are "testing" you, to see if you can handle the ridicule . . . to see if you are "one of them." He says the comments will cease after you've been on the job for a while—"once you prove yourself."

Word gets out that you complained about the comments to the supervisor, and you begin to feel increasingly isolated among the prison officer ranks. The officers stop making comments to your face, but they also stop speaking to you unless communication is absolutely necessary. You can sense that the officers are making derogatory comments behind your back. Although you're not a quitter, it becomes increasingly difficult for you to continue working in such an atmosphere.

Questions

1. Do you believe the situation would have improved if instead of contacting your supervisor you ridiculed the male officers?
2. Should the supervisor have reacted differently?
3. What steps, if any, can you take in this instance to improve your working conditions?
4. Was it appropriate for you to complain about the comments, or should you have simply brushed them off?

KEY TERMS

acquaintance rape

Civil Rights Act of 1964

collateral damage

culture

double marginality

Equal Employment Opportunity Act of 1972

feminist movements

gender

marital rape

Nineteenth Amendment

prison play-families

reintegration

sentencing guidelines

sex

DISCUSSION QUESTIONS

1. Why have females become increasingly involved in the criminal justice system?
2. What barriers do females face with regard to being accepted as police officers? What can be done to address these barriers?
3. Discuss the differences between males and females as they relate to: (1) courtroom personnel and (2) defendants being sentenced.
4. What are the distinctive needs of females undergoing correctional supervision?
5. What can prison officials do to reduce the harms on children with incarcerated parents?

FOR FURTHER READING

Adler, F. *Sisters in Crime*. New York: McGraw-Hill, 1975.

Barberet, R. *Women, Crime and Criminal Justice: A Global Enquiry*. London: Routledge, 2014.

Chesney-Lind, M., and L. Pasko. *The Female Offender: Girls, Women, and Crime*, 3rd ed. Thousand Oaks, CA: Sage, 2013.

George, E. *A Woman Doing Life: Notes from a Prison for Women*, 2nd ed. New York: Oxford University Press, 2014.

Muraskin, R. *Women and Justice: It's a Crime*, 5th ed. Upper Saddle River, NJ: Pearson, 2012.

NOTES

1. Roslyn Muraskin, "Ain't I a Woman?" in *It's a Crime: Women and Justice* (Upper Saddle River, NJ: Prentice Hall, 2007), 2–12.

2. Ibid.

3. B. R. Price and Natalie J. Sokoloff, "Preface," in *The Criminal Justice System and Women: Offenders, Prisoners, Victims & Workers*, 3rd ed. (New York: McGraw-Hill, 2004), xiii–xxii.

4. Susan F. Sharp and Kristen Hefley, "This Is a Man's World . . . Or Least That's How It Looks in the Journals," *Critical Criminology* 15 (2007): 3–18.

5. Ibid.

6. L. A. Hughes, "The Representation of Females in Criminological Research: A Content Analysis of American and British Journal Articles," *Women & Criminal Justice* 16 (2005): 1–28.

7. Federal Bureau of Investigation, "Arrests, by Sex, 2014—Table 42," *Crime in the United States, 2017*, U.S. Department of Justice. Accessed August 13, 2019, at: https://ucr.fbi.gov/crime-in-the-u.s/2017/crime-in-the-u.s.-2017/topic-pages/tables/table-42

8. Federal Bureau of Investigation, "Ten-Year Arrest Trends, by Sex, 2008–2017—Table 33." *Crime in the United States, 2017*, U.S. Department of Justice. Accessed August 13, 2019, at: https://ucr.fbi.gov/crime-in-the-u.s/2017/crime-in-the-u.s.-2017/topic-pages/tables/table-33

9. E.g., Darrell Steffensmeier and Jennifer Schwartz, "Contemporary Explanations of Women's Crime," in Price and Sokoloff, *The Criminal Justice System and Women*, 113–26.

10. Ibid.

11. Fred E. Jandt, *An Introduction to Intercultural Communication: Identities in a Global Community*, 6th ed. (Thousand Oaks, CA: Sage, 2010), 240.

12. C. Mastony, "Was Chicago Home to the Country's 1st Female Cop?" *Chicago Tribune*, September 1, 2010. Available at: http://articles.chicagotribune.com/2010-09-01/news/ct-met-first-police-woman-20100901_1_female-officer-police-officer-female-cop

13. Michael D. Lyman, *The Police: An Introduction*, 4th ed. (Upper Saddle River, NJ: Pearson Prentice Hall, 2010).

14. Shelley S. Hyland and Elizabeth Davis, *Local Police Departments, 2016: Personnel*. U.S. Department of Justice, Bureau of Justice Statistics NCJ 252835, 5.

15. A. M. Schuck, "Female Representation in Law Enforcement: The Influence of Screening, Unions, Incentives, Community Policing, CALEA, and Size," *Police Quarterly* 17, no. 1 (2014): 54–78.

16. Federal Bureau of Investigation, "Full-Time Law Enforcement Employees—Table 74," *Crime in the United States, 2011*, U.S. Department of Justice. Accessed May 24, 2016, at: https://www.fbi.gov/about-us/cjis/ucr/crime-in-the-u.s/2011/crime-in-the-u.s.-2011/tables/table_74_full-time_law_enforcement_employees_by_population_group_percent_male_and_female_2011.xls

17. Connor Brooks, *Federal Law Enforcement Officers, 2016—Statistical Tables*, U.S. Department of Justice, Bureau of Justice Statistics, 2019, NCJ 251922, 6.

18. D. M. Schulz, "Women Special Agents in Charge: The First Generation," *Policing: An International Journal of Police Strategies & Management* 32 (2009): 675–93.

19. D. M. Schulz, *Breaking the Brass Ceiling: Women Police Chiefs and Their Paths to the Top* (Westport, CT: Praeger, 2004).

20. H. H. Yu, "An Examination of Federal Law Enforcement: An Exploratory Analysis of the Challenges They Face in the Work Environment," *Feminist Criminology* 10, no. 3 (2015): 259–78.

21. See Eugene A. Paoline III and William Terrill, "Women Police Officers and the Use of Coercion," *Women & Criminal Justice* 15, no. 3/4 (2004): 97–119, for elaboration on the ability of women to perform as police officers.

22. Paoline and Terrill, "Women Police Officers."
23. Ibid.
24. J. Hunt, "Police Accounts of Normal Force," in V. Kappeler (ed.), *The Police and Society*, 3rd ed. (Prospect Height, IL: Waveland, 1999), 306–24.
25. Paoline and Terrill, "Women Police Officers."
26. P. B. Hoffman and E. R. Hickey, "Use of Force by Female Police Officers," *Journal of Criminal Justice* 33 (2005): 145–51.
27. S. E. Martin, "'Outsiders Within' the Station House: The Impact of Race and Gender on Black Women Police," *Social Problems* 41 (August 1994): 383–84, 389.
28. Ibid; also G. T. Felkenes and J. R. Schroeder, "A Case Study of Minority Women in Policing," *Women and Criminal Justice* 4 (1993): 65–89.
29. S. L. Miller, K. B. Forest, and N. C. Jurik, "Lesbians in Policing: Perceptions and Work Experiences Within the Macho Cop Culture," in Price and Sokoloff (2004), *The Criminal Justice System and Women*, 511–25.
30. International Association of Women Police, "Past & Present, 1915–Today." Accessed July 4, 2016, at: http://www.iawp.org/history/pastpresent.htm
31. E. Davis and A. Whyde, *Contacts Between the Police and the Public, 2015*. U.S. Department of Justice, Bureau of Justice Statistics, 2011, NCJ 251145.
32. Ibid.
33. Ibid.
34. Coramae M. Mann, "Minority and Female: A Criminal Justice Double Bind," *Social Justice* 16 (1989): 95–114.
35. Ibid.
36. Cassia Spohn and Dawn Beichner, "Is Preferential Treatment of Female Offenders a Thing of the Past? A Multisite Study of Gender, Race, and Imprisonment," *Criminal Justice Policy Review* 11, no. 2 (2000): 149–84. See also C. C. Spohn and J. W. Spears, "Gender and Case-Processing Decisions: A Comparison of Case Outcomes for Male and Female Defendants Charged with Violent Felonies," *Women & Criminal Justice* 8 (1997): 29–59.
37. Marian R. Williams, "Gender and Sentencing: An Analysis of Indicators," *Criminal Justice Policy Review* 10, no. 4 (1999): 471–90.
38. Spohn and Beichner, "Preferential Treatment."
39. Ibid.
40. Tracy L. Snell, *Capital Punishment, 2016*. U.S. Department of Justice, Bureau of Justice Statistics, 2018, NCJ 251430, 7.
41. Darrell Steffensmeier and Chris Hebert, "Women and Men Policy Makers: Does the Judge's Gender Affect the Sentencing of Criminal Defendants?" *Social Forces* 77, no. 3 (1999): 1163–96.
42. A. E. Laffey and A. Ng, "Diversity and Inclusion in the Law: Challenges and Initiatives, American Bar Association, May 2, 2018. Accessed August 13, 2019, at: https://www.americanbar.org/groups/litigation/committees/jiop/articles/2018/diversity-and-inclusion-in-the-law-challenges-and-initiatives/; American Bar Association, "Charting Our Progress: The Status of Women in the Profession Today," *A Current Glance at Women in the Law* (Chicago, IL: American Bar Association, 2016). Accessed at: http://www.americanbar.org/content/dam/aba/marketing/women/current_glance_statistics_may2016.authcheckdam.pdf
43. S. Zaratsky, "The Law Schools Where the Most Women Enrolled as Students (2019)," *Above the Law* (2019, February 5). Accessed August 13, 2019, at: https://abovethelaw.com/2019/02/law-school-most-women/

44. R. L. Abel, "The Transformation of the American Legal Profession," *Law & Society Review* 20, no. 1 (1986): 7–18.

45. J. Gramlich, "Trump Has Appointed a Larger Share of Female Judges than Other GOP Presidents, but Lags Obama, *Pew Research Center*, October 2, 2018. Accessed August 13, 2019, at: https://www.pewresearch.org/fact-tank/2018/10/02/trump-has-appointed-a-larger-share-of-female-judges-than-other-gop-presidents-but-lags-obama/

46. National Association of Women Judges, *2018 US State Court Women Judges*. Accessed August 13, 2019, at: https://www.nawj.org/statistics/2018-us-state-court-women-judges

47. R. Spill and K. Bratton, "Clinton and Diversification of the Federal Judiciary," *Judicature* 84 (2001): 256–61.

48. Gramlich, "Trump Has Appointed."

49. Vault Career Intelligence, *Vault/MCCA Law Firm Diversity Survey Report*, Minority Corporate Counsel Association and Vault, 2016. Available at: http://www.mcca.com/_data/global/downloads/research/reports/VaultMCCA_Survey-2015-v03.pdf

50. American Bar Association, *Visible Invisibility: Women of Color in Law Firms—Executive Summary* (Chicago, IL: American Bar Association, 2006).

51. Steffensmeier and Hebert, "Women and Men Policy Makers."

52. D. W. Neubauer and H. F. Fradella, *America's Courts and the Criminal Justice System*, 12th ed. (Boston, MA: Cengage, 2017), 140.

53. Steffensmeier and Hebert, "Women and Men Policy Makers."

54. J. Crawford, "Alternative Sentencing Necessary for Female Inmates with Children," *Corrections Today* (June 2003): 8–10.

55. M. J. E. Danner, "Three Strikes and It's *Women* Who Are Out," in Muraskin, *It's a Crime*, 723–33.

56. J. Belknap, *The Invisible Woman: Gender, Crime, and Justice*, 2nd ed. (Belmont, CA: Wadsworth, 2001).

57. Meda Chesney-Lind, *The Female Offender: Girls, Women, and Crime* (Thousand Oaks, CA: Sage, 1997).

58. B. R. Price and Natalie J. Sokoloff, *The Criminal Justice System and Women: Offenders, Prisoners, Victims & Workers*, 3rd ed. (New York: McGraw-Hill, 2004).

59. Jennifer Bronson and E. Ann Carson, *Prisoners in 2017*. U.S. Department of Justice, Bureau of Justice Statistics, April 2019, NCJ 252156; William J. Sabol, Todd D. Minton, and Paige M. Harrison, *Prison and Jail Inmates at Midyear 2006*, U.S. Department of Justice, Bureau of Justice Statistics, June 2007, NCJ 217675; E. A. Carson, *Prisoners in 2014*, U.S. Department of Justice, Bureau of Justice Statistics, 2015, NCJ 248955.

60. Zhen Zeng, *Jail Inmates in 2017*. U.S. Department of Justice, Bureau of Justice Statistics, 2019, NCJ 251774, 4.

61. Bronson and Carson, *Prisoners in 2017*, 17.

62. Z. T. McGee, E. Joseph, I. Allicott, T. A. Gayle, A. Barber, and A. Smith, "From the Inside: Patterns of Coping and Adjustment Among Women in Prison," in Muraskin, *It's a Crime*, 507–27.

63. Susan W. McCampbell, "Gender-Responsive Strategies for Women Offenders," *American Jails* (September/October 2005): 39–41, 43–46; 43.

64. General Accounting Office, *Women in Prison: Issues and Challenges Confronting U.S. Correctional Systems* (Washington, DC: U.S. Department of Justice, 1999).

65. Ibid.

66. Ibid.

67. F. Adler, G. O. W. Mueller, and W. S. Laufer, *Criminal Justice: An Introduction*, 6th ed. (New York: McGraw-Hill, 2012), 335–36.

68. K. S. Van Wormer and C. Bartollas, *Women and the Criminal Justice System*, 2nd ed. (Boston, MA: Allyn & Bacon, 2007).

69. J. Diaz-Cotto, *Gender, Ethnicity, and the State: Latina and Latino Prison Politics* (Albany: State University of New York Press, 1996).

70. "For Some Mothers in Prison, a Sentence Doesn't Mean Separation," National Public Radio, February 22, 2015. Accessed at: http://www.npr.org/2015/02/22/388262646/for-some-mothers-in-prison-a-sentence-doesnt-mean-separation

71. Diane F. Reed and Edward L. Reed, "Mothers in Prison and Their Children," in Price and Sokoloff, *The Criminal Justice System and Women*, 261–73.

72. E.g., B. Bloom and D. Steinhart, *Why Punish the Children? A Reappraisal of the Children of Incarcerated Mothers in America* (San Francisco: National Council on Crime and Delinquency, 1993); S. H. Fishman, "Impact of Incarceration on Children of Offenders," *Journal of Children in Contemporary Society* 15 (1983): 89–99.

73. McGee et al., "From the Inside."

74. L. E. Glaze and L. M. Maruschak, *Parents in Prison and Their Minor Children*, U.S. Department of Justice, Bureau of Justice Statistics, 2008, NCJ 222984.

75. Jessica Pishko, interview by Arun Rath, All Things Considered, *National Public Radio*, February 22, 2015. Accessed at: http://www.npr.org/2015/02/22/388262646/for-some-mothers-in-prison-a-sentence-doesnt-mean-separation

76. E.g., C. F. Hairston, "Family Ties During Imprisonment: Important to Whom and for What?" *Journal of Sociology and Social Welfare* 18, no. 1 (1991): 87–104; N. E. Schaefer, "Prison Visiting Policies and Practices," *International Journal of Offender Therapy and Comparative Criminology* 35, no. 3 (1991): 263–75.

77. D. Johnston, "Intervention," in *Children of Incarcerated Parents*, ed. K. Gabel and D. Johnston (New York: Lexington Books, 1995), 199–236.

78. Luana Ross, "Resistance and Survivance: Cultural Genocide and Imprisoned Native Women," in Price and Sokoloff, *The Criminal Justice System and Women*, 235–47.

79. J. B. Morton, *Working with Women Offenders in Correctional Institutions* (Lanham, MD: American Correctional Association, 2004).

80. McGee et al., "From the Inside."

81. Danielle Kaeble, *Probation and Parole in the U.S., 2016*, U.S. Department of Justice, Bureau of Justice Statistics, 2015, NCJ 251148, 17.

82. Lauren E. Glaze, and Thomas P. Bonczar, *Probation and Parole in the United States, 2005*, U.S. Department of Justice, Bureau of Justice Statistics, November 2006, NCJ 215091.

83. Kaeble, *Probation and Parole in the U.S., 2016*, 24; Glaze and Bonczar, *Probation and Parole*; Kaeble et al., *Probation and Parole*, 7.

84. Marsha Bailey, "Georgia Parole Officers Confront Language and Cultural Barriers," *Corrections Today* (December 1991): 118, 120–21.

85. Ibid.

86. Criminal Justice Institute, *The Corrections Yearbook* (Middletown, CT: Author, 1998).

87. J. J. Stephan, *Census of State and Federal Correctional Facilities, 2005*, U.S. Department of Justice, Bureau of Justice Statistics, 2008, NCJ 222182.

88. DataUSA.com, "Probation Officers & Correctional Treatment Specialists," 2019. Accessed August 13, 2019, at: https://datausa.io/profile/soc/probation-officers-correctional-treatment-specialists; Federal Bureau of Prisons, "Staff Gender," 2019. Accessed at: https://www.bop.gov/about/statistics/statistics_staff_gender.jsp; Z. Zeng, *Jail Inmates in 2017*. U.S. Department of Justice, Bureau of Justice Statistics, 2019, NCJ 251774.

89. M. R. Pogrebin and E. D. Poole, "The Sexualized Work Environment: A Look at Women Jail Officers," *The Prison Journal* 77 (March 1997): 41–57.

90. John Irwin, *The Warehouse Prison: Disposal of the New Dangerous Class* (Los Angeles, CA: Roxbury, 2005).

91. J. Pollock, *Women, Prison and Crime*, 2nd ed. (Belmont, CA: Wadsworth, 2002).

92. N. Jurik, "An Officer and a Lady: Organizational Barrier to Women Working as Correctional Officers in Men's Prisons," *Social Problems* 32 (1985): 375–88.

93. Mary V. Leftridge Byrd, "African-American Women in Corrections," in C. Smalls (ed.), *The Full Spectrum: Essays on Staff Diversity in Corrections* (Lanham, MD: American Correctional Association, 2004), 105–116.

94. Irwin, *The Warehouse Prison*.

95. Ibid.

96. Van Wormer and Bartollas, *Women and the Criminal Justice System*.

97. Tekla S. Miller, "Woman Warden's Assignment Offered Rewarding Challenges," *Corrections Today* (December 1991): 110–11.

98. Van Wormer and Bartollas, *Women and the Criminal Justice System*

99. Ibid.

100. Van Wormer and Bartollas, *Women and the Criminal Justice System*.

101. Ilene R. Bergsmann, "ACA Women in Corrections Committee Examines Female Staff Training Needs." *Corrections Today* (December 1991): 106, 108–109.

102. Byrd, "African-American Women in Corrections."

CHAPTER 8

THE LGBT COMMUNITY AND THE CRIMINAL JUSTICE SYSTEM

CHAPTER OBJECTIVES

After reading this chapter, you should be able to:

- Describe the characteristics of the lesbian, gay, bisexual, and transgender (LGBT) populations in the United States
- Describe the history of the LGBT movement in the United States
- Understand hate crimes and the nature of victimization for LGBT people
- Discuss the issues and challenges in the criminal justice system in dealing with LGBT people. This includes gay police officers, juror bias against gays, and issues relating to prison experiences.

  - "I was standing on the street talking with some friends and a police officer approached me. She asked me for my ID and I gave it to her. She took a picture of my ID and sent it to the sixth precinct. The dispatcher told her my record was clear, but instead of letting me go, she said she wanted to look inside my purse. I didn't know my rights then or I would not have consented to the search. When she looked inside she saw two condoms. She called the precinct back and asked for a police car to come to her location. I asked her, 'Why are you locking me up? I can't carry condoms?' She replied, 'You are getting locked up for prostitution.' I was taken to the precinct and put in with the men. I was seventeen years old. For my community, it is not only being put at risk for HIV, STDs, or unwanted pregnancies, but having to be harassed and assaulted by police officers for being transgender or queer."[1]
  - "I spent three and a half years in federal prison on a drug charge. As a Black-trans woman, I experienced sexual violence while in prison. When I went to tell the prison staff, I was told that if I reported the assault the only place he could house me was in the SHU, which is isolation. I knew that being housed there would prevent me from participating in the drug program that was allowing me to qualify for early release and I would not be able to attend school programs that I was involved in. I chose to keep

quiet about what was happening to me so that I could be part of the program and be released from prison eighteen months early."[2]

- "I was jailed and eventually sentenced to a ten-year state prison term for aggravated assault on a police officer with a deadly weapon or dangerous instrument—the deadly weapon was my 'HIV-infected saliva.' After a six-year appeal, the charge was vacated by the New York State Court of Appeals and I was released. I remained on parole until 2014, where I was not allowed to leave my small county without my parole officer's permission. I cannot drive and was under a 9:00 pm curfew. I lost my health insurance and now rely on Medicare and Medicaid. I find myself having to explain my criminal history over and over again, from applying for housing to registering for classes at my local college. All of these things are a consequence of being charged with an HIV-related crime. I never realized the stigma attached to those with HIV and especially those who also have a criminal record."[3]

PUBLIC ATTITUDES ABOUT LESBIAN, GAY, BISEXUAL, AND TRANSGENDER PEOPLE

According to recent research by the National Opinion Research Center (NORC), an independent research organization affiliated with the University of Chicago, public attitudes toward gays and lesbians are changing. Based on the available evidence, the position of gays and lesbians in the United States has improved in recent decades.

For example, in 2017 in the United States, 61 percent of Americans support same-sex marriages, with 31 percent opposing it. Younger generations have higher levels of support for same-sex marriage, whereas many older Americans have only recently become supportive of same-sex marriage. Among other demographic variables, such as religious affiliation, race, gender, and political affiliation, a few trends should become clear.

Among Catholics and White mainline Protestants, about 60 percent support same-sex marriage, but the percentage is much lower among Black Protestants and White evangelical Protestants. Politically, approximately 75 percent of Democrats and Democratic-leaning Independents favor same-sex marriage, and even though only about 44 percent of Republicans support it, as with other groups these numbers have increased in the past decade as well. Approximately 62 percent of Whites and 51 percent of Blacks support same-sex marriage, along with 58 percent of Hispanics. Additionally, 66 percent of women and 57 percent of men favor same-sex marriage.[4]

These trends are quite different from what was seen in 2005. During that time, public opinion polls revealed that Americans were divided on same-sex marriage and the acceptance of homosexual people. A 2005 *USA Today*/CNN/Gallup poll found that, when asked whether same-sex relations between consenting adults should be legal, 48 percent agreed while 46 percent disagreed. Experts note that some of the factors relating to the general tolerance toward gay couples in general and same-sex marriages in particular involve a U.S. Supreme Court case that struck down anti-sodomy laws. Additionally, corporations have also become more accepting of the homosexual lifestyle.

For instance, Walmart expanded anti-discrimination protection to gay workers, while the Walt Disney Company changed its policy regarding the Fairy Tale Wedding program to include gay couples. Disney's prior policy was that only couples with a valid marriage license could purchase the service, which ranges in cost from $8,000 to more than $45,000. Disney Parks and Resorts Spokesman Donn Walker said, "We believe this change is consistent with Disney's long-standing policy of welcoming every guest in an inclusive environment. We want everyone who comes to celebrate a special occasion at Disney to feel welcome and respected."[5] Others see the change in acceptability of same-sex marriages as a function of the growing visibility of gays in the media, politics, and as cultural leaders.[6]

Still another issue relates to how LGBT people and people living with HIV (referred to here as PLWHIV) are involved in the criminal justice system. According to a recent national study, about 73 percent of all LGBT people and PLWHIV surveyed have had face-to-face contact with police officers during the past five years. About 5 percent report having spent time in jail or prison, a much higher rate than the 3 percent of the general U.S. adult population.[7] In fact, according to some advocacy groups, there is a consistent pattern of discrimination against LGBT and PLWHIV that is similar to many of the other minority groups discussed in this textbook. Like their African American, Hispanic, Native American, Asian, and elderly counterparts, part of the challenge of the disproportionate involvement in the criminal justice system can be understood in the context of issues relating to employment, education, social services, healthcare, and responses to violence. The difference, perhaps, between these other groups and LGBTs and PLWHIV, is that there may be less attention paid to their plight and less advocacy in terms of policy changes.[8]

In this chapter we will focus on how homosexuality affects the criminal justice system. While homosexual individuals are sometimes victimized because of their lifestyle, in what are known as hate crimes, there are other dimensions of this phenomenon as well, such as how the system perceives and responds to LGBTs and PLWHIV, and what are the internal challenges facing gay police officers within the system.

Disney has always maintained a level of sensitivity toward LGBT people.

OPERATIONALIZATION OF TERMS: GAY VERSUS HOMOSEXUAL

On one hand, defining homosexuality seems simple. Part of the difficulty in defining a topic like homosexuality, however, relates to the distinction between a person's behavior and their identity. Teenagers, for example, might vandalize an abandoned piece of property but are normally obedient and considerate of others. Or they might experiment with drugs but are not really drug abusers. This distinction between behavior and identity is found in the discussion of homosexuality. While people may engage in homosexual behavior, this does not mean they have taken on a homosexual identity.

The word **homosexual** first appeared in German in an 1869 political pamphlet by Karl Kertbeny intended to protest the inclusion of Prussian sodomy statutes in the German constitution. The term coincided with the discovery of an extensive network of gay males in European and North American cities. While it is not clear which came first, the discovery of a group of men with same-sex attractions or the label to identify them, by the mid-twentieth century, "homosexual" was frequently used to identify this segment of the population. The term also became compared to heterosexuality, which initially was understood to be connected to a desire for sexual contact with both sexes. Over time, however, "heterosexual" came to mean a desire for sexual contact exclusively with members of the opposite sex.[9]

The phrase **sexual orientation** is used to describe a sexual attraction toward people either of the same gender, the opposite sex, or both. The question of when someone is considered a heterosexual, homosexual, or bisexual is difficult to answer. Determining one's sexual orientation is not simply a matter of observing their behavior, since there is evidence that many heterosexuals have had homosexual encounters and vice versa. This runs counter to conventional wisdom, since many people believe that engaging in homosexual activity is evidence that a person must be a homosexual. However, there is substantial evidence to suggest this is not the case.[10]

For example, Alfred Kinsey's controversial study in the late 1940s of American males, and his study of American females in the 1950s, found that 37 percent of the males and 13 percent of females in his sample had had at least one homosexual encounter. So when does a man who has had a sexual encounter with another man become classified as homosexual? The problem is further complicated by the fact that research shows that many people engage in sexual experimentation before confining themselves to one type of sex partner. An added complication relates to a person's thoughts as well as their behaviors. What if a person is a heterosexual but has sexual fantasies about a homosexual encounter? How does one label that person? Sigmund Freud, for example, argued that one's sexuality is determined by their thoughts and images when becoming sexually aroused. Thus, a man who has same-sex fantasies while having sex with his wife would be classified as a homosexual even though there is nothing in his behavior that would indicate homosexual tendencies.

There is also the problem of what one might call **situational homosexuality**. These are instances in which homosexual behavior occurs between two otherwise heterosexual individuals. In this type of situation, homosexual behavior is contingent upon the environment in which a person finds themself. Examples would include prisons, ships at sea, monasteries and convents, or even boarding schools. Moreover, situational homosexuality consists of behavior that ranges from sexual experimentation, such as what might be found on a college campus, to prison rape. Even more complicated is the notion of **bisexuality**, where the person is attracted to both sexes. Like homosexuality, this sexual orientation has been stigmatized by both heterosexuals and homosexuals, making bisexuals feel pressured to "choose" one sexual preference or another.

The psychiatric literature on sexuality presents several theories about what "causes" homosexuality. According to some theorists, homosexuality is a regression to Freud's oral stage of development, meaning that most families of homosexual individuals are characterized by an overprotective mother and an absent father or that homosexual persons fear a dominant mother in the pre-Oedipal stage.[11] Other experts have suggested that homosexuality may be an expression of nonsexual problems, such as a fear of adult responsibility, or it may be triggered by various sexual experiences, such as an enjoyable homosexual encounter at an early age. Theories to explain lesbianism include memories of abusive relationships with men or disappointing heterosexual relationships.[12]

There may also be cultural factors at work to explain homosexuality. The need to fit in may drive some people into a particular orientation when their preferences are for members of the same sex. Thus, it is not clear how one goes about choosing a sexual orientation. It may be that people choose heterosexuality because they are attracted to the opposite sex or it may be that they feel pressured to be "normal" even though their thoughts, fantasies, and attractions are toward people from the same sex. Others may choose a homosexual orientation because they feel the need to be honest with who they are and in what they believe. Still others may not be able to decide and therefore choose bisexuality.

An added problem is that the research is not clear about whether sexual orientation is an actual choice or not. Some researchers have explored whether or not there is a biological connection to homosexuality. This is a very controversial topic, with biologists on one side and religious groups on the other. Biological proponents argue that homosexuality might be related to hormonal imbalances in the mother during pregnancy.[13] Others argue that homosexuality might be related to brain functioning.[14] Some research suggests that the hypothalamus in homosexual men is between 25 percent and 50 percent smaller than in heterosexual men.[15] Other studies have shown that homosexual men react differently to human pheromones than heterosexual men. Whatever the explanation, most theorists agree that homosexual orientation tends to arise at an early age.[16]

DIFFERENCES BETWEEN MALE AND FEMALE HOMOSEXUALITY

The incidence of female homosexuality appears less often than that of males. Female homosexuality is also much less visible. This is largely due to American social customs such as the greater tolerance for two females to hold hands in public, to dance, to kiss, or to share an apartment. Consequently, Americans are less likely to ascribe homosexuality to females than to males, making it much easier for females to conceal it if they choose to do so.

Lesbians tend to have fewer sexual partners than do male homosexuals. For example, while most males have "cruised," looking for sex with strangers, fewer than 20 percent of lesbians have done so. Lesbians tend to avoid the bar scene and tend to look for continuing, durable relationships. This may partly explain why male homosexuals, who tend to have numerous partners, have a larger representation in the numbers of AIDS cases. This is not to say that homosexual men do not form lasting gay relationships, it simply means that male homosexuals are more likely than females to "hook up" for casual sex.[17]

The term "LGBT" refers to the collective group of homosexual individuals who identify themselves as either lesbian, gay, bisexual, or transgender. It is a designation that reflects the larger community rather than a specific group. In this chapter, the terms "LGBT" and "gay/homosexual" will be used interchangeably to reflect the larger discussion, the history of the development of this movement, and some consideration to those who may be less informed about the recent stigma connected to the term "homosexual." Included, although not necessarily directly, are those individuals who are living with HIV/ AIDS. While not all LGBT individuals suffer from this illness, some that do fall into one of these classifications. Thus, people living with HIV, or PLWHIV, are incorporated into the larger discussion since they, too, often experience some levels of discrimination and mistreatment.

THE HISTORY OF HOMOSEXUALITY AND GAY IDENTITIES IN THE UNITED STATES

The general pattern of how American culture has perceived homosexuality over the sweep of history is best summarized by a transition from a sinful-conduct view, to a disease model, to the development of gay identities.[18] Churches have been largely responsible for the overall condemnation of homosexuality. In early America, colonial ministers spoke of an angry God who would rain fire and brimstone and destroy this segment of the population much in the same way He destroyed Sodom and Gomorrah. Citing scripture that deplores homosexuality, the distaste for homosexuality was a very powerful element in holding people accountable for their actions. Bible scripture also justified the harsh punishment inflicted on homosexual people. In every colony, sodomy was a capital offense while other homosexual acts, such as lewdness between women, were punished with whippings and fines.[19]

After the American Revolution, although Enlightenment philosophy largely dictated how laws were created, there was resistance to removing sodomy statutes as "crimes against nature." As time went on, legislatures and courts included a wider range of activities, such as oral sex between men and sexual activity between women. In the late nineteenth century, the medical profession diagnosed homosexuality as a form of mental illness. The development of Freudian psychoanalysis led many physicians and psychiatrists to conclude that homosexuality was an acquired affliction that required medical treatments, some of which were barbaric and torturous. Examples included electroshock therapy, lobotomy, hysterectomy, and castration.[20]

The development of psychiatry during this period also reinforced the medical model used to understand and treat homosexuality. Reflecting the attitudes, values, and beliefs about homosexuality at the time, many states enacted sexual psychopath laws to regulate consensual sex among same-sex partners. This medical model translated into criminal behavior for some adults. Not only were homosexual individuals perceived to be in need of treatment, and consequently more likely to spend time in mental institutions, but district attorneys often used the sexual psychopath laws to criminally prosecute them.[21]

Despite these risks, in the late nineteenth century, some people began to organize their lives around a homosexual orientation. At first certain parks, streets, and bathhouses became meeting places for men. Bars and clubs also appeared in or near **red-light districts,** or centers for prostitution, in major cities. As a result, a hidden urban gay subculture began to be seen in the 1920s and 1930s.[22]

After World War II ended, many men returned to the cities rather than going home to small towns. This, in turn, allowed many cities to begin to see an increase in the number of gay bars in the 1940s.[23] In the 1950s, during the time of the Cold War, not only were communists a threat to the American way of life, Senate investigations portrayed homosexuals in the same way. In fact, this perception was so pervasive that President Dwight D. Eisenhower issued an executive order barring gay men and lesbians from all federal jobs. In response, state and local governments followed suit, as did many companies in the private sector. The FBI created a surveillance program against homosexual individuals, and local police departments conducted undercover operations in gay bars, making mass arrests on a regular basis. Wichita, Dallas, Memphis, and Seattle were among the cities that most intensely attacked the gay community, averaging one hundred misdemeanor charges against gay men and lesbians per month.[24]

In the 1960s, influenced perhaps by the successful protests against other causes, such as the civil rights movement and the Vietnam War, the gay community began to

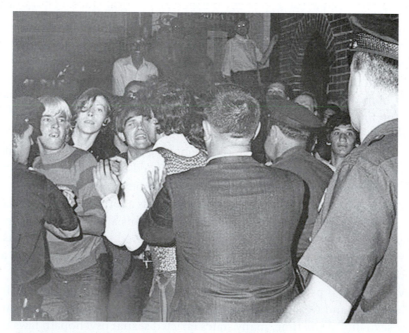

The Stonewall rebellion is a landmark moment in the history of the gay community's attempt to secure equal protection under the law.

organize politically. By 1969, nearly fifty gay-rights organizations existed in the United States, with membership running in the thousands. Then, on June 27, 1969, at the Stonewall Inn, a gay bar in New York City's Greenwich Village, the police conducted a raid. This time, members of the gay community resisted and violence broke out between citizens and the police. The angry response from patrons resulted in three nights of rioting and violence in the city. The Stonewall incident also spawned the "Gay power" movement. A massive grassroots gay liberation movement began, similar to those of Blacks, women, and college students of that era.

Like their militant counterparts, gay people challenged the public's perception of them, and the way they were treated by the larger society, with the proclamation that gays lived "alternative" rather than "deviant" lifestyles. The phrase "coming out of the closet" was born during this time to solidify their identity and value to the larger society. By 1973, there were almost eight hundred gay and lesbian organizations in the United States. By 1990, the number was several thousand.[25]

This politicization of the gay community resulted in changes in legislation, public policy, and the way gay people were perceived by American society. Not only did half the states decriminalize homosexual behavior over the next twenty years, but public and political pressure reduced the number of police raids, harassment, and arrests as well. Many cities included sexual orientation in their civil rights statutes, and in 1974 the American Psychiatric Association removed homosexuality from its list of mental illnesses. In 1975, the Civil Service Commission eliminated the ban on the employment of gays for federal jobs. In short, the gay and lesbian world was no longer hidden from public view. Gay individuals were very visible: there were gay businesses, political clubs, community centers, and even gay candidates running for public office.[26]

However, the "coming out" experience and identity was not universally welcomed. Mainstream society still had difficulty adjusting to the visible and militant presence of gays. The late 1970s and 1980s were a turbulent time for this community. Singer Anita Bryant, most known for her commercials regarding orange juice, began an anti-gay campaign in Dade County, Florida. The basis of her efforts was her opposition to equal rights for gays. Building off of her efforts, by the 1980s a conservative, Christian-based anti-gay movement had begun. Fundamentalist ministers such as Jerry Falwell, who formed the Moral Majority, Inc., worked with other groups to oppose homosexuality.

The threat of the AIDS epidemic in the early 1980s intensified anti-gay groups' efforts against homosexuality, this time from a public health perspective. However, the threat of AIDS also galvanized the homosexual community. As a result, many gay organizations were created to address the practical consequences of infection with the disease as well as its treatment. While initially perceived as a catastrophic event in the pursuit of equality for gays, AIDS was actually instrumental in shaping and changing the gay rights movement.[27]

The current issue in the gay rights movement focuses primarily on same-sex marriage. Although the issue of legalizing gay marriage was decided by the U.S. Supreme Court in the case of *Obergfell v. Hodges*,[28] the backlash against gay people can still be seen in the ways that they are victimized and discriminated against in the criminal justice system.

CHECKPOINT

- While the current climate in the United States shows that most Americans favor same-sex marriages and general support of LGBT populations, there is also a long history of mistreatment of this group. In addition, there is some controversy surrounding the definition of terms and how—or if—it can be definitively determined whether homosexuality is a biological phenomenon or a social choice.

LGBT PEOPLE AND THE CRIMINAL JUSTICE SYSTEM

HATE CRIMES AND VICTIMIZATION

On April 23, 1990, Congress passed the Hate Crime Statistics Act, which mandated that data be collected "about crimes that manifest evidence of prejudice based on race, religion, sexual orientation, or ethnicity." Management of this data was given to the FBI and the Uniform Crime Reporting program. The first report on hate crimes was issued in that same year, entitled *Hate Crime Statistics 1990: A Resource Book*, which drew from data in eleven states.

In 1994, Congress augmented the Hate Crime Statistics Act by passing the Violent Crime and Law Enforcement Act of 1994. This act expanded the scope of the Hate Crime Statistics Act by including bias against persons with disabilities. In 1996, Congress further expanded its efforts to understand and prevent hate crimes by passing the Church Arson Prevention Act. It also mandated that hate crime data become a permanent part of the Uniform Crime Reporting program.[29]

Methods of Collecting Hate Crime Data

In an effort to provide comprehensive coverage of hate crime information, the program merged the normal Uniform Crime Report information submitted by law enforcement agencies with hate crime data. The types of information reported include offense type, location, bias motivation, victim type, number of offenders, and the race of the offender.[30]

There are a number of challenges involved in the collection of information on hate crimes. For instance, because motivation is subjective, it is difficult to know whether a crime resulted from an offender's bias or some other factor. Additionally, even if the offender was biased toward a particular group or individual, their actions do not necessarily qualify as a hate crime. The only way an act is considered a hate crime is if the investigation into the incident reveals sufficient evidence to conclude that the offender's actions were motivated in some way by their bias.

As was mentioned, part of the data collected in the investigation of hate crimes consists of the crimes known to the police as a normal part of the UCR program. This includes **crimes against persons**, or violent crimes. Examples include murder and non-negligent manslaughter, forcible rape, assault, and intimidation. **Crimes against property**, or economic crimes, include burglary, larceny-theft, motor vehicle theft, vandalism, and arson.

Hate-crime legislation is an important component of protection for the gay community.

For those agencies that participate in the National Incident-Based Reporting System (NIBRS) an additional category is added, **crimes against society**, which include offenses such as gambling, prostitution, drugs, and weapons violations.[31]

Incidents and Offenses

The UCR program collects data about single-bias and multiple-bias hate crimes. For each offense reported, the police must indicate the motivation or bias on which it is based. A single-bias incident occurs when one or more offenses within the same incident are motivated by the same bias. A multiple-bias incident occurs when more than one offense occurs in the incident and at least two offenses are motivated by different biases. This means that there can be more incidents than offenses because for each incident, multiple crimes may occur.[32]

For instance, if a gay man is in a bar and a homophobic male attacks him, steals his wallet, and, as he leaves the bar, vandalizes the gay man's car, three separate crimes occurred: an assault, a robbery, and vandalism. However, because all three offenses were based on the fact that the victim was gay, the UCR would consider that a single-bias (sexual orientation) incident. In the same scenario, if the gay man is on a date with a Black man, and during the course of the same events, the offender shouts a racial slur at the Black man and threatens to kill both of them, now there is an assault, a robbery, threatening, and vandalism. For the purposes of data collection, that would be a multiple bias incident since two different types of bias are present: racial bias and sexual orientation bias.

Of the 16,149 agencies that participate in the hate crime program, 2,040 reported the occurrence of 7,175 hate crime incidents in 2017. These incidents involved 8,126 offenses, 8,493 victims, and 6,307 offenders.[33]

What the Data Show

The UCR program's analysis of the 8,437 offenses in 2017 showed a number of easily identifiable trends. That is, when hate crimes occur, they seem to consistently occur against particular groups. For instance, overall, approximately 58 percent of hate offenses were racially motivated; 22 percent were motivated by religious bias, and 16 percent occurred due to sexual-orientation bias. The data also reveal that the majority of hate crimes—63 percent—consisted of crimes against persons, while 37 percent were crimes against property (the designation of crimes against society accounted for only 1 percent of hate crime offenses).[34]

Of the racially based hate crime offenses in 2017, nearly 49 percent were the result of anti-Black bias and another 18 percent were motivated by anti-White bias. About 11 percent were anti-Hispanic, about 6 percent were against Native Americans, and the remainder was divided up between multiple race groups. Religious bias, which represents about 20 percent of all hate crimes, consists of 58 percent anti-Jewish motivations. About 18 percent were anti-Islamic, about 5 percent were anti-Catholic, another 3 percent were anti-Protestant, and the remainder was divided among other groups.[35]

With regard to sexual orientation, in 2017, there were 1,303 crimes overall, with gender identity bias incidents comprising 131 incidents. Of the latter, 118 were against transgender victims. Overall, approximately 58 percent of sexual orientation crimes were biased against gay males. Another 24 percent were generically anti-gay–motivated and about 12 percent targeted female homosexuals. Finally, there is disability bias. Recall that Congress included bias against disabled people in the hate crime statistics in 1994. Only 128 offenses in 2017 were based on disability, with 93 of them being against mentally disabled victims.

In terms of the type of victimization, about 27 percent of the offenses in 2017 consisted of intimidation while another 27 percent consisted of vandalism to property, and approximately 32 percent consisted of some type of assault, either a simple assault or one of a serious and aggravated nature.

Of the 6,307 known hate crime offenders in 2017, 51 percent were White, 21 percent were African American, and Hispanics represented about 8 percent of offenders. The remaining percentages were primarily unknown race or multiple race categories. Finally, in terms of the age of the offender, in the vast majority of cases—83 percent—offenders were over the age of 18.[36] Of the reported hate crime incidents in 2017, about 27 percent occurred in or near residences or homes. About 17 percent occurred on highways, roads, alleys, or streets, and about 8 percent happened at schools or colleges. Another 13 percent occurred in other locations, such as public buildings or churches.[37]

CHECKPOINT

- While the definition of a hate crime has been determined by federal legislation, the most recent data show that hate crimes in the United States consist primarily of anti-Black, anti-Jewish, anti-Hispanic, and anti–gay-male bias. The majority of events consisted of intimidation or assault and frequently occurred in or near the victim's home. Offenders tend to be male and White, although Blacks comprise about 20 percent of the offender population as well, and most offenders are adults.

GAY BASHING

On October 7, 1998, Matthew Shepard, a twenty-one-year-old student at the University of Wyoming, met Russell Henderson and Aaron McKinney in a bar in Laramie, Wyoming. Around midnight, Shepard asked the two men for a ride home. Subsequently, Shepard was robbed, severely beaten, and tied to a fence in a remote area, where he was left to die. About eighteen hours later, a bicyclist discovered Shepard, barely alive. Shepard suffered a fractured skull and had severe brain damage. Shepard never regained consciousness and died four days later. Police then arrested Henderson and McKinney.

There was an outcry of sympathy for Matthew Shepard. While he was in the hospital, candlelight vigils were held across the country. Moreover, people in the entertainment industry responded by making films about the case and writing songs in support of Shepard as a way of expressing their outrage over what had happened.

Both defendants attempted to use the "gay panic defense," arguing that they were driven temporarily insane by Shepard's sexual advances toward them. Henderson subsequently pleaded guilty and agreed to testify against McKinney to avoid the death penalty. In exchange, he received two consecutive life sentences. The jury found McKinney guilty of two counts of felony murder. As deliberations on whether to execute McKinney began, Shepard's parents intervened, which resulted in McKinney receiving two consecutive life terms without the possibility of parole.

The two defendants were not charged with a hate crime, since Wyoming had no such statute. A year after the trial, the Wyoming legislature introduced such a bill, but it was defeated on a 30-30 tie in the Wyoming House of Representatives.

Is Hate Crime Legislation Really Necessary?

Some researchers contend that hate crime legislation is not only unnecessary but it sets in motion a double standard of accountability that can create a host of problems. These problems stem largely from the way hate crime legislation is interpreted. Critics also contend that many state legislatures have passed laws to expand the general categories of hate crimes. As one author noted, "ethnic intimidation" legislation, which was originally targeted for people who are gay and transgender, have now expanded to include groups such as the elderly and people with disabilities. These "special status" crimes can include categories such as blindness, sensory handicap, involvement in human or civil rights activities, or even marital status or political affiliation."[38]

The main argument against hate crime laws is that they are unnecessary. The logic behind the legislation in the first place, opponents argue, was that hate crimes are worse than other forms of violence against a particular group of people. However, critics contend that some advocacy groups exaggerate the extent of hate crimes, creating a climate of fear about persecution, exploitation, and victimization that requires greater protection by the law. As evidence of this claim, one commentator noted that

> a careful look at hate crimes data shows that such crimes are a tiny fraction of major violent crimes and that many "hate crimes" are nonviolent personal conflicts. The federal Hate Crimes Reporting Act of 1990 requires that "intimidation" be included as a reported crime. This category, which consists of threats that are never carried out, accounts for 56 percent of the FBI's annually reported hate crimes against persons. In 2001, the FBI reported that there were 9,730 hate crime incidents. The fact that there were over 11,849,006 crimes reported to the police in 2001 suggests that less than one percent (0.09 percent) of personal or property crimes is a hate crime in the United States.[39]

In 2017, a similar trend showed that there were 8,437 hate crimes out of a total of 8,941,407 offenses known to the police. This, too, consists of less than 1 percent of all personal and property crimes (0.09 percent). In general, then, some experts contend that a special category of hate crimes is not needed since existing criminal law adequately protects victims. As evidence, one opponent to hate crimes argues that

> Wyoming has no hate crime laws but the killers of Matthew Shepard were sentenced to life in prison without parole and would have been sentenced to death, but for the request of Shepard's parents. Likewise, when James Byrd was dragged to his death by three men in Texas, the Texas criminal justice system reacted with its characteristic severity; two of the killers are on death row and the third was sentenced to life imprisonment. A hate crimes law in Texas could not have increased their punishment by one iota, nor could it have deterred their acts any more than the existence of the death penalty did.[40]

As evidence of the problems in highlighting hate, or bias, in crimes, consider the case in which a man and his wife were camping at an Ohio campground. The couple played their radio too loudly, disturbing the family in the next campground. When the park ranger told the couple to turn the radio down, they complied, but fifteen minutes later they turned it up again. The husband who was asked to lower his radio then yelled that he ought to shoot the campers at the next campsite. During his diatribe toward his fellow campers, the man used the word "nigger" and another racial epithet. He did not take any steps to carry out his threat, nor did he act in a violent way. While the man should have been prosecuted for disturbing the peace and making a threat, he was convicted of a hate crime felony and sentenced to a year-and-a-half in prison. If he had not said those words, his offense would have been a misdemeanor, subject to a sentence of perhaps no jail time or up to six months.[41]

Another potential problem with hate crimes, say critics, is that while ordinarily laws regarding harassment, disturbing the peace, and other forms of minor misbehavior require some fact finding about the offender's behavior, hate crime legislation often requires judges to determine a person's motives, their opinions, and whether they acted upon statements made, either in the present or in the past.

Critics of hate crimes point out that once the government begins to identify some groups for special treatment, it is difficult to determine which groups should or should not be given the same consideration. For instance, the number of women with a divorced spouse who stalks them is greater than the number of gays who are attacked because of their sexual orientation; however, no such special crime is identified for domestic violence. Why does one group merit special consideration? If it is based on extensive harm or violence, should women and other groups have similar protections?

Finally, critics of hate crime legislation argue that these statutes infringe upon freedom of thought. To punish someone because of their bad political thoughts or because of their inappropriate political words expressed during a crime, is to punish them more because of the beliefs they hold.

CHALLENGES FOR LGBT PEOPLE AND PLWHIV IN THE CRIMINAL JUSTICE SYSTEM

While the issues discussed in previous sections provide a broad context of understanding relating to how this group is affected by policies and practices within the criminal justice system, it would be a mistake to think of gays as a homogenous group. What is consistent, however, is that gender and sexuality impact law enforcement practices, interactions with court personnel and its operation. Additionally, the correctional system has a host of issues and challenges related to gender and sexuality. Each agent of the criminal justice system will be considered next, along with how sexuality impacts practitioners within the system as well.

LGBT PEOPLE/PLWHIV AND THE POLICE

Much of the literature regarding the relationship between LGBTs or PLWHIV and the police suggests that there may be a different set of standards used to stop and search these suspects than those used with the general public. For example, as one study pointed out, it is common for LGBT people, and particularly women and youth, to be perceived as involved in sex work. As such, police in some jurisdictions use possession of condoms as evidence supporting arrests for prostitution-related offenses.[42] Another study pointed out that LGBT people and PLWHIV are often targets of harassment by the police. Transgender people of color in particular are three times more likely to be victims of harassment and assault than non-transgender people. However, according to the National Coalition of Anti-Violence Programs, about half of the survivors who reported the violence to the police also reported incidents of police misconduct.[43]

In a recent national survey of LGBT people, a quarter of respondents who had recently had contact with the police reported at least one type of misconduct or harassment, including false arrests and verbal or physical assault by officers. Moreover, LGBT people of color were five times more likely to be asked about their immigration status by police officers than White survey respondents.

In light of these studies, it should not be surprising that many LGBT respondents in the study were uncomfortable seeking the help of the police should they need it.[44] Yet, given the nature of their existence, where homelessness, poverty, and other social challenges serve to marginalize this group, the likelihood of victimization for those same individuals is much higher than for the rest of the population. In fact, one study found that, over the past decade, the police have been among the top three categories of offenders against LGBT people.[45] As was mentioned, many LGBT youth are homeless or housing-challenged—by one estimate, LGBT youth make up 40 percent of all homeless youth in the United States.[46] As a result, LGBT people are impacted by police sweeps as well as by laws that address the use of public spaces. According to one report, about half to two-thirds of homeless LGBT in New York reported that they had been stopped, searched, threatened with arrest, or falsely arrested by police, compared to only 25 percent of LGBT youth who live in their own apartments.[47]

Further, challenges exist when LGBT people are arrested. According to the National Prison Rape Elimination Commission, as well as reports by human rights organizations, women and

LGBT people in police custody often experience unlawful searches and sexual assaults while in detention. Some of these searches and assaults, either on the street or in lockup, are ostensibly for the purpose of assigning a gender to detainees, but it is a short step from that to abuse.[48]

GAY POLICE OFFICERS

The idea of the police being a subculture is not new and has been well documented.[49] For our purposes, a **subculture** may be defined as the meanings, values, and behavior patterns unique to a particular group in a given society. Entry into the police subculture begins with a process of socialization whereby recruits learn the values and behavior patterns characteristic of experienced officers. The development and maintenance of attitudes and values by police officers have both positive and negative implications.

In addition to a certain **homogeneity**, or similarity in attitudes, values, and beliefs in policing, many experts have argued that law enforcement embraces ideas of masculinity, strength, and bravery, with femininity being equated with weakness. It should not be surprising, then, to realize that there is also a tendency for police officers to be homophobic, particularly towards gay males. Essentially there are two issues relating to the relationship between gays and police officers. The first relates to how heterosexual police officers treat gay suspects, victims, and citizens, while the second focuses on the way gay police officers are treated by their law enforcement colleagues.

Homophobia and Policing

While **gay bashing**, or unprovoked attacks on people with gay identities, remains a fundamental problem for this group, one area of concern relates to the way police officers treat gay and lesbian victims. Recall the recent surveys, where many LGBT people have claimed harassment, threats, and misconduct by police officers. In fact, many police officers have observed the differential treatment at times.

One study showed that officers believe that a correlation exists between general attitudes toward gays and lesbians and actual discriminatory behavior. Between 30 percent and 40 percent of officers indicate that gays and lesbians will not be treated the same or will not be taken as seriously as heterosexuals by the larger society. Although the study points out that this might be an improvement over how gay people have been treated in the past, the implication is that problems will still be evident for gays and lesbians and they will remain relatively easy targets for harassment.[50]

Another study examined police officers' responses to incidents of domestic violence involving same-sex couples compared to opposite-sex couples. Although members of the gay and lesbian community believe that police officers respond differently to same-sex couples, this study offered four versions of a scenario depicting an incident of domestic violence to which two imaginary police officers responded. The study found that the sexual orientation of the couple played a role in how the officers handled the situation. While this study could not predict how officers would respond to an actual incident, the findings do raise a number of questions about traditional law enforcement interactions with same-sex couples.[51]

Homophobia Within Policing

Historically, gay police officers felt that they could not reveal their sexual orientation among colleagues since law enforcement is known to be male-dominated and portrays a macho image. Gay officers feared embarrassment, harassment, or isolation if their sexual identities became known. In the past, one of the attractions to law enforcement as a career was the sense of brotherhood and camaraderie. To be excluded from that community, particularly since police officers often feel isolated from the larger society, would make it difficult for officers to function effectively. It also meant that officers might not receive assistance in emergency situations from their fellow officers. Thus, many homosexual officers felt they could not reveal their identities and had to hide behind a more macho image.

Some of the early research on homosexuality in policing suggested there was a lot of truth to these perceptions. For instance, in perhaps one of the most thoughtful books on the subject of gay police officers, Steven Leinen interviewed forty-one gay officers from the New York City Police Department (NYPD). In the vast majority of cases, homosexual officers described the fear of being discovered by other officers as well as the struggles of passing themselves off as heterosexuals.[52]

More recently, in response to court cases, many police departments that had previously refused to hire known homosexuals and did not offer any type of support mechanisms for gay cops began to develop programs to address their needs. There appear to be mixed findings about how gay police officers are treated. On one hand, there appears to be evidence that officers remain hostile toward gay officers. Being an openly gay officer once meant being subject to overt ridicule, including anti-gay graffiti painted on an officer's locker or having their uniform soaked in urine. Like much of the overt racism against Blacks, outright anti-gay behavior in law enforcement has become more subdued. However, there is some evidence that discriminatory treatment remains. One study of the San Diego Police Department found that while having openly gay and lesbian officers does not undermine the effectiveness of the department, some forms of discrimination and harassment do exist. This means that openly gay officers face a number of challenges.[53]

Two groundbreaking court decisions made it easier for gay officers to publicly proclaim their sexual orientation. In *Romer v. Evans* in 1996, the U.S. Supreme Court struck down a Colorado constitutional amendment that denied gay men and lesbians anti-discrimination protections. Some legal experts argued that this case cleared the way for other states to protect gay employees. In 2003, the U.S. Supreme Court struck down anti-sodomy laws, which essentially took away termination-for-cause options for police departments. Prior to 2003, departments could refuse to hire gays and could fire officers who came out because they were presumed to be engaging in illegal behavior.[54]

Some gay officers have successfully sued police departments for discriminating against them. For instance, a California Highway Patrol officer won $1.5 million in damages after other officers used derogatory names to describe him and urinated on his uniform and stuffed it in his locker. In 1993 a Los Angeles Police Department (LAPD) officer sued the department and settled once the department agreed to create anti-gay harassment policies. He sued the department again in 1996 for failure to implement those policies. In 2005, a New Jersey police officer sued his department for failing to protect him from taunts and harassment by his coworkers.

Additionally, if the number of gay police officers is any indication of a willingness to reject traditional views of homosexuality in law enforcement, there may be reason for optimism. Gays and lesbians have become an increasingly larger part of policing over the past two decades. In fact, some departments have actively recruited gay officers, particularly in areas heavily populated by gays and lesbians.

While the law has granted gays some protections, there remains a considerable level of fear among gay officers. While some officers argue that being gay is less stigmatizing than ever before, pointing to the creation of liaison officers between departments and the gay community[55] as well as the creation of gay officers' associations in many agencies across the country, other officers contend that problems occur even when departments seem to be attempting to minimize the effects of homophobia in their organizations. Gay officers argue that they are still the target of harassment and jokes, and, perhaps most importantly, other officers will not provide them "backup" on calls for service.[56]

There is also the issue of the type of homosexuality to consider. Some male officers feel that lesbians in policing are more likely to be accepted, partly, they say, because of their common interest in women. As one gay female officer put it, "It's plain to me that it's much easier for women to be accepted. We work mainly with men and are treated like one of the guys. They'll joke around with you, like saying 'check out that hot chick over there.'"[57]

Some gay officers believe that their sexual orientation is actually an asset in the performance of their duties. One study in a Midwestern police department found that gay officers viewed themselves as particularly qualified to work with marginal groups, largely because they understand the implications and consequences of being stigmatized by the larger society. Officers in this study described the double marginality they experience: as police officers they are prevented from being fully integrated into the larger community and they are also gay, which creates a host of problems in terms of their place in the larger culture.[58]

Other gay officers believe that sexual orientation matters less than people think in policing. Rather, these officers argue that acceptance by non-gay officers has more to do with professional competency. There may be some empirical support for this perception. One study found that gay officers balance the stigma of "homosexual" with the value of being a "good cop." This study found that officers did not view themselves in terms of their being men, women, or even homosexual or heterosexual. Rather, they believed that officers who worked hard and proved themselves to be competent were more likely to be accepted by other officers. This study also found that gay officers viewed their sexual orientation as a professional asset rather than as a liability in dealing with the public.[59]

To be designated a "good cop," police officers must have professional skills that are needed to survive the work environment. Among police officers, a good cop was characterized by the following general terms:

- An officer who backs up a partner and co-workers in emergency situations
- An officer who covers up co-workers' indiscretions or misconduct at work, or at the very least, does not betray a fellow officer who is accused of having engaged in misconduct

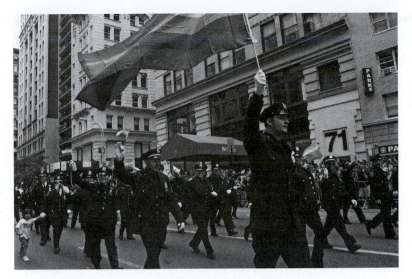

Increasingly, more gay police officers feel free to publicly celebrate their sexual orientation.

- An officer who is a risk-taker and not afraid to deviate from departmental rules to get the job done
- An officer who shares in the workload, especially in the handling of routine or tedious jobs; and who does not look for others to do his or her work.[60]

A fascinating dimension to the study of gay police officers is the fact that the issue of stigmatization, discriminatory practices, and the lack of legal protections are rather unique to American policing. Other countries, particularly the United Kingdom, have dealt with the issue of homosexuality in law enforcement for some time. One example of this acceptance is the popularity of the Gay Police Association (GPA) in England. Formed in 1990, it has grown into a formidable agency with members in all of the police forces in England. Focusing on policy development, hate crimes, victim care, and training in cultural diversity, the GPA has been a leader not only on issues relating to homosexuality but also for those with physical disabilities, minority groups, and women. Other studies in England point to the ways in which police officers are treated as compared to those in the United States.[61]

CHECKPOINT

- Both within policing as well as during officer encounters with citizens, there is a documented pattern of differential treatment involving members of the LGBT community. Much of the literature regarding the relationship between LGBTs or PLWHIV and the police suggests that there may be a different set of standards used to stop and search LGBT suspects than that used with the general public. Within policing there are an increasing number of gay police officers who have brought lawsuits against departments for their failure to provide equal protection of their civil rights.

THE COURTS AND LGBT PEOPLE

The courts also appear to have some difficulty in dealing with the gay community. Some scholars argue that the status of homosexual people in society is reflected in the kind of treatment they receive from the courts. This is particularly true with regard to jury bias. The jury is one of the most important parts of the legal system in this country and it is required to be composed of a fair cross-section of the population. If a jury is biased against gays, a defendant might be convicted for being homosexual rather than for the crime they have committed. Further, jury bias against gays can raise questions about the credibility of a gay witness despite the fact that this should have no bearing on whether they are telling the truth. Bias against gays can also result in reduced sentences against an offender who victimizes a gay person since the jury might perceive the victim as deserving of what happened to them.[62] Thus, the composition of juries, their perceptions of homosexuality, and how sexuality factors into jury decisions all play a pivotal role in understanding the relationship between gays and the justice system.

Perhaps one of the most obvious instances of jury bias relates to the ways defendants are treated who victimize gay people. One controversial legal aspect of homophobia occurred in the 1990s, called the **homosexual advance theory**, in which courts allow a nonviolent homosexual advance to constitute sufficient provocation to incite a reasonable man to "lose his self-control and kill in the heat of passion, thus mitigating murder to manslaughter." The homosexual advance theory is different from self-defense in that it does not attempt to justify the behavior of the offender. Rather, the theory states that it is a mitigating factor that should reduce the severity of the crime. While not all courts allow this theory to be introduced in homicide cases, the fact that some do raises concerns that perhaps some juries and judges allow their individual preferences on sexuality to interfere with equality of justice.[63]

For example, in *Schick v. State* (570 N. E. 2d 918 [Ind. Ct. App. 1991]), the defendant, Schick, claimed that after being propositioned by a man for sex, Schick had attacked him, knocking him to the ground. When Schick had stopped hitting and kicking the man, he heard "gurgling noises" coming from the man's chest. Schick took the man's wallet and left the scene. The man later died. At trial, Schick argued that he had been so repulsed by being propositioned by another man that he had lost control. The jury found Schick not guilty of murder while attempting to commit robbery, but he was convicted of voluntary manslaughter.

In other cases, however, the homosexual advance played no part in the decision at trial. For example, in *State v. Volk* (421 N.W. 2d 360 [Minn. Ct. App. 1988]) the defendant was convicted of second-degree murder after the trial court refused to give a manslaughter instruction to the jury. Volk allegedly was hitchhiking with his friend, who testified that they had planned to pose as prostitutes, pick up a gay man, and rob him. They found the victim at a store, and he invited Volk and his friend to his apartment. Volk allegedly hit the victim over the head with a liquor bottle and tied him up. When Volk's friend left to search the victim's car for money, the victim freed himself, attacked Volk, and during the fight Volk shot him twice. At trial Volk argued that, in part, he was revolted by the victim's homosexual advance and this should serve, like intoxication and exhaustion, as a mitigating factor in the crime. The court found that there "was no provocation sufficient to elicit a heat of passion response." The court further found that a reasonable person finding themselves in such circumstances would have simply walked away from the scene.

These cases show how divided the courts are in deciding which set of circumstances warrant the homosexual advance criteria as a mitigating factor. The most important point with regard to the homosexual advance theory is that if juries are allowed to use a homosexual advance as a mitigating factor in the commission of a crime, courts reinforce the idea that gay men do not have the same protections afforded to nonhomosexual men in the criminal justice system.[64]

While the homosexual advance theory remains controversial, where there is greater agreement about the likelihood of jury bias against homosexual individuals is found in the selection process. This is not to say that all juries are biased against gay people; however, there is greater concern over how and in what ways jury bias can creep into the process, causing a host of problems in the administration of justice. The main question surrounding *voir dire*, or the jury selection process, concerns jurors' sexuality and how such information should be used.

In some cases, sexual orientation is one of the main issues presented to the jury, such as in cases of hate crimes or sexual discrimination. Thus, in those cases where sexual orientation is a central issue, potential jurors' attitudes toward homosexuality may affect whether attorneys can select an impartial jury. What is less clear is whether jurors should be questioned about homosexuality when sexual orientation is not an issue in the case but where the defendant or the victim is gay. Considering that jury bias against gays plays a crucial role in the outcome of such cases, is it fair for a court to ask individual jurors about their sexual orientation, or is it an invasion of privacy?

The courts have indicated that jurors have some privacy rights when being asked to serve on juries. It appears that two conditions must be met if a juror can legitimately be asked about his or her sexual orientation. First, it must be clear that sexual orientation–related bias might bear on deliberations. As was mentioned, in those cases involving hate crimes or sexual discrimination suits, clearly the jurors' sexual orientation is a significant factor in the case. However, in those cases where the victim or the defendant is gay but there is no legal question about sexual orientation, it is unlawful for attorneys to ask jurors about their own sexuality.

The second condition relates to the first in that it is an invasion of privacy to ask jurors about their own sexuality when any bias against gays could be discovered simply by asking jurors about their attitudes toward homosexuality. In other words, the attorney cannot circumvent a juror's right to privacy under the guise of trying to determine juror bias by starting with a round of questions about how they feel about homosexuality and then asking them about their own sexual orientation. The best way to avoid jury bias against gays appears to be to allow the questioning of jurors about their attitudes toward homosexuality in general.

Some experts believe that an unbiased jury will not allow evidence of sexuality of the victim or the defendant to affect the outcome of the case. They will not care if the defendant in a rape case is gay or if the murder victim made a homosexual advance.[65] Jury bias and homophobia by court personnel sometimes affect decision-making. While the courts have never provided a constitutional protection of a jury of one's peers (meaning that a gay person cannot ask for a jury made up of only other gay people), they have provided that a jury will come from a cross-section of the population, and there are steps that can be taken to minimize the bias many people feel toward gay defendants and victims.

CHECKPOINT

- As it relates to the courts, there is some evidence of a credibility issue for members of the LGBT community. The homosexual advance theory is one strategy that continues to demonstrate that members of this group are not seen as credible witnesses during courtroom testimony as well as providing a defense strategy for those who may be accused of hate crimes based on sexual orientation.

LGBT PEOPLE AND PRISON LIFE

Certain places, such as prisons, induce situational homosexual behavior, which includes acts of homosexuality by people who do not otherwise practice it. The first ethnographic study of sex by male inmates was conducted in 1934. Joseph Fishman, a former inspector for federal prisons, found that inmates engaging in homosexual activity were divided into different categories based on whether or not the behavior was coerced or consensual.[66]

In the late 1950s, Gresham Sykes wrote a book on prison life entitled *The Society of Captives*. Sykes describes the process by which a person becomes socialized into prison life. He refers to it as **prisonization**. It is a social and physical transformation of the individual in an effort to compensate for the pains of imprisonment, one of which relates to sexual behavior. Sykes argues that being deprived of heterosexual outlets leads the prison inmate to find ways to alleviate the stress associated with it.[67]

Building on Sykes's and Fishman's work, research in the 1970s on prison life included homosexual behavior. The findings of several studies resulted in a number of typologies to describe participants who engage in homosexual activities. The first is the **queen**. Inmates and staff use the term to refer to a male inmate who prefers male sexual partners. The queen is not really engaged in situational homosexual behavior, for "she" would prefer male partners in prison or on the outside. To attract partners, the queen exaggerates aspects of female sexuality. She may take on a feminine nickname and let her hair grow long, wear jewelry, makeup etc. The queen is accorded some social status in the prison, but not much.

The second type of participant is called the **punk**. This group of homosexual inmates are accorded one of the lowest statuses in the institution. Punks are despised by inmates who see homosexual behavior as the result of either weakness in the face of pressure or a willingness to sacrifice one's manhood to obtain goods and services. There are essentially two types of punks: **canteen punks**, who perform oral or anal sex in exchange for candy, cigarettes, or other items purchased at the prison store or canteen, and **pressure punks**, who are inmates that submit to homosexual behavior because they have been threatened or raped by other prisoners. There are generally two ways to become a pressure punk. An inmate may offer help of some sort to a new inmate or "fish." If the fish accepts the offer, he then becomes indebted to his benefactor. The second way is to rig a gambling game so that the fish loses. In either case, when the debt is called, the fish cannot usually pay, so the inmate demands sex as payment. This leaves the fish with two choices: fight the inmate or submit to the sexual advance. Anyone who submits must continue to do so for the rest of his prison term.

The third type of participant in prison is called the **wolf** or **jocker**. This type of inmate is viewed by his colleagues as a "man." To remain a "man" and still engage in homosexual acts, the jocker has to present an image of exaggerated toughness. So the jocker uses force: he rapes. The more violence that surrounds his sexual acts, the more he is seen as masculine. To maintain his status, he must also keep his sexual acts emotionless and impersonal. It is not uncommon for a wolf to "own" a punk and to prostitute him much in the same way a pimp uses a female prostitute on the street.[68]

As was mentioned, early research on situational homosexual behavior indicated that men in single-sex environments such as the military, correctional institutions, boarding schools, or remote work sites have been known to engage in sexual activities with one another yet maintain a heterosexual identity. The behavior was simply defined as a response to the deprivation or lack of mixed-sex interactions. The general belief was that most men who engage in this type of activity would return to heterosexual sexual activities once they return to a mixed-sex environment.

The early explanations for homosexual behavior in prison focused on environmental influences—that is, that the social structure of the prison produces and promotes homosexual behavior. First, the lack of female companionship may drive some men toward homosexual behavior, particularly if this type of behavior is tolerated by prison officials and understood as necessary by other inmates.

Another factor relating to prison homosexuality is idleness. Without opportunities to work or engage in distracting activities, some research suggests that homosexual behavior is more likely. Another reason for homosexual behavior in prisons relates to overcrowding. Currently, many prisons exceed their maximum capacity for inmates. Overcrowding means more inmates per cell, less privacy, and the greater likelihood of inmates acting upon their sexual urges. Finally, experts note that when prisons prohibit pornography or conjugal visits, which can act as release methods for prisoners to achieve some of their sexual desires, the incidence of homosexual behavior and prison rape increases. Currently, only a few states allow conjugal visits in their correctional facilities.[69]

Another significant issue with regard to homosexual behavior in prisons relates to HIV/AIDS. Clearly, the spread of sexually transmitted diseases is an important area of concern for all institutions, particularly those that house violent inmates, where prison rape is more common. While abstinence is clearly the most effective method to prevent the transmission of HIV/AIDS or other sexually transmitted diseases, this is less likely to occur in prison. The other primary method to prevent the spread of diseases is through safe-sex practices. However, many prison officials are reluctant to promote safe sex since it suggests that they are supplying condoms to inmates for the purpose of engaging in prohibited behavior inside the institution.[70]

While the subject of coerced sexual behavior in prison has been studied extensively, consensual homosexual behavior has been largely ignored in the literature. Most of the research on this subject focuses on the formation of surrogate families in female prisons. What appears to be missing from the literature is research on masturbation and consensual sex among males in prison. While these two practices appear to be vastly more common than prison rape or some type of coerced sex, only a few studies exist on consensual homosexual activity in U.S. male prisons, four of which were conducted in the 1980s or early 1990s. The general findings of these studies showed that the vast majority of inmates masturbated on a regular basis and if consensual homosexual behavior occurred, inmates who considered themselves heterosexuals almost always took on the masculine role in the interaction, while the feminine role was associated with being a gay or bisexual person.[71]

A more recent study explored the dynamics of these activities in an attempt to understand how and in what ways the prison environment induced changes in one's sexual identity both inside the institution as well as once the inmate was released. The findings of this study showed that race significantly affected an inmate's decision to engage in homosexual behavior. Whites were more likely to engage in homosexual activity than non-Whites. Additionally, White inmates were more likely to be targeted for sexual approaches than non-White inmates. The explanation for this may be that non-White inmates perceive homosexual activity as a threat to their identity as both males and heterosexuals. In fact, there are some studies that show that Black inmates are more likely to rape White inmates while incarcerated.[72]

It is important to note that whether or not inmates remain involved in homosexual activity after their release is unclear. While the prison environment can explain why some inmates engage in homosexual activity, whether as consensual partners or due to the threat of violence, what is unclear is what happens after they are released.[73]

WOMEN, HOMOSEXUALITY, AND PRISON LIFE

The early research on same-sex behavior among female inmates suggested that, in an effort to replace lost family roles, "pseudo families" or kinship networks dominated life in women's prisons. The relationships formed in prison dominated social life for inmates, and the social structure it created simulated life outside prison walls. "Marriages," "divorces," "infidelity," and other evidence of family drama were found in prisons among women.[74] Although the relationships women form in prison continue to reflect early research trends discovered in the 1960s, 1970s, and even 1980s, there is some evidence that these types of prison relationships have diminished in recent years. One researcher noted that while female offenders still participate in "pseudo families" and form homosexual relationships with other inmates, it is not considered acceptable, nor is it practiced by all inmates.[75]

The dynamics of social interaction among female inmates suggests that the move away from rehabilitation as a philosophy of punishment, which has been replaced with a more punitive orientation, has had an impact on the types of social relationships inmates form with each other. Rather than forming caring relationships, or extended networks of quasi-families, female inmates are more reluctant than before to become involved with others. Preferring instead to "doing time" alone, many female inmates are beginning to resemble their male counterparts in that they prefer to avoid common areas in the prison and rely only on a few trusted friends. This is done in an attempt to survive an increasingly violent and unstable environment in women's prisons.

Some of the changes in female inmates' relationships are structural: in the past, women's institutions were designed to be more conducive to social interaction. The cottage system of the 1960s was designed to facilitate a more rehabilitative approach to women largely because it was felt that if the prison environment were more like a home than a cell, inmates would be more successful in being rehabilitated. With the change in orientation from rehabilitation to an emphasis on punishment, many women's prisons now resemble male prisons. Additionally, prisons are less isolating than in the past. Inmates can continue to be influenced by the larger culture through television, movies, radio, visits with family members and, in some cases, conjugal visits.

This makes the aforementioned "pains of imprisonment" different from what they were in the past. It also negates the need for a single unifying inmate subculture that provides surrogate roles for inmates to emulate the outside. Thus, inmates simply do not need the same types of relationships they did in the past, and given the wider diversity of female offenders entering prisons, there is less cohesiveness and there are greater levels of violence. Consequently, while homosexual relationships still occur in women's prisons, their need and pervasiveness have declined.[76]

For LGBT people and PLWHIV, prison life presents additional challenges. For instance, a 2009 study found that transgender prisoners experience sexual victimization at a rate thirteen times higher than non-transgender prisoners.[77] This is what led to the National Prison Rape Elimination Commission to mandate that correctional facilities take more pronounced steps to protect this segment of the inmate population from harm. While the violence and victimization that occur in prison have been well documented, the issues related to protecting and providing adequate care for LGBTs and PLWHIV are significant, and many correctional institutions are limited in their ability to provide adequate care.

The solution by many correctional facilities has been to place LGBT people and PLWHIV in solitary confinement for their protection. However, such a practice results in a lack of access to mail, job opportunities, and programs while incarcerated. Some reports indicate that LGBT people remain in protective custody for years, meaning that they are likely to serve much of their sentence in isolation and are more likely to serve the maximum time since they are not eligible for good-time credit and early release.[78]

Another dimension relating to the incarceration of LGBT people and PLWHIV relates to immigration. According to one estimate, there are at least 267,000 undocumented LGBT

immigrants in the United States. While an exact figure cannot be determined, it is estimated that a significant percentage of those detained in immigration detention and holding facilities are LGBT people.[79]

Further, because of changes in immigration policy in the United States, the number
of persons detained by immigration officials has dramatically increased in recent years.
Advocates estimate that almost 70 percent of the 420,000 persons detained by Immigration
and Customs Enforcement (ICE) were held in state and local facilities. While the same
issues for LGBT immigrants occurs for natives, meaning the discrimination, use of solitary confinement, and so on, there is the added challenge of filing a claim for asylum
during the one-year window, which impacts nearly 20 percent of those people fleeing
persecution.[80]

SUMMARY

There can be little doubt that the debate over gay identity and same-sex marriage in this
country remains controversial. Public opinion polls in past years showed a general tolerance for gay lifestyles, and, more recently Americans have been found to be more willing
to grant gays equal rights. Evidence of the intolerance of gays is seen throughout American
history and it was only in the 1960s, with the famous Stonewall incident, that the gay community began to assert itself and organize politically in an effort to change people's understanding of the gay lifestyle. Despite the apparent progress, gays remain a stigmatized
and victimized group. Hate crime legislation, which was enacted in 1990 to provide additional protection against offenders motivated by a racial, religious, or sexual orientation
bias, made it a federal crime to victimize gays. Despite the small number of crimes, the
symbolic importance of hate crime legislation is an important illustration of the position
of gay people in America.

The gay community has also experienced discrimination and other problems when
gay people have entered certain professions such as law enforcement. Like the society as a
whole, while it appears progress is being made in terms of equal treatment, gay police officers still encounter problems in their profession. Similarly, when homosexual individuals
find themselves in court, whether as defendants, victims, or witnesses, a number of unique
challenges are presented. Juror bias in particular is perhaps the greatest problem in the
courts in the administration of justice for gay people.

Finally, homosexual behavior in prison has been a long-standing problem. Prison rape
as well as consensual sex have created numerous problems for prison officials, particularly
as it relates to sexually transmitted diseases such as HIV/AIDS. Additionally, the changing
nature of prison life for women, with a greater emphasis on punishment rather than rehabilitation, has also affected the nature of social interaction. The nature of gay relationships
in women's prisons historically took on the characteristics of pseudo-families, with less
violence and more cooperative roles. As the philosophy of punishment shifted to a model
in prison with an emphasis on punishment, the prevalence of pseudo-families appears to
have decreased. Female inmates now resemble their male counterparts in terms of their
relationships to other inmates.

YOU MAKE THE CALL

HATE CRIMES

Consider the following scenario. Debate the pros and cons of all options and decide what you would do.

You are a criminal defense attorney who has been asked to represent two youths who engaged in "gay bashing" against a homosexual male. The two defendants, both males, were propositioned by the victims in a bar near a college campus. In response to the solicitation by the victim, your clients brought the victim to a motel under the guise of a romantic encounter but once the three arrived, the two youths attacked the victim, beating him with fists, feet, and clubs. The victim sustained serious injuries and was in a coma for ten days. The two suspects were arrested a few days after the assault and contacted you to represent them. You have taken a strong and very public stance against gay people and same-sex marriage. You have also tried to influence Congress to repeal hate crime legislation, stating that it unfairly discriminates against some types of victims. This public stance was the main reason the two suspects contacted you to represent them.

Questions

1. Do you agree to represent the two suspects or turn them down? Why?
2. If you agree to represent the two suspects, could you separate your personal biases against gays and adequately represent them?
3. Do you think your public (and personal) stance on homosexuality will adversely affect the jury? If so, in what ways?
4. Should there be a different standard of justice on the basis of race, religious beliefs, or sexual orientation? Why or why not?
5. Would you use the homosexual advance theory in this case? Why or why not?

KEY TERMS

bisexuality
canteen punk
crimes against persons
crimes against property
crimes against society
gay bashing
homogeneity
homosexual advance theory
homosexuality
jocker

pressure punk
prisonization
punk
queen
red-light district
sexual orientation
situational homosexuality
subculture
voir dire
wolf

DISCUSSION QUESTIONS

1. Do you think the change in the structure of women's prisons, where they now resemble male institutions, has affected the nature of social interaction and sexual behavior? Is this a good thing, or does it present more serious problems for prison officials?
2. As homosexual behavior continues to gain some level of acceptability in society, do you think the police subculture will become more tolerant of gay police officers? Why or why not?
3. Do you think that jurors are biased against gay people? What do you think about the homosexual advance theory—should offenders' responsibility be reduced for the crime they committed if the victim made a sexual advance toward them?
4. Why do you think many Americans are opposed to same-sex marriage? Is it simply based on religion, or are gays perceived as a threat in some ways?
5. Some people argue that if a person engages in homosexual behavior, then they must be a homosexual. Do you think there is really a difference? Why or why not?

FOR FURTHER READING

D'Emilio, J. *Sexual Politics, Sexual Communities: The Making of a Homosexual Minority in the United States 1940–1970*. New York: Basic Books, 1983.

Katz, J. *Gay American History*. New York: Avon Books, 1978.

Leinen, S. *Gay Cops*. Brunswick, NJ: Rutgers University Press, 1993.

Sykes, G. *The Society of Captives: A Study of a Maximum Security Prison*. Princeton, NJ: Princeton University Press, 1958.

Owens, B. *In the Mix: Struggle and Survival in a Women's Prison*. Albany, NY: State University of Albany Press, 1989.

NOTES

1. Z. Ford, "Five Stories of LGBT People Being Unfairly Treated by the Criminal Justice System," Think Progress, 2014. Available at: http://thinkprogress.org/lgbt/2014/05/07/3435157/5-stories-of-lgbt-people-being-unfairly-treated-by-the-criminal-justice-system/

2. Ibid.

3. Ibid.

4. *Majority of Public Favors Same-Sex Marriage, but Divisions Persist*, Pew Research Center, U.S. Politics & Policy, May 14, 2019. Available at: https://www.people-press.org/2019/05/14/majority-of-public-favors-same-sex-marriage-but-divisions-persist/

5. G. Gentile, "Disney Opens Weddings to Gay Couples," Associated Press, April 6, 2007.

6. Susan Page, "Poll Shows Backlash on Gay Issues," *USA Today*, May 20, 2005.

7. Lambda Legal, "Protected and Served? Survey of LGBT/HIV Contact with Police, Prisons, Courts and Schools," Fact Sheet, 2014.

8. C. Hanssens, A. C. Moodie-Mills, A. J. Ritchie, D. Spade, and U. Vaid, *A Roadmap for Change: Federal Policy Recommendations for Addressing the Criminalization of LGBT People and People Living with HIV* (New York: Center for Gender and Sexuality Law, Columbia Law School, 2014).

9. C. J. Summers, ed., *An Encyclopedia of Gay, Lesbian, Bisexual, Transgender, and Queer Culture* (Chicago, IL: Glbtq, Inc., 2004).

10. Ibid.

11. Cheshire Calhoun, "Separating Lesbian Theory from Feminist Theory," *Ethics* 104, no. 3 (April 1994): 558–81.

12. Ibid.

13. Mark J. Stern, "Born This Way?" *Slate*, June 28, 2013. Available at: http://www.slate.com/articles/health_and_science/science/2013/06/biological_basis_for_homosexuality_the_fraternal_birth_order_explanation.html

14. Dick. F. Swaab, "Sexual Orientation and Its Basis in Brain Structure and Function," *Proceedings of the National Academy of Sciences* 105, no. 30 (July 2008). Available at: http://www.pnas.org/content/105/30/10273.full

15. Simon LeVay, "A Difference in Hypothalamic Structure Between Heterosexual and Homosexual Men," *Science* 253, no. 5023 (August 1991): 1034, Available at: https://www.ncbi.nlm.nih.gov/pubmed/1887219

16. Ibid.

17. C. Grov, T. J. Parsons, and D. S. Bimbi, "Cruising for Sex Among Gay and Bisexual Men: Different Venues, Different Risks," *Journal of Sex Research* (February 2006).

18. J. D'Emilio, *Sexual Politics, Sexual Communities: The Making of a Homosexual Minority in the United States 1940–1970* (New York: Basic Books, 1983).

19. Ibid.

20. Ibid.

21. J. Katz, *Gay American History* (New York: Avon Books, 1978).

22. D'Emilio, *Sexual Politics*.

23. Katz, *Gay American History*.

24. D'Emilio, *Sexual Politics*.

25. Ibid.

26. Katz, *Gay American History*.

27. D'Emilio, *Sexual Politics*.

28. Obergfell v. Hodges, 576 U.S. ___2015.

29. Federal Bureau of Investigation, "Hate Crime Statistics 2017," Uniform Crime Reports, U.S. Department of Justice, 2018. Available at: https://ucr.fbi.gov/hate-crime/2017/topic-pages/incidents-and-offenses

30. Ibid.

31. Ibid.

32. Ibid.

33. Ibid.

34. Ibid.

35. Ibid.

36. Ibid. https://ucr.fbi.gov/hate-crime/2017/topic-pages/tables/table-9.xls

37. Ibid. https://ucr.fbi.gov/hate-crime/2017/topic-pages/tables/table-10.xls

38. D. Kopel, "Hate Crime Laws: Dangerous and Divisive," Independence Institute, January 13, 2003.

39. Ibid.

40. Ibid.

41. Ibid.

42. Hanssens et al., *A Roadmap for Change*.

43. *Report on Lesbian, Gay, Bisexual and Transgender, Queer, and HIV-Affected Hate Violence in 2012*, National Coalition of Anti-Violence Programs, June 3, 2013. Available at http://www.avp .org/storage/documents/ncavp_2012_hvreport_final.pdf

44. Lambda Legal, "Protected and Served?"

45. National Coalition of Anti-Violence Programs, *Report*.

46. *HRC Issue Brief: Housing and Homelessness*, Human Rights Campaign, 2012. Available at: http://www.hrc.org/files/assets/resources/HousingAndHomeless_Document.pdf; see also A. Greenblatt, "In Some Cities, Gays Face Greater Risk of Becoming Homeless," National Public Radio, August 7, 2013. Available at: http://www.npr.org/2013/08/06/209510271/in-some-cities-gays-face-greater-risk-of-becoming-homeless

47. *All Our Children: Strategies to Prevent Homelessness, Strengthen Services and Build Support for LGBTQ Youth*, New York Commission for Lesbian, Gay, Bisexual, Transgender, and Questioning Youth, June, 2010. Available at: http://www.nyc.gov/html/om/pdf/2010/pr267_10_report.pdf

48. Just Detention International, *PREA and Police Lockups*, May 2015. Available at: https://www.prearesourcecenter.org/sites/default/files/library/lapdblueprint.pdf

49. See, e.g., E. Bittner, *The Functions of Police in Modern Society* (Chevy Chase, MD: National Clearinghouse for Mental Health, 1970); G. Kirkham, *Signal Zero* (New York: Ballentine, 1970); Milton Rokeach, Martin Miller, and Hohn Snyder, "The Value Gap Between Police and Policed," *Journal of Social Issues* 27 (1971): 155–71; William Westley, *Violence and the Police: A Sociological Study of Law, Custom, and Morality* (Cambridge, MA: MIT Press, 1970).

50. M. Bernstein and C. Kostelac, "Lavender and Blue: Attitudes about Homosexuality and Behavior Toward Lesbians and Gay Men Among Police Officers," *Journal of Contemporary Criminal Justice* 18, no. 3 (2002): 302–28.

51. J. Younglove, M. G. Kerr, and C. J. Vitello, "Law Enforcement Officers' Perceptions of Same Sex Domestic Violence: Reason for Cautious Optimism," *Journal of Interpersonal Violence* 17, no. 7 (2001): 760–72.

52. S. Leinen, *Gay Cops* (Brunswick, NJ: Rutgers University Press, 1993).

53. A. Belkin and J. McNichol, "Pink and Blue: Outcomes Associated with the Integration of Openly Gay and Lesbian Personnel in the San Diego Police Department," *Police Quarterly* 5, no. 1 (2002): 63–95.

54. T. Henneman, "A Gun and Badge for Gays: Becoming an Openly Gay Police Officer Used to Mean Facing Harassment and Rejection. Now Departments Across the Country Are Actively Seeking Gay Recruits," *The Advocate: The National Gay and Lesbian News Magazine,* May 9, 2006.

55. See, e.g., the Washington DC Metropolitan Police Department's Gay Liaison Unit, January 11, 2016. Available at: https://mpdc.dc.gov/page/lesbian-gay-bisexual-and-transgender-liaison-unit-lgbtlu

56. Henneman, "A Gun and Badge for Gays."

57. Keegan, "Gay Police Officers."

58. S. Miller, K. B. Forest, and N. C. Jurik, "Diversity in Blue: Lesbian and Gay Police Officers in a Masculine Operation," *Men and Masculinities* 5, no. 4 (2003): 355–85.

59. K. A. Myers, K. B. Forest, and S. L. Miller, "Officer Friendly and the Tough Cop: Gays and Lesbians Navigate Homophobia and Policing," *Journal of Homosexuality* 47, no. 1 (2004): 17–37.

60. Leinen, *Gay Cops,* 79.

61. M. E. Burke, *Coming Out of the Blue: British Police Officers Talk About Their Lives in "The Job" as Lesbians, Gays and Bisexuals* (London: Cassell, 1993).

62. H. C. Brunelli, "The Double Bind: Unequal Treatment for Homosexuals Within the American Legal Framework," *Boston College Third World Law Journal* 20, no. 1 (2001).

63. R. Minson, "Homophobia in Manslaughter: The Homosexual Advance as Insufficient Provocation," *California Law Review* 80 (1992): 133. See also J. Dressler, "When Heterosexual Men Kill Homosexual Men: Reflections on Provocation Law, Sexual Advance, and the Reasonable Man Standard," *Journal of Criminal Law and Criminology* 85 (1995): 726.

64. Brunelli, "The Double Bind."

65. Ibid.

66. C. Hensley, J. Wright, R. Tewksbury, and T. Castle, "The Evolving Nature of Prison Argot and Sexual Hierarchies," in R. Tewksbury (ed.), *Behind Bars: Readings in Prison Culture* (Upper Saddle River, NJ: Prentice-Hall, 2006), 421–29.

67. G. Sykes, *The Society of Captives: A Study of a Maximum Security Prison* (Princeton, NJ: Princeton University Press, 1958).

68. A. I. Ibrahim, "Deviant Sexual Behavior in Men's Prisons," *Crime and Delinquency* 20, no. 1 (1974): 38–44. See also L. Bowker, *Prison Victimization* (New York: Elsevier North Holland, 1980).

69. C. Hopper, "The Evolution of Conjugal Visiting in Mississippi," *The Prison Journal* 69, no. 1 (1989):103–109.

70. C. Saum, H. Surratt, J. Inciardi, and R. Bennett, "Sex in Prison: Exploring the Myths and Realities," *The Prison Journal* 75, no. 4 (1995): 413–30.

71. See, e.g., P. Naccis and T. Kane, "Sex and Sexual Aggression in Federal Prisons." *Federal Probation* 47, no. 4 (1983): 31–36; Saum et al. "Sex in Prison"; R. Tewksbury, "Measures of Sexual Behavior

in an Ohio Prison," *Sociology and Social Research* 74, no. 1 (1989): 34–39; W. Wooden and J. Parker, *Men Behind Bars: Sexual Exploitation in Prison* (New York: Plenum, 1982).

72. L. Carroll, *Hacks, Blacks and Cons* (Lexington, MA: D. C. Heath, 1974).

73. C. Hensley, R. Tewksbury, and J. Wright, "Exploring the Dynamics of Masturbation and Consensual Same-Sex Activity Within a Male Maximum Security Prison," in Tewksbury, *Behind Bars*, 97–109.

74. J. Pollock, *Counseling Women in Prison* (Thousand Oaks, CA: Sage, 1998).

75. B. Owens, *In the Mix: Struggle and Survival in a Women's Prison* (Albany, NY: State University of Albany Press, 1989).

76. K. Greer, "The Changing Nature of Interpersonal Relationships in a Women's Prison," in Tewksbury, *Behind Bars*, 110–28.

77. National Coalition of Anti-Violence Programs, *Report*.

78. Ibid.

79. See Gary Gates, "LGBT Adult Immigrants in the United States." The Williams Institute, UCLA School of Law, 2013. Available at: https://williamsinstitute.law.ucla.edu/research/census-lgbt-demographics-studies/us-lgbt-immigrants-mar-2013/

80. National Coalition of Anti-Violence Programs, *Report*.

CHAPTER 9

THE ELDERLY AND THE CRIMINAL JUSTICE SYSTEM

CHAPTER OBJECTIVES

After reading this chapter, you should be able to:

- Describe the characteristics of the elderly population in the United States
- Understand victimization patterns for the elderly
- Describe the types of activities elderly criminals commonly engage in
- Discuss the challenges elderly criminals and inmates pose for the criminal justice system

There can be little doubt that the population in the United States is getting older. According to *the Statistical Abstract of the U.S.*, in 2005 there were approximately 36 million people age sixty-five and over, which represented about 13 percent of the population. In 2016, the most current data available, that number is over 49 million, which is about 15 percent of the U.S. population. While there are problems in determining what constitutes "elderly," the generally accepted age category is sixty-five and older. As a result of improvements in health and medicine, people are living longer in this country. According to the U.S. Census Bureau, the life expectancy of an American in 1960 was 69.7 years, in 1990 it was 75.4 years, and in 2016, it was 78.9 years.[1] Additionally, all of the age categories one might use to describe the elderly—fifty-five and over, sixty-five and over, and seventy-five and over—witnessed dramatic increases in size since 1980. The fifty-five-and-over category increased by 42 percent, the sixty-five-and-over category increased by 44 percent, while the seventy-five-and-over category witnessed an 82 percent increase.

This explosive growth is expected to continue. According to the U.S. Census Bureau, by 2050, the population of people age sixty-five years and over will almost double its size in 2016, to 98.2 million. The Census Bureau has included a new category, eighty-five years and over, in making its projections for the next fifty years. In fact, by 2050, the Census Bureau expects that the surviving baby boomers will be over the age of eighty-five.[2] The implications of the population getting older means that the elderly population will become more racially and ethnically diverse and programs like Social Security and Medicare, as well as healthcare providers, families, and businesses, will all be affected by this trend. The Census Bureau notes that the majority of the sixty-five-and-older group were married (58 percent), while 26 percent were widowed, and 26 percent were divorced. About 81 percent in this age category were high school graduates, and 24 percent had a college degree. Only about 9 percent of the sixty-five-and-over age group were living below the poverty line.[3] The low poverty rate among the elderly is primarily due to Social Security benefits. Without programs like Social Security, most experts believe that about half of the elderly would be poor.[4]

In 2017, 23 percent of persons age sixty-five and over were members of racial or ethnic minority populations—9 percent were African-Americans (not Hispanic), 4 percent were Asian or Pacific Islander (not Hispanic), 0.5 percent were Native American (not Hispanic), 0.1 percent were Native Hawaiian/Pacific Islander (not Hispanic), and 0.7 percent of persons age sixty-five and over identified themselves as being of two or more races. Persons of Hispanic origin (who may be of any race) represented 8 percent of the older population.[5]

In general, then, the population as a whole is getting older, the numbers of people considered elderly is growing, and they are living longer. Recent estimates indicate that life expectancy at age sixty-five was 15.2 years in 1972 and rose to 19.1 years in 2010. For those turning eighty-five, the life expectancy for someone reaching that age was 5.5 years in 1972. However, in 2010, this had risen to 6.5 years. Much of the advance in mortality is driven by improvements in healthcare, but there is also an argument to be made for health behavior changes, such as reductions in the number of people suffering from obesity and smoking.[6] There can be little doubt that as the elderly population continues to grow, the social and economic issues that an they represent are considerable. One of those costs relates to healthcare; another relates to crime.

BABY BOOMERS, GENERATION X, AND GENERATION Y

After World War II ended, the United States experienced an explosion of births, nearly 76 million from 1946 to 1964. Sociologists define the people born during those years as **baby boomers**. This group represents about 28 percent of the U.S. population and is responsible for some of the most dramatic changes in American history. From the Vietnam War protests to the civil rights movement to the rise of feminism and the hippie movement, baby boomers have been at the center of the debate, discussion, and social change. This group, many of whom turned sixty years old in 2006, comprises some of the country's leading politicians, entertainers, and social activists. Baby boomers have also been referred to as the "Me" generation for their emphasis on narcissism and individual pleasure. In fact, this group has fundamentally altered the way in which the elderly are understood in American society. Not content to simply age gracefully like their parents, this group has remained healthy and active into their retirement years. As a result, baby boomers have changed the way most Americans conceive of normal aging.[7]

Baby boomers focused on their careers and on leisure activities, and many delayed having children or remained childless. As a result, an anticipated second baby boom generation did not occur. The subsequent generation, clearly smaller in size, consisting of about 41 million, were born roughly between 1968 and 1979. These are often referred to as **Generation X** (Gen Xers). Many experts argue that this group has often been ignored and misunderstood, a disheartened generation.[8] Gen Xers are generally marked by their lack of optimism for the future and an absence of trust in traditional values. During the early 1990s, the media portrayed Gen Xers as a group of overeducated, underachieving "slackers," who are more concerned with tattoos and body piercings, and who spawned the grunge music movement.

Gen Xers grew up during the end of the Cold War, the Reagan administration, and witnessed the economic depression of the 1990s. Many members of this generation watched as their parents coped with the loss of their careers and jobs due to outsourcing, deindustrialization, and corporate mergers. This had a profound impact on many Gen Xers, who realized that company loyalty and sacrifices to get ahead did not always pay off. As a result, many Gen Xers did not take advantage of their education or talents and ended up in jobs in the lowest paying sectors of the market, including many minimum wage jobs. This lack of stability in the job market left many Gen Xers with a strong sense of cynicism about their lives, their future, and the country as a whole. This group is also generally critical of the baby boomer generation, whom many Gen Xers look upon as self-centered and impractical.[9]

Generation Y (Gen Yers), those born approximately between 1977 and 1994, make up over 20 percent of the U.S. population, or 70 million people. This generation is a large one and they are likely to have a significant impact on this country's social and economic landscape in the future. Generation Y is characterized by three main elements. First, members are comfortable and tolerant of the racial and ethnic diversity around them and feel comfortable interacting with people outside their own ethnic group.

Second, one of the most noted trends in the Generation Y segment of the population is that for parents of Generation Y children, much of the family focus is on them. That is, unlike parents of Generation X, parents of Generation Y kids are very involved in the daily lives and decisions of their children. Parents often help Gen Yers plan their achievements, take part in their daily activities, and strongly encourage their children to succeed. This encouragement by parents makes members of the Y Generation believe they can accomplish anything. Their relationships with their parents also make it more likely for Gen Yers to feel they can always return home to their parents for support and assistance.

Third, an important characteristic of this generation is that its members are technologically savvy—Gen Yers tend to be more sophisticated in their computer skills than previous groups. This is largely due to being exposed to and using technology at an early age. For instance, according to the Pew Research Center, 95 percent of teens have access to a smartphone and 45 percent say they are online almost constantly.[10] This generation is ambitious and have high expectations of themselves and those around them. It also means the individuals in this group are accustomed to instant gratification and tend to be overly confident. They are also often characterized as those who are willing to cheat, if necessary, to achieve their goals. On the positive side, this group is very adaptable in a variety of settings, they are efficient at multitasking, and they possess the technological skills and educational talents to achieve significant goals.[11]

CHECKPOINT

- There is little doubt that the population in the United States is getting older. Such a trend presents a host of challenges for society, ranging from health care issues to employment, as well as criminal behavior, both as victims and as offenders. Generational differences, such as those between baby boomers and millennials, create social tensions, as those groups see the world from very different vantage points.

THE ELDERLY AND CRIME

Since the early 1970s some attention has been paid to the relationship between crime and the elderly.[12] The majority of this focus has been on fear of crime as well as elderly victimization. While conventional wisdom has been that the elderly are at the greatest risk of becoming the victims of crime, research has consistently shown that they have the lowest rates of actual victimization.[13] However, fear itself can be seen as a form of victimization, and the elderly, along with females, express the highest levels of fear. Moreover, the consequences of actual victimization can be more severe for the elderly than for other age groups because of their physical limitations as well as their limited economic ability to recover from financial losses sustained by crime.

ELDERLY VICTIMS

As a general rule, as a person ages, rates of victimization tend to decline. According to the U.S. Department of Justice Office of Victims of Crime, in 2015 elderly persons—those over the age of sixty-five, generally experience less violence and fewer property crimes than younger persons. Property crime provided the greatest threat to those age sixty-five or older. Elderly persons had substantially lower victimization rates of violent crime (5.2 victimizations per 1,000 persons) compared to younger people over age twelve (18.6 victimizations per 1,000 persons). The trend of victimization for people over the age of sixty-five has been steadily declining: 6.8 victimizations per 1,000 persons in 1995 to 5.2 in 2015.[14]

While the victimization rates for the elderly are generally much lower than for the rest of the population, in 2017 the rates increased from 2015 (see Table 9.1).[15]

While the elderly are much less likely to experience victimization by either a violent crime or a property crime, they are about as likely to report such crimes to the police. According to the NCVS and the Office of Victims of Crime, only about 45 percent of violent crimes against the elderly are reported to the police.[16]

ELDER ABUSE

Another type of victimization concerns elder abuse. No one knows exactly how many older Americans are abused, neglected, or exploited each year; part of the reason for this has to do with the problems of defining elder abuse. Additionally, there is no uniform reporting system, rendering any type of comprehensive national database difficult to obtain. A study

**TABLE 9.1   RATES OF VICTIMIZATION FOR VIOLENT AND
SERIOUS VIOLENT CRIMES**

Age Group	Violent Victimization		Serious Violent Victimization	
	2015	2017	2015	2017
12–17	31.3	33.5	7.8	10.4
18–24	25.1	34.7	10.7	18.3
25–34	21.8	26.3	9.3	8.5
35–49	22.6	20.1	7.8	7.4
50–64	14.2	16.3	5.7	4.4
65 and older	5.2	6.5	1.5	1.8

Source: Rachel Morgan and Jennifer L. Truman, *Criminal Victimization 2017*. U.S. Bureau of Justice Statistics, 2018. Available at: https://www.bjs.gov/content/pub/pdf/cv17.pdf

funded by the National Institute of Justice of more than seven thousand elders living in a community found that approximately one in ten reported experiencing at least one form of elder mistreatment in the past year. The study found that financial exploitation by a family member had occurred in the past year by about 5 percent of participants.[17] Another NIJ funded study of abuse in assisted living facilities found that verbal and psychological abuse were the most common forms of abuse reported by care workers.[18] Finally, in another study, based on both staff accounts of incidents and responses by residents themselves, there appears to be an increasing trend toward elder mistreatment by patients themselves in residential care facilities.[19]

Like many crimes, elder abuse often goes unreported. According to the National Center on Elder Abuse, for every case of elder abuse, neglect, or exploitation, or self-neglect reported to authorities, about five more go unreported.[20] Additionally, the types of abuse vary. One type involves financial exploitation. This is usually the result of some sort of confidence game or fraud committed against the elderly. According to one study, the overall reporting of financial exploitation is about one in twenty-five cases, which translates into about five million financial abuse victims each year.[21]

Another type of elderly victimization is physical abuse. A study of nursing homes found that among seven types of abuse, physical abuse was the most common type reported.[22] The National Center on Elder Abuse found that older women were far more likely than men to suffer from physical abuse or neglect—almost two-thirds (65.7 percent) of elder abuse victims were women. This study also found that 43 percent of abuse victims were age eighty or older. The abusers in this study were primarily females (52.7 percent) and three-fourths of offenders were under age sixty. About half of the perpetrators of elderly abuse were members of the victim's family—a third of the perpetrators were adult children and another 21 percent were other family members. Spouses or intimate partners accounted for only 11 percent of the total number of offenders. According to the study, caregiver neglect accounted for about 20 percent of all neglect cases.[23]

Elder abuse is one of the most underreported crimes.

Part 1

ELDERLY OFFENDERS

Q2 While a great deal of attention has been given to elderly victims, relatively little has been offered on elderly offenders. The image of the elderly offender is filled with stereotypes and misinformation. Because people think of the elderly as infirm or limited in mobility, it is relatively easy to conclude that these individuals commit relatively "harmless" crimes, such as shoplifting or other nonviolent acts. However as was mentioned, there is no consensus in determining when someone is considered "elderly." Most people use sixty-five years old as the cutoff point. This is the usual retirement age, the point at which one is eligible for Social Security benefits, pensions, retirement income, Medicare, and so on. But the number is rather arbitrarily designated. Additionally, the agencies that collect data on crime vary considerably in their **operationalization** of age, or how they define it for the purpose of analysis.

For example, the FBI, in their analysis of crime statistics, uses "65 and over" as the uppermost category in arrest data, but they include fifty-five-to-fifty-nine and sixty-to-sixty-four age groups as well. Other agencies in the criminal justice system, such as the Federal Bureau of Prisons, use forty-five as their cutoff point, while some state systems use sixty. More recently, some states have taken to using the degree of disability in their definition rather than chronological age. An added problem is that the elderly population tends to overlap with two other special-needs categories: the chronically ill and terminally ill.[24]

In general, the criminal justice system often classifies those fifty-five and over as elderly. Opinions vary as to why this is the case, but many researchers contend that the reason for the differences has to do with collapsing intervals in order to have enough people in the respective categories.[25] However, this variability makes it difficult to compare information about elderly criminals from one study to the next.

To complicate the problem further, some researchers relate age categories to the type of crime committed. For instance, "joyriding" tends to be committed by teenagers. If a person thirty-five years of age is arrested for joyriding, for the purpose of statistical analysis, he or she could be defined as an elderly offender, largely because people in this age group typically do not engage in this type of activity. As a result of these problems, most researchers rely on the chronological categorization of age, but even here, problems emerge.[26]

The classification based on age is but one part of the problem. There is also the problem of defining a crime. When people typically talk about the "crime problem" they are referring to street crime. Using this definition, crime statistics reflect the image that crime tends to be a young, minority, male phenomenon. However, this is an overly simplistic definition of crime since it does not take into account white-collar or organized crime, nor does it include professional criminals, most of whom tend to be older. While crime is generally considered a "young man's game," it is important to account for when, and under what circumstances, the elderly become involved in criminal activity. As was mentioned, according to the Uniform Crime Reports, which classifies arrests by age, there are three general categories to use in assessing elderly criminals: fifty-five to fifty-nine, sixty to sixty-four, and sixty-five and older. Given the problems of operationalizing the term "elderly," for the purpose of this chapter, all three categories will be used.

AGING MOBSTER, 96, SENTENCED

Ninety-six-year-old Albert "The Old Man" Facchiano, a "made member" of the Genovese crime family, the nation's largest and most powerful Mafia family for decades, pleaded guilty to charges of racketeering, conspiracy, and jury tampering. According to prosecutors, Facchiano supervised robberies, money laundering, bank fraud, and stolen merchandise from 1994 to 2006. He also pled guilty to trying to locate and intimidate a government witness in New York in 2005. Facchiano became one of the oldest criminals to plead guilty to federal crimes and one of the oldest to have committed crimes at such an advanced age. During the court hearing, Facchiano used a special headset to hear questions from the U.S. District Court judge. When asked by the judge, "Is your mind okay?" Facchiano eventually responded "Oh yes, I can't hear, but I can understand, your honor." Facchiano's attorney stated that his client sees a doctor four times a week, suffers from back pain and a host of other ailments. While the charges against Facchiano carried a prison sentence of up to thirty years and $500,000 in fines, by pleading guilty, prosecutors recommended Facchiano serve house arrest, citing that any form of incarceration would be a form of capital punishment (Source: "Chinky still an old-school gangster at 96," *The Guardian*, March 5, 2007. Available at: https://www.theguardian.com/world/2007/mar/05/usa.richardluscombe)

CHECKPOINT

- There is little question that the population in the United States is getting older. As it relates to crime, the elderly remain one of the smallest segments of the victim population, particularly of violent crimes, but elder abuse and victimization continue to occur. As more people become involved in assisted living or nursing care, the likelihood of an increase in elder abuse increases.

Elderly Criminals and the Criminal Justice System

While the research on elderly criminals is relatively small, it is worth noting that each phase of the criminal justice system is confronted with the challenges presented by elderly criminals. For the police, there is ample research that the age of the suspect, along with other factors, plays a role in how the officer evaluates a situation. However, this applies mostly to young offenders—few, if any, police departments provide training on how to deal with elderly suspects. However, it could be that some officers might take a more lenient view of elderly offenders, particularly if the crime is not a serious one. But what about the elderly criminal who continues to commit crimes without any remorse or concern for the victims? Or when a respectable citizen who is elderly commits a crime such as a sex crime against a minor, a crime involving the sale of drugs, or even a DUI charge? While it may be that conventional wisdom assumes that the elderly are given a more gentle touch when they engage in minor offenses, not all suspects are, or should be, treated the same.[27]

Similarly, as it relates to how the courts deal with elderly criminals, while the decision to pass sentence should include factors such as the seriousness of the crime, the suspect's criminal record, and other factors relating to the activity, should the age of the offender and/or his or her declining health also be factors to consider at the sentencing stage? Like the challenges facing the police, the issue is anything but clear—some argue that older offenders should know better, while opponents think that these things should be mitigating factors in an offender's sentence. The research on the role of age of the offender at sentencing is mixed—the general conclusion is that the age of the offender, if they are elderly, should be considered a mitigating factor for minor charges, such as shoplifting.[28]

Where the issue of elderly offenders becomes most significant is at the incarceration stage. While the number of studies on elderly criminals remains small, particularly after the 1980s, the most recent research continues to focus on the challenges of older inmates and the economic costs to states that are responsible for their healthcare. As a result of the harsh sentences in the 1980s and 1990s, many offenders have remained in prison for an extended period of time. The deleterious effect of prison life in general, coupled with whatever other problems inmates brought with them to prison, are the subject of considerable debate and present challenges to correctional institutions that were not designed to be ADA compliant or to contain the medical facilities necessary to treat chronically ill and aging inmates.[29] Yet, that is exactly what is occurring and many states wrestle with how to provide an adequate standard of care and to provide some level of protection to medically and/or emotionally disabled inmates.

What is interesting about the research on this population during the 1980s was that many experts were looking at elderly criminals as the onset of a social problem.[30] In their seminal text, *Constructing Social Problems*, John Kitsuse and Malcom Spector state that **claimsmaking** is a fundamental aspect of how social problems are defined in a given society.[31] When people, particularly experts, assert that an event or phenomenon is problematic for a society, the process of making a claim occurs, and a social problem is created. This same process occurred in the literature on elderly criminals. Because it seemed logical at the time, and because many researchers were pointing to the inevitability of an increase in elderly offenders, many criminal justice researchers and sociologists were convinced of the validity of these claims. As an illustration, the authors of one of the most comprehensive texts on the subject of elderly criminals offered this prediction:

> It is a rare opportunity to see a social problem coming with enough lead time to do something about it. We are very sure that the demographic balance of our population will shift so that more people will be in the upper age ranges. As this occurs, the elderly crime problem can only assume a more important position on our list of domestic problems. It seems particularly appropriate to begin developing policies of control and prevention right now.[32]

However, just as the research in the 1980s intensified in anticipation of a significant social problem, the research nearly stopped in the 1990s. As was mentioned, while some assessment of this subject continues, it is usually much more focused on the effects of incarceration rather than the incidence of elderly crime.[33] Few studies make reference to the expectations of a decade earlier. However, this is not to say that what was discovered during this time period was flawed—a great deal was learned about the range of activities of many elderly offenders.

At first glance, the dramatic decrease in the number of studies suggests a wavering interest in the topic, which could be taken as evidence that the elderly crime wave failed to occur. However, a better indicator of the accuracy of this prediction would be an analysis of arrest statistics much in the same way that they were conducted in the 1980s. One study, for example, analyzed arrest statistics from the Uniform Crime Reports between 1964 and 1979, and found a dramatic increase of arrests for serious crimes among those fifty-five years old and older.

The findings of this study showed a significant increase in the percentage of elderly arrests for property crime, motor vehicle theft, and sex offenses, especially when compared to the rest of the offender population. The conclusion drawn from this study was that while the elderly constitute only a small part of the total arrests, there was every reason to expect the number of elderly arrests to increase dramatically as the entire population grew older.[34] An analysis of the Uniform Crime Reports arrest statistics was done from 1990 to 1994 in an effort to assess these predictions over time. The findings from this study

TABLE 9.2   VIOLENT AND PROPERTY CRIME ARRESTS BY AGE GROUP, 2007 AND 2017

	2007			2017		
	55–59	60–64	65 and over	55–59	60–64	65 and over
Violent Crime	7,321	3,380	3,024	13,677	6,549	5,104
Property Crime	16,998	7,049	5,638	29,721	13,474	8,741
Total Arrests		451,071			407,496	

Source: U.S. Department of Justice, Federal Bureau of Investigation (2018). *Crime in the United States 2017.* Table 38. Available at: https://ucr.fbi.gov/crime-in-the-u.s/2017/crime-in-the-u.s.-2017/topic-pages/tables/table-38

showed that the percentage of arrests for the population had increased from 1990 to 1994, but the overall arrest rate for elderly offenders had decreased by 5 percent.[35]

In 2007 there were 7,321 arrests for violent crime in the 55–59 age group, 3,380 for those aged 60–64, and 3,024 for those aged 65 and over. These numbers nearly doubled in every category in 2017. In 2017, the number of violent crimes for those aged 55–59 was 13,677, for those aged 60–64 years of age, the number was 6,549, and for those aged 65 and over, the number of violent crime arrests was 5,104. A similar trend was seen for property crimes across age groups as well.[36]

Thus, the current trends in crime committed by the elderly, as well as the types of crimes, are somewhat supported from what was known in the 1980s. Recall that the research predicted that the number of offenders would increase as the population got older, and the data seem to suggest that arrests are on the upswing.[37]

TYPES OF OFFENSES COMMITTED BY THE ELDERLY

SHOPLIFTING

As was mentioned, the image of the elderly criminal strikes most people as incongruous with their understanding of crime in society. When Americans think of elderly criminals, it is not uncommon to envision a rather passive and benign type of offender: one who does not injure his or her victims and commits economic crimes rather than violent ones. Shoplifting is one type of crime that fits this image. It is passive, it does not usually lead to injuries to bystanders, and one does not need a great deal of dexterity or mobility to commit it.

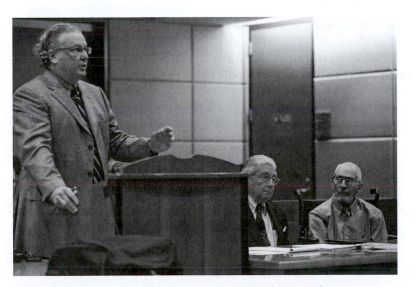

Because of the complexity of the issues involving elderly criminals, some advocates promote the idea of a separate court system for this population.

Many people also attempt to deflect the culpability of the elderly offender by offering exculpatory reasons for committing this act, such as economic hardship or lack of intent. In other words, elderly shoplifters are simply those people who forget to pay for their purchases and then are apprehended when they attempt to leave the premises. Loneliness is also used as an explanation by some scholars, in that the elderly criminal is in need of contact with others and, like a young child, steals for the attention they receive.[38]

But what do we really know about elderly shoplifters? One of the few studies of this population examined 191 first-time offenders in Florida who agreed to participate in a court-ordered diversion program. In trying to answer the question that elderly shoplifters steal because they are poor, researchers in this study collected data on the offenders' income, occupation, and whether or not they owned a home. With regard to income, the median monthly income level was approximately $7,500 and about half of those cases (45 percent) derived their incomes from three or more sources: interest from savings, stocks and bonds, and Social Security benefits. Most were white-collar workers, professionals, and administrators in their former careers. Moreover, 83 percent of offenders owned their place of residence. Thus, the vast majority of elderly shoplifters in this study were home-owners and had sufficient resources, which runs counter to the indigent argument.

Additionally, of the objects stolen, the most common were clothing items and cosmetics rather than subsistence or need-based items such as food or drugs. Researchers in this study also attempted to document the "lack of intent" explanation, where shoplifting cases by the elderly were due to forgetfulness rather than intention. While there are instances where people innocuously take items and forget to pay for them, this explanation loses much of its validity when multiple items are taken. That is, most people can understand forgetting one item, but the intent to shoplift becomes more credible as the number increases. In this study, about half (48 percent) of the cases involved two or three stolen items.

Finally, as was mentioned, a popular explanation for elderly shoplifting involves loneliness. In these cases, the elderly offender is isolated from social interaction and craves attention. However, the findings of this particular study showed that approximately 70 percent of the offenders did not live alone, and 65 percent were married. In addition, approximately 80 percent indicated that they have family members or close friends living in the area. Other tests of social isolation given to offenders supported the conclusion that the offenders were not stealing due to loneliness or feeling isolated from the larger community.[39]

TABLE 9.3   LARCENY-THEFT BY AGE, 2007 AND 2017

	2007			2017		
	55–59	60–64	65+	55–59	60–64	65+
Larceny-Theft	14,432	6,128	3,024	24,872	11,609	7,806
Total Arrests	897,626			750,750		

Source: U.S. Department of Justice, Federal Bureau of Investigation (2018). *Crime in the United States 2017*. Table 38. Available at: https://ucr.fbi.gov/crime-in-the-u.s/2017/crime-in-the-u.s.-2017/topic-pages/tables/table-38

In sum, the research on the elderly shoplifter, while still quite scant, runs counter to popular understanding of why these individuals engage in this type of criminal activity. They are not indigent, are not without other resources, and appear to have adequate social and emotional support networks. Moreover, elderly shoplifters do not appear to be retaliating against businesses they patronized. In fact, many rated the establishments from which they had stolen rather high in terms of the services they provide.

While no formal category of shoplifting exists in official statistics, according to the Uniform Crime Reports, there has been a dramatic increase in the number of arrests for crimes like shoplifting (see Table 9.3). Similar to the trends noted in violent crime and property crime arrests, the data for larceny among each elderly category witnessed substantial increases. In 2007, for example, there were 14,432 arrests for those aged 55–59; 6,128 arrests for larceny for those aged 60–64; and 3,024 larceny arrests for those aged 65 and older. In 2017, those numbers in each category nearly doubled.[40]

HOMICIDE

While relatively few homicides occur in the United States each year, the number and proportions of violent crime committed by the elderly remains less than 2 percent on any given year, according to arrest statistics from the Uniform Crime Reports.[41]

While a great deal of attention is given to older victims of homicide, information is generally lacking on older homicide offenders. In the quest to demystify some of the notions about this topic, one study examined elderly homicide using *Supplemental Homicide Reports* by the Federal Bureau of Investigation to profile elderly homicide offenders. The study showed that, like the fluctuation in the overall homicide rate, the rate for the elderly is not stable across jurisdictions. As a result, the elderly offender is affected by the same sociological factors that create different murder rates among younger adults from state to state.

Some experts argue that elderly offenders would be more likely to kill those of their own age than offenders in other categories. Some of the research on this topic shows that many young homicide offenders kill people older than they are as a result of robberies or the commission of other felonies.[42] Since the data show that the elderly are not as likely to be involved in these kinds of activities, one might conclude that older people *would* be more likely to kill within their own age group. However, the data suggest that the opposite is true. According to the Uniform Crime Reports for 2017, people in the sixty-to-sixty-four and sixty-five-to-seventy-four groups were actually less likely to kill someone their own age and about 21 percent of those age fifty and over kill victims of the same age.

Finally, it was argued that elderly offenders would be more likely to use firearms than offenders in other age groups. The logic, of course, is that since the elderly are not as strong as younger people, they would be more likely to use a gun to commit the crime. Twenty years ago a study found that this was supported by the data: elderly offenders were more likely to use firearms than the nonelderly. In the mid-1990s, another study of elderly homicide offenders was conducted in Detroit.[43] Many of the trends identified in the initial study of elderly homicide remained constant almost ten years later. This study found that older homicide offenders were more likely to use firearms in the commission of a crime than their younger counterparts. The author of this study also found that "Proportionally

TABLE 9.4 HOMICIDE BY AGE, 2007 AND 2017

	2007			2017		
	55–59	60–64	65+	55–59	60–64	65+
Homicide	175	77	83	226	115	114
Total Arrests		10,082			9,516	

Source: U.S. Department of Justice, Federal Bureau of Investigation (2018). *Crime in the United States 2017*. Table 38.
Available at: https://ucr.fbi.gov/crime-in-the-u.s/2017/crime-in-the-u.s.-2017/topic-pages/tables/table-38

fewer homicides perpetrated by older persons appear to be committed between 8:00 pm and 1:59 am. For some reason, the elderly are less inclined to kill late at night than are the nonelderly."[44]

An analysis of homicide statistics from 1976 to 2004 revealed that only about 8 percent of offenders age fifty and older used a firearm to commit a homicide.[45] These data suggest that elderly homicide offenders are not significantly different in many ways from other types of murderers, although some of the practical aspects of committing the crime account for some differences in their rates. For instance, unlike younger offenders, older killers commit many of their crimes within their own residences. This may be due to a variety of reasons, but perhaps the most significant is that elderly people tend to spend more time at home than in public or commercial establishments. Finally, the low incidence of murders by the elderly may have something to do with the shorter life span of violent individuals. Some research suggests that people with predispositions toward violence are less likely to reach the age of fifty-five and thus are at lower risk to become an elderly offender. Thus, while it is true the elderly commit fewer homicides, in general the patterns are similar to younger offenders.

The most recent data available on elderly homicide show some changes in the fifty-five-to-fifty-nine age group category. According to the Uniform Crime Reports, in 2007, there were approximately 335 elderly arrests for homicide. This includes 175 for offenders in the fifty-five-to-fifty-nine age category, 77 in the group aged sixty to sixty-four, and 83 for those sixty-five and older. However, the overall number increased 36 percent in 2017 to a total of 455. The distribution of arrests for each category was 226, 115, and 114, respectively (see Table 9.4).[46]

SEX OFFENSES

As with other crimes, stereotypical images exist about elderly sex offenders that interfere with an accurate understanding of this phenomenon. Some people believe, for instance, that sexual offenses involving children are the most often committed by old men.[47] The media has also created a climate in which the image of a sexual predator is an elderly man, likely a Catholic priest, who preys upon innocent children. In fact, there is a great deal of distortion of sex offenses among the elderly and the pedophilia of priests in particular. Much of what has been called pedophilia is actually non-forcible sex among older boys, not child abuse or sexual assault as has been portrayed in the media. This trend does not suggest that pedophilia is acceptable or that what some priests have done is appropriate.

TABLE 9.5   SEX CRIMES BY AGE, 2007 AND 2017

	2007			2017		
	55–59	60–64	65+	55–59	60–64	65+
Sex Crimes	2,024	1,313	1,436	2,005	1,367	1,491
Total Arrests		62,756			37,850	

Source: U.S. Department of Justice, Federal Bureau of Investigation (2018). *Crime in the United States 2017*. Table 38. Available at: https://ucr.fbi.gov/crime-in-the-u.s/2017/crime-in-the-u.s.-2017/topic-pages/tables/table-38.

However, the media's distorted image does suggest that perhaps the elderly are not as involved in sex offenses as is commonly believed.[48]

One study attempted to synthesize the information on the subject by examining eighty-six old and young sex offenders ("young" was defined as thirty years old or younger, while "old" was defined as those sixty years or older). The results were that elderly offenders had more stability in terms of their marital status, occupational income, and ties to the community. Younger sexual offenders were more likely to have higher education levels, a history of drug and alcohol abuse, and were likely to have a sexual encounter with a child in a public place, such as a local park. Elderly offenders were more likely to be a passive recipient in the exchange with a child and to engage in this activity in the privacy of their own home.[49]

In virtually all of the cases, there was some sort of relationship between the victim and the offender, and the nature of the activity was usually nonviolent. This study and others have found that mental disorders, organic brain dysfunctions such as dementia and delirium, as well as neurosis, personality disorders, and alcoholism are much more common among the elderly than younger offenders.[50]

For the purposes of analysis, according to the Uniform Crime Reports, sex crimes include all activities except prostitution and forcible rape. While this covers a wide range of activities, the data suggest that this trend decreased considerably in 2017, but remained relatively stable for elderly offenders. The total number of the elderly arrested for sex offenses in 2007 was 62,756. This included 2,024 for those fifty-five to fifty-nine and 1,313 arrests in the sixty-to-sixty-four category. For those age sixty-five and over, the number of arrests was 1,436. In 2017, the total number of arrests for sex offenses was 37,850, a decrease of approximately 39 percent. This included 2,005 in the fifty-five-to-fifty-nine category, 1,367 in the sixty-to-sixty-four group, and 1,491 in the over-sixty-five category (see Table 9.5). While the number of arrests remained relatively stable for all elderly categories, the total number of arrests in all age categories for this crime decreased sharply.[51]

DRUNK DRIVING

Unlike other forms of elderly crime, the evidence on the relationship between alcohol use and criminal activity among the elderly has a larger empirical foundation. The questions and controversy surrounding this type of criminal behavior stems largely from whether or not elderly people drink more than young people—while some experts argue that older people drink to alleviate feelings of isolation, emotional loss, or to derive some sense of satisfaction in life, others contend that the incidence of these types of crimes decreases with age.[52]

TABLE 9.6   DUI AND DRUNKENNESS ARRESTS BY AGE, 2007 AND 2017

	2007			2017		
	55–59	60–64	65+	55–59	60–64	65+
DUI	32,610	15,929	12,059	41,058	23,147	17,915
Drunkenness	15,716	6,437	3,994	20,247	9,690	5,447
Total Arrests:	451,055			289,608		

Source: U.S. Department of Justice, Federal Bureau of Investigation (2018). *Crime in the United States 2017*. Table 38. Available at: https://ucr.fbi.gov/crime-in-the-u.s/2017/crime-in-the-u.s.-2017/topic-pages/tables/table-38

Alcohol-related arrests, such as driving while intoxicated and public drunkenness, account for the majority of criminal behavior of people fifty-five or older. Other research on alcohol-related crime by the elderly has shown that the majority of offenders are males with long-term, chronic drinking problems and equally long histories of crime while under the influence of alcohol.[53] However, there are also data that suggest that older people generally drink less than their younger counterparts. In fact, in contrast to these prevailing theories, some studies suggest that the very old, those seventy-five or older, are more likely to abstain from alcohol altogether.[54] While there remains a great deal of debate about this issue, the research suffers from methodological problems and often lacks comparability with other studies. However, the weight of the evidence suggests that the problem of alcohol-related crime by the elderly is not of epidemic proportions. While the data show that if older people are arrested for crimes, they are very likely to be alcohol-related ones, it is still the case that alcohol-related offenses, such as drunk driving and public drunkenness, account for only a small percentage of all reported arrests of older adults.[55]

According to the Uniform Crime Reports in 2007, there were over a million arrests for driving under the influence (DUI). This breaks down into 32,610 for those in the fifty-five-to-fifty-nine age category, 15,929 for those sixty to sixty four, and 12,059 for those 65 and over. In 2017, there were 82,120 DUI arrests of the elderly. This includes 41,058 in the fifty-five-to-fifty-nine age group, 23,147 in the sixty-to-sixty-four age group, and 17,915 in the over-sixty-five category. Public drunkenness also witnessed an increase between 2007 and 2017. There were 26,147 elderly arrests for public drunkenness in 2007 compared to 35,384 arrests for that crime in 2017, about a 35 percent increase (see Table 9.6).[56]

CHECKPOINT

- A number of common myths persist about elderly offenders that run counter to the actual data on offending patterns. For instance, despite the notion that "dirty old men" are involved in the sexual exploitation of children, the data suggest that elderly offenders are much more likely to engage in drunk driving or other minor forms of crime. Elderly offenders are much less likely to be involved in violent crimes as well.

FORMAL REACTIONS TO THE ELDERLY CRIMINAL

It should be clear at this point that the "problem" of elderly crime is really not a problem in terms of the actual numbers of offenders or offenses. It is unlikely, either now or perhaps even in the future, that an "elderly crime wave" will occur. Despite their limitations and flaws, the Uniform Crime Reports have consistently shown that elderly criminals do not represent a significant crime problem. Perhaps the problem should not be understood in terms of its volume or magnitude but in terms of its uniqueness. The fact that elderly individuals commit various types of crime, including violent offenses, raises a number of questions about the pursuit of justice, the goals of punishment, and the purpose of the criminal justice system.

The problem is somewhat similar to the juvenile justice system in that society recognizes young people as being different from adults when they commit criminal acts. Consequently, this system has a different philosophy from the adult system: one that tempers the culpability of the offender while still holding youth accountable. Add to the fact that since most of the recent research focuses on the particular problems elderly criminals encounter when they are processed through the system,[57] many criminal justice experts have argued that perhaps one way to alleviate these problems is to establish a separate system for the elderly, or what is sometimes referred to as a **geriatric court**.[58]

Proponents of this type of change argue that elderly criminals are inherently different from other-age criminals and merit special consideration in the justice process. Moreover, the pains of punishment are more taxing on elderly offenders. Advocates of the geriatric court also contend that there should be a more lenient attitude by the courts in sentencing, a more lax approach by law enforcement, and a sympathetic approach to punishment by the correctional institutions. The logic, of course, is that neither society nor the individual benefits from the unilateral treatment of offenders. What good does it serve society, for example, if a sixty-five-year-old man is given a thirty-year prison sentence? The same punishment to a fifteen-year-old does not end his life; however, in the former case, this sentence for an elderly criminal may in fact be a form of capital punishment. Moreover, since the legal precedent for a separate system has already been established for juveniles, and the particular needs and problems of older offenders are similar to those of juveniles (in terms of vulnerability and risks, as well as the issue of rehabilitation), why not create a separate system?

It may very well be that a geriatric court can lead to improvements in meeting the needs of the elderly population. While the answers to these questions cannot be found without additional and extensive research, the idea of a geriatric court requires an examination of many current policies and practices involving the administration of justice.

On the other hand, opponents of this approach argue that distinctions of crime cannot be based on chronological age. In other words, a person is ultimately responsible whether they are eighteen years old or eighty. In this model, one that clearly fits within the **just deserts** philosophy, which argues that every person is equally responsible for their actions and should be punished according to what they have done, the symbolic and practical consequences of taking a lenient attitude toward the elderly may encourage other potential offenders to commit crime.

Finally, as was mentioned, while there is much left to be done in terms of understanding elderly crime, the vast majority of the research has focused on how and in what ways offenders are forced to cope with the pains of imprisonment. This includes the organizational and logistical problems faced by correctional institutions with an increasingly older inmate population. The problems are many, quite diversified, and they will likely increase with time. Thus, the handling of elderly inmates, both in terms of physical safety as well as healthcare, will likely remain a central feature in the study of elderly offenders.

ELDERLY INMATES

As part of a "get tough" approach to crime that began over thirty years ago, the number of offenders sentenced to long prison sentences has resulted in an increase in the number of elderly inmates. This development comes at a time when prison populations in recent years are decreasing, reflecting a shift in thinking of the purpose and value of incarceration for offenders. However, for those remaining, the pains of imprisonment along with the increased health-related problems presents challenges for correctional officials. In fact, at the end of 2016, fewer people were in prison than any year in almost two decades. However, during that same period, the number of inmates age fifty-five or older increased by 280 percent (see Figure 9.1).[59]

The National Institute of Corrections estimated the annual cost of incarcerating those fifty-five or older who have chronic and terminal illnesses to be two to three times that for

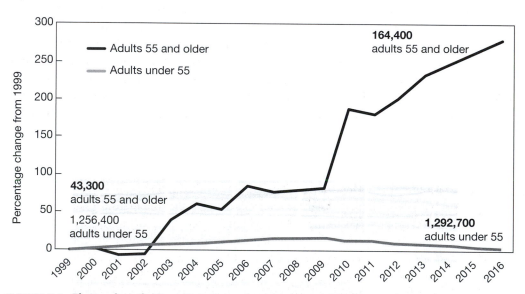

FIGURE 9.1 The number of older prisoners grew by 280%, 1999–2016. Percentage change in sentenced adults by age group.

Note: The Bureau of Justice Statistics estimates the age distribution of prisoners using data from the Federal Justice Statistics Program and statistics that states voluntarily submit to the National Corrections Reporting Program. State participation in this program has varied, which may have caused year-to-year fluctuations in the Bureau's national estimates, but this does not affect long-term comparisons. From 2009 to 2010, the number of states submitting data increased substantially, which might have contributed to the year-over-year increase in the national estimate between those years.

Source: Bureau of Justice Statistics

all other inmates. However, the Office of Inspector General found that federal institutions with high percentages of aging inmates spend five times more per inmate on medical care and fourteen times more per inmate on medication.

The National Institute of Corrections uses age fifty due to the stress of incarceration and the lack of appropriate healthcare prior to and during incarceration.[60] The real problem with the aging of the inmate population relates to escalating healthcare costs. In 2018, according to a study by the Pew Charitable Trusts, the cost of incarcerating an aging inmate population was an estimated $16 billion per year, including $3 billion in medical care. While it costs taxpayers approximately $34,000 per year on average to incarcerate a non-elderly prisoner, it costs over $68,000 to care for an elderly prisoner. Moreover, the problem appears to be getting worse. By one estimate, by 2030, nearly a third of the entire prison population in the United States, nearly 400,000 inmates, will be elderly.[61]

The most common health-related problems elderly inmates experience include incontinence, respiratory illnesses, cardiovascular disease, and chronic problems such as arthritis, high blood pressure, prostate problems, and ulcers. Elderly inmates also suffer from typical age-related illnesses such as cognitive impairment, reduced vision and hearing, loss of physical strength, and emotional disorders.[62]

The special circumstances surrounding the incarceration of elderly inmates also create a number of challenges for correctional institutions. For example, older inmates have greater healthcare needs, may require a number of structural changes in the facility to accommodate them, such as single beds instead of bunk beds, fewer inmates per cell, and even the creation of geriatric units within the prison. Healthcare needs also require correctional institutions to either establish or contract comprehensive healthcare services.[63] Even the day-to-day stressors and risks associated with institutional life are exceptionally

One of the most pressing issues in corrections is providing healthcare to an aging inmate population.

hard on elderly offenders. Elderly inmates also require more protection by correctional officers from younger predators.

Across the country, some states are attempting to address the escalating healthcare costs for elderly inmates. For example, at least sixteen states have established separate facilities to house older inmates, and many are offering hospice care for dying prisoners. In Texas, for example, about two hundred inmates over the age of sixty-five receive round-the-clock care. The state of Nebraska offers nursing home living for some inmates while Oklahoma is also creating a separate unit for older inmates.[64]

In California, where there are 172,000 prisoners in the state system, the problem has become acute, with jails releasing convicted felons because of overcrowding. In the state prisons, inmates are stacked three-high in cells and housed in hallways and converted gyms. Some California prisons are even 200 percent to 300 percent over capacity. In order to provide space for inmates, some facilities have had to rent cell space from other, less crowded prisons. As prison officials struggle to find solutions to the problems of overcrowding, they are faced with a 70 percent **recidivism rate**, which is also known as the re-offending rate. This means that 70 percent of the inmates convicted of a crime will commit another one within three years of release. California's recidivism rate is currently the highest in the nation.

In California, the number of prisoners fifty-five and older has doubled since 1997, with almost 20,000 prisoners over age fifty and almost 750 over seventy years old. In fact, California, Texas, and Florida combined accounted for 43 percent of the nation's entire elderly prison population in 2013.[65] As one expert on prisons noted, there is evidence that prisoners are physiologically ten years older than their chronological age. This means that inmate needs are increasing, as are the costs of their incarceration.[66] Because of this, some have suggested that the best way to alleviate overcrowding in prison would be to release the inmates who pose the least risk to the community. Given that recidivism rates generally drop around the age of thirty and continue to fall after that, an argument can be made that releasing elderly criminals makes sense in that they are least likely to commit another crime against the community.[67]

As the current research tries to show, there are a number of practical issues surrounding elderly inmates. These range from the pragmatic difficulties of maneuvering a wheelchair in a prison cell to the importance of improved healthcare facilities. For example, it seems obvious that planners did not foresee—and perhaps could not have foreseen—these issues when prisons were being constructed ten, twenty, or even forty years ago. Prison cells were simply not designed for offenders who were limited in mobility. However, the realities of incarcerating older inmates, as well as caring for those who become ill, needs to be incorporated into the design and construction of new facilities. While this will increase the costs, it may be one of the consequences of punishing older offenders or keeping people incarcerated for long periods of time.

Related to the issues surrounding elderly inmates are several philosophical and pragmatic questions raised by many criminal justice scholars. David Newman, a noted expert on elderly crime, makes an interesting point about the practical problems for police officers who encounter elderly criminals. He questions whether handcuffing or shackling a seventy-five-year-old is really in line with the goals of the criminal justice system. Newman also questions whether or not booking procedures, including fingerprinting, photographing, and lineups, are really necessary and appropriate for seventy-year-old suspects. In addition, Newman argues against monetary bail as the only way elderly offenders can be released while awaiting trial. He asks, "Are they likely to flee? Do many or most elderly offenders really need to be jailed or imprisoned?"[68] In short, Newman calls into question the issue of whether or not the criminal justice system effectively addresses the problems of elderly offenders.

While Newman raises some interesting points, does this mean chronological age should play a part in these issues? There are many instances in which exceptions are made for all types of offenders. If the person is violent, whether they be elderly or not, one would think that the safety of the arresting officers, the citizens of that community, and the well-being of the individual offender would override any embarrassment or humiliation the particular suspect might feel. In short, it is not clear whether older offenders should be given special considerations with regard to the early stages of the justice process. Where there is stronger support in Newman's argument is where it concerns the pragmatic problems of being imprisoned. Given that cells are not designed for the elderly, this presents a number of problems for the correctional institution as well as the inmate.

The subject of elderly criminals presents one of the most interesting juxtapositions of the disciplines of criminology, criminal justice, and gerontology. Despite the fact that it has not grown in the way the research had predicted, the issues and problems surrounding this phenomenon will continue to have an impact on the understanding and perceptions of aging in American society as well as how and in what ways crime influences social life.

SUMMARY

This chapter explored the phenomenon of elderly crime. There can be little doubt that as the population gets older, the number of people involved in crime, whether as victims or as offenders, will likely increase. Baby boomers—those born between 1946 and 1964—represent the newest group of elderly in this country. As a generation, they have redefined the face of America with the civil rights movement and protests against the Vietnam War, and they represent some of the leading figures in politics, economics, and social activism. As this generation becomes older, it is likely that they will also redefine the criteria used to evaluate the concept of aging. Generation X, or Gen Xers, are those individuals born between 1968 and 1979. This group is generally considered an underachieving generation that is critical of the self-indulgence of baby boomers, and who grew up amid a host of social problems in the 1980s and 1990s. Generation Y is the latest group of young people in this country, born approximately between 1977 and 1994; they are characterized by their willingness to embrace cultural diversity, are educationally and technologically sophisticated, and have a strong sense of self including feelings of entitlement, self-confidence, and impatience in climbing the ladder of success.

Conventional wisdom concerning elderly crime typically focuses on elderly victimization. As this chapter has shown, the elderly are the least likely to be victimized of any other age group, but this should not be interpreted to mean that the elderly are not victimized. There is a great deal of empirical evidence on elder abuse as well as research on elderly offenders.

Early predictions of an "elderly crime wave," based largely on population and demographic shifts, have failed to materialize. However, the research on elderly criminals, found primarily in official crime statistics, shows that elderly crime is not as frequent as crime committed by younger offenders; however, it is sufficient to warrant more attention. Generally speaking, most of the elderly crime noted in the data relates to minor forms of crime, usually alcohol-related or some type of larceny. Despite noted cases where elderly criminals commit violent acts, these instances are relatively rare.

Where most of the research interest on elderly criminals has focused has been in the area of incarceration and prison life in general. As inmates are sentenced to longer prison terms, issues relating to healthcare and the overall quality of life for inmates become a topic of keen interest to researchers.

YOU MAKE THE CALL
ELDERLY CRIMINALS

Consider the following scenario. Debate the pros and cons of all options and decide what you would do.

You are a federal judge who has received an appeal from a sixty-five-year-old inmate, who was convicted of murdering his terminally ill wife. Knowing that she was going to endure extraordinarily painful treatments, the man, overcome with emotion, decided to throw his wife off of the balcony of his ten-story apartment. Upon conviction, he received a thirty-year sentence for his crime, but he appealed on the basis that this constituted cruel and unusual punishment. The reason for this, obviously, is that such punishment is, effectively, a death sentence given his age. The public is supportive of a merciful approach, particularly given the fact that the offender's crimes, while heinous, merit some consideration.

Questions

1. What do you do?
2. Should there be a different standard of justice on the basis of the man's age?
3. Should the way the man killed his wife factor into the sentencing decision?
4. Does the public's sentiment toward the man merit consideration? Why or why not?

KEY TERMS

baby boomers
claimsmaking
Generation X
Generation Y

geriatric court
just deserts
recidivism rate

DISCUSSION QUESTIONS

1. Do you think a geriatrics court would be helpful in the processing of elderly offenders? Could it be used in a similar fashion as the juvenile justice system? Why or why not?
2. What responsibility does the government have to provide comprehensive healthcare to elderly inmates? Should correctional agencies be forced to meet serious and chronic healthcare needs of elderly inmates, or should they only be responsible for routine care or emergencies?
3. In what ways do you think the baby boomer generation will change the way the elderly are perceived? Is this characterization of baby boomers seen in a positive or negative light?

4. How is elder abuse different from child abuse? Should offenders be given the same punishments as child abusers? How do you think elder abusers would be perceived in prison compared to child abusers?

5. Given the role that alcohol plays in elderly crime, do you think society should be able to restrict its use among the elderly in the same way it limits access for minors? Why or why not?

6. Given the public's perception of elderly criminals, what steps can you think of to help merchants prevent the elderly from shoplifting?

FOR FURTHER READING

Zemke, R., C. Raines, and B. Filipczak. *Generations at Work: Managing the Clash of Veterans, Boomers, and Xers and Nexters in Your Workplace*. New York: American Management Association, 2000.

Castle, N. *Examination of Resident Abuse in Assisted Living Facilities. Final Report to the National Institute of Justice*. 2013. Grant number 2010-IJ-CX-00223.

Shimkus, J. *The Graying of America's Prisons: Corrections Copes with Care for the Aged*. Washington, DC: National Commission on Correctional Healthcare, 2007.

Newman, E. S., D. J. Newman, and M. L. Gerwitz. *Elderly Criminals*. Cambridge, MA: Oelgeschlager, Gunn, and Hain, 1984.

Wolfgang, M. *Patterns of Criminal Homicide*. Philadelphia: University of Pennsylvania Press, 1958.

NOTES

1. Andrew Roberts, Stella Ogunwole, Laura Blakeslee, and Megan Rabe, "A Snapshot of the Fast-Growing U.S. Older Population," U.S. Census Bureau, October 30, 2018. Available at: https://www.census.gov/library/stories/2018/10/snapshot-fast-growing-us-older-population.html

2. Sandra L. Colby and Jennifer M. Ortman, "Projections of the Size and Composition of the U.S. Population 2014 to 2060." U.S. Census Bureau, March 2015. Available at: https://www.census.gov/content/dam/Census/library/publications/2015/demo/p25-1143.pdf

3. U.S. Census Bureau, *Aging and Disability: 2017 Profile of Aging Americans*, U.S. Department of Commerce, April 2018. Available at: https://acl.gov/sites/default/files/Aging%20and%20Disability%20in%20America/2017OlderAmericansProfile.pdf

4. Ibid.

5. Ibid.

6. Ibid.

7. U.S. Census Bureau, *Oldest Baby Boomers Turn 60*, Facts for Features, U.S. Department of Commerce, 2014 (Washington, DC: U.S. Government Printing Office, 2014).

8. Deborah Rothberg, "Generation Y for Dummies," *eWeek*, August 24, 2006. Available at: http://www.eweek.com/c/a/IT-Management/Generation-Y-for-Dummies

9. R. Zemke, C. Raines, and B. Filipczak, *Generations at Work: Managing the Clash of Veterans, Boomers, and Xers and Nexters in your Workplace* (New York: American Management Association, 2000).

10. Monica Anderson and Jingjing Jiang, "Teens, Social Media and Technology 2018." Pew Research Center, May 31, 2018. Available at: https://www.pewresearch.org/internet/2018/05/31/teens-social-media-technology-2018/

11. Ibid.

12. See, e.g., L. J. Siegel, *Criminology* (New York: West Publishing, 2005); G. M. Sykes and F. T. Cullen, *Criminology* (New York: Harcourt Brace and Jovanovich, 2005).

13. J. Livingston, *Crime and Criminology* (Englewood Cliffs, NJ: Prentice-Hall, 1992); F. Adler, G. O. W. Mueller, and W. S. Laufer, *Criminology* (New York: McGraw-Hill, 1995).

14. *Crime and Victimization Fact Sheet*, U.S. Department of Justice, Office of Victims of Crime, 2018. Available at: https://ovc.ncjrs.gov/ncvrw2018/info_flyers/fact_sheets/2018NCVRW_OlderAdults_508_QC.pdf

15. R. Morgan, *Crimes Against the Elderly, 2003–2013*, U.S. Department of Justice, Bureau of Justice Statistics, November 2014. Available at http://www.bjs.gov/content/pub/pdf/cae0313.pdf

16. Rachel Morgan and Jennifer Truman, *Criminal Victimization, 2017*, Bureau of Justice Statistics, December 2018, NCJ 252472. Available at: https://www.bjs.gov/content/pub/pdf/cv17.pdf

17. R. Acierno, M. Hernandez-Tejada, W. Muzzy, and K. Steve, *Final Report: The National Elder Mistreatment Study*, National Institute of Justice, grant no. 2007-WG-BX-009, March 2008, document no. NCJ 226456.

18. N. Castle, *An Examination of Resident Abuse in Assisted Living Facilities* (final report), National Institute of Justice, grant number 2010-IJ-CX-00223, March 2013, document no. 241611.

19. M. Lachs, J. A. Teresi, and M. Ramirez, *Documentation of Resident to Resident Elder Mistreatment in Residential Care Facilities. Final Report to the National Institute of Justice* (final report), grant number 2009_IJ-XC-0001, April 2014, document no. 246429.

20. National Center on Elder Abuse, *National Elder Abuse Incidence Study* (Washington DC: U.S. Government Printing Office, 2005).

21. J. Wasik, "The Fleecing of America's Elderly," *Consumer's Digest* (March/April 2000).

22. R. Acierno, M. A. Hernandez, A. B. Amstadler, H. S. Resnick, S. K. Muzzy, and D. G. Kilpatrick, "Prevalence and Correlates of Emotional, Physical, Sexual, and Financial Abuse and Potential Neglect in the United States: The National Elder Mistreatment Study," *American Journal of Public Health* 100, no. 2 (2010): 292–297.

23. National Center on Elder Abuse, Elder Abuse Statistics, 2018. Available at: https://ncea.acl.gov/What-We-Do/Research/Statistics-and-Data.aspx#08

24. J. Shimkus, *The Graying of America's Prisons: Corrections Copes with Care for the Aged* (Washington, DC: National Commission on Correctional Healthcare, 2007).

25. See, e.g., D. J. Newman, "Elderly Offenders and American Crime Patterns," in E. S. Newman, D. J. Newman, and M. L. Gerwitz, *Elderly Criminals* (Cambridge, MA: Oelgeschlager, Gunn, and Hain, 1984), 3–16.

26. Ibid.

27. R. H. Aday and J. J. Krabill, "Aging Offenders in the Criminal Justice System," *Marqueet Elder's Advisor* 7, no. 2 (2006). Available at: http://scholarship.law.marquette.edu/elders/vol7/iss2/4

28. See, e.g., Aday and Krabill, "Aging Offenders"; C. Cushall and K. Adams, "Responding to Older Offenders: Age Selectivity in the Processing of Shoplifters," *Criminal Justice Review* 1, nos. 1 and 4 (Fall 1983); G. Feinberg and D. Khosla, "Sanctioning Elderly Delinquents," *Trial* (1985): 46, 47–49.

29. See, e.g., Aday and Krabill, "Aging Offenders"; J. Rudolf, "Elderly Inmate Population Soared 1,300 Percent Since 1980s: Report," *Huffington Post*, June 13, 2012; Shimkus, *The Graying of America's Prisons*; H. Deluca, "Managing Elderly Inmates: It's More Than Just Time," in R. P. McNamara and D. E. Redburn (eds.), *Social Gerontology* (Westport, CT: Auburn House, 1997), 209–20.

30. Newman et al., *Elderly Criminals*.

31. Malcolm Spector and John I. Kitsuse, *Constructing Social Problems* (Piscataway, NJ: Transaction Publishers, 2000).

32. Newman et al., *Elderly Criminals*, 209.

33. See, e.g., G. Jones, M. Connelly, and K. Wagner, *Aging Offenders and the Criminal Justice System* (College Park: Maryland State Commission on Criminal Sentencing, 2001); M. T. Harrison, "True Grit: An Innovative Program for Elderly Inmates," *Corrections Today Magazine* 68, no. 7 (2006): 46–49; S. Wallace, "Health Status of Federal Inmates: A Comparison of Admission and Release Medical Records," *Journal of Prison and Jail Health* 10, no. 2 (1992): 133–51; L. Long, "A Study of Arrests of Older Offenders: Trends and Patterns," *Journal of Crime and Justice* 15, no. 2 (1992): 157–75.

34. D. Shichor, "The Extent and Nature of Lawbreaking by the Elderly: A Review of Arrest Statistics," in Newman et al., *Elderly Criminals*, 17–32.

35. Federal Bureau of Investigation, *Crime in the United States 2007*, U.S. Department of Justice, September 2008. Available at: https://ucr.fbi.gov/crime-in-the-u.s/2007; see also *Crime in the United States 2017*, U.S. Department of Justice, Fall 2018. Available at: https://ucr.fbi.gov/crime-in-the-u.s/2017/crime-in-the-u.s.-2017/topic-pages/tables/table-38

36. Ibid.

37. Federal Bureau of Investigation. *Crime in the United States 2004*, U.S. Department of Justice. Available at: https://ucr.fbi.gov/crime-in-the-u.s/2004/crime-in-the-u.s.-2004; and *Crime in the United States 2014*. Available at: https://ucr.fbi.gov/crime-in-the-u.s/2014/crime-in-the-u.s.-2014

38. D. Curran, "Characteristics of the Elderly Shoplifter and the Effect of Sanctions on Recidivism," in W. Wilbanks and P. K. Kim (eds.), *Elderly Criminals* (New York: University Press of America, 1984), 123–42.

39. G. Feinberg, "Profile of the Elderly Shoplifter," in Newman et al., *Elderly Criminals*, 35–50.

40. *Crime in the United States 2004* and *Crime in the United States 2014*.

41. Ibid.

42. See, e.g., A. Blum and G. Fisher, "Women Who Kill," in I. L. Kutash, S. B. Kutash, and L. B. Schlesinger and Associates (eds.), *Violence: Perspectives on Murder and Aggression* (San Francisco: Jossey-Bass, 1979); A. Goetting, "Patterns of Homicide Among the Elderly," *Violence and Victims* 7, no. 3 (1992): 203–15; S. J. Hucker and M. H. Ben-Aron, "Violent Elderly Offenders: A Comparative Study," in Wilbanks and Kim, *Elderly Criminals*, 69–82; R. A. Silverman and L. W. Kennedy, "Relational Distance and Homicide: The Role of the Stranger," *Journal of Criminal Law and Criminology* 78 (1987): 272–308; W. Wilbanks and D. D. Murphy, "The Elderly Homicide Offender," in Newman et al., *Elderly Criminals*, 79–92; M. Wolfgang, *Patterns of Criminal Homicide* (Philadelphia: University of Pennsylvania Press, 1958); M. A. Zahn and P. C. Sagi, "Stranger Homicides in Nine American Cities," *Journal of Criminal Law and Criminology* 78 (1987): 377–97.

43. Goetting, "Patterns of Homicide," 203–15.

44. Ibid., 212.

45. Federal Bureau of Investigation, *FBI Supplementary Homicide Reports 1976–2004*, Department of Justice (Washington, DC: U.S. Government Printing Office, 2005).

46. *Crime in the United States 2004* and *Crime in the United States 2014*.

47. S. J. Hucker, "Psychiatric Aspects of Crime in Old Age," in Newman et al., *Elderly Criminals*, 67–78.

48. See, e.g., Ames and Houston, "Legal, Social, and Biological Definitions," 333–42; J. Briere and M. Runtz, "University Males' Sexual Interest in Children: Predicting Potential Indices of 'Pedophilia' in a Nonforensic Sample," *Child Abuse and Neglect* 13, no. 1 (1989): 65–75.

49. Hucker and Ben-Aron, "Violent Elderly Offenders," 69–82.

50. See, e.g., E. Revitch and R. Weiss, "The Pedophiliac Offender," *Diseases of the Nervous System* 23, no. 2 (1962): 1–16; J. Mohr, R. E. Turner, and M. B. Jerry, *Pedophilia and Exhibitionism* (Toronto: University of Toronto Press, 1964).

51. *Crime in the United States 2004* and *Crime in the United States 2014*.

52. See, e.g., C. Burnett and S. T. Ortega, "Elderly Offenders: A Descriptive Analysis," in W. Wilbanks and P. K. Kim, *Elderly Criminals*, 17–40.

53. See, e.g., United States Department of Justice, *Jailing Drunk Drivers: Impact on the Criminal Justice System* (Washington, D.C: U.S. Government Printing Office, 1984); D. Calahan, *Problem Drinkers* (San Francisco: Jossey-Bass, 1970).

54. See, e.g., U.S. Department of Justice, *Jailing Drunk Drivers*; J. H. Atkinson, "Alcoholism and Geriatric Problems, I and II," *Advances in Alcoholism* 11, nos. 8–9 (1981): 1–13; E. Gomberg, *Drinking and Problem Drinking Among the Elderly* (Ann Arbor, MI: Institute for Gerontology, University of Michigan, 1980).

55. Ibid.

56. *Crime in the United States 2004* and *Crime in the United States 2014*.

57. See, e.g., P. C. Kratcoski and S. Babb, "Adjustment of Older Inmates: An Analysis by Institutional Structure and Gender," *Journal of Contemporary Criminal Justice* 6, no. 4 (1990): 264–81; R. H. Aday, "Golden Years Behind Bars: Special Programs and Facilities for Elderly Inmates," *Federal Probation* 58 (21): 47–54; Long, "A Study of Arrests," 157–75; Wallace, "Health Status of Federal Inmates," 133–51.

58. See, e.g., for instance A. J. Abrams, "Foreword," in Newman et al., *Elderly Criminals*.

59. Matt McKillop and Alex Boucher "Aging Prison Population Drives Up Costs," Pew Research Center, February 20, 2018. Available at: https://www.pewtrusts.org/en/research-and-analysis/articles/2018/02/20/aging-prison-populations-drive-up-costs

60. "Reports on Elderly Prisoners Spur Call for Reforms," *Prison Legal News*, 2014. Available at https://www.prisonlegalnews.org/news/2014/may/19/reports-elderly-prisoners-spur-call-reforms/

61. See, e.g., "The Rising Costs of Incarcerating the Elderly," *The Crime Report*, May 17, 2018. Available at: https://thecrimereport.org/2018/05/17/the-rising-cost-of-punishing-the-elderly/

62. Shimkus, *The Graying of America's Prisons*.

63. C. M. Lemieux, T. B. Dyeson, and B. Castiglione, "Revisiting the Literature on Prisoners Who Are Older: Are We Wiser?" *Prison Journal* 82, no. 4 (2002): 440–58.

64. K. Leonard, "Is Medicaid the Answer to Crushing Health Care Costs for Inmates?" *U.S. News and World Reports*, May 19, 2015. Available at: https://www.usnews.com/news/articles/2015/05/19/is-medicaid-the-answer-to-crushing-health-care-costs-for-inmates; Pew Charitable Trusts, *Managing Prison Health Care Spending*, October 2013. Available at: http://www.pewtrusts.org/~/media/legacy/uploadedfiles/pcs_assets/2014/pctcorrectionshealthcarebrief050814pdf.pdf; C. W. Johnston and N. O. Alozie, "Effect of Age on Criminal Processing: Is There an Advantage to Being Older?" *Journal of Gerontological Social Work* 34, no. 4 (2001): 65–82.

65. Prison Legal News, 2014. Reports on Elderly Prisons.

66. Jonathan Turley, "Release Elderly Inmates," *Los Angeles Times*, October 7, 2006. See also Office of Inspector General, *The Impact of an Aging Inmate Population on the Federal Bureau of Prisons*, U.S. Department of Justice, February 2006. Available at: https://oig.justice.gov/reports/2015/e1505.pdf; Florida Institute of Government, Project on Accountable Justice, *Florida's Aging Inmate Population* (March 2015). Available at: http://www.iog.fsu.edu/paj/documents/Florida%20Aging%20Prisoners%20March%2027%202015.pdf

67. Ibid.

68. Newman et al., *Elderly Criminals*.

CHAPTER 10

JUVENILES AND THE CRIMINAL JUSTICE SYSTEM

CHAPTER OBJECTIVES

After reading this chapter, you should be able to:

- Define juvenile delinquency and *parens patriae*
- Trace society's historical development of the juvenile justice system
- Discuss crime data as they relate to juveniles, particularly African Americans, Hispanic/Latino Americans, Asian Americans, and Native Americans
- Describe current social policies related to addressing the disproportionality of minority involvement in the juvenile justice system

A review of any major news outlet regularly offers stories about young offenders who commit violent acts. Also included are stories about children who are victimized by adults, other youth, and a host of other forms of maltreatment. Still other websites and blogs offer opinions about the failure of the juvenile justice system to protect society from hard-core violent offenders. Often, positions are presented about why the United States should disband the entire juvenile justice system and treat young offenders who commit crimes like adults. Other accounts point to the disproportionality of minority youth who are arrested, convicted, and incarcerated for their involvement in crime. Like their counterparts in the adult criminal justice system, minorities in the juvenile justice system face many distinct challenges.

In many ways, some of the same trends we see with adult minorities in the criminal justice system can be applied to juveniles, but there are a number of significant differences. Societal attitudes about juveniles are different, and there is ample evidence that the current juvenile justice system adequately deals with the problem of juvenile misbehavior. However, a "get tough" approach to crime in the United States during the 1980s and 1990s impacted all types of offenders. What we have seen for the past twenty years has been a steady decline in delinquency offending, similar to what we have seen in the adult population.

Victimization patterns are different for juveniles simply based on the types of crimes that are committed against them, where they occur, and how they are prevented. In addition to different types of offenses and forms of victimization, American attitudes about children and youth in general require us to think differently about juvenile crime. As mentioned, while there is an element within society that views serious juvenile offenders as miniature adults, for the most part juvenile crime is qualitatively different from adult crime and is handled in a different manner. Perhaps most importantly, some of the trends remind us that there are a host of factors beyond race and ethnicity that impact juvenile delinquency.

In this chapter we will examine the juvenile population in the United States as well as how delinquency is defined and addressed by the justice system. Since there are crimes that only youths can commit, such as status offenses, we explore these activities as well.

DEFINITIONS OF JUVENILE DELINQUENCY

Juvenile delinquency is a complex issue that requires a thorough understanding of the physical, social, economic, legal, and political context in which it occurs. Delinquency also encompasses a wide range of activities, making it difficult to define. How one defines delinquency has much to do with how it is measured, understood, and addressed. Sometimes we apply the legal definition. Although this definition works to standardize the behaviors associated with delinquency to some degree, it is not always inclusive of what the general public believes delinquency to be.

In most states, the legal definition of delinquency consists of behavior that violates the criminal code and is committed by youth who have not reached the age of majority (in the U.S., this is usually eighteen).[1] Because each state has its own definition of delinquency, there is wide variation in the age at which youths remain under the jurisdiction of the juvenile court. Historically, many states have failed to distinguish between youths who commit criminal acts and youths who are victims of abuse, neglect, or other mistreatment who commit criminal acts.[2] With the passage of federal legislation separating minor offenders from serious ones—most notably, the Juvenile Justice and Delinquency Prevention Act—many states began to distinguish between delinquents and **status offenders**, that is, those who engage in activities that could only be committed by youths, such as truancy, running away, or underage drinking.[3]

Legally, delinquent acts are those for which youths can be arrested and sentenced—a process referred to in juvenile court as **adjudication**. While legal definitions provide narrower designations for delinquent acts, others define delinquency much more broadly. Parents and siblings, for example, may use the term "delinquent" to define a wide array of behaviors, such as refusing to complete household chores, hanging out with people they think are troublemakers, or listening to rap music. The way that youths dress and talk, and the people with whom they associate do not necessarily mean they are breaking any laws. While parents may complain to social workers, counselors, or even probation officers, these types of behaviors are not likely to be considered delinquent acts by the juvenile justice system.

HISTORY OF JUVENILE DELINQUENCY IN THE UNITED STATES

The law has historically differentiated juveniles from adult offenders, but the degree of that distinction has varied during different eras and for many reasons. In early U.S. history, the law was heavily influenced by the common law of England, which governed the American colonies.

One of the most important English lawyers of the time was William Blackstone, whose *Commentaries on the Laws of England*, first published in the late 1760s, was read widely by the nation's founders.[4] Blackstone identified two criteria by which to hold someone accountable for a crime. First, the person had to have a "vicious will," the intent to commit a crime. Second, the person had to commit an unlawful act. If either the will or the act was lacking, no crime had occurred.[5]

Blackstone felt that there were groups of people who were incapable of committing a crime based on these two criteria. One group consists of infants, or children who are too young to fully understand their actions. Those under the age of seven were classified as infants and could not be guilty of a felony or serious crime such as burglary, kidnapping, or murder. Children over the age of fourteen were said to be able to understand the significance of their actions and so were treated like adults if found guilty of a crime.[6]

For Blackstone and his contemporaries, the ages between seven and fourteen were more difficult to categorize, because children in this age range were generally presumed incapable of committing crimes. If, however, children appeared to understand the difference between right and wrong, then they could be convicted and suffer the full consequence, such as a prison sentence, or even the death penalty in a capital crime.[7]

NINETEENTH-CENTURY UNITED STATES

In the early nineteenth century, the United States experienced significant social and economic changes as a result of the Industrial Revolution. Economic growth, coupled with immigration, urbanization, and industrialization, had an adverse effect on many families. Many poor families had to migrate from farms to cities and take jobs in factories in order to survive. Many children were forced to work long hours in those same factories to help their families. Child labor laws were developed to prevent the exploitation of children, but because parents were working long hours, many children did not receive adequate supervision, which led to a rise in neglect and abuse of children, as well as increases in crime and delinquency.

During this time, several reform movements emerged in an effort to protect children. One of the earliest came in New York City, which had many orphans, runaways, and throwaway children. To remedy the problem, Reverend Charles Loring Brace, who established the **Children's Aid Society** to help homeless children, came up with an innovative idea. Believing that one of the main reasons for juvenile crime stemmed from the negative influence of the urban environment, Brace created **orphan trains**, which transported city youths to rural farms, where families assumed custody of and responsibility for them as apprentices.

At regularly scheduled dates, farming families would go to their local train stations and select orphaned children to live with them. The children and their families had one year to decide whether they would stay together. At the end of the year, if either party decided to part ways, the child would be returned to the Children's Aid Society and board the next train, to be selected by a family in another location.[8]

The orphan trains strategy was a popular one, since many families were moving west and could use help operating their farms. It also provided orphans with a family environment and got them away from dangers found in cities. Unfortunately, some host families considered orphans to be little more than cheap labor, and so treated them harshly. While the practice of shipping children to unknown families was questionable, with some evidence that this was yet another form of exploitation by adults, some experts cite success stories associated with the experience.[9]

Another attempt to address juvenile crime and child exploitation was the **child-saving movement**, which consisted primarily of philanthropists and social reformers who felt that the exploitation of children ultimately resulted in juvenile crime and a host of other problems. Child savers attempted to enact laws that would allow children to be placed in reformatories or other institutions. As with the orphan trains, the thought was that if children were placed in country settings where they could be taught the value of hard work, away from the negative influences of the city, their lives could be improved.

Unfortunately, the noble goal of creating a better life for children often resulted in youths being warehoused in institutions where they were treated poorly and their needs were not met. Some experts note that the child savers were unrealistic in their efforts to reform troubled youths. The false expectation that urban, immigrant children would easily and willingly adopt rural Protestant values often resulted in misbehavior.[10]

For those youths who did not participate in orphan trains or reside in institutions in rural areas, **houses of refuge** were created. The first house of refuge opened in New York in 1825 as a facility exclusively for children. By the 1840s, an additional fifty-three houses had been built around the country. Houses of refuge did not limit their services to children who had committed crimes. They were also homes for poor children, orphans, and any children thought to be incorrigible or wayward. The average number of children in a house was two hundred, but some, like the New York House of Refuge, housed over one thousand youths at any given time.[11]

Orphan trains, houses of refuge, and other organizations attempted to remove delinquents from the deleterious conditions of the city.

As the needs of children surpassed the ability of the houses of refuge to safely care for them, with problems such as overcrowding, deplorable living conditions, and reports of abuse by staff, training schools were developed in the mid-nineteenth century. **Training schools** were larger facilities that placed a greater emphasis on education and vocational training. Consistent with contemporary thinking at the time, the city was the source of temptation, and a rural setting would offer youths a simpler and more virtuous way of life. Such thinking led to many of the new facilities being built outside of cities.[12]

Although the twentieth century brought the development of individualized diagnosis and treatment, new kinds of rehabilitative therapy, and improved educational programming, the training school model of concentrating large numbers of juvenile offenders in one institution has persisted.[13]

DELINQUENCY IN THE EARLY TWENTIETH CENTURY

In the late nineteenth century, in response to continuing problems associated with juvenile delinquency, child neglect, and the exploitation of children, the child savers and other reformists attempted to establish a separate court for juveniles. In 1899, after years of development and months of compromise, the Illinois legislature passed a law permitting counties in the state to designate one or more of their circuit court judges to hear all cases involving dependent, neglected, and delinquent children younger than age sixteen. The law stipulated that these cases were to be heard in a special courtroom that would be designated as the juvenile courtroom, generally referred to as the juvenile court. Thus, the first juvenile court in Cook County, Illinois, was not a new court but a division of the existing circuit court with original jurisdiction over juvenile cases.

By 1910, thirty-two states had established juvenile courts and/or probation services. By 1925, all but two states had followed Illinois's lead in creating a separate court for juveniles. Borrowing from British thinking, the doctrine *parens patriae* (literally, "parent of the nation"; essentially, the state as parent) served as the foundation for the state to intervene and to provide protection for children whose parents did not provide adequate care or supervision.[14]

In line with their "parental" role, juvenile courts tried to focus on the best interests of children. They emphasized an informal, nonadversarial, and flexible approach to cases—there were few procedural rules that the courts were required to follow. Cases were treated as civil (noncriminal) actions, and the ultimate goal was to guide juvenile offenders through adolescence to become responsible, law-abiding adults. The juvenile court could, however, order that young offenders be removed from their homes and placed in juvenile reform institutions as part of their rehabilitation program.[15]

In subsequent years, most juvenile courts had exclusive jurisdiction over all youths under age eighteen who were charged with violating criminal laws. Only if the juvenile court decided to waive its jurisdiction in a case could a child be transferred to criminal court and tried as an adult. **Transfer** decisions were made on a case-by-case basis, using a "best interests of the child and public" standard.[16]

By this stage in the development of the juvenile court, there were significant differences in the juvenile and adult criminal court systems. The focus of the juvenile court was on the offender, not on the offense, and the juvenile court could be much more flexible and informal than the adult criminal court. Additionally, the focus was on rehabilitation rather than punishment. There was a wide range of options available to judges at the sentencing phase: judges were not limited to punitive sanctions stemming from the particular offense.[17]

DELINQUENCY IN THE 1960s–1970s

In the 1950s and 1960s, treatment strategies available to juvenile justice professionals were called into question. Although the goal of rehabilitation through **individualized justice**— the basic philosophy of the juvenile justice system—was not in question, professionals were concerned about the growing number of juveniles who were being institutionalized indefinitely in the name of treatment. In a series of decisions beginning in the 1960s, the U.S. Supreme Court required that juvenile courts become more formal, like the criminal courts.[18]

Formal hearings were required in waiver situations, and delinquents facing possible confinement were given protection against self-incrimination and rights to receive notice of the charges against them, to present and question witnesses, and to have an attorney present during the proceedings. The burden-of-proof standard for adjudication changed from merely a preponderance of evidence to the much more rigorous proof beyond a reasonable doubt. The Supreme Court, however, still held that there were enough "differences of substance between the criminal and juvenile courts . . . to hold that a jury is not required in the latter."[19]

Take, for example, the case of Morris Kent, whose circumstances set precedent in the landmark Supreme Court decision known as *Kent v. the United States*, 383 U.S. 541 (1966). Kent first entered the juvenile court system at the age of fourteen, following several housebreakings and attempted thefts. Two years later, his fingerprints were found in the apartment of a woman who had been robbed and raped. Detained and interrogated by police, he admitted to the crimes. Kent's mother hired a lawyer, who arranged for a psychiatric examination of the boy. The examination concluded that Kent suffered from "severe psychopathology" and recommended that he be placed in a psychiatric hospital for observation.[20]

The juvenile court judge had authority to **waive jurisdiction** in Kent's case to a criminal court, where Kent would be tried as an adult. Kent's lawyer opposed the waiver and offered to prove that if Kent was given proper hospital treatment, he would be a candidate for rehabilitation. The juvenile court did not respond to the motions made by Kent's lawyer and, without a hearing, waived jurisdiction to adult court.[21]

The U.S. Supreme Court ruled that Kent was entitled to a hearing and to a statement of the reasons for the juvenile court's decision to waive jurisdiction. The majority of the justices also expressed concerns that the juvenile courts were not living up to their potential and speculated "that there may be grounds for concern that the child receives the worst of both worlds [in juvenile courts]: that he gets neither the protections accorded to adults nor the solicitous care and regenerative treatment postulated for children."[22]

A year after the Kent decision, the case of *in re Gault* 387 U.S. 1 (1967) was heard by the U.S. Supreme Court and fundamentally changed the way juvenile courts processed cases. Gault, a fifteen-year-old Arizona boy, was accused of making an indecent phone call to a neighbor. The victim, who recognized Gault's voice, called the police. Officers arrived at Gault's home and took him into custody, without leaving notice to Gault's parents that their son had been arrested. Before Gault's adjudication hearing, neither Gault nor his parents received notification of the specific charges against him. At the hearings, there were no sworn witnesses, and no record was made of the proceedings. Not even the neighbor who had made the complaint about the phone call was present.[23]

At the end of the hearings, the judge committed Gault to Arizona's State Industrial School until he turned twenty-one, a six-year sentence. An adult convicted of using vulgar or obscene language would have received a maximum penalty of a $50 fine and imprisonment for no more than two months. Gault's parents argued that he had been denied due process of the law and that his constitutional rights to a fair trial had been violated. The case eventually made its way to the Supreme Court, which ruled in Gault's favor.[24]

While the U.S. Supreme Court was protecting the constitutional rights of juveniles accused of committing crimes, Congress was attempting to determine the types of crimes and offenders that warranted special attention. In 1968, Congress passed the **Juvenile Delinquency Prevention and Control Act**, recommending that children charged with noncriminal (status) offenses be handled outside the court system. A few years later, Congress passed the **Juvenile Justice and Delinquency Prevention Act of 1974**, which prohibited states from incarcerating status offenders and required them to detain juvenile offenders in separate facilities from adult offenders.[25]

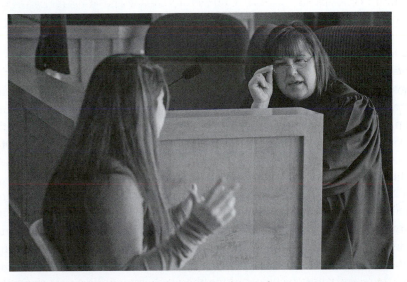

Most youths who enter the juvenile justice system tend not to return as repeat offenders.

DELINQUENCY FROM THE 1980s INTO THE NEW MILLENNIUM

During the 1980s and 1990s, many politicians and policy makers asserted that not only were instances of serious juvenile crime increasing, but the juvenile justice system was too lenient with offenders. In response, many states attempted to limit the authority of the juvenile courts over some types of delinquents. Changes included mandatory waivers and/or sentences for certain offenses, and a reduction in protections normally afforded to juveniles, such as having confidentiality laws, fingerprinting and photographing suspects during booking procedures, using a juvenile's prior record at the sentencing stage of the process, and allowing juvenile hearings to be open to the public.

Over the past forty years, the media have painted a picture of juveniles as violent and chronic offenders, and many policymakers and politicians claim that delinquency is out of control. But the vast majority of juvenile offenders are not violent, nor are they chronic in their misbehavior, and the juvenile justice system appears to be able to adequately deal with the challenges they present to their respective communities.[26] Ample research also suggests that incarceration does not rehabilitate juvenile offenders.[27] Instead, it may contribute to the delinquency problem, as youths are more likely to commit additional crimes after being incarcerated.[28]

CHECKPOINT

- The history of juvenile delinquency has shown that at one point, delinquents were treated like miniature adults. Later, with the child-saving movement, delinquents were seen as individuals in need of treatment. However, many of the constitutional protections offered to adult criminals were not initially extended to juveniles. This resulted in a series of Supreme Court decisions that guided criminal justice officials in the processing of juvenile offenders. In the 1980s, as part of a larger "get tough" approach to crime, there was a more intentional effort to arrest and detain juveniles, largely due to the fear of youth who committed violent crimes.

THE JUVENILE POPULATION

According to recent data, in 2018 there were approximately 74 million children and youth under the age of eighteen in the United States, representing about 23 percent of the total population. Estimates show that this number is expected to increase to about eighty million by 2050. However, because of declining birth rates and the overall aging of America, children have represented a decreasing percentage of the overall population. According to some data, children represented 36 percent of the population in 1960, 26 percent in 1990, and 23 percent in 2016. By 2050, children will represent about 20 percent of the U.S. population.[29]

As mentioned, from the outset it is important to note that most youths do not engage in delinquent acts, and if they do, the situation is handled long before the juvenile justice system becomes involved. However, even when youths are referred to the system for formal processing, there are a host of places along the way where a diversion or resolution can occur. Given all this, most who progress through the system do not return as repeat offenders. This finding alone should raise questions about the arguments made that the juvenile justice system is ineffective—perhaps what is needed is a more in-depth understanding of the types of offenders the juvenile justice system is designed to handle—it is not focused on the hard-core offenders. Let's look at the role of juveniles in the justice process, both as victims and as offenders. What we will find is that the trends noted in previous chapters regarding a race and ethnicity disproportionality exists among juveniles as it does with adults.

JUVENILE VICTIMS

Of all the discussions of background factors that contribute to crime, such as poverty, poor educational achievement, abuse, neglect, and others, most researchers use these variables to explain adult criminality. Moreover, race and ethnicity play important roles in understanding the disproportionality found in the crime data. However, a closer look at these data shows that experiences such as exposure to violence at an early age, being neglected or abused, or poor academic achievement are all early-onset factors for adult offenders. They also contribute to a juvenile's engagement in crime. Thus, while one could make the argument, as has been done in virtually every chapter in this book, that discriminatory practices against certain groups results in an increased frequency of involvement in the criminal justice system, we could also say that many of the same background factors are crucial to understanding delinquency patterns.

According to the National Center for Juvenile Justice and the Office of Juvenile Justice and Delinquency Prevention, in their 2014 report, *Juvenile Offenders and Victims: 2014 National Report*, child maltreatment occurs "when a caretaker [a parent or substitute] is responsible for, or permits, the abuse or neglect of a child." The maltreatment can result in actual physical or emotional harm, or it can place the child in danger of physical or emotional harm. The acts include physical abuse (an act that caused or could have caused physical injury to a child), sexual abuse (involvement of a child in sexual activity, either forcefully or without force), emotional abuse (verbal threats or emotional assaults, willful cruelty or exploitation), physical neglect (disregard of a child's physical needs, including failure to seek healthcare, inadequate supervision, food, hygiene, or clothing), emotional neglect (inadequate affection, exposing a child to domestic violence or other inattention to emotional or developmental needs), or educational neglect (permitting chronic truancy or inattention to educational needs)."[30]

According to a 2017 report from the U.S. Department of Health and Human Services, the youngest children are the most vulnerable to maltreatment. Nationally, about 29 percent of victims are younger than three years old. The victimization rate is highest for children younger than a year old, at 25.3 per 1,000 children in the population of the same age. This is more than double the rate of victims who are a year old (11.7 per 1,000 children). Victims who are two or three years old have victimization rates of 11.0 and 10.4 victims per 1,000 children, respectively. In general, the rate of victimization decreases as the child's age increases.[31]

The percentages of child victims are similar for boys (48.6 percent) and girls (51 percent). The sex is unknown for 0.4 percent of victims. Most victims are one of three races or ethnicities—White (44.6 percent), Hispanic (22.3 percent), or African-American (20.7 percent). The racial distributions for all children in the population are 50.7 percent White, 25.2 percent Hispanic, and 13.7 percent African-American,. For 2017, American-Indian or

Alaska Native children have the highest rate of victimization at 14.3 per 1,000 children in the population of the same race or ethnicity; and African-American children have the second highest rate at 13.9 per 1,000 children.[32]

The 2017 data show that three-fourths (74.9 percent) of victims are neglected, 18.3 percent are physically abused, and 8.6 percent are sexually abused. In addition, 7.1 percent of victims experience such "other" types of maltreatment as threatened abuse or neglect, drug/alcohol addiction, and lack of supervision.

Generally speaking, maltreatment rates vary by parents' employment status and economic situations. That is, children with an unemployed parent or those with parents not working have a higher risk of experiencing maltreatment compared to children who have one or both parents in the labor force. Similarly, children who lived in families with low household incomes, below $15,000 per year, or those who received food stamps, public housing, or any type of public assistance, were five times more likely to be maltreated in some way, three times more likely to be abused, and seven times more likely to be neglected than children who did not live in these types of families.[33]

Similarly, children who lived with two married biological parents fared much better than children who live in single-parent families or in adoptive or step-parent families. In fact, children living with two married biological parents have the lowest rates of maltreatment of any group, whereas children who lived with a single parent, or those who had a cohabitating partner, have the highest maltreatment rates.[34]

According to the Department of Health and Human Services, neglect was the most common form of maltreatment for victims, a trend that has remained consistent for the past several decades. While children are often the victims of more than one type of maltreatment, if they are separated into independent categories, 75 percent of all victims experienced neglect, whereas about 18 percent experienced physical abuse, 9 percent were sexually abused, 8 percent were emotional maltreated, and 10 percent experienced some other form of maltreatment.[35]

The breakdown of this trend is that just over 51 percent of maltreatment victims are girls and most victims were White (44.8 percent), followed by Black (21.9 percent) and Hispanic (21.4 percent). Asian/Pacific Islanders, along with American Indian/Alaska Natives, accounted for about 1 percent each. Black children had the highest maltreatment rates (14.6 per 1,000), which is about twice the rate of White children (7.8 per 1,000). Although they only accounted for a small percentage of reported maltreatment victims, American Indian/Alaska Natives had victimization rates higher than 10 per 1,000.[36]

The overwhelming majority of maltreatment offenders are parents of the victims. The 2017 data show that about 92 percent of victims are maltreated by one or both parents. Sixty-nine percent of victims are maltreated by a mother, either acting alone (41 percent) or with a father and/or nonparent (28 percent). About 14 percent of victims are maltreated by a perpetrator who was not the child's parent, including a relative or partner of the parent. The National Child Abuse and Neglect Data System recognized over 700,000 unique offenders of child maltreatment. Women are disproportionately represented in these statistics—they accounted for more than half (54 percent) of maltreatment offenders. Further, nearly half of offenders were White, 20 percent were Black and 18 percent were Hispanic. Not too surprisingly, this distribution is similar to the race profile of victims of maltreatment.[37]

Most offenders of child neglect are parents.

Other types of victimization relate to a child's exposure to violence. According to the National Survey of Children's Exposure to Violence, 61 percent of youth surveyed had been either victims of or witnesses to violence in the prior year, with nearly half (46 percent) reporting being victims of assault in the past year. About 25 percent report being victims of robbery, vandalism, or theft. About 13 percent report being physically bullied within the last year. Overall, about 6 percent of youth stated they have been sexually victimized in the past year, with the age group fourteen to seventeen being the most common one to experience this.[38]

Homicide is one of the leading causes of juvenile deaths in the United States. According to the National Center for Injury Prevention and Control, homicide is the fourth leading cause of death for children ages one to eleven, and it is the third leading cause of death for juveniles ages twelve to seventeen. An estimated 1,450 persons under age eighteen were murdered in the United States in 2010, about 10 percent of all persons murdered that year. Nearly half of these victims were Black, while 47 percent were White and 3 percent were either American Indian or Asian. Given that White youth comprise 76 percent of the U.S. resident juvenile population in 2010, while Blacks represented 17 percent, the murder rate for Black youth was nearly five times the rate for White youth.

As it relates to suicides, the suicide rate among ten- to nineteen-year-olds rose 56 percent between 2007 and 2016, with greater increases for females than males. Suffocation, firearms, and poisoning accounted for more than 92 percent of all suicide deaths in 2016. Unlike two decades earlier, where firearms were a leading cause of suicide, today suffocation is the leading cause of suicide among children and adolescents. Still, firearms play an important role in suicides, with the Centers for Disease Control and Prevention (CDC) reporting their use as the leading method for males age ten to nineteen, whereas suffocation was the leading method for females. The number of suicide deaths by poisoning, primarily involving opioid drug overdoses, was higher for females than for males. Last year, the CDC reported that suicide rates among fifteen- to nineteen-year-old girls doubled between 2007 and 2015, reaching a forty-year high.[39]

JUVENILE OFFENDERS

While the image of the hard-core, violent juvenile offender is popular in the media and perhaps colors the public's images about delinquents in general, the reality is that the vast majority of offenders in the juvenile justice system do not return to it, and most offenders in general never enter the system in the first place. This suggests a very different portrait of juvenile delinquents, as well as the overall effectiveness of the juvenile justice system. Additionally, the range of activities in which youths become involved that might be classified as criminal vary substantially—it could be a fight at school, vandalizing someone's property, underage drinking and/or smoking tobacco, illicit drug use, or it can be a more serious crime such as gang activity or violent crime. For the purposes of this discussion, we will focus on the more serious crimes since they are most likely to demonstrate a more pronounced racial and ethnic distribution. At every stage of the juvenile justice process, we see evidence of a similar type of disproportionality to that which we saw in chapters for adult minorities.

CHECKPOINT

- Juveniles represent about one-fourth of the U.S. population, and this number has continued to decline in recent decades. This is due to low birth rates along with an aging population. As victims, much of the data focus on neglect and abuse, including sexual abuse of children. The data show that over three-fourths of child maltreatment involves neglect and the majority of the offenders are the child's parents and relatives. As offenders, there is a misperception of juvenile delinquents—that they are hardened criminals who commit violent crimes. In reality, most youth who enter the juvenile justice system do not return, which suggests that the system is working to prevent youth from becoming adult offenders.

JUVENILES AND THE POLICE

When examining the crime data presented by the Uniform Crime Reports, it is important to note that arrest information is divided by race and by ethnicity. That is, there is one table that captures arrest information for Whites, Blacks, Asians, Native Americans, and those from Hawaii and the Pacific Islands. There is another table that contrasts arrests for Hispanics and Latinos, comparing it to non-Hispanics/Latinos.[40]

In 2017, according to the Uniform Crime Reports, there were a total of 625,099 arrests for individuals under the age of 18. This is a significant decline from 2010, when there were 1,642,500 juvenile arrests. However, in examining some of the demographic trends, little difference is found among those groups who were arrested during either period. For instance, in 2010, 66 percent of juveniles arrested were White, with Blacks representing 31 percent of all arrests. In 2017, 62 percent of all juveniles arrested were White and 35 percent were Black. In presenting these data, the Uniform Crime Reports divides arrests by race (White, Black, Asian) and also by ethnicity (Hispanic/Latino compared to non-Hispanic/Latino). In the latter case, the percentages are slightly different because the total number of arrests made varies. In 2017, for example, there were a total of 466,450 arrests by ethnicity, of which 101,762 were classified as Hispanic/Latino. This represented about 22 percent of all arrests by ethnicity. Non-Hispanic/Latino comprised about 78 percent of all arrests. This division applies for specific crimes as well as for all arrests, and the trends noted in 2017 are similar to those in 2010.[41]

Of course, these proportions vary according to the type of crime committed, but on balance, what we see is a fairly consistent portrait of juvenile arrests in the United States. For instance, for those arrested under the age of eighteen, White juveniles accounted for about two-thirds of rape arrests, whereas Black juveniles made up over two-thirds of robbery arrests. Similarly, nearly 75 percent of White juveniles were arrested for arson, while only about 24 percent of Black juveniles were arrested for this crime. Arrests for homicide were higher among Black juveniles than Whites (66.6 percent vs. 37.7 percent), and more Whites were arrested for aggravated assault than Black juveniles (54.2 percent vs. 42.5 percent).[42]

The ratio of White-Black arrests for rape was 2 to 1, with Whites comprising 1,970 arrests for this crime compared to 925 for Black juveniles. Hispanic/Latinos represented 489 rapes, far lower than for either Whites or Blacks. The robbery ratio for Blacks to Whites was 2.5 to 1. The juvenile arrest rate for robbery has seen a consistent decline since 2000. In 2010, the rate for Black youth was ten times the rate for White youth, fifteen times the rate for Native American youth, and nineteen times the rate for Asian youth. In 2017, the robbery ratio of White to Native Americans was close to 73 to 1, and it was 23 to 1 for White to Asian youth. This trend still applies despite dramatic declines in the number of overall arrests.[43]

Interestingly, arrests for aggravated assault have continued to decrease since their peak in 1994, by as much as 53 percent in 2010. However, what is noted in the data, including in 2017, is the increase in the number of females arrested for this crime. There may be several explanations for this, but as one author noted, the reason may have to do with a modification of policy that encouraged arrests of females, particularly for domestic violence situations. Similar trends are noted for simple assaults. This trend can also be attributed to policy changes, where many schools have enacted zero-tolerance policies, which result in arrests for incidents that would normally be handled informally.[44]

Schools provide unique settings for juveniles as they spend much time there, and they are the setting for much delinquency and related activities. Researchers assessed the impact of various protective measures, such as law enforcement, security policies, and school/neighborhood characteristics on school violence with consideration of the racial composition of schools and grade levels. The researchers noted that minority schools often faced higher levels of reported violence and had a heavier law enforcement presence. The enhanced law enforcement efforts at predominantly minority schools had mixed or counterproductive results for reducing school violence, leading the researchers to suggest that the environments in which the schools are located and the characteristics or culture of the schools should be considered in efforts to reduce violence on campus.[45] The increased presence of law enforcement at schools results in many behaviors that were once handled informally becoming part of a youth's official record, and contributes to the "**school-to-prison pipeline**," which refers to the increasing patterns of students having contact with the justice system as a result of more punitive approaches to addressing school-related problems.

For some youths, gang life is a means of survival.

Ultimately, with regard to arrests, there appears to be a consistent trend of disproportionality with regard to African Americans and Whites. While Whites still represent the majority of arrests for most crimes, minorities, particularly African Americans and Hispanics, are overrepresented in the arrest data.

CHECKPOINT

- The arrest data on juveniles show that juvenile crime has been decreasing over the past twenty years. The data also indicate that, in absolute numbers, there are far more White youth arrested for virtually all crimes than any other minority. However, African Americans, like their adult counterparts, are disproportionately represented in the data, with Blacks being, on average, twice as likely to be arrested as Whites.

JUVENILES AND THE COURTS

A 2018 report, *Juvenile Court Statistics*, provides information on delinquency and status offense cases handled by juvenile courts, including demographic profiles of the trends in the volume and characteristics of court activity. U.S. courts with the authority to hear juvenile cases handled approximately 850,500 cases in 2016 in which a youth was charged with a delinquency offense. The overall trends have been downward; with a decrease of about 49 percent of cases between 2005 and 2016. Specifically, property crimes decreased by 54 percent; public order crimes decreased by 51 percent, person crimes by 44 percent, and drug offenses by 42 percent between 2005 and 2016.[46]

In terms of a demographic distribution, overall males represented about 72 percent (614,900) of cases handled by juvenile courts in 2016, while females represented about 28 percent. The average annual decrease in the male and female delinquency caseloads was very similar for all offense types between 2005 and 2016. Both males and females had increases in drug offenses, but the change was slightly larger for females than males for cases (3 percent vs. 1 percent). Both groups saw increases in person crimes, with males witnessing a 3-percent increase between 2005 and 2016 while females witnessed a 4-percent increase. Both males and females saw decreases in property crimes between 2005 and 2016 (3 percent for males and 5 percent for females), while both groups saw small decreases (1 percent each) for public order crimes (see Table 10.1).[47]

In 2016, Black juveniles represented about 15 percent of the juvenile population and about a third of all delinquency cases. White youth made up 56 percent of the juvenile population and about 43 percent of all delinquency cases. Similarly, American Indians represented about 2 percent of the population and about 2 percent of cases, whereas Asian youth represented about 5 percent of the juvenile population and 1 percent of delinquency cases. These percentages were about the same ten years earlier, indicating that the disproportionality problem is a chronic one in the juvenile court system (see Table 10.2).[48]

TABLE 10.1   PERCENTAGE OF DELINQUENCY CASES BY GENDER, 2005–2016

2016	Male	Female
Person Crimes	28%	32%
Property Crimes	34%	32%
Drug Offenses	13%	11%
Public Order Crimes	25%	26%
2005	**Male**	**Female**
Person Crimes	25%	28%
Property Crimes	37%	37%
Drug Offenses	12%	8%
Public Order Crimes	26%	27%

Source: Sarah Hockenberry and Charles Puzzancherra, *Juvenile Court Statistics 2016*, U.S. Department of Justice, Office of Justice Programs, Office of Juvenile Justice and Delinquency Prevention, August 2018. Available at: https://www.ojjdp.gov/ojstatbb/njcda/pdf/jcs2016.pdf

TABLE 10.2   RACE AND DELINQUENCY CASES

Race	Total Delinquency	Person	Property	Drugs	Public Order
White	43%	40%	44%	55%	40%
Black	36%	42%	36%	20%	37%
Hispanic	18%	15%	17%	22%	21%
Amer. Indian	2%	2%	2%	2%	1%
Asian	1%	1%	1%	1%	1%

Source: Nina Hyland, "Delinquency Cases in Juvenile Court 2014," *Juvenile Justice Statistics*, U.S. Department of Justice, Office of Justice Programs, Office of Juvenile Justice and Delinquency Prevention, January 2018. Available at: https://www.ojjdp.gov/pubs/251107.pdf

The racial disparity in delinquency cases varied across offense categories. White youth accounted for a larger proportion of drug offense cases (55 percent) than any of the other offense categories. In contrast, Black youth were involved in only 20 percent of drug offense cases, accounting for a larger proportion of person offense cases (42 percent) than any other offense category. Hispanic youth are about as likely to be involved in drug offenses and public order crimes, while Asian and American Indian youth accounted for a small proportion of all cases.

The rate at which Black youth were referred to juvenile court for a delinquency offense was more than three times the rates for White and Hispanic youth. The rate at which referred cases were petitioned for formal processing was greater for Black youth than for White youth and greater than the rate for Hispanic youth. Once adjudicated, cases involving Black or Hispanic youth were more likely to result in residential placement than cases involving White youth (28 percent and 43 percent, respectively). Conversely, adjudicated cases involving White youth were more likely to result in probation than cases involving Black or Hispanic youth (5 percent and 4 percent).[49]

Interestingly, until 2016, information on Hispanic involvement in delinquency cases was not well known, despite the growth of the overall Hispanic population in the United States. In a recent publication titled *Delinquency Cases Involving Hispanic Youth 2013*, researchers from the National Center on Juvenile Justice explored the participation of Hispanic youth in juvenile court. The findings of the study, based on a sample of cases, showed that Hispanic youth accounted for 26 percent of all cases processed in 2013. Property and public order offense cases each accounted for about one-third of the Hispanic delinquency caseload during that time period, and younger teens, those under the age of sixteen, accounted for about half of the caseload. The study concluded that, compared with White youth, Hispanic youth were 20 percent more likely to be referred to juvenile court and equally as likely to have their cases handled formally. Once adjudicated, Hispanic youth were as likely as White youth to be placed on probation, but 30 percent more likely to be ordered to out-of-home placement.[50]

However, given that most adjudicated delinquency cases result in either residential placement or formal probation as a disposition, one question this data may raise is whether or not there is a racial distribution regarding this outcome. The data indicate that White youth were less likely than Black youth or American Indian youth to be ordered to residential placement as a result of a finding of adjudication of delinquency. However, there are many factors to consider when making a decision to place a youth in a residential facility, including criminal history, severity of the offense, and other factors.[51]

What should policymakers do about these apparent disparities? In 1988, Congress passed an amendment to the Juvenile Justice and Delinquency Prevention Act that required states to address the problem of disproportionality, particularly as it relates to confinement. Known as DMC, for disproportionate minority confinement, this amendment was expanded in 2002, which required states to create systems to reduce the problem of minorities who come into contact with the juvenile justice system. That is, measuring disparity can occur at multiple points in the system and can build upon itself in terms of the severity of outcomes. The research suggested that disparity is most pronounced at arrest, and as youth continue through the system, the differential treatment they receive is cumulative—disparity at arrest impacts disparity treatment in the court system, and so on.[52]

RELATIVE RATE INDEX

To address these problems, in 2010 the Office of Juvenile Justice and Delinquency Prevention created the Relative Rate Index (RRI) to measure disparities across the stages of the system by comparing rates of juvenile justice contact experienced by different groups of youth. The RRI includes the size of each subgroup (White, Black, Asian, etc.) at each stage and compares it to the preceding stage that occurred before it.

The idea is to quantify the nature of the decisions at each point and then compare the decisions in an effort to identify any influence disparity at one point impacts the next phase. While imperfect and given that not all states contribute to the database, the idea of having some sort of index or indicator of disparity is an important step in uncovering the reasons why disparity exists in the system as well as identifying specific "sticking points" for certain groups. In 2010, RRI data show that Black youth were arrested for delinquency offenses at more than twice the rate for White youth; and the diversion rate (meaning a case is diverted from further processing) for Black and other minority groups was less than the rate for White offenders. In general, there is more disparity for Black juveniles at arrest, detention, and waiver to criminal court than at other stages of the juvenile justice process.[53]

CHECKPOINT

- As is the case with arrest data, the number of youths who are brought to juvenile court has consistently decreased over the past several years. Similar to trends found in the past, the vast majority of offenders are male, although females have become more involved in juvenile court than in the past for certain crimes. Additionally, there is racial disparity within the number of petitioned cases—where Blacks are much more likely than Whites to be brought to juvenile court and to have their cases adjudicated as delinquent.

JUVENILES AND CORRECTIONS

The emphasis on individualized justice as a guiding philosophy of the juvenile justice system lends itself to a variety of resolutions to delinquent behavior. While most cases are handled informally and do not even come to the attention of the juvenile justice system, when they do, solutions such as probation and other less punitive measures are often provided. These are sometimes referred to as community-based programs and can include forestry camps, wilderness programs, mentoring programs, and other alternative measures. While they have their place and some have been shown to be notably effective in reducing repeat delinquent behavior, in other cases the offense committed by the juvenile is too serious to warrant such an approach.

In these instances, more formal detention is required. Institutional facilities are generally designed to serve youths awaiting a detention or adjudication hearing or those who were committed to detention by a juvenile court or some other administrative body, such as a social service agency. Youths referred to detention facilities under these circumstances are sometimes called **voluntary placements** because either their parents turned them over to a social service agency or the agency placed them because they committed delinquent acts but were not formally adjudicated. However, voluntary placements are rare, consisting of less than 1 percent of all detained youth.[54] Far more common are situations in which a judge orders a youth to a residential facility for committing a delinquent act. There are a wide range of options for institutional detention, including reception centers, ranches and forestry camps, boot camps, traditional training schools, and adult prisons.

According to Child Trends data, the rates and number of juveniles in residential placement have consistently decreased for more than twenty years. In 2015, there were 48,043 juveniles in residential placement, which calculates to a rate of about 152 juveniles per 100,000 population. This is far lower than the 356 per 100,000 rate in 1997 (see Figure 10.1). The rate fell roughly equally among Whites, Blacks, and Hispanics (55 to 70 percent). Over that same period, rates for Asian youth fell the most (88 percent), while rates for American Indians fell the least (47percent).[55]

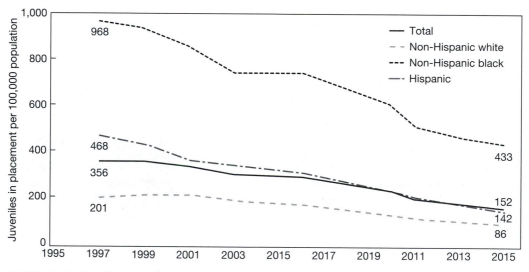

FIGURE 10.1 Juveniles in residential placement per 100,000 population, by race and Hispanic origin: Selected years, 1997–2015

The Census of Juveniles in Residential Placement collects data from all juvenile residential custody facilities in the United States, asking for information on each youth assigned a bed in the facility on the last Wednesday in October. Residential facilities include detention centers, shelters, reception/diagnostic centers, group homes, boot camps, ranch/wilderness camps, residential treatment centers, and long-term secure facilities. Rates are calculated per 100,000 juveniles ages ten through the upper age of each state's juvenile court jurisdiction. *Source:* M. Sickmund, T. J. Sladky,! Kang, and C. Puzzanchera *Easy Access to the Census of Juveniles in Residential Placement* [Data tool], Office of Juvenile Justice and Delinquency Prevention (OJJDP), 2017. Retrieved from http://www.ojidp.gov/oistatbb/ezacirp/.

The vast majority of juveniles in residential placement—about 95 percent—were there because of a delinquency or criminal charge. In 2015, the most recent data available, Asian youth had the lowest rates of juvenile residential placement among males (38 per 100,000 population). Hispanic males had a rate of 237 per 100,000, followed by American Indian males (384 per 100,000), and Black males (746 per 100,000).[56]

As in the case of males, Black females and American Indian adolescents had the highest rates of residential placement (110 and 134 per 100,000, respectively). Non-Hispanic White females were also less likely to be in residential placement (32 per 100,000 in 2015) than Hispanic females (44 per 100,000). Non-Hispanic Asian females were the least likely to be in residential placement, with a rate of 7 per 100,000.[57]

In some cases, especially for serious offenders, juveniles can be sent to training schools or state institutions for longer periods of detention. They can also be sent to adult prisons, depending on a number of factors. The main difference between an adult prison and a training school is that there is a greater emphasis placed on rehabilitation and counseling in the juvenile facility. However, the emphasis on maintaining order and control of individual behavior is relatively the same in both places.[58]

In juvenile facilities, there is an emphasis placed on altering the individual's behavior so that he or she does not commit additional crimes in the future. It is often difficult to assess the success of programs with this goal in mind since participants have committed serious offenses or are repeat offenders. Thus, this group represents perhaps the worst of the delinquency population, making success a relatively difficult concept to evaluate. The fact that many serious offenders go on to adult careers in crime is not necessarily an indication that such programs are ineffective—it may be that the population they serve is the most difficult to change.[59]

Whether they look like prisons or college campuses, or even when attempts are made to create a home environment, training schools, which are being used increasingly in the United States to house juveniles, are an expensive way to handle delinquent youths. This is particularly true given the fact that only a small percentage of youths sentenced to secure detention have committed a violent crime. The vast majority of offenders have committed

One unintended consequence of detention for some youths is that incarceration actually improves their standard of living.

property crimes, such as burglary or larceny-theft.[60] In addition to the expense, like their adult counterparts, overcrowding has become problematic for juvenile training schools, and gangs are becoming a feature of the training school landscape.[61]

Short-Term Facilities

In addition to long-term secure facilities, a youth can be placed in a short-term one as well. Essentially, there are two types of short-term facilities: those that house youths awaiting adjudication or dispositional hearings, which are similar in many ways to jails, and short-term facilities for adjudicated offenders. Examples of the latter are boot camps, forestry camps, or ranches. Part of the problem with this type of approach is that they offer little in the way of therapy nor do they contribute to correcting the behavior that caused youths to be arrested in the first place.

Additionally, there is no follow-up care from this type of program; youths are simply sent back to the environments and neighborhoods from which they originally came with few tools to cope with the problems that got them into trouble. While the popularity of boot camps peaked around the mid-1990s, with several hundred programs operating across the country, the evaluations of these programs demonstrated that they do little in the way of long-term positive effects. In sum, given their short duration, the absence of consistency of the message after residents leave the program, and few opportunities for youths to understand the significance of what happened to them during the process, this type of intervention falls quite short of the mark in terms of changing youths' behavior.[62]

INSTITUTIONAL LIFE FOR DELINQUENTS

Everyone responds to stress in different ways: some confront it head-on, others withdraw, and still others develop a variety of coping mechanisms. The sad truth is that while detention is supposed to be a place where constructive work can occur despite the coercive setting, for many youths, time spent in a detention facility actually improves their social standing, a term sociologists refer to as **upward social mobility**. The reason for this is that many youths come from dysfunctional families, where living arrangements are chaotic, and going to jail or prison is actually an improvement in their quality of life since they are provided with shelter, food, and clothing, something often lacking at home.[63]

Still, despite its potential social benefits, institutional life can be quite unsettling for youths. Not only must they adapt to an inflexible structure, where their freedom, meals, and time are regulated by others, perhaps for the first time in their lives, but oftentimes, youths also must confront a wide range of issues brought out during therapy sessions.[64]

Institutionalized youths are also likely to suffer from underdeveloped social and communication skills, which often translate into anti-social behavior. Because the structure of the institution forces youths to interact with others, juveniles need a great deal of encouragement and support as they begin to learn how to effectively deal with others.[65] There are also a number of other issues, such as coping with various forms of mental illness and suicidal tendencies.

MENTAL ILLNESS AND DETENTION

Many youths enter the prison system suffering from a host of emotional and psychological disorders. One meta-analysis of the literature on psychological and mental disorders in juvenile detention facilities found that adolescents, particularly boys, were ten times more likely to suffer from psychosis than the general population. Girls in detention were most often diagnosed with major depression, and males were more likely to be diagnosed with ADHD, conduct disorders, bipolar disorder, and other illnesses.[66] According to some studies, between 50 percent and 90 percent of youths in confinement suffer from conduct disorders, about half suffer from attention deficit disorder, 40 percent suffer from anxiety disorders, nearly 50 percent are substance abusers, 80 percent suffer from affective disorders, and between 1 percent and 5 percent have a psychotic disorder.[67] All of these figures are higher for detained youth than for those in the general population.[68] These problems can result in disciplinary issues while incarcerated as well as limit youths' participation in programs designed to address their disorders. One of the challenges facing most public institutions is the provision of such services. While this may not seem to be that important at first glance, in that youths are increasingly being detained for the purposes of accountability and punishment rather than treatment, the end result is likely a higher rate of recidivism once they are released.

SUICIDE AND INSTITUTIONALIZED YOUTH

The risk of suicide is an important factor in how youths are treated while detained. According to the surgeon general of the United States, youth suicide in the general population is a national tragedy and a major public health problem.[69] A recent national survey found that more than three million youths are at risk for suicide each year, with 37 percent of surveyed youths reporting that they had attempted suicide during the previous twelve months.[70]

Despite the fact that youth suicide in the general population is considered a major public health problem, comparable research has not been conducted regarding juvenile suicide in confinement.[71] A review of the literature on suicide among detained juveniles shows only a few studies on this topic, but the information available suggests that self-harm and suicide attempts happen rather frequently in juvenile correctional facilities. For example, according to one study, more than 11,000 juveniles are estimated to engage in more than 17,000 incidents of suicidal behavior in juvenile detention facilities each year.[72]

The research also shows that White youths appear to attempt suicide in confinement or think about it more often than African American, Hispanic, or Asian youths.[73] It should be noted that while isolation often occurs in detention centers as a disciplinary measure, as well as a safety precaution to prevent victimization, it can also be an important factor in suicide. Further, a report by the Office of Juvenile Justice and Delinquency Prevention notes that youths sent to secure detention facilities are unlike the vast majority of offenders who come to the attention of the juvenile justice system. As such, they bring with them unique problems, behaviors, and perspectives that may put them at a higher risk for extreme behavior such as suicide. This underscores the need for staff working in confined environments to receive additional training on handling these types of offenders.[74]

DELINQUENCY, DETENTION, AND PUBLIC POLICY

Not only do the fears and concerns about serious juvenile offenders translate into practices and programs that focus more on punishment than on treatment, what is available to youths who have been detained is also limited by the public's perception of who they are and what they need. The research suggests that detention does little to effectively rehabilitate youths, and perhaps the need for accountability supersedes any therapeutic benefit. What is missing from the discussion, however, are the long-term effects of the "get-tough" approach to delinquents. Similar to adult offenders, eventually inmates must be released, and in the absence of effective methods to reintegrate them into society (e.g., life skills, job training, housing, healthcare), it is likely that those who have experienced incarceration will return to the justice system. The same can be said for juveniles who have been detained; the difference is that their criminal careers have the potential to be much longer than their older counterparts. At the same time, there may not be effective alternatives to detention for serious and violent juvenile offenders, leaving incarceration—perhaps in adult facilities—the only viable option for some states.

SUMMARY

This chapter explored the history of the treatment of juveniles who committed delinquency as well as the development of the juvenile justice system in the United States. Included in the discussion was an assessment of the disproportionality of minorities for juveniles, either as victims or as offenders. Like their adult counterparts, African American and Hispanic juveniles are more likely than White youth to be involved in each stage of the juvenile justice process, from arrest, to adjudication, to sentencing, to detention. Also included in the discussion about juveniles was the influence of emotional disorders and suicidal tendencies for detained youth. From a public policy standpoint, the issue of the overall "get tough" approach to crime, popular since the 1980s, has impacted how the general public views juveniles, despite the fact that most youths who enter the juvenile justice system do not return. The remaining small number of hard-core, violent juvenile offenders has shaped public policy in all aspects of the juvenile system, with a greater emphasis on treating youth like adults for many offenses.

YOU MAKE THE CALL
ZERO-TOLERANCE POLICIES AND DELINQUENCY

You were recently hired as an elementary school teacher in an inner-city urban area. As part of the school's zero-tolerance policy, you were instructed by your principal to call the police in the event that students engage in fighting or combative behavior. As you are supervising the cafeteria at lunch, a group of students gathers in a circle to observe a fight between two males. You make your way over to the location where the fight is taking place and separate the two young men, one of whom is White and the other Black. The White student begins to protest that he was only defending himself and that he wants to press charges against his African American colleague. The other youth is silent and says nothing to anyone. A more experienced teacher is present who tells you to have the office call the police. When they arrive, the officers place the Black youth in custody and take a statement from the White youth, but do not place him in handcuffs. You notice this and ask the officers about it—they inform you that they plan to bring the African American youth to the station for processing. When you ask why, the officers are a bit evasive, stating only that they believe the African American initiated the fight. Given that you were

(continued)

(continued)

the only one who really saw what happened, you wonder how the officers could know that.

Questions

1. Do you think the officers are being fair in the assessment of the confrontation? If so, why?
2. Do you think you should try to persuade the officers to take both youths into custody until the matter is resolved?
3. Why do you think the African American youth remained silent throughout the experience while the White youth made the case that he was the victim?
4. Do you think the African American youth will be formally processed through the juvenile justice system? Why or why not?
5. What can you do as a teacher to address this issue?

KEY TERMS

adjudication

child-saving movement

Children's Aid Society

houses of refuge

individualized justice

juvenile delinquency

Juvenile Delinquency Prevention and Control Act

Juvenile Justice and Delinquency Prevention Act of 1974

orphan trains

parens patriae

school-to-prison pipeline

status offenders

training schools

transfer

upward social mobility

voluntary placements

waive jurisdiction

DISCUSSION QUESTIONS

1. What are some of the primary differences between the juvenile justice system and the adult system?
2. Do you think that the juvenile justice system should be abolished and all offenders handled by the adult system? Why or why not?
3. Why is *parens patriae* such an important feature of the juvenile justice system? How does it operate in practice?
4. What is it about the life of many delinquents that suggests that detention is actually an improvement in their standard of living?
5. How do the statistics about the disproportionality in the adult system compare to what is seen among juveniles who enter the juvenile justice system?
6. What do you think about the connection between juvenile detention and suicide and mental illness?

FOR FURTHER READING

McNamara, R. H. *The Lost Population: Status Offenders in America*. Durham, NC: Carolina Academic Press, 2008.

O'Connor, S. *Orphan Trains*. Boston: Houghton Mifflin, 2001.

Tanenhaus, D. S. *Juvenile Justice in the Making*. New York: Oxford University Press, 2005.

Marrus, E. *Children and Juvenile Justice*. Durham, NC: Carolina Academic Press, 2007.

NOTES

1. Robert H. McNamara, *Juvenile Delinquency: Bridging Theory to Practice* (New York: McGraw-Hill, 2013).
2. Juvenile Justice and Delinquency Prevention Act of 1974, P.L. 93–415, 88 Stat. 1109.
3. See Robert H. McNamara, *The Lost Population: Status Offenders in America* (Durham, NC: Carolina Academic Press, 2008).
4. See A. W. Simpson, *Blackstone's Commentaries on the Laws of England* (New York: Nabu Press, 2010).
5. Ibid.
6. Ibid.
7. Ibid.
8. See, e.g., S. O'Connor, *Orphan Trains* (Boston: Houghton Mifflin, 2001).
9. Ibid.
10. Ibid.
11. D. S. Tanenhaus, *Juvenile Justice in the Making* (New York: Oxford University Press, 2005).
12. Ibid.
13. E. Marrus, *Children and Juvenile Justice* (Durham, NC: Carolina Academic Press, 2007).
14. See, e.g., the Center on Juvenile and Criminal Justice at http://www.cjcj.org/juvenile/justice/juvenile/justice/overview
15. Tanenhaus, *Juvenile Justice.*
16. Ibid.
17. Marrus, *Children and Juvenile Justice.*
18. H. N. Snyder and M. Sickmund, *Juvenile Offenders and Victims 2006: A National Report.* U.S. Department of Justice, Office of Justice Programs, Office of Juvenile Justice and Delinquency Prevention, 2006. Available at: https://www.ojjdp.gov/ojstatbb/nr2006/
19. Ibid.
20. Kent v. United States, 383 U.S. 541 (1966).
21. Ibid.
22. Ibid.
23. Ibid.
24. Ibid.
25. Ibid.
26. Marrus, *Children and Juvenile Justice.*
27. See R. A. Mendel, *Less Hype, More Help: Reducing Juvenile Crime: What Works and What Doesn't* (Washington, DC: America Youth Forum, 2002); also B. Krisberg, *Juvenile Justice: Redeeming Our Children* (Los Angeles: Sage, 2005); D. L. Mackenzie, *What Works in Corrections* (Boston: Cambridge University Press, 2006), 271–303.
28. Ibid.
29. ChildTrends.org. "Appendix 1—Number of Children Under 18 in United States as a Percentage of the Population," *Child Trends Databank*, November 2018. Available at: https://www.childtrends.org/indicators/number-of-children
30. M. Sickmund and C. Puzzanchera, eds., *Juvenile Offenders and Victims: 2014 National Report* (Pittsburgh, PA: National Center for Juvenile Justice, 2014).
31. U.S. Department of Health and Human Services, *Child Maltreatment 2017*, Administration on Children, Youth and Families, Administration for Children and Families, 2018. Available at: https://www.acf.hhs.gov/cb/resource/child-maltreatment-2017
32. Ibid.
33. Ibid.

34. Ibid.

35. Ibid.

36. Ibid.

37. Ibid.

38. Ibid.

39. Fiza Pirani, "What's Killing America's Teens? Inside the CDC's New Mortality Report," *Atlanta Journal Constitution*, June 1, 2018. Available at: https://www.ajc.com/news/national/what-killing-america-teens-inside-cdc-new-mortality-report/OeNlRXFCJqxZz5H7LsL5zJ/

40. Federal Bureau of Investigation, *Crime in the United States 2017*—Table 43B, U.S. Department of Justice, 2018. Available at: https://ucr.fbi.gov/crime-in-the-u.s/2017/crime-in-the-u.s.-2017/topic-pages/tables/table-43

41. Ibid.

42. Ibid.

43. Federal Bureau of Investigation (2018), *Crime in the United States 2017*. Available at: https://ucr.fbi.gov/crime-in-the-u.s/2017/crime-in-the-u.s.-2017/topic-pages/tables/table-43

44. McNamara, *Juvenile Delinquency*.

45. C. Crawford and R. Burns, "Reducing School Violence: Considering School Characteristics and the Impacts of Law Enforcement, School Security, and Environmental Factors," *Policing: An International Journal of Police Strategies & Management*39, no. 3 (2016): 456–77.

46. Sarah Hockenberry and Charles Puzzancherra, Juvenile Court Statistics 2016, U.S. Department of Justice, Office of Justice Programs, Office of Juvenile Justice and Delinquency Prevention, August 2018. Available at: https://www.ojjdp.gov/ojstatbb/njcda/pdf/jcs2016.pdf

47. Ibid.

48. Nina Hyland, "Delinquency Cases in Juvenile Court 2014," *Juvenile Justice Statistics*, U.S. Department of Justice, Office of Justice Programs, Office of Juvenile Justice and Delinquency Prevention, January 2018. Available at: https://www.ojjdp.gov/pubs/251107.pdf

49. Ibid.

50. Sarah Hockenberry and Charles Puzzanchera, *Delinquency Cases Involving Hispanic Youth 2013*, U.S. Department of Justice, Office of Justice Programs, Office of Juvenile Justice and Delinquency Prevention, November 2016. Available at: http://www.ncjj.org/pdf/249915.pdf

51. Sickmund and Puzzanchera, *Juvenile Offenders and Victims*.

52. Ibid.

53. Ibid.

54. Ibid.

55. "Juvenile Incarceration," Child Trends, July 1, 2016. Available at: https://www.childtrends.org/indicators/juvenile-detention

56. Ibid.

57. Ibid.

58. See S. M. Taroola, E. F. Wagner, J. Rabinowitz, and J. L. Tubman, "Understanding and Treating Juvenile Offenders: A Review of Current Knowledge and Future Directions," *Aggression and Violent Behavior* 7, no. 2 (2002): 125–43.

59. See R. Haapanen, L. Britton, and T. Croisdale, "Persistent Criminality and Career Length," *Crime and Delinquency* 53, no. 1 (2007): 133–55.

60. Sickmund and Puzzanchera, *Juvenile Offenders and Victims*.

61. Ibid.

62. See D. L. Mackenzie, *What Works in Corrections: Reducing the Criminal Activities of Offenders and Delinquents* (Cambridge, MA: Cambridge University Press, 2006).

63. For some inmates, life improves substantially when they are incarcerated, insofar as their immediate needs are met. For an interesting discussion of the economics of incarceration, see Vera Institute of Justice, *The Unintended Consequences of Incarceration*, 1996. Available at: http://archive.vera.org/sites/default/files/resources/downloads/uci.pdf

64. See, e.g., M. Petersen-Badali and C. J. Koegl, "Juveniles' Experiences of Incarceration: The Role of Correctional Staff in Peer Violence," *Journal of Criminal Justice* 30, no. 1 (2002): 41–49.

65. Ibid.

66. S. Faze, H. Dole, and N. Angstrom, "Mental Disorders Among Adolescents in Juvenile Detention and Correctional Facilities: A Systematic Review and Meta Regression Analysis of 25 Surveys," *Journal of American Academy of Child and Adolescent Psychiatry* 48, no. 9 (2008): 1010–19.

67. R. Otto, J. Greenstein, M. Johnson, and R. Friedman, "Prevalence of Mental Disorders Among Youth in the Juvenile Justice System," in J. K. Cocozza (ed.), *Responding to the Mental Health Needs of Youth in the Juvenile Justice System* (Seattle, WA: National Coalition for the Mentally Ill in the Criminal Justice System, 1992), 7–48; J. Eden and R. Otto, "Prevalence of Mental Disorders Among Youth in the Juvenile Justice System," *Focal Point* (Spring 1997): 1–18.

68. See, e.g., J. Coosa and K. Skiwear, "Youth with Mental Health Disorders: Issues and Emerging Responses," *Juvenile Justice* 7, no. 1 (2000): 3–13.

69. R. H. Carmona, *Suicide Prevention Among Native American Youth*. Testimony of Surgeon General Before the Indian Affairs Committee, U.S. Senate, June 15, 2005. Department of Health and Human Services, *The Surgeon General's Call to Action to Prevent Suicide, 1999* (Washington, DC: U.S. Department of Health and Human Services, 1999).

70. Substance Abuse and Mental Health Services Administration, *Summary of Findings from the 2000 National Household Survey on Drug Abuse*, NHSDA Series: H-13, DHHS Publication No. SMA 01-3549. (Rockville, MD: U.S. Department of Health and Human Services, 2001).

71. L. Hayes, "Prison Suicide: An Overview and a Guide to Prevention," *The Prison Journal* 75, no. 4 (1995): 431–55; L. M. Hayes, *Suicide Prevention in Juvenile Correction and Detention Facilities: A Resource Guide* (South Easton, MA: Council of Juvenile Correctional Administrators, 1997).

72. D. Parent, V. Leiter, S. Kennedy, L. Livens, D. Wentworth, and S. Wilcox, *Conditions of Confinement: Juvenile Detention and Corrections Facilities* (Washington, DC: Office of Juvenile Justice and Delinquency Prevention, 1994).

73. T. Kempton and R. Forehand, "Suicide Attempts Among Juvenile Delinquents: The Contribution of Mental Health Factors," *Behaviour Research and Therapy* 30, no. 5 (1992): 537–41. N. Alessi, M. McManus, A. Brickman, and L. Grapentine, "Suicidal Behavior Among Serious Juvenile Offenders," *American Journal of Psychiatry* 141, no. 2 (1984): 286–87.

74. Lindsay M. Hayes, *Juvenile Suicide in Confinement: A National Survey*, Open-file report NJC 213691, U.S. Department of Justice, Office of Justice Programs, Office of Juvenile Justice and Delinquency Prevention, 2009. Available at: https://www.ncjrs.gov/pdffiles1/ojjdp/213691.pdf

INTERNAL ISSUES IN THE CRIMINAL JUSTICE SYSTEM AND MULTICULTURALISM

CHAPTER 11

POLICING AND MULTICULTURALISM

CHAPTER OBJECTIVES

After reading this chapter, you should be able to:

- Understand how the historical development of policing relates to current concerns regarding multiculturalism
- Understand the extent, nature, and need for multiculturalism among police personnel
- Recognize how police practices exist with regard to multiculturalism, and how those actions affect police-community relations and perceptions of the police
- Understand the significance of police-community relations

In January 2017, the U.S. Department of Justice (DOJ) announced that it had found probable cause to believe that the Chicago Police Department engaged in a pattern or practice of use of excessive force, including deadly force, which violated the Fourth Amendment. The DOJ further noted that the pattern of unreasonable force predominantly impacted Black and Latino neighborhoods. Similarly, in 2015 the DOJ identified a pattern of clear racial disparities and discriminatory intent in the Ferguson (Missouri) Police Department.

These DOJ findings emerged during a time when various other acts of seemingly biased and unprofessional policing had caused many in society to reconsider the role of the police, police practices, police training, police-community relations, and a host of other issues related to policing. Police practices have undergone increasing scrutiny, as tensions between the police and certain groups in society (primarily minority groups) have suffered from the exposure of questionable police practices, including but not restricted to racial profiling and seemingly wrongful deaths.

The nature of police work, including regular social interaction with varied groups, sometimes results in claims of officer misbehavior. Put simply, police practices are sometimes controversial, and failure to recognize cultural diversity is sometimes a primary contributing factor. Scholars have noted that: "Some of the most problematic encounters involving the police occur between White police officers and minority citizens. Encounters between the police and Blacks, Hispanics, Native Americans, and, increasingly, Asians indicate that a good deal of hostility remains as a result of racist attitudes, historical distrust, and past discrimination."[1] The diverse culture in which policing is practiced requires officers to maintain, at minimum, a base-level recognition and understanding of cultural differences in order to ensure justice, personal safety, and the safety of others.

The police are the primary agents of formal social control in our society. Charged with the dubious and vague tasks of "serving and protecting," officers must find a balance between controlling and preventing crime, and preserving individual rights. It could be argued that too often the police sacrifice individual rights for the sake of crime control, and vice versa. Finding an approach that suits everyone is much easier said than done.

Modern police practices largely reflect the roots of historical policing. In their insightful and thorough work, *Police in a Multicultural Society*, authors David and Melissa Barlow discuss the historical evolution of policing and tie it to modern police practices.[2] They comment on police practices such as **underpolicing**, which involve the police denying "equal protection to racial and ethnic minorities in the United States by failing to protect them from violent racist actions by Whites, by declining to ensure their basic human rights, and by inadequately responding to problems of crime and neglect in minority neighborhoods."[3] Barlow and Barlow also discuss **overpolicing**, which involves "the oppressive and often brutal treatment of marginalized groups by police."[4] These styles of policing highlight the historical and recent conflict between police and underrepresented groups in society.

Throughout this book there are numerous accounts of how multiculturalism affects policing. This chapter focuses specifically on how policing came to be, why it exists, and how diversity and multiculturalism have shaped modern policing. Included is discussion of policing, and multiculturalism as it pertains to critical issues in policing. Of particular interest is the history of policing, police personnel issues, police practices and behavior, and police-community relations. As demonstrated throughout this book, police officers, as the primary gatekeepers to the criminal justice system, should be well-versed in recognizing and understanding cultural diversity.

HISTORICAL POLICING

Much of what police do today is similar to what was done when formal policing began. In other words, policing has not changed much in the roughly 190 years of its existence. There have been alterations and developments in the manner in which policing exists and occurs. However, there have been few, if any, major changes to policing in general. With regard to policing in the United States, the activities and practices of the earliest periods of policing largely reflect those found in England. The following discussion of the history of policing maintains a primary focus on diversity and multiculturalism.

THE ROOTS OF U.S. POLICING

The history of formal policing dates back to the development of the Metropolitan Police, the name for the police department established in London in 1829 and organized by Sir Robert Peel.[5] Prior to formal policing, social control was primarily the responsibility of the citizens. Citizens lived communally for several reasons, including the need for enhanced farming practices and for safety and security. With regard to the latter, it became evident to citizens that there was strength in numbers. Under what was known as the **Frankpledge system**, or the practice of informal social control in which community members protected one another, citizens raised the **hue and cry** upon being victimized.[6] Raising the hue and cry, or call to arms, generated a response from every able-bodied male in attempts to bring the offenders(s) to justice. Failure to respond to the hue and cry could result in punitive sanctions. Citizens also protected one another through night watch and day ward systems in which constables and/or citizens were expected to watch out for danger—whether it be in the form of weather, fires, or individuals. Such informal social control was initially effective given the small population sizes and the homogeneity of groups living communally.

The need for formal social control became evident as small towns became large cities and England began transitioning from an agrarian society to one focused on industrialism. Numerous individuals migrated to cities in hopes of great success, only to find a great deal of social disorganization, poverty, and difficulty in attaining their goals. Many individuals abandoned their lifestyles and belongings in their attempt to find success in the big city, only to find limited opportunities and great difficulties upon their arrival. The increased cultural diversity during this transitional period also contributed to the difficulties. No longer could informal social control (e.g., fellow citizens) serve the purposes of law enforcement. The need for formal social control (e.g., policing) became increasingly evident as rioting occurred, and populations and culture conflict significantly increased in the cities as industrialization took hold.

London magistrate Sir Henry Fielding is credited with creating the **Bow Street Runners**, a precursor to the first formal police department.[7] Fielding noticed the frequency with which particular individuals were brought into his court and decided something needed to be done. Mind you, bringing someone to justice during this time (circa 1750) was not as easy as it is today. Citizens had to hire private security to bring the accused before the court, or do it themselves. Fielding decided to hire individuals to seek law violators in the Bow Street region of London, and paid a sum of money to those who brought suspects before the court. The limitations of this approach are clearly evident (e.g., unethically bringing forth suspects in efforts to make money); however, the Bow Street Runners helped cleanse the area of much crime, and inspired the **Metropolitan Police Act**, which was passed in 1829. This act led to the first formal police department, the Metropolitan Police, led by Sir Robert Peel. Peel's approach was very reactive and centered on serving the public. Much of what Peel proposed is evident in the community policing approaches found in many of today's police departments. His principles generally emphasized crime prevention, police cooperation with the public, and police professionalism.

The London police initially were not well accepted by Londoners, who believed that their rights were being violated. To proactively seek law violators and monitor societal behavior was a new practice at the time, and not all citizens appreciated the perceived intrusion. Such public disapproval of policing would eventually subside as citizens recognized that the police provided citizens with protection. Such frustration in public approval of the police was a sign of things to come, as throughout the history of policing we've seen peaks and valleys regarding public approval of police and police actions. The development of policing in England would mirror the development of policing in the United States, and the Metropolitan Police would provide a blueprint for all police practices.

HISTORICAL U.S. POLICING

Policing in the United States developed in much the same manner as policing in England. Informal social control in which citizens protected one another, and relied on the hue and cry and the watch and ward system, was used prior to the development of large cities. Formal policing emerged in areas where small towns grew into larger ones. Cities along the eastern seaboard were among the first to have formal police departments, as settlers eventually recognized the need for formal law enforcement. Formal policing would soon extend across the entire country, as settlers moved west and small towns grew into large ones.

SLAVE PATROLS AND BLACK CODES

Policing in Southern states, however, took a notably distinct approach compared to elsewhere in the United States. The roots of policing in the South are found in the **slave patrols** used in the Southern states and colonies prior to and following the Revolutionary War. Slave patrols are considered by some as the first American police departments[8] and were established as early as the 1740s. By 1750 every Southern colony maintained a slave patrol.[9] The patrols were tasked with preventing slave revolts and apprehending runaway slaves. The large population of slaves in the South prompted plantation owners to create special codes of laws and, subsequently, special forces to ensure that slaves abided by the laws. These laws, for instance, prevented slaves from having weapons, leaving plantations without permission, gathering in groups, and resisting punishment.[10] Southern states also made it legal for any White freeman to stop, search, and apprehend any Black person, regardless of whether or not they were a slave.[11] Most states and colonies permitted slave patrols to enter any slaves' dwellings, punish slaves who were away from their plantations, and search, punish, and perhaps even kill slaves found to be in violation of the slave code.[12]

The emancipation of the slaves did not provide an end to the enhanced levels of social control faced by African Americans in the South. Southern states circumvented the emancipation by creating **Black codes**, laws designed to nullify the rights granted to the newly freed slaves. Among the restrictions found in Black codes were the prohibition of interracial marriage, renting land in urban areas, preaching the gospel without a license, and assuming any occupation other than servant or farmer unless the newly freed slave paid a tax. The mission of Southern police departments was to protect the White population from the violent threats of slaves, and later, freed slaves.[13] The **Civil Rights Act of 1866**, passed by Congress despite President Johnson's veto, was targeted to address the Black codes by defining all persons born in the United States, with the exception of Native Americans, as national citizens who were to enjoy specific rights. These rights included permission to make contracts, bring lawsuits, and enjoy the full and equal benefit of the law.[14]

THREE ERAS OF POLICING

The history of policing in the United States has been categorized into three eras: the political era, the reform era, and the community era (see Table 11.1).[15] While the history of a complex institution such as policing can be difficult to categorize into three periods, there are several identifiable characteristics of these eras, particularly as they relate to multiculturalism. While such a categorization provides for interesting discussion of the historical intervals of policing, it is argued that the categorization fails to consider the development of policing with regard to segregation, slavery, discrimination, and racism,[16] factors which have undoubtedly influenced modern U.S. policing. To understand our police requires an understanding of the barriers they've overcome, the obstacles they've provided, and their relationship to the communities they serve.

The Political Era

The **political era of policing** (1840–1930) is characterized by police officers establishing intimate relationships with the community and politics heavily influencing police departments and police practices. The police had limited technology during this time, thus they walked beats which encouraged police-community interaction. In addition to crime control, officers provided a significant amount of general services to the public and relied on their problem-solving skills, as there was no radio to call for backup and no police car to provide rapid assistance.

Police practices during this period were also influenced by politics, with those holding political power rewarding those who supported them during their candidacy and when in office. The "spoils system" was evident during this period and certainly influenced who worked for the police department and in what capacity they served. **Patronage**, or the practice of politicians rewarding friends, created police departments that often reflected the communities they served.[17] For instance, the Irish Americans began appointing their friends as police officers once the Irish Americans began to win political power.[18]

Police officers during the political era were not exempt from the lack of cultural sensitivity existent at the time, and minority police officers were treated differently from White officers. For instance, Black officers were prohibited from patrolling in predominantly White areas, were required to call a White officer to arrest a White suspect, and were given

TABLE 11.1   THREE ERAS OF U.S. POLICING

The Political Era (1840–1930)

The Reform Era (1930–1980)

The Community Era (1980–present)

assignments in high-crime, predominantly minority neighborhoods. The virtual absence of Black police officers resulted in less police attention and protection in areas heavily populated by minorities.[19] Other racial and ethnic groups, as well as women, were also underrepresented, if not absent, from early police departments. Society in general at this time was largely unaware of the impending social unrest that would result from cultural insensitivity.

Police corruption was problematic during the political era, especially during the years of **Prohibition** (1919–1933), which criminalized the sale, transport, or manufacturing of alcohol. It was during Prohibition when police officers sometimes took advantage of "favors" offered in exchange for them looking the other way while alcohol was served. Prohibition had a significant impact on the history of policing, particularly with regard to police corruption and public perceptions of the police because officers were charged with enforcing an unpopular law.

Race riots and racial disorder, especially in New York City, Boston, and Philadelphia, also significantly shaped policing during the political era, as departments developed and assumed the responsibility of quelling the disturbances. Unfortunately, little professional training existed for addressing civil disorders. The level of violence accompanying the unrest was sometimes agitated by officers too quickly resorting to violence. Civil disorder would not end with the political era.

The Reform Era

The **reform era of policing** (1930–1980), also known as the progressive era, was a time when police-community relations suffered and police became increasingly reliant upon technology and overly concerned with efficiency. It was during the reform era that police departments began heavily using police cars to enhance overall police practices. Although the automobile and other technological advances (e.g., the two-way radio) enhanced policing, police-community relations suffered as officers became distant from the public. Officers were no longer primarily walking beats and interacting with the public. Instead, they largely focused on crime fighting. The "just the facts, ma'am" approach to policing may have initially enhanced the efficiency of crime control, but it did very little for police-community relations, which became problematic during this period.

Several turbulent incidents occurred during the reform era, which in turn impacted policing. Many of these events have direct relationships with policing a multicultural society. Among the happenings was the civil rights movement, which began in the late 1950s and set in motion a series of actions that would change policing, and more generally, society.

The civil rights movement initially began as a grassroots effort to highlight economic, political, and social inequality in the United States. Blacks who chose to protest were confronted by police officers who were typically White males with limited training in how to confront such collective action. The officers' actions in handling protest marches and general civil disobedience often aggravated the situation.[20] The assassinations of several prominent figures such as Martin Luther King Jr., Malcolm X, President Kennedy, and Medgar Evers contributed to the unrest during this period, as did the protest of those opposed to the war in Vietnam. Police were charged with handling, among other responsibilities, a series of race and antiwar demonstrations. The underrepresentation of African Americans and other minorities in policing contributed to clashes between the groups and certainly played a role in the hundreds of riots that occurred between 1966 and 1971. The unrest further separated the police from the public and created danger for officers, as police practices such as providing public protection sometimes generated collective violence in the form of rioting. We've seen several similar incidents in more recent times.

A wave of riots occurred between 1964 and 1968 due in part to tensions between the police and the Black community. Many of the riots followed a situation involving police.[21] For instance, the New York City riot began following the shooting death of a Black teenager by an off-duty police officer. The Watts, California, riot was initiated by a traffic stop.[22] Rioting during this time was largely perpetuated by negative public attitudes toward the police, the lack of preparedness of police to address civil unrest, and racial tensions between Blacks and Whites.[23] Racially selective policing exacerbated protest demonstration most significantly in areas with strained police-minority community relations.[24] The potential harm and costs of such unrest was alarming. For instance, the week-long rioting in Detroit in 1967 resulted in forty-three deaths and roughly $40 million in property damage. In 1966, forty-three riots were identified in major urban areas across the United States.[25] These numbers say little about the damage done to police-community relations.

The lack of police training, particularly with regard to addressing cultural diversity, contributed to the police being seen by many as the enemy. A confusing array of social movements, including the emerging drug culture, contributed to the problems faced by police.[26] Officers were commonly referred to as "pigs," and the isolation that was emerging between police and society was enhanced by the overall social unrest of the times. The White male police officers tasked with maintaining the peace in the predominantly minority urban ghetto faced numerous challenges, especially in light of the officer's symbolic representation of power and control. Many angry and frustrated Blacks viewed the police as symbolic of a criminal justice system that had been largely unresponsive to their needs.[27] To compound the situation, an increasing number of viewers across the United States could watch the events in the comfort of their own homes as televisions were becoming increasingly common in households.

The tension and conflict between police and minority groups led to intense focus on the problems underlying the social unrest. Prominent among the national commissions formed to examine the situation and to offer recommendation for change was the 1965 **President's Commission on Law Enforcement and Administration of Justice** (also known as the President's Crime Commission).[28] The commission focused on enhancing professionalization of policing and police officers by hiring greater diversity in policing and encouraging departments to become more community-oriented. Another commission, the **National Advisory Commission on Civil Disorders** (also known as the Kerner Commission), was created to study the causes behind the rioting. The commission identified a series of issues that contributed to the collective violence, including unequal justice, institutional racism, unemployment, and discrimination. With regard to policing, the Kerner Commission noted the lack of Black police officers, inadequate training and supervision, brutal and abrasive police conduct, and poor police-community relations.[29] The police during this period faced criticism from every direction.

Police practices were also the target of several landmark Supreme Court decisions made during this period. The decisions restricted police powers and provided greater rights to defendants. Beginning in the 1950s, several Court decisions under the direction of Supreme Court Justice Earl Warren influenced police-community relations and the lives of many individuals from underrepresented groups. The Supreme Court ruled in cases such as *Mapp v. Ohio*,[30] which extended the **exclusionary rule**, or the prohibition of introducing in court illegally seized materials, to apply in all courts and jurisdictions in the United States. The Court also ruled in *Gideon v. Wainwright*[31] that all defendants charged with a felony are entitled to legal representation, and in *Miranda v. Arizona*[32] that any evidence obtained by police during a custodial interrogation cannot be used in court unless the suspect is informed of his or her basic rights before the interrogation. In *Terry v. Ohio*[33] the Court clarified the law surrounding when a police officer can stop and question a person. These cases restricted police discretion and provided numerous protections to individuals.

The reform era was influential in the history of U.S. policing. Police officers initially shifted their focus away from interacting with the public, yet, at the end of the era they were forced to confront violent reactions. Many of these reactions resulted from what were perceived as intrusive and/or biased police practices. It was also a time when police departments were forced to reassess their relationship with the community. In turn, many departments recognized the need to get back in touch with the roots of policing and begin to once again more positively interact with citizens.

The Community Era

The **community era of policing**, which began around 1980 and continues today, involves efforts by the police to reconnect with the public primarily through the adoption of the **community policing** philosophy. Clearly defining community policing, however, is not easily done. The problems associated with defining community policing largely stem from the different approaches to community policing taken by various departments, and the difficulties departments face when implementing the community policing philosophy. Generally, the term has been defined as "a philosophy that promotes a decentralized organizational design; a proactive approach to policing that encourages partnerships and problem-solving to address public concerns."[34]

Community policing is by no means solely focused on public relations at the expense of crime fighting. One can easily recognize how the community era of policing combines the positive elements of the political era with the strengths of the reform era. Getting back in touch with citizens and doing so in an effective manner, for instance, through problem-oriented policing, highlights one of the strengths of community policing. **Problem-oriented policing**, a component of community policing, involves a four-step approach to addressing specific crimes in the community. These steps include scanning communities to identify problems, analyzing the nature and extent of the problems, responding to the problems, and assessing whether or not the problems have been properly addressed. It can

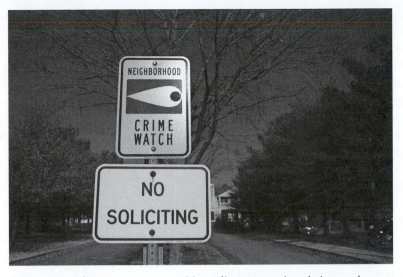

Community policing encourages positive police-community relations and encourages citizens to take a more active role in crime fighting. Neighborhood Watch programs are an example.

be stated with confidence that police getting back in touch with the public while maintaining a concern for crime control was needed in light of events occurring during the latter part of the reform era.

Regardless of its strength and good intentions, community policing has not solved society's problems, and not all departments have adopted a community-oriented approach. Because some departments have adopted the philosophy on a piecemeal basis, and it is difficult to measure a philosophical approach to policing, it remains unclear whether or not community policing meets all of its goals. We do know that the approach improves police-community relations, which certainly provides optimism for police as they continuously operate in an increasingly multicultural society. The Bureau of Justice Statistics reported that in 2013, roughly 68 percent of local police departments had a mission statement that included a community policing component.[35] The percentage has increased from 2003, when only 47 percent of departments mentioned community policing in their mission statements.[36]

Despite the progress made with regard to police-community relations following the reform era, many of the issues that contributed to the rioting in the 1960s remain.[37] The 1992 riots in Los Angeles following the acquittal by a mostly White jury of the Los Angeles Police Department (LAPD) officers seen beating Black motorist Rodney King sent a message that racial tensions had not disappeared. The riot, which led to forty-three deaths, was perpetuated by economic tensions of residents in South Los Angeles and historical strains in police-community relations, especially with regard to claims of officers engaging in racial profiling and excessive force against minorities. The **Christopher Commission**, assembled in the wake of the Rodney King incident in response to claims of LAPD officer misbehavior, stated in its report that "there is a significant number of officers in the LAPD who repetitively use excessive force against the public and persistently ignore the written guidelines of the Department regarding force."[38] They added that "the problem of excessive force is aggravated by racism and bias" and noted that "failure to control (problem) officers is a management issue that is at the heart of the problem."[39]

Later, rioting in Cincinnati began in April 2001 following the fatal shooting of nineteen-year-old Timothy Thomas by a White Cincinnati police officer. Similar to other riots, the riot stemmed from tension among the minority community and police. Fifteen Black males under the age of forty were killed by Cincinnati police officers between 1995 and 2001, compared zero males from other races during the same period. Claims of officers engaging in racial profiling with regard to traffic stops also contributed to the violence. The police argued that they were doing their job and reacted in an appropriate manner, yet protestors claimed that the police were biased and unjust. The rioting, which lasted three days, resulted in hundreds of thousands of dollars in property damage and over eight hundred arrests.

These and related incidents have occurred throughout the history of the police. More recently, in July 2014, Eric Garner was killed on Staten Island (in New York) due to a chokehold used by an officer. The death was ruled a homicide. A month later, the fatal shooting of Michael Brown by a Ferguson (Missouri) police officer set off a series of protests around the country, with the primary focus on police misusing their powers against minorities. During the same month of Mr. Brown's death, Freddie Gray died while in police custody in Baltimore (Maryland), which further ignited the social unrest. Similar incidents were brought to the public's attention during this tumultuous period, including a shooting death caught on video in South Carolina and the police shooting of twelve-year-old Tamir Rice, who was playing with a toy pistol when police shot him.

These incidents were followed by several other shootings of Black males by White officers, including those in Minnesota, Florida, and Louisiana. The tension and frustration generated by the shootings led to several acts of retaliation against the police, including a 2016 incident in Dallas (Texas) in which five police officers were killed by a gunman. The shootings occurred at the conclusion of a peaceful Black Lives Matter march in the city, as citizens bound together to protest the shootings. The officers were accompanying the protestors. Ten days later, a gunman killed three law enforcement officers in Louisiana in what was again believed to be an act of retaliation against the police for the shootings. These incidents have been followed by other, albeit less controversial, acts involving the police arguably misusing their power.

The short history of policing in the United States is rife with conflict between police and society. Much of the conflict involves members of underrepresented groups who feel that the police overstep the boundaries of procedural law, which dictates how the police are to use their powers. To be sure, negative police-citizen interactions are often brought to the public's attention. It is rare that society hears how an officer successfully overcame cultural barriers and quelled a situation. Perhaps public opinion of police-minority contacts would improve if we heard more about the successes. Arguably, many of the previously discussed

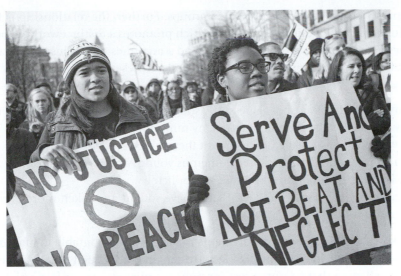

Police practices can be very controversial. Several high-profile shootings generated a series of protests and acts of retaliation against police officers following the events, which drew national attention.

problems with regard to police-community relations were intensified and/or perpetuated by the historical lack of minority representation in policing. In response, efforts have been made to better diversify police departments.

CHECKPOINT

- The roots of policing in the United States are grounded in England, including the use of informal social control and the Frankpledge system.
- The evolution of policing in the United States followed what occurred in England, as formal policing emerged when small towns grew into large cities and informal social control broke down.

- Slave patrols and Black codes, as they existed primarily in Southern states, were among the earliest forms of policing and formal social control in the United States.
- Policing in the United States has been categorized according to the Political, Reform, and Community eras.

POLICE PERSONNEL ISSUES

Police departments are regularly hiring new officers. The expansion of local-level policing duties to address terrorism and homeland security has also led to the increased need for officers. The challenges of recruiting and selecting officers who maintain awareness of cultural diversity pose several difficulties for local law enforcement agencies.

Historically, White males have been overrepresented on police forces across the United States, meaning that non-Whites and females have been largely underrepresented. Part of the problematic relationship departments and officers have with the public stem from the limited representation of underrepresented groups. Further, the relationship is hampered by the influences of the **police subculture**, which promotes a distinct working personality that encourages solidarity, authoritarianism, and sometimes the exclusion of females and minority officers. The causes of the historical underrepresentation of minority people in policing include:

- Minority individuals were not aggressively sought by police departments until the 1980s.
- Police work has not been attractive to many minorities.
- Minority individuals have reason to doubt they will be accepted in policing.
- For social rather than racial reasons, numerous young African Americans have a criminal record, limiting their options for a career in policing.
- Many educationally better-qualified Blacks have sought and taken more attractive employment opportunities.[40]

The lack of diversity in some departments may also be attributable to biased selection practices. For instance, in 2019 the U.S. Department of Justice sued the Baltimore County government, alleging that a written test for police applicants was unfairly biased against African Americans who applied. The test, it was argued, included questions that were not related to the position of being a police officer.[41]

Much has been done to increase the diversity of police departments. Addressing issues pertaining to the demographic makeup of officers is necessary for effective policing in a multicultural society. Among other contributions, increased diversity in policing promotes tolerance of different groups and helps defuse historical concerns regarding the underrepresentation of particular cultures in policing. Legislation and affirmative action programs influenced police departments to increase diversity and proactively seek and hire candidates from underrepresented groups.

LEGISLATING DIVERSITY IN POLICING

Title VII of the **Civil Rights Act of 1964** prevents governments, unions, employment agencies, and private employers with fifteen or more employees from discriminating based on color, race, sex, religion, or national origin. The **Equal Employment Opportunity Act of 1972** extended the 1964 act to state and local governments and placed further restrictions on hiring practices. Table 11.2 depicts other influential acts that promoted equal employment opportunities for women and minorities. A series of **affirmative action** programs designed to promote the hiring of minority applicants accompanied these and related pieces of legislation.

Historically, police departments have needed greater female and minority representation. Recall that the National Advisory Commission on Civil Disorders reported that poor police-minority relations were prominent among the causes underlying the rioting. As noted below, there's been notable success in this area as the number of females and racial minorities working in police departments steadily increased following passage of the Equal Employment Opportunity Act of 1972.[42]

Government agencies that receive public funds and all private employers must have affirmative action plans. Affirmative action plans require employers to: (1) conduct a census

TABLE 11.2   PROMOTING EQUAL EMPLOYMENT OPPORTUNITIES

Equal Pay Act, 1963—Prohibited unequal pay for men and women who performed the same work.

Age Discrimination in Employment Act of 1967—Prohibited employment discrimination against those over age forty.

Executive Order, 1969—Prevented the federal government from using gender as a qualification for hiring.

Crime Control Act, 1973—Ensured that police departments didn't discriminate against women in hiring practices by threatening to withhold funding should departments do so.

Americans with Disabilities Act, 1990—Prevented agencies from discriminating against any person otherwise qualified for a job because of a disability.

Family and Medical Leave Act of 1993—Required employers with fifty or more employees to grant eligible employees with up to twelve weeks of unpaid, job-secured leave for medical and family reasons.

of current employees, (2) identify underutilization or concentration of minorities and women, and (3) develop a recruiting plan to correct any underutilization.[43] Affirmative action plans have undoubtedly shaped the look of today's police departments.

Failure to comply with affirmative action policies could result in an agency facing civil suits from the parties excluded and a loss of funding from major grant bodies. Affirmative action policies are controversial in that they generate charges of **reverse discrimination**, or claims that minorities are being hired at the expense of those in the majority. Further, some individuals from underrepresented groups are being hired as "**tokens**" or officers who received their position solely because of affirmative action policies.[44] In policing, tokens were often treated differently by those in the majority race and gender, which often led to discrimination in assignments and evaluations, exclusion from the police culture, and harassment.[45]

INTEGRATING POLICING

Many police agencies seek to establish a department that reflects, from a race and ethnicity standpoint, the community in which they operate. Doing so helps gain the public's trust and confidence in the police, and better enables individuals from minority groups to provide insight from different backgrounds and cultures into policing. Bilingual officers provide important contributions to policing in situations in which language barriers pose problems. However, only about 40 percent of local police departments had bilingual or multilingual personnel in 2016, and only about 10 percent of officers spoke two or more languages.[46]

Departments have become increasingly diverse, yet there have been—and there remain, to some extent—particular obstacles associated with hiring members of minority groups. Prominent among the obstacles are: (1) police departments failing to make their job searches extensive enough to attract the most qualified individuals to the job, (2) some African Americans failing to possess the minimum qualifications for the position, and (3) many African Americans possessing a negative impression of police officers and police work.[47] One could claim that outright discrimination against underrepresented groups in hiring practices contributed in some part to the failure. These difficulties are not restricted to African Americans, as individuals from many minority groups historically have experienced difficulty obtaining and retaining positions in policing.

Both females and racial and ethnic minorities have become increasingly represented in policing. For instance, roughly 27 percent of local police officers were members of a racial or ethnic minority in 2016, compared to 15 percent in 1987. The biggest increase has been with regard to the hiring of Latino or Hispanic officers. From 1997 to 2016 the percentage of Hispanic or Latino local police officers increased from 8 percent to 13 percent (a 61-percent increase). Black or African American officers comprised roughly 11 percent of local officers in 2016, which was an increase from 1987, when only 9 percent of officers were Black or African American.[48] Figure 11.1 highlights recent changes in the makeup of police departments.

Females remain largely underrepresented in policing, although their representation has increased. In 2017, females comprised roughly 14 percent of local police officers compared to 1987, when only 8 percent were female.[49] Though women have made progress in law enforcement and many agencies have taken action to eliminate and reduce occupational barriers, much work remains.[50]

Compared to the U.S. population in general, African Americans are not notably underrepresented in policing anymore. Particularly, in 2016 African Americans comprised 13 percent of the U.S. population, and 11 percent of all local police officers. Hispanics

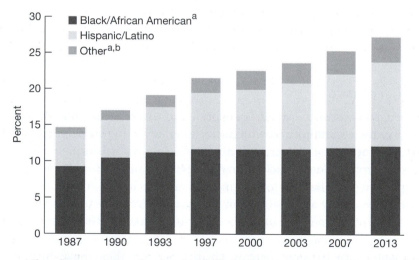

FIGURE 11.1 Minority representation among full-time sworn personnel in local police departments, 1987–2013

Note: Figure includes all years for which data were collected.

[a]Excludes persons of Hispanic or Latino origin.

[b]Includes Asian, Native Hawaiian, or other Pacific Islanders; American Indian or Alaska Natives; and persons identifying two or more races.

Source: Brian A. Reaves, *Local Police Departments, 2013: Personnel, Policies and Practices*, U.S. Department of Justice, Bureau of Justice Statistics, 2015, NCJ 248677.

and Latinos are somewhat underrepresented, as they comprised 17.8 percent of the U.S. population, but only 13 percent of local police officers. Females remain largely underrepresented relative to their presence in society, due in large part to issues such as workplace harassment, family issues, recruitment and selection biases, females generally not being interested in a career in policing, and the general non-acceptance of females in policing.

Comparing the demographics of the United States to the demographics of policing provides some insight regarding the inclusiveness of policing, but it also masks some problems. Of particular concern are cities in which African Americans and members of other minority groups remain underrepresented in policing. For instance, the Ferguson Police Department, which was at the center of a controversy in 2015 following the shooting death of Michael Brown, had fifty-three officers on its force, four of whom were Black. Ferguson's population was 66 percent Black.[51] Another example involves Baltimore County and Baltimore City, which have higher percentages of white officers compared to the demographics of the county and city. Eighty percent of the officers in Baltimore County in 2019 were White, compared to only 57 percent of the county's population. The police force in the city of Baltimore was 45 percent White; however, Whites comprise only 28 percent of the city's population.[52]

There is limited information regarding Hispanic police officers and officers from other cultural backgrounds simply because it is only recently that policing has become more diversified. We do know that the Hispanic population in the United States is increasing and their presence in police departments is beginning to keep pace. Hispanics in the United States come from various areas and bring with them diverse cultural backgrounds. Of particular importance to police is the ability of Hispanic officers to speak Spanish and to better understand different cultures.

Hispanics have faced many of the same limitations as other underrepresented groups in policing, including difficulties in gaining employment with police departments. The historical underrepresentation of Hispanics in policing can be attributed to the language barrier, the belief that many Hispanics may not wish to become police officers, and Hispanics not being sought after by police departments.[53]

Other minority groups have much to offer policing, although their presence in police departments has been relatively limited. For instance, Asian Americans and gay and lesbian officers offer specific contributions that assist police work. Asian American officers, akin to Hispanic officers, offer insight into different cultures, and help address language barriers, although they are poorly represented in police departments across the United States. This is due, in part, to the lack of Asian Americans applying for police positions, given the influences of parents who may not wish for their children to seek this line of work given the limited professionalism of policing in their homelands.[54]

The number of gay and lesbian officers is difficult to determine as many departments do not ask about sexual orientation, and officers may mask the fact that they are members of these groups out of concern for differential treatment. The historical mistreatment and underrepresentation of LGBT officers may be dissipating, as some departments have made proactive efforts to hire gay and lesbian officers. These efforts are particularly evident in

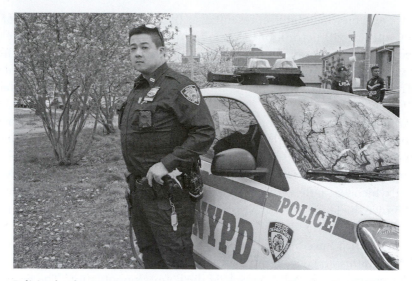

Policing has become increasingly diverse, as departments have made notable efforts to hire officers from historically underrepresented groups.

cities where there are large gay and lesbian populations, including Key West (Florida), where the police chief openly admitted that he is gay. The strengths and contributions of other underrepresented groups in policing are discussed throughout this book.

STEPS TO DIVERSIFY POLICING

Departments actively recruit in minority communities to increase their diversity. In doing so, they may use special officer recruitment efforts to attract females and racial and ethnic minorities. They may also use special recruitment efforts to attract multilingual persons.[55]

Departments may offer incentive pay to bilingual officers with the intent to address existing and potential cultural and communication problems. Qualified individuals are often available, but departments sometimes face difficulty finding, attracting, and hiring them. If faced with difficulties, it is argued that departments should not lower their standards to find suitable minority candidates. Instead, they should suspend hiring practices to do more effective targeted recruiting.[56] Departments may enhance their search practices when faced with obstacles in hiring. Advertising in minority-specific media outlets, utilizing religious and community groups, and employing the services of bilingual recruiters can help departments become more diverse. **Market segmentation**, or marketing practices "focused on a subset of prospects to identify individuals who will provide the greatest return for the efforts,"[57] is common in many occupations, including policing. For instance, researchers found that distributing information about position openings in areas where people of color live, work, and play helped address the lack of diversity among local law enforcement agencies.[58]

Retaining and promoting underrepresented groups in policing is critical for diversifying a department. Too often women and minorities in policing, and many other occupations, experience the **glass ceiling**, or an abstract barrier preventing certain groups and/or individuals from moving beyond entry-level positions. The lack of minority promotion in policing is well documented in the research literature: for instance, about one in eight local police officers were female in 2016; however, only about 3 percent were police chiefs, 7.5 percent were intermediate supervisors, and 9.7 percent were sergeants or first-line equivalents. Further, about 90 percent of police chiefs in local police departments were White.[59] Organizational factors such as discrimination, challenging work schedules that interfere with family life, and the fear of being identified as a "token" appear to continue to prevent females from seeking more supervisory positions.[60] It is assumed that there will be more diversity among the higher ranks of law enforcement as time progresses, as it is only somewhat recently that departments have become increasingly diverse, and years of service are required for promotions and assuming command positions.

Recent developments suggest hope for a more positive future regarding the promotion of underrepresented groups in policing. For instance, females serve as police chiefs in several major cities, women have directed several prominent federal law enforcement agencies (e.g., the DEA, Secret Service, and U.S. Marshals Service), and Beverly Harvard became the first African American female to head a large municipal police department in 1994.

One cannot overlook the problems within police departments stemming from historical failures to diversify. Affirmative action policies, the civil rights movement, and the demand for increased diversity in policing following the 1960s riots all contributed to greater multiculturalism in our police departments. Evidence of the progress is noted in minority officers approaching representation in policing commensurate with their representation in society. Police departments are to be commended for their actions with regard to more culturally sensitive hiring practices.

As noted in Table 11.3, there are many organizations and associations that promote the interests of women and cultural/racial/ethnic groups in policing. These organizations and

TABLE 11.3   EXAMPLES OF ORGANIZATIONS AND ASSOCIATIONS PROMOTING INTERESTS OF WOMEN AND CULTURAL/RACIAL/ETHNIC GROUPS IN POLICING

Gay Officers Action League

Hispanic National Law Enforcement Association

International Association of Women Police

Irish American Police Officers Association

National Asian Peace Officers' Association

National Association of Black Law Enforcement Executives

National Center for Women and Policing

National Coalition of Italian American Law Enforcement Organizations

National Latino Peace Officers Association

National Native American Law Enforcement Association

Polish American Police Association

associations provide officers opportunities to share concerns, issues, and related aspects of the job with officers of similar backgrounds from around the country and sometimes internationally.

CHECKPOINT

- Various legislative acts have been passed to help diversify police departments.
- Police departments in the United States have become increasingly diverse.

- Various recruitment and marketing efforts are used to encourage members of specific demographic groups to join the ranks of policing.

POLICE PRACTICES

Recent incidents involving controversial police practices in Ferguson, New York, Baltimore, and other cities once again directed societal attention toward policing. Accounts of poor relations between the police and various minority groups, and reports of controversial police practices, are continuously brought to public attention. It could be argued that such practices have long occurred, although we hear about them more frequently due in part to the increased accessibility and use of technology, such as cell phones with video cameras that have increasingly documented questionable and unprofessional police practices. The use of cameras provides a new layer of accountability for police officers who may wrongfully enforce the law, and officers who may subscribe to the **blue wall of silence**, which is the unwritten rule among officers to not report other officers' wrongful behavior. Cameras also provide protection for officers and the public, as video footage can provide powerful evidence of both good and bad police practices.

Having special powers to actively enforce social control puts police in a notably difficult position. The profession has progressed with regard to the methods, strategies, and overall practices employed by departments and officers, yet controversy remains. Police field practices pose the greatest sources of tension between minorities and police.[61] Among the most important types of police practices that contribute to the tension are:

- Delays in responding to calls for service
- Verbal abuse, such as the use of racially offensive epithets or other forms of disrespect
- Excessive stopping, questioning, and frisking of African-American citizens
- Discriminatory patterns of arrest and traffic citations
- Excessive use of physical force
- Excessive use of deadly force
- Systematic underenforcement of the law and the failure to protect law-abiding citizens[62]

This list is significant and identifiable in modern policing. To what extent each practice exists is unknown. Research on policing has largely increased following the research revolution of the 1960s when substantial government funding was allocated toward police sciences, yet it remains unclear to what extent police behave differently toward various groups in society.

Among the more recent controversial police practices involved the New York Police Department's stop-and-frisk program, which largely targeted high-crime areas and hot spots of crime. Some argue that the policy contributed to reductions in crime, while others argued that it violated individual rights. The policy, which began in the 1990s, involved stopping suspicious people and questioning them about their activities. It also involved searching them for weapons or contraband. An analysis of the practice found that the police increasingly stopped citizens, most of whom were African American or Hispanic. The police found nothing illegal and took no further action in the large majority (89 percent) of the stops.[63]

There is ongoing debate regarding whether police treat groups differently. For instance, consider the following scenario. *A young man steals a cellphone from a department store. The police catch the suspect as he enters the parking lot of the store and arrest him.*

Seems pretty straightforward. The police did their job. Now, let's alter the variables a bit. Suppose the young man is ten years old and admitted stealing the phone so he could buy food for his younger sister. His mother is always away from home and his father is in prison. His sister was painfully hungry. What should the police do in this case? What would you do? Arrest him? Give him a stern lecture? Hold his mother accountable? There are no easy answers to these questions. The young man obviously had good intentions, but went about his business in an inappropriate manner. Should his motive, age, or race influence police practices? Police officers are often required to use their discretion and are criticized when they use it poorly or not in accord with community standards.

Consider the following findings extracted from two Bureau of Justice Statistics reports with regard to traffic and street stops, and police use of nonfatal force.

Traffic and street stops:

- Of the individuals involved in traffic and street stops, Blacks were less likely than Whites to believe the police behaved properly during the stop.
- Drivers pulled over by an officer of the same race or ethnicity were more likely than drivers pulled over by an officer of a different race or ethnicity to believe that the reason for the traffic stop was legitimate.
- White drivers were both ticketed and searched at a lower rate than Black and Hispanic drivers.[64]

Police use of nonfatal force:

- Blacks were more likely to experience nonfatal force during their most recent contact with police than Whites and Hispanics.
- Blacks were far more likely than Hispanics and Whites to experience nonfatal force during street stops.
- Traffic stops involving an officer and driver of different races were more likely to involve force than traffic stops involving an officer and driver of the same race.
- Blacks were twice as likely as Whites to experience force during contacts involving a personal search.[65]

These findings suggest that certain groups, particularly African Americans, are more likely to be treated punitively by the police (as emphasized in Chapter 3 of this book). Of course, we must consider the context of police-citizen encounters; for instance, it may be the case that the police acted appropriately during a particular encounter, and it was the actions of the individuals they stopped and used force against that warranted the more punitive behavior. Or, it may be the case that the police misuse their powers by treating groups differently. Arguably, it is a combination of both, although it is difficult to discern the extent to which one factor plays a more significant role than the other.

American policing has become increasingly militarized in nature, largely due to federal funding. Special Weapons and Tactics (SWAT) teams have become increasingly common among police departments, and their use has been subject to little scrutiny. A report by the American Civil Liberties Union (ACLU) noted that SWAT teams, which were created primarily to deal with emergency situations such as hostage, barricade, and shooter situations, have commonly been used to search suspect's homes for drugs. Analyzing over eight hundred SWAT deployments among twenty law enforcement agencies, the ACLU noted that most (79 percent) of the incidents involved the use of a SWAT team to search someone's home, with more than 60 percent of the cases involving a search for drugs.

The report further noted that the use of paramilitary tactics and weapons largely impacted people of color. For instance, 42 percent of the people affected by a SWAT deployment to execute a search warrant were Black, and 12 percent were Latino. The report noted that SWAT deployments involving drug searches primarily involved people of color, while deployments in hostage or barricade scenarios (which constituted 7 percent of all deployments) primarily involved Whites.[66] These numbers add support to the argument that different styles of policing may exist for different groups. To address the continued militarization of the police, in May 2015 President Obama banned the federal government from providing some military-style equipment to local police departments, and put stricter controls on other weapons and gear provided to law enforcement. These restrictions were designed to prevent law enforcement agencies from misusing or overusing the items, which are often viewed as militaristic in nature, and to prevent further damage to the tenuous police-community relations in some areas.

POLICE DISCRETION

Police discretion, which involves officer decision-making, is evident in all aspects of police practices and at times is recognized as a necessary evil. Discretion is necessary in policing as officers are consistently faced with difficult situations involving multiple variables. It can be harmful when police misuse their discretion, regardless of whether it is intentional or accidental. While police training provides the nuts and bolts for doing the job, no amount of formal training can ever fully prepare officers to properly handle all situations they encounter. Much of what is learned in policing comes from on-the-job experience.

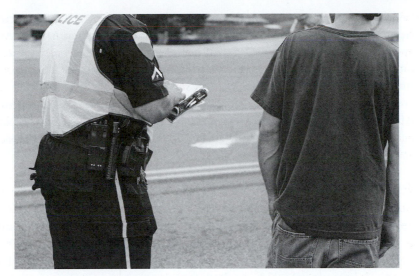

Police officers maintain a great deal of discretion throughout the course of each shift. We expect them to always make the correct choices, and they do so appropriately the large majority of the time. There are times, however, when discretion is misused.

It is hoped that an officer's formal training and street experience encourage him or her to properly exercise discretion. With the goal of better understanding police practices, researchers categorized the factors that influence an officer's use of discretion. These factors include: (1) organizational influences (e.g., guidance from the department), (2) situational characteristics (e.g., time of day, presence of witnesses, race of suspect), (3) officer characteristics (e.g., male or female, minority or nonminority), and (4) neighborhood or community influences (e.g., poor or wealthy community). The research literature contains many accounts of how these factors influence police practices. Ultimately, many variables influence policing.

Organizational Variables

Several organizational factors influence police discretion, including the professionalism or bureaucratic nature of the department, the size of the department, supervision levels, and the rotation of officers.[67] There is evidence that connects how closely a department adopts a militaristic style to how officers police. Researchers found that officers in more bureaucratic departments tend to focus more on law and order rather than providing general services.[68] Another study found that an officer's continued presence in a neighborhood promoted community relations and an understanding of community problems.[69]

Situational Factors

Situational factors are closely related to police practices. Factors such as suspect characteristics and behaviors, and the characteristics of the settings in which police and citizens interact, provide the most powerful explanations of police violence.[70] Of particular interest with regard to policing in a multicultural society are findings that African Americans are overrepresented in arrests, use of force, and police shootings. Currently there exist two explanations for the disproportionality: (1) African Americans commit a disproportionate amount of crime, and (2) police treat African Americans more punitively than they treat other groups. Both explanations address the disproportionate level of interactions between African Americans and police, and both have been used as excuses, explanations, and justifications for racial profiling. To what extent each contributes to the disproportionality is open for debate.

Officer Characteristics

Officer characteristics, in general, are not strong predictors of officer discretion and behavior. With regard to police violence, a National Institute of Justice report stated with modest confidence that "use of force appears to be unrelated to an officer's personal characteristics, such as age, gender, and ethnicity."[71] However, some research suggests that officer race is related to arrest practices,[72] but others found no relation.[73] One study found that African American officers are overrepresented in police shootings, but the notable level of deployment of African American officers in predominantly minority neighborhoods likely accounts for the differences.[74] A study of police use of force in predominantly minority communities suggested that patrol officer education was related to their use of force, as officers with higher levels of education less frequently used force, and used lower levels of force compared to patrol officers with lower levels of education.[75]

Earlier research suggested that Black officers were less lenient to Black suspects than were White officers.[76] More recent work in this area, however, found no strong evidence that African American or Hispanic officers police differently than White officers. Minority officers may find interacting with minority suspects more difficult in that the officers may be viewed as representing a biased criminal justice system that imposes its will upon minority groups. It was argued that Black officers sometimes suffer from **double marginality**, meaning that they are viewed as traitors by some in the Black community, while White officers may distrust them as colleagues.[77] Nevertheless, Black officers report that their on-duty relationships with White officers are satisfactory and they are confident that their White partners would back them up if needed.[78]

Neighborhood and Community Influences

There is a significant need to consider neighborhood-related variables when discussing policing and multiculturalism. For example, the research literature covering police use of deadly force highlights the impact of neighborhood or community variables on police discretion. Further, the literature highlighting inequities in wealth distribution suggests that income inequalities among groups promote instability in the social order. Responses to the instability in social order sometimes involve the use of force or coercion by the dominant class.[79] It is argued that the economic power maintained by some individuals and groups provides the basis for formal social control, for instance, as income inequality appears to be the strongest explanation for police killings.[80]

Population variation also appears to influence police use of deadly force. It is well established in the criminology literature that population stability typically results in greater intimacy among members of society. Conversely, social disorganization prompts instability. Aside from stability, the presence of particular minority groups appears to influence police practices. Research suggests that cities with more African Americans have higher police killing rates of African Americans.[81]

Police practices range from simple police-citizen verbal exchanges to police use of deadly force. Police use of deadly force is obviously the most scrutinized aspect of policing and generates much concern with regard to policing in a multicultural society. Two explanations are offered for police killings: (1) political threat explanations, which suggest that such acts are more likely to occur where racial or economic differences are greater, because of the threat resultant from the divisions between the groups, and (2) reactive explanations, which suggest that police killings are more likely to occur in areas experiencing high violent crime rates, or where officers must respond to urban conditions such as enhanced levels of poverty, thus making their job more difficult.[82] These explanations facilitate understanding the influences of neighborhood and community variables with regard to police practices in a multicultural society.

The rate of African Americans shot or killed by police far exceeds the rate for Whites. However, as noted, there remains debate as to why this is the case. Several researchers subscribe to the belief that police discretion or "differential policing" largely explains the disproportionality. Others hold that racial imbalance is a reflection of the struggles associated with being a member of a disadvantaged class, including social inequality and economic deprivation. Such a situation is evidenced in the extensive research literature which suggests that lower-class suspects receive harsher treatment from the police. Looking to the future of policing, author David Bayley argued in his article "Policing in America: Social Science and Public Policy in America" that the possibility of group violence in the United States is real, largely as a result of inequities in race, class, and ethnicity.[83] The civil unrest we've more recently witnessed in response to questionable police practices, such as racial profiling and seemingly wrongful deaths, provides evidence for his claim. (For further discussion of these events, see Chapter 3, "African Americans and the Criminal Justice System.")

Many examples throughout this book highlight the complexities and controversial practices involved with policing a multicultural society. This chapter highlights but a few of the many facets of police practices. As noted in Chapter 14 ("Preparing for Multiculturalism in the Criminal Justice System: Training and Policy"), it is perhaps with more efficient and effective training and policies that police can overcome the many obstacles and challenges they face on a daily basis. Further, police practices can be enhanced through stronger relations with the communities they serve.

CHECKPOINT

- Police practices are primarily influenced by police discretion. The factors that influence officer discretion include organizational variables, situational factors, officer characteristics, and neighborhood and community influences.

POLICE-COMMUNITY RELATIONS

Police-community relations have become increasingly important, as departments seek to gain the trust of the communities they serve. Doing so has become notably difficult in light of the aforementioned events around the United States in which many citizens perceived that the police misused their powers, particularly against less powerful groups. Strong police-community relations, which provide the foundation for many community-policing efforts, generally enable the police to more effectively perform their job, assist with crime-reporting practices, facilitate crime-prevention efforts, facilitate effective communication between groups, and encourage more individuals to consider careers in policing.

Most people in society are supportive of the police. There are, of course, segments of society that are less supportive of the police, and have less confidence in them. Police-community relations have been controversial throughout history, particularly in light of the suggestion that "The police have had a long history of discriminating against members of minority groups because of their own prejudices, ignorance, or official responsibility for enforcing laws that restricted some people's civil rights (such as segregation laws). Numerous civil disturbances in the United States have been precipitated by police behavior considered inappropriate or offensive by minority groups."[84] Various factors have hampered police-community relations. For instance, the war on drugs has had notable impacts on many minority communities, as has the increased militarization of the police, and decreased civil liberties in a time of concerns for homeland security and immigration.

There are discernable trends with regard to public approval of and confidence in the police. Generally, Americans are supportive of the police, although there are notable differences in levels of support for and confidence in the police among groups, and the levels of support fluctuate on a regular basis. Several Gallup polls offer insight into the nature of police-community relations. Results from these polls suggest that Black Americans are not particularly supportive of the police compared to other groups, and do not maintain confidence in them. For instance, a 2015-2017 Gallup poll found that 30 percent of Blacks noted that the they had a great deal or quite a lot of confidence in police, compared to the national average of 54 percent who felt the same way. Hispanics (45 percent) and Whites (61 percent) reported far more confidence in the police than did Blacks.[85]

Muslim Americans have received increased attention from the police following the 2001 terrorist attacks against the United States. Members of these groups have increasingly been the targets of hate crimes, and police have more closely monitored them out of concerns for homeland security. As such, there have been concerns regarding their civil rights and the suspicion they generate within their communities. They have requested additional law enforcement attention, and departments have responded by providing protection and training officers with regard to Muslim beliefs and traditions in efforts to minimize misunderstandings.[86]

A comprehensive literature review of empirical studies that have examined perceptions and attitudes of police across ethnic and racial groups noted that individuals who identified themselves as Black, non-White, or Hispanic were more likely to maintain negative perceptions of the police than self-identified Whites. Hispanics tended to have more negative views of the police than Whites, yet more positive views than Blacks.[87] Many reasons explain the differences among groups with regard to perceptions of the police, including that historical targeting of African Americans based on the stereotype that they are dangerous or otherwise violent criminals, and because the murders or abuses of innocent victims by police are more visible in Black communities compared to other groups.[88]

Immigration, both legal and illegal, has also provided challenges for police officers. New immigrants bring with them various cultural beliefs that may conflict with the norms of the dominant groups in the United States, and they may have pre-established perceptions of policing based on practices in their homeland. Illegal immigrants warrant specific attention given their status as being in the United States illegally, and local police are often placed in the difficult position of enforcing laws that seem controversial. The lack of clear and consistent federal, state, and local laws regarding how to respond to illegal immigration places police officers, who are at the front line of addressing issues pertaining to illegal immigration, in particularly difficult situations.

Evidence of the rift in the relationship between some minority groups and the police is noted with the 2013 "Black Lives Matter" activist movement in the United States that originated following the 2013 acquittal of George Zimmerman after he shot African American teenager Trayvon Martin. The movement gained greater attention after the 2014 deaths of two unarmed African Americans (Michael Brown in Ferguson, Missouri, and Eric Garner in New York City) and the failure of grand juries to indict the officers involved in the shootings. The group campaigns against police brutality against African Americans.

Blue Lives Matter, a countermovement to Black Lives Matter, was created to raise awareness and encourage assistance to the police and their families as they endure difficult times. The group advocates making the killing of police officers a hate crime, which was influential in Louisiana becoming the first state to do so. The legislation was passed in 2016, and other states have followed their lead.

In light of several events which highlighted the rifts between local police and some communities they serve, President Barack Obama signed an executive order establishing the Task Force on 21st Century Policing in December 2014. The task force was charged with finding best practices and providing recommendations on how police practices can promote effective crime fighting while building public trust. Among other contributions, the task force identified six areas of recommendation for policing. The areas include:

- Building trust and legitimacy (e.g., treating people with respect, and being neutral in decision-making)
- Policy and oversight (e.g., working with community members to create strategies in high-crime areas to reduce crime by improving relationships, and promoting community engagement and cooperation)
- Technology and social media (e.g., striving to identify new technology to assist with policing, and finding best practices to use social media)
- Community policing and crime reduction (e.g., developing and adopting policies and strategies that promote the importance of community engagement with regard to public safety)

- Training and education (e.g., encouraging the federal government to support the development of partnerships with training facilities to promote consistent standards for high quality training)
- Officer wellness and safety (e.g., being wary of the harmful effects of policing on officers, and proactively addressing potential problems)[89]

These areas are certainly important to the future of policing, and several have direct implications for policing in a diverse society. Particularly, the need to build trust and legitimacy, for effective policy and oversight, for community policing and crime reduction, and for enhanced training and education can all serve to better improve police-community relations, and ultimately enhance policing.

In 2014, the U.S. Department of Justice (DOJ) issued a report which noted that the Cleveland Division of Police (CDP) regularly violated Fourth Amendment protections by engaging in a pattern or practice of use of excessive force, including deadly force. This finding was similar to the aforementioned DOJ report involving the Chicago Police Department. The Cleveland Police Department reached an agreement with the DOJ, which focused on "building community trust, creating a culture of community and problem-oriented policing, officer safety and training, officer accountability, and technological upgrades." Among the provisions of the agreement were the creation of the Community Police Commission, which consists of representatives from the community and various police personnel, the integration of bias-free policing principles to all levels of the organization, including training of officers and supervisors, and the development of a recruiting policy and strategic recruitment plan in efforts to attract well-qualified applicants from a broad cross-section of the community.[90] Each of these provisions highlights the importance of multiculturalism in policing.

Police departments must consider future developments with regard to multiculturalism and demographic changes. For instance, the percentage of Hispanics is expected to continue increasing in the United States, and departments must be prepared for the change. Another demographic change involves an increasingly older U.S. population. People are living longer, healthier lives, and the police must be prepared to respond to the special needs of an increasingly aging population. Such needs include dementia, deterioration of driving skills, elder abuse, and self-neglect. Training and preparing officers to best respond to these and related issues will facilitate police-community relations and result in more effective police practices.

Steps have been taken to address the concerns of older populations. The National Association of Triads, a partnership created by the American Association of Retired Persons (AARP), the International Association of Chiefs of Police (IACP), and the National Sheriffs' Association (NSA), seeks to promote adult safety and reduce the fear of crime among the elderly. Triads involving partnerships between the police and senior citizens exist in many communities, and assist older residents through education, offering support, uniting agencies, and offering opportunities for volunteers to become involved in policing.

CHECKPOINT

- The majority of people in the United States support the police, although there are differences among demographic groups. Many steps have been taken and proposed to build strong relations between the police and the public.

SUMMARY

The news media are filled with stories involving police practices. Unfortunately, we often hear of the negative aspects of policing and failure to prevent crime. For instance, we rarely hear of the police officer who arrested the drunk driver and possibly saved several lives, or the officer who successfully defused a sticky situation verbally instead of violently. Instead, we hear of the officer who was arrested or the officer accused of racial profiling. To be sure, these events occur and should not be tolerated. However, those reading this chapter should bear in mind that most police officers abide by the law and are professional in their practice. Most are not racist, biased, or hateful. They perform a difficult and controversial job that grants them special powers and often places them in the spotlight. Unfortunately, the negative actions of a few officers are often reflected on all. As a society, one of our primary goals with regard to social control remains to identify and remove from policing those who fail to appropriately do their job.

YOU MAKE THE CALL

ETHICAL POLICING?

Consider the following scenario. Debate the pros and cons of all options and decide what you would do.

You're an African American rookie police officer patrolling a community heavily populated by Hispanic Americans. There is ongoing tension between the police and Hispanic American residents in the area following claims of police abuse of young Hispanic males. You stop a car that made an illegal U-turn in the street. The car pulls over. You notice three young Hispanic males in the car as you approach the vehicle. The driver rolls down the window and you smell marijuana. The driver seems agitated that you pulled him over and begins making claims of racial profiling. You're somewhat sympathetic to his claims as you've personally seen officers profile minority drivers. The others in the car chime in. You ask the driver to step out of the car and he refuses, claiming he wants a lawyer. You call for backup. As you're making the call, the three individuals step out of the car in what you perceive to be an aggressive manner. They're angry and not listening to your commands. Your backup is three minutes away. You reach for your baton and command the individuals to get on the ground. They refuse and move toward you. Their aggressive demeanor prompts you to use your baton on them. Your backup arrives as you wrestle with the suspects. You and the other officers successfully place the suspects in custody. The suspects claim you targeted them based on their ethnicity, used excessive force by using a baton, and said derogatory terms during the tussle. You don't recall saying anything of that nature, and believe you were fully justified in your actions.

Questions

1. How should your supervisor respond to the claims that you used derogatory terms?
2. How could you have prevented this incident from escalating into violence?
3. To what extent do you believe the tensions in the community contributed to the unfortunate outcome of this incident?
4. What steps, if any, should the police chief take to ensure that an incident such as this does not occur again? What should you do, if anything?

KEY TERMS

affirmative action

Black codes

blue wall of silence

Bow Street Runners

Christopher Commission

Civil Rights Act of 1866

Civil Rights Act of 1964

community era of policing

community policing

double marginality

Equal Employment Opportunity Act of 1972

exclusionary rule

Frankpledge system

glass ceiling

hue and cry

Market segmentation

Metropolitan Police Act

National Advisory Commission on Civil Disorders

overpolicing

patronage

police discretion

police subculture

political era of policing

President's Commission on Law Enforcement and Administration of Justice

problem-oriented policing

Prohibition

reform era of policing

reverse discrimination

slave patrols

tokens

underpolicing

DISCUSSION QUESTIONS

1. Discuss significant events in the history of policing that contributed to current problematic relations between underrepresented groups and the police.
2. Identify the three eras of policing and discuss the impact of each on public perceptions of the police.
3. What significant events have helped diversify police forces?
4. Identify and discuss the four categories of variables that influence police discretion. How do these factors affect policing in a multicultural society?
5. What steps do you believe are most important in building and maintaining strong police-community relations?

FOR FURTHER READING

Barlow, David, and Melissa Hickman Barlow. *Police in a Multicultural Society: An American Story*, 2nd ed. Long Grove, IL: Waveland Press, 2018.

Palmer, Darren, Michael M. Berlin, and Dilip K. Das, eds. *Global Environment of Policing*. Boca Raton, FL: CRC Press, 2012.

Perez, D. W. *Paradoxes of Police Work*, 2nd ed. Clifton Park, NY: Cengage, 2011.

Skolnick, J. *Justice Without Trial: Law Enforcement in a Democratic Society*. New York: John Wiley & Sons, 1966.

Wells, S. K., and B. L Alt. *Police Women: Life with the Badge*. Westport, CT: Prager, 2005.

NOTES

1. S. M. Cox, W. P. McCamey, and G. L. Scaramella, *Introduction to Policing*, 2nd ed. (Thousand Oaks, CA: Sage, 2014), 324.
2. David Barlow and Melissa Hickman Barlow, *Police in a Multicultural Society: An American Story*, 2nd ed. (Long Grove, IL: Waveland Press, 2000).

3. Ibid., 53.

4. Ibid, xii.

5. Philip Smith, *Policing Victorian London* (London: Greenwood Press, 1985).

6. Craig Uchida, "The Development of the American Police: An Historical Overview," in R. Dunham and G. Alpert (eds.), *Critical Issues in Policing: Contemporary Readings*, 2nd ed. (Prospect Heights, IL: Waveland Press, 1993), 16–32.

7. Philip Stead, *The Police of Britain* (New York: Macmillan, 1985).

8. W. Marvin Dulaney, *Black Police in America* (Bloomington: Indiana University Press, 1996).

9. Ibid.

10. Linda S. Miller and Karen M. Hess, *Community Policing: Partnerships for Problem Solving*, 4th ed. (Belmont, CA: Wadsworth, 2005).

11. James A. Fagin, *Criminal Justice*, 2nd ed. (Boston, MA: Allyn and Bacon, 2007).

12. Miller and Hess, *Community Policing*, 9.

13. Fagin, *Criminal Justice*.

14. Hubert Williams and Patrick V. Murphy, "The Evolving Strategy of Police: A Minority View," U.S. Department of Justice, National Institute of Justice, No. 13 (January 1990).

15. George L. Kelling and Mark H. Moore, "From Political to Reform to Community: The Evolving Strategy of Police," in Jack R. Greene and Stephen D. Mastrofski (eds.), *Community Policing: Rhetoric or Reality* (New York: Praeger Publishers, 1991), 3–25.

16. Williams and Murphy, "The Evolving Strategy."

17. Samuel Walker and Charles M. Katz, *The Police in America*, 7th ed. (New York: McGraw-Hill, 2011), 31.

18. Ibid.

19. Williams and Murphy, "The Evolving Strategy."

20. Miller and Hess, *Community Policing*.

21. Walker and Katz, *The Police in America*, 42.

22. Ibid.

23. Anthony D. Perez, Kimberly M. Berg, and Daniel J. Myers, "Police and Riots, 1967–1969," *Journal of Black Studies* 34, no. 2 (2003): 153–82.

24. Ibid, 177.

25. Michael D. White, *Current Issues and Controversies in Policing* (Boston, MA: Allyn and Bacon, 2007).

26. Miller and Hess, *Community Policing*, 12.

27. Williams and Murphy, "The Evolving Strategy," 11.

28. Miller and Hess, *Community Policing*, 13.

29. National Advisory Commission on Civil Disorders, *Report of the National Advisory Commission on Civil Disorders* (New York: Bantam Books, 1967).

30. Mapp v. Ohio, 367 U.S. 643 (1961).

31. Gideon v. Wainwright, 372 U.S. 335 (1963).

32. Miranda v. Arizona, 384 U.S. 436 (1966).

33. Terry v. Ohio, 392 U.S. 1 (1968).

34. R. G. Burns, *Policing: A Modular Approach* (Upper Saddle River, NJ: Pearson, 2013), 8.

35. Brian A. Reaves, *Local Police Departments, 2013: Personnel, Policies, and Practices*, U.S. Department of Justice, Bureau of Justice Statistics, 2015, NCJ 248677, 8.

36. Matthew J. Hickman and Brian A. Reaves, *Local Police Departments, 2003*, U.S. Department of Justice, Bureau of Justice Statistics, 2006, NCJ 210118, 19.

37. Perez et al., "Police and Riots," 179.
38. *Report of the Independent Commission on the Los Angeles Police Department*, July 9, 1991, p. iii.
39. Ibid., iv.
40. David L. Carter and Louis A. Radelet, *The Police and the Community*, 6th ed. (Upper Saddle River, NJ: Prentice Hall, 1999), 298–99.
41. Pamela Wood and Wilborn P. Nobles III, "Justice Department Accuses Baltimore County of Racial Bias in Police Hiring," *Washington Post*, August 28, 2019. Available at: https://www.washingtonpost.com/local/public-safety/justice-department-accuses-baltimore-county-of-racial-bias-in-police-hiring/2019/08/28/f0c9d398-c9b0-11e9-a4f3-c081a126de70_story.html
42. Robert H. Langworthy and Lawrence P. Travis III, *Policing in America: A Balance of Forces*, 2nd ed. (Upper Saddle River, NJ: Prentice Hall, 1999), 244.
43. Walker and Katz, *The Police in America*.
44. H. B. Grant and K. J. Terry, *Law Enforcement in the 21st Century*, 4th ed. (Upper Saddle River, NJ: Pearson, 2017).
45. Ibid.
46. Shelley S. Hyland and Elizabeth Davis, *Local Police Departments, 2016: Personnel*, U.S. Department of Justice, Bureau of Justice Statistics, October 2019, NCJ 252835, 9.
47. Michael D. Lyman, *The Police: An Introduction*, 4th ed. (Upper Saddle River, NJ: Pearson, 2010), 96.
48. Shelley S. Hyland and Elizabeth Davis, *Local Police Departments, 2016: Personnel*, 6.
49. Reaves, *Local Police Departments, 2013*, 4; DataUSA.com, "Police Officers," 2019, accessed August 14, 2019 at: https://datausa.io/profile/soc/333050/#demographics.
50. H. H. Yu, "Overcoming Tokenism and Gender Barriers: The Critical Role of Nongovernmental Organizations for Women in Federal Law Enforcement," *The Police Chief* (January 2015): 50.
51. Y. Alcindor and N. Penzenstadler, "Police Redouble Efforts to Recruit Diverse Officers," *USA Today*, January 21, 2015. Available at: http://www.usatoday.com/story/news/2015/01/21/police-redoubling-efforts-to-recruit-diverse-officers/21574081/
52. Pamela Wood, "Across the Board, Baltimore Area Police Departments Are Much Whiter than the People They Serve," *Baltimore Sun*, September 11, 2019. Available at: https://www.baltimoresun.com/maryland/bs-md-pol-police-diversity-20190911-2zozdposu5hebo6tnkxjjcb7ji-story.html
53. Burns, *Policing*, 316.
54. J. S. Dempsey and L. S. Forst, *An Introduction to Policing*, 7th ed. (Clifton Park, NY: Cengage, 2014), 209.
55. B. A. Reaves, *Hiring and Retention of State and Local Law Enforcement Officers, 2008—Statistical Tables*. U.S. Department of Justice, Bureau of Justice Statistics, 2012, NCJ 238251, 13.
56. White, *Current Issues*.
57. Burns, *Policing*, 104.
58. Charles P. Wilson, Shirley A. Wilson, and Mary Gwann, "Identifying Barriers to Diversity in Law Enforcement Agencies," *Journal of Ethnicity in Criminal Justice*, 14, no. 4 (2016): 231–53.
59. Hyland and Davis, *Local Police Departments, 2016: Personnel*, 7.
60. John A. Shjarback and Natalie Todak, "The Prevalence of Female Representation in Supervisory and Management Positions in American Law Enforcement: An Examination of Organizational Correlates," *Women & Criminal Justice*, 29 (2019): 129–47.
61. Kenneth J. Peak and Ronald W. Glensor, *Community Policing and Problem Solving: Strategies and Practices*, 2nd ed. (Upper Saddle River, NJ: Prentice Hall, 1999), 218–20.
62. Ibid.

63. Jennifer Fratello, Andres F. Rengifo, and Jennifer Trone, *Coming of Age with Stop and Frisk: Experiences, Perceptions, and Public Safety Implications* (New York: Vera Institute of Justice, 2013).

64. L. Langton and M. Durose, *Police Behavior During Traffic and Street Stops*, U.S. Department of Justice, Bureau of Justice Statistics, 2013, NCJ 242937, 1.

65. S. Hyland, L. Langton, and E. Davis, *Police Use of Nonfatal Force, 2002–2011*. U.S. Department of Justice, Bureau of Justice Statistics, 2015, NCJ 249216, 1.

66. American Civil Liberties Union, *War Comes Home: The Excessive Militarization of American Policing*, June 2014. Available at: https://www.aclu.org/sites/default/files/assets/jus14-warcomeshome-report-web-rel1.pdf

67. Laure Weber Brooks, "Police Discretionary Behavior: A Study of Style," in R. G. Dunham and G. P. Alpert (eds.), *Critical Issues in Policing: Contemporary Readings* (Long Grove, IL: Waveland, 2005), 89–105.

68. J. Skolnick, *Justice Without Trial: Law Enforcement in a Democratic Society* (New York: John Wiley & Sons, 1966).

69. S. Mastrofski, "Policing the Beat: The Impact of Organizational Scale on Patrol Officer Behavior in Urban Residential Neighborhoods," *Journal of Criminal Justice* 9 (1981): 343–58.

70. Ronald Burns and Charles Crawford, "Situational Determinants of Police Violence," in R. Burns and C. Crawford (eds.), *Policing and Violence* (Upper Saddle River, NJ: Prentice Hall, 2002), 76.

71. National Institute of Justice, Executive Summary. *Use of Force by Police: Overview of National and Local Data*. U.S. Department of Justice, 1999, Bureau of Justice Statistics, NCJ 176330, viii.

72. L. Sherman, "Causes of Police Behavior: The Current State of Quantitative Research," *Journal of Research in Crime and Delinquency* 17 (1980): 69–100.

73. R. E. Worden, "Situational and Attitudinal Explanations of Police Behavior: A Theoretical Reappraisal and Empirical Assessment," *Law and Society Review* 23 (1989): 667–711.

74. R. Geller and K. Karales, *Split Second Decisions: Shootings of and by the Chicago Police* (Chicago: Chicago Law Enforcement Study Group, 1981).

75. C. Chapman, "Use of Force in Minority Communities Is Related to Police Education, Age, Experience, and Ethnicity," *Police Practice and Research* 13, no. 5 (2012): 421–36.

76. N. Alex, *Black in Blue: A Study of the Negro Policeman* (New York: Appleton-Century-Crofts, 1976).

77. Ibid.

78. Cox et al., *Introduction to Policing*.

79. D. Jacobs and R. O'Brien, "The Determinants of Deadly Force: A Structural Analysis of Police Violence," *American Journal of Sociology* 103 (1998): 837–62.

80. D. Jacobs and D. Britt, "Inequality and the Police Use of Deadly Force," *Social Problems* 26 (1979): 403–12.

81. Jacobs and O'Brien, "The Determinants of Deadly Force."

82. Ibid.

83. David Bayley, "Policing in America: Social Science and Public Policy in America," *Society* (Nov./Dec. 1998): 16–19.

84. R. Roberg, K. Novak, G. Cordner, and B. Smith, *Police and Society*, 6th ed. (New York: Oxford University Press, 2015), 98.

85. Jim Norman, *Confidence in Police Back at Historical Average*, Gallup, July 10, 2017. Available at: https://news.gallup.com/poll/213869/confidence-police-back-historical-average.aspx

86. Dempsey and Forst, *Introduction to Policing*, 325–26.

87. J. H. Peck, "Minority Perceptions of the Police: A State-of-the-Art Review," *Policing: An International Journal of Police Strategies and Management* 38, no. 1 (2015): 173–203; Kevin L. Nadal, Kristin C. Davidoff, Neil Allicock, Christine R. Serpe, and Tanya Erazo, "Perceptions of Police, Racial Profiling, and Psychological Outcomes: A Mixed Methodological Study," *Journal of Social Issues*, 73(4): 808–30.

88. Nadal et al., "Perceptions of Police," 824.

89. *Final Report of the President's Task Force on 21st Century Policing* (Washington, DC: Office of Community Oriented Policing Services, 2015).

90. U.S. Department of Justice, "Justice Department Reaches Agreement with City of Cleveland to Reform Cleveland Division of Police Following Finding of a Pattern or Practice of Excessive Force" (press release), May 26, 2015 (updated August 4, 2015). Available at: http://www.justice.gov/opa/pr/justice-department-reaches-agreement-city-cleveland-reform-cleveland-division-police

CHAPTER 12

COURTS AND MULTICULTURALISM

CHAPTER OBJECTIVES

After reading this chapter, you should be able to:

- Discuss how pretrial processes maintain potential biases against underrepresented groups
- Identify potential biases working against minorities with regard to the manner in which prospective jurors are identified and the manner in which jurors are ultimately selected
- Discuss the steps of a trial, including areas where the prosecution may have an unfair advantage
- Identify how sentencing practices and sentencing structures have contributed to the overrepresentation of minorities in prison
- Explain why we need diversity among the courtroom personnel and identify whether race influences judicial practices

The U.S. criminal court system consists of state and federal courts. State courts process those charged with state violations. Federal courts process those accused of committing federal offenses. The U.S. Supreme Court, the highest court in the land, hears cases from both state and federal courts. Most criminal case processing occurs in state courts. Multiculturalism plays a significant role in our court systems given the large number of defendants processed each year.

In their book *American Cultural Pluralism and Law*, Jill Norgren and Serena Nanda note that as the United States increasingly diversifies, "it faces a fundamental tension: on one hand there is the need to create national institutions, including law, which unify culturally different groups, and on the other, the need to protect human rights by allowing some degree of religious, personal, cultural, and local political autonomy."[1] They add that "law . . . is one of the most important mechanisms for addressing this inevitable tension between the needs of the nation-state for some growing consensus around a dominant set of cultural values and institutions, and the needs of groups to enact and increase their autonomy."[2] U.S. courts interpret, create, and apply criminal and civil law, and are particularly vulnerable to the previously described tensions.

Increased diversity in the courtroom perpetuates interpersonal misunderstandings. For example, the verbal and body language of non-English speaking defendants and witnesses are sometimes misinterpreted by English-speaking courtroom personnel. In response, courts have become increasingly sensitive to the needs of those unable to speak English.[3] Some suggest holding trials in Spanish should a defendant choose to do so.[4]

In a newspaper article titled "Courts Asked to Consider Culture," author Richard Willing commented on the role of culture in U.S. courts, suggesting that "Immigrants with roots in Africa, Asia, and other non-Western cultures are winding up in America's courts after being charged with crimes for acts that would not be offenses in their home countries."[5] Incidents involving animal sacrifices, ritual mutilations, and other customs of foreign cultures are increasingly showing up in our courts, leading to the suggestion that the courts permit defendants from non-Western backgrounds to offer a "cultural defense" in response to being charged with a crime.[6] Cultural defenses have been reluctantly allowed in court, although, as Willing notes, "Exceptions have come when groups have been able to argue that their religious as well as cultural rights have been violated."[7]

Research addressing felony defendants in large urban counties found an overrepresentation of Blacks and an underrepresentation of Whites entering criminal court. Black defendants accounted for 45 percent of those entering courts on felony charges, while Whites constituted 30 percent of those charged with felony offenses, and 24 percent were

The U.S. Supreme Court is the highest court in the United States. It is an appellate court that it hears cases that originate in both state and federal courtrooms.

Hispanic. Of particular interest is the finding that over half (55 percent) of those under age eighteen and entering felony court were Black males. Black males were also largely over-represented (37 percent) among the felony defendants who were age forty or older when entering criminal court. Males were far more likely than females to end up in felony court (83 percent compared to 17 percent).[8]

The following discussion of multiculturalism in the courts is organized according to the stages of criminal case processing in criminal courts. The discussion begins with a look at multiculturalism in the events occurring at the initial appearance, followed by discussion of preliminary/grand jury hearings, arraignments, trials, sentencing, and appeals. This chapter concludes with discussion of the diversity of those working in our courts. Due to their overrepresentation in the courts, African Americans are the focus of much discussion regarding multiculturalism and the courts.

INITIAL APPEARANCE

At the **initial appearance**, also referred to as the first appearance, defendants are:

- Brought before the court
- Informed of the formal charges against them
- Advised of their rights, including the right to retain a lawyer or have one appointed to them
- Possibly granted pretrial release
- Made aware of the upcoming steps in their case

In general, felony criminal case processing is more complicated than misdemeanor processing. The difference stems from the more severe or harmful circumstances typically involved in felonies than in misdemeanors. The more severe penalties associated with felonies also contribute to the differences in the resources devoted to each type of case. Misdemeanor processing often begins and ends with the initial appearance. Felony processing is more drawn out and more likely to involve the steps occurring after the initial appearance.

NOTICE OF CHARGES

Decisions to charge a defendant and the nature of the charges are sometimes controversial. Prosecutors typically examine the evidence provided to them following an arrest and preliminary investigation and use their discretion to determine whether or not to file charges. If they choose to file charges, they must then determine what charge(s) to file. Prosecutors depend heavily on police reports and input from those involved with the incident to make their assessment. The power to make several key decisions, especially as they relate to filing charges, offers avenues for prosecutorial abuse of discretion.

Prosecutors primarily rely on the strength of the evidence in their decisions to file charges against a defendant. However, there is evidence that variables such as race and ethnicity may play a role in this stage of criminal justice processing. Several studies found that African American and Hispanic suspects were more likely than White suspects to face criminal charges. An evaluation of thirty-four research studies that considered the decision to charge found inconsistent results, as some suggested that minorities were the recipients of more punitive practices, while other studies suggested they weren't.[9] In their assessment of race and the decision to charge, authors Walker and colleagues noted that "there is compelling evidence of racial *disparity* in charging and plea bargaining" (italics in original) and further added that the "disparity frequently reflects racial discrimination."[10]

COUNSEL AND THE INITIAL APPEARANCE

Defendants entering court are commonly represented by counsel. Very few defendants choose to represent themselves. Counsel comes in two forms: private counsel secured by the defendant and state-provided counsel. In *Gideon v. Wainwright* the U.S. Supreme Court ruled that all who enter our courts have the right to counsel at all critical stages of the criminal justice process.[11] Prior to *Gideon*, only defendants in federal courts had the right to counsel, as decided in *Johnson v. Zerbst*.[12]

State-issued counsel is provided in the forms of assigned counsel and public defenders. Both groups are tasked with providing legal representation to **indigent defendants**, those who cannot afford representation. The **assigned counsel** approach involves the court appointing indigent cases to practicing attorneys. Attorneys are assigned indigent cases in return for a statutorily determined fee. In many cases, these attorneys have a caseload in their private practice that generates more income than the indigent cases. The statutorily prescribed fee for indigent representation is far below what attorneys earn in their private practices. Such a situation may result in attorneys devoting greater attention to their private practices than to the assigned cases, given the need for private entities to generate profit for their financial survival.[13]

Although most U.S. counties use the assigned counsel system, most defendants are represented by **public defenders** who work in offices that exist solely to provide indigent representation. Public defenders face many challenges, including responsibility for large caseloads and limited resources. Their offices are primarily located in large urban cities where large volumes of criminal cases require their services.

Racial and ethnic minorities are more likely than Whites to receive state-issued counsel upon entering court.[14] The economic differences between minorities and nonminorities significantly contribute to this finding. It is important to take the limitations of indigent representation very seriously, as public defenders and appointed counsel face several challenges in providing quality defense. Those representing the poor are threatened by a lack of financial support, large caseloads, and questionable training and supervision.[15] Indigent defendants are often represented by overworked, underpaid, and unqualified attorneys.[16] Prosecutors typically have more resources than indigent-defense attorneys, thus putting defendants with fewer means at a clear disadvantage.

The Supreme Court requires that indigent defendants receive "effective assistance," but the standard for "effectiveness" is subjective. The subjectivity of the term is evident in cases where lawyers representing the indigent showed up in court drunk or fell asleep during the proceeding yet were deemed effective.[17] Those purchasing the services of private attorneys can shop around and determine for themselves who they wish to represent them, but indigent defendants are provided attorneys by the state. Such a situation has resulted in inexperienced lawyers with limited knowledge of the complex law pertaining to capital punishment trials representing some indigent defendants facing the death penalty.[18] Nevertheless, the research literature has not consistently demonstrated that those represented by public defenders receive harsher sentences than those who use private counsel.[19]

PRETRIAL RELEASE

Arrestees are sometimes detained following arrest and prior to trial. The severity of the offense for which they've been arrested largely determines whether or not they are detained. Those arrested for the more serious offenses and posing the greatest threats to society are most likely to be detained. While detained, most arrestees will be granted **pretrial release** at their initial appearance. Pretrial release can be secured monetarily, as in the case of bail, or nonfinancially, such as release on recognizance, which involves the accused being released with no financial obligations but with a promise, in writing, to appear at all later court hearings. Judges typically determine whether or not the accused will be released prior to trial, as well as the nature of the release. Among the considerations related to the nature of one's pretrial release are ensuring that the defendant will stay out of trouble while released and will return to court for further processing.

Judicial discretion in setting or denying bail and the circumstances surrounding release generates controversy. Judges typically consider a variety of factors in the release decision, such as the seriousness of the offense, the defendant's criminal record, their likelihood of returning to court, and their anticipated behavior should they be released. Part of the controversy involves the uncertainty of how variables such as race, gender, and ethnicity influence judicial discretion. Studies observing the effect of race on bail-setting decisions provide contradictory results. Much has improved with regard to the unfair treatment of racial minorities who are arrested and detained; however, evidence suggests that some judges still consider race and other extralegal variables with regard to decisions concerning bail.[20] For instance, one study found that Blacks and Latinos, at both arrest and prior to trial, were more likely than Whites to be denied bail and detained in urban courts and county jails across the United States.[21]

Research suggests that Black and Hispanic detainees are more likely than Whites to be detained in jail while awaiting trial.[22] Other research found that Hispanics received significantly higher bail amounts than their African American and White counterparts.[23] Financial bail poses more of a challenge to the poor than it does to those with financial means. The inability to secure release provides many challenges for defendants, including the increased likelihood of being found guilty, and a longer sentence.[24]

CHECKPOINT

- The primary functions of the initial appearance are to notify the defendant of the charges and their right to counsel, and determine whether pretrial release will be granted and under what conditions if so.
- There is evidence suggesting that White defendants receive more favorable treatment than other groups with regard to the charges filed against them.

- All defendants are entitled to representation, although the effectiveness of state-provided indigent representation has been questioned.
- Defendants may be granted pretrial release at the initial appearance, and evidence suggests that Whites generally receive more favorable treatment.

PRELIMINARY HEARING/GRAND JURY

A preliminary hearing or grand jury hearing is required in felony cases due to the more severe circumstances associated with felonies than with misdemeanors. Preliminary hearings differ from grand jury hearings in several ways, although their primary goal remains the same: to determine if the accused should remain in the system. **Preliminary hearings** involve a prosecutor demonstrating to a judge why charges have been filed and justification for continued processing. The prosecutor bears the burden of demonstrating guilt.

Grand jury hearings are also used to determine if continued case processing may be necessary. Grand jurors are laypersons selected to serve on the jury. In grand jury hearings jurors basically replace the judge used in a preliminary hearing. The grand jury's task is to determine if the prosecutor's case is strong enough to warrant an **indictment**. An indictment is the charging document used by grand juries to suggest that enough evidence exists to proceed with case processing. Grand juries are also permitted to engage in evidence collection of their own, should they choose to do so. Some states rely on preliminary hearings; others use grand juries or both types of hearings.

It is argued that preliminary hearings and grand jury hearings are somewhat insignificant in criminal case processing due to the unfair advantage maintained by prosecutors. While there are no implications of racism or cultural bias with regard to grand jury and preliminary hearings, defendants are arguably at a disadvantage in both types of hearings.

Let's consider grand jury hearings as a potential setting for bias or discrimination. Prosecutors maintain great discretion in jurisdictions that use grand jury hearings. They are the only legal officers permitted in the room when grand jury members consider evidence.[25] Prosecutors assess what types of evidence will be presented to grand juries, which undoubtedly influences grand jury decisions to indict. The absence of defendants during grand jury hearings typically works to their disadvantage, as does the low level of proof required (probable cause) for an indictment. Other factors influencing the outcomes of grand jury hearings include the need for only one-half to two-thirds of grand juror votes to find probable cause in most states, the permissible use of hearsay evidence in grand jury deliberations, and the effective screening practices on behalf of prosecutors who drop cases they perceive as unworthy of grand jury consideration. In light of these variables, it is understandable why a grand jury indictment is referred to as little more than a rubber stamp.[26] While the advantages provided to the prosecution by no means exemplify overt racism, the disproportionate number of minority defendants, particularly African Americans, entering our courts is most directly affected.

CHECKPOINT

- Preliminary and grand jury hearings are designed to ensure that there is enough evidence to proceed in a case against the accused.

ARRAIGNMENT

An **arraignment** is the step in criminal case processing when the accused is formally notified of the charges against them, and they enter a plea. At an arraignment, defendants enter a plea, pretrial motions are offered, and **discovery** may occur. Discovery is the sharing of information among the attorneys with the goal of helping attorneys adequately prepare their cases. None of these steps has proven challenging with regard to multiculturalism. Nevertheless, one must remember that the use of discretion inherent during the arraignment and throughout all stages of adjudication could pose problems for underrepresented groups entering our courts.

It is not until the arraignment that felony defendants enter a plea. As noted earlier, misdemeanor processing is more informal than felony processing. Thus, defendants charged with a misdemeanor often have their cases disposed of more quickly. Many individuals charged with a misdemeanor enter a plea upon first entering the court. Felony cases are typically more formal; a defendant's case may come up in court several times prior to the individual entering a plea.

Defendants typically enter one of three pleas during the arraignment: guilty, not guilty, or *nolo contendere*. Most who enter our courts enter a guilty plea after having engaged in **plea bargaining**, or an exchange between the prosecution and defense which would encourage a guilty plea in exchange for a benefit for the defendant. Defendants sometimes enter a plea of *nolo contendere*, or "no contest," which has the legal effect of a guilty plea. Defendants may choose to enter a plea of *nolo contendere* instead of admitting guilt in attempt to cooperate with the court (through essentially pleading guilty), but they do not wish to directly admit guilt. Pleading "no contest" is sometimes done in cases in which a forthcoming civil trial may occur between the defendant and the victim and/or their family. The civil trial would be brief and perhaps unnecessary if a defendant had earlier admitted guilt in criminal court, as evidence used in the criminal court case (e.g., the admission of guilt) could be introduced in the civil case. Defendants sometimes enter a *nolo contendere* plea out of principle; they do not believe they are guilty, yet they are attracted to the benefits of the plea bargaining negotiations. Defendants may stand mute or refuse to recognize the court, which is typically done when one is protesting the actions of the criminal justice system. The court recognizes standing mute as a "not guilty" plea.

Plea bargaining is continuously replacing the criminal trial. Pleading guilty facilitates case processing and rewards defendants. By eliminating the need for a trial through pleading guilty, defendants generally receive reduced sentences or other beneficial treatment by the court (e.g., a less-stigmatized type of crime). Roughly 90 to 95 percent of felony defendants plead guilty, many of whom are minorities. Similar to other steps of the adjudication process, there is evidence that African Americans are treated differently, for instance as they appear to be less likely than Whites to receive a reduced charge and shorter or reduced sentences.[27]

The level of justice inherent in plea bargaining is a topic of scholarly debate. To be sure, our court system would collapse if all defendants who entered a courtroom requested a jury trial or even a **bench trial** in which the judge serves as both judge and jury. Our court system simply does not have the resources to provide everyone a trial. Plea bargaining encourages certain individuals to admit guilt when they are innocent. Further, there's evidence of discriminatory practices with regard to the deals offered and the opportunities to engage in plea bargaining.[28] Defendants have no right to plea bargaining; it occurs only when both attorneys agree to an arrangement and a judge approves the deal.

Research regarding the impact of race on plea bargaining suggests that bias does exist. For instance, using data on plea bargaining in relation to misdemeanor marijuana cases, researchers found that, compared to Whites, Black defendants were less likely to be offered reduced charge offers, and Latino and Black defendants were more likely to receive custodial sentence offers. These disparities, however, were primarily explained through evidence, legal factors, court actor characteristics, and arrest circumstances. After removing these controls, Black defendants were still more likely than Whites to receive custodial sentence offers. Given the large role of plea bargaining, biases in this aspect of the court process have significant impacts on minority representation in prison and other correctional sanctions.[29]

Pleading not guilty means one is willing to go to trial. In preparation for the trial, attorneys may begin, at the arraignment, offering **pretrial motions**. These motions help ensure that each side's interests are recognized by the court. Among the more common motions are:

- Motion to dismiss—typically filed by the defense in hopes that the case will be dismissed, for example, based on due process violations or insufficient evidence.
- Motion to determine the competency of the accused to stand trial—designed to protect mentally ill persons from improperly being held responsible for their acts.
- Motion to suppress evidence obtained through an unlawful search or seizure—designed to protect a defendant's Fourth Amendment rights.
- Motion to suppress a confession, admissions, or other statements made to the police—protects against violation of the suspect's legal rights.
- Motion to require the prosecution to disclose the identity of a confidential informant—enables the defense to better understand the sources of information and evidence to be used against them.

- Motion for a change of venue—offered in attempt to relocate the setting for a trial with the goal of ensuring that a fair verdict can be rendered. This motion is sometimes offered in response to pretrial publicity.
- Motion for a continuance—provides attorneys more time to prepare their case.

These motions are presented to a judge and can be a determining factor in the outcome of a case. For example, should a judge deny a defendant's motion to suppress illegally obtained evidence, a defense attorney may wish to initiate plea negotiations since their likelihood of winning a case may be severely diminished. The discretion inherent in judicial decisions to grant or deny particular motions provides further evidence of the need for cultural awareness in the criminal justice system.

CHECKPOINT

- The primary functions of an arraignment are to allow the defendant to enter a plea, and begin entering pretrial motions if the case is headed to trial.

TRIALS

The events involved with criminal trials largely reflect our society's quest for justice. The formality associated with the criminal trial, including much of the symbolism found in the courtroom (e.g., the judge's robe and gavel), suggests that justice will be served. History suggests, however, that our courts suffer from several limitations, not the least of which is the desire of attorneys to "win" cases as opposed to finding justice. Further, there's evidence of the differential treatment of certain groups that enter our courts. While the modern-day criminal trial is certainly more civil than earlier forms of seeking justice, there is great room for improvement. For example, the substantial levels of prosecutorial and judicial discretion inherent in trials have, on occasion, generated ethical concerns and questions of misbehavior.

Judges and prosecutors play significant roles in the adjudicatory process. Judicial discretion is evident in many areas, especially in bench trials where judges serve as both judge and jury. Judges are also influential with regard to certain sentencing decisions, their directions to jurors, the decision to allow or disallow evidence to be introduced or objections to be acknowledged, and many other areas. Prosecutorial discretion at trial includes decisions such as whether or not to introduce particular pieces of evidence and whether continued case processing is warranted. Among the key decisions made by the defense at trial are whether or not to put the suspect on the stand and what type of defense, if any, they should offer. Defense attorneys represent the accused and typically don't have to prove much of anything; their client enters court under a presumption of innocence until proven guilty.

Trials involve a series of events (see Figure 12.1) that have generated controversy with regard to multiculturalism. Trials begin with the selection of jurors, followed by opening statements, the presentation of evidence, closing arguments, the judge's charge to the jury,

> Jury Selection → Opening Statements → Presentation of Evidence → Judge's Charges
> → Jury Deliberations → Verdict

FIGURE 12.1 Steps in a criminal trial

jury deliberations, and the jury offering a verdict. If found guilty, the defendant is sentenced or a sentencing hearing is scheduled for a later date.

JURY SELECTION

Jury selection has an influence on the outcome of many criminal trials. The selection of jurors and unethical jury behavior have unfortunately hampered the effectiveness of jury trials. For instance, we sometimes hear statements such as "he was convicted by an all-White jury," suggesting that race may have impacted the jury's decision. Further, as noted in Chapter 8, victim characteristics appear to influence jury decision-making. It is argued that Whites are more punitive in cases involving defendants of color,[30] especially when Whites constitute the majority of the jury.[31] A study of jury composition in North Carolina found that jury pools with greater numbers of White males were more likely to convict Black male defendants than White defendants. It was also noted that jury pools with higher proportions of Black males were more likely to acquit all defendants, especially Black men.[32]

There are many arguments for having diverse juries. To begin with, jury members from diverse backgrounds provide broader views and experiences, and are more reflective of the communities in which trials are conducted. Diverse juries also have the potential to sensitize other jury members to the potential for prejudice[33] and discourage attorneys from using stereotypical arguments and other biased arguments.[34] Further, excluding racial and ethnic minorities from serving on juries denies members of these groups the opportunity to participate in the judicial process and reduces their confidence in the legal system,[35] and diverse juries tend to deliberate longer and have higher quality discussions of cases than do all-White juries.[36] This occurs despite the fact that members of some groups (e.g., Asian Americans)[37] exhibit lower levels of participation during jury deliberations than members from other groups.

Controversy with regard to jury selection and multiculturalism exists primarily in the manner in which potential jurors are identified and the process of questioning jurors known as *voir dire*. A series of changes in jury selection practices attempted to overcome the historical underrepresentation of minorities and other groups; however, racial discrimination in the selection of jurors remains problematic.[38]

CONSTRUCTING THE VENIRE

States use various means to assemble a jury pool, or **venire**, from which prospective jurors will be selected and questioned. Voter registration lists are most commonly used, and are often supplemented with driver's license lists, automobile registration lists, and property tax rolls. The **Federal Jury Selection and Service Act of 1968** prohibited the exclusion of individuals based on religion, race, gender, national origin, or economic status. The ability of currently used lists to adequately provide a cross-section of society has been questioned by scholars. Minorities and low-income individuals are less likely than their counterparts to be identified for jury selection, as they are less likely to own property or cars, be registered voters, or have a driver's license. Further, minorities and the poor are more likely than their counterparts to switch residences[39]; thus, they are less likely to receive a **summons**, a document informing an individual of their call to jury duty.

An example of the limitations of current jury selection practices is found in research in a southeastern district in the United States, which noted that the selection process systematically Whitened juries, which produced frequently all-White juries or ones that contained only one minority member. It was noted that the limitations associated with minority groups receiving summonses were the primary reason, a problem that was compounded by racial disparities in the use of peremptory strikes and removals for cause. The researcher suggested the use of a broader range of sources to identify potential jurors, encouraging or requiring employers to pay full days' wages to those who are called to jury duty, and addressing language barriers to assist those for whom English is a second language.[40] Consideration and the implementation of these practices widens the pool of potential jurors and increases the likelihood of adequate representation of all groups.

Those targeted for potentially serving on a jury are required to report to a particular location on a specified date for jury duty. At this point, names will be randomly selected and prospective jurors will be instructed to report to a specific courtroom for questioning

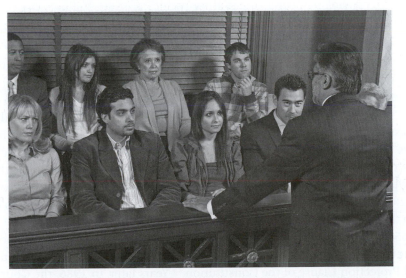

Jury selection is an integral part of the adjudication process. In light of claims that juries lack diversity, efforts have been made to ensure greater representation of members from all groups on juries.

regarding their suitability to serve. Accordingly, not all who are included in the venire will be selected for participation on a jury. Potential jurors may not even make it to *voir dire*, and others will be excused following *voir dire*. Some will be excluded due to legal stipulations surrounding participation on a jury. Virtually all states have provisions requiring jurors to be U.S. citizens, residents of the locality, a certain minimum age, and able to understand English.[41] Most states do not permit convicted felons or insane persons from serving. Certain states maintain statutory exemptions for select individuals (e.g., government officials, lawyers) who are excused.[42] These restrictions have implications for creating culturally diverse juries. Excluding those unable to understand English, non–U.S. citizens, and convicted felons (who are disproportionately minority) all pose problems in a multicultural society. It is argued that all jury venires should be reflective of the community in efforts to select more representative juries. Some judges require this, and those that do not, it is argued, should insist upon it.[43]

VOIR DIRE

Voir dire is the final step in jury selection. During this process, prospective jurors are questioned by a judge and/or attorneys to determine their suitability for serving on a jury. The questioning seeks to identify whether jurors have any familiarity with the primary actors in the case, the individual's beliefs or attitudes regarding specific issues that may arise in the trial, and any other matters that may influence the prospective juror's ability to render a fair decision in the case. Unsuitable jurors are dismissed by the defense attorney or the prosecution during *voir dire* via one of two manners: challenges for cause and peremptory challenges. These options are designed to promote the assemblage of an unbiased jury.

Attorneys who wish to eliminate a juror because of an identifiable bias, or a juror's apparent inability to judge a case fairly, file a **challenge for cause** motion. The judge rules on the motion and, if sustained, the prospective juror is dismissed. Judges assessing the appropriateness of a challenge for cause demonstrates the presence of judicial discretion in jury selection. **Peremptory challenges**, on the other hand, generate much greater controversy with regard to multiculturalism in U.S. courts.

Peremptory challenges, similar to challenges for cause, enable attorneys to eliminate seemingly unfit or inappropriate members of the jury pool. Attorneys typically do not need to justify using a peremptory challenge. They are provided an unlimited number of challenges for cause, but they are limited in the number of peremptory challenges they can use. Controversy surrounds the use of peremptory challenges, leading author David Neubauer to state that "based on hunch, prejudice, knowledge of psychology, or pseudoscience, attorneys use peremptory strikes—without having to give a reason—to eliminate the jurors they feel might not vote for their side."[44]

In 1965 the Supreme Court ruled in *Swain v. Alabama* that a prosecutor who used peremptory challenges to remove all six African Americans in the jury pool did not violate the Equal Protection Clause of the Constitution.[45] Years later, in 1986, the Court ruled in *Batson v. Kentucky* that a prosecutor's use of peremptory challenges may not include the dismissal of members of the jury pool based solely on their race.[46] The Court ruled that doing so was in violation of the Equal Protection Clause found in the Fourteenth Amendment. Despite the positive intentions of the *Batson* decision to enhance jury selection practices, the decision hasn't eliminated the use of race-based peremptory strikes.[47] In *Batson* the Court sought to retain a great deal of the freedom inherent in peremptory challenges, while excluding challenges based strictly on race. In turn, attorneys have much freedom in their use of peremptory challenges as courts must accept any explanation for exclusion that is not race-based.[48]

Additional Supreme Court cases[49] following *Batson* have sought to prevent the use of peremptory challenges as a means of violating the Equal Protection Clause; however, there is evidence that the challenges continue to be used in a discriminatory manner.[50] Minorities continue to be excluded from juries, as lawyers offer spurious reasons for the dismissal of minority individuals.[51] In discussing the jury selection practices as a barrier to the participation of racial and ethnic minority in trials, Professor Jennifer Hunt noted: "Despite the prohibition on race-based peremptory challenges, there is considerable evidence that they continue to be used in a discriminatory manner."[52] As a result, there is an overrepresentation of White middle- and upper-class jurors and an underrepresentation of the poor and racial minorities.[53]

Recent reform in the pretrial stages of adjudication, such as reconsideration of the sources via which potential jurors are identified, has reduced discrimination, and it has become less likely that minority defendants will be tried by an all-White jury.[54] Attorneys seek to assemble a jury that will view a case according to the attorney's interest. Put simply, jury selection is sometimes more about winning a case than seeking justice. To be sure, discrimination exists with regard to both prosecutors and defense attorneys, as the practices of using peremptory challenges to eliminate minorities from a jury pool could just as easily be used to eliminate Whites from a jury. The bottom line is that racial, ethnic, and cultural considerations are prevalent in jury selection. Such is the nature of seeking justice in a multicultural society.

THE BODY OF THE TRIAL

Scarce scholarly attention has addressed multiculturalism as it pertains to select steps of a trial. Limited attention has focused on the impact of various cultural groups with regard to opening statements, the presentation of the evidence, closing arguments, and the judge's charge to the jury. These important stages often impact the outcome of criminal cases.

Once the trial stage is set, attorneys offer opening statements. The prosecution typically offers the initial opening statement to the jury (or the judge, depending on whether it's a bench or jury trial), followed by the defense. It could be argued that being permitted to make the "first impression" with the jury is an unfair advantage for the prosecution. However, someone has to go first, and the prosecution seems suitable given their task of having to prove guilt. Opening statements permit attorneys to outline their case for the jury.

Potential obstacles for attorneys during opening statements include understanding the background of the jury and being able to effectively speak in comprehensible terms.

Attorneys are encouraged to avoid "legal speak" and to recognize that the jury may not have a large working vocabulary. These suggestions hold true throughout all stages of a trial.

Both the prosecution and the defense present evidence following opening statements. The presentation of evidence can be controversial in several ways. Some public defenders don't have the resources to thoroughly investigate their cases. As mentioned earlier, public defenders are often overworked and have limited resources. The impact of their situation may be evident during the presentation of the evidence. For instance, technology is influencing our courtrooms, and those with greater resources can sway juries with impressive technology-based presentations. Limited resources also hamper a public defender's ability to locate witnesses or to obtain other helpful information.

Notable judicial and attorney discretion exists with regard to the presentation of evidence. For example, judges may allow or disallow particular pieces of evidence to be introduced. Legal guidelines certainly assist with judicial discretion, as judges must abide by a code of conduct. The failure of judges to properly use their discretion, for example regarding the introduction of key evidence, can be grounds for a case to undergo appeal. Cases are sometimes won or lost depending on a judge's decision regarding the introduction of key pieces of evidence.

Among the many decisions they face at trial, defense attorneys must decide whether or not to put the defendant on the stand. Juries would seemingly like to hear from the defendant,[55] but it may not be strategically advantageous for the defense if the defendant is not an effective communicator. Defense attorneys should assess both at trial and during *voir dire* whether or not a jury will be receptive to their client. Cultural differences could certainly influence whether or not a defendant takes the stand.

At trial, defendants offer one of two defenses. They may offer an **alibi** that suggests that they did not commit the crime (e.g., they were in another location at the time of the crime), or defendants may also offer an **affirmative defense**, in which they admit to committing the action in question but assert that they have legal justification for having done so. Entering an affirmative defense requires defendants to demonstrate that their action was justified. Self-defense, insanity, coercion, and entrapment are affirmative defenses. Although not widely used, the defense "**Black rage**" attempts to provide legal justification for criminal behavior by some African Americans frustrated by oppression resulting from living in a White-dominated society.

Closing arguments are offered once the defense and prosecution present their evidence and cross-examination of that evidence is completed. Closing arguments allow attorneys to make a final impression on the jury by recapping their arguments.

Following closing arguments, the judge prepares the **charge to the jury**, a written document that explains how the law applies to the case. Charges to the jury are typically assembled in an informal conference involving the judge and trial attorneys. The charge generally:

- Reminds the jury of the prosecution's responsibility to prove guilt beyond a reasonable doubt
- Provides procedural directions for deliberations

- Identifies evidence that may or may not be considered during deliberations
- Lists the options of verdicts for jury consideration

Cultural differences and general familiarity with trial procedure and the law are of importance at this point. It is important for judges to provide clearly defined and readable instructions for jury members. Scholars have questioned the ability of jurors to clearly understand the directions provided by judges.[56] In turn, there have been calls for improving jury instructions. Providing visual aids to jury members[57] and offering instructions in multiple languages are among the suggestions for improvement.

Juries leave the courtroom and begin deliberating upon receiving the judge's instructions. A foreperson is elected by the jury, or one is appointed by the court prior to deliberations. This individual presides over jury deliberations and ultimately reads the verdict in the courtroom. One stronghold of jury deliberations is the secrecy involved. No outsiders are permitted in deliberations. The secrecy prohibits much understanding of the dynamics involved in deliberations. What we know about jury deliberations comes mostly from mock juries, interviews of jurors following their dismissal, and the questions asked during deliberations.[58] Research on jury decision-making suggests that jurors are sometimes influenced by implicit biases with regard to minority defendants.[59] Such biases are subtle, making them difficult to identify or address.

Unanimity is not necessary in non-capital cases although most jurisdictions require it. Federal cases must be unanimous. It can be challenging to have a group of strangers from various cultural backgrounds come to agreement. Juries may be requested to further deliberate if they cannot initially reach a verdict, or a judge may rule the case a mistrial, causing preparation for a new trial with new jurors to begin. Juries sometimes fail to reach agreement due to **jury nullification**, which is the practice of jurors acquitting particular defendants despite strong evidence suggesting guilt.

JURY NULLIFICATION

Jury members are charged with assessing the facts of the case and rendering a verdict. Juries are permitted to acquit even when the facts of the case suggest they convict in what is known as **jury nullification**. Jury nullification enables the community to actively participate in criminal law enforcement. It is rooted in English common law,[60] and is sometimes used in cases where the jury believes a prosecutor enforced an unpopular law or a jury sympathizes with the defendant. Jury nullification has become controversial as several prominent African American scholars encouraged Blacks to acquit other Blacks due to perceived mistreatment of African Americans by the courts and, more generally, the criminal justice system.

Former U.S. attorney Paul Butler commented on the power involved with jury nullification. He suggested that African American jurors should consider jury nullification in cases involving victimless, nonviolent offenses (e.g., drug possession). He argued that White jurors have historically engaged in jury nullification, and that Black jurors should follow suit. He adds that jury nullification would generate controversy and call into question the existing problems in the use of juries. Such attention could lead to methods of correcting the injustices faced by African Americans and other minorities.[61] Butler's comments are controversial and have generated critical responses. It is argued that race-based jury nullification further damages race relations, has moral implications, and generates greater racial discrimination.[62]

ENHANCING JURY TRIALS

The limitations inherent in the selection of juries have led to suggestions of alternatives, or enhancements of current practices. Professional juries, which involve full-time, trained, salaried professional jurors, purportedly address many of the problems associated with the use of laypersons serving as jurors. Professional jurors would provide the benefits of dependability, knowledge, and equity. Allowing jury members to write notes during the trial and participate more in trials by posing questions to witnesses are also feasible options for enhancing jury trials. Some California courts present jurors with notebooks containing trial exhibits and legal papers to help them render a fair verdict.[63] Other courts provide legal instructions to jurors before trial, instead of at the conclusion of the trial, to enable them to better understand their roles.

The need for effective verbal and nonverbal communication is evident throughout the trial. Attorneys must be clear and concise when addressing the court, especially in communication with jurors who have limited experience in legal terminology or courtroom procedures. As noted earlier, communication is largely conveyed nonverbally. Accordingly, the ability to speak clearly and "visually appeal" to those in the courtroom are important. This point should be noted by defense attorneys who should prepare their clients for trial, but preparing defendants for trial is much easier said than done. Defendants are often unfamiliar with legal terminology and the overall legal culture of the courtroom. Enhanced use of interpreters and an overall needs assessment related to enhancing jury practices would help.

Much of the needed change with regard to trials and, more generally, our criminal justice system stems from the misuse of individual discretion. As evidenced throughout this book, discretion is inherent in the criminal justice system. Although most criminal justice professionals use their discretion in a very professional manner, there remains controversy when one makes decisions that appear to, or are intended to, negatively impact certain groups.

CHECKPOINT

- Jury trials involve a series of steps designed to determine the fate of the accused. Jury nullification can impact trials, and several suggestions have been offered to improve trials.
- Selecting a representative, objective jury is important for the administration of justice.
- Several steps are taken to ensure that the venire is reflective of the community in which the case is being heard.

- The body of the trial involves the presentation of evidence.
- Jury nullification enables community members to express their views regarding specific laws and/or policies.
- Assisting jurors with the trial process has much potential to improve the adjudication process.

SENTENCING

What purposes are to be served through criminal sentences? The primary purposes of criminal sanctions include offender rehabilitation, retribution, deterrence, and incapacitation. **Rehabilitation** involves attempts to "cure" or "fix" the ills leading to the offender's behavior. **Retribution**, or punishment, adopts the "eye for an eye" approach. **Deterrence** seeks to dissuade the offender (specific deterrence) or society in general (general deterrence) from engaging in acts for which the offender is being punished. **Incapacitation** involves physically preventing one from committing similar criminal acts in the future. Incarceration is the most widely used form of incapacitation. Each sentence has a purpose or perhaps several purposes. For instance, a judge who orders an offender to life in prison without the possibility of parole is intent on incapacitation and retribution. The drug offender who receives treatment is targeted for rehabilitation.

Does our justice system treat various groups differently? The answer to that question largely depends on who is asked. A 2016 Gallup poll found that over three-fourths (76 percent) of Blacks noted that the American justice system is biased against Blacks, yet only 45 percent of Whites concurred.[64] Historically, the groups most affected by the courts are the ones most likely to be critical of justice-based practices.

DISCRIMINATORY SENTENCING?

Early research on the sentencing of minorities suggested discrimination in the types of sentences and sentence severity, but recent research produced conflicting findings. For example, the research literature provides conflicting results regarding the possibility of discrimination regarding Native Americans sentenced in court. Several studies find that Blacks receive harsher sentences than Whites, while other findings suggest that the opposite is true. Still, some findings suggest no differences in sentencing practices with regard to race.

If sentencing practices are unbiased, why is there disparity in the percentages of minorities entering our prisons? An obvious response to this question concerns socioeconomic status. While race may not be evident in sentencing decisions, one's socioeconomic status certainly influences the likelihood of being punished. The disparity with which minorities are punished in our courts is explained, in large part, by unfavorable social conditions faced by many minorities. Further, the structures under which individuals are sentenced appear to unfavorably influence poor minorities. Thus, discrimination may not be evident in the actions of those imposing sentences; instead it may be located within the structural components of criminal sentencing. In commenting on how we can move forward with regard to sentencing practices, Professor Cassia Spohn noted: "Theoretically informed and methodologically rigorous research identifying the racial effects of charging and sentencing policies and practices is critically important to efforts to reform the system and reduce racial disparities and disproportionality."[65]

SENTENCING STRUCTURES

Sentencing is perhaps the most controversial aspect of courtroom practices, primarily because of the extensive amount of discretion inherent in this part of criminal case processing. We can easily view the penalties received by various individuals in relation to their demographics, the crime(s) they committed, and their criminal history. Historically, judges maintained wide latitude in sentencing practices. Beginning in the late 1960s and early 1970s conservatives and liberals, albeit for different reasons, agreed that sentencing reform was needed. The indeterminate sentencing structure that existed provided too much discretion. Both liberals and conservatives agreed consistency was needed, as conservatives pointed to judges giving sentences that were too lenient, while liberals believed punishments were too harsh. It was agreed that determinate sentencing would reduce disparity and alleviate discrimination.[66]

A number of states have adopted **determinate sentencing** practices that involve offenders receiving a specific amount of time to be served based on the crime for which they were convicted. Determinate sentencing differs from indeterminate sentencing, which relies on parole board determinations regarding an offender's readiness for reentry to society. Instead of relying on discretionary release from a parole board, offenders processed in jurisdictions using mandatory release are free to leave prison upon expiration of their sentence minus "good time." **Good time** is time taken off a prison sentence for good behavior. Determinate sentencing was designed to reduce discretion in the courts and help ensure equal treatment for all.

Since the 1980s legislatures have created commissions to look into sentencing practices. Among the developments are **sentencing guidelines**, which are used by some states. The guidelines provide a risk assessment of the offender based on current offense and past history. The ultimate goal is to ensure justice with limited discretion. However, sentencing guidelines prompt controversy due to the belief that they are harsh, haven't reduced disparities, and are too rigid and complex.[67] The federal government introduced sentencing guidelines in 1984; however, it ceased using them following the U.S. Supreme Court's 2005 decision in *United States v. Booker*.[68] In *Booker*, the Court noted that the guidelines violated the Sixth Amendment and made the guidelines advisory, meaning that federal judges must consider, but are not required to use, them. State guidelines are less controversial than the federal provisions, as states have made adjustments to accommodate particular cases and provide judges a sense of discretion as needed.

Sentencing guidelines appear to shift discretion from judges to prosecutors, who determine the charges. Consideration of prior criminal record in sentencing guidelines leaves minorities at a disadvantage compared to nonminorities, who are less likely to have a criminal history.[69]

Legislators responded to public sentiment that prison sentences are too lenient by imposing **mandatory minimum sentencing**. Mandatory minimums require offenders convicted of certain offenses to be sentenced to prison for no less than a specified term of years, and nonprison sentences (e.g., probation) are not an option. Mandatory minimum sentences are typically imposed on violent offenders. Similar to sentencing guidelines, mandatory minimum sentencing has generated criticism. African Americans are disproportionately convicted under these laws, primarily due to their overrepresentation in drug offenses and the disparity in sentences given to offenses involving crack cocaine.[70] "Three strikes and you're out" penalties have been the topic of much controversy with regard to sentencing practices.

Between 1993 and 1995 many states imposed varied versions of **"three strikes and you're out"** sentencing targeted toward repeat offenders. The legislation demonstrates the public's disdain for crime and an attempt to target those who seem undeterred by criminal law and punishment. Three-strikes laws vary among the states that use them, with offenders in certain jurisdictions facing life sentences following a third felony. The idea behind the legislation and its application are popular, yet implementation of the legislation has posed several problems, especially for minorities.[71] One researcher commented on the "draconian results" associated with the penalties, in which some offenders have received notably stringent penalties for minor offenses.[72] Further, one cannot ignore the influence of the legislation on many offenders who are aging out of crime and don't commit a third offense until late in their criminal careers. The costs associated with the laws are also problematic as offenders serve longer sentences. Further, three-strikes laws arguably increase the risks for police officers as "two-strike" defendants being pursued by officers may be willing to attempt escape at all costs.[73]

In his article "The Impact of Federal Sentencing Reforms on African Americans," author Marvin D. Free Jr. commented on the influences of sentencing practices in stating that "neither mandatory minimum sentences nor the guidelines have been effective in eliminating racial disparity in sentencing in federal court."[74] The disparity is affected by drug laws, especially with regard to crack cocaine. Selective law enforcement on the streets also impacts the disparity.[75] Recent sentencing reform involving determinate sentencing and sentencing guidelines has reduced the likelihood of overt discrimination in the courts, yet discriminatory sentencing practices have not disappeared.

There are various reasons why African American and Hispanic defendants receive harsher penalties than their White counterparts. First, differences in sentence severity could be explained by African Americans and Hispanics committing more serious crimes, and having more serious criminal histories than Whites. They could be explained through economic discrimination, with poor defendants (typically minorities) receiving differential treatment in the courts. Third, blatant racial or ethnic discrimination on behalf of those involved in sentencing could explain the disparity. Or, the disparities could be due to contextual discrimination in the sense that minorities are treated differently upon being sentenced for certain crimes (e.g., violent crimes).[76] Each explanation has merit, and combined they largely explain the disparity in sentencing. The first argument, that minorities commit more serious crimes and are thus punished more severely than Whites, is the only one of the four that doesn't involve some form of discrimination.

Disparities and discrimination evident in the sentencing of minorities to the death penalty are covered in Chapter 3 of this book. As suggested earlier, evidence suggests that racial minorities have disproportionately received capital punishment. Accordingly, in his book *No Equal Justice*, author David Cole states, "Virtually every study of race and the death penalty has concluded that, all other things being equal, defendants who kill

White victims are much more likely to receive the death penalty than those who kill Black victims."[77] This statement is supported by others; for instance, as one researcher noted, the existing research suggests that jurors often make more punitive judgments of defendants from other ethnic and racial groups, and are more likely to impose death sentences in cases involving White victims and Black or Latino defendants.[78] Recent efforts to reform the application of the death penalty, beginning with the 1972 Supreme Court case *Furman v. Georgia*,[79] provide perhaps the best evidence of the discrepancies found in its application.

Sentencing reform efforts are further noted by the federal government passing the Formerly Incarcerated Reenter Society Transformed Safety Transitioning Every Person Act, or **FIRST STEP Act** in 2018. The legislation was created to address sentencing concerns and help ensure that released offenders do not recidivate. The legislation permitted about 2,600 offenders serving life sentences for crack cocaine convictions the chance to petition the court for a reduced sentence, and allowed federal judges to not adhere to mandatory minimum sentencing guidelines for offenders who had no criminal histories. Among other provisions, the act also eased the severity of the federal "three strikes" rule. In particular, the mandatory life sentence penalty was changed to a twenty-five-year sentence, and serious drug felonies that previously warranted an automatic twenty-year minimum sentence were reduced to fifteen years.[80] The legislation disproportionately impacted certain groups, as over 91 percent of the individuals whose sentences were reduced in the four months after the Act was passed were African American, and 98 percent were male.

The preceding discussion of multiculturalism and sentencing, and more generally our court system, has focused primarily on African Americans and Hispanics. This is not to disregard the plight of many other underrepresented groups who enter our courts. The research in this area, especially with regard to sentencing, focuses primarily on Blacks, with less information on Hispanics and even less information on other groups.

CHECKPOINT

- The primary functions of sentences include retribution, deterrence, rehabilitation, and incapacitation.
- There is conflicting evidence with regard to whether certain groups receive more favorable sentences than others.

- Various efforts have been made to ensure fairness in sentencing, and to ensure that habitual offenders serve more punitive sentences.

APPELLATE COURTS

Defendants have the right to appeal following their conviction. Defendants also have the right to counsel during the appellate stage. Accordingly, U.S. courts can be categorized based on their trial and appellate jurisdiction. Among other functions, appellate courts help protect defendants' rights according to state or federal constitutions, criminal court procedural law, and substantive law.

Most criminal cases do not involve an appeal given the large percentage of cases settled by plea bargaining. Defendants forfeit their right to appeal following the admission of guilt. Appeals involve the legal aspects of the trial, often focusing on issues such as the introduction of illegally seized evidence, improper jury instructions, and denial of counsel or a fair trial.[81]

Many of the same limitations faced by underrepresented groups in the trial court jurisdiction appear in the appellate court system. Discretion is inherent in the appellate process, and historical evidence suggests that groups have received differential treatment. For example, researchers found that a defendant's race significantly influenced an appellate court's decision to uphold a trial court's decision in which a judge departed from the sentence recommended by guidelines.[82]

High levels of judicial and attorney discretion exist in the appellate courts. For instance, discretion is involved with appellate court judges determining the significance of alleged errors at trial. The **harmless error doctrine** holds that a trial court decision will not be overturned based on small, insignificant errors that appear to have small or no impact on the trial. The term "harmless" is certainly subjective and open to interpretation by appellate judges.

CHECKPOINT

- Appellate courts provide oversight for trial courts. Many of the same challenges faced by underrepresented groups in trial courts exist in appellate courts.

MULTICULTURALISM AND COURTROOM PERSONNEL

Thus far this chapter has focused predominantly on the role of underrepresented groups who enter our courts. What about members of the various cultural groups working in our courts? Have minorities assimilated into the courtroom workgroup? Are they treated differently? Do they act in contrast to others? Progress has been made toward increasing the diversity of those working in our court system. Affirmative action programs have increased the presence of historically underrepresented groups, and it is anticipated that greater representation is forthcoming.

The lack of diversity working in the courts is well documented in the research literature. Systematic discrimination targeting females and minorities in the legal arena has been endemic in the United States.[83] Such discrimination has occurred formally, for instance via the choices and actions of courts, legislatures, law schools, and bar associations to disallow or discourage minorities from entering the legal profession, and informally through mistreating minorities in the legal field.[84]

Despite much progress, females and members of some racial and ethnic groups remain underrepresented as judges. For instance, in 2017, only about 32 percent of judges were female, and Hispanics or Latinos (6.7 percent) and Asians (1.2 percent) were underrepresented relative to their presence in the U.S. population. Blacks or African Americans constituted about 13 percent of judges, which is about representative of their presence in the United States.[85] These percentages suggest that greater diversity is needed on the bench. Further disparity exists with regard to the percentages of lawyers. Only about 6.1 percent of lawyers were Hispanic in 2017, followed by African American (5.5 percent) and Asian (4.9 percent) attorneys. Females (37.4 percent) were also underrepresented.[86] The percentages of women and minority associates and partners at law firms have grown over time, although these groups still remain underrepresented in these positions.[87]

Why are minorities underrepresented as professionals in the courts? Edward Chen, the first Asian Pacific American judge appointed to the federal bench for the Northern District of California—despite the significant number of Asian Pacific Americans in the area— noted that the lack of diversity in the judiciary is attributable to several factors. Prominent among the factors are the lack of diversity in the pool of experienced attorneys, the influences of political ties negatively affecting minorities, the limited access of networking for minorities, and overall hampered career opportunities.[88]

Progress has been made in diversifying the courts, particularly the federal courts. During his terms in office, President Barack Obama made great efforts to diversify the federal courts. Roughly 60 percent of his appointments were non-White males. As of 2014, there were ten openly gay judges on the federal bench, all of whom were appointed by President Obama.

Why do we need greater diversity in the courts? To begin with, greater diversity promotes greater cultural sensitivity and comprehension of the varied issues addressed in the courts. Courtroom personnel may be able to recognize differences within their objective context, as opposed to at face value. Further, greater diversity promotes respect for the courts from underrepresented groups. Minorities are more likely than Whites to view

MULTICULTURALISM IN THE WORKFORCE

Failing to promote a multicultural workforce is costly in many aspects. The courts play an integral role in ensuring that employees are treated in a fair and just manner both within and outside of the criminal justice system. Several cases highlight the important role of the courts in ensuring diversity and equal treatment in the workforce, including one involving the large brokerage firm Merrill Lynch. The company agreed to pay $160 million to settle a racial bias lawsuit originated by a longtime broker of the company who accused the company of providing better opportunities and more compensation for White employees. The case grew to include over 1,200 brokers.

In a different case, New Jersey Transit, which is the state's public transportation organization, agreed to pay $3.65 million to settle a racial discrimination lawsuit. The suit was filed by seven current and former employees who claimed that they were subjected to racial insults by supervisors. The plaintiffs claimed that they were paid less than their White coworkers and were victims of unfair treatment while working for the organization. The agreement to settle the case came less than four years after New Jersey Transit spent $5.8 million to settle a similar discrimination lawsuit filed by minority police officers who were employed by the organization.

In 2019, Google agreed to settle a class-action lawsuit that alleged age bias. The company was accused of systematically discriminating against older people, and agreed to pay $11 million to more than two hundred job seekers over age forty who had applied for and were denied positions with the company. As part of the settlement, Google will be required to train management and employees regarding age bias, create a committee that focuses on age diversity, and ensure that age-related complaints are fully investigated. Other companies, such as Facebook and IBM, have also been accused of age discrimination, a phenomenon that appears to recently be part of the employment climate regardless of industry.[89]

Unfortunately, these are but a few of the many cases in which workers must rely on the law to ensure a safe and bias-free workplace.

the courts with apprehension. Past discriminatory practices could be mended, in part, if it appeared that our court system isn't primarily staffed with non-minorities. Used in this context, the term **"symbolic representation"** refers to making our courts more representative of all groups.[90] In other words, the perceived legitimacy of the courts would be enhanced through greater diversity among courtroom personnel.

There is also evidence that judges may be biased in their decision-making. For instance, researchers surveyed judges in a northeastern state in the United States regarding their beliefs as to why there exist racial disparities in the criminal justice system. In other words, they were asked why racial minorities are overrepresented in the system. Most judges attributed the disparities, in part, to differential treatment by judges and/or other criminal justice officials, while some attributed the disparities to the negative impacts of poverty and different offending rates among

Females and racial and ethnic minorities have increasingly assumed positions as attorneys and judges, yet they remain underrepresented in these key courtroom positions. Pictured is Supreme Court Justice Sonia Sotomayor.

racial groups.[91] The differential treatment explanation incorporates implicit and overt discrimination by those tasked with enforcing the law, including police officers, judges, prosecutors, and probation officers.[92] Still, other research analyzed approximately half a million court cases in Texas and found that the race or ethnicity of a judge was not related to sentencing decisions.[93]

As noted in Table 12.1, there are many organizations and associations that promote the interests of women and cultural/racial/ethnic groups in the courts. These organizations and associations provide workers opportunities to share concerns, issues, and related aspects of the job with officers of similar backgrounds from around the country.

Recent efforts to promote diversity on the bench have resulted in greater representation of minority judges and an opportunity to better understand the behaviors of minority judges in the courtroom. There is conflicting research regarding the practices of minority and nonminority judges. One study found that African American and White judges considered case and offender information similarly when imposing punishment decisions. Black judges were more likely than White judges to impose a prison sentence on both Black and White offenders. The more punitive approach taken by Black judges may be attributable to their perceptions of themselves as "tokens" or it may be that they maintain greater sensitivity to the harms associated with crime.[94]

TABLE 12.1   EXAMPLES OF ORGANIZATIONS AND ASSOCIATIONS PROMOTING INTERESTS OF WOMEN AND CULTURAL/RACIAL/ETHNIC GROUPS IN THE COURTS

American Bar Association Commission on Women in the Profession

American Bar Association Commission on Racial and Ethnic Diversity in the Profession

American Bar Association Council on Racial and Ethnic Justice

Hispanic National Bar Association

National Asian Pacific American Bar Association

National Conference of Women's Bar Association

National LGBT Bar Association

Native American Bar Association

National Association of Women Lawyers

Researchers found conflicting results when comparing the sentencing and incarceration practices of Black and White judges. White judges were more likely than Black judges to treat White defendants leniently. Little discrimination was found with regard to sentence severity. However, White judges treated Black and White defendants equally severely. Black judges treated Black defendants more leniently than White defendants.[95] With regard to gender, earlier research found that female judges were more likely than male judges to treat male and female defendants equally.[96]

Research on judicial practices in Detroit identified few differences with regard to race and judicial behavior. There were notable similarities in the sentencing practices of both Black and White judges, with race offering limited significant predictive powers with regard to judicial sentencing practices. It was found that both Black and White judges sentenced Black defendants more severely than their White counterparts.[97] The similarities in sentencing practices could be attributed to the judicial recruitment process, which produces a somewhat homogeneous judiciary with regard to judicial practices. The socialization practices of judges and others working in the criminal justice system certainly influence the behaviors of those in the field.[98]

Defendants should and do consider cultural factors in choosing a bench or jury trial. For instance, given public sentiment, an Arab-American charged with robbery shortly after the September 11, 2001, terrorist attacks may have had a better chance of receiving a fair trial absent a jury. However, one cannot discard the elevated level of judicial discretion inherent in bench trials. It is presumed that judges are better able than jurors to put aside personal beliefs in favor of professionalism.

CHECKPOINT

- Despite much progress, racial and ethnic minorities remain underrepresented as employees working within the courts.

SUMMARY

While this discussion of the U.S. court system and multiculturalism centers on criminal courts, one cannot overlook the accomplishments of federal civil courts in shaping state and local criminal justice practices with regard to diversity. Several areas of federal civil legislation have important consequences for criminal justice officials. The more significant legislation relates to:

- Civil rights violations, which enables individuals to sue civilly city or state employees who deprive them of their constitutional rights
- Equal employment opportunities, which prohibits discrimination based on race, color, religion, sex, age, or national origin
- Sex discrimination
- Discrimination against the disabled, which protects Americans with disabilities from discrimination in employment and the use of public facilities and services

Steven Vago, author of the book *Law and Society*, stated that "racism is embedded in the system and proponents recognize that its elimination is impossible but at the same time they insist that an ongoing struggle to countervail racism must be carried out."[99] To be sure, disparity and discrimination in the courtroom are not restricted to one's race; gender, ethnicity, culture, and socioeconomic factors influence discretionary practices at all stages of the system. As an example, minority women face special concerns upon entering the criminal justice system, particularly given their high rates of poverty and unemployment, and the increased likelihood of them being single parents. Unfortunately, the plight of minority women who enter our courts has been the subject of scant research efforts. What we do know about this group suggests differential treatment of minority women in the courts and throughout the criminal justice system.[100]

Much has changed in our courts, as numerous reforms directed at leveling the playing field for minorities and all groups have influenced courtroom practices and personnel. Nevertheless, much work remains. It is hoped that recognizing and highlighting the problems and accomplishments provides an impetus for continued progress.

YOU MAKE THE CALL
COURTROOM CONTROVERSY

Consider the following scenario. Debate the pros and cons of all options and decide what you would do.

You're a public defender assigned to represent a defendant who is charged with fifteen counts of animal cruelty involving the sacrificing of cats. The defendant claims the sacrifices were part of his religious practices, and he is not guilty of anything illegal. He cites his constitutional right to freedom of religion. Professionally, you have an obligation to provide appropriate representation for your client. Personally, you're an animal lover and have four cats. You're familiar with the judge presiding over this case. She also loves animals.

The prosecuting attorney in this case is a member of the People for the Ethical Treatment of Animals (PETA).

Questions

1. Does your client enter court at a disadvantage?
2. Will you be able to put aside your personal feelings and provide effective counsel for the accused?
3. Should you decline to defend the client (if possible) and/or request a new judge?
4. Do you encourage your client to plea bargain, request a bench trial, or take his chances with a jury trial?

KEY TERMS

affirmative defense

alibi

arraignment

assigned counsel

bench trial

Black rage

challenge for cause

charge to the jury

determinate sentencing

deterrence

discovery

Federal Jury Selection and Service Act of 1968

FIRST STEP Act

good time

grand jury hearing

harmless error doctrine

incapacitation

indictment

indigent defendant

initial appearance

jury nullification

mandatory minimum sentencing

nolo contendere

peremptory challenge

plea bargaining

preliminary hearing

pretrial motion

pretrial release

public defender

rehabilitation

retribution

sentencing guidelines

summons

symbolic representation

"three strikes and you're out" sentencing

venire

voir dire

DISCUSSION QUESTIONS

1. Identify and discuss the steps of the trial. Which step do you believe involves the greatest area of controversy with regard to discrimination? Why?

2. Identify how judicial, prosecutorial, and defense attorney discretion influences the outcome of court cases.

3. How are jurors selected? Does this process seem fair to you? Discuss why or why not.

4. How have recent sentencing reform efforts failed to eliminate disparity in sentencing? What steps would you take to improve sentencing practices?

5. Are racial and ethnic minorities adequately represented among the courtroom personnel? If not, what steps could be taken to diversify our courts?

FOR FURTHER READING

Baer, J. A., and L. F. Goldstein. *The Constitutional and Legal Rights of Women: Cases in Law and Social Change*, 3rd ed. New York: Oxford University Press, 2006.

Benforado, A. *Unfair: The New Science of Criminal Injustice*. New York: Crown, 2015.

Neubauer, D. W., and H. F. Fradella. *America's Courts and the Criminal Justice System*, 12th ed. Boston, MA: Cengage, 2017.

Ramirez, L. F., ed. *Cultural Issues in Criminal Defense*. Huntington, NY: Juris, 2010.

Walsh, A., and C. Hemmens. *Law, Justice, and Society*, 4th ed. New York: Oxford University Press, 2016.

NOTES

1. Jill Norgren and Serena Nanda, *American Cultural Pluralism and Law* (New York: Praeger, 1988), 1.
2. Ibid.
3. Norgren and Nanda, *American Cultural Pluralism.*
4. Gaye Tuchman, "Let's Hold Trials Here in Spanish," *New York Times,* August 28, 1979, A17.
5. Richard Willing, "Courts Asked to Consider Culture," *USA Today,* May 25, 2004, 3A.
6. Ibid.
7. Ibid.
8. B. A. Reaves, *Felony Defendants in Large Urban Counties, 2009—Statistical Tables.* U.S. Department of Justice, Bureau of Justice Statistics, 2013, NCJ 243777.
9. B. Kutateladze, V. Lynn, and E. Liang. *Do Race and Ethnicity Matter in Prosecution? A Review of Empirical Studies* (New York: The Vera Institute, 2012).
10. S. Walker, C. Spohn, and M. Delone, *The Color of Justice: Race, Ethnicity, and Crime in America,* 5th ed. (Belmont, CA: Wadsworth, 2012).
11. Gideon v. Wainwright, 372 U.S. 335 (1963).
12. Johnson v. Zerbst, 304 U.S. 458 (1938).
13. Frank Schmalleger, *Criminal Justice Today: An Introductory Text for the Twenty-First Century* (Upper Saddle River, NJ: Prentice Hall, 2005), 392–93.
14. Caroline W. Harlow, *Defense Counsel in Criminal Cases.* U.S. Department of Justice, Bureau of Justice Statistics, November 2000, NCJ 179023.
15. Bennett L. Gershman, "Themes of Injustice: Wrongful Convictions, Racial Prejudice, and Lawyer Incompetence," in Lisa Stolzenberg and Stewart J. D'Alessio (eds.), *Criminal Courts for the 21st Century* (Upper Saddle River, NJ: Prentice Hall, 1999), 360.
16. David Cole, *No Equal Justice: Race and Class in the American Criminal Justice System* (New York: The New Press, 1999), 89.
17. Ibid., 64.
18. Ibid., 76.
19. Walker et al., *The Color of Justice.*
20. Ibid.
21. T. Schlesinger, "Racial and Ethnic Disparity in Pretrial Criminal Processing," *Justice Quarterly* 22 (2005):170–92.
22. Victor E. Kappeler and Gary W. Potter, *The Mythology of Crime and Criminal Justice,* 4th ed. (Long Grove, IL: Waveland, 2005), 274.
23. K. B. Turner and James B. Johnson, "A Comparison of Bail Amounts for Hispanics, Whites, and African Americans: A Single County Analysis," *American Journal of Criminal Justice* 30, no. 1 (2005): 35–53.
24. M. T. Phillips, *Pretrial Detention and Case Outcomes. Part 2: Felony Cases* (New York: New York City Criminal Justice Agency, 2008); M. Sacks and A. R. Ackerman, "Bail and Sentencing: Does Pretrial Detention Lead to Harsher Punishment?" *Criminal Justice Policy Review* 25, no. 1 (2014): 59–77.
25. Ronald G. Burns, *The Criminal Justice System* (Upper Saddle River, NJ: Prentice Hall, 2007), 41.
26. D. W. Neubauer and S. S. Meinhold, *Judicial Process: Law, Courts, and Politics in the United States,* 7th ed. (Boston, MA: Cengage, 2017), 225.
27. L. Devers, *Plea and Charge Bargaining: Research Summary,* U.S. Department of Justice, Bureau of Justice Assistance, 2011, 3.

28. Walker et al., *The Color of Justice*; see 229–31 for discussion of race and plea bargaining decisions.

29. B. L. Kutateladze, N. R. Andiloro, and B. Johnson, "Opening Pandora's Box: How Does Defendant Race Influence Plea Bargaining?" *Justice Quarterly* 33, no. 3 (2016): 398–426.

30. S. R. Sommers, "Race and the Decision Making of Juries," *Legal and Criminological Psychology* 12, no. 2 (2007): 171–87.

31. M. Lynch and C. Haney, "Mapping the Racial Bias of the White Male Capital Juror: Jury Composition and the 'Emphatic Divide,'" *Law and Society Review* 45, no. 1 (2011): 69–102.

32. Francis X. Flanagan, "Race Gender, and Juries: Evidence from North Carolina," *Journal of Law and Economics*, 61 (2018): 189–214.

33. S. R. Sommers and O. O. Adekanmbi, "Race and Juries: An Experimental Psychology Perspective," in G. S. Park and S. Jones (eds.), *Critical Race Realism: Intersections of Psychology, Race, and Law* (New York: The New Press, 2008), 78–93.

34. H. Fukurai and R. Krooth, *Race in the Jury Box: Affirmative Action in Jury Selection* (Albany: State University of New York Press, 2003).

35. Ibid.

36. J. S. Hunt, "Race, Ethnicity, and Culture in Jury Decision Making," *Annual Review of Law and Social Science* 11 (2015): 269–88.

37. E. Y. Cornwell and V. P. Hans, "Representation Through Participation: A Multilevel Analysis of Jury Deliberations," *Law & Society Review* 45, no. 3 (2011): 667–98.

38. Cole, *No Equal Justice*, 101.

39. Ibid.

40. J. M. Gau, "A Jury of Whose Peers? The Impact of Selection Procedures on Racial Composition and the Prevalence of Majority-White Juries," *Journal of Crime and Justice* 39, no. 1 (2016): 75–87.

41. D. W. Neubauer and H. F. Fradella, *America's Courts and the Criminal Justice System* (Boston, MA: Cengage, 2017), 361.

42. Ibid.

43. P. A. Joy and K. C. McMunigal, "Racial Discrimination and Jury Selection," *Criminal Justice*, 31(2): 43–45.

44. Neubauer and Fradella, *America's Courts*, 363.

45. Swain v. Alabama, 380 U.S. 202 (1965).

46. Batson v. Kentucky, 476 U.S. 79 (1986).

47. Cole, *No Equal Justice*, 120; Joy and McMunigal, "Racial Discrimination and Jury Selection."

48. Ibid.

49. Edmonson v. Leesville Concrete Company, No. 89–7743, 500 U.S. 614 (Sup. Ct. 1991); Miller-El v. Dretke, No. 03–9659, 545 U.S. 231 (Sup. Ct. 2005); Snyder v. Louisiana, No. 06–10119, 552 U.S. 472 (Sup. Ct. 2007).

50. Hunt, "Race, Ethnicity, and Culture."

51. Gershman, "Themes of Injustice," 359.

52. Hunt, "Race, Ethnicity, and Culture"; Flanagan, "Race Gender, and Juries," 212.

53. Walker et al., *The Color of Justice*.

54. Ibid.

55. Burns, *The Criminal Justice System*, 56.

56. E.g., R. Dattu, "Illustrated Jury Instructions," *Judicature* 82, no. 2 (Sept./Oct. 1998): 79; see also W. D. Foglia, "They Know Not What They Do: Unguided and Misguided Discretion in Pennsylvania Capital Cases," *Justice Quarterly* 20, no. 1 (2003): 187–211.

57. Dattu, "Illustrated Jury Instructions."

58. Burns, *The Criminal Justice System*, 58.

59. J. Kang et al., "Implicit Bias in the Courtroom," *UCLA Law Review* 59 (2012): 1124–86.

60. Walker et al., *The Color of Justice.*

61. Paul Butler, "Racially Based Jury Nullification: Black Power in the Criminal Justice System," *The Yale Law Journal* 105, no. 3 (Dec. 1995): 677–725.

62. Randall Kennedy, *Race, Crime, and the Law* (New York: Vintage, 1997).

63. R. Willing, "Courts Try to Make Jury Duty Less of a Chore," *USA Today*, March 17, 2005, 17A–18A.

64. Frank Newport, "Public Opinion Context: Americans, Race and Police," Gallup, July 8, 2016. Available at: https://news.gallup.com/opinion/polling-matters/193586/public-opinion-context-americans-race-police.aspx

65. Cassia Spohn, "Race, Crime, and Punishment in the Twentieth and Twenty-First Centuries,", *Crime and Justice* 44, no. 1 (2015): 49–97, p. 92.

66. Neubauer and Fradella, *America's Courts.*

67. M. Tonry, "The Failure of U.S. Sentencing Commission's Guidelines," *Crime and Delinquency* 39 (1993): 131–49.

68. United States v. Booker, 543 U.S. 220 (2005).

69. Marvin D. Free Jr., "The Impact of Federal Sentencing Reforms on African Americans," *Journal of Black Studies* 28, no. 2 (1997): 268–86.

70. Ibid.

71. Cole, *No Equal Justice.*

72. Ibid., 147.

73. Ibid.

74. Free, "The Impact," 283–84.

75. Ibid.

76. Free, "The Impact," 286.

77. Cole, *No Equal Justice*, 132.

78. Hunt, "Race, Ethnicity, and Culture."

79. Furman v. Georgia, 408 U.S. 238, 245 (1972).

80. J. George, "What's Really in the First Step Act," *The Marshall Project*, November 16, 2018. Available at: https://www.themarshallproject.org/2018/11/16/what-s-really-in-the-first-step-act; K. Schallhorn, "What Is the First Step Act? Five Things to Know About the Criminal Justice Reform Law," Foxnews.com, December 19, 2019. Available at: https://www.foxnews.com/politics/what-is-first-step-act-5-things-to-know-about-the-criminal-justice-reform-law

81. Burns, *The Criminal Justice System*, 67–68.

82. J. J. Williams, "Predicting Decisions Rendered in Criminal Appeals," *Journal of Criminal Justice* 19 (1991): 463–69.

83. Mark S. Hurwitz and Drew Noble Lanier, "Explaining Judicial Diversity: The Differential Ability of Women and Minorities to Attain Seats on State Supreme and Appellate Courts," *State Politics and Policy Quarterly* 3, no. 4 (2003): 329.

84. Ibid.

85. Bureau of Labor Statistics, "Household Data Annual Averages," Table 11. Available at: https://www.bls.gov/cps/cpsa2018.pdf

86. Ibid.

87. A. Cuyler, "Diversity in the Practice of Law: How Far Have We Come?" *GP Solo* 29, no. 5 (2012). Accessed at: http://www.americanbar.org/publications/gp_solo/2012/september_october/diversity_practice_law_how_far_have_we_come.html

88. Edward M. Chen, "The Judiciary, Diversity, and Justice for All," *California Law Review* 91 (2003): 1109–24.

89. Jack Kelly, "The IBM Age Discrimination Lawsuit Sheds Light on a Harrowing Employment Trend," *Forbes.com*. Accessed August 19, 2019, at: https://www.forbes.com/sites/jackkelly/2018/09/18/the-ibm-age-discrimination-lawsuit-will-shed-light-on-this-harrowing-trend/#6a33058c5ce1; Jack Kelly, "Google Settles Age Discrimination Lawsuit, Highlighting the Proliferation of Ageism in Hiring, *Forbes.com*. Accessed August 19, 2019, at: https://www.forbes.com/sites/jackkelly/2019/07/23/google-settles-age-discrimination-lawsuit-highlighting-the-proliferation-of-ageism-in-hiring/#37808d55c67d

90. Susan Welch, Michael Combs, and John Gruhl, "Do Black Judges Make a Difference?" *American Journal of Political Science* 32, no. 1 (1988): 126–36.

91. M. Clair and A. S. Winter, "How Judges Think About Racial Disparities: Situational Decision-Making in the Criminal Justice System," *Criminology* 54, no. 2 (2016): 332–59.

92. K. Beckett, K. Nyrop, and L. Pfingst, "Race, Drugs, and Policing: Understanding Disparities in Drug Delivery Arrests," *Criminology* 44 (2006):105–37; C. C. Spohn, "Racial Disparities in Prosecution, Sentencing, and Punishment," in S. M. Bucerius and M. Tonry (eds.), *Oxford Handbook of Ethnicity, Crime, and Immigration* (New York: Oxford University Press, 2013).

93. Claire S. H. Lim, Bernardo S. Silveira, and James M. Snyder Jr., "Do Judges' Characteristics Matter? Ethnicity, Gender, and Partisanship in Texas State Trial Courts," *American Law and Economics Review* 18, no. 2 (2016): 302–57, p. 340.

94. Darrell Steffensmeier and Chester L. Britt, "Judges' Race and Judicial Decision Making: Do Black Judges Sentence Differently?" *Social Science Quarterly* 82, no. 4 (2001): 749–64.

95. Welch et al., "Do Black Judges Make a Difference?" 126.

96. John Gruhl, Susan Welch, and Cassia Spohn, "Women as Policy Makers: The Case of Trial Judges," *American Journal of Political Science* 25 (1981): 308–22.

97. Cassia Spohn, "The Sentencing Decisions of Black and White Judges: Expected and Unexpected Similarities," *Law & Society Review* 24, no. 5 (1990): 1197–216.

98. Ibid.

99. Steven Vago, *Law and Society*, 7th ed. (Upper Saddle River, NJ: Prentice Hall, 2003), 71.

100. Coramae Richey Mann, "Minority and Female: A Criminal Justice Double Bind," *Social Justice* 16, no. 4 (38) (1989): 95–114. Available at: http://www.jstor.org/stable/29766503

CHAPTER 13

CORRECTIONS AND MULTICULTURALISM

CHAPTER OBJECTIVES

After reading this chapter, you should be able to:

- Recognize the significance of multiculturalism with regard to institutional corrections
- Identify and discuss the significance of cultural diversity as it relates to prison life
- Understand the challenges associated with incarceration
- Recognize the importance of cultural diversity as it pertains to community corrections
- Understand the significance of ensuring that correctional staff is aware of and tolerant of cultural diversity

Enforcing formal social control over those convicted of crimes is no easy task, and current correctional practices in the United States generate controversy. The controversy largely stems from the lack of directed goals with regard to many correctional practices, the limited capacity of correctional practices to "correct" human behavior, and the problems stemming from the multicultural makeup of our correctional system. With regard to the latter, it is well documented that the demographics of those under correctional supervision are unlike the demographics of society in general. The diversity within our correctional system, coupled with controversial correctional practices, makes for interesting study and is the focus of this chapter.

It is argued that heterogeneous countries, in which citizens differ based on race, ethnicity, religion, and other traits, are more punitive in nature than are homogenous countries. Support for this argument is found in imprisonment rates in the 1990s during which the United States, Russia, and South Africa led all other nations in the rate of incarceration. All three countries faced difficulties related to multiculturalism, compounded in the case of Russia and South Africa by changing government regimes. Law and punishment were increasingly used to formally control the disorder and conflict found in these countries.[1]

In recent years the United States has increasingly relied on incarceration and punishment as means to address crime, although this practice does appear to be slowing to some extent, as the incarceration rate has declined slightly since 2007. The "get tough" approaches witnessed from the 1980s through the 2000s have disproportionately impacted many lower-income minority communities which have suffered in numerous ways. While it is argued that imprisonment and overall correctional practices help protect society, we must remember that most offenders eventually return to the same communities and environments in which they committed their offenses. Some may have been "corrected"; however, there are many who return to society to face the same difficulties as they did prior to correctional intervention. Their problems are often amplified in various ways, not the least of which involves being labeled a "criminal," or "ex-con."

The status change from accused to offender leads to those under correctional supervision being viewed as criminals. In other words, upon being convicted they lose their status as "innocent until proven guilty." Offenders are often recognized by society as law violators who must be punished. Accordingly, our correctional system deals with individuals maintaining the lowest status of all who enter the criminal justice system. Upon release these same individuals will continue to be looked down upon by society. This is but one of the many challenges faced by those entering corrections.

The complexities of more frequently interacting with diverse groups and individuals are another difficulty faced by those under correctional supervision. Prison inmates face many struggles associated with being incarcerated, including contending with cultural biases. The situation is enhanced in jails where the classification of inmates is less of a concern than in prisons. To increase the likelihood of success in community corrections, probationers, parolees, and the officers who supervise offenders in the community must overcome cultural differences. Discussion of multiculturalism and corrections becomes more important as the number of individuals under correctional supervision increases and subsequently diversifies.

This chapter addresses multiculturalism and corrections by focusing on the main components of corrections: institutionalization in the forms of prisons and jails, and community corrections in the forms of probation and parole. This discussion is preceded by an observation of the organization and structure of corrections and some characteristics of those under correctional supervision. The chapter concludes with a look at how cultural diversity impacts correctional staff.

THE ORGANIZATION OF CORRECTIONS

The organization of correctional agencies is complex in nature, due to the varied approaches comprising corrections and the different practices adopted by the fifty states and the federal government. Perhaps the best way to summarize the organization of corrections is to begin with observation of corrections at the federal level and follow with examination of how states primarily organize their correctional practices.

As of 2019, the **Federal Bureau of Prisons** within the Department of Justice operated 122 institutions and twenty-two community corrections offices, and contracted with eleven private companies to run private correctional institutions. The bureau oversaw roughly 177,000 federal inmates. Included in these facilities are detention centers, which, similar to jails, hold those awaiting trial. The approximately 39,000 employees responsible for the day-to-day functioning of the bureau are spread throughout the United States.[2] The **U.S. Probation and Pretrial Services System** is responsible for several tasks, not the least of which is assisting the federal courts with pretrial practices and supervising federal probationers. The **U.S. Parole Commission** oversees federal parolees.

The organization of state correctional facilities is more complex, as each state designs its organizational structure. **Prisons** are state-run correctional facilities administered by the executive branch of each state government. They hold inmates serving sentences of one year or more. **Jails** hold detainees awaiting trial and those sentenced to incarceration for less than a year. In most states, jails are operated by county-level officials, mostly sheriff's departments. The organization of **probation** and **parole**, both forms of **community corrections** in which offenders are supervised in the community, is more elaborate. Among the issues of concern with regard to probation is whether it should be organized in a centralized or decentralized manner, meaning administered by state government or the judiciary, and whether it should be combined with parole services.[3] States vary in their approach to these issues, as they consider what works best with regard to their resources and culture. Parole is administered by state parole boards, which may or may not work in conjunction with probation services. State correctional systems oversee far more offenders than the federal system, as most crimes are prosecuted at the state level.

CHECKPOINT

- Correctional practices are very decentralized in the United States. Federal correctional authorities address federal cases, while various state and local correctional agencies address other offenses.

THE CORRECTIONAL POPULATION

Corrections in the United States took an interesting turn beginning in the early 1980s. Crime control became a primary focus, and greater use of incarceration was a significant part of the approach. Enhanced focus on incarceration increased the number of incarcerated by nearly 3.8 million between 1974 and 2001.[4] The increase has continued to a large extent; at year-end 2016 there were roughly 6.6 million adults under some form of correctional supervision, despite recent, slight decreases in the correctional population. An estimated one in thirty-eight adults (roughly 2.6 percent of persons age eighteen or older in the U.S.) was under some form of correctional supervision as of year-end 2016.[5] Much of the increased reliance on corrections to address crime was felt by minority groups.

The U.S. Bureau of Justice Statistics (BJS) provides the most accurate demographic account of prison and jail inmates. Reports show that over 2.1 million persons were incarcerated in the United States at the end of 2016, with prisons holding over two-thirds of that population.[6] Of particular interest with regard to incarceration are the overrepresentation of African Americans, the aging prison population, and the increased percentage of female offenders. Particularly, as of year-end 2017, the imprisonment rate was 568 prisoners per 100,000 U.S. residents. The rate for African Americans was 1,549.[7] With regard to age, the number of prisoners age fifty-five or older in state or federal prisons increased 280 percent from 1999 to 2016.[8]

Prisons maintain very diverse populations that provide challenges for all who work or stay in them.

Although females are far less likely than males to end up in prison (they account for only 7 percent of all prisoners), their presence in prison is growing. The rate of growth for female prisoners has been twice as high as it has been for males since 1980.[9]

Probation is the most frequently used criminal sanction. A recent BJS report noted that over 3.6 million probationers were supervised in the community at year-end 2016, most of whom were male (75 percent). The percentage of female probationers increased from 20 percent in 2000 to 25 percent, and most probationers were White (55 percent), followed by Black (28 percent) and Hispanic probationers (14 percent).[10]

The parole population at year-end 2016 was roughly 874,800, with males again accounting for the greatest percentage (87 percent). Of particular interest with regard to multicultural issues is the percentage of Blacks on parole (38 percent), which is largely disproportionate to their representation in the United States. Hispanics constituted 15 percent of those on parole as of the end of 2016.[11]

These numbers provide an overview of those incarcerated and those on probation and parole. They say little of why these individuals ended up under correctional supervision or the difficulties they face. Nonetheless, the numbers provide a foundation for examination of multiculturalism as it relates to corrections. Knowing who is incarcerated or being supervised in the community facilitates discussion of the multicultural issues existent within corrections.

CHECKPOINT

- The correctional population increased steadily from the 1980s until relatively recently. African Americans remain overrepresented among the correctional population, and the percentages of older inmates and female inmates have each increased.

INCARCERATION

Incarceration, or the physical detention of an inmate, exists primarily in two forms: prison and jail. These institutions have much in common, yet they differ in several ways. Prominent among the differences is the length of sentence served by those incarcerated. Jails typically hold those serving a sentence of less than one year, while prisons hold those serving sentences of a year or more. Another significant difference is the clientele. Jails hold the unconvicted awaiting trial and those convicted of crimes. Prisons do not hold unconvicted individuals. The demographics of jail and prison inmates are somewhat similar in the sense that one typically does not get to prison without having first entered jail. Accordingly, many of the issues associated with prisons are found in jails, and vice versa.

Inmates face numerous difficulties upon being incarcerated. The challenges are so severe that several guidebooks for surviving prison life are available.[12] The loss of liberty, goods and services, autonomy, heterosexual relationships, and security are prominent among the deprivations faced by the incarcerated.[13] In his book *The Warehouse Prison*, John Irwin identifies some of the main sources of harm in the modern warehouse prison, where inmates are stockpiled much like merchandise stored in a department store warehouse. Particularly, Irwin cites the troubles associated with health and disease, psychological damages, and **prisonization**,[14] or an inmate's adaptation to the prison culture. Each of these issues makes prison life profoundly different from life outside of prison.

Female inmates face additional challenges, including concerns related to privacy, separation from their children, pregnancy, clothing and hygiene, a loss of dignity, effective programming, mental and physical health/damage, strict enforcement of prison rules, and psychological and physical safety.[15] Needless to say, institutionalization generates significant changes and demands, including forced daily interaction with individuals from diverse cultures.

Inmates from different ethnic and religious groups often have a dislike for each other, which sometimes leads to violent encounters and promotes greater separation among the groups.[16] Author Todd Clear and his colleagues noted that, "reflecting tensions in U.S. society, many prisons are marked today by racially motivated violence, organizations based on race, and voluntary segregation by inmates by race whenever possible."[17] For twenty-five years, California prisons segregated tens of thousands of inmates according to racial lines during their first sixty days in custody. The policy was designed to reduce racially motivated violence. In 2005 the state ended its practice of doing so. Ultimately, jail and prison administrators need to strategically house inmates within facilities and recognize that cultural factors influence staff and inmate safety and well-being.

Violence among inmates is of utmost concern for correctional officials. Prison rape is often mentioned with regard to prison violence, as the nature of institutionalization seems ripe for such attacks. Same-sex, regimented institutions such as prison tend to precipitate sexually deviant behavior.[18] It appears that inmate race is related to sexual violence in prison. It was found that Whites comprised 70 percent of victims of inmate-on-inmate prison and jail sexual violence; yet, they were the perpetrators in only 45 percent of such incidents. Blacks constituted 18 percent of the victims and 39 percent of the perpetrators of such attacks. Females are particularly vulnerable to sexual violence in prison, as the same research noted that between 2009 and 2011, females represented about 7 percent of all state and federal prison inmates, yet accounted for 22 percent of inmate-on-inmate victims and 33 percent of staff-on-inmate victims.[19] The **Prison Rape Elimination Act**, passed in 2003, was designed to address prison rape through developing standards to prevent incidents of sexual violence in prison, including a zero-tolerance policy, emphasizing research, and information gathering. Violence in prisons and jails extends beyond sexual attacks, and factors such as overcrowding, improper classification, and race relations certainly underlie much of the violence in prison.

PRISON

You're driving along the highway after having a few too many drinks. The next thing you know you wake up in a jail cell inhaling an odor you've never smelled, nor do you care to ever again. With a heavy head, you listen to the rumblings of the other jail inmates, none of whom seem to be like you, and none of whom seem overly friendly. Eventually, a jailer approaches your cell, only to tell you that last night you crossed the highway dividing line and killed a passing driver. Your heart drops into your stomach as you realize what you've done. Then, you realize the potential consequences of your actions, not the least of which involves taking an innocent victim's life and the fact that you're not, nor perhaps will you ever be, prepared for prison life.

You initially think and hope you'll receive a sentence of probation, as you've never been in trouble before. But, killing someone? That's pretty serious. Perhaps you can plea bargain for only a few years in prison. Still, you're not "prison material." What will you do upon entering prison, and how will you protect yourself? What about your family? What will you do upon exiting prison?

Prison life poses many difficulties for those who enter. Consider the scenario described above. Picture the offender as a middle-class, White male enrolled in college. How do you perceive this individual faring in prison? How do you envision this individual will be upon exiting prison? Would you perceive the situation differently if the offending drunk driver was an African American male with a criminal history? Do you believe that person would have an easier time adjusting to prison life and life after prison? How would you fare in prison?

The detrimental effects of going to prison extend beyond the incarcerated individual. Families may struggle in response to the absence of a parent, and society in general may experience the effects of prisonization once an individual returns to the community following incarceration. It is not unreasonable to expect that inmates will bring some effects of prison life back into society upon their release.

The impacts of incarceration are many. Of particular interest is the absence of a parent. This concern notably influences Black communities; research on incarcerated parents found that Black children in the United States were seven-and-a-half times more likely than White children to have a parent in prison. Hispanic children were two-and-a-half times more likely than White children to have a parent in prison.[20] The absence of a parent poses numerous challenges for all young children, particularly in relation to accountability, financial support, and overall family stress.

Life in prison is full of many challenges, including the potential for much cultural misunderstanding and conflict.

Have you ever visited a prison? If so, did you consider racial, ethnic, and cultural issues as they pertain to social control? If you haven't visited a prison and are interested in criminal justice, you are encouraged to do so. Among the many interesting things you'll notice in prison is the diverse population under formal social control. Further, you'll notice a prisoner lifestyle that is likely much different from the one you live.

Prison Life

The prison life observed in most institutions differs from life on the outside in many facets. Prominent among the differences are the presence of a particular inmate subculture, recognition of the need to balance constitutional rights with concerns for safety and security, the enhanced influences of gang members, and the notable concerns surrounding the spread of communicable diseases. These and related issues continuously challenge prison officials, and the impact of those issues will increase as we rely on imprisonment as a primary form of social control.

Researchers have identified a subculture among prisoners that maintains characteristics different from society in general. For instance, **ultramasculinity**, or an emphasis on being strong, is a priority.[21] The **inmate code**, which involves the norms and values developed and stressed in prison, encourages toughness, insensitivity, and disdain and manipulation of fellow inmates and the prison staff. The inmate code generally varies among institutions, as does inmate commitment to the code. Nevertheless, a notable trend among institutions is the social organization of inmates along racial and ethnic lines.[22] White inmates, with few exceptions, associate with White inmates, Blacks with Blacks, and Hispanics with Hispanics.[23]

Prison staff trainees often ask why prisons accommodate a large number of religions.[24] The simple answer to the question involves respect for inmates' First Amendment right to religious freedom. Federal and state legislation may further define the religious freedoms of inmates, and prison systems have policies and procedures designed to ensure that constitutional and statutory religious rights are recognized. The American Correctional Association's standards for accreditation require that inmates be provided the right to practice religion. Such practices should be considered with concern for institutional order and safety.

Religion offers an avenue of solidarity among inmates, provides a mechanism of adjustment to incarceration for some individuals,[25] and encourages rehabilitation and overall self-improvement. Religion also provides avenues of differences among inmates and staff and sometimes generates struggles in regards to multiculturalism. The Black Muslim movement and concerns from Native Americans with regard to their religious freedoms in prisons were certainly among the factors influencing how correctional officials recognize religious practices in prison. Over the years we've seen religion play an integral role in prison organization and overall prison practices.

Many prisons permit access to religion as a form of rehabilitation. The U.S. penal system, however, has its roots in Judeo-Christian concepts of punishment and rehabilitation. Christianity is promoted and provided to Native Americans ahead of their own traditions. Judeo-Christian–based rehabilitation centers around an individual reflecting upon their own misbehavior. This contrasts the Native American belief system which involves all people, animals, and elements that constitute the universe as an interrelated force. They believe that the community contributed to some of the individual's wrongdoings, thus self-reflection and individual counseling is limited. It is argued that more effective rehabilitative approaches for Native Americans, one more in line with their cultural beliefs, would involve Native spiritual leaders to counsel inmates and the use of **sweat lodges**, which are used by many Native Americans.[26] The lodges are small huts in which ceremonies are held to cleanse spirits in a religious rite of purification and penance.

Researchers have commented on the changing nature of gangs in prisons as a new generation of inmates is incarcerated. The more-established gangs remain active in prison, although several new groups have emerged largely in response to older gang members dropping out of gang life, being segregated from the rest of prison, or going undercover.[27] These newer gangs, much like their predecessors, are heavily influenced by race and ethnicity. Table 13.1 depicts the major prison gangs and their affiliated race/ethnicity.

TABLE 13.1   MAJOR PRISON GANGS

Name	Race/Ethnicity
Neta	Puerto-Rican/Hispanic
Aryan Brotherhood	White
Black Guerrilla Family	Black
Mexican Mafia	Mexican-American/Hispanic
La Nuestra Familia	Mexican-American/Hispanic
Texas Syndicate	Mexican-American/Hispanic

Source: Florida Department of Corrections (n.d.), "Major Prison Gangs," *Gang and Security Threat Group Awareness.* Available at: https://www.libraryindex.com/pages/2531/Characteristics-Inmates-PRISON-GANGS.html

CULTURAL SOLIDARITY AMONG PRISON GANGS

Prison gangs increase the likelihood of violence in prison and strongly define the social structure of prison life. Gangs in prison are organized along hierarchical lines, and typically have a creed or motto, symbols signifying membership, and a constitution that guides member behavior. Further, prison gangs are divisive, adversarial factions that are largely structured along racial and ethnic lines. They are more commonly found in male prisons.

The organization of prison gangs along racial and ethnic lines demonstrates the solidarity and commitment associated with various cultural groups. Examples of the divisive nature of prison gangs is found in Hispanic inmates assembling into gangs such as the Mexican Mafia and the Nuestra Familia, Black inmates belonging to the Black Guerilla Family, and White inmates being actively involved in the Aryan Brotherhood. The organization of gang-involved inmates according to race and ethnicity suggests that multiculturalism is not well accepted among inmates.[28]

The exclusivity and secrecy associated with prison gangs prohibits in-depth understanding of prison gangs in general. At face value, however, there is little doubt that prison gang members typically associate with those from a similar racial or ethnic background. While it is admirable that prison gang members remain committed to their ancestral heritage, aligning themselves with others simply based on race or ethnicity does little toward the advancement of multiculturalism. Almost all inmates who enter prison will return to society. Unfortunately for some former inmates, their time in prison will have been spent festering dislike and hatred for others simply based on race or ethnicity. These feelings will likely remain within the individual as they readjust to life outside prison, making it less likely that society will adopt a true appreciation of multiculturalism.

Prison life provides an excellent opportunity to test the effectiveness of pro-multicultural programs. For instance, the divisive nature of inmates among racial and ethnic lines and the captive audiences found in prisons provide ample opportunities for prison officials to "test" or "experiment" with programs that promote diversity. Promoting multiculturalism in prison has many benefits, not the least of which involves the decreased likelihood of violent behavior.

To be sure, street and prison gangs are largely intertwined; involvement in gang life doesn't necessarily cease upon incarceration. Pressures emanating from gang involvement on the inside or outside of prison provide numerous difficulties for any attempts to correct criminal behavior. With regard to multiculturalism, the organization and practices of prison gangs certainly highlight the significance of race and ethnicity.

Prison life is challenging to say the least. Protecting oneself from exploitation or attack is indeed significant. Protection from disease and illness are also of concern. Consider the "cold and flu" season that occurs each winter. Both colds and the flu seem to spread quite easily, affecting large numbers of persons. Now, consider a communicable disease in prison, where individuals are confined to an institution and aren't always able to purchase over-the-counter drugs to address the ill effects of the disease.

Now, let's up the ante a bit. Let's change the communicable disease from colds and the flu to the human immunodeficiency virus (HIV) or AIDS. We most certainly need to alter our scenario in response, particularly with regard to the methods of transmitting these harmful diseases. Sharing colds and the flu is much more easily done than is transmitting HIV or AIDS. Nevertheless, inmates are at a much greater risk of obtaining and transmitting the diseases given their increased involvement in particular activities associated with transmission, including sharing dirty hypodermic needles (which have been smuggled into the facility or made from items such as pens) and engaging in unprotected sex. Absent from this discussion is the effects of other communicable diseases such as various types of hepatitis and the more easily transmitted tuberculosis.

In 2015, there were forty-five AIDS-related deaths in state prisons, the lowest number since 1991, when data was first collected. Nevertheless, African American inmates seem to be more affected by the deadly disease than other inmates. Twenty-three of those forty-five deaths involved Black inmates, followed by White inmates (18). Further, the rate of AIDS-related deaths for Black prison inmates has historically been higher than it is for other groups.[29] The Centers for Disease Control and Prevention noted that the situation is more pronounced in jails, where African American men are five times as likely as White males and twice as likely as Hispanic/Latino men to be diagnosed with HIV.[30] The impact of AIDS on African Americans is not restricted to prisons, as African Americans both within and outside of prison have a higher rate of contracting the disease than others. The fact that African Americans are overrepresented in the criminal justice system contributes to the need to recognize and treat infected individuals. The above-noted findings provide guidance for corrections officials charged with the safety and well-being of inmates.

These health and safety concerns as they relate to prison most certainly also apply to all other aspects of corrections. Those on probation and parole and those incarcerated in jail face many of the same challenges. Jail inmates face particular challenges due to the limited amount of testing, treatment, and classification of inmates. Individuals charged with supervising offenders with communicable diseases face specific challenges, particularly as they relate to the need for face-to-face contacts, confidentiality, offenders maintaining employment, and preventing inmates from engaging in sexual contact with others.

Multiculturalism and Challenges in Prison

The North Carolina Department of Public Safety removed the book *The New Jim Crow: Mass Incarceration in the Age of Colorblindness* from its list of books banned from state prisons in January 2018. The book has sold over a million copies and has garnered much public attention in light of its coverage of racial disparities in sentencing policies and the notable effects of mass incarceration upon African Americans. The book presents mass incarceration as a continuation of the tradition of racial discrimination in the United States. North Carolina's decision to remove the ban on the book came about two weeks after authorities in New Jersey made the same decision. Both groups had been pressured by the American Civil Liberties Union, which claimed that banning the book was shameful, wrong, and unconstitutional.

Prisons are full of demands, not the least of which involves the need to control a diverse group of seemingly dangerous individuals. The increasingly diverse nature of corrections poses particular difficulties, several of which are identified and discussed below. Critical issues with regard to multiculturalism and prisons involve specific needs of select groups, counseling methods that must consider cultural diversity, and overall correctional approaches designed to address cultural needs.

Many of the challenges stemming from living in a multicultural society result from society often categorizing individuals based on a particular label, trait, or characteristic. Consider, for instance, the term "inmate." Many in society assume that most inmates are similar simply because they broke the law and were convicted of a crime. Yet, there are notable differences among inmates that need to be recognized before we can expect significantly positive results from incarceration or any other type of correctional intervention.

Individuals maintain several roles, belong to specific groups, and are categorized and/ or stereotyped accordingly. Of particular interest in prisons and, more generally, corrections, is categorizing individuals as Hispanic. It is argued that the disaggregation of the term "Hispanic" is needed in correctional institutions in light of the diversity of the groups comprising the term. The classification of all Hispanics into one group blurs a great deal of cultural diversity.[31] Groups classified under the label "Hispanic," including Mexicans, Puerto Ricans, and Cubans, show notable differences with regard to offense characteristics, criminal records, family backgrounds, and personal characteristics.[32] Prison officers and others throughout the criminal justice system should recognize the distinct characteristics of those comprising the term "Hispanic."

Perhaps one of the most effective means of observing how multiculturalism impacts corrections requires observation of how particular groups exist, coexist, and function while incarcerated. Researchers suggest that there are differences between Black and White prison inmates, perhaps due to Blacks facing discrimination from those involved in all steps of the criminal justice system.[33] Particularly, researchers have identified differences among inmates, with Black inmates more likely than White inmates to engage in conflicts with other inmates and the staff.[34] Blacks were also more likely than Whites to engage in conduct that attracted the attention of prison administrators. Racial biases on behalf of prison staff and administrators may contribute to the differential.[35]

Research on racial differences among inmates further suggests that White inmates experience higher levels of fear and stress than Black inmates, and it appears that White inmates have more positive perceptions of prison officers than do their minority counterparts. It was found that Black **exmates**, those released from prison, were significantly more likely than White exmates to perceive that prison officers use too much force on inmates. Further, Whites were more likely than Blacks to believe they were treated "pretty good" in prison, and were almost twice as likely as Black or Hispanic exmates to disagree with the suggestion that prison officers treated them as if they were less than human.[36]

Race, however, is not the only variable of concern with regard to multiculturalism in corrections. Consider the prison experience of a transgender individual. Given the emphasis on masculinity in male prisons, what obstacles does the transgender male inmate face? Further, what challenges does this inmate pose for prison officials? At the very least, determination of what prison the inmate is sent to and the classification of the inmate are of notable significance. The inmate's right to treatment must also be considered. Should this treatment include hormones used to maintain one's transgender appearance?

Transsexual people who haven't had genital surgery are typically classified according to their birth sex, regardless of how long they've lived as the opposite sex. Those who have had genital surgery are typically classified and housed based on their reassigned sex.[37] Some transsexual inmates are permitted to maintain their hormone treatments while in prison. Until 2010, the U.S. Bureau of Prisons provided hormones at whatever levels were maintained prior to incarceration. The policy was changed following a lawsuit, and the agency now includes transgender women who had not started hormone therapy until after their incarceration.[38]

Homosexuality in prison poses particular difficulties for corrections officials. The extent of homosexual activity varies by prison and by the methods used to assess such behavior. Inmates report higher levels of homosexual activity than are recognized in official accounts.[39] Nevertheless, a common approach in response to homosexual activity is to do nothing or pretend it doesn't exist. This approach is limited in the sense that it may neglect nonconsensual acts of homosexuality, and it may lead to sexual discrimination claims by heterosexual inmates who may argue for conjugal visits.[40] In other words, it could be argued that heterosexual inmates are subject to sexual discrimination when they're prevented from having sexual relations while LGBT inmates are not. Other policy approaches to homosexuality in prison include providing condoms to promote safe sex, permitting conjugal visits, and the more radical approaches of establishing mixed-sex prisons (yet refraining from any physical contact), permitting homosexual activity, and promoting safe-sex practices through education.[41]

Native Americans face particular problems upon entering the correctional system. As an example, Native American culture differs from the dominant culture in that maintaining eye contact may convey disrespect.[42] As noted elsewhere in this book, failure to maintain eye contact when communicating can play an integral role in miscommunication. Further, some Native Americans view being under correctional control as an extension of their ancestral experiences.[43] Many institutions limit participation in Native American healing ceremonies to individuals who are enrolled in federally recognized tribes. This policy neglects Native Americans' First Amendment right to freedom of religion and the fact that not all tribes are recognized by the federal government. The possession of items considered sacred by Native Americans is also problematic for the incarcerated and prison officials. Eagle feathers, bear claws, pipes, and other artifacts may be viewed by correctional officers as potential safety and health risks.[44] Further, Native Americans reared in traditional manners are prompted to learn through experience, which isn't always possible while incarcerated. In turn, some of the Native American culture is lost when young adults are incarcerated.[45] Gayl Edmunds, Program Director for the Indian Alcoholism Treatment Service in Wichita, Kansas, commented on the problems faced by Native Americans in the correctional system in stating that a "total lack of understanding and often, respect, for American Indians' spiritual beliefs and practices, has created fertile ground for an ethnic community that feels misunderstood, disenfranchised, and powerless."[46]

Traditional counseling methods in prison are targeted toward the White middle-class, which poses challenges for those from diverse backgrounds. Such counseling may neglect diverse beliefs, values, experiences, and behaviors maintained by the varied groups that enter prison.[47] The concentration is often focused on helping inmates adapt to the dominant culture, while neglecting multiculturalism.

The term "corrections" suggests that some form of correcting is being done. Treatment is not the primary concern of many prisons these days, as punishment and deterrence have become increasingly popular. Nevertheless, counseling and therapeutic approaches are found in most, if not all, prisons. Selecting a treatment approach that suits all offenders is challenging to prison officials. Particularly, inmates come from diverse backgrounds and face many obstacles. A single approach to treating the ills of all inmates will not work. Accordingly, prison officials must identify and adopt the most effective approach for each individual, something that is easier said than done.

Puerto Rican inmates, as an example, face particular challenges with regard to counseling. Puerto Rican cultural issues as they pertain to time, relationships and friends, morality, responsibility and decision-making require recognition on behalf of counselors to consider how to shape their counseling efforts. For instance, cultural influences prompt Puerto Rican inmates to believe moral issues are to be discussed only with family members, while in the dominant culture morality is often a public issue.[48] Recognition of these and related issues can only serve to enhance the counseling of inmates.

The formal and social organization of inmates highlights the significance of the classification and day-to-day functions of inmates. Multiculturalism is certainly on the minds of prison administrators who must determine, among other things, who should share a cell with whom, and what groups should eat or recreate at the same time. Failure to consider inmate hostility toward particular groups contributes to a disruptive prison. However, it could be argued that isolating inmates of different backgrounds for the sake of safety discourages tolerance and acceptance of different groups and perpetuates the associated problems.

JAIL

Jails have been described by some as "poorhouses of the twentieth century,"[49] "festering sores," "cesspools of crime," "teeming houses of horror," and "the ultimate ghetto."[50] These terms were offered decades ago, but it appears they remain accurate.[51] In contrast to prisons, jails are the least understood and least frequently studied component of the criminal justice system[52]; yet, the significance of jails to the criminal justice system cannot be understated. Particularly:

- More people pass through jail than through prison.
- Critical decisions are often made while inmates remain in jail or are released on bond.
- Jail-related experiences often influence inmates' minds.
- Jail arguably imposes the cruelest means of punishment in the United States.[53]

Jails have a constantly changing population and much potential for cultural misunderstanding and conflict. Jail officials can eliminate their need to engage in physical forms of social control through greater understanding of cultural differences. Entering jail can be a traumatic experience for anyone who may soon realize that they face an unpleasant environment. Their reaction can be violence directed toward themselves (e.g., suicide) or others, including jail officials and/or other inmates. Effective assessment of an individual's dangerousness is facilitated through better understanding those who enter jail.

Effectively assessing individuals requires recognition of cultural backgrounds. Behaviors or responses that seem dangerous may be attributable to cultural practices.

Cultural practices seemingly influence assessment practices regarding the suicidal risks of American Indians placed in jail. Particularly, researchers found that American Indians are discomforted by the interview process involved in screening practices concerning jail inmate suicide. Many American Indians considered the screening intrusive and feared the repercussions of admitting a propensity to harm themselves. These, and related reactions, were not found among non-Indian counterparts. Part of the American Indian reactions and responses to the suicide risk screening is attributed to the American Indian concept of respect, which discourages prying into the innermost thoughts and feelings of others as is done in suicide screening.[54]

Jails differ from prisons in several ways. Among the differences are the higher turnover rate of inmates, the enhanced control over inmates, and the limited influence of an inmate subculture found in jails.[55] Much of the research literature on incarceration focuses on life in prison, in contrast to the scant study of jails.[56] One area of neglect is research on violence in jails.[57] What is known, however, suggests that many of the same factors influencing prison violence affect violence in jails. Particularly, overcrowding, poorly trained correctional staffs, acts of social injustice, and offender personalities are among the factors influencing jail violence.[58] Inmate age also influences behavior, as younger inmates are generally more unruly than their older counterparts. Researchers found mixed results with regard to inmate misconduct and race,[59] although it appears that Black inmates are more often written up for misconduct than are other groups. The disproportionality is possibly the result of reactions to perceived mistreatment, including closer scrutinization of Black inmates by correctional officials.[60]

For some individuals, entering jail is a traumatic experience. The ones most influenced by jail placement may be most vulnerable to treatment. Accordingly, jails sometimes have chaplains, clergy, and related individuals who interact with inmates in attempts to make the most of a difficult situation. These groups are also present in prisons, however their influence on jail inmates is of importance given the vulnerability of some inmates. Among the benefits of providing religious faith and spirituality in jails (and prisons, for that matter) are positive influences on character development, recovery from various types of addiction, and overall transformation and rehabilitation.[61] Providing jail chaplains or clergy who recognize different faiths provides for a more effective jail experience[62] and demonstrates the significance of concerns for multiculturalism in the criminal justice system.

CHECKPOINT

- Incarceration primarily consists of placement in prison or jail. Various issues pertaining to multiculturalism exist within both.
- Compared to jails, prisons house inmates serving longer periods of incarceration. Prison life, including the influences of the prison subculture and gangs, is rife with challenges related to diversity and multiculturalism.
- Jails house the convicted serving short periods of confinement, and the unconvicted awaiting trial. Many of the same issues pertaining to diversity and multiculturalism in prisons are recognized in jails.

COMMUNITY CORRECTIONS

Community corrections involves correctional supervision provided outside an institution. Community corrections personnel are expected to rehabilitate, monitor, and manage offenders outside of strict institutional settings. The practice is traced back to the pre-revolutionary colonial period, although at that time the community was not viewed as either a cause of crime, or an avenue to correct criminal behavior.[63] Today, community corrections is used largely to reduce prison overcrowding. Correctional practices in the community include probation, parole, halfway houses, residential centers, and work furloughs.

Correctional supervision in the community is preferred by most offenders and is often used by courts and correctional personnel as an incentive toward good behavior. While offenders typically view community supervision as preferable to incarceration, they do remain aware that misbehavior could result in (re)commitment to prison or jail. Determining who receives community corrections involves discretion and opens opportunities for differential treatment of various groups. The situation is perhaps best summarized by researchers Todd Clear and Harry Dammer, who note:

> Where there is discretion, there is the possibility of abuse of decision-making authority. Judges, parole boards, and program administrators are human. When they consider an offender for a community program in place of incarceration, they are looking for attributes that give reason to believe the offender will succeed in that program. It is not difficult to imagine that some of those attributes might be correlated with social statuses we think are not permissible for them to use. The most significant problems have to do with race and ethnicity.[64]

Clear and Dammer comment on the difficulties faced by Black Americans in the criminal justice system, who are more likely than their White counterparts to be unemployed, be less educated, be younger, be less skilled, and have a more serious criminal record. These characteristics could result in a partiality that involves biases in selecting clients for community corrections.[65]

Gender discrimination is also apparent with regard to community corrections programs. Aside from having some different needs or concerns than males undergoing community corrections (e.g., a female is more likely to be a single parent), females also face difficulties stemming from community corrections programs that often structure their strategies toward males.[66] This could result in an emphasis on surveillance and control at the expense of support, the latter being of greater importance to females than males.[67]

Probation and parole are the most frequently used forms of community corrections. The terms "probation" and "parole" are often used to refer to the same thing: supervision in the community. However, they differ in several ways. Probation is a front-end strategy in which judicial bodies place conditions on offenders in lieu of incarceration. Parole is a back-end strategy, in that it is imposed following a period of incarceration. Many of the challenges of dealing with multiculturalism and probationers are evident with regard to parolees, as both require supervision in the community. Recognizing cultural differences in the manner in which supervision is conducted benefits both the supervising agents and the individuals under supervision.

PROBATION

Probation practices in the United States are traced back to 1841 when shoemaker John Augustus assisted minor offenders. Augustus would offer to supervise offenders in the community. Probation is defined as conditional freedom offered by a judicial officer to an alleged or adjudged offender, provided the individual abides by certain conditions of behavior. Conditions of probation may involve offenders submitting to random drug tests, obeying curfews, reporting to a probation officer on a regular basis, and/or avoiding particular individuals or locations. Judges may impose a prison sentence upon an offender following a guilty verdict and subsequently suspend the sentence in lieu of probation. The offender would be accountable for their actions and subject to additional penalties should they commit another crime. Should they violate the terms of their probation, or commit what is referred to as a **technical violation**, they would serve the suspended sentence of incarceration. Technical violations involve infractions committed by those on probation or parole that are not necessarily illegal, but they violate the terms of the probation or parole agreement. Signing a contract or changing residences without permission are two of the more recognizable types of technical violations.

Investigation and supervision are at the heart of probation. Investigation involves preparing and presenting a presentence investigation report to judges involved in sentencing hearings. Supervision involves what most people associate with probation: supervising offenders in the community. The difficulties associated with the supervisory component of probation is perhaps best summarized by author Todd Clear and his colleagues, who identify the informal nature of the supervisory aspect of probation "as a complex interaction between officers (who vary in style, knowledge, and philosophy) and offenders (who vary in responsiveness and need for supervision) in a bureaucratic organization that imposes significant formal and informal constraints on the work."[68]

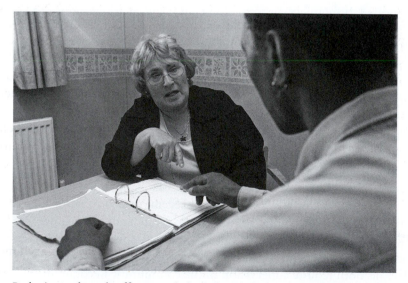

Probation and parole officers regularly work with diverse populations in ensuring that offenders are properly supervised in the community.

The supervision of probationers generally consists of three primary components, including the probation officer establishing a relationship with the offender and defining the roles of the probationer and probation officer; the officer and offender establishing supervision goals to assist the offender with complying with the conditions set by the court; and the officer deciding how the probation period will be terminated (e.g., early termination, expiration of sentence, revocation).[69] Perhaps the most significant aspect of probation involves enforcing the terms of probation. Enforcement of probationer behavior requires probation officers to properly process cases in which probationers commit new offenses or technical violations. The discretion inherent in this aspect of the job provides probation officers the power to involve or avoid judicial intervention when dealing with minor infractions. In other words, probation officers use their discretion to formally or informally confront problematic situations. They may also choose to ignore the problem. An officer's level of discretion decreases as the severity of the violation increases.

Is it possible for probation officers to use their discretion in an unfair and biased manner through bringing minor infractions of particular groups to the attention of the courts, yet not doing so for other groups? Absolutely. How often this happens is unknown, although it could be argued that one time is too many. Discretion to involve or avoid contact with judges provides an avenue for the differential treatment of probationers. Probation officers working in a jurisdiction where judges closely follow the probation revocation recommendations of the probation officer maintain notable influence on the outcome of the revocation hearing. Officers possessing a solid understanding and appreciation of different cultures reduce the likelihood that probationers will be treated unfairly.

Research on probation revocation practices found that young Black male individuals received the harshest penalties, while Hispanics and Whites were generally treated the same. Further, one's employment status at the time of their probation violation seemed to offer no support for young Black males since employed young Black males received harsher treatment than their White unemployed counterparts. The lack of statutory or administrative guidelines permits wide judicial discretion with regard to probation revocation.[70]

An offender's response to the supervision they're provided influences the effectiveness of their probation sentence. Put simply, how probationers respond to a probation officer's supervisory powers greatly affects their likelihood of successfully completing the terms of their probation. How the roles of probationers and probation officer are initially established influences supervision practices, and differences among cultures dictate that different approaches to establish and enforce "supervisor–supervised relationships" are needed.

The diverse nature of the individuals entering our correctional agencies dictates that corrections personnel maintain a keen awareness of cultural differences, for instance, as they relate to transgender and transsexual persons. Many probation officers will at some point encounter a transgender person. Those who lack knowledge about transgenderism feel less confident than those with more knowledge in dealing with specific issues as they pertain to transgenderism.[71] Privacy and confidentiality are primary among the issues raised when dealing with transgender probationers. The need to understand a person's transgender status becomes important for presentence investigation reports, particularly if the punishment may involve incarceration.[72] Probation officers must appropriately confront their own perceptions of transgenderism when dealing with these individuals, and recognize that transgender individuals have higher rates of psychological and substance abuse problems than their counterparts.[73] The difficulties associated with the social isolation of many transgender individuals are compounded by probation officers not overly familiar with support networks for transgender persons.[74]

The vast number of individuals entering probation comes from diverse cultures. The extensive and diverse caseloads maintained by probation officers require staff recognition of multicultural issues. Cross-cultural barriers provide a primary impediment to constructing an effective officer-client relationship.[75] Diversifying probation officer staffs is a step in the right direction, as these individuals provide many contributions to offender supervision in the community. However, there remains a significant need to ensure that field officers recognize, consider, and appreciate cultural differences. Sincerity, high service energy, knowledge of a client's culture, resourcefulness, and a nonjudgmental attitude are characteristic of a culturally competent probation officer.[76] Having a solid grasp of the innuendos of multiculturalism and actively questioning one's assumptions regarding particular groups undoubtedly contribute to the effectiveness of probation officer supervision.

RELEASE FROM PRISON AND PAROLE

Inmates are released from prison conditionally or unconditionally. Those released under conditions face community supervision for a specified time upon exiting prison. **Conditional release** can involve **discretionary release**, for instance when a parole board grants an inmate parole, or inmates can receive **mandatory release** in states that have abandoned traditional parole practices in favor of **"good time"** practices. States using mandatory release eliminate parole board discretion through a policy in which inmates earn time off of their prison sentence through various incentives, such as behaving appropriately in prison and taking advantage of self-improvement programs. Individuals released unconditionally have "maxed out" or served their entire sentence and are released from prison without conditions or supervision in the community.

Unlike probationers, parolees have spent time in prison and face particular obstacles. Prominent among the difficulties faced by those released from prison are: the influences of prisonization; being labeled a "former prisoner"; losing the right to vote, hold public office, or sign contracts in some states; and surviving without much state support. The need to find employment and re-establish ties with family and community members pose particular problems for some parolees. The financial cutbacks in many prisons have contributed to some inmates failing to address the factors leading to their incarceration. Financial concerns have led some prisons to reduce the number of counseling and treatment opportunities for inmates.

The increased number of prisoners beginning in the 1980s generated an increased focused on **reentry**, or an inmate's return to society. Providing support for inmates who are reentering society contributes to their avoiding a return to prison. Government and private groups have emerged in efforts to assist former inmates. For instance, the Ban the Box campaign emerged in the late 1990s in the United States when civil rights groups and advocates sought to encourage employers to remove the box that asks job applicants if they have a criminal record. As of 2016, over forty-five cities and counties have altered their hiring practices in public employment to limit the negative impacts of asking about arrest or conviction records.[77]

While the challenges of parole apply to all groups, cultures, and individuals, the disproportionate number of African American prisoners in the United States results in enhanced struggles for this group. One could argue that failing to address the initial causes underlying the incarceration and the difficulties of adjusting to parole perpetuate the overrepresentation of Blacks in prison and the criminal justice system in general.

Parole board members in most states are typically appointed by a governor for a fixed period of time. Members primarily assess inmate suitability for parole and assist with parole policy development. Participation on a parole board requires thorough knowledge of crime, justice, and human behavior, and recognition and appreciation of cultural diversity. A preparole investigation report, similar to a presentence investigation report, containing vital information regarding the potential parolee assists parole board members with their decision. Parole board member discretion in determining whether or not to grant an inmate parole is notable for any discussion of multiculturalism in corrections.

Those currently released on parole are being supervised by parole officers emphasizing *surveillance* over *assistance* even though both components are essential to parole. It is argued that inmates are receiving longer prison sentences coupled with limited pre-release or rehabilitation programs. This problem is compounded by the increased level of disorganization and disadvantages in the communities to which inmates are returning, inmates' families being less likely to support them upon their release, and fewer available social services for parolees.[78]

Parole officers supervise parolees and are influential in determining who is brought to the attention of the court following parole violations. Their duties are quite similar to those provided by probation officers. Parole officers provide law enforcement services and social services primarily through ensuring that parolees abide by the terms of their parole agreements and referring parolees to social services as needed.

A person's parole can be revoked following the commission of a new offense or a technical violation of an individual's parole agreement. As noted, parole officers use their discretion to decide whether or not to pursue revocation of parole, an issue of particular significance with concern for multiculturalism.

Aside from parole or maxing out, inmates are released from prison via other means. Inmates may be granted **clemency**, which permits legislative action to reduce the severity of one's punishment, waive the punishment associated with a crime, or exclude certain individuals from prosecution of a specific crime. Clemency comes in the form of pardons, amnesty, commutations, and reprieves. **Pardons** involve the restoration of a former inmate's rights and privileges. **Amnesty** is similar to pardons, although it involves groups of people instead of individuals. Granting rights and privileges to illegal aliens is an example of amnesty. **Commutations** involve shortening or changing an inmate's prison sentence, for instance when one becomes terminally ill or death sentences are switched to sentences of life in prison. They may also be used for other reasons; for instance, President Barack Obama commuted the sentences of over 1,900 inmates, many of whom were released as it was believed they were the victims of particularly harsh sentences. **Reprieves** involve the postponement of a sentence and are typically associated with delaying an execution. The decision to grant clemency is often influenced by several individuals. The extent to which cultural diversity influences such decisions remains unknown. Given historical use of discretion in the criminal justice system, it can be stated with modest confidence that multicultural issues play a role in this decision-making.

CHECKPOINT

- Many offenders are supervised in the community, largely under probation supervision.
- Probationers are monitored in the community and face various restrictions on their freedoms.

- Inmates are released from prison in various ways, and most are supervised in the community for a period of time upon their release. Akin to probationers, they face numerous restrictions during the course of their supervision.

CORRECTIONAL STAFF

Commenting on the difficulties of working with a correctional staff, Deputy Secretary Mary Leftridge Byrd of the Pennsylvania Department of Corrections stated, "The convergence of public expectation, responsibilities of correctional professionals, and demands of the correctional environment, coupled with the cultural influence of the large world, creates incredible dynamics."[79] The hands-on approach of correctional professionals evident throughout corrections requires directed attention toward multiculturalism.

DIVERSITY AND CORRECTIONAL STAFF

Several trends have impacted the correctional workforce. Prominent among the trends are the increased number of privately operated prisons, the continued introduction of technology, the imposition of standards on correctional facilities by outside agencies, and changes in the workforce demographics.[80] With regard to the latter, the demographic changes involve increases in the number of female and minority correctional staff.

Diversity among correctional staff was limited until about thirty to forty years ago. The infamous 1971 rioting at the Attica Correctional Facility in New York was largely encouraged by inmate perceptions of the correctional staff's inability and failure to recognize and respect varying cultures, ethnic backgrounds, and religious practices and rights.[81] The lack of multicultural awareness contributing to the rioting is evidenced by the staff's seeming lack of concern for religious beliefs. As noted by author Howard Abadinsky:

> Attica had a large number of Black Muslims (members of the Nation of Islam) who had difficulty with a prison diet that was heavy with pork. Muslims also objected to the lack of ministers. Correctional officials would not allow the ministers, many of whom had prison records, into Attica. Black Muslims spent their recreation time in the yard engaging in worship and highly disciplined physical exercise. The correctional staff, which never understood the Black Muslims, was quite fearful of this group, who exhibited military-type discipline and remained aloof from both staff and other inmates.[82]

Accordingly, Black Muslims played a significant role in the rioting that ensued.

The close contact between inmates and correctional staff mandates the need for all to maintain an understanding and appreciation of diversity.

Since the time of the Attica prison riot there has been increased representation of various ethnic and racial minority groups among correctional staffs, and the benefits have become obvious to corrections professionals. The opportunities of diverse groups to work together in correctional settings facilitate staff interaction and learning from one another. Creating a diverse correctional staff also encourages inmates to recognize that the criminal justice system does not solely consist of middle-class White men who don't understand cultural diversity.

Prisons were historically built in rural locations, often in areas with homogenous populations from which staff members were drawn. The inmates placed in these institutions, however, often hailed from urban, more heterogeneous areas.[83] Such a situation clearly encourages culture-based conflict. Differences between the traditional rural-White prison officer and the urban-minority prisoner still exist in some states, although they have largely diminished in large, more urban states.[84] Creating a diverse staff provides several challenges, like encouraging minority workers to move to rural locations; minorities finding employment in more attractive public service and private industry positions; and the unwillingness of some minorities to work in a system they view as racist.[85] Equal-opportunity programs have assisted in diversifying correctional staff; however, working in prisons where racial and ethnic tensions contribute to an already challenging situation discourages some minorities from seeking such work.

Non-Whites, particularly African Americans, have increasingly assumed prison staff positions. Unfortunately, they've faced many obstacles working in prison. Early on, resentment from White officers, many of whom hailed from rural backgrounds, was complemented by the perception that Black prison officers would be more sympathetic to inmates, particularly Black inmates.[86] But Black and Latino officers were eventually accepted into the prison officer culture. Inmates currently recognize little difference among White and non-White officers.[87] It is projected that females and minorities will increasingly join correctional staffs and bring their cultural beliefs and backgrounds into an arena that has long been secluded from such input.

There are some groups that continue to face obstacles with regard to being accepted into the prison officer culture. For instance, in 2018 a transgender correctional officer received a $500,000 settlement to end her lawsuit against the California Department of Corrections and Rehabilitation. The lawsuit was based on claims by the officer that she was forced to comply with a male dress code and her colleagues verbally tormented her. As part of the agreement she agreed to not seek employment in a state prison in the future.[88]

There is sometimes an assumption among inmates that cultural similarities will outweigh prison officer responsibilities and commitment to the job.[89] In other words, some inmates feel that prison officers will provide favoritism to inmates from cultures similar to their own. Determining the extent to which prison officers let cultural influences dictate their actions is difficult, if not impossible. However, we would be foolish to believe that cultural influences are completely unrelated to officer discretion.

Research has produced mixed results with regard to the differences among correctional officer attitudes and practices. Some suggest that minority officers assume more punitive attitudes toward inmates than do White officers.[90] Other studies suggest the opposite[91] or argue that there's no difference between the groups.[92] Some suggest that African American correctional officers are more likely than their White counterparts to support rehabilitative practices and are more likely to perceive the current court system as too harsh.[93]

CHECKPOINT

- Correctional staffs have become increasingly diversified in terms of race, ethnicity, and gender.

- Historically, members of underrepresented groups have had difficulty in being accepted among the ranks of correctional personnel.

SUMMARY

None of the many facets of corrections is exempt from multicultural concerns. The diversity within our correctional system warrants significant societal attention. What type of attention is needed and what can society do? Being tolerant of diversity would break down many barriers between cultural groups. Trying to understand the many cultural lifestyles found in society may help us better understand why people commit crime and how we can correct their behavior.

Cultural intolerance has existed for some time. So has the inability of correctional practices to fully correct. These statements, taken together, do not imply that becoming tolerant of other cultures will substantially change corrections. There are far too many variables involved with correctional practices to suggest that enhanced tolerance is the solution to solving crime. However, understanding the uniqueness of individuals and groups certainly plays a significant role in correcting human behavior.

What can we expect with regard to multiculturalism and corrections in the near future? The increased presence of females and minorities on correctional staffs suggests a more diverse correctional workforce. Such diversity will seemingly coincide with an increasingly diverse correctional population. Demographic trends suggest increased minority representation in the larger society, and statistical trends suggest greater representation of minorities under correctional supervision. It is hoped that the continuous search for alternatives to crime can someday eliminate the need for correctional intervention.

YOU MAKE THE CALL
PROBATION OFFICER CHALLENGES

Consider the following scenario. Debate the pros and cons of all options and decide what you would do.

You became a probation officer because you like to help people and you appreciate the spontaneity associated with the job. As an African American male, you face particular challenges when visiting your clients, especially those who live in predominantly nonminority neighborhoods. On one occasion you were (wrongfully) stopped by police who claimed you had failed to come to a complete stop at a stop sign as you approached a probationer's home. Personally, you believe the officers were engaging in racial profiling. You decided not to let it bother you. However, three weeks later, officers (again wrongfully) stopped you in the same neighborhood claiming that you had failed to signal during a lane change. Again, you believe the officers were targeting you because you're a Black man in a predominantly White neighborhood. To make matters worse, you often receive suspicious looks from the citizens in the community, and have had the police slowly drive by and monitor your actions as you've walked toward your probationer's home. Your probationer is a blatant racist who has no respect for you and on several occasions has filed claims of

impropriety about you. You like the job, but you begin to wonder whether the hassles are worth it.

Questions

1. Should you simply explain to the police officers why you're in the neighborhood, ignore the unjustified stops, or report the wrongful actions of the police to the police department or some other official agency?

2. Should you request to be removed from this client's case, in light of the disturbance your presence causes in the neighborhood?

3. Should you attempt to enlighten the probationer's racist attitude, adopt a more punitive approach toward him, or ignore his shortsighted racist behavior?

4. Do you believe your continuous presence as a probation officer of color in the neighborhood helps or hinders efforts toward multiculturalism? In other words, do you believe it is a positive experience for citizens to have diversity in their surroundings?

KEY TERMS

amnesty
clemency
community corrections
commutation
conditional release
discretionary release
exmates
Federal Bureau of Prisons

good time
incarceration
inmate code
jail
mandatory release
pardon
parole
prison

Prison Rape Elimination Act
prisonization
probation
reentry
reprieve

sweat lodges
technical violation
ultramasculinity
U.S. Parole Commission
U.S. Probation and Pretrial Services System

DISCUSSION QUESTIONS

1. How are correctional agencies organized? Do you believe that a centralized approach to corrections (e.g., in the form of one unified correctional system) would be more effective than our fragmented approach?
2. Discuss the difficulties of being incarcerated.
3. What particular challenges do Native Americans face upon incarceration?
4. Why is concern for multiculturalism of significance to probation and parole officers? What steps can be taken to address these concerns?
5. Why is it important for correctional agencies to incorporate cultural diversity into their staffs?

FOR FURTHER READING

Alexander, M. *The New Jim Crow: Mass Incarceration in the Age of Colorblindness*. Jackson, TN: New Press, 2010.

Bauer, S. *American Prison*. New York: Penguin Press, 2018.

Schmidt, C. *If You Don't Laugh You'll Cry: The Occupational Humor of White Wisconsin Prison Workers*. Madison: University of Wisconsin Press, 2017.

Stojkovic, S. (ed.). *Prisoner Reentry: Critical Issues and Policy Directions*. New York: Palgrave Macmillan, 2017.

Sykes, Gresham M. *The Society of Captives*. Princeton, NJ: Princeton University Press, 1958/2007.

NOTES

1. Burk Foster, *Corrections: The Fundamentals* (Upper Saddle River, NJ: Prentice Hall, 2006).
2. Federal Bureau of Prisons, "About Us." Available at: https://www.bop.gov/about/
3. T. R. Clear, M. D. Reisig, and G. F. Cole, *American Corrections*, 11th ed. (Boston, MA: Cengage, 2016).
4. Thomas P. Bonczar, *Prevalence of Imprisonment in the U.S. Population, 1974–2001*. U.S. Department of Justice, Bureau of Justice Statistics, August 2003, NCJ 197976, 3.
5. D. Kaeble and M. Cowhig, *Correctional Populations in the United States, 2016*, U.S. Department of Justice, Bureau of Justice Statistics, April 2018, NCJ 251211, 1.
6. Ibid., 2.
7. Jennifer Bronson and E. Ann Carson, *Prisoners in 2017*, U.S, Department of Justice, Bureau of Justice Statistics, 2019, NCJ 252156, 9.
8. Matt McKillop and Alex Boucher, "Aging Prison Populations Drive Up Costs, *Pew*, February 20, 2018. Accessed August 20, 2019 at: https://www.pewtrusts.org/en/research-and-analysis/articles/2018/02/20/aging-prison-populations-drive-up-costs
9. The Sentencing Project, *Fact Sheet: Incarcerated Women and Girls*, 2019. Available at: https://www.sentencingproject.org/publications/incarcerated-women-and-girls/
10. D. Kaeble, *Probation and Parole in the United States, 2016*, U.S. Department of Justice, Bureau of Justice Statistics, 2018, NCJ 251148, 17.
11. Ibid., 24.

12. E.g., Jeffrey Ian Ross and Stephen C. Richards, *Behind Bars: Surviving Prison* (Indianapolis IN: Alpha, 2002); Jim Hogshire, *You Are Going to Prison* (Port Townsend, WA: Loompanics Unlimited, 1994).

13. Gresham M. Sykes, *The Society of Captives* (Princeton, NJ: Princeton University Press, 1958).

14. John Irwin, *The Warehouse Prison: Disposal of the New Dangerous Class* (Los Angeles, CA: Roxbury, 2005).

15. Barbara Owen, "The Case of Women: Gendered Harm in the Contemporary Prison," in J. Irwin (ed.), *The Warehouse Prison: Disposal of the New Dangerous Class* (Los Angeles, CA: Roxbury, 2005), 264–89.

16. Daniel Moriarty, "Training Detention Officers to Understand Inmate Behavior," *Corrections Today* (Dec. 1991): 72, 74–75.

17. Clear et al., *American Corrections*, 281.

18. Niyi Awofeso, "Managing Homosexuality in Prison: A Brief Review of Policy Options," *American Jails* (Jan./Feb. 2005): 79–81.

19. A. J. Beck and R. R. Rantala, *Sexual Victimization Reported by Adult Correctional Authorities, 2009–2011*, U.S. Department of Justice, Bureau of Justice Statistics, 2014, NCJ 243904, 1.

20. L. E. Glaze and L. M. Maruschak, *Parents in Prison and Their Minor Children*, U.S. Department of Justice, Bureau of Justice Statistics, 2008, NCJ 222984, 2.

21. Don Sabo, Terry A. Kupers, and Willie London, "Gender and the Politics of Punishment," in Don Sabo, Terry A. Kupers, and Willie London (eds.), *Prison Masculinities* (Philadelphia, PA: Temple University Press, 2001), 3.

22. E.g., Sabo et al., "Gender and the Politics of Punishment"; Ross and Richards *Behind Bars*.

23. Ross and Richards, *Behind Bars*.

24. Doris Woodruff-Filbey, "Religious Diversity: A Kaleidoscope of Faiths," in C. Smalls (ed.), *The Full Spectrum: Essays on Staff Diversity in Corrections* (Lanham, MD: American Correctional Association, 2004), 53–64.

25. S. Walker, C. Spohn, and M. DeLone, *The Color of Justice*, 5th ed. (Belmont, CA: Wadsworth, 2012).

26. J. Saleem, "Native American Spirituality in the United States Prison System: Part 2: Legal Restrictions on Spirituality," MulticulturalFamilia.com, March 6, 2012. Available at: http://www.multicultural-familia.com/2012/03/06/native-american-spirituality-in-the-united-states-prison-system-part-2-legal-restrictions-on-spirituality/

27. Geoffrey Hunt, Stephanie Riegel, Tomas Morales, and Dan Waldorf, "Changes in Prison Culture: Prison Gangs and the Case of the 'Pepsi Generation,'" *Social Problems* 40, no. 3 (1993): 398–409.

28. B. Foster, *Corrections: The Fundamentals* (Upper Saddle River, NJ: Prentice Hall, 2006).

29. Laura M. Maruschak and Jennifer Bronson, *HIV in Prisons, 2015—Statistical Tables*, U.S. Department of Justice, Bureau of Justice Statistics, 2017, NCJ 250641.

30. Centers for Disease Control and Prevention, *HIV Among Incarcerated Populations*, 2015. Accessed online at: http://www.cdc.gov/hiv/group/correctional.html

31. D. J. Martinez, "Hispanics Incarcerated in State Correctional Facilities: Variations in Inmate Characteristics Across Hispanic Subgroups," *Journal of Ethnicity in Criminal Justice* 2, no. 1/2 (2004): 119–31.

32. Ibid.

33. Craig Hemmens and James W. Marquart, "Friend or Foe? Race, Age, and Inmate Perceptions of Inmate-Staff Relations," *Journal of Criminal Justice* 28 (2000): 297–312.

34. Ibid.

35. T. J. Flanagan, "Correlates of Institutional Misconduct Among State Prisoners," *Criminology* 21 (1983): 29–39.

36. Hemmens and Marquart, "Friend or Foe?"

37. See Farmer v. Brennan, 511 U.S. 825, 829 (1994); Farmer v. Haas, 990 F.2d 319, 320 (7th Cir. 1993).

38. J. Keenan, "Getting Hormones and Surgery for Transgender Prisoners," *The Atlantic*, August 23, 2013. Available at: http://www.theatlantic.com/health/archive/2013/08/getting-hormones-and-surgery-for-transgender-prisoners/278998/

39. Awofeso, "Managing Homosexuality."

40. Ibid.

41. Ibid.

42. Gary Cesarz and Joyce Madrid-Bustos, "Taking a Multicultural World View in Today's Corrections Facilities," *Corrections Today* (December 1991): 68, 70–71.

43. Willliam G. Archambeault, "The Web of Steel and the Heart of the Eagle: The Contextual Interface of American Corrections and Native Americans," *The Prison Journal* 83, no. 1 (2003): 3–25.

44. Ibid.

45. Ibid.

46. Gayl R. Edmunds, "American Indians," in C. Smalls, *The Full Spectrum*, 82.

47. Edil Torres Rivera, Michael P. Wilbur, and Janice Roberts-Wilbur, "The Puerto Rican Prison Experience: A Multicultural Understanding of Values, Beliefs, and Attitudes," *Journal of Addictions and Offender Counseling* 18, no. 2 (1998): 63–78.

48. Ibid.

49. R. Goldfarb, *Jails: The Ultimate Ghetto* (Garden City, NY: Doubleday, 1975), 29.

50. J. Thompson, "The American Jail: Problems, Politics, and Prospects," *American Journal of Criminal Justice* 10 (1986): 205.

51. See, e.g., Michelle Mark and Associated Press, "Report: New York's Biggest Jail Has a Huge Problem with Sexual Abuse." Businessinsider.com, June 21, 2016. Available at: http://www .businessinsider .com/ap-apnewsbreak-report-assails-nyc-jails-sex-abuse-response-2016-6.

52. R. Kiekbusch, "Misinformation About the American Jail and Our Duty to Inform," *American Jails* (March/April 1999): 119.

53. J. Irwin, *The Jail: Managing the Underclass in American Society* (Berkeley: University of California Press, 2013), xxii.

54. A. R. Gonzalez, T. A. Henke, and S. V. Hart, "American Indian Suicides in Jail: Can Risk Screening Be Culturally Sensitive?" U.S. Department of Justice, Office of Justice Programs, June 2005, NCJ 207326, 4.

55. J. D. Senese and D. B. Kalinich, "A Study of Jail Inmate Misconduct: An Analysis of Rule Violations and Official Processing," *Journal of Crime and Justice* 15, no. 1 (1993): 131–47.

56. R. Burns, "Assessing Jail Coverage in Introductory Criminal Justice Textbooks," *Journal of Criminal Justice Education* 13, no. 1 (2002): 87–100.

57. P. F. McManimon Jr., "Correlates of Jail Violence," *American Jails* (May/June 2004): 41–43, 45–47.

58. M. Braswell, S. Dillingham, and R. Montgomery Jr., *Prison Violence in America* (New York: Anderson, 1985).

59. McManimon, "Correlates of Jail Violence."

60. E. D. Poole and R. M. Regoli, "Race, Institutional Rule Breaking, and Disciplinary Decision Making in Prison," *Law and Society Review* 14, no. 4 (1980): 931–46.

61. Robert Toll, "How a Multifaith Chaplaincy Program Operates in a County Detention Facility," *American Jails* (January/February 2004): 19–24.

62. Ken Kerle, "Religion and Jails," *American Jails* (May/June 2004): 5. See also Toll, "How a Multifaith Chaplaincy Program Operates."

63. Mark C. Dean-Myrda and Francis T. Cullen (1998). "The Panacea Pendulum: An Account of Community Response to Crime," in *Community Corrections: Probation, Parole, and Intermediate Sanctions*, ed. J. Petersilia (New York: Oxford University Press, 1998), 3–18.

64. Todd R. Clear and Harry R. Dammer, *The Offender in the Community* (Belmont, CA: Wadsworth, 2000), 40.
65. Ibid.
66. Ibid.
67. Ibid.
68. Clear et al., *American Corrections*, 209.
69. Ibid.
70. Michael Tapia and Patricia M. Harris, "Race and Revocation: Is There a Penalty for Young, Minority Males?" *Journal of Ethnicity in Criminal Justice* 4, no. 3 (2006): 1–25.
71. Lindsey Poole, Stephen Whittle, and Paula Stephens, "Working with Transgendered and Transsexual People as Offenders in the Probation Service," *Probation Journal* 49, no. 3 (2002): 227–32.
72. Ibid.
73. Ibid.
74. Ibid.
75. Robert A. Shearer and Patricia Ann King, "Multicultural Competencies in Probation: Issues and Challenges," *Federal Probation* 68, no. 1 (June 2004): 3–9.
76. M. Sanders, "Building Bridges Instead of Walls: Effective Cross-Cultural Counseling," *Corrections Today* 65, no. 1 (2003): 58–59.
77. Ban the Box, "About: The Ban the Box Campaign," 2016. Available at: http://bantheboxcampaign .org/about/#.WFfj7XeZPEY
78. R. P. Seiter and K. R. Kadela, "Prisoner Reentry: What Works, What Does Not, and What Is Promising," *Crime & Delinquency* 49, no. 3 (2003): 360–88.
79. Mary V. Leftridge Byrd, "African-American Women in Corrections," in Smalls, *The Full Spectrum*, 115.
80. Portia Hunt, "Correctional Officers Need Cultural Diversity Training," in Smalls, *The Full Spectrum*, 127–55.
81. Joe W. Booker Jr., "Staff Equality: A Welcomed Addition to the Correctional Workplace," *Corrections Today* (1999): 95.
82. H. Abadinsky, *Probation & Parole: Theory & Practice*, 12th ed. (Upper Saddle River, NJ: Pearson, 2015), 79.
83. Booker, "Staff Equality."
84. Irwin, *The Warehouse Prison*.
85. Scott Camp, William G. Saylor, and Kevin N. Wright, "Racial Diversity of Correctional Workers and Inmates: Organizational Commitment, Teamwork, and Workers' Efficacy in Prisons," *Justice Quarterly* 18, no. 2 (2001): 411–27.
86. Byrd, "African American Women."
87. Ibid.
88. Adam Ashton, "Transgender California Prison Guard Receives $500,000 to Settle Discrimination Case," *Sacramento Bee* (2019, July 9). Available at: https://www.sacbee.com/news/politics-government/ the-state-worker/article232412212.html
89. Ana T. Aguire, "Latinos in Corrections: One View," in Smalls, *The Full Spectrum*, 65–74.
90. J. B. Jacobs and L. Kraft, "Integrating the Keepers: A Comparison of Black and White Prison Guards in Illinois," *Social Problems* 25 (1978): 304–18.
91. N. Jurik, "Individual and Organizational Determinants of Correctional Officer Attitudes Towards Inmates," *Criminology* 23 (1985): 523–39.
92. B. M. Crouch and G. P. Alpert, "Prison Guards' Attitudes Towards Components of the Criminal Justice System," *Criminology* 18 (1982): 227–36.
93. John A. Arthur, "Correctional Ideology of Black Correctional Officers," *Federal Probation* 58 (1994): 57–65.

CHAPTER 14

PREPARING FOR MULTICULTURALISM IN THE CRIMINAL JUSTICE SYSTEM: TRAINING AND POLICY

CHAPTER OBJECTIVES

After reading this chapter, you should be able to:

- Understand the role of education with regard to training
- Describe the types of training provided for criminal justice professionals
- Explain why training alone cannot prepare criminal justice personnel for the many diversity-related challenges they will encounter
- Demonstrate how criminal justice policies have impacted less powerful groups in society
- Explain the benefits of maintaining a global perspective with regard to policy-making

In June 2016, the Kentucky Commissioner of Corrections declared that prison policies that banned inmate mail that dealt with or promoted homosexuality were unacceptable. The policy, which was believed to unfairly target gay inmates, was later rescinded. A few months earlier, the city of Allentown (Pennsylvania) paid $100,000 to settle a lawsuit regarding a police officer's use of a stun gun against a fourteen-year-old girl. The lawsuit contained allegations of excessive force by a police officer, improper training, and deficient policies. These accounts are reflective of the importance of training and policy in the criminal justice system. Diversity and the need for tolerance and understanding of differences among individuals and groups pose many notable challenges for the criminal justice system. Evidence demonstrating the need for greater preparedness and understanding of differences are found everywhere—on the news, in other countries, in workplaces, and so on. This chapter addresses the training received by criminal justice officials with regard to diversity and related concepts, and highlights policy as it relates to diversity, tolerance, understanding of others, and acceptance.

To be sure, overcoming the challenges associated with diversity is not easy. The history of the United States is rife with accounts of individuals being treated differently based solely on skin color, cultural beliefs, appearance, age, sexual orientation, and related factors. To simply state that additional training and/or policies will solve all of our problems is shortsighted. Nevertheless, educating and training our criminal justice professionals, and creating policies that are inclusive as opposed to exclusive, will contribute much toward improving the system and society in general.

TRAINING AND MULTICULTURALISM

In 2018, the New York Police Department signed a $4.5 million contract with a firm that will train all of the department's officers with regard to implicit bias. In 2016, the U.S. Department of Justice required over 33,000 federal agents and prosecutors to undergo training designed to prevent unconscious bias from affecting their law enforcement decisions. Similar training requirements have been introduced in many justice-based agencies, as training is believed to be a primary means by which bias and discrimination can best be addressed.

Training, similar to formal education, seeks to impart knowledge and skills on an individual in preparation for future endeavors. It could be argued that enhanced training for all criminal justice officials could solve many problems associated with the intersection of multiculturalism and justice-based practices. It could also be argued that solid training wouldn't solve the problems. Such is the nature of trying to change human behavior. Consider a college-level criminal justice class, for example. Some students will comprehend all of the material and earn an "A" in the course. Others will get much (70–79 percent) of the information and earn a "C." Other students will get very little out of the course, and some will fail to receive credit. The students who earned a "C" or an "A" both passed the class. They've demonstrated their ability to grasp much or perhaps all of the material. However, does comprehending "much" of the material mean that you're trained in this area? And does one's ability to pass exams and/or write papers necessarily demonstrate overall comprehension of the material? Many of the challenges found in training college students are evident in training criminal justice officials.

Properly training criminal justice professionals is vital to the success of justice-based practices. Training, of course, is difficult, primarily because it seeks to alter human behavior. Training will not change everyone, but the notably large amount of resources regularly devoted to training criminal justice practitioners suggests that we rely on it heavily, and it must have many benefits. Some training programs and requirements are more effective than others, and the key to successful training is finding what works and for whom. The importance of training is noted, for instance, in the body of research which suggests that training can have positive, significant effects upon the interactions between probation officers and their clients, and can contribute to lower offender failure rates.[1]

Cultural differences and other diversity-related issues have been at the core of many problems and controversies in the criminal justice system. Evidence is noted with the **Black Lives Matter** activist movement in the United States that originated after the 2013 acquittal of George Zimmerman, who shot and killed Trayvon Martin, an African American teenager. The movement received greater attention following the 2014 deaths of two unarmed African Americans (Michael Brown in Ferguson, Missouri, and Eric Garner in

New York City) and the failure of grand juries to indict the officers involved in the shootings. The group campaigns against police brutality against African Americans.

In general, cultural diversity training should include four primary components: awareness of one's own cultural influences, understanding of other cultures, comprehension of the emotional challenges faced in recognizing and understanding diversity, and the basic skills needed to appropriately address cultural differences.[2] It is argued that a weakness in any of these components hampers understanding of cultural diversity. Self-reflection through examination of one's own cultural influences and understanding the emotional challenges with regard to diversity facilitates individuals' overcoming personal biases they may have toward other groups.

There are two basic approaches taken with respect to multicultural skills development: culture-specific and culture-general training. **Culture-specific training** addresses the practices, beliefs, and traits of particular cultural groups. **Culture-general training** emphasizes the flexibility, skills, and knowledge that would apply to understanding an array of cultures.[3] Research with regard to these approaches found that the culture-general model, interactive training methods, and trainer qualifications hold viable potential for positive training impacts.[4] These findings provide guidance for future training practices.

Cultural diversity and awareness training for criminal justice practitioners should, at minimum, address:

- Communication skills
- Understanding and recognizing bias
- Racism, bigotry, discrimination, and the like
- Understanding and appreciating various (or, if possible, most or all) cultures
- Understanding the benefits and challenges of diversity and its relationship to justice-based practices
- Action steps to confronting multicultural challenges

Agencies faced with limited resources should tailor their training to focus primarily on the groups within their jurisdiction. For example, probation officers working in an area with a large number of Native Americans should familiarize themselves with Native American culture.

Cultural sensitivity and diversity training are generally imposed on line workers, but it is also very important for administrators and supervisors to be culturally sensitive, and to take remedial actions with those who are not. Supervisors and administrators heavily influence the agencies and departments they oversee, since they are largely involved in the recruitment, selection, and training of employees. Further, their practices help establish how discretion will be used, and largely shape the overall organizational culture. Diversity is one of the more substantial issues in the workplace, yet many employers are ill-prepared to address it. The problem appears in part because many managers grew up isolated from other cultures. Accordingly, it is imperative that cultural sensitivity training be provided to all who work in criminal justice.

In discussing the importance of fairness and neutrality with regard to race and policing, police administrators Kessee and Nila noted that "the goal of effective diversity training is not simply to check the box and meet mandatory requirements, but rather to create long-lasting transformative change."[5] Ultimately, training should be designed to have long-lasting effects that shape the individual in a positive manner. The benefits of training should be emphasized to all employees, and efforts should be made to continuously engage trainees. Disinterested or bored trainees are less impressionable than those who are actively engaged in the training practices.

THE ROLE OF EDUCATION

Education is an important aspect of training. It promotes critical thinking skills, the incorporation of theory, and ethical considerations. Education is primarily concerned with learning about something, while training is much broader and encompasses learning about something and *doing* it. Consider police academies, for example. Officers must attend police academies to become sworn officers. At the academy (as discussed later in this chapter), officers have classroom sessions in which they are educated about important aspects of policing, and they engage in field activities in which they practice what they were taught. Their training continues after the academy, for instance in the form of **field training** in which they patrol the streets under the guidance of an experienced colleague.

One of the more notable shifts in the focus of higher education involves greater consideration for diversity and multiculturalism.[6] There exist many ways to cover these topics in the classroom, and the issues covered by general university-level training regarding diversity and multiculturalism range from understanding basic concepts to interpretation of advanced statistical analyses regarding race and gender. Unfortunately, most university

Classroom education is an important component of formal training. It alone, however, is not enough to ensure that those who work in criminal justice are prepared for their positions.

students will get only one course on multiculturalism.[7] Similar to those who have taken only one semester of a foreign language, students taking only one course in multiculturalism will have a broad overview of the topic but lack substantial comprehension of the many-faceted aspects of the topic. It is not uncommon for instructors teaching a sensitive topic such as diversity or multiculturalism to sacrifice complexity for morality.[8]

Teaching about diversity, multiculturalism, and tolerance should not be restricted to university settings. Changing stereotypical images and discriminatory practices requires teaching at an early age. The onus is on both public and private educational institutions from kindergarten through college to address tolerance and diversity, as today's students are tomorrow's professionals.[9] Recognizing and incorporating the many significant accomplishments of individuals from various cultures encourages young, impressionable students to embrace multiculturalism; however, additional work is required.

The goal in teaching multiculturalism is to structure one's mind toward tolerance and acceptance of a diverse society. To do so, it is important to observe historical events that shaped current thought. Throughout this book we've commented on the historical treatment of various cultures and groups both within and outside of the criminal justice system. Teaching about diversity and multiculturalism, particularly to students of criminal justice, requires a holistic approach that encompasses, in addition to historical events, various social, political, economic, demographic, and related considerations. In other words, we can't simply consider the role of various cultures in the criminal justice system without recognizing the significance of political influences, the effects of poverty, the impact of racist attitudes, and the changing nature of our society's population.

In discussing an approach to incorporating multiculturalism into the criminal justice curriculum, researcher William Calathes argues that cultural pluralism, intergroup relations, demography, and involvement constitute the theoretical component of multiculturalism. He adds that such topics are often neglected in traditional criminal justice textbooks.[10] At the very least, concepts that highlight the contextual nature of diversity within the system should be emphasized in any discussion of multiculturalism within the criminal justice system.

Calathes argues that a multicultural approach to criminal justice would help students recognize the "present and future eventualities" and assist students in obtaining the critical thinking skills and ability to work, teach, and engage in research from that perspective.[11] Calathes offers a series of steps that would promote teaching multiculturalism in the criminal justice curriculum. Included among his suggestions are:

- Informing students of the experiences of different cultures as they relate to life both within and outside of the criminal justice system
- Teaching from the perspective of the subjects
- Emphasizing the relationship between law and politics, including examination of the power differentials in society
- Teaching students to recognize various cultures, with particular concern for racism and oppression
- Preparing students to understand the problems of different groups and conflicts between groups[12]

Students are often taught critical thinking skills to encourage them to consider all possibilities with regard to problem-solving. Critical thinking skills promote consideration of alternatives or solutions, and discourage individuals, including those within the criminal justice system, from acting in a manner simply because "that's the way it's always been done." Such skills could be useful in efforts to enhance our justice systems with regard to diversity and the need for understanding different groups.

Teaching tolerance for diversity should not be restricted to schools. Parents, coaches, mentors, and other role models need to stress the importance of recognizing and appreciating other groups. For instance, athletic coaches are often in ideal situations to stress teamwork among individuals from different backgrounds. The lesson that individuals need to work as a team could be generalized to society with the goal of encouraging athletes (and others) to recognize the beneficial contributions from diverse individuals. The same idea holds true for band leaders, church group facilitators, and others. There are many avenues where progress can be made with regard to accepting and appreciating diverse individuals and groups.

TRAINING AND LAW ENFORCEMENT

The police are considered the "gatekeepers to the criminal justice system," as they are involved with the initial steps of the criminal case processing. The police interact with citizens more frequently than any other component of the criminal justice system, and they largely shape the public's perception of justice-based practices. As such, police training is important for numerous reasons. Failing to properly train officers could result in negative police-community relations, wasted resources, dangers to the public, the failure to properly address society's problems, and lawsuits. With regard to the latter, counties and municipalities can face litigation if it is believed they are in violation of federal statute Title 42, United States Code, Section 1983, which allows individuals to hold government employees and in some cases their employers accountable for violation of rights under the U.S. Constitution. With regard to police training, individuals who believe they were treated improperly by the police can claim that their rights were violated by a failure to adequately train officers.[13] The importance of both training and education is noted in a study which found that enhanced employment screening tests, higher departmental education requirements, and increased field training requirements were associated with a reduction in use-of-force complaints.[14]

All states have mandated training for police officers. The requirements for the minimum standards of training, and general guidance for police training, are provided by state organizations typically called **Police Officers Standards and Training Commissions** (POSTs). In addition to establishing minimum standards, POSTs typically provide training criteria for police officers and seek means, for instance through research, to improve police training practices. As an example, the Louisiana Peace Officer Standards and Training Council develops training standards for peace officers in Louisiana. Among other contributions, the Council develops and evaluates the curriculum of mandatory basic training courses for peace officers in the state.[15]

Cultural sensitivity training, also known as cross-cultural training, for police officers largely emerged in the 1980s. The increased focus on cultural sensitivity training was designed to improve police-community relations and address citizen complaints of police officers misusing their powers against underrepresented persons in the community.[16] Although such training largely emerged in the 1980s, there has been a historical need for sensitivity training. For example, the 1967 Kerner Report suggested that poor police-community relations were at the root of much civil unrest.

Cultural sensitivity training is imperative for today's police officers. Ideally, training should alter officer behavior, generate alternative solutions to problematic or confrontational situations, and encourage officers to adopt the values and ideals of the department.[17] With regard to the latter, one must assume and hope that the values and ideals of the department are based on tolerance and cultural sensitivity. The shift in policing toward greater interaction with the public in the form of community-oriented policing necessitates greater emphasis on personal communication skills, and tolerating and appreciating diversity. Accordingly, many departments and police academies have enhanced their focus on cultural sensitivity training. As noted in Chapter 11, the *Task Force on 21st Century Policing* included training and education among its six areas of recommendations to improve police practices and build public trust. In emphasizing training as it relates to interacting with diverse groups, the report noted:

> One specific method of increasing the quality of training would be to ensure that Peace Officer and Standards Training (POST) boards include mandatory Crisis Intervention Training (CIT), which equips officers to deal with individuals in crisis or living with mental disabilities, as part of both basic recruit and in-service officer training—as well as instruction in disease of addiction, implicit bias and cultural responsiveness, policing in a democratic society, procedural justice, and effective social interaction and tactical skills.[18]

Among the issues surrounding sensitivity training are gaining an understanding, recognition, and respect for the various groups and cultures in society. Training must consist of more than a briefing or cursory examination at the academy, or generic comments offered at roll call. Such training must be ongoing and reinforced by fellow officers and superiors who should also have notable appreciation of cultural diversity. Further, cultural sensitivity training is more effective when various groups outside of policing, for example civic leaders, offer input regarding their expectations and an overview of their cultural beliefs and practices.

It would be difficult for police officers, especially those in large cities where diversity is most prominent, to have a thorough understanding of all cultural beliefs and practices. Fortunately, community policing strategies emphasize police-citizen interaction, in part, by having officers consistently work in specific jurisdictions. In other words, maintaining an officer's presence in a particular neighborhood or community becomes important for officers to grasp the local culture as they become better able to understand those in the community. Learning how to grasp the local culture and how to respect cultural diversity are among the many topics addressed at the police academy.

Pre-service training for officers begins at the police academy. The academy teaches officers the technical skills required for the job, indoctrinates cadets into the social world of policing, and identifies those unfit for a career in policing. At the police academy officers spend time on law, practical skills, human relations, criminal investigations, patrol procedures, the structure and practices of policing, and more generally the criminal justice system. Officers will later be provided in-service and field training to keep them fresh and abreast of changes throughout their careers, and help them apply what they learned at the academy, respectively.

Data from the U.S. Bureau of Justice Statistics regarding local and state police training in 2013 notes that officers received an average of 843 hours of classroom instruction, and an average of 521 hours of field training. On average, special jurisdiction police agencies required the largest number of hours (1,075), followed by county police (1,029) and municipal police (936 hours). Municipal police departments required the highest average number of field training hours (630).[19] These and related findings are noted in Table 14.1.

The same report includes information regarding the special topics included in state and local law enforcement training academies, as well as the percentages of agencies that include such topics.[20] Many of these topics are of particular interest to the many groups

TABLE 14.1   DURATION OF BASIC TRAINING PROGRAMS IN STATE AND LOCAL LAW ENFORCEMENT TRAINING ACADEMIES, BY TYPE OF ACADEMY, 2013

Type of Academy	Average Length in Classroom	Mandatory Field Training Component			Average Length (hrs.)[a]
		Total	For All Recruits	Agency Specific	
All types	843 hrs.	81%	37%	44%	521
State POST	650	38	14	24	250
State police/highway patrol	878	94	76	18	455
Sheriff's office	706	90	37	53	506
County police	1,029	100	76	24	479
Municipal police	936	97	71	26	630
4-year college/ university	903	68	15	53	321
2-year college	822	71	14	57	332
Technical school	703	65	0	65	~
Special jurisdiction	1,075	100	69	31	493
Multiagency/regional	827	95	36	60	185

Note: Detail may not sum to total due to rounding.

"~" = Not applicable.

[a]Excludes field training segments that were not overseen by academies.

[b]Peace Officer Standards and Training.

Source: Bureau of Justice Statistics, "Census of Law Enforcement Training Academies, 2013."

discussed in this book. The findings can be viewed as both encouraging and discouraging; for instance, it is encouraging that the majority of academies address issues such as domestic violence, hate crimes/bias crimes, and elder abuse. However, the finding that only three hours on average are devoted to topics such as hate crimes/bias crimes and elder abuse, and that fact that only 78 percent and 73 percent include this as part of the training could be viewed as discouraging. These and related findings are noted in Table 14.2.

In discussing his many years of teaching cultural diversity and ethics to law enforcement groups, Daniel Carlson, author of the book *When Cultures Clash*, suggested that training on topics such as ethics or cultural diversity is not popular among police officers. He states, "Very often in the heat of these classes, officers bemoan the fact that while they are 'forced' to endure training designed to improve police-citizen interactions, no such training exists for citizens." The officers argue that the public needs to better understand policing and police officers.[21] There is certainly merit to this argument, as policing arguably has a distinctive culture of its own. The dilemma exists in that it is a "give-and-take" situation that requires effort from both sides.

So what exactly is cultural sensitivity training for police officers? Should coverage of hate or bias crime be included in such training? Departments have responded to concerns surrounding hate crimes, in part by training officers and administrators to understand how to identify hate crimes. Should cultural sensitivity training also include teaching officers to recognize the differences between those with physical ailments from the intoxicated? In discussing the best practices to improve police relations with transgender individuals, scholar Jan Redfern noted that "police departments should consider sensitivity training of

TABLE 14.2 SPECIAL TOPICS INCLUDED IN BASIC TRAINING PROGRAMS IN STATE AND LOCAL LAW ENFORCEMENT TRAINING ACADEMIES, 2013

Subject Area	Percent of Academies with Training	Average Number of Hours of Instruction per Recruit*
Domestic violence	98	13
Mental illness	95	10
Sexual assault	92	6
Crimes against children	90	6
Domestic preparedness/terrorism	85	9
Gangs	82	4
Victim response	80	5
Hate crimes/bias crimes	78	3
Sexual harassment	75	3
Elder abuse	73	3
Clandestine drug labs	67	4
Human trafficking	64	3
Cyber/internet crimes	57	3

*Excludes academies that did not provide this type of instruction.

Source: Bureau of Justice Statistics, Census of Law Enforcement Training Academies, 2013.

law enforcement professionals to increase awareness and appreciation of gender diversity, to avoid personal biases and assumptions, and to avoid costly litigation from civil rights violations." Such training, Redfern argues, would assist officers by improving interactions and communications in assisting or arresting transgender individuals.[22]

Cultural sensitivity is a complex phenomenon that is created and shaped in individuals during their upbringing. What is taught in the police academy and supplemented on the streets also contributes to how officers react to multiculturalism. Police training is an ongoing process, as evidenced during an officer's probationary period following graduation from the academy. Many departments use **field training officer programs**, which pair new officers with experienced ones. Field training officers teach new officers the practical aspects of police work, building upon and reinforcing what was taught at the academy, and acclimate the officers to the department's and community's values.[23] It is at this point in the officer's new career that they gain a foundation of skills, knowledge, and expectations that shape their future. Pairing new officers with culturally sensitive officers enhances policing in many ways. Continued in-service training should reinforce earlier training and expose officers to developments in policing.

MULTICULTURALISM AND COURTROOM PERSONNEL TRAINING

The nature of the training for the primary actors (i.e., judges, prosecutors, and defense attorneys) in the courtroom is much different from that in policing and corrections. Judges, prosecutors, and defense attorneys are primarily trained through law school and on-the-job experience. Training in policing and corrections is more formal in nature, for instance as corrections officers and police officers attend training academies and must complete a specified number of training courses or hours. Individuals interested in practicing law typically attend law school, and from there either join private law firms or become public defenders or assistant district attorneys. Judges primarily have years of experience as practicing attorneys, and are elected or appointed to their positions.

Police officer training is particularly important given the frequency with which officers engage the public and the seriousness of the encounters they sometimes face.

Law schools provide an academic view of the law, with emphases in particular areas. The courses a law school student takes during their first year are typically prescribed, and students are often permitted to study particular areas of law in their latter two years. These areas include criminal law, contract law, corporate law, and tax law, among others. Students typically spend three years studying various aspects of law, following which they must pass a bar exam to practice law in the state in which they took the exam.

In discussing the importance of law school students understanding civil rights issues, law professor Tamara Lawson noted that "it is optimal for students to take a specialized course in Race-in-the-Law, Critical Race Theory, or Civil Rights, but many students are unable to take such a course either due to their schedules, their university's offerings, or their lack of interest in the subject." Professor Lawson suggested that discussions of civil rights should be incorporated into the core curriculum, which would enable all law school students to have a better understanding of diversity and civil rights.[24]

New assistant district attorneys are generally granted much freedom with regard to how they handle their cases, and office policies are typically general and vague in nature. New attorneys are encouraged to observe and ask questions of the more experienced attorneys, a socialization process that helps them better understand the expectations of the position.[25] Historically, training for new assistant district attorneys was primarily conducted through on-the-job learning. It was not uncommon for recently hired attorneys to be placed in the courtroom on their first day of employment. This has changed in recent years, as prosecutors' offices have incorporated more systematic training for new employees. Such training may include introducing the new employee to the different divisions

Much of the formal training for attorneys occurs in law school. Judges are often former practicing attorneys who attended law school. The schools are increasingly incorporating experiential education to better prepare law students for a career in the courts.

of the office, and having them attend different courtroom proceedings where they closely observe how experienced prosecutors handle cases.[26]

Similar to the training for new assistant district attorneys, training for new public defenders has largely consisted of learning through working in the courts and learning as one handles cases. This has been supplemented by some public defenders working closely with more experienced attorneys and formal training programs.[27] In noting its support for training new public defenders, the American Bar Association highlighted the importance of training and continued legal education in Principles 6 and 9 of its *Ten Principles of a Public Defense Delivery System*. Principle 6 notes:

- **Defense counsel's ability, training, and experience match the complexity of the case.** "Counsel should never be assigned a case that counsel lacks the experience or training to handle competently, and counsel is obligated to refuse appointment if unable to provide ethical, high-quality representation."

Principle 9 notes:

- **Defense counsel is provided with and required to attend continuing legal education.** "Counsel and staff providing defense services should have systematic and comprehensive training appropriate to their areas of practice and at least equal to that received by prosecutors."[28]

Statewide administrative offices regularly develop, update, and offer elaborate training and education programs for new judges. These programs also provide formal training for experienced judges, and may last several weeks and cover a wide range of topics.[29] For instance, the "New Jersey Judicial Education Program" provides training and guidance for new and experienced judges, in part by keeping them abreast of developments in the law and judicial administration.[30]

Educational qualifications for appellate and general jurisdiction judges in the state courts are largely established by state constitutional provisions. Some states give the legislature the power to set or expand on the criteria. Other states have no specific educational requirements established by statute. Although most states require a judge in courts of general jurisdiction to be a qualified attorney, over half of all states permit non-attorneys to become judges in their lower-courts. In many cases there are no educational requirements to preside over the lower courts, or the requirement may be a high school diploma or a GED. Permitting non-attorneys to become judges helps address the problems encountered in rural areas where there are typically few attorneys.[31]

Law schools have responded to the lack of hands-on experience of law school students through offering more skills-oriented classes in their curricula. The schools have increasingly added problem-based learning and community-engaged learning activities designed to better prepare students for employment in the field.[32] For instance, law professor Charlotte Alexander wrote about the hands-on experience law students receive in a course at Georgia State University College of Law in which students are paired with an attorney in solo practice or a small law firm. The fieldwork exposes students to the realities of practicing law, including the ethical decision-making practices, practice management tools, and general skills needed to be an attorney. The students are matched with attorneys who practice law in subject areas that the students anticipate entering, and the fieldwork begins with an interview of the attorney and observation of them at work. This course is one of many similarly designed courses increasingly being offered at law schools around the United States, in efforts to ensure that new attorneys are prepared for practicing law.[33]

MULTICULTURALISM AND CORRECTIONAL STAFF TRAINING

In the late 1970s, the American Correctional Association (ACA) Commission on Accreditation established the first training standards for corrections workers. Among other contributions, the commission set standards for positions within corrections, identified training topics, set specified numbers of pre-service and annual training hours, and established specific basic administrative policy support requirements for training programs.[34] States built upon the initial work of the ACA, and almost all states today require at least one hundred hours of pre-service training for correctional officers working in institutions. Most states require at least two hundred hours of training.[35]

Aside from the ACA, other associations in corrections offer models of professionalism designed to advance the field. Among them are the American Probation and Parole Association and the American Jail Association. These groups offer principles, guidance, and support for correctional workers and administrators. They offer training opportunities, host seminars and meetings, advertise position openings, and publish literature designed to advance correctional practices. They may also lobby legislative bodies to further a particular cause.

Training requirements for correctional officers vary among jurisdictions and institutions. State administrative agencies typically establish the standards and requirements. Standard training typically includes use of force and restraints, weapons, self-defense, first aid and CPR, report writing, testifying in court, defusing hostile situations, interpersonal communications, gang intelligence, and law.

Probation and parole officers have similar training requirements as those who work in institutions.[36] For instance, the Nevada Department of Public Safety Training Division offers training for probation and parole officers in the state, requiring them to complete 480 hours of classroom and field training during their first year of work. The training covers areas such as legal liability issues, ethics, personnel matters, department policies and procedures, and statutes.[37]

Correctional agencies typically do not have the resources to train all staff regarding the cultural differences of the incarcerated. Accordingly, training resources must be used wisely. Employees working with special populations, such as the elderly or mentally impaired, receive specific sensitivity training. The correctional population includes large numbers of offenders from these two groups, as well as many other groups that require special attention. An analysis of state correctional officer training academies found that about 72 percent provided training that directly focused on LGBTQ offenders, and roughly 46 percent addresses elderly offenders. The average amount of training hours focused on these groups was about 2.2 and 1.7, respectively.[38] The finding that a minority of states provided training for the elderly warrants attention given the large and increasing number of elderly offenders. Employees assuming leadership roles in the institution receive more advanced training in diversity.[39]

In the end, exposing all staff members to as many cultural differences as feasible contributes to more effective correctional practices. Correctional leadership needs to promote tolerance and cultural diversity among the officers and encourage officers to develop the interpersonal skills necessary to operate in a multicultural institution, or work in community corrections. Effective communication skills are necessary for working in corrections since poor communication is a major source of problems.[40] The ability to speak a second language can largely contribute to a correctional or any other criminal justice officer's effectiveness. Bilingual or multilingual prison officers provide much needed safety and security in institutions with great diversity.[41] Considering cultural context in the course of communicating ultimately promotes a more effective work environment.

The use of community resources to assist correctional staff is important in many ways, particularly in cases in which there exists a notable lack of familiarity with a particular culture. Incorporating input from volunteers, guest speakers, professional associations, and specific interest groups demonstrates to correctional staff and the individuals they supervise that the agency respects cultural diversity. The onus is on correctional agencies to proactively identify means by which they can send a message of tolerance to all individuals with whom they associate.

One difficulty associated with multicultural awareness training involves a method or technique of assessing awareness or knowledge with regard to cultural diversity.[42] In other words, how do we know if someone (e.g., a probation officer) is prepared to supervise individuals from diverse cultures? Part of correctional officer training involves role-play, in which cadets act as unruly inmates demonstrating cultural idiosyncrasies that test the correctional officials' ability to properly respond. The actor's cadet colleagues learn methods of responding appropriately to the challenges. Communication skills, including interpreting and using nonverbal communication, are stressed, as is the need to recognize and appreciate culture-related symbolism. While these and related training skills will not end culture conflict throughout correctional systems, they certainly will help alleviate tensions among correctional officials and those under correctional supervision.

Correctional officers maintain a great deal of discretion in their day-to-day functions. Determining whether to confront troubling situations with formal or informal methods is one example of this discretion. Improper use of discretion could explain why inexperienced prison officers are more likely than their experienced counterparts to be assaulted by inmates.[43] Violent inmate reactions may be spurred by perceptions of injustice. Sensitivities to race, age, and crime-related factors of individual inmates undoubtedly factor into how corrections officers use their discretion.[44] Training officers to properly consider such extralegal factors, as well as continuous reinforcement of that training, should be of primary concern to correctional administrators.

Institutional administrators play a significant role in promoting cultural diversity. Proper recruitment, selection, and training contribute to recognizing and promoting multiculturalism in corrections. The organizational culture of the institution or agency should be one in which cultural diversity is among the primary concerns. Failure to recognize diversity results in a much greater likelihood of violence and related negative consequences. Promoting cultural tolerance among staff members is significantly important for administrators, as failure to properly resolve situational conflicts and misunderstandings is related to:

- Lost productivity
- Increased isolation of staff members
- Enhanced suspicion and distrust among staff members
- Increased staff turnover
- More disgruntled employees
- Overall negative changes in the climate of the correctional institution[45]

THE LIMITATIONS OF TRAINING

Despite the many benefits of training, there are some limitations. As referenced earlier, changing human behavior is sometimes difficult. The question is asked whether training is too heavily focused on critical incidents that occur relatively infrequently (e.g., shootings) at the expense of the kinds of situations that occur more frequently (e.g., interacting with diverse groups).[46] The following common issues and limitations are inherent in police training, although most apply to training for many other important positions in the criminal justice system:

- Program content—programs might not cover significant areas (e.g., rape, human relations)
- Training facilities and equipment—the lack of adequate facilities in which to train
- Part-time training instructors and directors—full-time personnel with no other job duties should be provided
- Full-time attendance—officers who work and attend the academy face many difficulties
- Training prior to exercising power—this prevents untrained officers from working the streets
- Follow-up evaluation—training should occur at two-year intervals following initial pre-service training
- Field training officers—to evaluate the recruit's work in the field
- Quality control of instructors—instructors might not be effective teachers[47]

The significant role played by trainers cannot be ignored, and instructors are typically expected to teach in certain areas. Race, ethnicity, gender, cultural background, and related factors could influence trainer effectiveness, as it was noted, for instance, that White course facilitators discussing racial profiling are often easily dismissed by trainees who generally believe that the facilitator is unaware of life as an officer on the streets. Yet, a racial minority police officer who shares personal experiences of being harassed by the police generates notable attention.[48]

Despite the aforementioned and other limitations, training is an integral and vital aspect of employment in the criminal justice system. It could be argued, however, that we expect too much out of training. This dilemma presents a challenge for all employees who work in the criminal justice system, and will continue to do so until the limitations are addressed. At the most basic level, criminal justice practitioners are, first and foremost, human beings who were molded and shaped by various forces prior to entering the field. Various types of training may be expected to undo internal limitations or conflicts among individuals. Part of cultural sensitivity training involves "undoing" damage from the past and promoting tolerance. It is hoped that proper recruitment, selection, and training can provide criminal justice agencies with individuals who won't let personal conflicts affect their ability to properly perform their jobs. In sum, much progress has been made to address the limitations involved in training, although much work remains.

CHECKPOINT

- Pre-service and continued training are vital to the effective functioning of all components within the criminal justice system. Emphasis should be placed on training with regard to multiculturalism.
- Police officers undergo much training prior to beginning—and during—their careers. Cultural diversity training has become increasingly important in the field.

- Much of the formal training for attorneys and judges is provided in law schools and on the job.
- The training requirements for those who work in corrections vary according to jurisdiction and the nature of their position.
- Training is certainly important in all aspects of criminal justice; however, there are limitations regarding its effectiveness.

POLICIES AND MULTICULTURALISM

Similar to the earlier suggestion that training alone cannot solve all problems related to an increasingly diverse society, no policy or group of policies will completely fix the diversity-related challenges facing the criminal justice system. This, of course, is not to say that policy cannot change some things and have positive, lasting effects. **Policy** refers to decisions or actions that address particular issues or problems. **Public policy** is supported by public resources and enforced by the legal system. **Criminal justice policy** focuses on issues or problems pertaining to policing, courts, corrections, and related areas of formal social control.

Policies should not be established simply for the sake of making policy. There must be valid reasons to impose restrictions or offer guidance on human behavior. Effective policies directly address areas in which attention is needed. Policies are necessary for many reasons: they guide behavior, promote fair and just practices, and can serve as a deterrent. Their existence symbolizes concern for a particular issue. Of particular importance with regard to any policy are efforts to ensure that it is properly enforced. Failing to properly enforce or address a policy is harmful in many aspects, because policy becomes of little importance and has limited, if any, effect if there's no concern for it. Further, neglecting policies sends a message that the issue at the center of the policy is of limited importance.

With regard to the criminal justice system, one can simply consider findings from recent Gallup public opinion polls to identify the need for more effective policy. The following results highlight the many diversity-, justice-, and tolerance-related issues that challenge the United States today:

- For more than a decade prior to December 2014, no more than 5 percent of Americans had named racism or race relations as the top problem facing the United States, with the figure often measuring 0 percent. In December 2014 it was 13 percent. In July 2019 it was 7 percent.[49]
- Forty percent of Americans reported being worried a great deal about race relations in the United States in 2019. This is among the highest percentage since Gallup first asked the question in 2001.[50]
- In 2016, Blacks (53 percent) were far more likely than Whites (27 percent) to report that they worry a great deal about race relations in the United States.[51]
- In 2016, Whites (62 percent) were significantly more likely than non-Whites (39 percent) to note that they had a great deal or quite a lot of confidence in the police.[52]
- Forty-three percent of Americans harbored some degree of prejudice toward Muslims in 2015.[53]

Public perception of the criminal justice system is particularly low, as noted in Table 14.3.[54] The finding that only 22 percent of respondents had a great deal or quite a lot of confidence in the criminal justice system suggests that change is required. Such change may include altering some existing policies, eliminating others, and creating effective new ones.

TABLE 14.3   AMERICANS' CONFIDENCE IN US INSTITUTIONS, 2018

	Great deal/ Quite a lot %	Some %	Very little/ None (vol.) %	Net positive^ %
The military	74	20	5	+69
Small business	67	26	6	+61
The police	54	31	15	+39
The church or organized religion	38	33	27	+11
The presidency	37	18	44	-7
The U.S. Supreme Court	37	42	18	+19
The medical system	36	37	26	+10
Banks	30	46	22	+8
The public schools	29	44	27	+2
Organized labor	26	45	25	+1
Big business	25	43	30	-5
Newspapers	23	35	40	-17
The criminal justice system	22	41	36	-14
Television news	20	34	45	-25
Congress	11	39	48	-37

(vol.) = volunteered response; ^Net positive = "Great deal"/"Quite a lot" minus "Only a little"/"None" (vol.)

Results from this poll suggest that the general public is not as confident in the criminal justice system as it is in other institutions in the United States. Interestingly, the public has a relatively high level of confidence in the police. This finding, however, should be considered in light of the notable differences in levels of confidence in the police between Whites and racial and ethnic minorities, as noted earlier.

The history of criminal justice in the United States is filled with policies designed to address particular problems. Some of the more recognizable policies are those that pertain to drugs, capital punishment, guns, and sentencing. Despite the fact that policies are designed to address problems, and despite the many benefits that policies often provide, they are often subject to criticism. Some, and perhaps much, of the criticism has been voiced by less powerful groups in society, primarily because they are often the targets of criminal justice policies. For example, the punitive laws directed toward drug offenses involving crack cocaine in the 1980s and 1990s were believed to be targeted toward inner-city African American males. More generally, harsh penalties imposed on all drug offenses have been perceived to be directed toward many minority groups. Tougher sentencing policies have disproportionately impacted less powerful groups in society, leaving many to believe that they too were intentionally designed to punish groups as opposed to individuals.

Policies are subject to change, and proactive institutions, agencies, and organizations regularly create and update policies to address changes. The United States has recently experienced a change in many drug-related policies, as earlier efforts to confront drug use were viewed as overly harsh. As of 2019, thirty-three states had passed laws legalizing marijuana in some form, whether it be for medicinal or recreational purposes.

Criminal justice policies are often popular because we all wish to live in a crime-free society, and we generally want those who break the law to be punished for their actions. It is often politically popular to be tough on crime, and the interconnectedness of politics and criminal justice has contributed to increasingly punitive policies and practices. Consider the fact that several key criminal justice practitioners are elected to their positions in many places. For example, judges and sheriffs in many places are elected officials who often shape their political campaigns around the public's want for tough justice-based practices. What is overlooked in many instances are the repercussions or outcomes of tough policies and practices. For instance, tougher sentencing laws and practices result in higher levels of incarceration, which consumes public funding that could otherwise be used for education, healthcare, and related services. Tougher sentencing practices have also had a disproportionate impact on particular groups, including African Americans, and contribute to more children living in single-parent households and families living in poverty. Ultimately, an important, yet often overlooked, aspect of policies is the long-term effects the policy-related actions will have.

To be sure, policies are important in society. They have been the source of both criticism and many positive changes. No single policy is going to have all desired outcomes, and no policy is going to please everyone. Differences among groups, including varied interests, contribute to different perceptions of policies. Policies that may seem appropriate for one group are viewed with disdain by other groups. Policies should not consist of knee-jerk reactions to pressing problems, but instead should be well thought out, with particular concern for their effects. Agencies and organizations are constantly changing, and new organizational policies or procedures are typically met by resistance from those most affected.[55] Accordingly, the adoption of new policies requires explanation of—and justification for—the new policy to ensure buy-in.

Aside from the many high-profile policies found within justice-based practices, there are many policies that go unnoticed by much of society. Consider, for instance, the placement of halfway houses and other residential correctional facilities. As used by the criminal justice system, **halfway houses** are community-based facilities that enable offenders to reside in the community while remaining under relatively close supervision. Offenders are able to maintain employment and family ties, while being supervised and undergoing programming and counseling. The residences are, however, viewed by some groups and individuals as problematic, as they contribute to the concentration of offenders in a particular area, may be perceived as harmful by residents who live in close proximity to the facilities, may decrease property values, and generally impact quality-of-life issues for residents who live close by. Would you be excited to hear that the house next to yours has been turned into a halfway house? Thus, the question is often asked: Where should we place halfway houses?

The acronym **NIMBY** refers to "Not in my backyard," and relates to citizen concerns about the siting of something unpleasant or potentially dangerous in their vicinity. Such concerns are not restricted to the siting of criminal justice facilities; for instance, citizens have argued against the placement of hazardous waste facilities near their residences.[56] Nevertheless, there have been concerns over the location of many criminal and juvenile justice facilities, because having a prison as a neighbor is not appealing to a large number of people. The nature of community corrections becomes increasingly important, as offenders are not confined within prison walls and are supervised in the community.

In a study of the placement of residential facilities in Connecticut, researchers noted that halfway houses were significantly more likely to be located in non-White communities with high crime rates.[57] Related research has noted that such undesirable facilities are often located in areas where there is a concentration of less powerful groups. To be sure, there is no policy which states that such facilities will be placed in particular areas. The government officials tasked with locating halfway houses and related facilities undoubtedly consider a host of factors, including resources. Simply, it's less expensive to operate a facility in a low-income area. This predicament results in concerns for **social justice**, which is defined as a "perspective of justice that evaluates how a society provides for the needs of its members and the extent to which it treats its subgroups equally."[58]

Although policy does not dictate that undesirable correctional facilities are to be located in low-income areas, they often are. Policy, however, does dictate the use of halfway houses, and the siting of them contributes to controversy. While it may be less costly to locate halfway houses in low-income areas, the repercussions of doing so are many. Citizens in these areas may believe that they are being placed at a greater risk of victimization, and may view the placement of such facilities as another example of powerful individuals lacking a concern for social justice.

Community resistance to the placement of halfway houses provides an example of the widespread effects of policies. Halfway houses provide helpful services for offenders residing in the community, yet many residents do not wish to have them located in their communities.

The policy of using halfway houses and the associated difficulties in locating them are among the many policy-related concerns in criminal justice. This section does not provide a comprehensive account of which policies work, which policies do not, and which policies should be adopted. To do so with something as vast as criminal justice practices is notably burdensome. Instead, we seek to introduce readers to what constitutes a policy, and the need for considering diversity and related issues when issuing policy. Next we offer some examples of policies that offer promise for more successful justice-based actions, and recognize that there are many others in existence.

One of the more promising policy approaches in policing is the increased use of community liaison officers, who meet with residents and business owners to discuss crime and crime prevention efforts. These officers are ideally situated to interact with citizens in a nonconfrontational manner, share information with the community, and learn about issues that may hamper police and general criminal justice practices. The officers can better understand cultural and other diversity-related differences among the citizens, and they promote the benefits of the police departments. The use of such officers has increased with the incorporation of community policing, and the need for

TRANSGENDER BATHROOM DEBATE

Transgender activism became the focus of much national attention in 2016, especially in relation to the use of public restrooms. Several states introduced—and one passed—legislation with regard to transgender bathroom use. North Carolina's law requires all people to use the bathroom matching the sex on their birth certificate, and other states proposed legislation that would restrict which bathrooms transgender individuals could use. Several cities passed ordinances that require people to use restrooms based on their sex, as opposed to gender identity, and some schools have rules that require transgender students to use restrooms and locker rooms that match the sex listed on their birth certificates. These and forthcoming policies will continue to be addressed in the courts.

The primary rationale behind these policies is a concern for predators, who could prey on women and children in bathrooms. It is believed that some individuals may pretend to be transgender and would now have easy access to commit deviant and harmful acts. Critics argue that the policies are discriminatory in nature, and that transgender individuals pose little to no danger. Several large companies and other groups denounced the bathroom laws, including PayPal, which canceled plans to build a global operations center in North Carolina, resulting in the loss of millions of dollars and over four hundred jobs to the state. In addition to that, performing artists such as Bruce Springsteen canceled shows in the state to show their opposition to the law.

additional use of these officers is evident in the aforementioned polls regarding Black respondents' low level of confidence in the police.

Policies directed toward diversifying criminal justice agencies promote more effective justice-based practices. Many criminal justice agencies have adopted policies designed to diversify the workforce. As noted throughout this book, women and racial and ethnic minorities have been underrepresented in criminal justice agencies. Efforts have been taken to diversify the field, however much work remains. Among other benefits, a more diverse criminal justice workforce helps practitioners identify broader solutions, helps generate culturally sensitive solutions to problems, enhances trust between the agencies and the public, reduces discrimination, and encourages members of underrepresented groups to support criminal justice practices.

Similarly, policies directed toward building and maintaining positive work environments encourage more positive criminal justice practices. The term **organizational culture** refers to shared beliefs, values, and assumptions that influence how individuals behave in organizations. Much has been written about different cultures and subcultures, including the police subculture, and it appears that cultural organization has a significant impact on employee performances and behaviors. While it is easy to simply state that criminal justice agencies should create positive organizational cultures that value diversity and promote multiculturalism, it remains important that they do so. Policies that encourage tolerance, acceptance, understanding of different groups, and the like would contribute much to addressing many of the issues faced in the criminal justice system. Among the means to create a more positive organizational culture are recruiting, selecting, and hiring individuals who will treat all groups and individuals with respect. Effective training, as noted previously, also contributes to creating a positive organizational culture, as do specific programs designed to promote tolerance. For instance, the West Hartford (Connecticut) Police Department adopted a policy designed to assist officers when interacting with members of the LGBT community. Among other requirements, the policy notes that officers should use the person's preferred name as opposed to their legal name when interacting with them, and abide by the transgender person's request to be searched by an officer of a specific gender.[59]

Several incidents in which the police were accused of using too much force against racial and ethnic minorities have resulted in less positive perceptions of the police. For instance, the shooting of Michael Brown by a Ferguson (Missouri) police officer generated protests in the city and around the country. In discussing the significance of race in contemporary urban policing, authors Jones-Brown, Moran, King-Toler, and Sudula offered three policy recommendations designed to enhance policing, including public perceptions of the police. Particularly, they suggest making multicultural competency an integral part of policing policy and practice; prioritizing constitutionality, transparency, and accountability; and analyzing the effects of police policies on racial and ethnic minorities.[60] These suggestions, while offered with consideration of urban policing, could apply to all types of policing and all components of the criminal justice system.

CHECKPOINT

- Policies are decisions or actions that address particular issues or problems, and those who support and/or pass them must be aware of all policy implications, including those pertaining to multiculturalism.

GLOBAL PERSPECTIVES

Consideration of the justice-based practices in other countries could enable us to adopt pieces, or aspects, of those practices that could promote additional tolerance and fairness in our criminal justice system. Justice systems in the United States are based on English heritage; they closely resemble criminal justice practices in some countries and differ greatly from practices found in other countries. Our system has been refined over time as various reforms in policing, the courts, and corrections have regularly reshaped our justice-based practices.

Consideration of other country's systems of justice may provide avenues through which we could enhance our policies and practices. Four legal traditions are recognized in countries across the globe.[61] These categories include the common tradition, the civil tradition, the Islamic tradition, and the Eastern Asia tradition. The **common legal tradition** is found in the United States and other countries and is based on feudal practices, custom, and equity. The **civil legal tradition** is based on Roman and canon laws, and codification. The **Islamic legal tradition** is based on the Qur'an and Sunna, as well as the doctrine of consensus and reasoning by analogy. The **Eastern Asia legal tradition** is grounded in the principles of Confucianism, along with collectivism, context, and informalism. The two primary legal systems today are the common law and civil law systems. Common law systems are found primarily in North America and England, while the civil law system is most often found throughout the rest of the world today.[62] Consideration of policies in other countries with similar legal traditions, and perhaps even those that differ greatly from those found in the United States, has the potential to enhance our justice-based practices.

Studying justice systems is beneficial in many ways, as it facilitates a better understanding of other people and cultures and highlights avenues for improvement, especially with regard to policies. Further, it enables individuals to adopt a more global perspective of justice.[63] The need to better understand varying systems of justice and the ease with which transnational crimes can occur was highlighted by Thomas Friedman in his popular book *The World Is Flat: A Brief History of the Twenty-First Century*, in which he highlights how various societal changes, including those pertaining to communication and transportation, have impacted society in many important ways.[64] A primary benefit of globalization is the sharing of ideas and practices, which could benefit justice-based practices in the United States and abroad. The United States is certainly not the only country dealing with diversity-related issues both within and outside of its justice system. Identifying helpful and proven approaches to address the issues in other countries is a promising means by which to effectively address our issues.

Of particular importance when comparing international criminal justice systems is the need to consider what type of system is in place and the practices of the individuals in relation to the system. For instance, two countries may have similar criminal justice systems in design, but the laws may be applied with differing levels of severity and the use of discretion may differ. The system of justice in the United States is similar to what exists in England; however, the United States is viewed as being particularly more punitive than England and many other countries.

CHECKPOINT

- Consideration of global justice-based practices has much potential to enhance our criminal justice system. Understanding what works and what doesn't work in other countries could help improve our own criminal justice system.

SUMMARY

This chapter addressed two important issues that could help those who work in the criminal justice system in many ways: training and policies. Training is required of all criminal justice employees, and it helps prepare individuals for the situations they will encounter. Education is a very important component of training, but it alone cannot properly train an individual. Hands-on experience and guidance from supervisors and experienced colleagues are also important to one's training. Training requirements vary among the numerous positions in the criminal justice system; for instance, police officers and correctional officers attend training academies, while lawyers and judges attend law school and primarily learn from work experience and guidance. Training is limited in several ways; it cannot fully prepare individuals for what they will experience on the job.

Policies are created, implemented, and enforced with the goal of controlling behaviors. Criminal justice policy has been both very helpful and at times controversial. Many effective policies have been implemented, and their benefits often go unnoticed. The controversial policies draw the most attention. Fortunately, policies are flexible and can be altered to address unanticipated challenges. Policies can be imposed at the agency level (e.g., with regard to decisions to prosecute) or on a much larger scale, for example in the form of federal drug policies. Criminal justice agencies should consider policies from other countries in efforts to generate new, effective approaches that could possibly be implemented in the United States.

YOU MAKE THE CALL
TEACHING DIVERSITY

Consider the following scenario. Debate the pros and cons of all options and decide what you would do.

You're a new college faculty member at a historically African American university. As part of your teaching assignment, you've been asked to teach the upper-level undergraduate "Minorities and Crime" course. As a White male, however, you're a bit apprehensive. Sure, you know all about crime and took courses and researched minority issues, but you never anticipated such a challenge this early in your teaching career. Aside from having to be current on your knowledge of crime, you also have to discuss minority issues to a large group of minorities. On the first day of class, a young man in the audience asks how you can comment on minority issues, when you have absolutely no life experience being a minority. You hoped this wouldn't be an issue, but you are prepared to answer the question.

Questions

1. How will you build credibility with the predominantly African American students?
2. How will you structure the course? In other words, would you approach the course from the views of minority groups or the views of the majority? Or, would you attempt to provide an adequate balance between both?
3. How would you answer the student's question?
4. Discuss how the following teaching tools could assist with your situation:
   - Class discussion
   - Videos (what movies would you include?)
   - Guest speakers
   - Lecture

KEY TERMS

Black Lives Matter
civil legal tradition
common legal tradition
community liaison officers
criminal justice policy
culture-general training
culture-specific training
Eastern Asia legal tradition
field training
field training officer programs

halfway house
Islamic legal tradition
NIMBY
organizational culture
Police Officers Standards and Training Commissions
policy
pre-service training
public policy
social justice

DISCUSSION QUESTIONS

1. To what extent do you believe additional training for police officers will alleviate the problems we've seen with officers allegedly misusing their powers against African American males?
2. Should prosecutors and defense attorneys be required to attend a training academy, akin to what is required of police and corrections officers? Or, do you believe law school and on-the-job experience alone appropriately prepare attorneys for working in the courts?
3. Assume you are a city manager tasked with locating a new prison in your city. What factors will you consider in placing the facility? Will you select the areas where there will be the least amount of resistance?
4. What recent policy (since the 1980s) has most notably impacted the criminal justice system? Do you support this policy?
5. What do you believe are the limitations in looking to other countries for guidance with regard to criminal justice policy? Should the United States consider what policies work and which ones do not in other countries?

FOR FURTHER READING

Friedman, T. L. *The World Is Flat: A Brief History of the Twenty-First Century*. New York: Farrar, Straus, and Giroux, 2005.

Haberfeld, M. *Critical Issues in Police Training*, 3rd ed. Upper Saddle River, NJ: Pearson, 2013.

Reichel, P. L. *Comparative Criminal Justice Systems: A Topical Approach*. Upper Saddle River, NJ: Pearson, 2013.

Welsh, W. N., and P. W. Harris, *Criminal Justice Policy and Planning: Planned Change*, 5th ed. New York: Routledge, 2016.

Worrall, J. L. *Crime Control in America: What Works?* 3rd ed. Boston, MA: Pearson, 2014.

NOTES

1. C. T. Lowenkamp, A. M. Holsinger, A. W. Flores, I. Koutsenok, and N. Pearl, "Changing Probation Officer Attitudes: Training Experience, Motivation, and Knowledge," *Federal Probation* 77, no. 2 (2013): 54–58.
2. R. Brislin and T. Yoshida, *Intercultural Communication Training: An Introduction* (Thousand Oaks, CA: Sage, 1994).
3. Myrna M. Cornett-DeVito and Edward L. McGlone, "Multicultural Communication Training for Law Enforcement Officers: A Case Study," *Criminal Justice Policy Review* 11, no. 3 (2000): 234–53.
4. Ibid., 234.
5. T. Keesee and M. J. Nila, "Fairness and Neutrality: Addressing the Issue of Race in Policing," *The Police Chief*, 78 (2011): 34–39.
6. D. K. Magner, "Fewer Professors Believe Western Culture Should Be the Cornerstone of the College Curriculum," *Chronicle of Higher Education* (September 13, 1996): 12–13.
7. T. Platt, "Desegregating Multiculturalism: Problems in the Theory and Pedagogy of Diversity Education," *Social Justice* 29, no. 4 (2002): 41–46.
8. Ibid.
9. See C. M. Mann and M. S. Zatz, "A Fragile Future: Pitfalls and Possibilities," in C. R. Mann, M. S. Zatz, and N. Rodriguez (eds.), *Images of Color, Images of Crime*, 3rd ed. (Los Angeles, CA: Roxbury, 2006), 252–64.

10. W. Calathes, "The Case for a Multicultural Approach to Teaching Criminal Justice," *Journal of Criminal Justice Education* 5, no. 1 (1994): 1–14.

11. Ibid., 4.

12. Ibid., 9–11.

13. M. J. King, "'Deliberate Indifference': Liability for Failure to Train," *FBI Law Enforcement Bulletin* 74, no. 10 (October 2005): 22–31.

14. Ben Stickle, "A National Examination of the Effect of Education, Training, and Pre-Employment Screening on Law Enforcement Use of Force." (2016). *Justice Policy Journal*, Spring (2016): 1–15.

15. Louisiana Commission on Law Enforcement and Administration of Criminal Justice, "Peace Officer Standards and Training Council," November 27, 2016. Available at: http://www.cole. state.la.us/programs/post.asp

16. E. A. Thibault, L. M. Lynch, R. B. McBride, and G. Walsh, *Proactive Police Management*, 9th ed. (Upper Saddle River, NJ: Pearson, 2015).

17. Kenneth W. Flynn, "Training and Police Violence," in R. G. Burns and C. E. Crawford (eds.), *Policing and Violence* (Upper Saddle River, NJ: Prentice Hall, 2002), 127–46.

18. President's Task Force on 21st Century Policing, *Final Report of the President's Task Force on 21st Century Policing* (Washington, DC: Office of Community Oriented Policing Services, 2015), 4.

19. B. A. Reaves, *State and Local Law Enforcement Training Academies, 2013*. U.S. Department of Justice, Bureau of Justice Statistics, 2016, NCJ 249784, 4.

20. Ibid., 7.

21. Daniel P. Carlson, *When Cultures Clash: The Divisive Nature of Police-Community Relations and Suggestions for Improvement* (Upper Saddle River, NJ: Prentice Hall, 2003).

22. J. S. Redfern, "Best Practices to Improve Police Relations with Transgender Individuals," *Journal of Law Enforcement* 3, no. 4 (2013). Available at: http://jghcs.info/index.php/l/article/view/265/239

23. R. M. Getty, J. L. Worrall, and R. G. Morris, "How Far from the Tree Does That Apple Fall? Field Training Officers, Their Trainees, and Allegations of Misconduct," *Crime & Delinquency* 62, no. 2 (2016): 821–39.

24. T. F. Lawson, "Mainstreaming Civil Rights in the Law School Curriculum: Criminal Law and Criminal Procedure," *St. Louis University Law Journal* 54, no. 3 (2010): 838.

25. D. W. Neubauer and H. F. Fradella, *America's Courts and the Criminal Justice System*, 7th ed. (Boston, MA: Cengage, 2017).

26. Ibid.

27. P. E. Mann, "Progressing from Law School to J.D. to Public Defender, Training Is the Key," National Legal Aid & Defender Association, 2010. Available at http://www.nlada.net/library/articles/na_trainingisthekeyndli

28. *ABA Ten Principles of a Public Defense Deliver System*, American Bar Association, February 2002, 3. Available at: http://www.americanbar.org/content/dam/aba/administrative/legal_aid_indigent_defendants/ls_sclaid_def_tenprinciplesbooklet.authcheckdam.pdf

29. N. Sharp, "Judicial Formation: A Step Beyond Education or Training for New Judges," *Justice System Journal* 29, no. 1 (2008): 100–104.

30. New Jersey Courts, "Judicial Education," 2018. Available at: https://njcourts.gov/courts/education/education.html

31. W. E. Raftery, "Get Thee a Law Degree! More States Are Imposing Minimum Educational Requirements for Judges," *Judicature* 100, no. 2 (2016): 7–8.

32. J. S. Bard, "Practicing Medicine and Studying Law: How Medical Schools Used to Have the Same Problems We Do and What We Can Learn from Their Efforts to Solve Them," *Seattle Journal for Social Justice* 10 (2011): 135–209.

33. C. S. Alexander, "Learning to Be Lawyers: Professional Identity and the Law School Curriculum," *Maryland Law Review* 70, no. 2 (2011): 465–83.

34. H. E. Williamson, *The Corrections Profession* (Newbury Park, CA: Sage, 1990).

35. Alexander L. Burton, Jennifer L. Lux, Francis T. Cullen, William T. Miller, and Velmer S. Burton Jr., "Creating a Model Correctional Officer Training Academy: Implications from a National Study," *Federal Probation* 82, no. 1 (2018): 26–36.

36. F. Schmalleger and J. O. Smykla, *Corrections in the 21st Century*, 4th ed. (New York: McGraw-Hill, 2009).

37. Nevada Department of Public Safety, n.d., "Parole and Probation." Available at: http://npp.dps.nv.gov/Employment/Officer_Training/

38. Alexander et al., "Creating a Model Correctional Officer Training Academy."

39. Reginald A. Wilkinson, "Diversity in Correctional Management: An Essential Tool," in *The Full Spectrum: Essays on Staff Diversity in Corrections*, ed. C. Smalls (Lanham, MD: American Correctional Association, 2004), 117–25.

40. P. Hunt, "Correctional Officers Need Cultural Diversity Training," in Smalls, *The Full Spectrum*, 127–55.

41. A. T. Aguire, "Latinos in Corrections: One View," in Smalls, *The Full Spectrum*, 65–74.

42. R. A. Shearer, and P. A. King, "Multicultural Competencies in Probation: Issues and Challenges," *Federal Probation* 68, no. 1 (June 2004): 3–9.

43. P. C. Kratcoski, "The Implications of Research Explaining Prison Violence and Disruption," *Federal Probation* 52, no. 1 (1988): 27–32.

44. P. F. McManimon Jr., "Correlates of Jail Violence," *American Jails* (May/June 2004), 41–43, 45–47.

45. Linda Dillon, "Effective Communication Embraces Diversity," in Smalls, *The Full Spectrum*, 1–9.

46. S. Walker and C. M. Katz, *The Police in America*, 7th ed. (New York: McGraw-Hill, 2011).

47. Thibault et al., *Proactive Police Management*.

48. Carlson, *When Cultures Clash*, 61.

49. R. Rifkin, "Racism Edges Up Again as Most Important U.S. Problem," Gallup, July 16, 2015. Available at: http://www.gallup.com/poll/184193/racism-edges-again-important-problem.aspx?g_source=race&g_medium=search&g_campaign=tiles; Gallup, "Most Important Problems," 2019. Available at: https://news.gallup.com/poll/1675/most-important-problem.aspx

50. Gallup, "Most Important Problems," 2019.

51. J. Norman, "U.S. Worries About Race Relations Reach a New High," Gallup, April 11, 2016. Available at: http://www.gallup.com/poll/190574/worries-race-relations-reach-new-high.aspx?g_source=police&g_medium=search&g_campaign=tiles

52. F. Newport, "U.S. Confidence in Police Recovers from Last Year's Low," Gallup, June 14, 2016. Available at: http://www.gallup.com/poll/192701/confidence-police-recovers-last-year-low.aspx

53. M. Younis, "Perceptions of Muslims in the United States: A Review," Gallup, December 11, 2011. Available at: http://www.gallup.com/opinion/gallup/187664/perceptions-muslims-united-states-review.aspx

54. Gallup, "Confidence in Institutions," June 1–5, 2016. Available at: http://www.gallup.com/poll/1597/confidence-institutions.aspx

55. R. Maurer, "Using Resistance to Build Support for Change," *Journal for Quality and Participation*, 19, no. 3 (1996): 56–63.

56. M. J. Lynch, R. G. Burns, and P. Stretesky, *Environmental Law, Crime, and Justice*, 2nd ed. (El Paso, TX: LFB Scholarly, 2014).

57. S. E. Costanza, J. C. Kilburn Jr., and S. Vendetti-Koski, "Are Minority Areas Disproportionately Targeted for Halfway House Placement?" *Journal of Ethnicity in Criminal Justice* 11 (2013): 256–76.

58. B. A. Arrigo, *Social Justice/Criminal Justice: The Maturation of Critical Theory in Law, Crime, and Deviance* (Belmont, CA: Wadsworth, 1999), 282.

59. Associated Press, "West Hartford Police Department Adopts New LGBT Policy," *Washington Times*, August 15, 2016. Available at: http://www.washingtontimes.com/news/2016/aug/15/west-hartford-police-department-adopts-new-lgbt-po/

60. D. Jones-Brown, K. Moran, E. King-Toler, and S. Sudula, "The Significance of Race in Contemporary Urban Policing Policy," in K. Ismaili (ed.), *U.S. Criminal Justice Policy: A Contemporary Reader*, 2nd ed. (Burlington, MA: Jones & Bartlett, 2017), 21–61.

61. P. L. Reichel, *Comparative Criminal Justice Systems: A Topical Approach* (Upper Saddle River, NJ: Pearson, 2013).

62. H. Wallace and C. Roberson, *Principles of Criminal Law*, 3rd ed. (Boston, MA: Pearson Allyn & Bacon, 2006).

63. Reichel, *Comparative Criminal Justice Systems*.

64. T. L. Friedman, *The World Is Flat: A Brief History of the Twenty-First Century* (New York: Farrar, Straus, and Giroux, 2005).

CHAPTER 15

THE FUTURE OF DIVERSITY AND MULTICULTURALISM IN CRIMINAL JUSTICE: STRATEGIES FOR SUCCESS

CHAPTER OBJECTIVES

After reading this chapter, you should be able to:

- Understand the methods by which the future is forecasted
- Recognize the drivers that influence the future of multiculturalism and criminal justice
- Identify and discuss the critical issues challenging the future of multiculturalism and criminal justice
- Discuss the extent to which progress has been made with regard to multiculturalism and criminal justice

The future of multiculturalism and diversity, particularly as it relates to criminal justice, can be viewed from many perspectives. For instance, one could observe the positive changes, such as the increased presence of minority groups working within the system, and this could be one reason to have optimism about the future of the system. Conversely, differential treatment of groups still exists in the criminal justice system, contributing to the perception that multiculturalism and diversity are simply buzzwords for something not likely to occur in criminal justice or in society in general. How, exactly, will we know what the future holds for multiculturalism?

   This question can only be answered with time as the future plays out and we see what becomes of our increasingly diverse society. Yet, sitting back and waiting to see what happens (i.e., taking a reactive approach) is likely detrimental. Tomorrow's professionals are tasked with making society a better place, and doing so requires proactive efforts. Recognizing the nature and extent of the problems faced by our current justice system is the most appropriate place to begin. Accordingly, the preceding chapters have examined the hurdles and obstacles faced by different groups within the criminal justice system. The chapters have also examined how the criminal justice system has responded to an increasingly diverse society. Thus, the foundation for progress has been set. Now comes the tricky part: understanding what can be done.

FORECASTING THE FUTURE

Futurists are scientists who forecast future developments in society. Notice the term "forecast" is used in place of the term "prediction." **Forecasting** involves the use of scientific techniques regarding future developments. These developments can be topic- or discipline-specific (e.g., pertain solely to criminal justice) or more general in nature. **Predictions**, on the other hand, involve instinctual feelings (aka "gut feelings") that lack scientific validity. The difference between the terms is evidenced in your local news programming when meteorologists forecast the weather through the use of various models. Meteorologists offer weather forecasts based on scientific evidence as opposed to gut feelings. As we all know, however, the forecast is not always correct. While forecasting provides a more scientific-based assessment of future developments, there is certainly an element of uncertainty involved.

Forecasting the weather and forecasting what will become of multiculturalism and the criminal justice system seem quite different, and they are in many respects. Nevertheless, the incorporation of scientific methods makes both types of forecasting similar. Weather patterns are distinct from human behavior, yet science enables us to anticipate changes in the weather much like we anticipate changes in human behavior. As a social science, criminal justice is vulnerable to changes in human behavior. It differs from the hard sciences, such as chemistry where it is certain that the combination of particular substances will have a particular effect. Errors are more likely to occur in the social sciences given the varied nature of society in general.

Consider the changes that occurred following the terrorist attacks against the United States on September 11, 2001. Many forecasts made as late as September 10, 2001, were largely, and unexpectedly, impacted by the changes that ensued. The resulting reorganization of federal law enforcement agencies in the United States and an overriding concern for homeland security changed daily lives and significantly impacted the criminal justice system. For example, local law enforcement agencies now must maintain an intensified concern for homeland security and competing for scarce personnel resources as the wars in Iraq and Afghanistan required the services of qualified applicants.

Futurists use several techniques to forecast the future. Prominent among the methods are **quantitative analyses**, which involve the use of statistics and trends to anticipate changes in society. Demographers, for instance, observe population trends and offer input regarding the demographic nature of society in the forthcoming years. Forecasters and futurists also consider **qualitative approaches**, which largely involve examination of non-numerical trends and patterns in attempt to anticipate future developments and changes. Among the qualitative approaches to forecasting the future is the **Delphi method**, in which experts offer input regarding anticipated developments in their areas of expertise. For instance, a forecaster intent on using the Delphi method to anticipate the future of criminal behavior may seek input from experts in the fields of sociology, biology, demography, economics, and criminal justice. The collaborative efforts of professionals result in identification of anticipated changes in the future. Futurist Gene Stephens used the Delphi method when he surveyed police experts regarding the role of the police in the future. Briefly, the group agreed that better-educated police officers with enhanced interpersonal skills and an understanding of technology were needed for the future success of policing.[1] The use of **scenarios**, in which a narrative is used to describe anticipated future events, is another method utilized by forecasters. To be sure, there are other methods by which the future is forecasted. Advanced statistical analyses and the increased incorporation of technology in forecasting, specifically computers, have improved the accuracy of future expectations.

There is debate regarding which forecasting method is most effective; however, analyses of multiple forecasts of the future may show consistencies and offer substantial confidence. In addition to selecting a forecasting method, futurist researchers must select appropriate variables for their analyses. Of particular concern when forecasting are **drivers of the future**, or particular issues which have significant impacts on the future. Among the drivers of forecasting, particularly with regard to criminal justice, are economics, crime factors (e.g., the increasing amount of international and computer crime), demographics, technology, and politics. Timeframe is also of significance to forecasting, as researchers must consider how far into the future they're projecting. There are no restrictions on how far into the future one can forecast; however, the accuracy of the forecast generally decreases as one looks further ahead.[2]

FORECASTING MULTICULTURALISM IN THE CRIMINAL JUSTICE SYSTEM

So, what's expected with regard to multiculturalism and criminal justice? In this section we offer our analyses, using various forecasting methods, regarding the future of criminal justice with concern for multiculturalism. There are many limitations to our analyses, as we provide a simplified, broad forecast of the future. For instance, we provide general overviews of trend data and forego advanced statistical analyses of the many significant factors that drive changes in the criminal justice system. We leave the hardcore forecasting to futurist researchers. Our analyses, nevertheless, offer a general overview of expected changes and demonstrate how forecasting the future is conducted.

To begin, we must first consider a time frame. Let's look at anticipated changes in ten years. Next, we have to identify our method of forecasting the future. As mentioned, comparing the outcomes of multiple forecasting methods generally provides a greater level of confidence, thus, let's conduct both a qualitative and a quantitative approach. We also must consider what exactly we're trying to forecast. For instance, are we forecasting the anticipated increase or decrease in the number of minorities working in the criminal justice system? Or, are we interested in the projected number of offenders? Let's consider diversity and the anticipated number of prisoners.

In 1980 the incarceration rate in the United States was 139 inmates in state and federal prisons per 100,000 population.[3] In 2007 and 2008 the rate reached 510. The incarceration rate began consistently declining in 2009, and as of 2017 was at 440; the lowest it had been since 1997.[4] Based on this trend and the costs associated with incarcerating notably large numbers of individuals, it's relatively safe to suggest that the incarceration rate will continue to slowly decline in the next ten years, although it is doubtful that we will see the rates found in the early 1980s and prior. Despite the recent declines, there remain concerns with regard to multiculturalism and diversity.

Demographics are a primary driver of change in the criminal justice system with regard to diversity and multiculturalism. Data from the U.S. Census Bureau suggest that by 2044 over half of all Americans will belong to a minority group, and Hispanics will constitute nearly 28 percent of the U.S. population by the year 2060, up from 12.6 percent in 2000. The percentage of African Americans in the United States is expected to change as well, increasing from about 14 percent in 2016 to 19 percent by 2060, as is the Asian population (expected to increase from 7 percent to 11 percent).[5] Given that minorities are overrepresented in U.S. prisons and the percentages of minorities in society are expected to increase, one can anticipate continued minority overrepresentation in our prisons. Thus, the importance of studying diversity within the criminal justice system is even more pronounced and necessary now than ever before.

To be sure, this is a *very* simplistic quantitative forecast. Many other factors besides historical practices influence incarceration trends. True forecasting methods take much more into account and involve more advanced analyses. This example, however, is offered to broadly demonstrate how forecasting is conducted. In this chapter we offer an equally simplistic qualitative forecast regarding multiculturalism and incarceration. Again, hardcore qualitative forecasting involves much more analyses, consideration, and depth than the cursory examination we provide. Our analyses are based on recent developments in several areas that appear to have implications for the future of incarceration.

Here we discuss three significant societal trends that will likely impact the future of incarceration as it pertains to diversity and culture. Many other qualitative factors will certainly impact the nature and extent of U.S. incarceration. We've identified factors that we believe are among the most significant drivers of incarceration in the future, with particular concern for diversity and multiculturalism.

First, issues pertaining to homeland security will continue to result in the expansion of law enforcement. For better or for worse, ours is a time of enhanced social control primarily due to terrorist threats. Accordingly, enhanced law enforcement and other social control efforts will result in the continued overrepresentation of minorities in the criminal justice system, as these groups are continuously closely monitored by law enforcement.

Second, females and other minorities will continue to be more visible in the criminal justice system. For instance, Chapter 7 of this book highlighted the changing nature of the criminal justice system as females become more actively involved as arrestees/offenders and practitioners. As females become increasingly involved in everyday activities, it is expected that their presence in the criminal justice system will continue to increase.

No signs point to decreased involvement of racial and ethnic minorities in the criminal justice system. The continued overrepresentation of minorities, particularly African Americans, as suspects and offenders in the criminal justice system does not seem to be waning. The social factors that contribute to the increased incarceration among minority groups persist and are perhaps becoming even more pronounced than during the past thirty to forty years when incarceration rates notably impacted minority communities. Increased levels of poverty and single-parent families are prominent among the factors contributing to increased minority representation in the criminal justice system.

Third, the nature of U.S. incarceration in the coming years concerns the increasing frequency with which international crimes occur. Thomas L. Friedman's best-selling book *The*

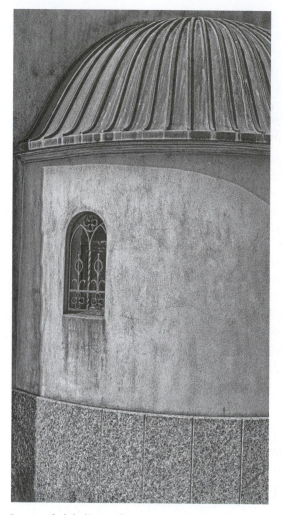

Increased globalism will require criminal justice practitioners to overcome many challenges, including language barriers. Having them understand key phrases, or even learning different languages, will contribute to more effective justice-based practices.

World Is Flat: A Brief History of the Twenty-first Century documents how increased globalization has impacted and will continue to impact the world.[6] Along these lines, it is anticipated that an increased amount of crime will have an international flavor as more opportunities for criminal behavior appear. In turn, criminal justice officials in the United States will have to continue working with other countries and promoting cooperative and collaborative efforts to ensure justice. Such efforts will result in the continued diversification of the system. For the purposes of our forecasting efforts, increased international crime will result in a greater need for multiculturalism in corrections. The need to recognize and react to various cultural backgrounds will increase as more offenders from around the globe enter our prisons.

Our forecasting efforts have targeted the future of incarceration with concern for multiculturalism. We could also observe the future of minority involvement as practitioners in the criminal justice system; and a variety of other, related issues. Regardless of our approach, the future of the criminal justice system and multiculturalism will be shaped by a variety of factors. Next, we turn our attention to several critical issues that affect and are expected to continue impacting the criminal justice system. The mere existence of these issues provides a discouraging commentary on the current state of tolerance for diversity and multiculturalism as it exists in society in general.

CRITICAL ISSUES AFFECTING MULTICULTURALISM AND CRIMINAL JUSTICE

Several critical issues hamper, and will continue to impact, efforts toward a multicultural society in the United States. These issues are not restricted to the United States; other countries face the same obstacles. Prominent among the issues impeding a completely multicultural society are racial profiling, hate crimes, immigration, and globalization.

RACIAL AND ETHNIC PROFILING

Racial and ethnic profiling are discussed in several chapters of this book, particularly in our focus on policing and multiculturalism. Police officers are often criticized for disproportionately targeting minority drivers in attempt to uncover drug trafficking. However, racial and ethnic profiling are not restricted to our roadways, as minorities have been unlawfully approached in their homes, while walking on public streets, at airports, in shopping areas, and in other places. An estimated 32 million Americans believe they have been subjected to racial profiling in their life-times.[7]

The practice of racial and ethnic profiling provides a gauge to determine society's concern for due process and crime control. Scholar Herbert Packer commented on these two competing models of criminal justice. The **crime control model of criminal justice** maintains an emphasis on expediency and reducing crime, yet such practices often occur at the expense of individual rights. The **due process model of criminal justice** is primarily concerned with respecting individual rights, yet doing so often comes at the expense of controlling crime.[8] In the United States, concern for homeland security and drug crimes has resulted in a criminal justice system focused on crime control that too often comes at the expense of individual rights. The notable concern about racial and ethnic profiling among minority communities provides evidence of this claim. Finding the proper balance between crime control and individual rights is often difficult in a multicultural, heterogeneous society such as the United States. A criminal justice system that recognizes and responds to multiculturalism is one that includes no racial or ethnic profiling. Future criminal justice practices will ideally be void of race-based and culture-based crime-fighting efforts.

Related to concerns for racial and ethnic profiling is implicit bias. Criminal justice agencies at all levels of government continue to try to identify, recruit, and train personnel who are bias-free. The existence of implicit bias, however, makes this difficult as it is often difficult to determine what exists inside an individual. Job candidates may appear bias-free during the selection process; however, subtle (and sometimes not so subtle) biased actions after being hired may be masked by the nature of the work. For instance, a patrol officer who disproportionately runs the license plates of Hispanic motorists out of a subconscious belief that the car was stolen may go unnoticed, despite the fact that the officer is stereotyping.

HATE CRIMES

In August 2019, Patrick Crusius allegedly drove over 600 miles to El Paso, Texas, and killed 22 people and injured 22 others when he fired an AK-47 at shoppers in a Walmart. Crusius, a 21-year-old white male, was charged with 90 federal hate crime charges in February 2020, and earlier pled not guilty to capital murder charges in state court. While surrendering to police after the incident, Crusius confessed to the shooting and stated that he was targeting Mexicans. He posted a long manifesto online minutes prior to the attack, stating that his actions were in response to "the Hispanic invasion of Texas."[9]

Hate crimes involve illegal actions that are motivated by hate and taken against particular groups. The term "hate crime" didn't exist prior to the 1980s and is sometimes used interchangeably with **bias crime**, which involves illegal acts taken against a group based on some form of bias. While the motivation, hate, is consistent in all hate crimes, the target and offender characteristics of hate crimes are not. The hatred or bias can be based on one's race, gender, religion, ethnicity, sexual orientation, disability, age, or political affiliation. Hate crimes are not, however, solely committed against minority groups, as White males have also been the targets of hate-motivated incidents. That an individual would be motivated to break the law based on hatred of a particular group suggests that not everyone is tolerant of diversity. The mere existence of hate crimes in society demonstrates that much work remains to be done with regard to creating a society that embraces multiculturalism.

Hate crime statistics, albeit controversial, speak loudly of the need for acceptance of multiculturalism. Victims reported over 7,100 hate crime incidents involving roughly 8,500 offenses in 2018. Most of the incidents were motivated by race/ancestry bias (about 60%), followed by religious bias (about 18%), sexual-orientation bias (about 17%), and gender-identity bias (about 2.2%). Most (about 66% percent) of the incidents were violent crimes, and intimidation (about 30%) was the most common offense.[10]

As discussed in Chapter 8, determining what, specifically, constitutes a hate crime is difficult. Similar to the difficulties found in courtrooms when attorneys attempt to determine whether or not the accused had the intent to commit a crime, determining one's motivation for committing a crime is not always easily done. Is the White supremacist who robs an African American female guilty of a hate crime? Yes, if he admits his motivation was hatred or his actions (e.g., verbal comments) suggest that hatred prompted the robbery. Otherwise, attorneys, judges, and jurors have to speculate or assume that the crime was not hate-motivated. Perhaps the African American female had simply provided the most opportune target for the offender.

Accordingly, one must consider hate crime statistics with caution, as there are several limitations to measuring hate crime. Particularly, the varied definitions of hate crime, the difficulty in determining a person's motivation, and the sometimes unreliable data-gathering methods of researchers, the government, and advocacy groups can distort the prevalence of hate crime in society. Authors James Jacobs and Kimberly Potter argue that there is no reliable evidence pointing to an increase in hate crimes. They suggest that the current hate crime movement is motivated by increased sensitivity to prejudice and bigotry.[11]

Hate crime laws provide enhanced penalties for offenders charged with crimes involving hate motivation. The ultimate goals are to promote tolerance and to recognize the benefits of diversity. The argument is that offenders who commit crime out of hatred or bias are morally worse, and thus more culpable, than those who engage in crime for other reasons. Hate crime laws are also justified on the grounds that hate crimes disproportionately impose injuries and harms to victims, have more substantial negative impacts on the community than do typical crimes, and facilitate the potential for retaliation and intergroup conflict. Hate crime legislation is intended to send a message that society is concerned about diversity and tolerance and, ultimately, deterring criminal behavior. Whether or not the goals of hate crime legislation are being reached is the subject of debate.[12] Hate crimes would not exist in a society that embraces multiculturalism. What current and future efforts are needed to eliminate or at the very least reduce hate crime incidents? This and related questions are addressed later in this chapter.

IMMIGRATION

The multicultural makeup of the United States is one of the many strengths of the country. Accordingly, the United States takes pride in its diversity. The excerpt from Emma Lazarus's poem "The New Colossus" engraved at the bottom of the Statue of Liberty speaks loudly:

> Give me your tired, your poor,
> Your huddled masses yearning to breathe free,
> The wretched refuse of your teeming shore.
> Send these, the homeless, tempest-tossed, to me:
> I lift my lamp beside the golden door.[13]

Despite these words, there is current debate regarding immigration into the United States. When discussing immigration, a distinction must be made between legal and illegal immigration. Legal immigration can be controlled by the government, in turn providing a monitor to protect over-population and the economic well-being of the country, among other things. Illegal immigration is a different matter. The government attempts to protect against illegal immigrants entering the country; however, doing so has been difficult and controversial. Too often discussions of immigration intermix references to both groups and the discussion becomes clouded. Currently, there is a particular concern with illegal immigration, which is making life more difficult for legal immigrants.

Illegal immigration attracts substantial attention given the illegal status of those who enter the country without permission. In the fight against illegal immigration, those opposed to immigration are joined by those opposed to law-breakers. The fight against illegal immigration extends from the federal government to local communities.

Critics of illegal immigration argue that the federal government hasn't done enough in response to the number of immigrants illegally entering the

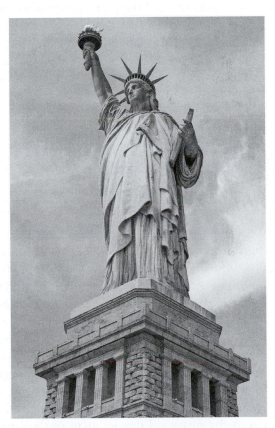

The Statue of Liberty is a symbol of freedom and the United States' willingness to accept all groups of people. Not everyone, however, can easily enter the country.

United States. Accordingly, state legislatures and local municipalities have taken action by considering and adopting an unprecedented number of measures to address the issue, and the 2016 election of Donald Trump as president of the United States further fueled discussions regarding immigration, as Trump adopted a tough stance toward immigration.

While much of the debate concerning immigration centers on illegal immigration, legal immigrants face particular challenges. For instance, from a criminal justice perspective, immigrants are victimized at rates similar to the general population, yet their rate of reporting victimization is much lower. The underreporting of criminal victimization of immigrants stems largely from the hardships associated with appearing in court, including language barriers, uncertainty regarding the U.S. criminal justice system, and general cultural differences.[14]

Among other effects, the failure to report crime fails to ensure the protection of all citizens and undermines the effectiveness of the criminal justice system. At the very least, it increases the likelihood of the offender committing further crime. Efforts have been made to address the underreporting by providing interpreters during court hearings and various victims outreach programs in communities heavily populated by immigrants.[15] It can be stated with confidence that the future of criminal justice and multiculturalism will be heavily impacted by immigration issues. A more extensive account of immigration is provided in Chapter 4.

Racial and ethnic profiling, hate crimes, and immigration concerns are not the only critical issues challenging efforts toward multiculturalism. These issues were discussed based on their relevance to the criminal justice system. Several other issues are affecting multiculturalism in the larger society. For instance, there has been and continues to be debate regarding prayer in schools. Should students be permitted to express their religious beliefs in a school setting?

Bigotry, prejudice, and bias are evident in many issues and at minimum hamper efforts toward tolerance. So what can be done? Are the immigration laws and reactions to our diverse society appropriate? The criminal justice system has, in the past, responded to discrimination and diversity-related issues. Efforts to eliminate or at least reduce discrimination in the criminal justice system are evident in actions such as sentencing guidelines, the 1970s decision to nullify existing capital punishment statutes, and an increased focus on diversity training among all criminal justice practitioners. However, attempts to limit or remove the impacts of discretionary actions by criminal justice professionals do not always reduce discriminatory practices. For instance, the manner in which capital punishment is used continues to be controversial insofar as poor minorities are more likely than their counterparts to face execution.[16]

Is there an "American culture" to which all groups in the United States must subscribe? Given the historical development of the United States (in which waves of immigrants landed on U.S. soil and helped build the country into what it is today) and failed efforts to change cultural beliefs, one could make a strong argument that tolerance of diverse cultures is needed. To be sure, culture conflict will continue. The goal is to eliminate, or at least minimize, the harms.

GLOBALISM AND INTERNATIONAL CRIME

Concerns for immigration in the United States and elsewhere largely stem from globalism. **Globalization** refers to the international integration of cultural, social, and economic issues among countries that have historically been distinct from one another. The increasingly international nature of crime and justice requires greater interaction among countries, particularly with regard to justice-based efforts. Simply, criminal justice agencies across the globe will need to be legally and procedurally prepared to confront such crimes.

The experienced and anticipated changes in the demographics and diversity in the United States largely stems from communication, travel, and commerce becoming increasingly global in nature. The ease with which one can travel to, or communicate with individuals in, other countries has diversified the United States, but it has also created several challenges. For instance, increased globalism contributes to increased levels of international crime, and jurisdictional issues cause concerns regarding extradition. Cooperation between countries, agencies, and justice officials will continue to become increasingly important. Criminal justice agencies will likely face an increasing number of challenging situations caused by increased globalism. Anticipating these changes and challenges will help officials prepare for and respond to them in the future.

In citing the need for our justice systems to prepare for the future, one researcher noted that "there's no question that terrorism, the growth of multicultural populations, massive migration, upheaval in age-composition demographics, technological developments, and globalization over the next three or more decades will affect the world's criminal justice systems."[17] This and related comments regarding the future of the criminal justice suggest that increasing change, including an increasingly diverse society, is indeed ahead for the United States.

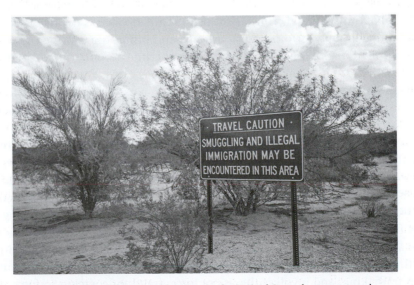

Concerns regarding illegal immigration in the United States have generated many enforcement actions at various levels of government. Finding an immigration policy that pleases all groups has long challenged government leaders.

Differences in laws, ideology, and justice-based practices among countries hamper efforts to address international crime. Increased globalism has, to some extent, enhanced levels of cooperation among different countries; however, much work remains. Among the biggest hurdles to overcome are conflict and change. Conflict among countries hampers justice-based efforts, and changes influence justice-based practices at differing rates and in various forms, as some countries are more advanced than others.[18]

International crime has historically involved organized crime and drug offenses, including piracy and White slavery among the earliest forms. International relations between involved countries often influenced the level of cooperation and ultimate resolutions of the cases.[19] Over time, however, international crimes have expanded in scope and occur more frequently. Crimes involving harms to the environment, gang crimes, weapons trafficking, and other crimes often associated with organized crime groups that were once viewed primarily as domestic concerns have become international in nature. The increased reliance of the internet and the associated vulnerabilities to criminal victimization, as well as human trafficking, have also expanded the scope and frequency of international crime.

Several incidents in the 1970s drew attention to the need for countries to better address global crimes. The expansion of the illegal drug trade, concerns about human trafficking and exploiting humans, and several terrorist attacks highlighted the increasingly international nature of crime.[20] International crime increased in the 1980s with trade and finance becoming increasingly international,[21] and the 2001 terrorist attacks against the United States prompted a more aggressive U.S. response to international crime concerns and homeland security in general.

International crimes are traditional forms of crime that cross borders of countries. They are difficult to detect, apprehend, and adjudicate due to the various countries involved, and while the public is more familiar with everyday street crime, it was noted that "the level of transnational crime affecting the United States is not inconsequential."[22] Organized crime groups, terrorists, drug cartels, and others are expected to continue to challenge criminal justice officials, as international crime becomes increasingly complex and occurs with greater frequency. For instance, various organized crime groups, including the Chinese triads, the Yakuza, La Cosa Nostra, Russian gangs, and Mexican and Colombian drug cartels, have engaged in international crime and have exploited weaknesses in international crime fighting efforts.

Among the more troubling forms of international crime is **human trafficking**, which involves "the involuntary movement of people across and within borders and typically involves coercion, deception, and violence," and is not legal anywhere in the world.[23] Human trafficking has become increasingly problematic in many countries and has been deemed "a major worldwide concern" and "likely one of the most egregious acts violating the most basic and fundamental human rights."[24] A recent report from the United Nations Office on Drugs and Crime noted that countries around the world are detecting and reporting more victims of human trafficking.[25] **Sex trafficking** is one of the more common forms of human trafficking, and involves the use of force, fraud, or coercion to force victims to perform commercial sex. It directly impacts more than four million victims globally each year, and profits from forced sexual labor are estimated to be $99 billion worldwide.[26]

Efforts to address human trafficking include specialized courts that focus directly on these cases. The Human Trafficking Intervention Courts in New York State are an example, as the statewide system of courts was created in large response to claims from criminal justice professionals and others that it is better to recognize prostitutes as victims instead of defendants or criminals. The view is largely the result of increased societal focus on human trafficking and exploitation of young girls in the United States. Upon determination by the court that a prostitute is a victim of human trafficking or sex trafficking, the defendant in the courts is provided protective services such as drug treatment, shelter, healthcare, job training, and education in efforts to prevent them from returning to the sex trade.[27]

Extradition involves a state surrendering an individual accused of a crime to the state in which the individual is accused, and is going to become increasingly used as globalism increases. The secretary of state in the United States is responsible for requesting the return of individuals from the United States who commit crimes and flee to other countries under the terms of extradition treaties the United States has with other countries. Such treaties, however, do not exist with all countries.

Efforts to better address globalism are evidenced in the 2002 creation of the **International Criminal Court** (ICC), which is a permanent international court that investigates, prosecutes, and tries individuals accused of committing the most serious crimes that are of concern to the international community. Those crimes include genocide, crimes against humanity, war crimes, and aggression. The creation of the ICC is certainly a positive step toward addressing international crime, but it has jurisdiction over only the most serious offenses. Many other international crimes occur outside the jurisdiction of the court, and it is anticipated that additional and new forms of international crime will occur in the future.

PROGRESS?

Arguably, criminal justice education has promoted assimilation, in contrast to multiculturalism, through adopting the idea that the United States is a melting pot.[28] Is the United States a "melting pot" that welcomes individuals from different backgrounds and promotes assimilation? Or is the term "salad bowl" better suited to describe the integration and interaction of different groups in society? Earlier interpretations of ethnic relations in the United States used the term melting pot, but more recently, the term salad bowl is used. Why? The melting pot metaphor conjures images of individuals molding together, or assimilating, in society. The salad bowl metaphor suggests that each individual retains their own flavor and integrity while contributing to the final product. References to cultural relations in terms of a salad bowl are another way of promoting multiculturalism.

Some sociologists actually use a "stew" metaphor instead of a salad, since, while there are distinct differences between the groups, inevitably the groups affect each other in profound ways and the groups shape the overall culture. The melting pot illustration was popular among the public but never really given any credence by the academic community, largely because of the racial and ethnic conflicts that have always existed.

The power differentials in a capitalistic society are such that those without means are more often brought to the attention of the criminal justice system. Whether or not the differential power structure encourages the less powerful to commit crime, or the criminal justice system disproportionately focuses on crimes of the lower class, it remains that the less powerful constitute the vast majority of our prison population. How do we change this unfavorable situation? The answer to this question involves radical changes in the sociocultural, socioeconomic, and sociopolitical makeup of the United States. Radical changes, however, are not beyond the capacity of any society. Consider the fact that Barack Obama, who is African American, recently served two terms as president of the United States (2009–2017), and in 2016 Hillary Clinton became the first woman to be nominated for president by a major political party.

If indeed we haven't seen progress with regard to diversity, multiculturalism, and tolerance in the criminal justice system, then what should we do? What changes are needed to improve the system? The answer to these questions is twofold, as we must consider increasing equity, diversity, and tolerance with regard to the accused and the offenders entering and within the system, in addition to those working within the system. Several authors have commented on the changes necessary for a more equitable system of criminal justice. For instance, scholars Coramae Richey Mann and Marjorie Zatz suggest that significant changes are needed in the major social institutions in the United States to erase the stereotype of people of color. Particularly, they cite changes needed in relation to housing, health, education, family, religion, political, and economic issues. Mann and Zatz argue that changes in these institutions will eradicate the negative stereotypical images of minorities as they pertain to crime.[29]

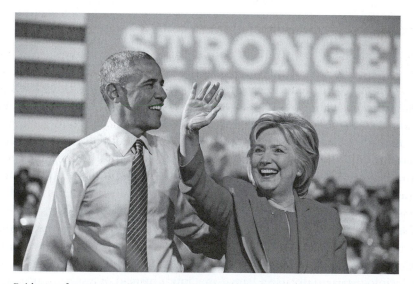

Evidence of progress in the United States with regard to diversity is found in politics, as members of historically underrepresented groups have made notable progress. There is, however, a need for continued progress in politics and other areas.

Author David Cole offers three promising and challenging solutions to address the inequities existent in today's criminal justice system. First, Cole argues that we must acknowledge that all are not equal before the law. The privileged still maintain a distinct advantage in many aspects of the criminal justice system. Second, Cole argues that we must restore the legitimacy of criminal law to eliminate or reduce the existing double standards. He cites the differential treatment of groups in many stages of the criminal justice system (as noted throughout this text) as evidence. Further legitimizing the criminal justice system would help address the existing disparities and bring to light charges of discrimination and differential treatment. Third, Cole argues that effective community-based responses to crime are needed at both the preventative and punitive stages.[30] His call for the further integration of the community in preventing and responding to crime is supported by many others, including those supporting community policing efforts, community courts, and community corrections.[31]

With regard to increasing the diversity of the criminal justice workforce, scholar Becky Tatum offers several suggestions to achieve and maintain diversity within the criminal justice system. Particularly, she encourages criminal justice organizations to:

- Understand that diversity enhances organizational effectiveness and success
- Continue practicing and promoting affirmative action policies
- Be committed to diversity
- Establish effective recruitment, selection, training, and promotion practices
- Create effective complaint policies and procedures to ensure that employees are not treated differently
- Evaluate progress and the results of policies and procedures[32]

To be sure, progress has been made with regard to multiculturalism in the criminal justice system. Despite existing problems, our system is fairer than it's been in the past, and the criminal justice workforce is more diverse than ever. However, the continued disintegration of affirmative action policies warrants mention. Affirmative action has played an integral part in diversifying the criminal justice workforce, although recent court rulings have limited its effectiveness. Further, affirmative action programs have not corrected the underlying causes of inequality and prejudice in many arenas.[33] Accordingly, the reduced impact of affirmative action and the general climate of intolerance in the United States may contribute to increased discriminatory practices.[34]

If progress has been made with regard to multiculturalism in criminal justice, then why the concern? The obvious answer is because there's more room for improvement. "Progress" refers to advancement and does not necessarily mean that success has been achieved. The concern regarding diversity and criminal justice relates to the work that remains, including greater sensitivity to diversity issues. Society is quite sensitive to culture-based issues. That we are more sensitive to such issues suggests that progress has been made and provides an ample opportunity for change. Nevertheless, the efforts pertaining to cultural sensitivity continue to highlight the existing challenges.

TECHNOLOGY AND POLICY

Policies are not always large-scale in nature. Departments and agencies have policies that guide employee practices. Failure to abide by the policies can lead to the dismissal of employees. The relatively recent, widespread incorporation of technology into our everyday lives has led to departments creating and refining policies regarding its use. The increased use of cell phones and social media has created new areas that require regulation in the workplace and have provided new means by which a lack of tolerance for diversity can be expressed. Inappropriate texting and emails, in particular, have resulted in the dismissal of criminal justice employees in several agencies.

Technology has the power to strongly influence our future; however, it also provides opportunities for misbehavior and intolerance. For instance, nine jail workers in New Jersey were terminated after the discovery of racist texts on their cell phones. The jailers exchanged over 5,700 text messages that contained inflammatory and racist comments that routinely targeted coworkers, inmates, superiors, and African Americans in general. In a different case, a Buffalo correctional officer resigned from his position after his department confronted him about derogatory comments he made on his Facebook page. Among other comments, the officer had threatened to shoot gay people. These are by no means the only accounts in which technology has provided a forum for hateful comments. Accordingly, departments are regularly revising their policies and guidelines with regard to texting, emails, and the use of social media.

Each time we hear that an LGBT candidate was denied an employment position in criminal justice based on his or her sexual orientation we believe we're taking a step backward. In many ways, such claims and actions are a step backward, but one could equally look at such claims as progress, since in years past we may not even have heard of the situation. The candidate may have simply accepted the discriminatory practice and moved on. Or, perhaps even worse, the candidate might not have applied for the position at all, out of a belief that they would be denied a position based on their sexual orientation. Hearing about discrimination can make the problem appear more prominent than it truly is; simultaneously, it sends a message that such practices are unacceptable.

Efforts toward multiculturalism are enhanced when individuals who have faced discrimination speak out about the mistreatment. Bringing the issue to light, in a nonconfrontational manner, draws attention. Such individuals must use caution, however, as exaggerated or elaborated stories often hamper efforts toward progress. The media can play a vital tool in helping victims of discrimination or mistreatment share their stories.

SUMMARY

One cannot consider the future without recognizing the impact of technology, although technological changes appear to have little impact on cultural relations. Nevertheless, the future of multiculturalism and the criminal justice system will be influenced by several changes in the larger society. Demographic trends will impact the system, as will the increased international nature of crime. The increasing separation of socioeconomic classes will continue to negatively impact multiculturalism and the criminal justice system, as will the ever-prominent crime control approach we've adopted.

All is not lost, however, as positive changes may be on the horizon. The changing demographics of society will dictate greater minority involvement as criminal justice practitioners, and this should promote positive changes to the system. Individuals from diverse backgrounds are increasingly assuming more powerful roles in public service, politics, and private business. While there may be current tensions between cultural groups (as evidenced in the anti-illegal immigration legislation), signs point toward greater recognition of diversity and increased acceptance of multiculturalism.

Changes in the criminal justice system begin with changes in people. The system is composed of and influenced by individuals from various backgrounds. The system, as designed on paper, is not biased, racist, or anti-multicultural. What's needed for acceptance of multiculturalism is tolerance among individuals in society. The problems and challenges faced by different cultures in the criminal justice system were created by people—including biased and unbiased people. The problems posed by the unbiased can be addressed through greater professionalism in criminal justice. Fortunately, many signs point to greater professionalism in the discipline. The problems posed by biased individuals are fixed through identifying and correcting the problems.

YOU MAKE THE CALL
PLANNING FOR THE FUTURE

Consider the following scenario. Debate the pros and cons of all options and decide what you would do.

You've just been promoted to Head of Research and Planning in the large municipal police department in which you work. While granting you the promotion, the police chief told you that she wants the department to become more proactive and better prepared for the future so the department is not in a reactionary mode. The chief mentioned that she wants you to focus on the future of several issues that currently challenge and are expected to continue to challenge the department. Particularly, she wants you to create short-, medium-, and long-term plans with regard to: (1) crime, (2) diversity in the community, and (3) intercultural relations.

You eagerly accept the position, and look forward to the challenges. You tell the chief that she has nothing to worry about, that you'll start immediately and do an exceptional job. In your mind, however, you have many uncertainties. Sure, you've worked in research and planning, but the department has historically brushed aside research efforts and forecasts of the future.

Questions

1. How will you begin the process of creating the various plans requested by the chief?
2. What methods of forecasting the future do you believe will be most effective in creating plans for the short-term? Medium-term? Long-term?
3. Who would you ask for help with regard to planning for the long-term?
4. What obstacles do you anticipate encountering as you create the plans?

KEY TERMS

bias crime
crime control model of criminal justice
Delphi method
drivers of the future
due process model of criminal justice
extradition
forecasting
futurists
globalization

hate crime
human trafficking
International Criminal Court
predictions
qualitative approaches
quantitative analyses
scenarios
sex trafficking

DISCUSSION QUESTIONS

1. Provide a scenario of the criminal justice system in the year 2075. Be sure to focus on issues pertaining to diversity, tolerance, and multiculturalism.
2. Compare and contrast the various methods of forecasting the future. Which do you believe offer the greatest accuracy? Why?
3. Discuss how racial profiling, immigration, and hate crimes will impact the future of multiculturalism and criminal justice.
4. Create an outline for an undergraduate-level course on multiculturalism and criminal justice. What topics would you include? How would you structure the course?
5. Identify and discuss three changes you believe are necessary for police departments, the courts, and correctional agencies to better welcome diversity among the ranks of practitioners.

FOR FURTHER READING

Frey, W. H. *Diversity Explosion: How New Racial Demographics Are Remaking America.* Washington, DC: Brookings Institution, 2015.

Parry, J. T., and L. S. Richardson, eds. *The Constitution and the Future of Criminal Justice in America.* New York: Cambridge University Press, 2013.

Simon, J. *Mass Incarceration on Trial: A Remarkable Court Decision and the Future of Prisons in America.* New York: The New Press, 2014.

Stuntz, W. J. *The Collapse of American Criminal Justice.* Cambridge, MA: Harvard University Press, 2011.

Zimring, F. E., and D. S. Tanenhaus, *Choosing the Future for American Juvenile Justice.* New York: New York University Press, 2014.

NOTES

1. G. Stephens, "Policing the Future: Law Enforcement's New Challenges," *The Futurist,* (March/April 2005): 51–57.
2. R. Burns, "The Future of Delinquency Prevention and Treatment," in M. D. McShane and F. P. Williams III (eds.), *Youth Violence and Delinquency,* vol. 3 (Westport, CT: Praeger, 2007), 171–85.
3. T. L. Snell, *Correctional Populations in the United States, 1993,* U.S. Department of Justice, Bureau of Justice Statistics, 1995, NCJ 156241, 9.
4. D. Kaeble, L. Glaze, A. Tsoutis, and T. Minton, *Correctional Populations in the United States, 2014,* U.S. Department of Justice, Bureau of Justice Statistics, 2015, NCJ 249513, 4; Jennifer Bronson and Ann Carson, *Prisoners in 2017,* U.S. Department of Justice, Bureau of Justice Statistics, 2019, NCJ 252156, 1.
5. S. L. Colby and J. M. Ortman, *Projections of the Size and Composition of the U.S. Population: 2014 to 2060,* United States Census Bureau, 2015. Available at: https://www.census.gov/content/dam/Census/library/publications/2015/demo/p25-1143.pdf; Jonathan Vespa, Lauren Medina, and David Armstrong, *Demographic Turning Points: Projections for the United States: 2020 to 2060.* Available at: https://www.census.gov/content/dam/Census/newsroom/press-kits/2018/jsm/jsm-presentation-pop-projections.pdf
6. T. L. Friedman, *The World Is Flat: A Brief History of the Twenty-First Century* (New York: Farrar, Straus, and Giroux, 2005).

7. "Threat and Humiliation: Racial Profiling, Domestic Security, and Human Rights in the United States," Amnesty International, 2004. Accessed August 6, 2007, at http://www.amnestyusa.org/racial_profiling/report/rp_report.pdf

8. H. L. Packer, *The Limits of the Criminal Sanction* (Stanford, CA: Stanford University Press, 1968).

9. Erin Coulehan, Katie Benner, and Manny Fernandez, "Federal Hate Crime Charges Filed in El Paso Shooting That Targeted Latinos," *NewYorkTimes.com*, February 6. Accessed online at: https://www.nytimes.com/2020/02/06/us/politics/el-paso-shooting-federal-hate-crimes.html.

10. Federal Bureau of Investigation, *2018 Hate Crime Statistic*. Accessed online at: https://ucr.fbi.gov/hate-crime/2018/topic-pages/incidents-and-offenses.

11. J. B. Jacobs and K. Potter, *Hate Crimes: Criminal Law and Identity Politics* (New York: Oxford University Press, 1998).

12. Ibid.

13. E. Lazarus, "The New Colossus," 1883.

14. R. C. Davis and E. Erez, *Immigrant Populations as Victims: Toward a Multicultural Criminal Justice System*, U.S. Department of Justice, Bureau of Justice Statistics, May 1998, NCJ 167571, 2.

15. Ibid.

16. M. Welch, *Punishment in America: Social Control and the Ironies of Imprisonment* (Thousand Oaks, CA: Sage, 1999).

17. N. Ritter, "Preparing for the Future: Criminal Justice in 2040," *National Institute of Justice Journal* 255 (2006): 8.

18. P. Andreas and E. Nadelmann, *Policing the Globe* (New York: Oxford University Press, 2006).

19. N. Gerspacher, "The History of International Police Cooperation: A 150-Year Evolution in Trends and Approaches," *Global Crime* 9, nos. 1–2 (2008): 169–84.

20. Andreas and Nadelmann, *Policing the Globe*.

21. P. Williams and E. Savona, "The United Nations and Transnational Organised Crime," *Transnational Organised Crime* 1, no. 3 (1995): 8–10.

22. J. A. Eterno, "Policing in the United States: Balancing Crime Fighting and Legal Rights," in J. A. Eterno and D. K. Das (eds.), *Police Practices in Global Perspective* (Lanham, MD: Rowman & Littlefield, 2010), 12.

23. S. Aguilar-Millan, J. E. Foltz, J. Jackson, and A. Oberg, "Global Crime Case: The Modern Slave Trade," *The Futurist* (2008): 45; K. Williams, "Human Trafficking: The Return of an Ancient Malaise and What Law Enforcement Can Do About It," *The Briefing* (August 2014): 1–3; National White Collar Crime Center.

24. A. L. Sciarabba and C. G. Sullivan, "Transnational Crime and the Law: An Overview of Current Practices," in Eterno and Das, *Police Practices*, 227.

25. UNODC, *Global Report on Trafficking in Persons 2018* (United Nations publication, Sales No. E.19.IV.2).

26. Cara Kelly, "13 Sex Trafficking Statistics that Explain the Enormity of the Global Sex Trade," *USAToday.com*, July 29, 2019. Available at: https://www.usatoday.com/story/news/investigations/2019/07/29/12-trafficking-statistics-enormity-global-sex-trade/1755192001/

27. W. K. Rashbaum, "With Special Courts, State Aims to Steer Women Away from Sex Trade," *New York Times*, September 25, 2013. Available at: http://www.nytimes.com/2013/09/26/nyregion/special-courts-for-human-trafficking-and-prostitution-cases-are-planned-in-new-york.html?_r=0

28. Welch, *Punishment in America*.

29. Coramae Richey Mann and Marjorie S. Zatz, "A Fragile Future: Pitfalls and Possibilities," in C. R. Mann, M. S. Zatz, and N. Rodriguez (eds.), *Images of Color*, 3rd ed. (Los Angeles, CA: Roxbury, 2006), 252–64.

30. David Cole, *No Equal Justice: Race and Class in the American Criminal Justice System* (New York: The New Press, 1999).

31. Among the many resources addressing community-based criminal justice are: T. Clear and E. Cadora, *Community Justice* (Belmont, CA: Wadsworth, 2003); V. E. Kappeler and L. K. Gaines, *Community Policing: A Contemporary Perspective*, 4th ed. (Cincinnati, OH: Anderson, 2005); and E. Lee, *Community Courts: An Evolving Model*, U.S. Department of Justice, Office of Justice Programs, October 2000, NCJ 183452.

32. B. Tatum, "Criminal Justice Personnel in the Twenty-First Century," in R. Muraskin and A. R. Roberts (eds.), *Visions for Change: Crime and Justice in the Twenty-First Century*, (Upper Saddle River, NJ: Prentice Hall, 2005), 670–83.

33. R. Thomas, "From Affirmative Action to Affirming Diversity," *Harvard Business Review* (March/April 1990): 107–17.

34. E. F. Morgan, "The Administration of Justice Based on Gender and Race," in Muraskin and Roberts, *Visions for Change*, 652–69.

GLOSSARY

ABOLITIONIST An individual who contended that slavery was morally objectionable.

ACQUAINTANCE RAPE An act of rape involving individuals familiar with one another.

ADJUDICATION The process in which it is determined whether a youth is responsible for the illegal act(s) with which he or she is charged.

AFFIRMATIVE ACTION Programs designed to promote the hiring of minority applicants.

AFFIRMATIVE DEFENSE A defense in which the defendant admits to committing the action in question but asserts that they have legal justification for having done so. Entering an affirmative defense requires the defendant to demonstrate that their action was justified. Self-defense, insanity, coercion, and entrapment are affirmative defenses.

ALIBI One of two types of defense that may be offered at trial (affirmative defense being the other). It states that the defendant did not commit the crime (e.g., they were in another location at the time of the crime).

ALIEN LAND ACT An act which prohibited anyone who was ineligible for citizenship to own land and which limited leases to three years. The land laws drove many first-generation Japanese into cities.

AMNESTY A type of clemency that restores rights and privileges of groups of people.

APPEARANCE The items worn by a person that signify that person's social status.

ARRAIGNMENT The step in criminal case processing when the accused is formally notified of the charges against them, he or she enters a plea, pretrial motions may be offered, and discovery may occur.

ASIAN INDIAN A term that represents a wide range of populations. India itself is a diverse nation with dozens of languages and ethnic enclaves.

ASSIGNED COUNSEL Court-appointed representation for indigent defendants. Attorneys are assigned indigent cases in return for statutorily determined fees.

ASSIMILATION The process by which a subordinate group takes on the characteristics of the dominant group and is eventually accepted as part of that group.

BABY BOOMERS A term to describe a segment of the population born in the years 1946 to 1964. This group represents about 28 percent of the U.S. population.

BARRIOS Concentrations of segregated areas or ghettos in the southwestern portion of the United States.

BATTLE AT LITTLE BIG HORN A battle fought in 1876 in which General George Custer and his men were defeated.

BATTLE OF WOUNDED KNEE The battle that extinguished the hope of the Sioux Nation of ever returning to a life of freedom.

BENCH TRIAL A trial in which a judge serves as both judge and jury.

BIAS CRIME An illegal act taken against a group based on bias.

BISEXUALITY A term used to describe an individual's attraction to both sexes.

BLACK CODES Laws designed to nullify the rights granted to the newly freed slaves. Among the restrictions found in Black codes were the prohibition of interracial marriage, renting land in urban areas, preaching the gospel without a license, and assuming any occupation other than servant or farmer unless the newly freed slave paid a tax.

"BLACK LIVES MATTER" An activist movement in the United States that originated after the 2013 acquittal of a Florida man in the shooting of an African American teenager. The group campaigns against police brutality against African Americans.

BLACK MIDDLE CLASS A term used to describe relatively affluent African Americans.

BLACK NATIONALISM The philosophy that encourages Blacks to see themselves as Blacks first rather than as Americans.

BLACK POWER A political movement that encouraged Blacks to create new institutions and emulate the political path followed by many European immigrant groups.

BLACK RAGE A defense offered in court which attempts to provide legal justification for criminal behavior by some African Americans frustrated by oppression resulting from living in a White-dominated society.

BLUE WALL OF SILENCE The unwritten rule among officers to not report other officers' wrongful behavior.

BOW STREET RUNNERS A precursor to formal policing, this group consisted of individuals who sought law violators in the Bow Street region of London. The runners were paid a sum of money for bringing suspects before the court.

BUREAU OF INDIAN AFFAIRS The primary regulatory arm of the federal government as it relates to Native Americans.

CANTEEN PUNK A prison inmate who performs oral or anal sex in exchange for candy, cigarettes, or other items purchased at the prison store or canteen.

CHALLENGE FOR CAUSE A motion through which attorneys may eliminate a potential juror because of an identifiable bias and/or an apparent inability to assess a case fairly.

CHARGE TO THE JURY A written document, prepared by a judge for a jury, that explains the parameters under which jurors may deliberate.

CHICANO An American of Mexican origin.

CHILD-SAVING MOVEMENT A movement that largely involved philanthropists and social reformers who felt that the exploitation of children ultimately resulted in juvenile crime and a host of other problems. They attempted to enact laws that would allow children to be placed in reformatories or other institutions.

CHILDREN'S AID SOCIETY A group, established by Reverend Charles Loring Brace, that helped homeless children.

CHINESE EXCLUSION ACT An act, passed in 1882, which outlawed Chinese immigration for ten years. It lasted in various forms for more than sixty years.

CHRISTOPHER COMMISSION A commission assembled in the wake of the Rodney King incident in response to claims of LAPD officer misbehavior. The commission identified several areas and instances of unethical behavior by LAPD officers.

CIVIL LEGAL TRADITION A justice system approach that is based on Roman and canon laws, and codification.

CIVIL RIGHTS ACT OF 1866 This act was targeted to address the Black Codes by defining all persons born in the United States, with the exception of Native Americans, as national citizens who were to enjoy specific rights. These rights included permission to make contracts, bring lawsuits, and enjoy the full and equal benefit of the law.

CIVIL RIGHTS ACT OF 1964 Prohibited discrimination in hiring on the basis of color, race, sex, religion, or national origin.

CIVIL RIGHTS MOVEMENT A movement designed to provide equal rights to minorities.

CLAIMSMAKING A fundamental aspect of how social problems are defined in a given society.

CLEMENCY Legislative actions which reduce the severity of one's punishment, waive the punishment associated with a crime, or exclude certain individuals from prosecution of a specific crime.

COLLATERAL DAMAGE   With regard to incarceration and children, it is the harms suffered by children of incarcerated parents.

COLLECTIVE CONSCIENCE   Shared beliefs and moral attitudes which contribute to unifying society.

COLOR GRADIENT   Distinctions in terms of group membership based on a light-to-dark skin continuum.

COMMON LEGAL TRADITION   A justice system approach that is found in the United States and other countries and is based on feudal practices, custom, and equity.

COMMUNITY CORRECTIONS   Correctional supervision in a community setting.

COMMUNITY ERA OF POLICING   An era of policing that began around 1980 and continues today. It involves efforts by the police to re-connect with the public primarily through the adoption of the community policing philosophy.

COMMUNITY LIAISON OFFICERS   A promising approach in policing in which designated officers meet with residents and business owners to discuss crime and crime prevention efforts.

COMMUNITY POLICING   A philosophical approach to policing that stresses creating and perpetuating a sense of community. It promotes positive police-citizen interaction and focuses on quality-of-life issues.

COMMUTATION   A type of clemency which involves shortening or changing an inmate's prison sentence.

CONCEALING ERRORS   Nondisclosure of errors that have been made in the preparation of a performance as well as steps that have been taken to correct these errors.

CONCEALING SECRET PLEASURES   Nondisclosure of activities engaged in prior to a performance or in past lives that are incompatible with a performance.

CONDITIONAL RELEASE   Release from prison accompanied by community supervision.

CONTINUUM OF FORCE   A concept that guides officer behavior with respect to use of force.

COURTROOM WORKGROUP   Individuals who work on a regular basis in a courtroom setting.

CRIME CONTROL MODEL OF CRIMINAL JUSTICE   A perspective on the administration of justice, as described by Herbert Packer, which maintains an emphasis on expediency and reducing crime.

CRIMES AGAINST PERSONS   Violent crimes, such as murder and non-negligent manslaughter, forcible rape, assaults, and intimidation.

CRIMES AGAINST PROPERTY   Economic crimes, such as burglary, larceny-theft, motor vehicle theft, vandalism, and arson.

CRIMES AGAINST SOCIETY   Often referred to as victimless crimes, these are crimes in which there is no easily discernable victim. These include offenses such as gambling, prostitution, drugs, or weapons violations.

CRIMINAL JUSTICE POLICY   Decisions or actions that address particular issues or problems pertaining to policing, courts, corrections, and related areas of formal social control.

CULTURAL FUSION   A goal of multiculturalism, where minority and majority groups come together to form an entirely new group.

CULTURE   Beliefs, values, norms, behaviors, and material goods that collectively constitute a people's manner of life. Culture shapes what we do and our personalities.

CULTURE-GENERAL TRAINING   Training that emphasizes the flexibility, skills, and knowledge that would apply to understanding an array of cultures.

CULTURE-SPECIFIC TRAINING   Training that addresses the practices, beliefs, and traits of particular cultural groups.

DAWES ACT   Legislation that made landowners of individual tribe members without consulting tribal leaders.

DELPHI METHOD   A qualitative approach to forecasting the future in which experts offer input regarding anticipated developments in their area of expertise.

DE-POLICING   A tactic employed by some officers who answer only high-priority calls instead of engaging in routine patrol.

DETERMINATE SENTENCING   Sentencing practices in which offenders receive a specific amount of time to be served based on the crime for which they were convicted.

DETERRENCE   Efforts to dissuade the offender (specific deterrence) or society in general (general deterrence) from engaging in acts for which the offender is being punished.

DISCOVERY The sharing of information among attorneys with the goal of helping them adequately prepare their case.

DISCREDITED STIGMA A type of stigma in which the actor assumes that the differences contributing to the stigma are known by the audience members or are evident to them.

DISCRETIONARY RELEASE Involves the use of discretion in the decision to release an inmate from prison. It most commonly refers to parole board decision-making.

DISCRIMINATION The unequal treatment of people based on their membership in a particular group.

DOUBLE MARGINALITY The challenges faced by minority officers who may be viewed as traitors by some in their community, while White officers may distrust them as colleagues.

DOWNWARD SOCIAL MOBILITY The movement of an individual or group into a diminished social class.

DRAMATURGICAL CIRCUMSPECTION The logistical planning involved in carrying out a performance. Examples include planning for emergencies, making only brief appearances, and preventing audience access to private information.

DRAMATURGICAL DISCIPLINE Concise preparation of a performance. It includes such things as having the presence of mind to avoid slips, maintaining self-control, and managing facial expressions and tone of voice in one's performance.

DRAMATURGY A view of social life as a series of dramatic performances like those performed on stage.

DRIVERS OF THE FUTURE Particular issues which have significant impacts on the future.

DUE PROCESS MODEL OF CRIMINAL JUSTICE A perspective on the administration of justice, as described by Herbert Packer, that is primarily concerned with respecting individual rights.

EASTERN ASIA LEGAL TRADITION A justice system approach that is grounded in the principles of Confucianism, along with collectivism, context, and informalism.

EMANCIPATION PROCLAMATION A proclamation and presidential executive order that freed slaves in the Confederacy.

ENDOGAMY The practice of marrying others with similar backgrounds.

ENVIRONMENTAL JUSTICE Attempts to treat all groups, regardless of race, ethnicity, or income, equally with regard to environmental protection and laws.

ENVIRONMENTAL RACISM The under-regulation of environmental laws, and the disproportionate placement of hazardous materials in minority neighborhoods.

EQUAL EMPLOYMENT OPPORTUNITY ACT OF 1972 This act extended the protections of women and other minorities to local governments.

ETHNICISM Emphases on ethnic identity. Preference for a particular ethnicity.

ETHNOCENTRIC The tendency to judge other cultures by the standards of one's own, thinking the latter is superior.

ETHNOCENTRISM Believing that one's culture or group is superior to others.

EXCLUSIONARY RULE Prohibits illegally seized materials from being introduced in court.

EXMATES Former prison inmates.

EXOGAMY The practice of marrying outside one's group.

EXPLICIT BIAS The biased beliefs or attitudes an individual maintains at a conscious level. The actions associated with this type of bias are apparent to the individuals and the audience.

EXPULSION The removal of groups from an area or territory.

EXTERMINATION A process where a government attempts to eliminate an entire group of people, either through relocation or violence.

EXTRADITION A state surrendering an individual accused of a crime to the state in which the individual is accused.

FEDERAL BUREAU OF PRISONS A bureau within the federal government that operates federal correctional institutions and community corrections offices across the United States.

FEDERAL JURY SELECTION AND SERVICE ACT OF 1968 This act provided greater equity in jury selection practices in that it prohibited the exclusion of individuals based on religion, race, gender, national origin, or economic status.

FEMINIST MOVEMENTS Social movements which generally promote the idea that males and females should be politically, socially, and economically equal.

FIELD TRAINING Police officer training which follows basic training and involves officers working under the guidance of an experienced colleague.

FIELD TRAINING OFFICER PROGRAMS Programs in which new officers are paired with experienced ones who teach new officers the practical aspects of the job, build upon and reinforce what was taught at the academy, and acclimate the officers to the department's and community's values.

FIRST STEP ACT Federal prison reform legislation passed in 2018 with the goal of reducing recidivism and the severity of some federal sentencing practices.

FORECASTING The use of scientific techniques to anticipate future developments.

FORT LARAMIE TREATY An agreement with the Sioux in which the U.S. government agreed to keep Whites from hunting or settling on the newly established Great Sioux Reservation, which included all of the land that is now South Dakota. In exchange, the Sioux relinquished most of the remaining land they occupied at that time.

FRANKPLEDGE SYSTEM The early English practice of informal social control in which community members protected one another.

FREEDOM SCHOOLS Private, all-White schools that enrolled an estimated 300,000 White children by 1970. Their development occurred with the intent of evading the *Brown* decision.

FUGITIVE SLAVE ACT Legislation which required that slaves who had escaped, even to a free state, be returned to their owners.

FUTURISTS Scientists who forecast future developments in society.

GAY BASHING Unprovoked attacks on people with gay identities.

GENDER A social characteristic that varies from one social group to another and refers to femininity or masculinity. It is a master status, as it cuts across all walks of life.

GENERATION X A term to describe the generation of individuals born between 1968 and 1979. Those born during the period are referred to as Gen Xers.

GENERATION Y A term to describe the generation of individuals born between approximately 1977 and 1994.

GENOCIDE The deliberate, systematic killing of an entire people group or nation

GERIATRIC COURT A distinct system of justice for the elderly.

GHOST DANCE RELIGION A religion that included dances and songs proclaiming the return of the buffalo and the resurrection of dead ancestors in a land free of White people.

GLASS CEILING An abstract barrier preventing certain groups and/or individuals from moving beyond entry-level occupational positions.

GLOBALIZATION The international integration of cultural, social, and economic issues among countries that have historically been distinct from one another.

GOING RATE The expected penalties associated with particular criminal offenses.

GOOD TIME Used in determinate sentencing structures, "good time" refers to the time eliminated from an offender's sentence for good behavior.

GRAND JURY HEARING A hearing used to determine if continued case processing is necessary. In grand jury hearings, jurors basically replace the judge used in a preliminary hearing. The grand jury's task is to determine if the prosecutor's case is strong enough to warrant an indictment.

GROUP GOALS Agreed-upon tasks or activities that a group seeks to complete or accomplish.

GROUP STRUCTURE The characteristics of a group. A group's structure is largely determined by group roles, and typically evolves in accordance with, or from, group norms and rules. The structure is vulnerable to change as norms, goals, and other factors impacting the group change.

HALFWAY HOUSE A community-based facility that enables offenders to reside in the community while remaining under relatively close supervision.

HARMLESS ERROR DOCTRINE A doctrine which holds that a trial court decision will not be overturned in an appellate court based on small, insignificant errors that appear to have limited or no impact on the trial outcome.

HATE CRIME An illegal action that is motivated by hate and taken against a particular group.

HATE SPEECH Communication that attacks individuals or groups on the basis of specific attributes, such as race, ethnicity, gender, sexual orientation, religion, or disability.

HETEROGENEOUS/HETEROGENEOUS SOCIETY Diverse in nature. A society in which people come from a wide range of backgrounds and experiences.

HMONG TRIBES Tribal groups that came together in the early 1860s under the label "Indochina" as the French colonized the region.

HOMOGENEITY Similarity in attitudes, values, and beliefs.

HOMOGENEOUS SOCIETY A society in which individuals share similar attitudes, values, and beliefs.

HOMOSEXUAL An individual attracted to those of the same sex.

HOMOSEXUAL ADVANCE THEORY The justification for courts to allow a non-violent homosexual advance to constitute sufficient provocation.

HOUSES OF REFUGE Facilities designed to house children who committed crimes, were poor, were orphans, or were thought to be incorrigible or wayward.

HUE AND CRY An early form of informal social control in which a call to arms generated a response from every able-bodied male in attempts to bring offenders to justice.

HUMAN SNAKES Individuals who leave China illegally.

HUMAN TRAFFICKING The involuntary movement of people across and within borders; it typically involves coercion, deception, and violence.

IMPLICIT BIAS Covert cognitive processes that shape attitudes and stereotypes while operating at a below-conscious level. The individual is not consciously aware of their biased behavior.

INCAPACITATION Physically preventing one from committing similar criminal acts in the future. Incarceration is the most widely used form of incapacitation.

INCARCERATION The physical detention of an inmate; it consists primarily of prison and jail.

INDIAN CLAIMS COMMISSION Although not an official U.S. court, the commission operates somewhat like one, in that lawyers present evidence for both sides in a disagreement. If the commission agrees with the tribe, it then determines the value of the land at the time it was illegally seized.

INDIAN HEALTH SERVICE An agency within the U.S. Department of Health and Human Services that is responsible for providing federal health services to American Indians and Alaskan Natives.

INDIAN REMOVAL ACT OF 1830 An act which called for the relocation of all Eastern tribes to west of the Mississippi River.

INDICTMENT The charging document used by grand juries to suggest that enough evidence exists to proceed with case processing.

INDIGENT DEFENDANT A defendant who cannot afford privately secured representation.

INDIVIDUALIZED JUSTICE Justice-based solutions that are fair and have the interests of the individuals involved in mind.

INITIAL APPEARANCE The stage of criminal case processing in which a defendant is brought before the court, informed of the formal charges against them, advised of their rights, possibly granted pretrial release, and made aware of the upcoming steps in their case.

INMATE CODE The norms and values developed and stressed in prison; it encourages toughness, insensitivity, and disdain and manipulation of fellow inmates and the prison staff. The code generally varies among institutions, as does inmate commitment to the code.

INSTITUTIONAL DISCRIMINATION The type of discrimination built into the structure of society.

INTERNATIONAL CRIMINAL COURT A permanent international court that investigates, prosecutes, and tries individuals accused of committing the most serious crimes that are of concern to the international community.

INVOLUNTARY MIGRATION The practice of bringing individuals to a new land against their will.

ISLAMIC LEGAL TRADITION A justice system approach that is based on the Qur'an and Sunna, as well as the doctrine of consensus and reasoning by analogy.

JAIL A place of confinement that holds detainees awaiting trial and those sentenced to incarceration for less than a year. In most states jails are operated by county-level officials, typically sheriff's departments.

JIM CROW An individual whose name is now associated with the label for the social, political, and legal separation of Whites and Blacks in all aspects of society.

JOCKER Also known as a "wolf," this type of prisoner is viewed by his fellow inmates as a "man." To remain a "man" and still engage in homosexual acts, the individual has to present an image of exaggerated toughness.

JURY NULLIFICATION The practice of jurors acquitting particular defendants despite strong evidence suggesting guilt.

JUST DESERTS A philosophy which argues that every person is equally responsible for their actions and should be punished according to what they have done.

JUVENILE DELINQUENCY Behaviors that violate the criminal code and are committed by youth who have not reached the age of majority (usually eighteen).

JUVENILE DELINQUENCY PREVENTION AND CONTROL ACT An act that recommended that children charged with noncriminal (status) offenses be handled outside the court system.

JUVENILE JUSTICE AND DELINQUENCY PREVENTION ACT OF 1974 An act that prohibited states from incarcerating status offenders and required them to detain juvenile offenders in separate facilities from adult offenders.

KINESICS Body language, including gestures, facial expressions, eye behavior, and body movements.

LATINO A term that refers to people and cultures of Latin America.

LOS BRACEROS Contracted workers who were allowed to enter the United States from Mexico due to the need for Mexican laborers.

MANDATORY MINIMUM SENTENCING A sentencing structure in which offenders convicted of certain offenses are to be sentenced to prison for no less than a specified term of years, and non-prison sentences (e.g., probation) are not an option. Mandatory minimum sentences are typically imposed on violent offenders.

MANDATORY RELEASE A policy in which inmates earn time off of their prison sentences through various incentives. Inmates are to be released when they've served the number of days they've been sentenced less good time.

MANNER A way of behaving that indicates what sort of role a person expects to play in a situation.

MARIELITOS A term which refers to individuals who were herded onto boats by Cuban authorities in Mariel, the fishing port west of Havana.

MARITAL RAPE The raping of one's spouse.

MARKET SEGMENTATION Marketing practices that target a subset of potential candidates to identify those who will likely provide the greatest return for the efforts.

MATERIAL CULTURE Objects that are real to the senses (e.g., a baton, handcuffs, a judge's gavel) and contribute to cultural identity.

MCJOBS Jobs in the lowest paying sectors of the market, including many minimum wage jobs.

MELTING POT A society that blends together a variety of backgrounds and cultures into a cohesive whole.

METROPOLITAN POLICE ACT Passed in 1829, an act that led to the first formal police department, the Metropolitan Police, led by Sir Robert Peel in London, England.

MODEL MINORITY MYTH The belief that Asian Americans constitute an ideal minority because they have endured political, economic, and social obstacles.

MULTICULTURALISM The embracing of cultural diversity.

NATIONAL ADVISORY COMMISSION ON CIVIL DISORDERS Also known as the Kerner Commission, this group was created to study the causes behind the 1960s rioting. The Commission identified a series of issues that contributed to the collective violence, including unequal justice, institutional racism, unemployment, and discrimination.

NATIONAL COUNCIL OF LA RAZA The largest Hispanic civil rights organization in the United States.

NATION OF ISLAM A religious, social, and political group that seeks to improve the mental, social, economic, and spiritual condition of Blacks.

NEGATIVE ATTRIBUTION African Americans developing a negative view of Whites that attributes evil motives and traits, due to the history of how Blacks have been treated.

NEOCOLONIALISM A type of dependence that arises when a country remains dependent on their dominators long after they separated from them politically.

NEORICAN A Puerto Rican who returns to the island after spending time away, typically in New York.

NIMBY An acronym that refers to "Not in my backyard," and relates to citizen concerns about the siting of something unpleasant or potentially dangerous in their vicinity.

NINETEENTH AMENDMENT Ratified by Congress in 1920, it gave women the right to vote.

NOLO CONTENDERE Also known as "no contest," this plea has the legal effect of a guilty plea. A defendant may choose to enter a plea of *nolo contendere* instead of admitting guilt in attempt to cooperate with the court when they do not wish to directly admit guilt.

NONMATERIAL CULTURE Shared beliefs and values which contribute to cultural identity; the social expectations individuals have for one another.

OPERATIONALIZATION The process of researchers defining terms and variables for the purpose of analysis.

ORGANIZATIONAL CULTURE Shared beliefs, values, and assumptions that influence how individuals behave in organizations.

ORPHAN TRAINS Trains used to transport city youths to rural farms, where families assumed custody of and responsibility for them as apprentices.

OVERPOLICING The oppressive and extensive use of formal social control against minority groups.

OVERSTAYER An individual admitted to a country on a temporary visa who either stays beyond the expiration of their visa or otherwise violates the terms of their admission.

PARDON A type of clemency which involves the restoration of a former inmate's rights and privileges.

PARENS PATRIAE Latin for "parent of the nation," this term refers to the power of the state to intervene and act as the parent of any child or individual who is in need of protection.

PAROLE Offender supervision in the community following a period of incarceration.

PATRONAGE The practice of politicians rewarding friends and/or acquaintances.

PERCEPTION The act of becoming aware or apprehending something via the senses.

PEREMPTORY CHALLENGE A motion through which attorneys can eliminate seemingly unfit or inappropriate members of the jury pool. Attorneys typically do not need to justify using a peremptory challenge, although they are limited in the number of peremptory challenges they can use.

PERSONAL FRONT Items of equipment that an audience identifies with performers and expects them to carry with them into the setting.

PLEA BARGAINING An exchange between the prosecution and defense designed to encourage a guilty plea in exchange for a benefit for the defendant.

POLICE DISCRETION Officer decision-making; it is evident in all aspects of police practices. It is necessary in policing as officers are consistently faced with difficult situations involving multiple variables.

POLICE OFFICERS STANDARDS AND TRAINING COMMISSIONS (POSTS) State organizations that establish minimum standards for policing, typically provide training criteria for police officers, and seek means to improve police training practices.

POLICE SUBCULTURE A distinct culture within policing that promotes a particular working personality that encourages solidarity, authoritarianism, and sometimes the exclusion of females and minority officers.

POLICY Decisions or actions that address particular issues or problems.

POLITICAL ERA OF POLICING An era (1840–1930) characterized by police officers seeking an intimate relationship with the community and politics heavily influencing police departments and police practices.

PREDICTIONS Evaluations of expected future developments based on instinctual feelings (or "gut feelings") that lack scientific validity.

PREJUDICE A negative attitude toward certain people based solely on their membership in a particular group.

PREJUDICED DISCRIMINATOR An individual who has negative feelings toward a particular group or groups and translates these sentiments into unequal and negative treatment of people in that group.

PREJUDICED NON-DISCRIMINATOR An individual who might be called a closet bigot; someone who is prejudiced against members of some groups but does not translate these attitudes into discriminatory practices.

PRELIMINARY HEARING A stage in criminal case processing in which a prosecutor demonstrates to a judge why charges have been filed and justifies continued processing.

PRE-SERVICE TRAINING Training which occurs prior to one's formal participation on the job. It typically begins at an accredited academy for police and corrections officers.

PRESIDENT'S COMMISSION ON LAW ENFORCEMENT AND ADMINISTRATION OF JUSTICE Also known as the President's Crime Commission, this group focused on enhancing professionalization of policing and police officers. It suggested hiring more members of minority groups and encouraging departments to become more community-oriented.

PRESSURE PUNK An inmate who submits to homosexual behavior because they have been threatened or raped by other prisoners.

PRETRIAL MOTION A motion offered in court prior to a trial in which an attorney seeks an order of the court. The motion is presented to a judge and can be a determining factor in the outcome of a case.

PRETRIAL RELEASE The release of a defendant prior to trial. Release can be secured monetarily, as in the case of bail, or non-financially, such as release on recognizance.

PRISON A correctional facility that incarcerates inmates serving sentences of one year or more.

PRISON PLAY-FAMILIES An aspect of the social structure of prisons in which inmates assume the roles of different family members. They are more common in female prisons than in male institutions.

PRISON RAPE ELIMINATION ACT An act passed in 2003 that was designed to address prison rape through developing standards to prevent incidents of sexual violence in prison, including a zero-tolerance policy, and emphasizing research and information gathering.

PRISONIZATION Inmate adaptation to prison culture. A social and physical transformation of the individual in an effort to compensate for the pains of imprisonment.

PROBATION Offender supervision in the community in lieu of incarceration.

PROBLEM-ORIENTED POLICING A four-step approach to addressing specific crimes in the community. The steps include scanning communities to identify problems, analyzing the nature and extent of the problem, responding to the problem, and assessing whether or not the problem is properly addressed.

PROHIBITION The period (1919–1933) in which the sale, transport, or manufacturing of alcohol was criminalized.

PROXEMICS The space between a communicator and his or her audience.

PUBLIC DEFENDER An attorney who works in an office that exists solely to provide indigent representation.

PUBLIC POLICY Decisions or actions that address particular issues or problems and are supported by public resources and enforced by the legal system.

PUNK A homosexual inmate with one of the lowest statuses in the institution. Punks are despised by inmates who see homosexual behavior as the result of either weakness in the face of pressure or a willingness to sacrifice one's manhood to obtain goods and services.

QUALITATIVE APPROACHES Consideration of non-numerical trends and patterns in attempt to anticipate future developments and changes.

QUANTITATIVE ANALYSES The use of statistics and trends to anticipate changes in society.

QUEEN A male inmate who prefers male sexual partners.

RACIAL PROFILING Recognizing individuals as suspects based merely upon race.

RACISM The belief in the innate superiority of one race over another that is exhibited in a group or individual's behavior.

RECIDIVISM RATE The rate related to which individuals commit an undesirable act after they have been treated or have experienced a negative consequence. It is also known as the re-offending rate.

RECONSTRUCTION A new social, political, and economic portrait of the South created after slavery was abolished.

RECONSTRUCTION ACT OF 1867 An act that required compliance with Reconstruction. According to the act, each Southern state was controlled by a military governor until a new state constitution could be written.

RED-LIGHT DISTRICT An area of a city frequented by prostitutes.

RED POWER MOVEMENT A movement that was similar to the Black Power movement for African Americans in that it attempted to gain economic, social, and political equality for Native Americans.

REENTRY An inmate's return to society.

REFORM ERA OF POLICING Also known as the progressive era, it was a time (1930–1980) characterized by police-community relations suffering and police becoming increasingly reliant on technology and overly concerned with efficiency.

REHABILITATION Attempts to "cure" or "fix" the ills leading to an offender's behavior.

REINTEGRATION The process of an offender reintegrating, or readjusting to life outside prison.

REPATRIATION A government-sponsored deportation program to send Chicanos back to Mexico.

REPRIEVE A type of clemency which involves the postponement of a sentence. Reprieves are typically associated with delaying an execution.

RESTRICTIVE COVENANTS A private contract between neighborhood property owners which stipulated that property could not be sold or rented to certain minority groups, thus ensuring minorities could not live in the area.

RETRIBUTION Punishment, or the "eye for an eye" approach.

REVERSE DISCRIMINATION The belief that efforts to remedy past mistakes in the treatment of minority groups are biased against members of the majority.

ROLE The behavior that is expected of an individual who maintains a particular status.

SANCTUARY LAWS Laws that prohibit police officers from inquiring about a suspect's immigration status.

SCENARIOS A method of forecasting the future in which narratives are used to describe anticipated future events and developments.

"SCHOOL-TO-PRISON PIPELINE" A term which refers to the increasing patterns of students having contact with the justice system as a result of more punitive approaches to addressing school-related problems.

SECESSION The process in which minority groups willingly depart from their country or for an opportunity to create their own society.

SEGREGATION The dominant group coexisting with a minority group, but with efforts made to limit contact between the dominant group and minority members.

SENTENCING GUIDELINES Guidelines used by some jurisdictions to provide consistency and parity in sentencing decisions. They involve a risk assessment of the offender based on current offense and past history.

SETOFFS Deductions from the money due equal to the cost of federal services provided to a tribe.

SETTING The physical scene that ordinarily must exist if the actors are to perform.

SEX The biological characteristics that distinguish males and females.

SEX TRAFFICKING The use of force, fraud, or coercion to force victims to perform commercial sex.

SEXUAL ORIENTATION A term used to describe a sexual attraction toward people either of the same gender, the opposite sex, or both.

SHOWING ONLY THE END PRODUCT Nondisclosure of all that precedes a particular performance.

SITUATIONAL HOMOSEXUALITY Instances in which homosexual behavior occurs between two otherwise heterosexuals.

SLAVE CODES Laws regulating slave behavior.

SLAVE PATROLS Considered by some as the first American police departments, they were established as early as the 1740s. The patrols were tasked with preventing slave revolts and apprehending runaway slaves.

SNAKEHEADS Chinese human smugglers who lead illegal immigrants across borders.

SOCIAL CONSTRUCTION OF RACE The concept in which every culture must determine which physical features are used to define membership in certain races.

SOCIAL CONSTRUCTION OF REALITY The process through which people mentally construct ideas about phenomena and thus create a reality.

SOCIAL GROUP Two or more individuals regularly interacting and feeling a sense of solidarity or common identity. Social groups typically share some norms and values while working to achieve common goals.

SOCIAL INTERACTION The process through which individuals act and react in relation to other individuals.

SOCIAL JUSTICE A perspective of justice that considers how a society provides for the needs of its members and the whether or not it treats its subgroups equally.

STATUS The social position maintained by an individual.

STATUS OFFENDERS Youth who violate the law by engaging in acts that are age-specific, such as truancy, running away, or underage drinking.

SUBCULTURE The meanings, values, and behavior patterns unique to a particular group in a given society.

SUMMONS A document informing an individual of their call to jury duty.

SWEAT LODGES Small huts in which Native American ceremonies are held to cleanse spirits in a religious rite of purification and penance.

SYMBOLIC ASSAILANT A particular individual who is perceived by a police officer to be a potential source of violence or an enemy to be reckoned with.

SYMBOLIC REPRESENTATION Making our courts more representative of all racial/ethnic groups.

SYMBOL An item used to represent something else.

TECHNICAL VIOLATION Misbehavior by a probationer or parolee that is not by itself a criminal offense and generally does not result in arrest. Serious technical violations or continuous misbehavior, however, while on probation or parole can result in re-incarceration.

TERMINATION ACT An act passed by Congress in 1953 which led to the termination of thirteen Native American tribes between 1945 and 1962.

The act also meant that certain tribes would lose tax-exempt status for their lands.

"THREE STRIKES AND YOU'RE OUT" SENTENCING A sentencing structure targeted toward repeat offenders. Three-strikes legislation demonstrates the public's disdain for crime and an attempt to target those who seem undeterred by criminal law and punishment. The laws vary among the states that use them.

TOKENS Individuals from underrepresented groups who were hired, or received their position, solely because of affirmative action policies, regardless of their ability to perform the job.

TRAINING SCHOOLS Facilities which replaced and supplemented houses of refuge. Compared to houses of refuge, training schools placed a greater emphasis on education and vocational training.

TRANSFER The relocation of a case from the jurisdiction of the juvenile court to an adult court.

TRIAD SOCIETY A group of leaders within the Chinese community responsible for setting boundaries and dictating most aspects of social life.

TRIAD SUBCULTURE The customs, beliefs, and practices of triad societies, which were created by ousted Chinese officials and the alienated poor in the seventeenth century in efforts to overthrow the government.

TRIBAL COURT A court of jurisdiction which allows tribes the authority to hear and decide cases relating to life on the reservation without interference of traditional U.S. courts.

ULTRAMASCULINITY A term denoting an exaggerated image of masculinity, which is a primary concern for many prison inmates. The inmate subculture emphasizes being strong.

UNDERPOLICING Actions not taken by the police to protect members of minority groups.

UNPREJUDICED DISCRIMINATOR A person who treats members of some groups unequally not because they have any personal animosity towards them but because it is simply advantageous to do so.

UNPREJUDICED NON-DISCRIMINATOR An individual who accepts other racial or ethnic groups both in belief and practice. They embrace the idea of difference, of cultural diversity as a healthy concept, and do not try to impose their own cultural and social ideas on others.

UPWARD SOCIAL MOBILITY Moving up a level in social status.

U.S. PAROLE COMMISSION The agency responsible for overseeing federal parolees.

U.S. PROBATION AND PRETRIAL SERVICES SYSTEM The agency responsible for, among other things, assisting the federal courts with pretrial practices and supervising federal probationers.

VENIRE A jury pool from which prospective jurors are selected and questioned.

VICARIOUS HASSLING Hassling individuals without cause. It is also the type of hassling that involves knowing someone who has experienced this type of treatment by the police.

VOCALICS Also known as paralanguage, it refers to vocal characteristics such as inflection, tone, accent, rate, pitch, volume, and vocal interrupters.

VOIR DIRE The process of questioning potential jurors regarding their suitability to serve on a jury.

VOLUNTARY MIGRATION The process involving people who willingly immigrate to a new country looking for a better life.

VOLUNTARY PLACEMENTS Youths referred to detention facilities because either their parents turned them over to a social service agency or the agency placed them because they committed delinquent acts but were not formally adjudicated.

VOTING RIGHTS ACT An act which encouraged Blacks to participate in the political process and prohibited discrimination with regard to voting rights.

WAIVE JURISDICTION The relocation of a case from the jurisdictions of the juvenile court to an adult court.

WOLF Also known as a "jocker," this type of prisoner is viewed by his fellow inmates as a "man." To remain a "man" and still engage in homosexual acts, the individual has to present an image of exaggerated toughness.

YAKUZA The Japanese version of organized crime.

YELLOW PERIL A fear-based "threat" that resulted in strict immigration laws and the imprisonment of Japanese American citizens.

CREDITS

CHAPTER 2: page 32, Photographerlondon/Dreamstime.com; page 36, Javier Sanchez Mingorance/123rf Photos; page 45 (left), Quorthon1/Shutterstock; page 45 (right), pkchai/Shutterstock; page 47, David Grossman/Alamy Stock Photo. CHAPTER 3: page 60, rawpixel/123rf Photos; page 71, Rommel Canlas/123rf Photos; page 83, csp_oneword/Fotosearch. CHAPTER 4: page 105, a katz/Shutterstock; page 107, Bettman/Getty Images; page 111, a katz/Shutterstock. CHAPTER 5: page 138, imtmphoto/123rf Photos; page 143, Everett Historical/Shutterstock; page 145, Associated Press. CHAPTER 6: page 168, Gabriel Olson/Getty Images; page 174, Andre Jenny/Alamy Stock Photo Chapter 7: page 194, B Christopher/Alamy Stock Photo; page 195, True Touch Lifestyle/Shutterstock; page 198, John Roman Images/Shutterstock; page 207, Skyward Kick Productions/Shutterstock. CHAPTER 8: page 227, Barcroft Media/Getty Images; page 235, Stacy Walsh Rosenstock/Alamy Stock Photo. CHAPTER 9: page 253, Ian Allenden/123rf Photos; page 257, Associated Press; page 265, Skyward Kick Productions/Shutterstock. CHAPTER 10: page 276, NY Public Library; page 279, Design Pics Inc/Alamy Stock Photo; page 283, Yakobchuk Viacheslav/Shutterstock; page 286, Monkey Business Images/Shutterstock; page 291, Saphoto/Shutterstock. CHAPTER 11: page 309, NikolayAP/Shutterstock; page 311, Rena Schild/Shutterstock; page 316, Ira Berger/Alamy Stock Photo; page 321, Photo TFoxFoto/Shutterstock. CHAPTER 12: page 334, Poet Sage Photos/Shutterstock; page 343, sirtravelalot/Shutterstock; page 355, dpa picture alliance/Alamy Stock Photo. CHAPTER 13: page 369, Lightfield Studios/Shutterstock; page 378, Janine Wiedel Photolibrary/Alamy Stock Photo; page 383, Marmaduke St. John/Alamy Stock Photo. CHAPTER 14: page 393, Free Wind 2014/Shutterstock; page 399, Vladimir Melnik/Shutterstock; page 400, wavebreakmedia/Shutterstock; page 409, Richard Cavalerri/Shutterstock. CHAPTER 15: page 422, Ikpro/Alamy Stock Photo; page 425, Vlad Ghiea/Alamy Stock Photo; page 427, Joe Vogan/Alamy Stock Photo; page 430, Evan El-Amin/Alamy Stock Photo.

INDEX

Page number suffixes indicate: f, figures; p, pictures; and t, tables.